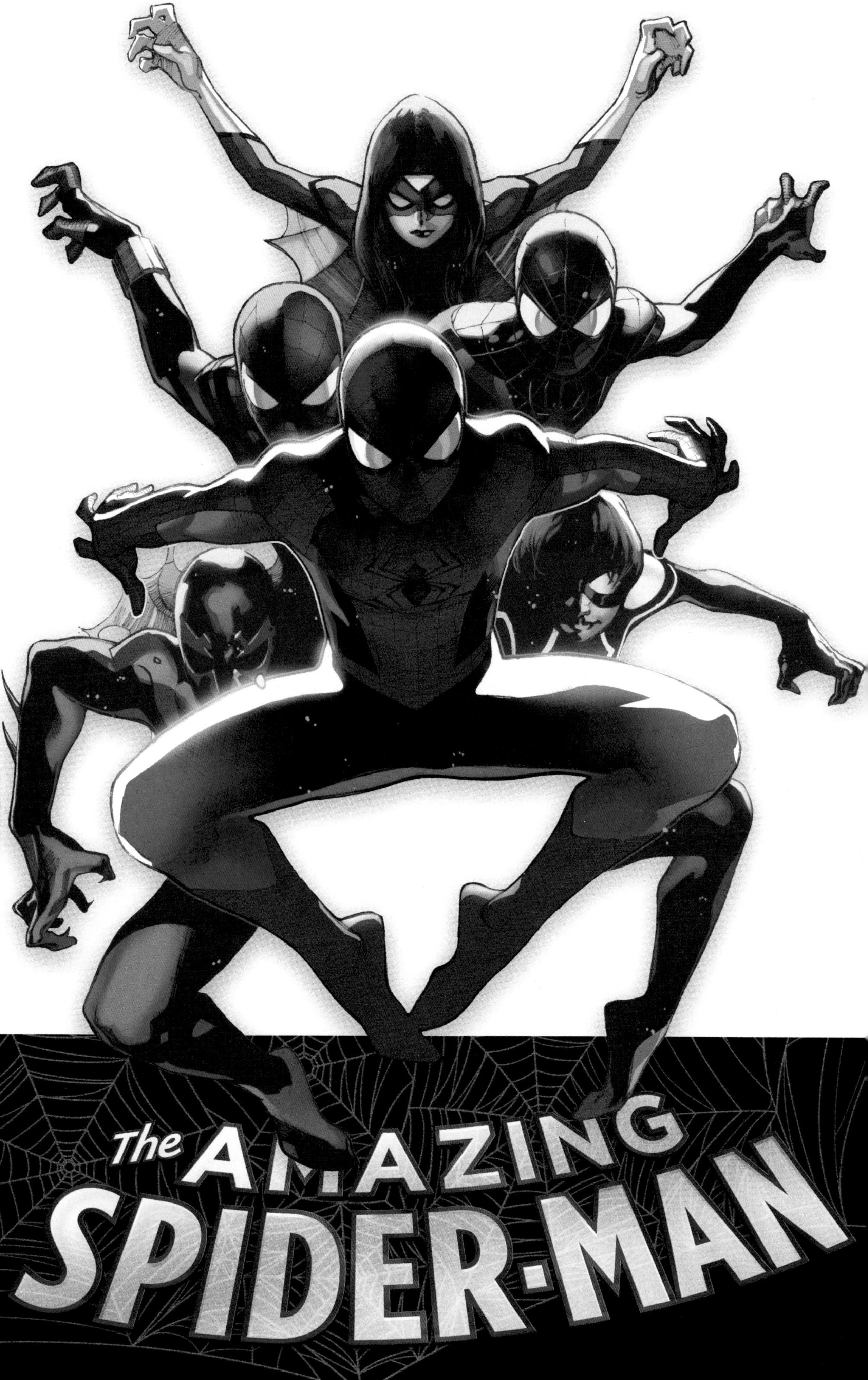
The AMAZING
SPIDER-MAN

COLLECTION EDITOR: **JENNIFER GRÜNWALD**
ASSISTANT EDITOR: **SARAH BRUNSTAD**
ASSOCIATE MANAGING EDITOR: **ALEX STARBUCK**
EDITOR, SPECIAL PROJECTS: **MARK D. BEAZLEY**
SENIOR EDITOR, SPECIAL PROJECTS: **JEFF YOUNGQUIST**
SVP PRINT, SALES & MARKETING: **DAVID GABRIEL**
BOOK DESIGNER: **ADAM DEL RE**

EDITOR IN CHIEF: **AXEL ALONSO**
CHIEF CREATIVE OFFICER: **JOE QUESADA**
PUBLISHER: **DAN BUCKLEY**
EXECUTIVE PRODUCER: **ALAN FINE**

AMAZING SPIDER-MAN VOL. 2. Contains material originally published in magazine form as AMAZING SPIDER-MAN #7-18, SUPERIOR SPIDER-MAN #32-33 and FREE COMIC BOOK DAY 2014 (GUARDIANS OF THE GALAXY) #1. First printing 2016. ISBN# 978-0-7851-9537-5. Published by MARVEL WORLDWIDE, INC., a subsidiary of MARVEL ENTERTAINMENT, LLC. OFFICE OF PUBLICATION: 135 West 50th Street, New York, NY 10020. **Printed in China.** ALAN FINE, President, Marvel Entertainment; DAN BUCKLEY, President, TV, Publishing and Brand Management; JOE QUESADA, Chief Creative Officer; TOM BREVOORT, SVP of Publishing; DAVID BOGART, SVP of Operations & Procurement, Publishing; C.B. CEBULSKI, VP of International Development & Brand Management; DAVID GABRIEL, SVP Print, Sales & Marketing; JIM O'KEEFE, VP of Operations & Logistics; DAN CARR, Executive Director of Publishing Technology; SUSAN CRESPI, Editorial Operations Manager; ALEX MORALES, Publishing Operations Manager; STAN LEE, Chairman Emeritus. For information regarding advertising in Marvel Comics or on Marvel.com, please contact Jonathan Rheingold, VP of Custom Solutions & Ad Sales, at jrheingold@marvel.com. For Marvel subscription inquiries, please call 800-217-9158. **Manufactured between 12/4/2015 and 2/15/2016 by R.R. DONNELLEY ASIA PRINTING SOLUTIONS, CHINA.**

10 9 8 7 6 5 4 3 2 1

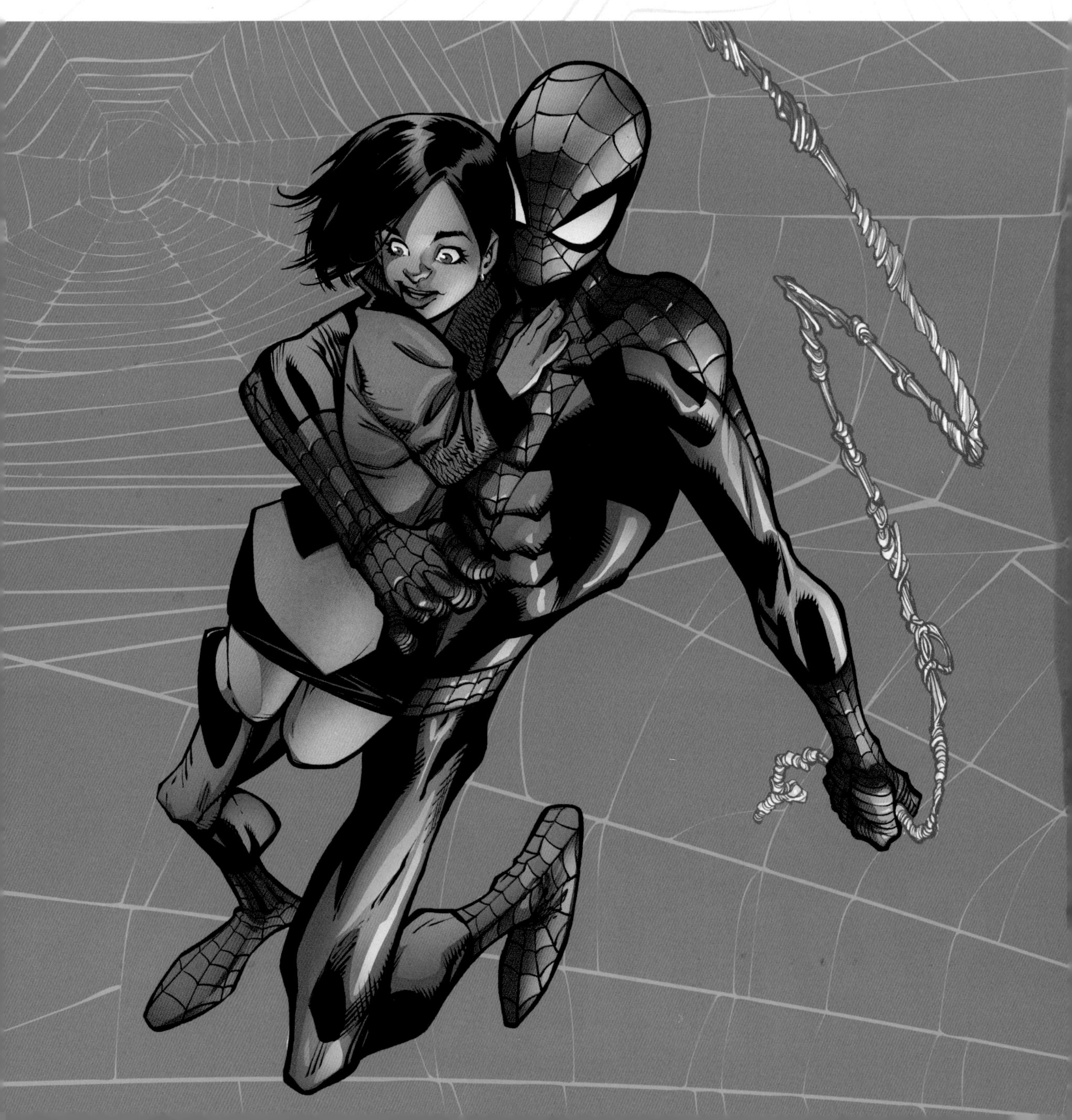

The AMAZING SPIDER-MAN

FREE COMIC BOOK DAY 2014

WRITER: **DAN SLOTT**
PENCILER: **GIUSEPPE CAMUNCOLI**
INKER: **JOHN DELL**

"STAGING GROUND"
COLORIST: **EDGAR DELGADO**
LETTERER: **VC's CORY PETIT**
EDITORS: **STEPHEN WACKER & ELLIE PYLE**

AMAZING SPIDER-MAN #7-8 & SUPERIOR SPIDER-MAN #32-33

PLOT: **DAN SLOTT** WITH **CHRISTOS GAGE** (SUPERIOR SPIDER-MAN #33)
SCRIPT: **CHRISTOS GAGE**
PENCILER: **GIUSEPPE CAMUNCOLI**

INKERS: **CAM SMITH** (AMAZING SPIDER-MAN #7-8)
& **JOHN DELL** (SUPERIOR SPIDER-MAN #32-33)
COLORIST: **ANTONIO FABELA**

"EDGE OF SPIDER-VERSE:
WEB OF FEAR"
WRITER: **DAN SLOTT**
PENCILER: **GIUSEPPE CAMUNCOLI**
INKER: **CAM SMITH**
COLORIST: **ANTONIO FABELA**

"EDGE OF SPIDER-VERSE:
MY BROTHER'S KEEPER"
WRITER: **DAN SLOTT**
PENCILER: **HUMBERTO RAMOS**
INKER: **VICTOR OLAZABA**
COLORIST: **EDGAR DELGADO**

"THE SPIDER-SANCTION"
WRITER: **CHRISTOS GAGE**
ARTIST: **ADAM KUBERT**
COLORIST: **RAIN BEREDO**

"BLACK SHEEP"
WRITER: **CHRISTOS GAGE**
ARTIST: **M.A. SEPULVEDA**
COLORIST: **RICHARD ISANOVE**

LETTERERS: **CHRIS ELIOPOULOS** WITH **VC's JOE CARAMAGNA** (SUPERIOR SPIDER-MAN #33)
COVER ART: **GIUSEPPE CAMUNCOLI, CAM SMITH & ANTONIO FABELA**
ASSOCIATE EDITOR: **ELLIE PYLE** | EDITOR: **NICK LOWE**

AMAZING SPIDER-MAN #9-15

WRITER: **DAN SLOTT**
PENCILERS: **OLIVIER COIPEL** (#9-11 & #14)
AND **GIUSEPPE CAMUNCOLI** (#12-15)
INKERS: **OLIVIER COIPEL** (#9-11), **CAM SMITH** (#12-15) &
WADE VON GRAWBADGER (#10-11 & #14) WITH **LIVESAY** (#11 & #14),
VICTOR OLAZABA (#11), **MARK MORALES** (#11) & **ROBERTO POGGI** (#15)

COLORIST: **JUSTIN PONSOR**
LETTERERS: **CHRIS ELIOPOULOS** WITH **VC's TRAVIS LANHAM** (#11)
COVER ART: **OLIVIER COIPEL & JUSTIN PONSOR** (#9-12),
**OLIVIER COIPEL, WADE VON GRAWBADGER &
JUSTIN PONSOR** (#13) AND **GIUSEPPE CAMUNCOLI,
CAM SMITH & JUSTIN PONSOR** (#14-15)

ASSISTANT EDITOR: **DEVIN LEWIS**
ASSOCIATE EDITOR: **ELLIE PYLE**
EDITOR: **NICK LOWE**

"SPIDER-VERSE: THE FEAST"
WRITER: **DAN SLOTT**
PENCILER: **GUISEPPE CAMUNCOLI**

INKER: **CAM SMITH**
COLORIST: **ANTONIO FABELA**
LETTERER: **VC's TRAVIS LANHAM**

AMAZING SPIDER-MAN #16-18

WRITERS: **DAN SLOTT**
& **CHRISTOS GAGE**
PENCILER: **HUMBERTO RAMOS**
INKER: **VICTOR OLAZABA**

COLORIST: **EDGAR DELGADO**
LETTERER: **CHRIS ELIOPOULOS**
COVER ART: **HUMBERTO RAMOS**
& **EDGAR DELGADO**

ASSISTANT EDITOR: **DEVIN LEWIS**
ASSOCIATE EDITOR: **ELLIE PYLE**
EDITOR: **NICK LOWE**

SPIDER-MAN CREATED BY **STAN LEE & STEVE DITKO**

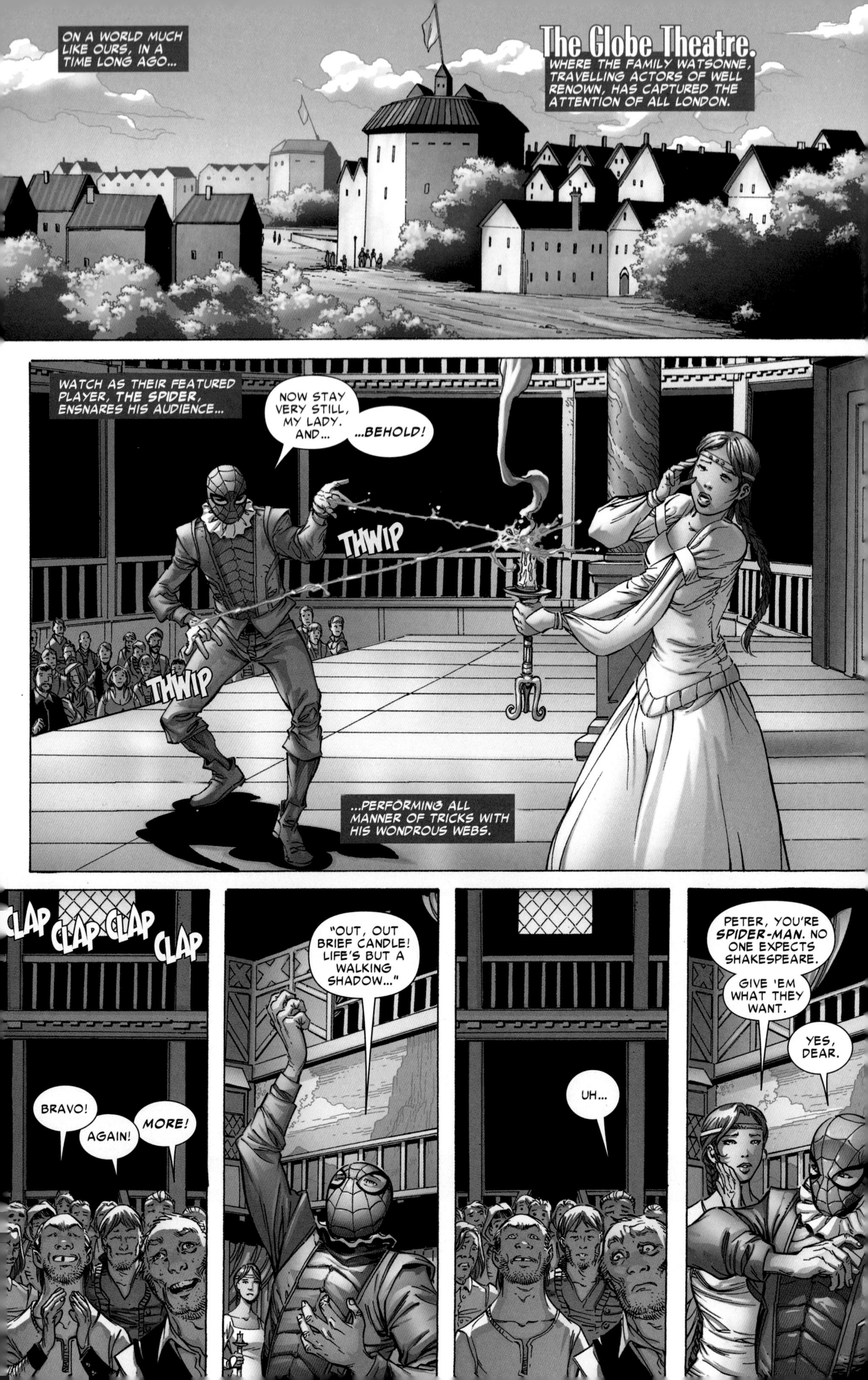

ON A WORLD MUCH LIKE OURS, IN A TIME LONG AGO...
The Globe Theatre.
WHERE THE FAMILY WATSONNE, TRAVELLING ACTORS OF WELL RENOWN, HAS CAPTURED THE ATTENTION OF ALL LONDON.
WATCH AS THEIR FEATURED PLAYER, THE SPIDER, ENSNARES HIS AUDIENCE...
NOW STAY VERY STILL, MY LADY. AND...
...BEHOLD!
THWIP
THWIP
...PERFORMING ALL MANNER OF TRICKS WITH HIS WONDROUS WEBS.
CLAP CLAP CLAP CLAP
BRAVO!
AGAIN!
MORE!
"OUT, OUT BRIEF CANDLE! LIFE'S BUT A WALKING SHADOW..."
UH...
PETER, YOU'RE SPIDER-MAN. NO ONE EXPECTS SHAKESPEARE.
GIVE 'EM WHAT THEY WANT.
YES, DEAR.

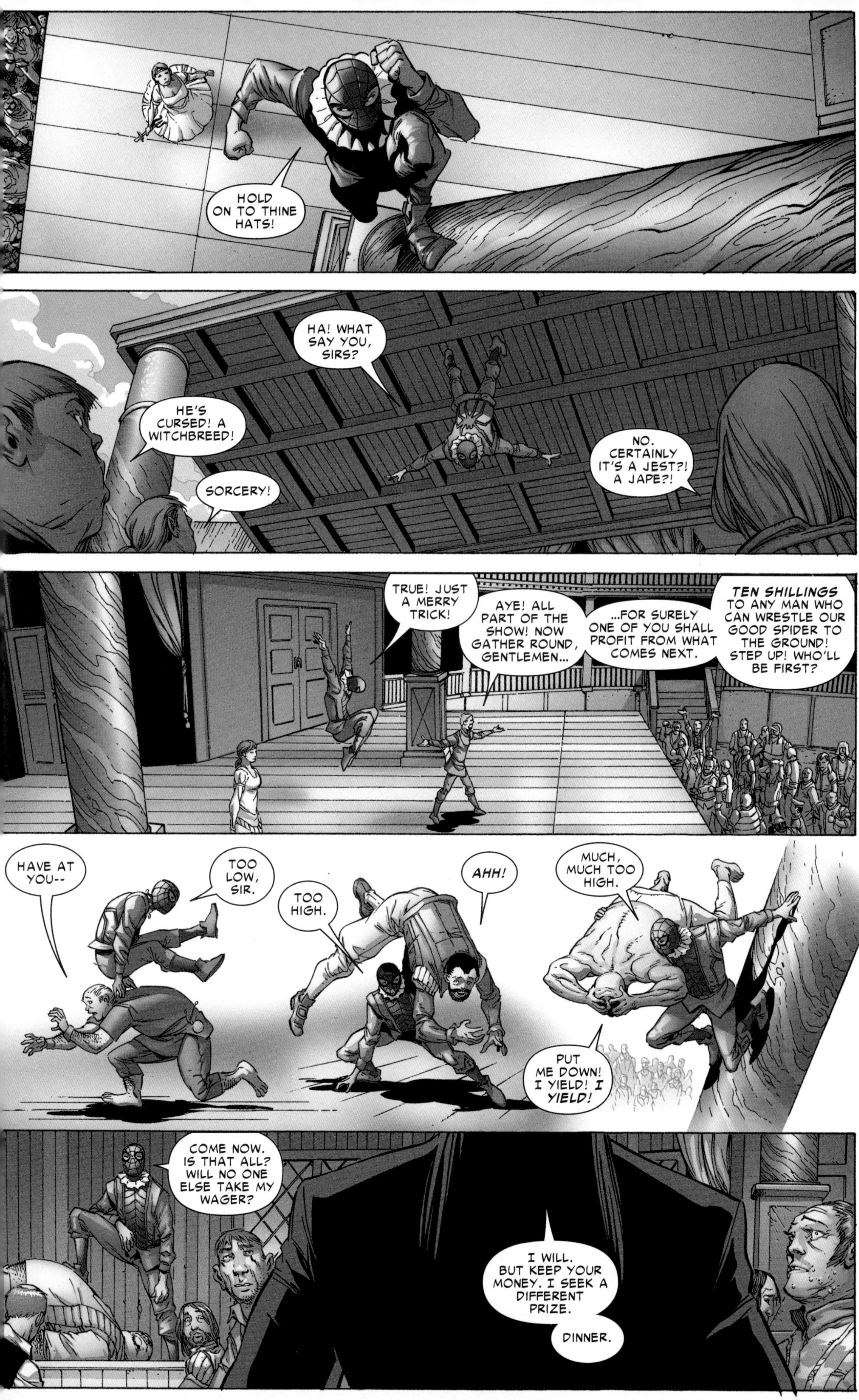
HOLD ON TO THINE HATS!
HA! WHAT SAY YOU, SIRS?
HE'S CURSED! A WITCHBREED!
SORCERY!
NO. CERTAINLY IT'S A JEST?! A JAPE?!
TRUE! JUST A MERRY TRICK!
AYE! ALL PART OF THE SHOW! NOW GATHER ROUND, GENTLEMEN...
...FOR SURELY ONE OF YOU SHALL PROFIT FROM WHAT COMES NEXT.
TEN SHILLINGS TO ANY MAN WHO CAN WRESTLE OUR GOOD SPIDER TO THE GROUND! STEP UP! WHO'LL BE FIRST?
HAVE AT YOU--
TOO LOW, SIR.
TOO HIGH.
AHH!
MUCH, MUCH TOO HIGH.
PUT ME DOWN! I YIELD! I YIELD!
COME NOW. IS THAT ALL? WILL NO ONE ELSE TAKE MY WAGER?
I WILL. BUT KEEP YOUR MONEY. I SEEK A DIFFERENT PRIZE.
DINNER.

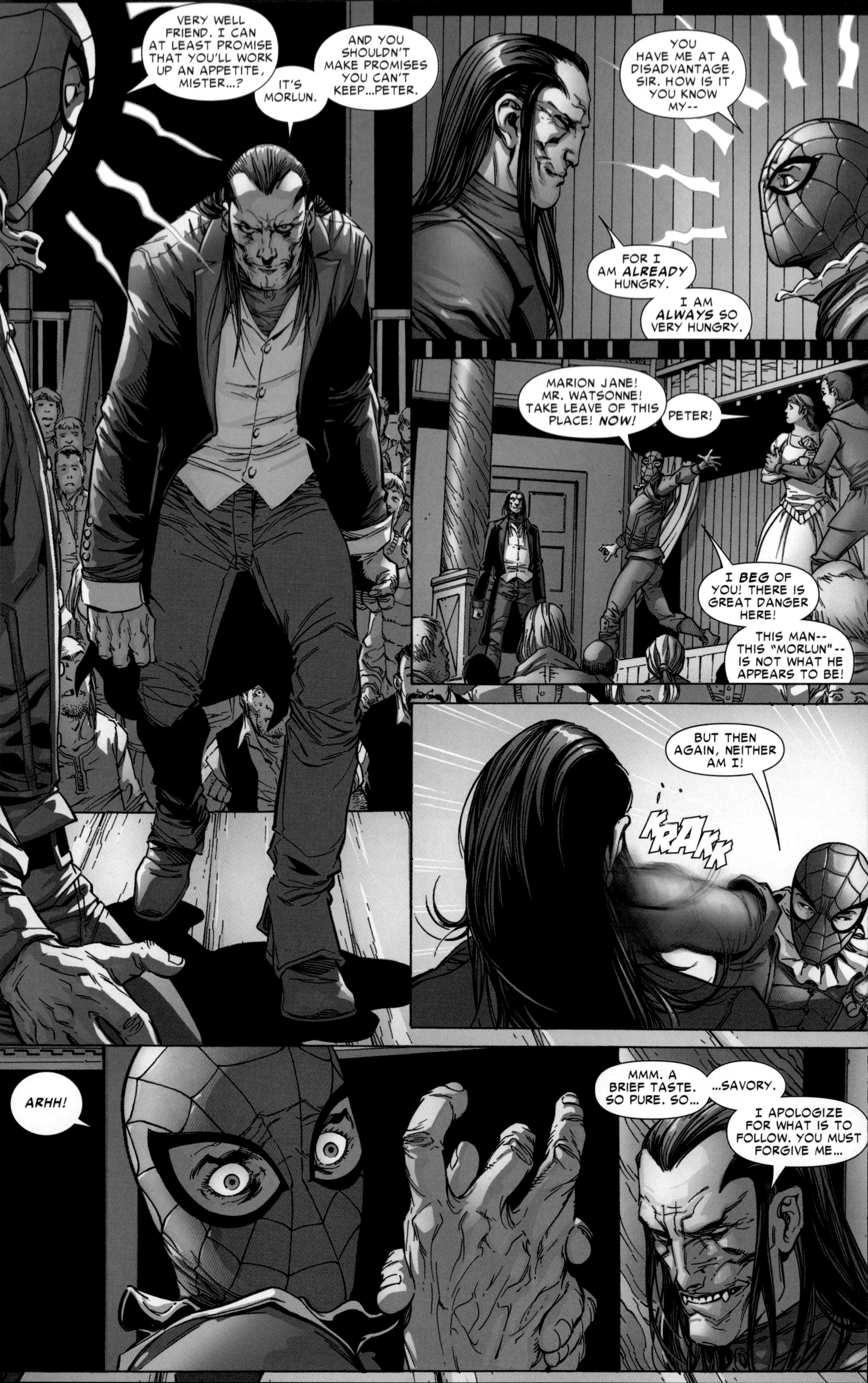
VERY WELL FRIEND. I CAN AT LEAST PROMISE THAT YOU'LL WORK UP AN APPETITE, MISTER...?
IT'S MORLUN.
AND YOU SHOULDN'T MAKE PROMISES YOU CAN'T KEEP...PETER.
YOU HAVE ME AT A DISADVANTAGE, SIR. HOW IS IT YOU KNOW MY--
FOR I AM ALREADY HUNGRY.
I AM ALWAYS SO VERY HUNGRY.
MARION JANE! MR. WATSONNE! TAKE LEAVE OF THIS PLACE! NOW!
PETER!
I BEG OF YOU! THERE IS GREAT DANGER HERE!
THIS MAN-- THIS "MORLUN"-- IS NOT WHAT HE APPEARS TO BE!
BUT THEN AGAIN, NEITHER AM I!
KRAKK
ARHH!
MMM. A BRIEF TASTE. SO PURE. SO...
...SAVORY.
I APOLOGIZE FOR WHAT IS TO FOLLOW. YOU MUST FORGIVE ME...

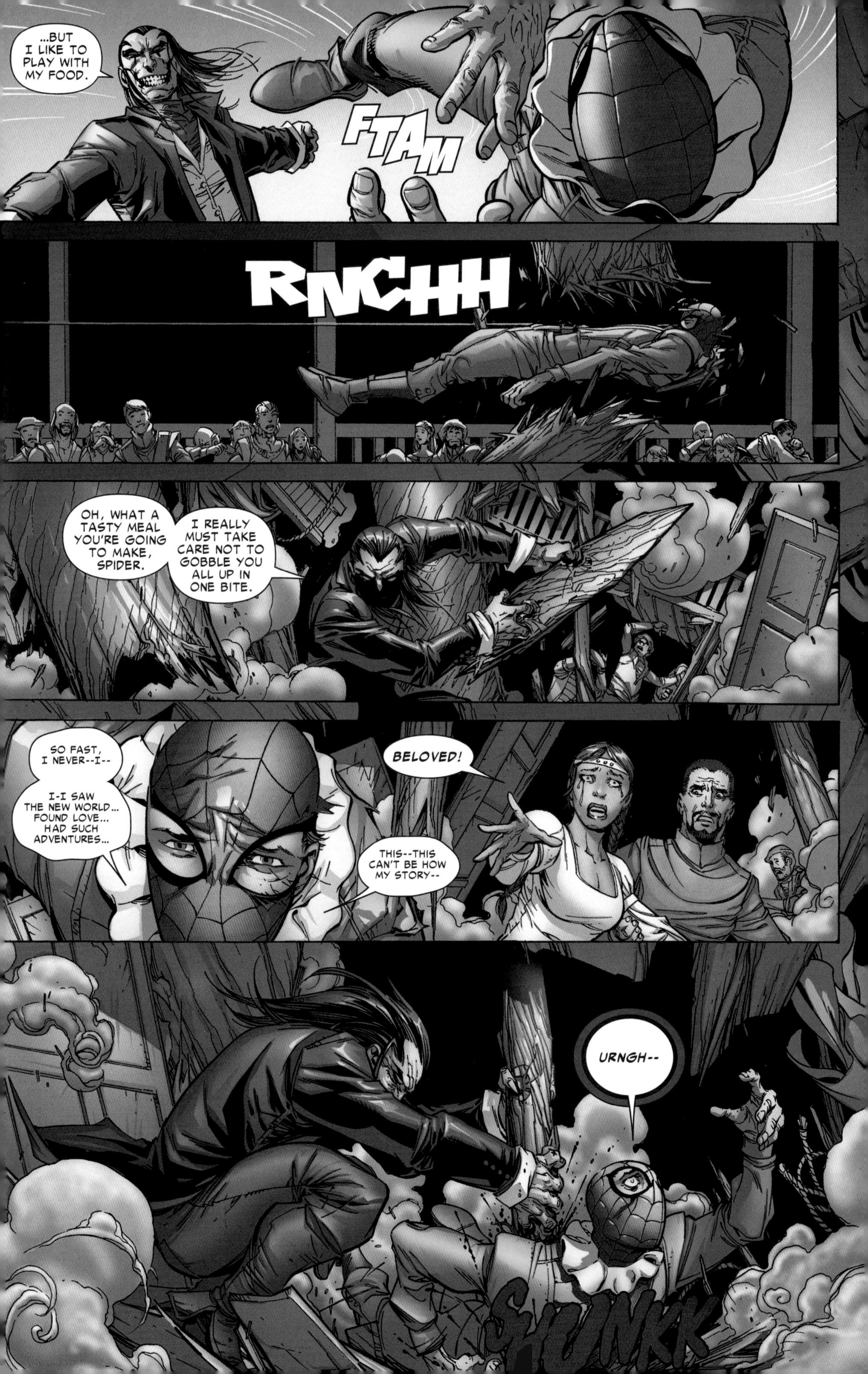
...BUT I LIKE TO PLAY WITH MY FOOD.
FTAM
RNCHH
OH, WHAT A TASTY MEAL YOU'RE GOING TO MAKE, SPIDER.
I REALLY MUST TAKE CARE NOT TO GOBBLE YOU ALL UP IN ONE BITE.
SO FAST, I NEVER--I--
I-I SAW THE NEW WORLD... FOUND LOVE... HAD SUCH ADVENTURES...
THIS--THIS CAN'T BE HOW MY STORY--
BELOVED!
URNGH--
SHUNKK

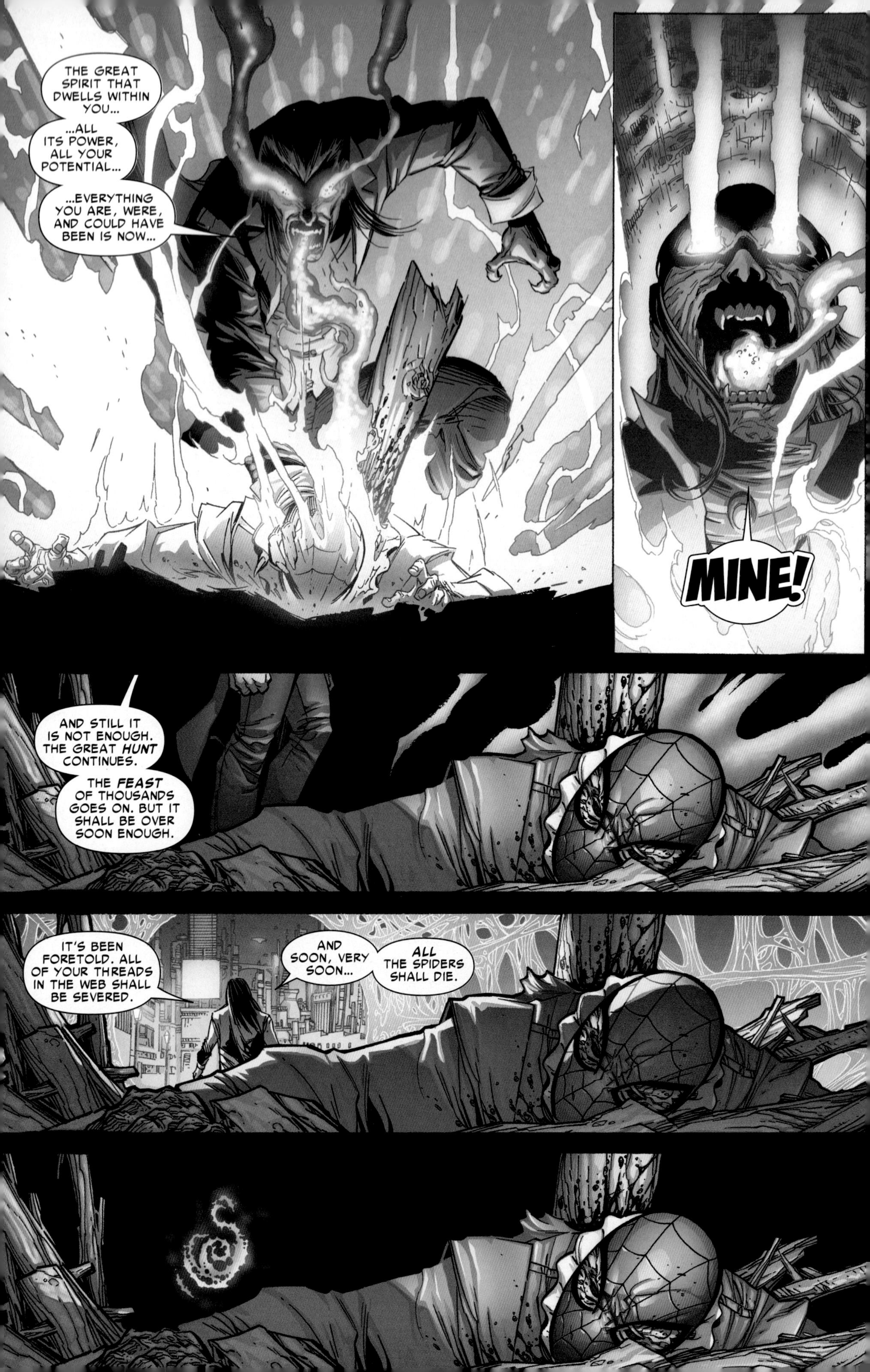
THE GREAT SPIRIT THAT DWELLS WITHIN YOU...
...ALL ITS POWER, ALL YOUR POTENTIAL...
...EVERYTHING YOU ARE, WERE, AND COULD HAVE BEEN IS NOW...
MINE!
AND STILL IT IS NOT ENOUGH. THE GREAT HUNT CONTINUES.
THE FEAST OF THOUSANDS GOES ON. BUT IT SHALL BE OVER SOON ENOUGH.
IT'S BEEN FORETOLD. ALL OF YOUR THREADS IN THE WEB SHALL BE SEVERED.
AND SOON, VERY SOON...
ALL THE SPIDERS SHALL DIE.

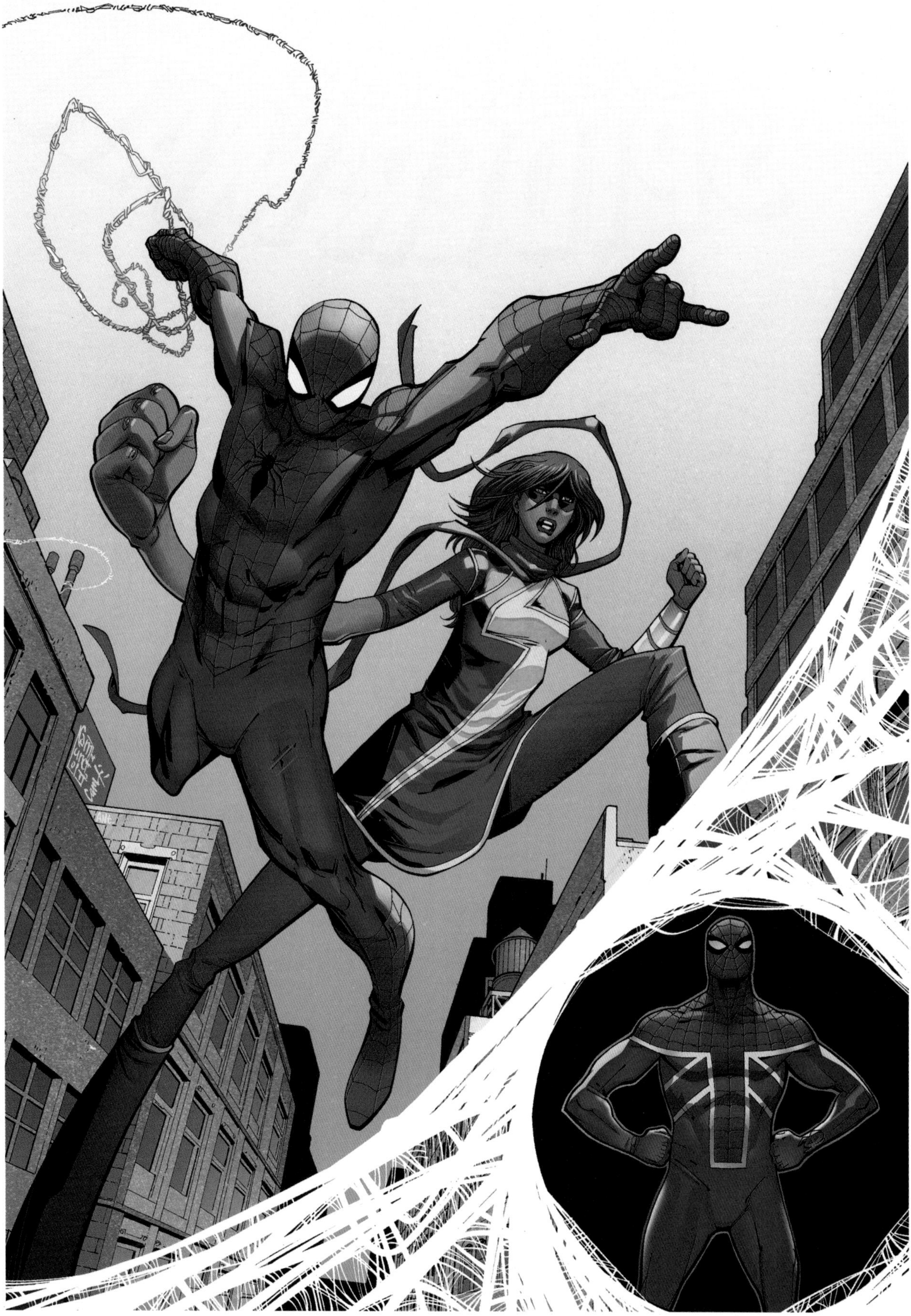

AMAZING SPIDER-MAN 7

Years ago, high school student PETER PARKER was bitten by a radioactive spider and gained the speed, agility, and proportional strength of a spider as well as the ability to stick to walls and a spider-sense that warned him of imminent danger. After learning that with great power there must also come great responsibility, he became the crime-fighting super hero…

the AMAZING SPIDER-MAN

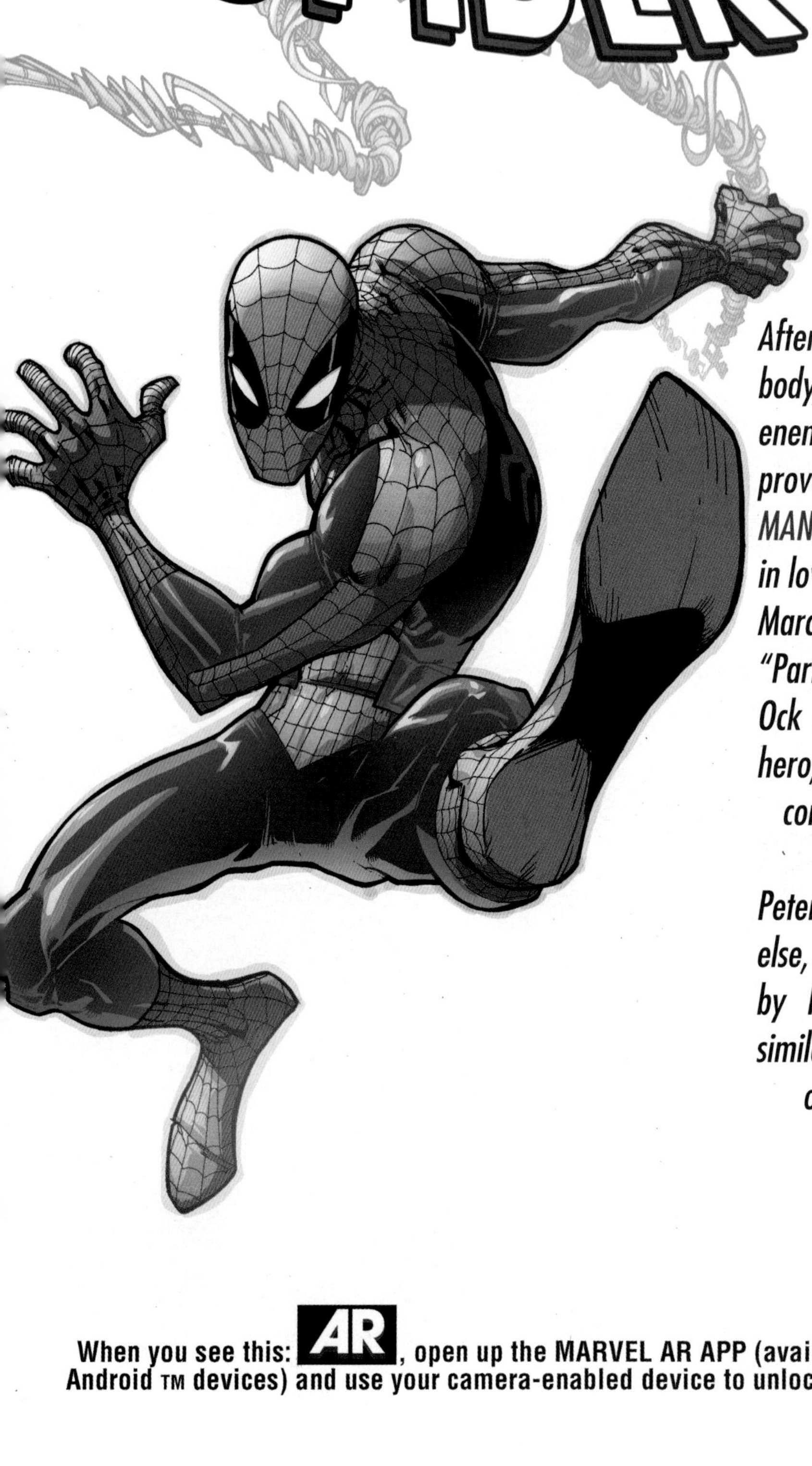

After swapping his mind into Peter's body, one of Spider-Man's greatest enemies, DOCTOR OCTOPUS, set out to prove himself the SUPERIOR SPIDER-MAN. He also completed Peter's PhD, fell in love with a woman named Anna Maria Marconi, and started his own company, "Parker Industries." But in the end Doc Ock realized that in order to be a true hero, he had to sacrifice himself and give control of Peter's body back to Peter.

Peter recently found out that someone else, Cindy Moon A.K.A. SILK, was bitten by his radioactive spider giving her similar powers to Peter. And that's not the only thing they have in common.

When you see this: AR, open up the MARVEL AR APP (available on applicable Apple ® iOS or Android ™ devices) and use your camera-enabled device to unlock extra-special exclusive features!*

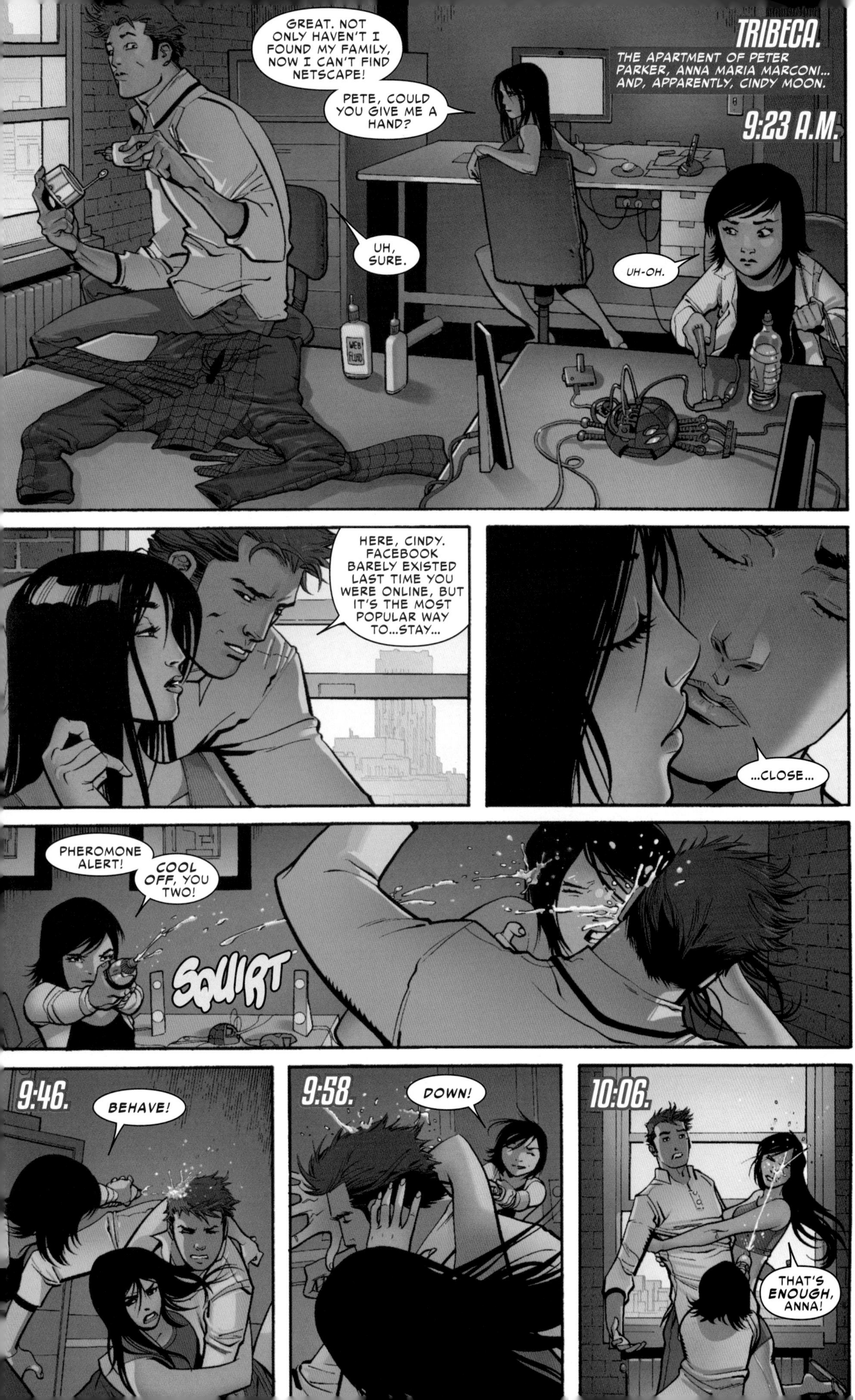
TRIBECA.
THE APARTMENT OF PETER PARKER, ANNA MARIA MARCONI... AND, APPARENTLY, CINDY MOON.
9:23 A.M.
GREAT. NOT ONLY HAVEN'T I FOUND MY FAMILY, NOW I CAN'T FIND NETSCAPE!
PETE, COULD YOU GIVE ME A HAND?
UH, SURE.
UH-OH.
WEB FLUID
HERE, CINDY. FACEBOOK BARELY EXISTED LAST TIME YOU WERE ONLINE, BUT IT'S THE MOST POPULAR WAY TO...STAY...
...CLOSE...
PHEROMONE ALERT!
COOL OFF, YOU TWO!
SQUIRT
9:46.
BEHAVE!
9:58.
DOWN!
10:06.
THAT'S ENOUGH, ANNA!

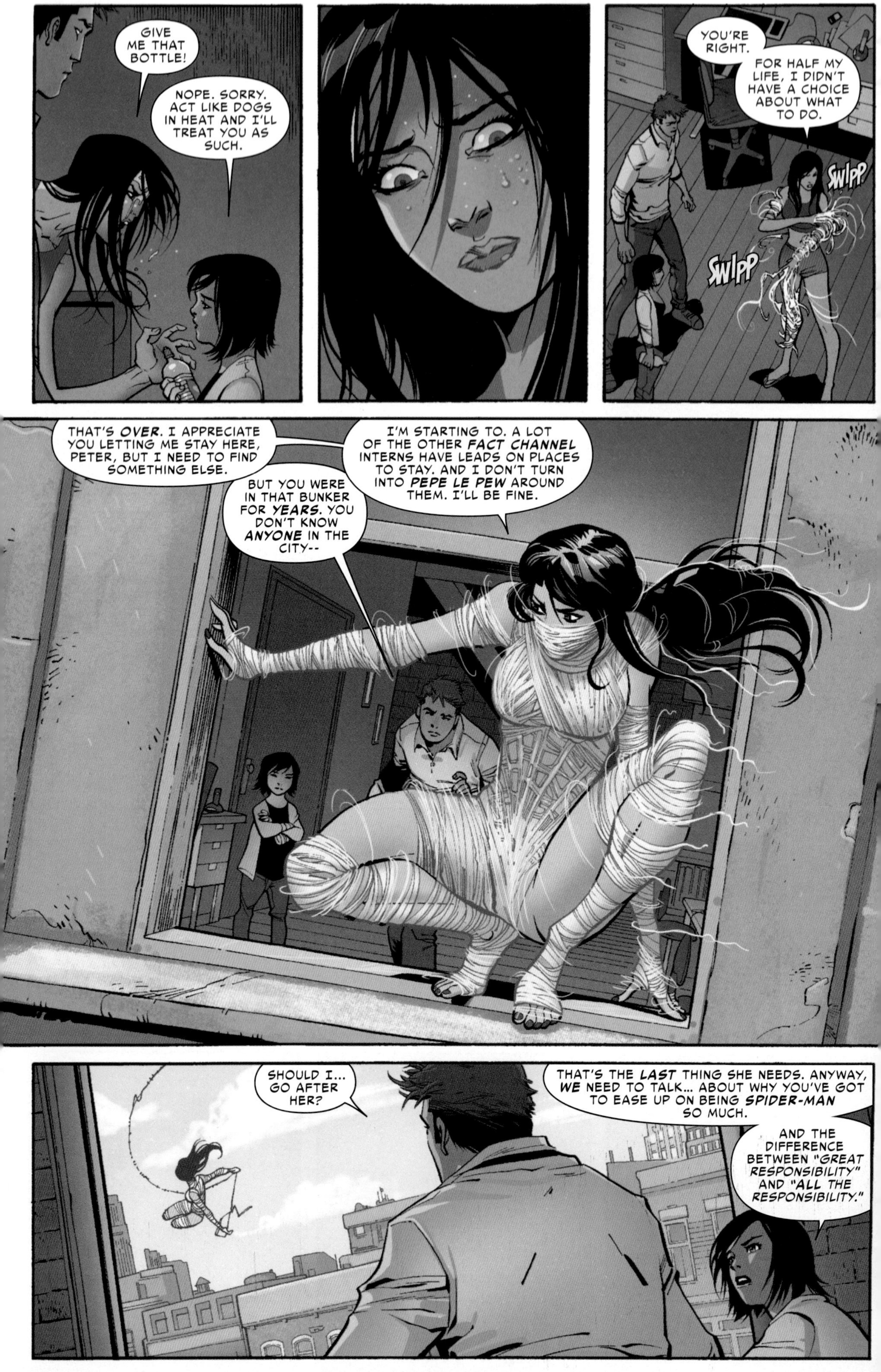
GIVE ME THAT BOTTLE!
NOPE. SORRY. ACT LIKE DOGS IN HEAT AND I'LL TREAT YOU AS SUCH.
YOU'RE RIGHT.
FOR HALF MY LIFE, I DIDN'T HAVE A CHOICE ABOUT WHAT TO DO.
SWIPP
SWIPP
THAT'S OVER. I APPRECIATE YOU LETTING ME STAY HERE, PETER, BUT I NEED TO FIND SOMETHING ELSE.
BUT YOU WERE IN THAT BUNKER FOR YEARS. YOU DON'T KNOW ANYONE IN THE CITY--
I'M STARTING TO. A LOT OF THE OTHER FACT CHANNEL INTERNS HAVE LEADS ON PLACES TO STAY. AND I DON'T TURN INTO PEPE LE PEW AROUND THEM. I'LL BE FINE.
SHOULD I... GO AFTER HER?
THAT'S THE LAST THING SHE NEEDS. ANYWAY, WE NEED TO TALK... ABOUT WHY YOU'VE GOT TO EASE UP ON BEING SPIDER-MAN SO MUCH.
AND THE DIFFERENCE BETWEEN "GREAT RESPONSIBILITY" AND "ALL THE RESPONSIBILITY."

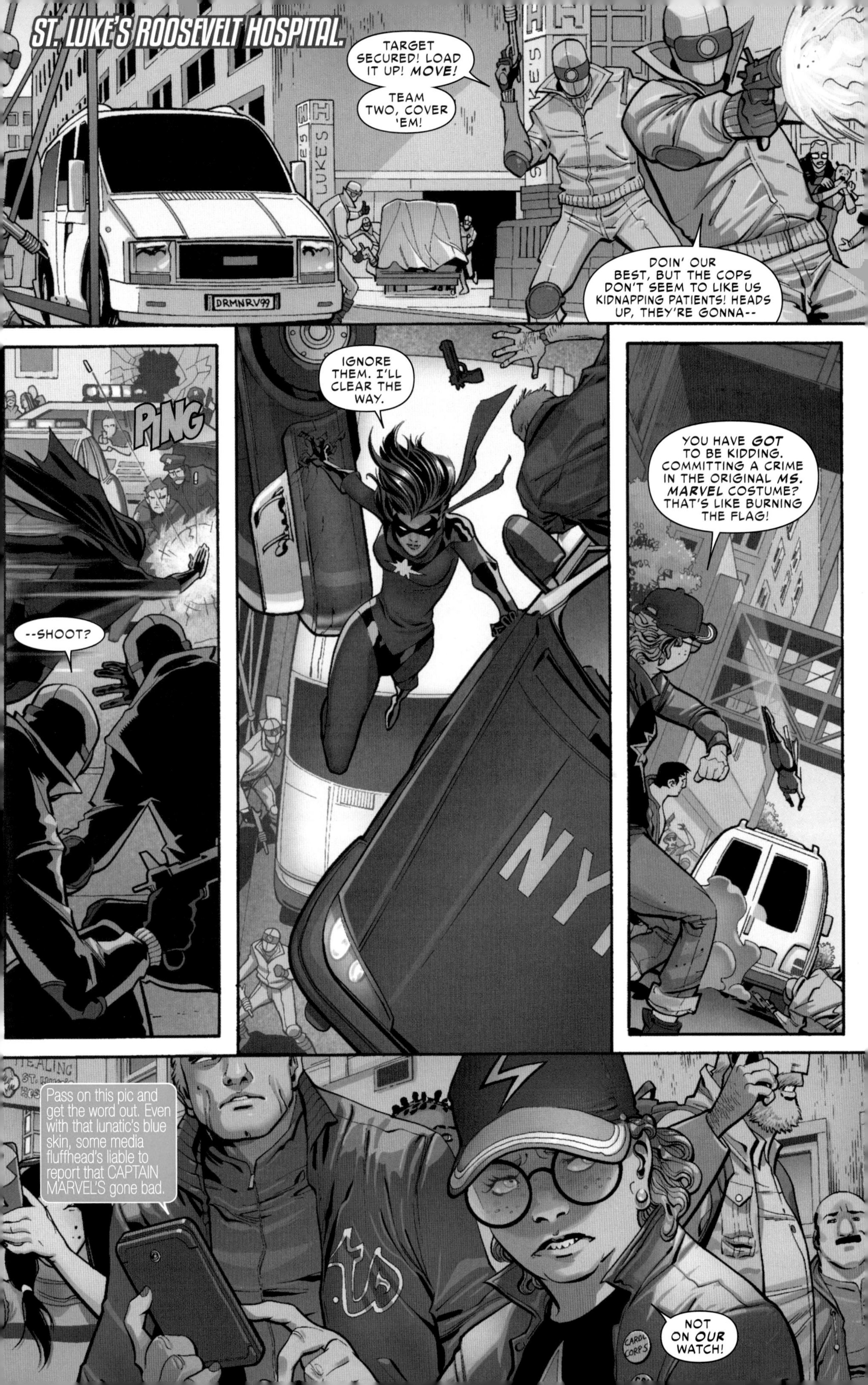
ST. LUKE'S ROOSEVELT HOSPITAL.
TARGET SECURED! LOAD IT UP! MOVE!
TEAM TWO, COVER 'EM!
DOIN' OUR BEST, BUT THE COPS DON'T SEEM TO LIKE US KIDNAPPING PATIENTS! HEADS UP, THEY'RE GONNA--
PING
--SHOOT?
IGNORE THEM. I'LL CLEAR THE WAY.
NY
YOU HAVE GOT TO BE KIDDING. COMMITTING A CRIME IN THE ORIGINAL MS. MARVEL COSTUME? THAT'S LIKE BURNING THE FLAG!
Pass on this pic and get the word out. Even with that lunatic's blue skin, some media fluffhead's liable to report that CAPTAIN MARVEL'S gone bad.
CAROL CORPS
NOT ON OUR WATCH!

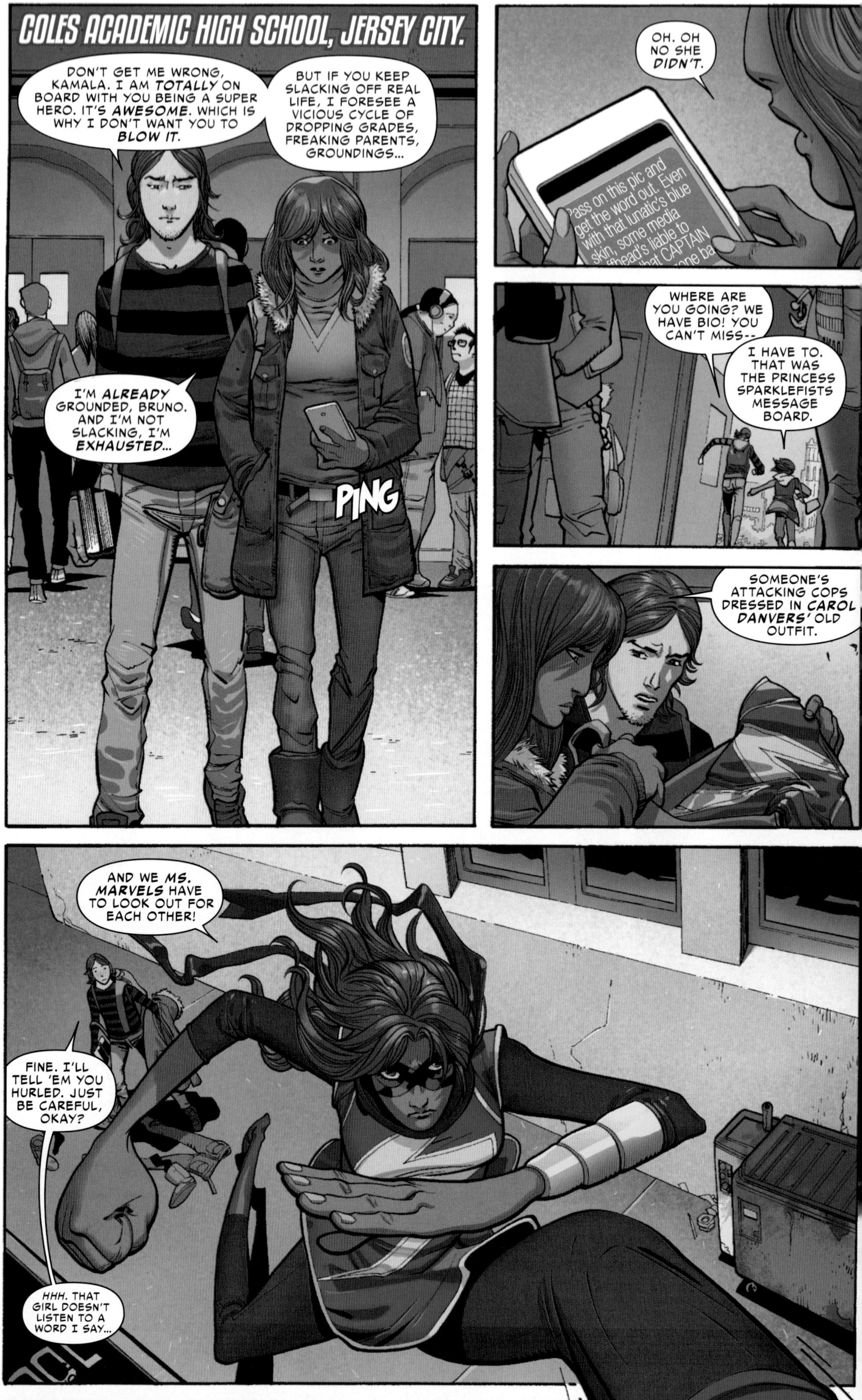
COLES ACADEMIC HIGH SCHOOL, JERSEY CITY.
DON'T GET ME WRONG, KAMALA. I AM TOTALLY ON BOARD WITH YOU BEING A SUPER HERO. IT'S AWESOME. WHICH IS WHY I DON'T WANT YOU TO BLOW IT.
BUT IF YOU KEEP SLACKING OFF REAL LIFE, I FORESEE A VICIOUS CYCLE OF DROPPING GRADES, FREAKING PARENTS, GROUNDINGS...
I'M ALREADY GROUNDED, BRUNO. AND I'M NOT SLACKING, I'M EXHAUSTED...
PING
OH. OH NO SHE DIDN'T.
Pass on this pic and get the word out. Even with that lunatic's blue skin, some media
WHERE ARE YOU GOING? WE HAVE BIO! YOU CAN'T MISS--
I HAVE TO. THAT WAS THE PRINCESS SPARKLEFISTS MESSAGE BOARD.
SOMEONE'S ATTACKING COPS DRESSED IN CAROL DANVERS' OLD OUTFIT.
AND WE MS. MARVELS HAVE TO LOOK OUT FOR EACH OTHER!
FINE. I'LL TELL 'EM YOU HURLED. JUST BE CAREFUL, OKAY?
HHH. THAT GIRL DOESN'T LISTEN TO A WORD I SAY...

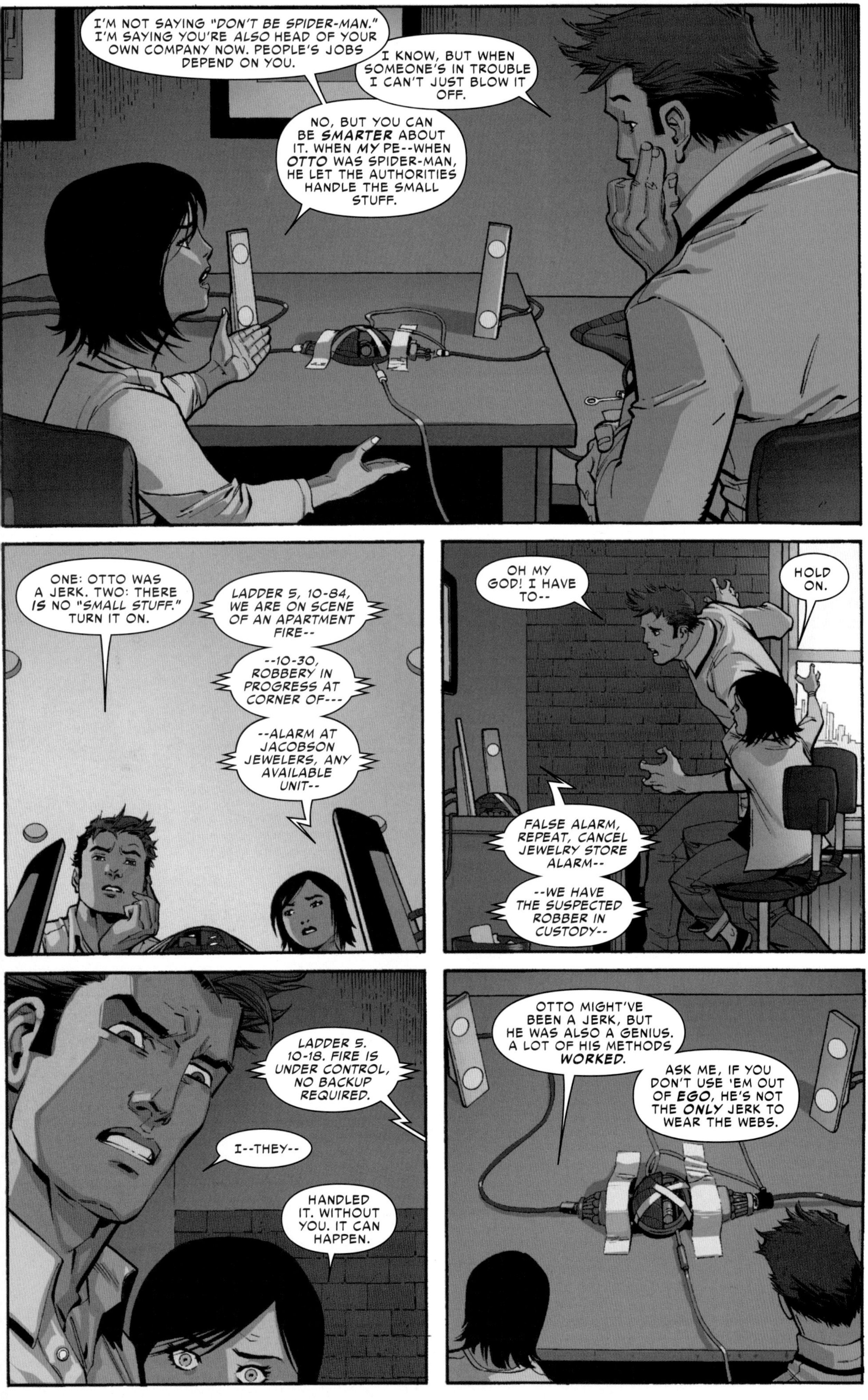
I'M NOT SAYING "DON'T BE SPIDER-MAN." I'M SAYING YOU'RE ALSO HEAD OF YOUR OWN COMPANY NOW. PEOPLE'S JOBS DEPEND ON YOU.
I KNOW, BUT WHEN SOMEONE'S IN TROUBLE I CAN'T JUST BLOW IT OFF.
NO, BUT YOU CAN BE SMARTER ABOUT IT. WHEN MY PE--WHEN OTTO WAS SPIDER-MAN, HE LET THE AUTHORITIES HANDLE THE SMALL STUFF.
ONE: OTTO WAS A JERK. TWO: THERE IS NO "SMALL STUFF." TURN IT ON.
LADDER 5, 10-84, WE ARE ON SCENE OF AN APARTMENT FIRE--
--10-30, ROBBERY IN PROGRESS AT CORNER OF---
--ALARM AT JACOBSON JEWELERS, ANY AVAILABLE UNIT--
OH MY GOD! I HAVE TO--
HOLD ON.
FALSE ALARM, REPEAT, CANCEL JEWELRY STORE ALARM--
--WE HAVE THE SUSPECTED ROBBER IN CUSTODY--
LADDER 5. 10-18. FIRE IS UNDER CONTROL, NO BACKUP REQUIRED.
I--THEY--
HANDLED IT. WITHOUT YOU. IT CAN HAPPEN.
OTTO MIGHT'VE BEEN A JERK, BUT HE WAS ALSO A GENIUS. A LOT OF HIS METHODS WORKED.
ASK ME, IF YOU DON'T USE 'EM OUT OF EGO, HE'S NOT THE ONLY JERK TO WEAR THE WEBS.

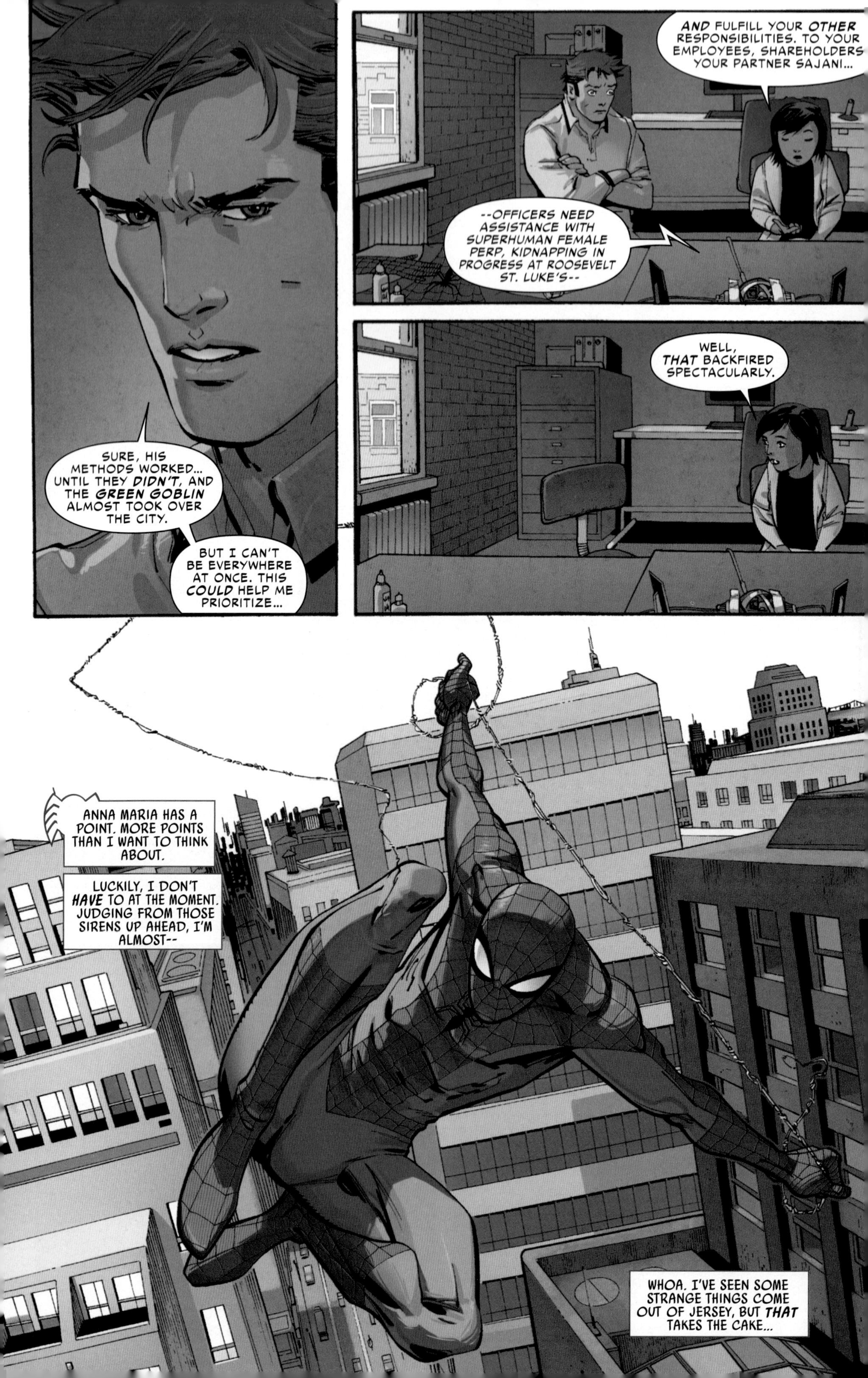

SURE, HIS METHODS WORKED... UNTIL THEY DIDN'T, AND THE GREEN GOBLIN ALMOST TOOK OVER THE CITY.
BUT I CAN'T BE EVERYWHERE AT ONCE. THIS COULD HELP ME PRIORITIZE...
AND FULFILL YOUR OTHER RESPONSIBILITIES. TO YOUR EMPLOYEES, SHAREHOLDERS YOUR PARTNER SAJANI...
--OFFICERS NEED ASSISTANCE WITH SUPERHUMAN FEMALE PERP, KIDNAPPING IN PROGRESS AT ROOSEVELT ST. LUKE'S--
WELL, THAT BACKFIRED SPECTACULARLY.
ANNA MARIA HAS A POINT. MORE POINTS THAN I WANT TO THINK ABOUT.
LUCKILY, I DON'T HAVE TO AT THE MOMENT. JUDGING FROM THOSE SIRENS UP AHEAD, I'M ALMOST--
WHOA. I'VE SEEN SOME STRANGE THINGS COME OUT OF JERSEY, BUT THAT TAKES THE CAKE...

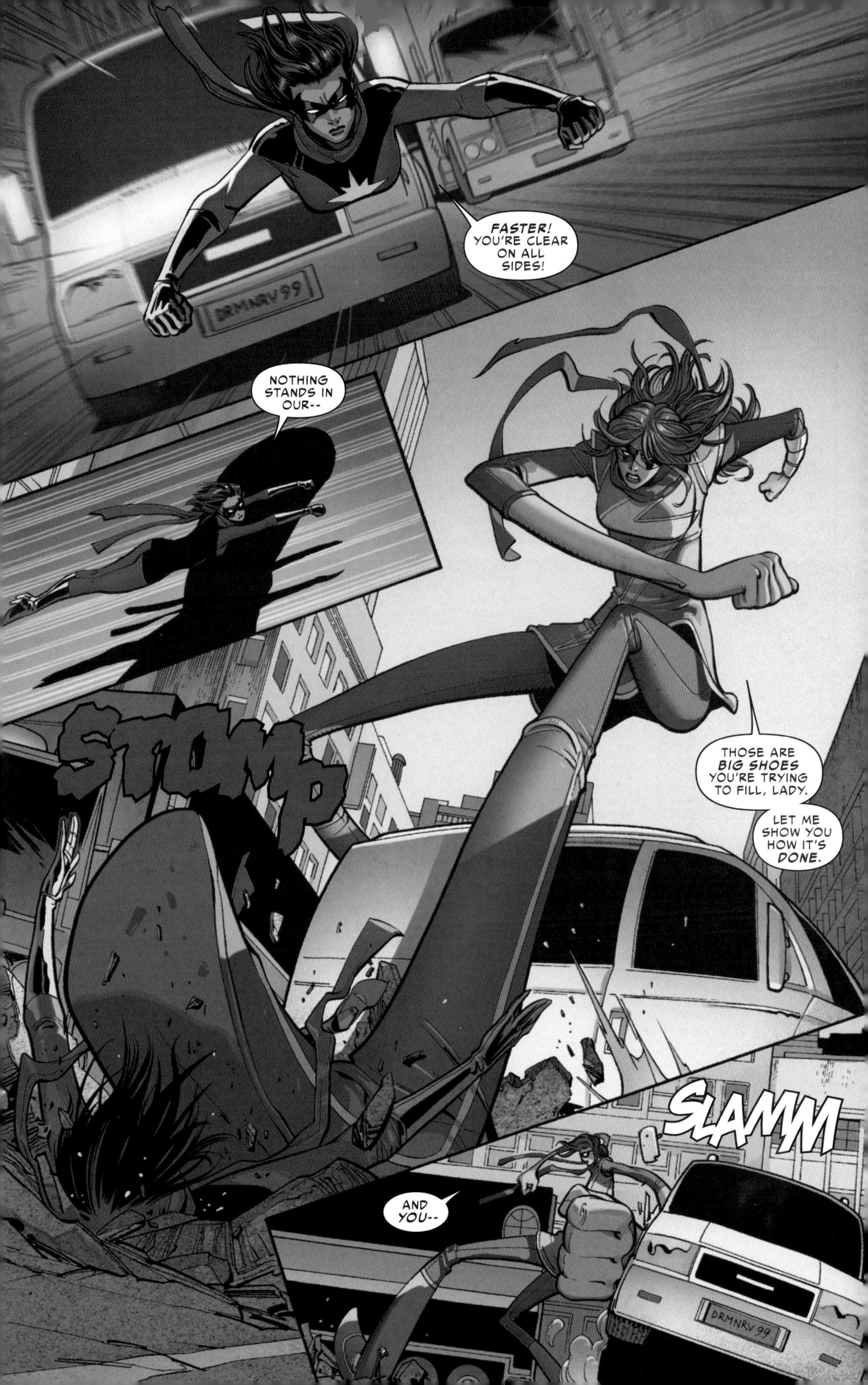
FASTER! YOU'RE CLEAR ON ALL SIDES!
DRMNRV 99
NOTHING STANDS IN OUR--
STOMP
THOSE ARE BIG SHOES YOU'RE TRYING TO FILL, LADY.
LET ME SHOW YOU HOW IT'S DONE.
SLAMM
AND YOU--
DRMNRV 99

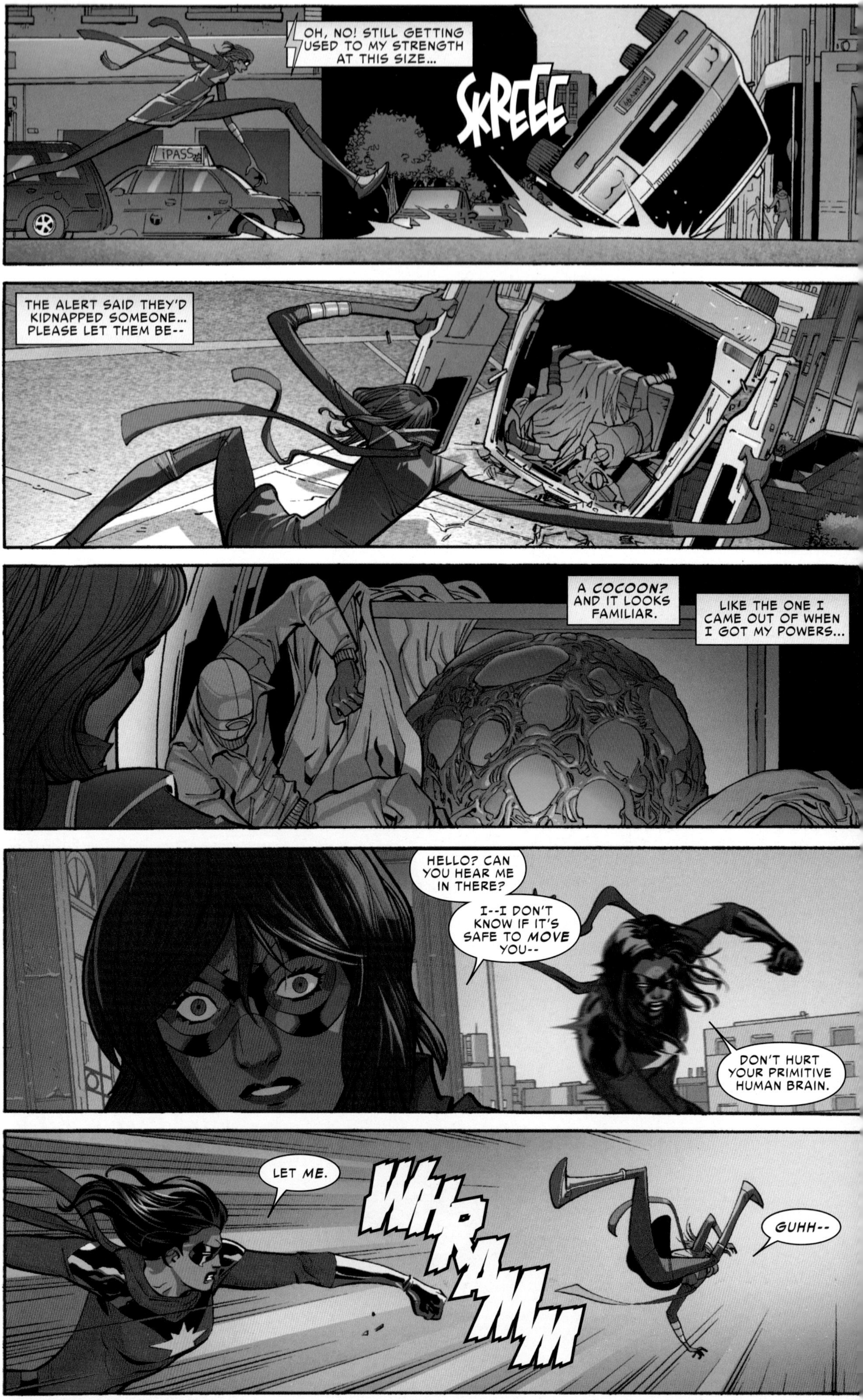
OH, NO! STILL GETTING USED TO MY STRENGTH AT THIS SIZE...
SKREEE
THE ALERT SAID THEY'D KIDNAPPED SOMEONE... PLEASE LET THEM BE--
A COCOON? AND IT LOOKS FAMILIAR.
LIKE THE ONE I CAME OUT OF WHEN I GOT MY POWERS...
HELLO? CAN YOU HEAR ME IN THERE?
I--I DON'T KNOW IF IT'S SAFE TO MOVE YOU--
DON'T HURT YOUR PRIMITIVE HUMAN BRAIN.
LET ME.
WHRAMMM
GUHH--

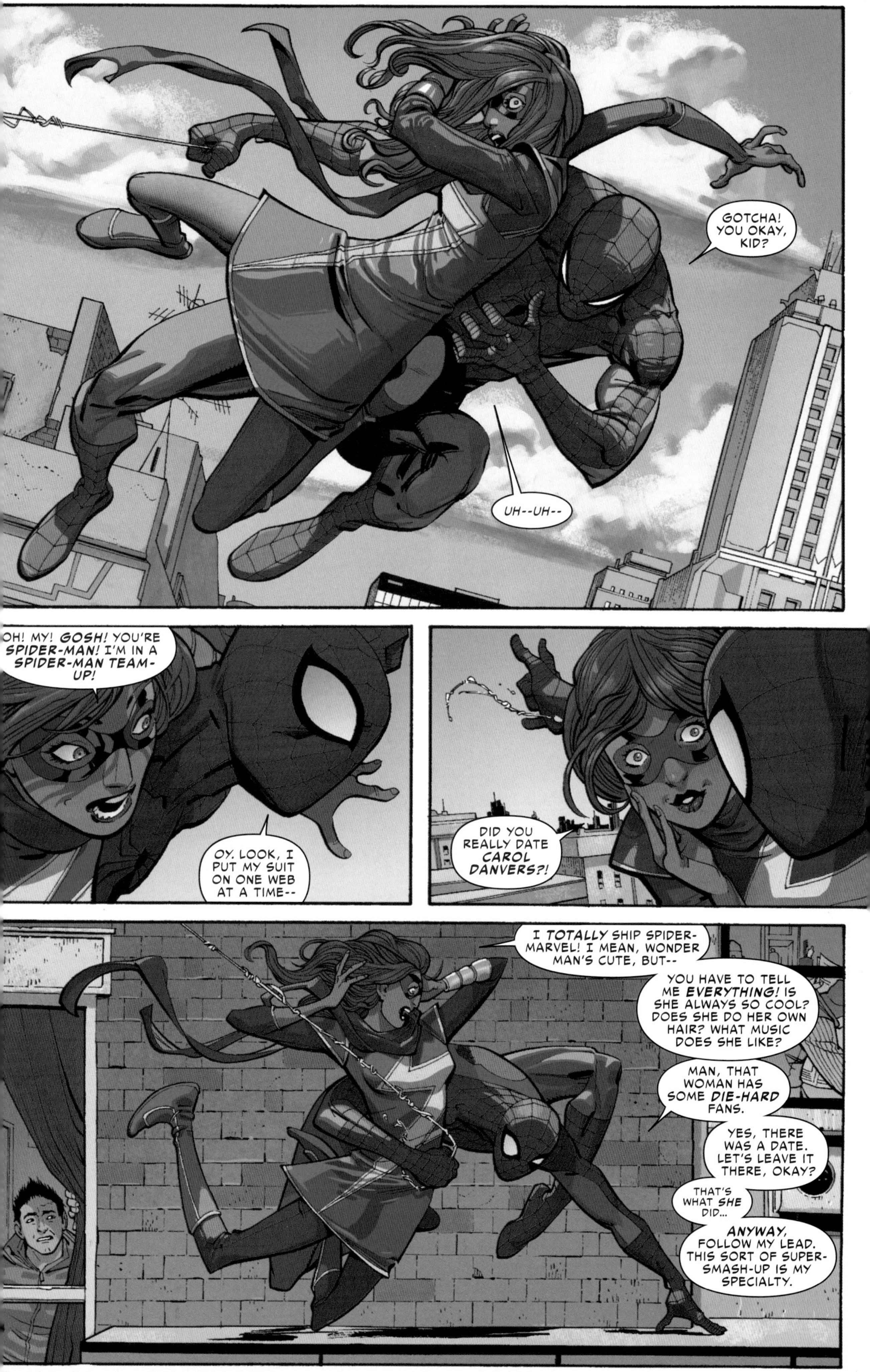
GOTCHA! YOU OKAY, KID?
UH--UH--
OH! MY! GOSH! YOU'RE SPIDER-MAN! I'M IN A SPIDER-MAN TEAM-UP!
OY. LOOK, I PUT MY SUIT ON ONE WEB AT A TIME--
DID YOU REALLY DATE CAROL DANVERS?!
I TOTALLY SHIP SPIDER-MARVEL! I MEAN, WONDER MAN'S CUTE, BUT--
YOU HAVE TO TELL ME EVERYTHING! IS SHE ALWAYS SO COOL? DOES SHE DO HER OWN HAIR? WHAT MUSIC DOES SHE LIKE?
MAN, THAT WOMAN HAS SOME DIE-HARD FANS.
YES, THERE WAS A DATE. LET'S LEAVE IT THERE, OKAY?
THAT'S WHAT SHE DID...
ANYWAY, FOLLOW MY LEAD. THIS SORT OF SUPER-SMASH-UP IS MY SPECIALTY.

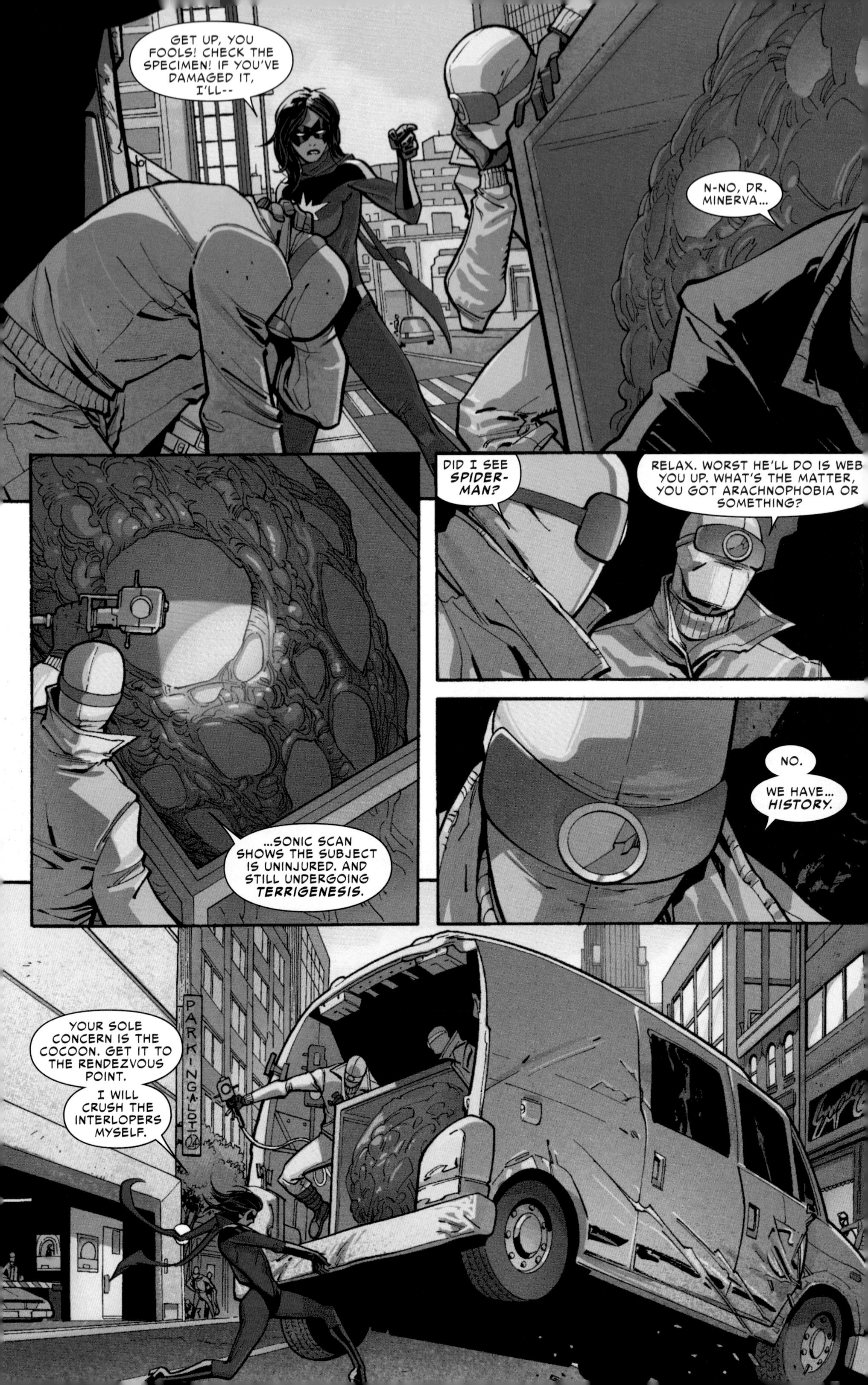
GET UP, YOU FOOLS! CHECK THE SPECIMEN! IF YOU'VE DAMAGED IT, I'LL--
N-NO, DR. MINERVA...
...SONIC SCAN SHOWS THE SUBJECT IS UNINJURED. AND STILL UNDERGOING TERRIGENESIS.
DID I SEE SPIDER-MAN?
RELAX. WORST HE'LL DO IS WEB YOU UP. WHAT'S THE MATTER, YOU GOT ARACHNOPHOBIA OR SOMETHING?
NO.
WE HAVE... HISTORY.
YOUR SOLE CONCERN IS THE COCOON. GET IT TO THE RENDEZVOUS POINT.
I WILL CRUSH THE INTERLOPERS MYSELF.
PARKING LOT
24

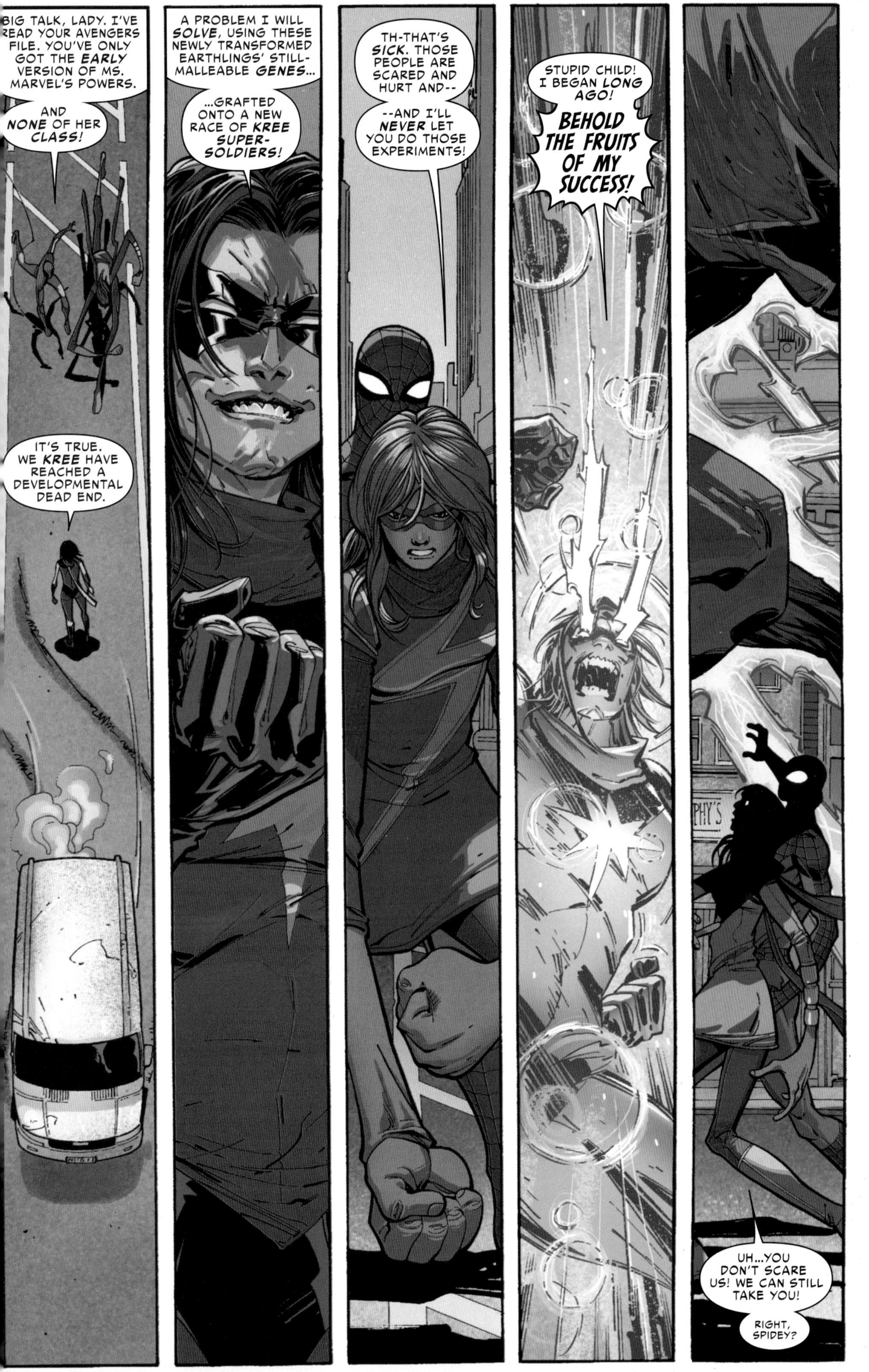
BIG TALK, LADY. I'VE READ YOUR AVENGERS FILE. YOU'VE ONLY GOT THE EARLY VERSION OF MS. MARVEL'S POWERS.
AND NONE OF HER CLASS!
IT'S TRUE. WE KREE HAVE REACHED A DEVELOPMENTAL DEAD END.
A PROBLEM I WILL SOLVE, USING THESE NEWLY TRANSFORMED EARTHLINGS' STILL-MALLEABLE GENES...
...GRAFTED ONTO A NEW RACE OF KREE SUPER-SOLDIERS!
TH-THAT'S SICK. THOSE PEOPLE ARE SCARED AND HURT AND--
--AND I'LL NEVER LET YOU DO THOSE EXPERIMENTS!
STUPID CHILD! I BEGAN LONG AGO!
BEHOLD THE FRUITS OF MY SUCCESS!
UH...YOU DON'T SCARE US! WE CAN STILL TAKE YOU!
RIGHT, SPIDEY?

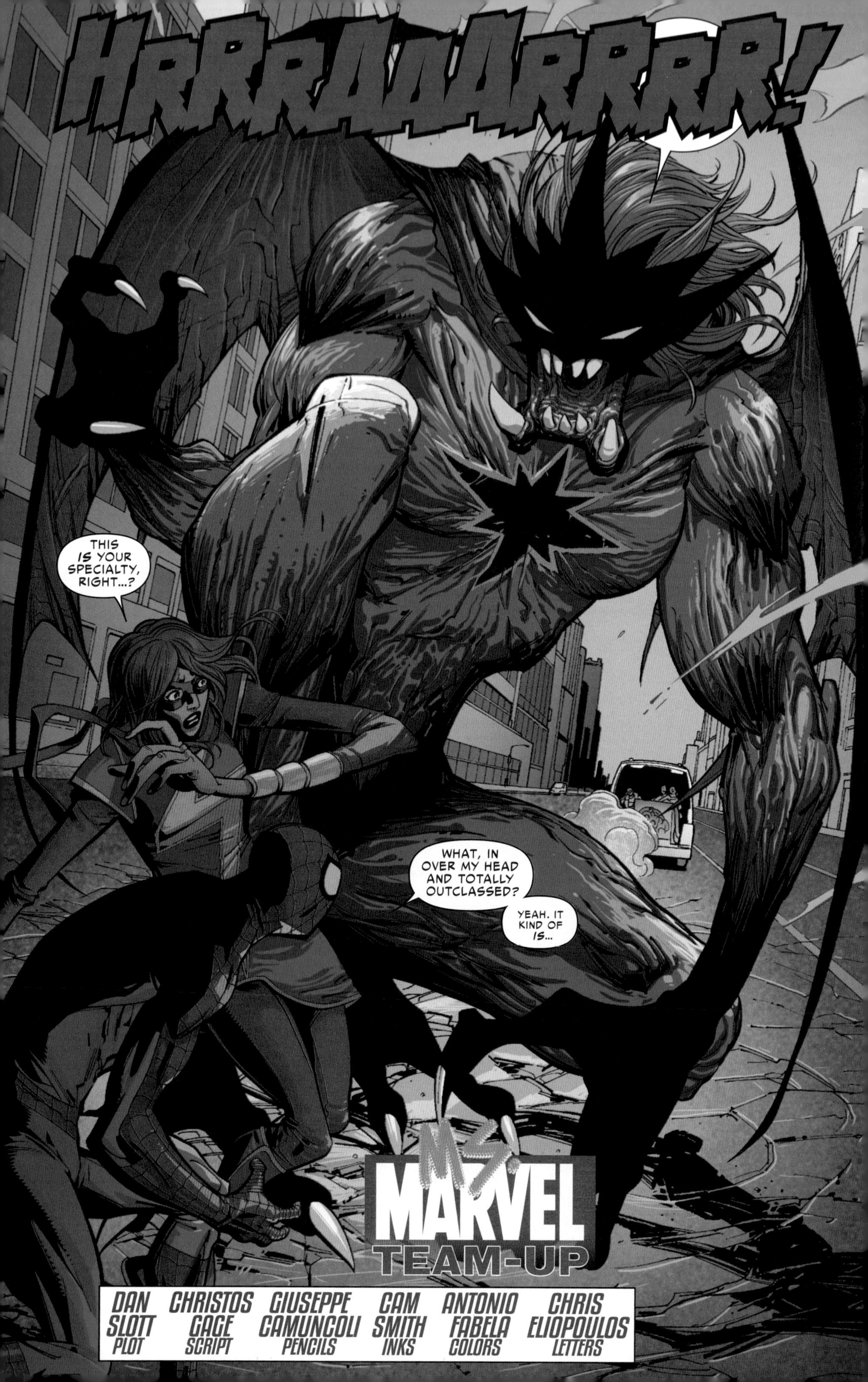
HRRRAWARRRR!
THIS IS YOUR SPECIALTY, RIGHT...?
WHAT, IN OVER MY HEAD AND TOTALLY OUTCLASSED?
YEAH. IT KIND OF IS...
MS. MARVEL TEAM-UP
DAN SLOTT PLOT
CHRISTOS GAGE SCRIPT
GIUSEPPE CAMUNCOLI PENCILS
CAM SMITH INKS
ANTONIO FABELA COLORS
CHRIS ELIOPOULOS LETTERS

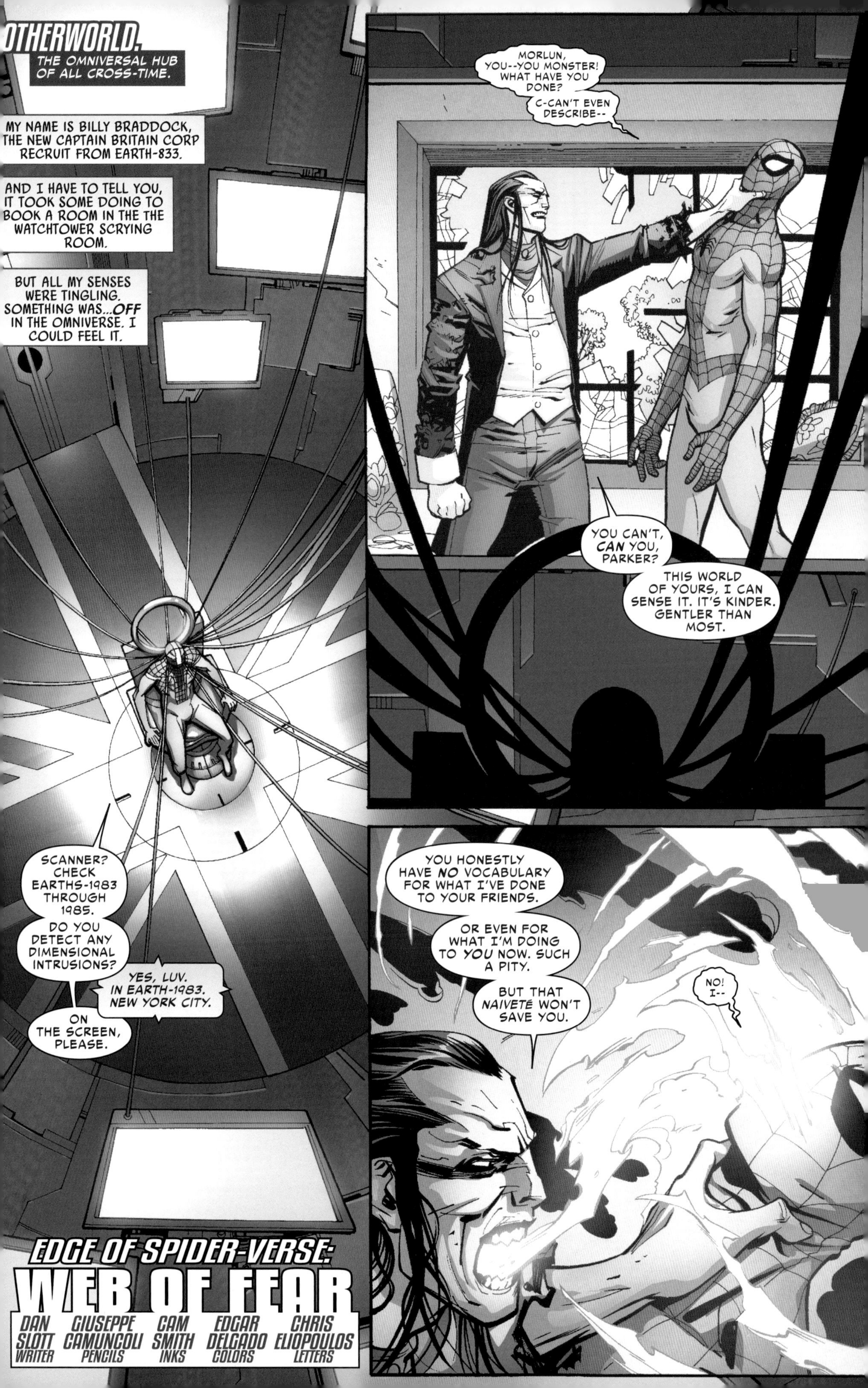
OTHERWORLD.
THE OMNIVERSAL HUB OF ALL CROSS-TIME.
MY NAME IS BILLY BRADDOCK, THE NEW CAPTAIN BRITAIN CORP RECRUIT FROM EARTH-833.
AND I HAVE TO TELL YOU, IT TOOK SOME DOING TO BOOK A ROOM IN THE THE WATCHTOWER SCRYING ROOM.
BUT ALL MY SENSES WERE TINGLING. SOMETHING WAS...OFF IN THE OMNIVERSE. I COULD FEEL IT.
SCANNER? CHECK EARTHS-1983 THROUGH 1985.
DO YOU DETECT ANY DIMENSIONAL INTRUSIONS?
YES, LUV. IN EARTH-1983. NEW YORK CITY.
ON THE SCREEN, PLEASE.
EDGE OF SPIDER-VERSE:
WEB OF FEAR
DAN SLOTT WRITER
GIUSEPPE CAMUNCOLI PENCILS
CAM SMITH INKS
EDGAR DELGADO COLORS
CHRIS ELIOPOULOS LETTERS
MORLUN, YOU--YOU MONSTER! WHAT HAVE YOU DONE?
C-CAN'T EVEN DESCRIBE--
YOU CAN'T, CAN YOU, PARKER?
THIS WORLD OF YOURS, I CAN SENSE IT. IT'S KINDER. GENTLER THAN MOST.
YOU HONESTLY HAVE NO VOCABULARY FOR WHAT I'VE DONE TO YOUR FRIENDS.
OR EVEN FOR WHAT I'M DOING TO YOU NOW. SUCH A PITY.
BUT THAT NAIVETÉ WON'T SAVE YOU.
NO! I--

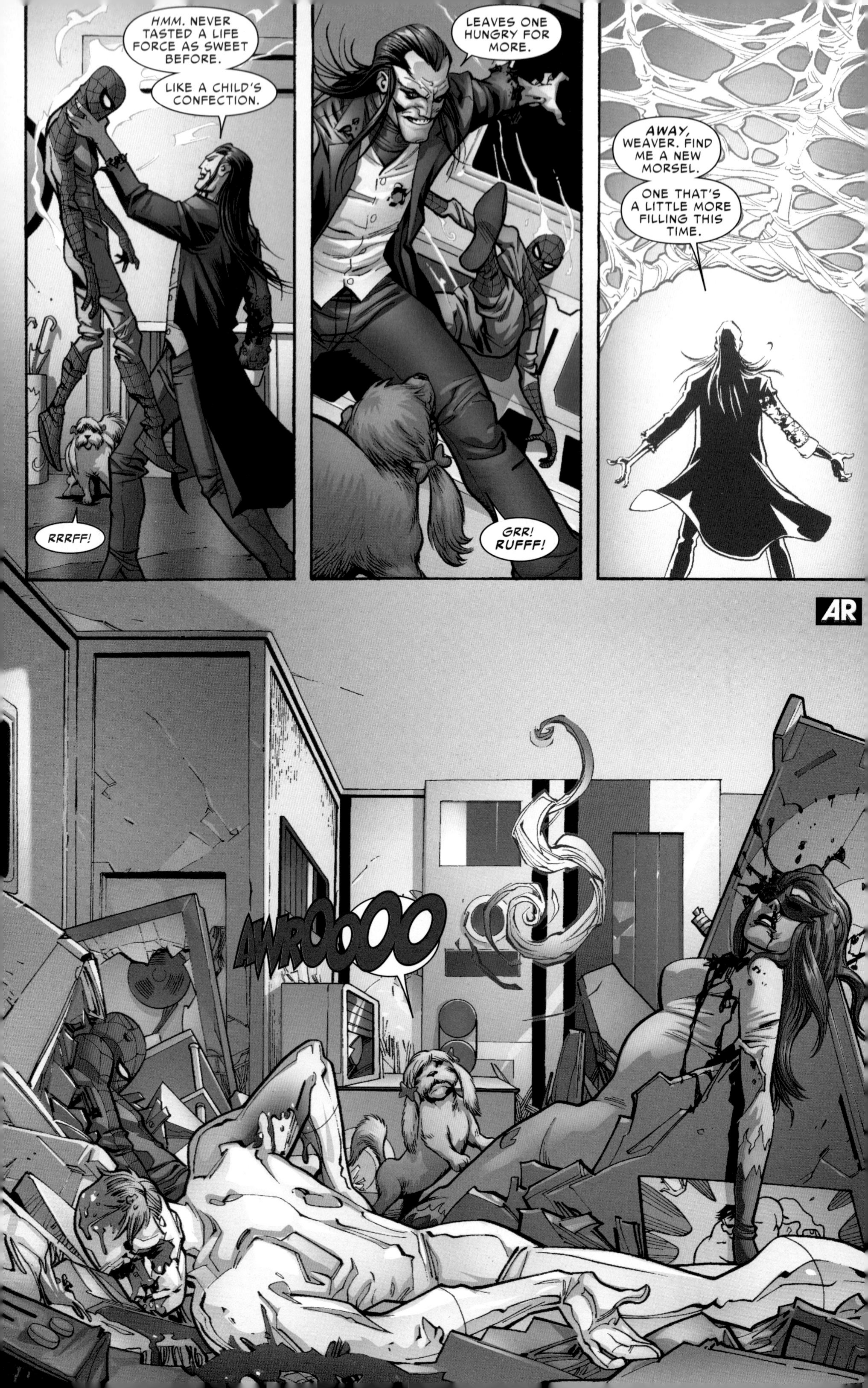
HMM. NEVER TASTED A LIFE FORCE AS SWEET BEFORE.
LIKE A CHILD'S CONFECTION.
RRRFF!
LEAVES ONE HUNGRY FOR MORE.
GRR! RUFFF!
AWAY, WEAVER. FIND ME A NEW MORSEL.
ONE THAT'S A LITTLE MORE FILLING THIS TIME.
AR
AWROOOO

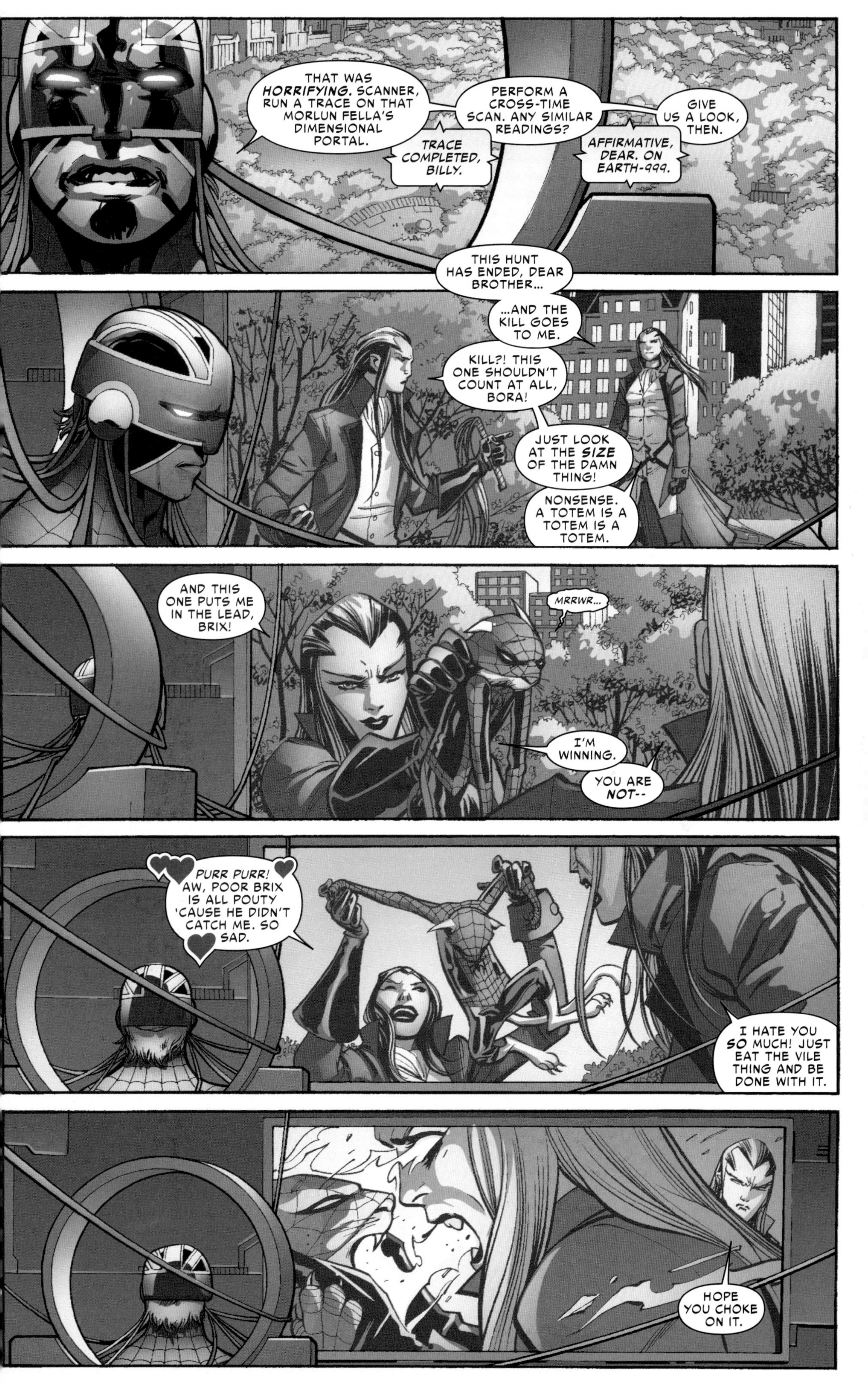
THAT WAS HORRIFYING. SCANNER, RUN A TRACE ON THAT MORLUN FELLA'S DIMENSIONAL PORTAL.
TRACE COMPLETED, BILLY.
PERFORM A CROSS-TIME SCAN. ANY SIMILAR READINGS?
AFFIRMATIVE, DEAR. ON EARTH-999.
GIVE US A LOOK, THEN.
THIS HUNT HAS ENDED, DEAR BROTHER...
...AND THE KILL GOES TO ME.
KILL?! THIS ONE SHOULDN'T COUNT AT ALL, BORA!
JUST LOOK AT THE SIZE OF THE DAMN THING!
NONSENSE. A TOTEM IS A TOTEM IS A TOTEM.
AND THIS ONE PUTS ME IN THE LEAD, BRIX!
MRRWR...
I'M WINNING.
YOU ARE NOT--
PURR PURR! AW, POOR BRIX IS ALL POUTY 'CAUSE HE DIDN'T CATCH ME. SO SAD.
I HATE YOU SO MUCH! JUST EAT THE VILE THING AND BE DONE WITH IT.
HOPE YOU CHOKE ON IT.

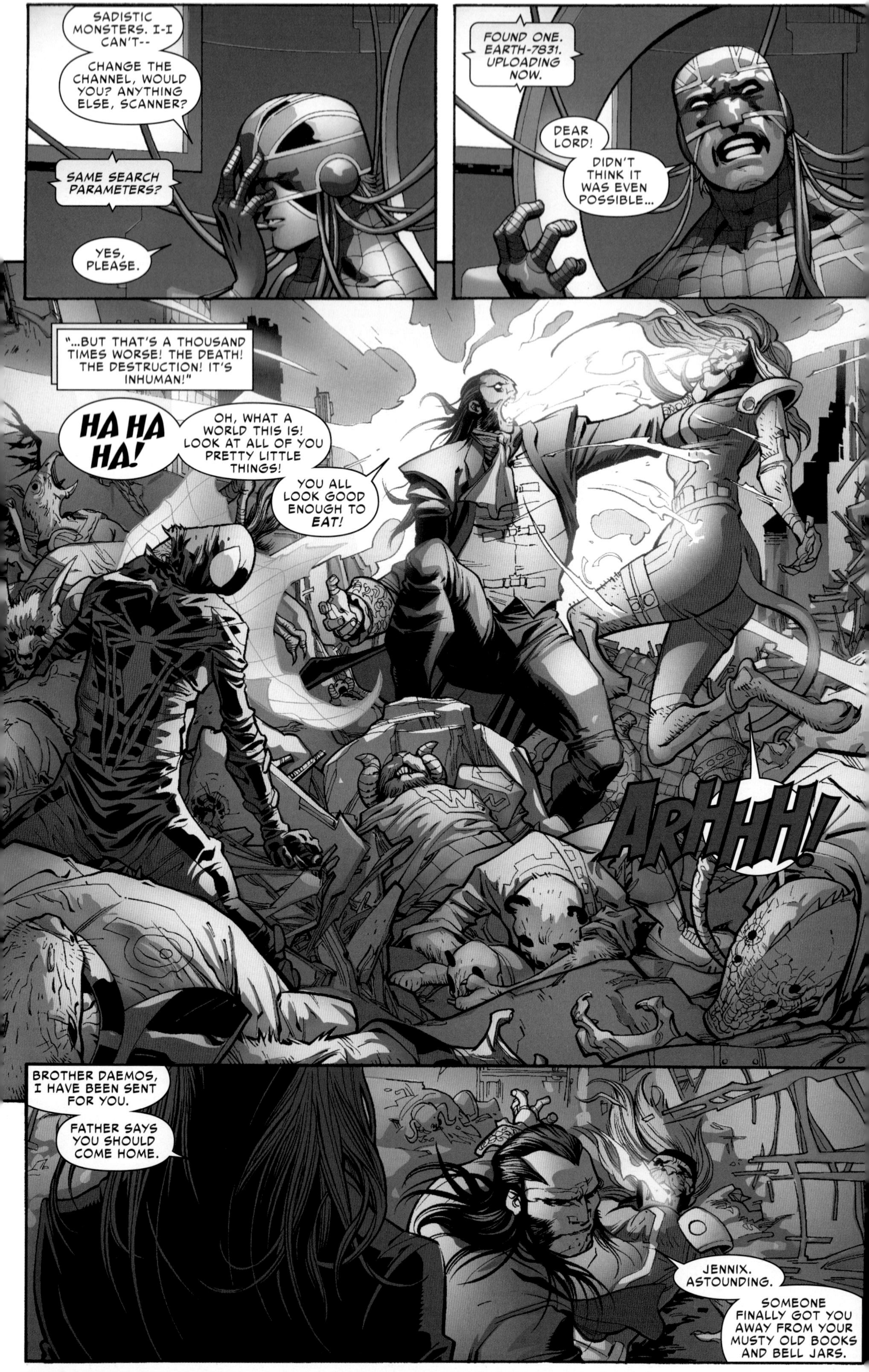
SADISTIC MONSTERS. I-I CAN'T--
CHANGE THE CHANNEL, WOULD YOU? ANYTHING ELSE, SCANNER?
SAME SEARCH PARAMETERS?
YES, PLEASE.
FOUND ONE. EARTH-7831. UPLOADING NOW.
DEAR LORD!
DIDN'T THINK IT WAS EVEN POSSIBLE...
"...BUT THAT'S A THOUSAND TIMES WORSE! THE DEATH! THE DESTRUCTION! IT'S INHUMAN!"
HA HA HA!
OH, WHAT A WORLD THIS IS! LOOK AT ALL OF YOU PRETTY LITTLE THINGS!
YOU ALL LOOK GOOD ENOUGH TO EAT!
ARHHH!
BROTHER DAEMOS, I HAVE BEEN SENT FOR YOU.
FATHER SAYS YOU SHOULD COME HOME.
JENNIX. ASTOUNDING.
SOMEONE FINALLY GOT YOU AWAY FROM YOUR MUSTY OLD BOOKS AND BELL JARS.

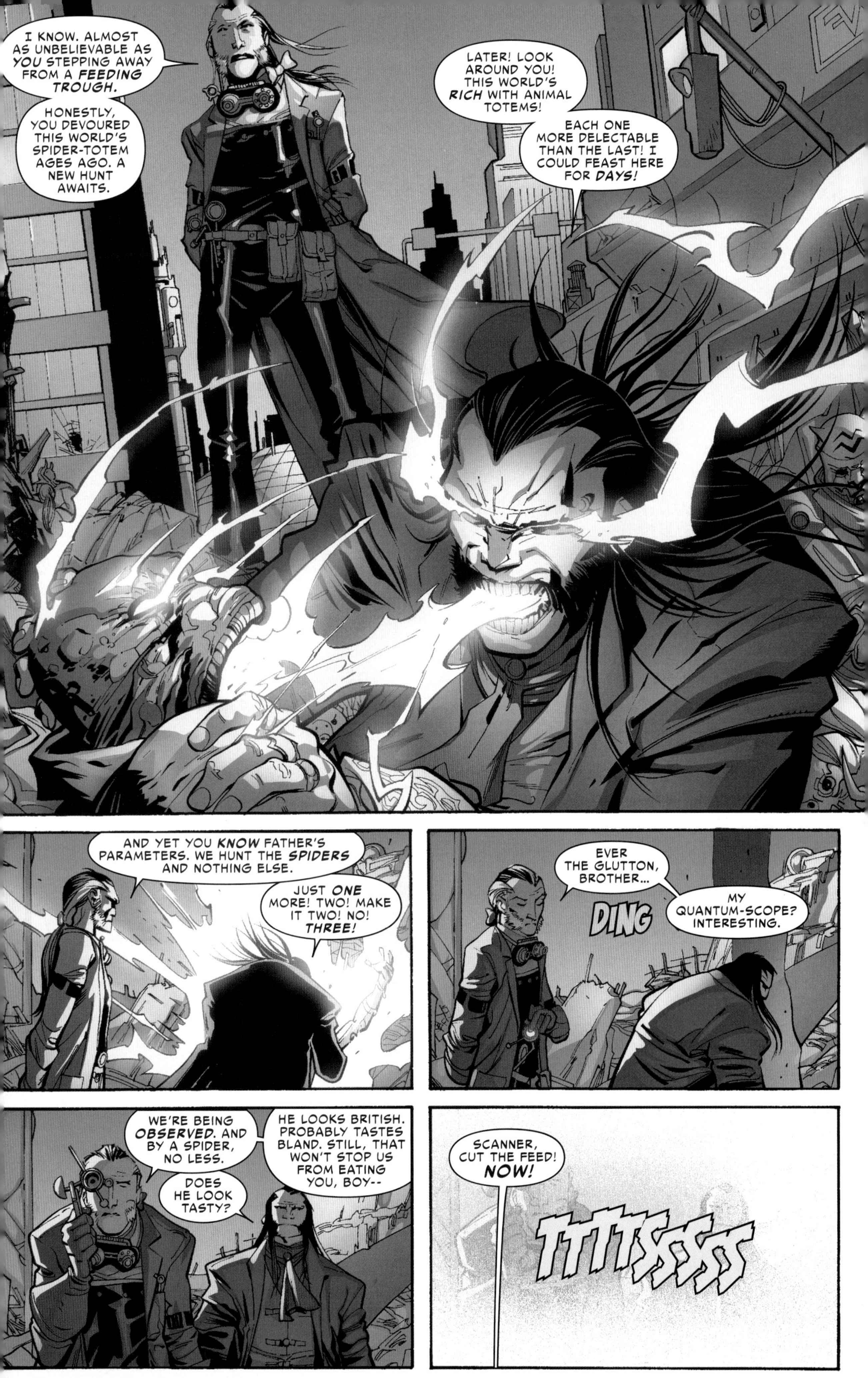
I KNOW. ALMOST AS UNBELIEVABLE AS *YOU* STEPPING AWAY FROM A *FEEDING TROUGH.*
HONESTLY, YOU DEVOURED THIS WORLD'S SPIDER-TOTEM AGES AGO. A NEW HUNT AWAITS.
LATER! LOOK AROUND YOU! THIS WORLD'S *RICH* WITH ANIMAL TOTEMS!
EACH ONE MORE DELECTABLE THAN THE LAST! I COULD FEAST HERE FOR *DAYS!*
AND YET YOU *KNOW* FATHER'S PARAMETERS. WE HUNT THE *SPIDERS* AND NOTHING ELSE.
JUST *ONE* MORE! TWO! MAKE IT TWO! NO! *THREE!*
EVER THE GLUTTON, BROTHER...
DING
MY QUANTUM-SCOPE? INTERESTING.
WE'RE BEING *OBSERVED.* AND BY A SPIDER, NO LESS.
DOES HE LOOK TASTY?
HE LOOKS BRITISH. PROBABLY TASTES BLAND. STILL, THAT WON'T STOP US FROM EATING YOU, BOY--
SCANNER, CUT THE FEED! *NOW!*
TTTTSSSSS

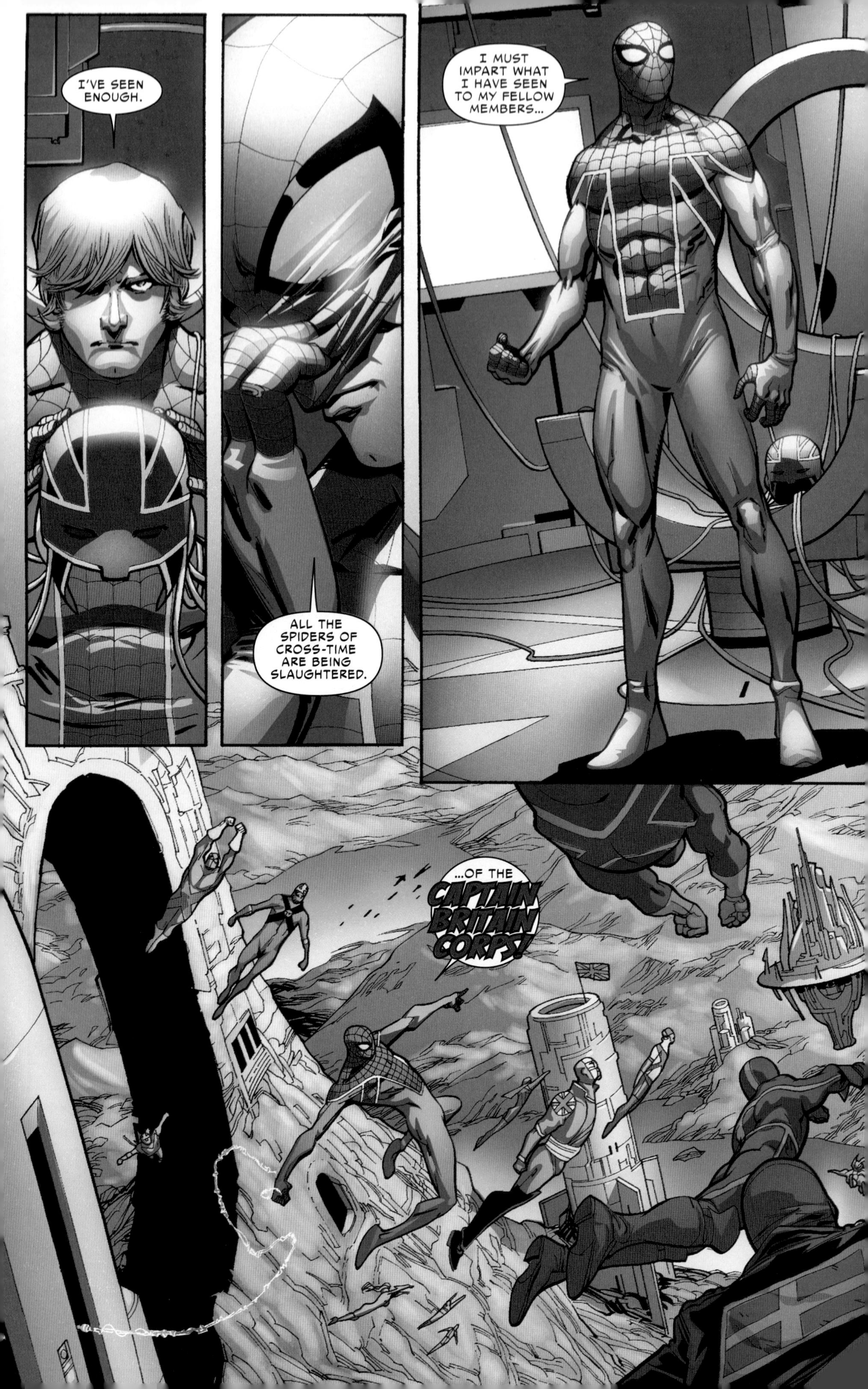
I'VE SEEN ENOUGH.
ALL THE SPIDERS OF CROSS-TIME ARE BEING SLAUGHTERED.
I MUST IMPART WHAT I HAVE SEEN TO MY FELLOW MEMBERS...
...OF THE CAPTAIN BRITAIN CORPS!

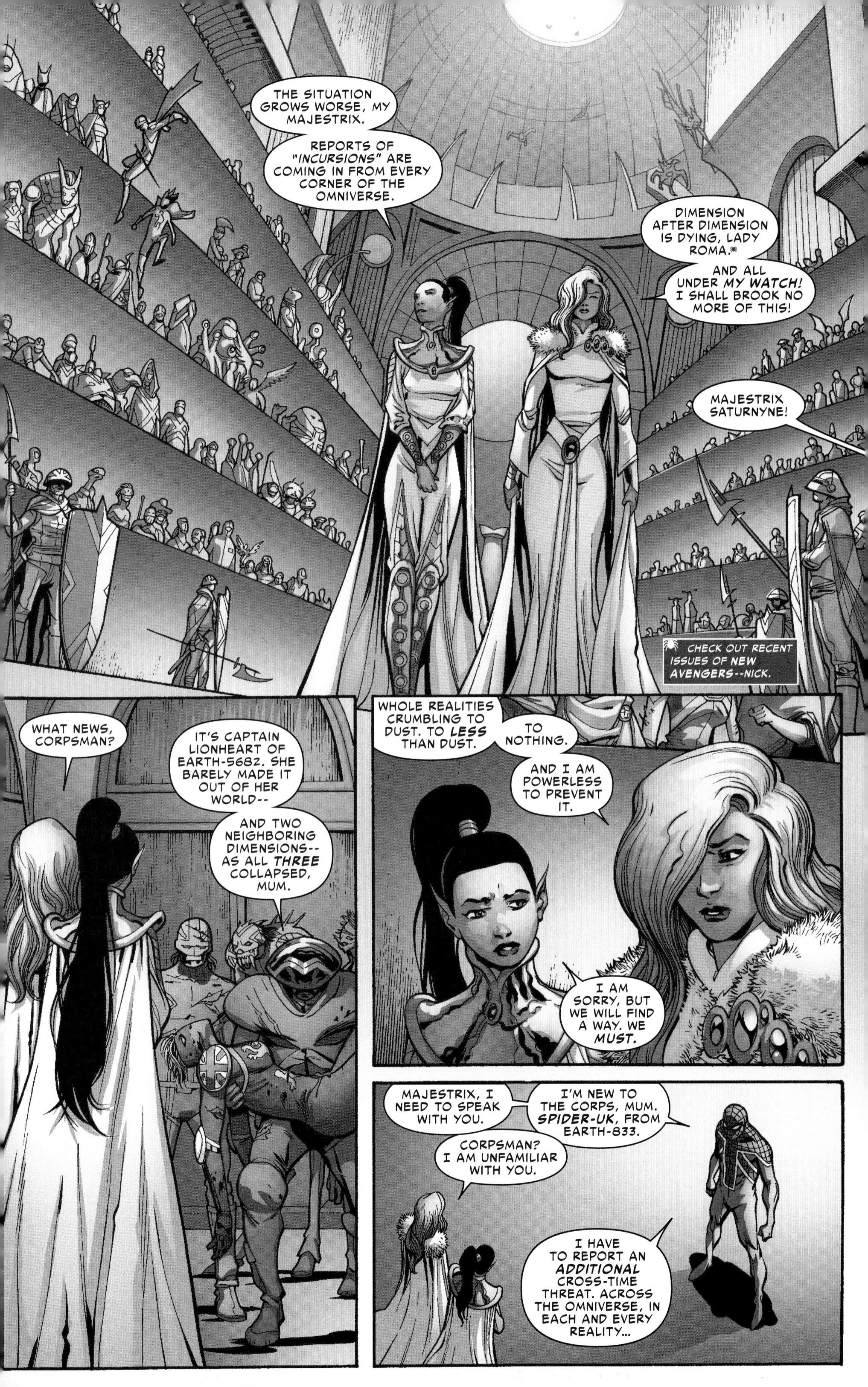
THE SITUATION GROWS WORSE, MY MAJESTRIX.
REPORTS OF "INCURSIONS" ARE COMING IN FROM EVERY CORNER OF THE OMNIVERSE.
DIMENSION AFTER DIMENSION IS DYING, LADY ROMA.
AND ALL UNDER MY WATCH! I SHALL BROOK NO MORE OF THIS!
MAJESTRIX SATURNYNE!
CHECK OUT RECENT ISSUES OF NEW AVENGERS--NICK.
WHAT NEWS, CORPSMAN?
IT'S CAPTAIN LIONHEART OF EARTH-5682. SHE BARELY MADE IT OUT OF HER WORLD--
AND TWO NEIGHBORING DIMENSIONS--AS ALL THREE COLLAPSED, MUM.
WHOLE REALITIES CRUMBLING TO DUST. TO LESS THAN DUST.
TO NOTHING.
AND I AM POWERLESS TO PREVENT IT.
I AM SORRY, BUT WE WILL FIND A WAY. WE MUST.
MAJESTRIX, I NEED TO SPEAK WITH YOU.
CORPSMAN? I AM UNFAMILIAR WITH YOU.
I'M NEW TO THE CORPS, MUM. SPIDER-UK, FROM EARTH-833.
I HAVE TO REPORT AN ADDITIONAL CROSS-TIME THREAT. ACROSS THE OMNIVERSE, IN EACH AND EVERY REALITY...

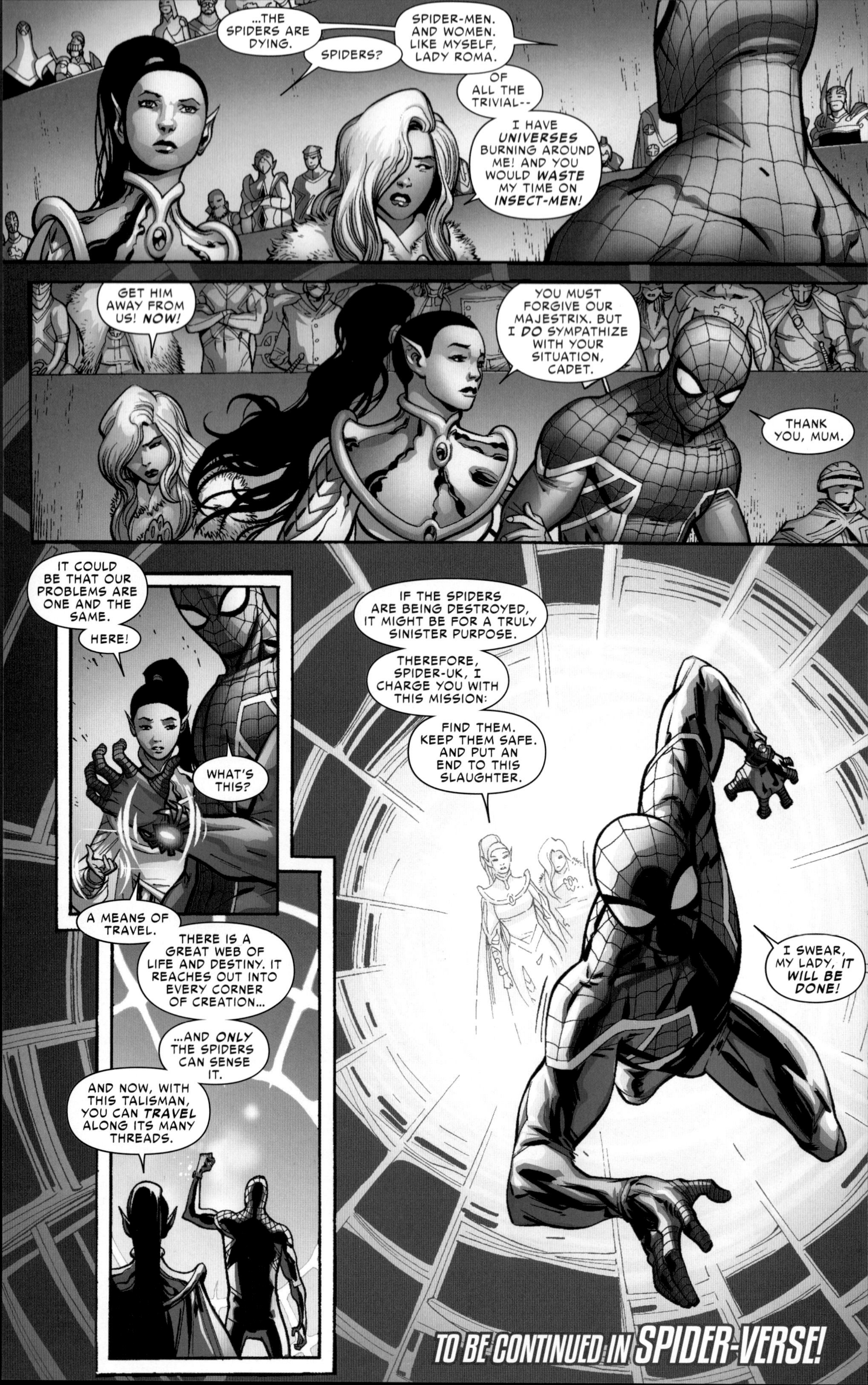
...THE SPIDERS ARE DYING.
SPIDERS?
SPIDER-MEN. AND WOMEN. LIKE MYSELF, LADY ROMA.
OF ALL THE TRIVIAL--
I HAVE UNIVERSES BURNING AROUND ME! AND YOU WOULD WASTE MY TIME ON INSECT-MEN!
GET HIM AWAY FROM US! NOW!
YOU MUST FORGIVE OUR MAJESTRIX. BUT I DO SYMPATHIZE WITH YOUR SITUATION, CADET.
THANK YOU, MUM.
IT COULD BE THAT OUR PROBLEMS ARE ONE AND THE SAME.
HERE!
WHAT'S THIS?
A MEANS OF TRAVEL.
THERE IS A GREAT WEB OF LIFE AND DESTINY. IT REACHES OUT INTO EVERY CORNER OF CREATION...
...AND ONLY THE SPIDERS CAN SENSE IT.
AND NOW, WITH THIS TALISMAN, YOU CAN TRAVEL ALONG ITS MANY THREADS.
IF THE SPIDERS ARE BEING DESTROYED, IT MIGHT BE FOR A TRULY SINISTER PURPOSE.
THEREFORE, SPIDER-UK, I CHARGE YOU WITH THIS MISSION:
FIND THEM. KEEP THEM SAFE. AND PUT AN END TO THIS SLAUGHTER.
I SWEAR, MY LADY, IT WILL BE DONE!
TO BE CONTINUED IN SPIDER-VERSE!

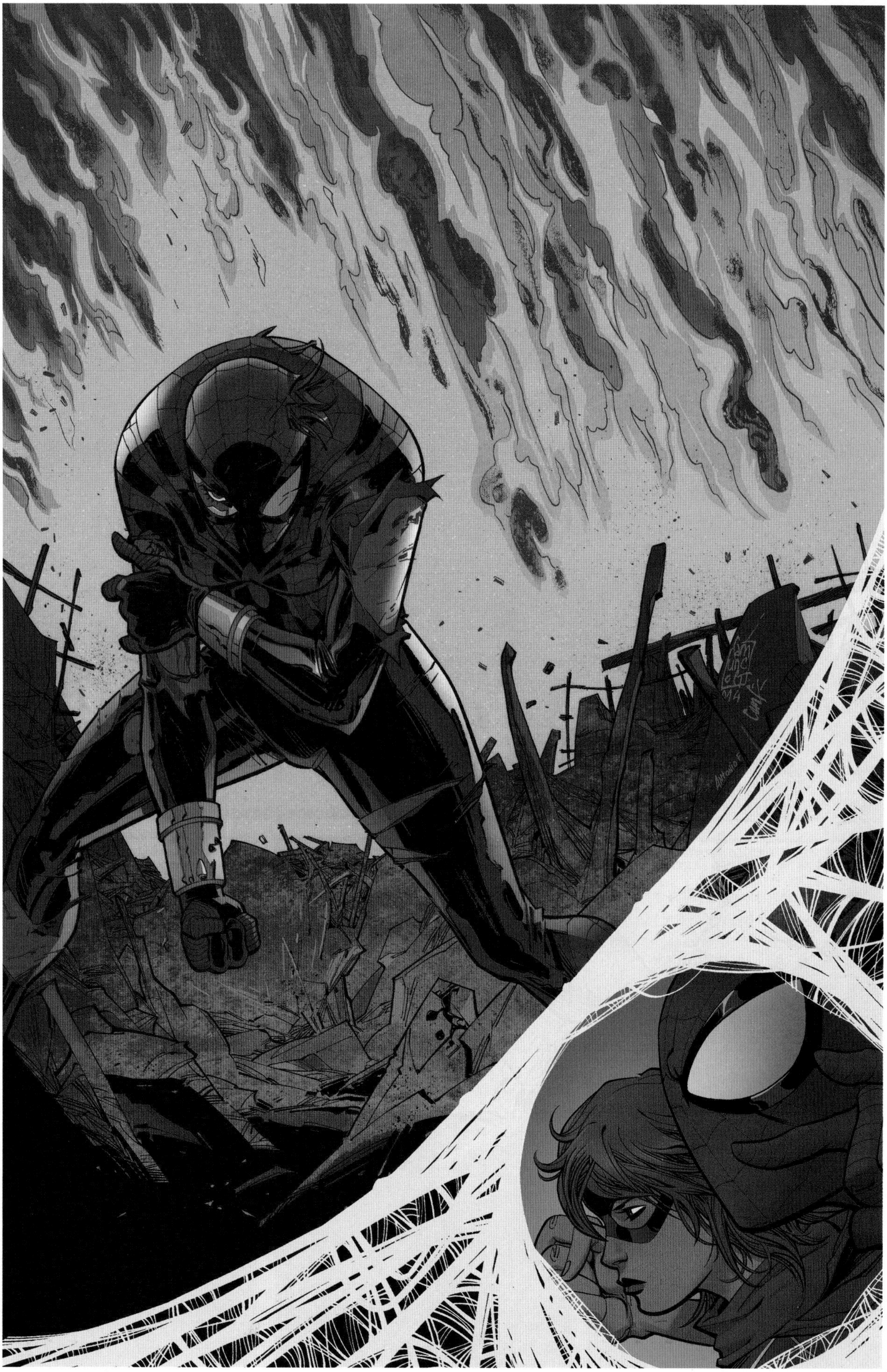

AMAZING SPIDER-MAN 8

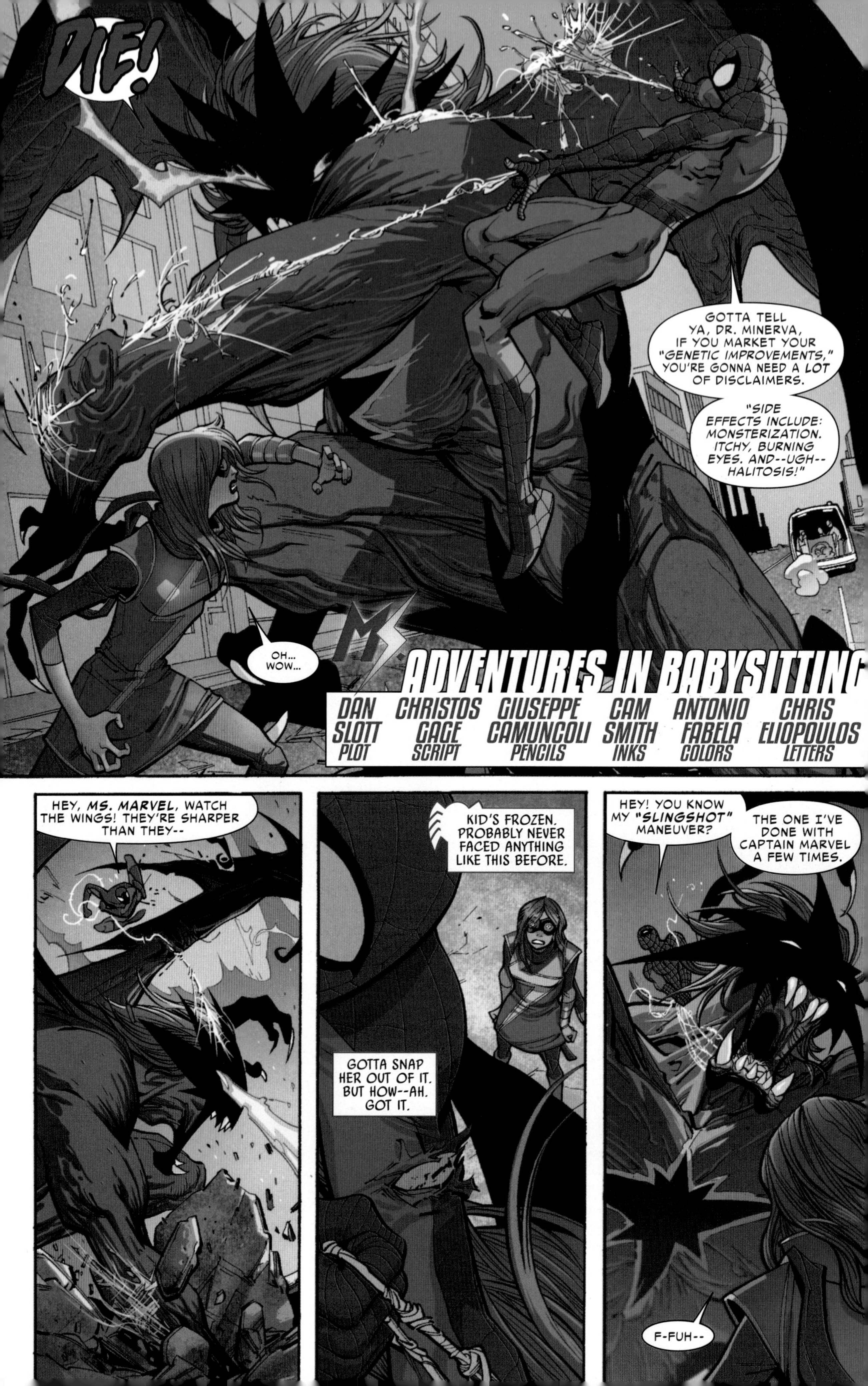
DIE!
GOTTA TELL YA, DR. MINERVA, IF YOU MARKET YOUR "GENETIC IMPROVEMENTS," YOU'RE GONNA NEED A LOT OF DISCLAIMERS.
"SIDE EFFECTS INCLUDE: MONSTERIZATION. ITCHY, BURNING EYES. AND--UGH--HALITOSIS!"
OH... WOW...
MS. ADVENTURES IN BABYSITTING
DAN SLOTT PLOT
CHRISTOS GAGE SCRIPT
GIUSEPPE CAMUNCOLI PENCILS
CAM SMITH INKS
ANTONIO FABELA COLORS
CHRIS ELIOPOULOS LETTERS
HEY, MS. MARVEL, WATCH THE WINGS! THEY'RE SHARPER THAN THEY--
KID'S FROZEN. PROBABLY NEVER FACED ANYTHING LIKE THIS BEFORE.
GOTTA SNAP HER OUT OF IT. BUT HOW--AH. GOT IT.
HEY! YOU KNOW MY "SLINGSHOT" MANEUVER?
THE ONE I'VE DONE WITH CAPTAIN MARVEL A FEW TIMES.
F-FUH--

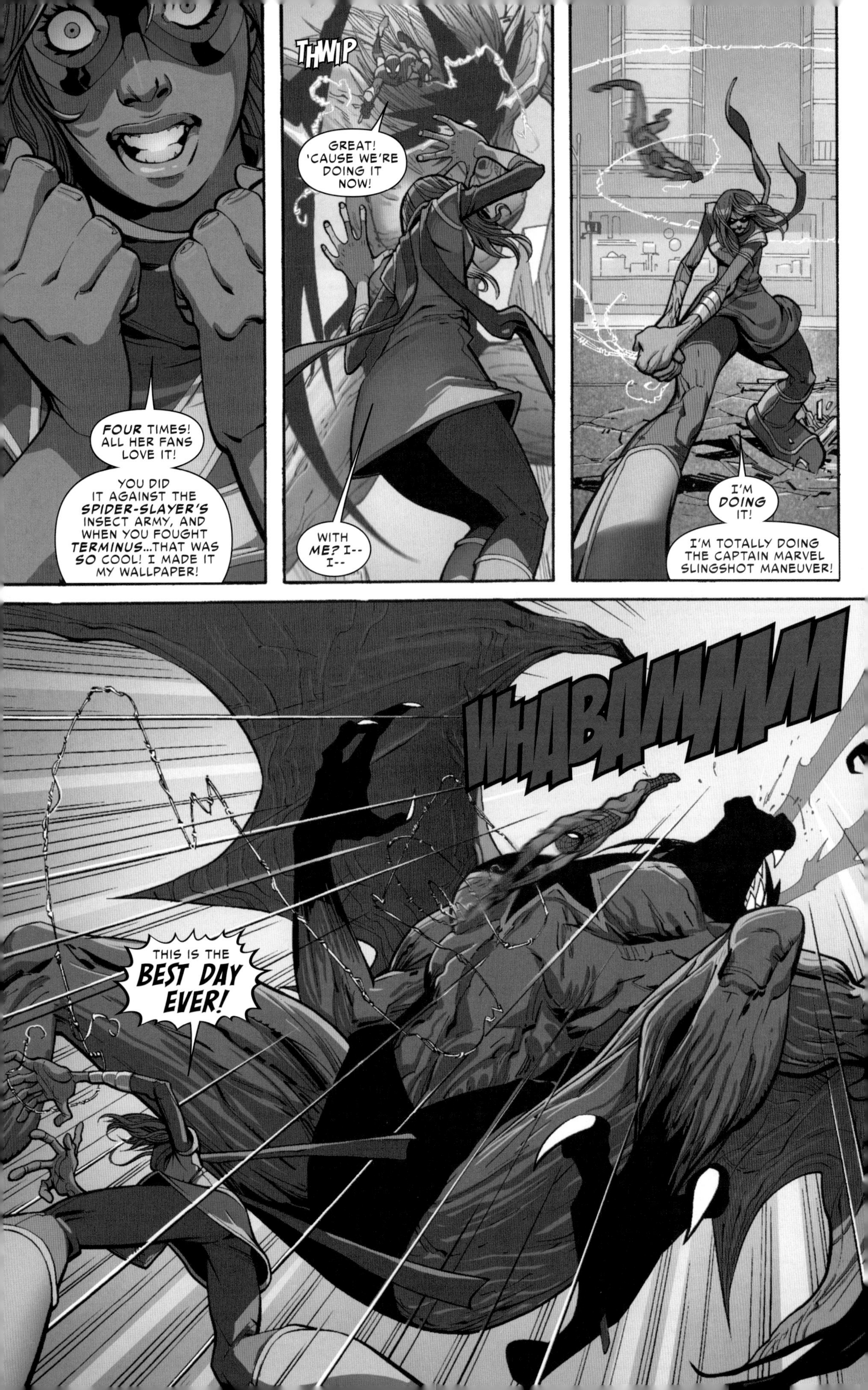
FOUR TIMES! ALL HER FANS LOVE IT!
YOU DID IT AGAINST THE SPIDER-SLAYER'S INSECT ARMY, AND WHEN YOU FOUGHT TERMINUS...THAT WAS SO COOL! I MADE IT MY WALLPAPER!
THWIP
GREAT! 'CAUSE WE'RE DOING IT NOW!
WITH ME? I-- I--
I'M DOING IT!
I'M TOTALLY DOING THE CAPTAIN MARVEL SLINGSHOT MANEUVER!
WHABAMMMM
THIS IS THE BEST DAY EVER!

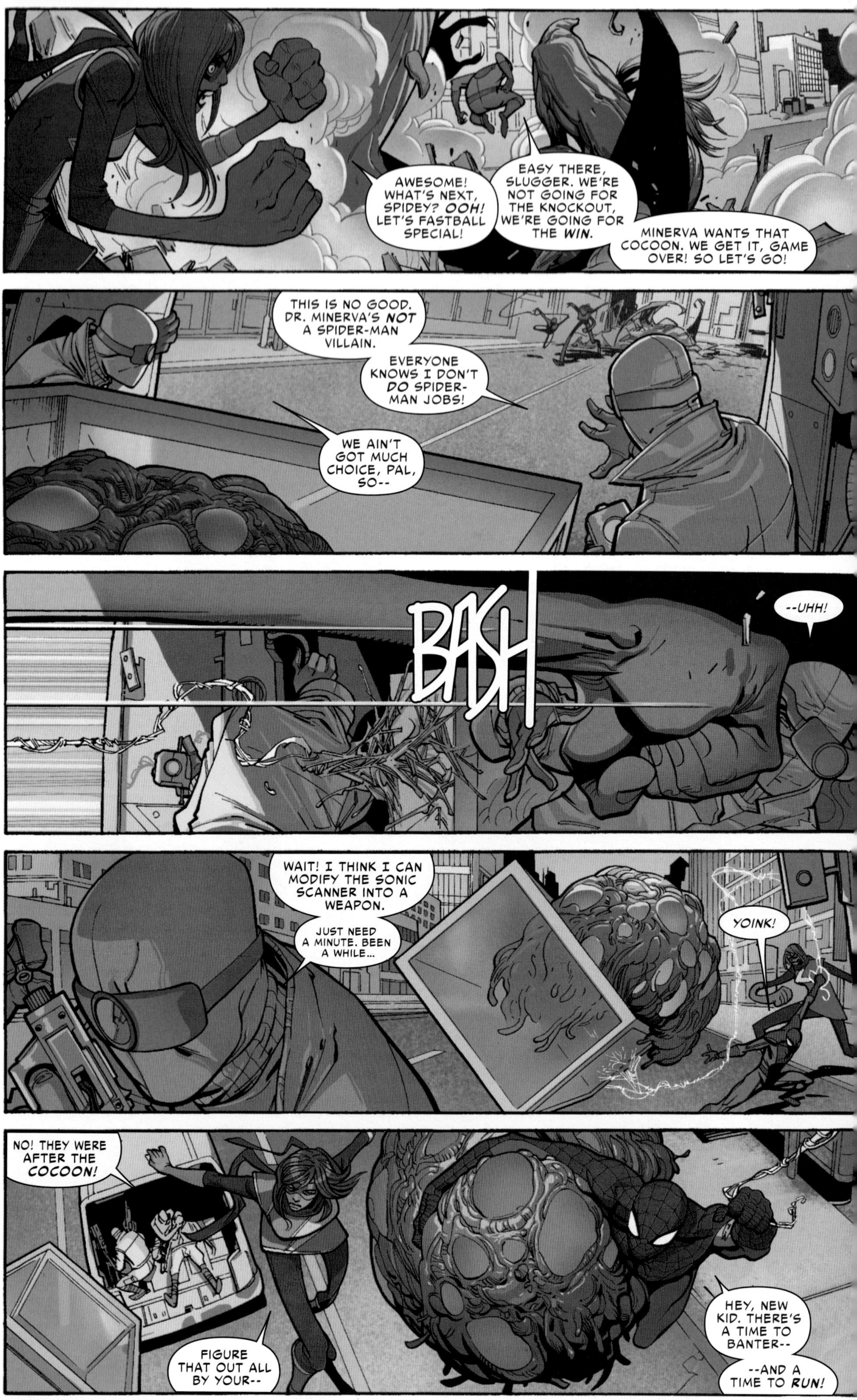
AWESOME! WHAT'S NEXT, SPIDEY? OOH! LET'S FASTBALL SPECIAL!
EASY THERE, SLUGGER. WE'RE NOT GOING FOR THE KNOCKOUT, WE'RE GOING FOR THE WIN.
MINERVA WANTS THAT COCOON. WE GET IT, GAME OVER! SO LET'S GO!
THIS IS NO GOOD. DR. MINERVA'S NOT A SPIDER-MAN VILLAIN.
EVERYONE KNOWS I DON'T DO SPIDER-MAN JOBS!
WE AIN'T GOT MUCH CHOICE, PAL, SO--
BASH
--UHH!
WAIT! I THINK I CAN MODIFY THE SONIC SCANNER INTO A WEAPON.
JUST NEED A MINUTE. BEEN A WHILE...
YOINK!
NO! THEY WERE AFTER THE COCOON!
FIGURE THAT OUT ALL BY YOUR--
HEY, NEW KID. THERE'S A TIME TO BANTER--
--AND A TIME TO RUN!

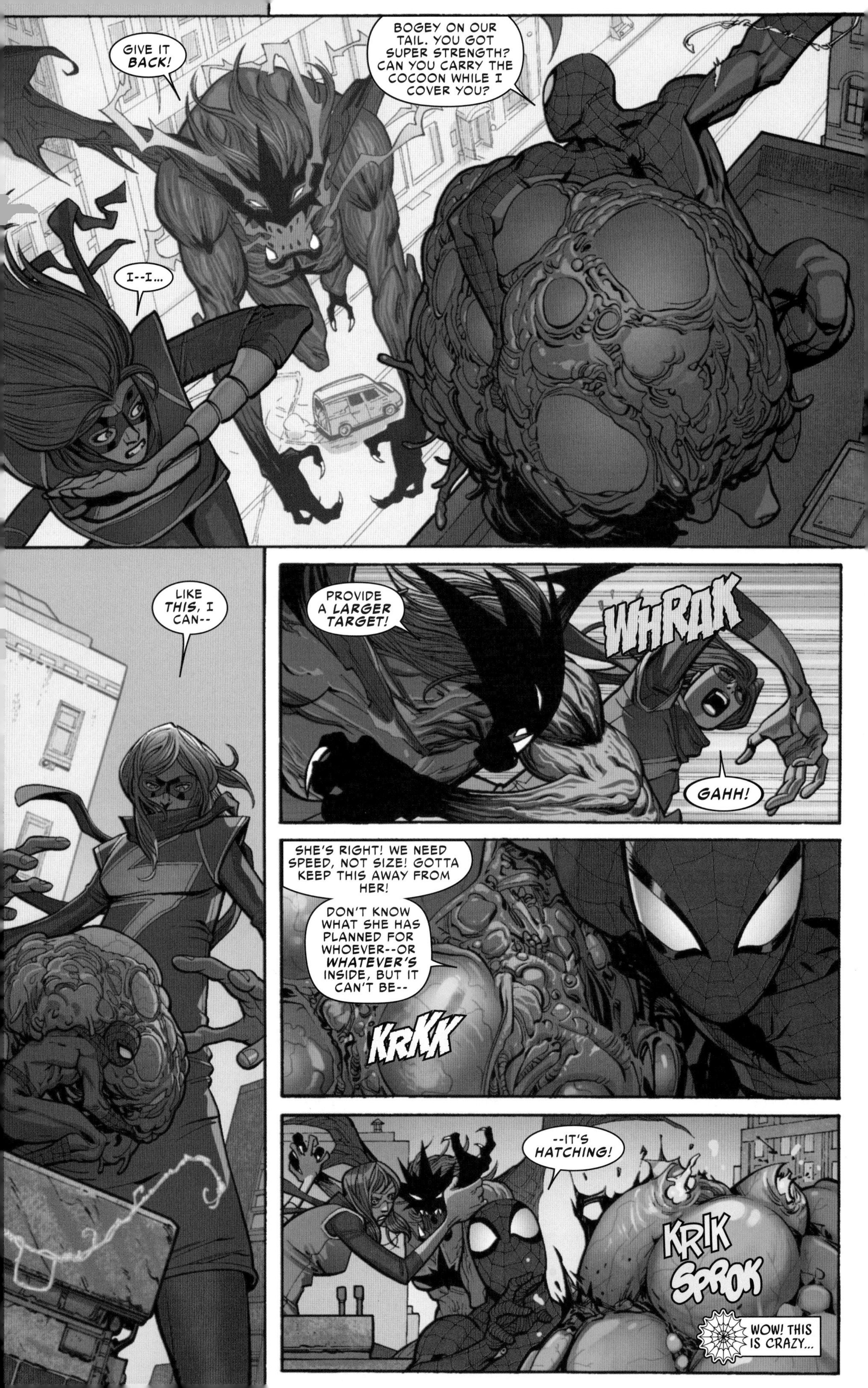
GIVE IT BACK!
BOGEY ON OUR TAIL. YOU GOT SUPER STRENGTH? CAN YOU CARRY THE COCOON WHILE I COVER YOU?
I--I...
LIKE THIS, I CAN--
PROVIDE A LARGER TARGET!
WHRAK
GAHH!
SHE'S RIGHT! WE NEED SPEED, NOT SIZE! GOTTA KEEP THIS AWAY FROM HER!
DON'T KNOW WHAT SHE HAS PLANNED FOR WHOEVER--OR WHATEVER'S INSIDE, BUT IT CAN'T BE--
KRKK
--IT'S HATCHING!
KRIK
SPROK
WOW! THIS IS CRAZY...

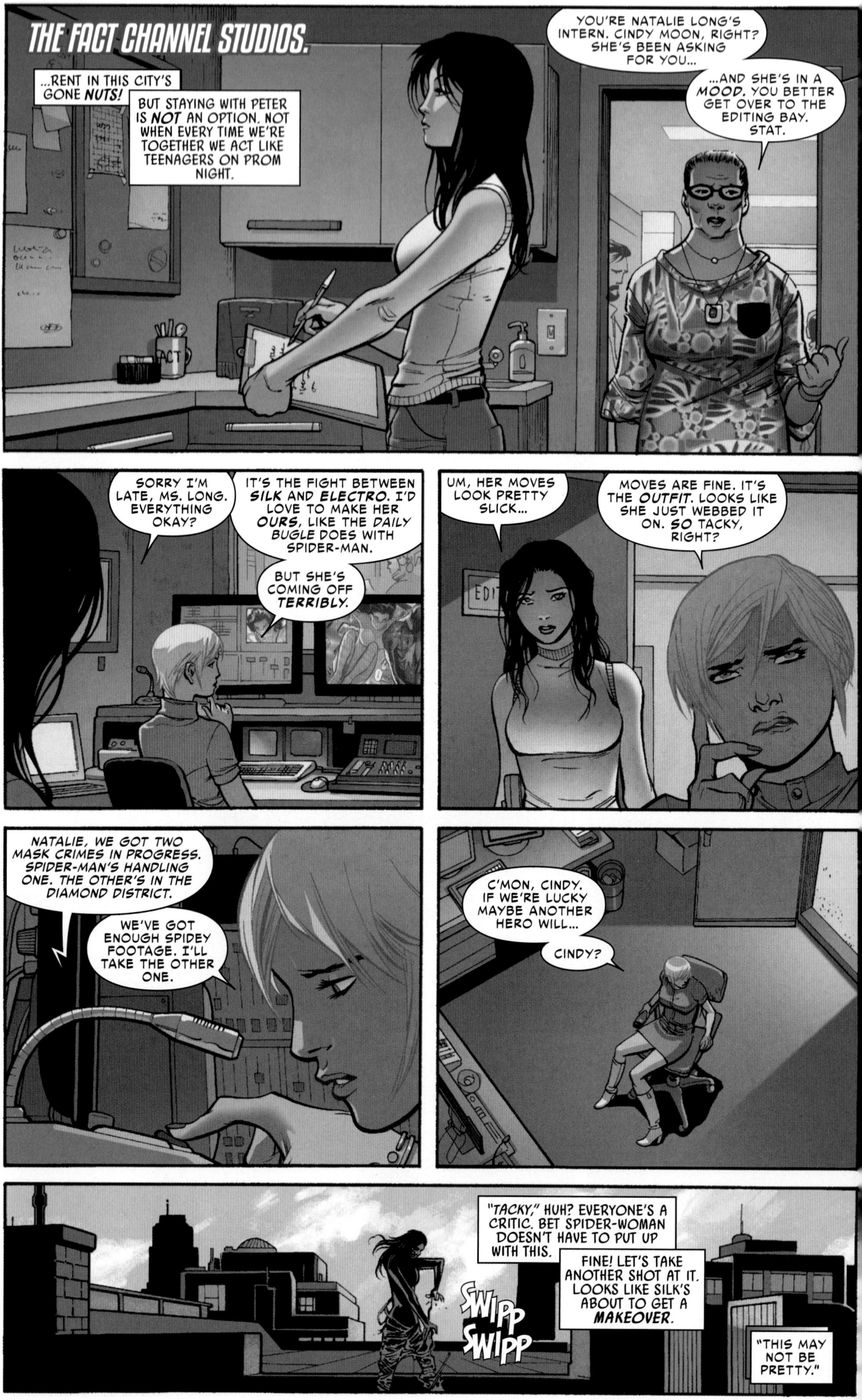
THE FACT CHANNEL STUDIOS.
...RENT IN THIS CITY'S GONE NUTS!
BUT STAYING WITH PETER IS NOT AN OPTION. NOT WHEN EVERY TIME WE'RE TOGETHER WE ACT LIKE TEENAGERS ON PROM NIGHT.
YOU'RE NATALIE LONG'S INTERN. CINDY MOON, RIGHT? SHE'S BEEN ASKING FOR YOU...
...AND SHE'S IN A MOOD. YOU BETTER GET OVER TO THE EDITING BAY. STAT.
SORRY I'M LATE, MS. LONG. EVERYTHING OKAY?
IT'S THE FIGHT BETWEEN SILK AND ELECTRO. I'D LOVE TO MAKE HER OURS, LIKE THE DAILY BUGLE DOES WITH SPIDER-MAN.
BUT SHE'S COMING OFF TERRIBLY.
UM, HER MOVES LOOK PRETTY SLICK...
MOVES ARE FINE. IT'S THE OUTFIT. LOOKS LIKE SHE JUST WEBBED IT ON. SO TACKY, RIGHT?
NATALIE, WE GOT TWO MASK CRIMES IN PROGRESS. SPIDER-MAN'S HANDLING ONE. THE OTHER'S IN THE DIAMOND DISTRICT.
WE'VE GOT ENOUGH SPIDEY FOOTAGE. I'LL TAKE THE OTHER ONE.
C'MON, CINDY. IF WE'RE LUCKY MAYBE ANOTHER HERO WILL...
CINDY?
"TACKY," HUH? EVERYONE'S A CRITIC. BET SPIDER-WOMAN DOESN'T HAVE TO PUT UP WITH THIS.
FINE! LET'S TAKE ANOTHER SHOT AT IT. LOOKS LIKE SILK'S ABOUT TO GET A MAKEOVER.
SWIPP SWIPP
"THIS MAY NOT BE PRETTY."

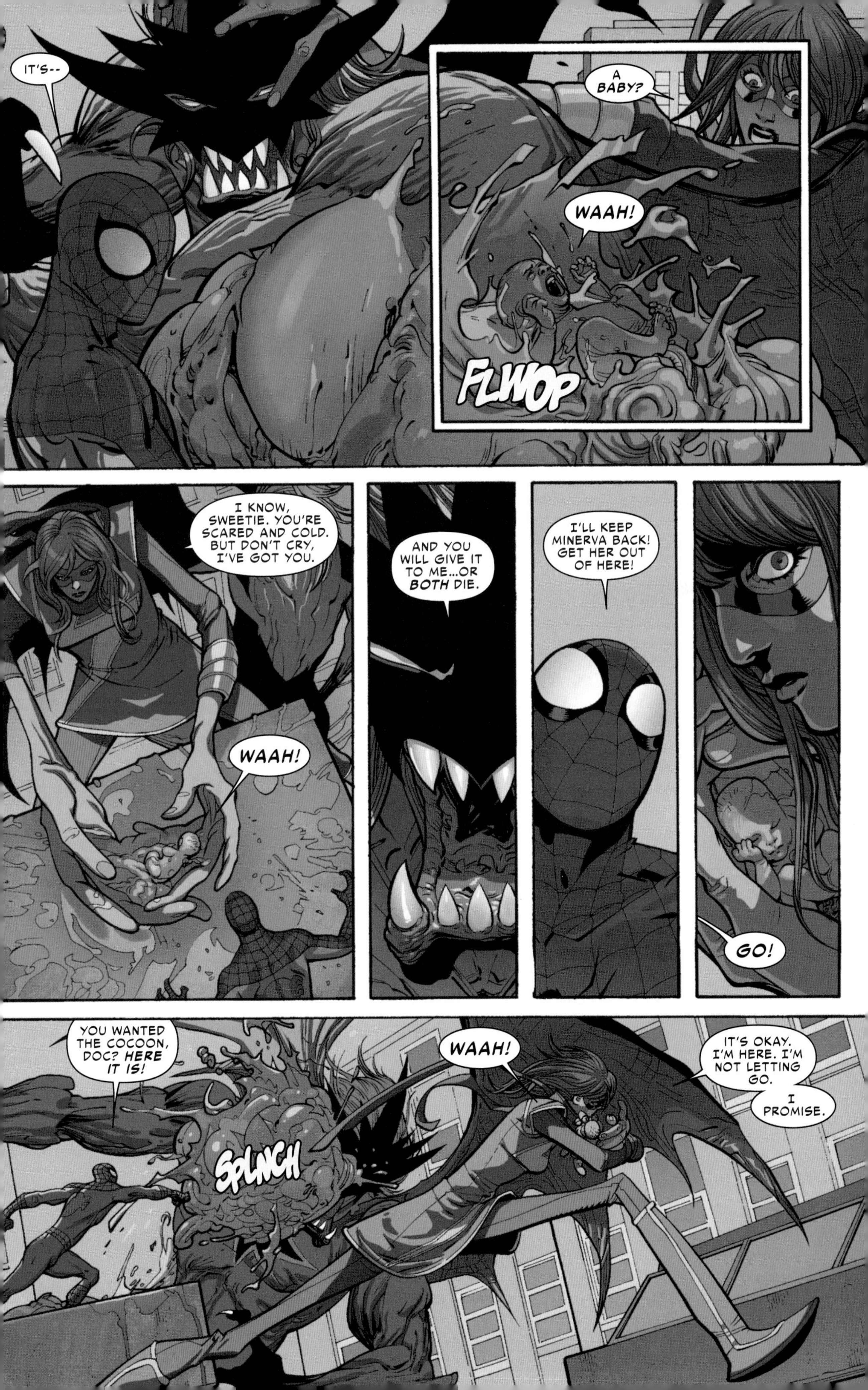
IT'S--
A BABY?
WAAH!
FLWOP
I KNOW, SWEETIE. YOU'RE SCARED AND COLD. BUT DON'T CRY, I'VE GOT YOU.
WAAH!
AND YOU WILL GIVE IT TO ME...OR BOTH DIE.
I'LL KEEP MINERVA BACK! GET HER OUT OF HERE!
GO!
YOU WANTED THE COCOON, DOC? HERE IT IS!
SPLNCH
WAAH!
IT'S OKAY. I'M HERE. I'M NOT LETTING GO.
I PROMISE.

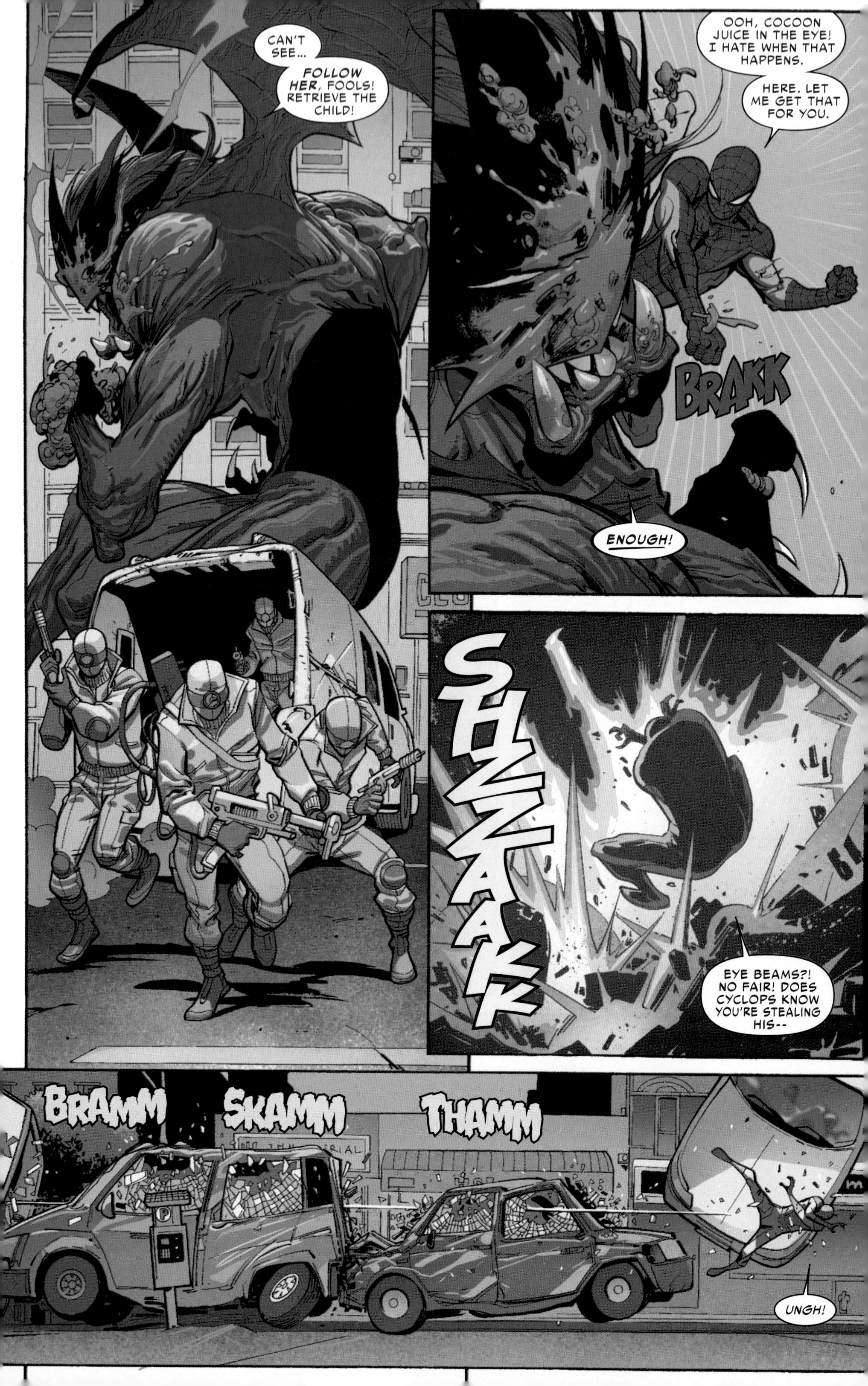

CAN'T SEE... FOLLOW HER, FOOLS! RETRIEVE THE CHILD!
OOH, COCOON JUICE IN THE EYE! I HATE WHEN THAT HAPPENS.
HERE. LET ME GET THAT FOR YOU.
BRAKK
ENOUGH!
SHZZAAKK
EYE BEAMS?! NO FAIR! DOES CYCLOPS KNOW YOU'RE STEALING HIS--
BRAMM
SKAMM
THAMM
UNGH!

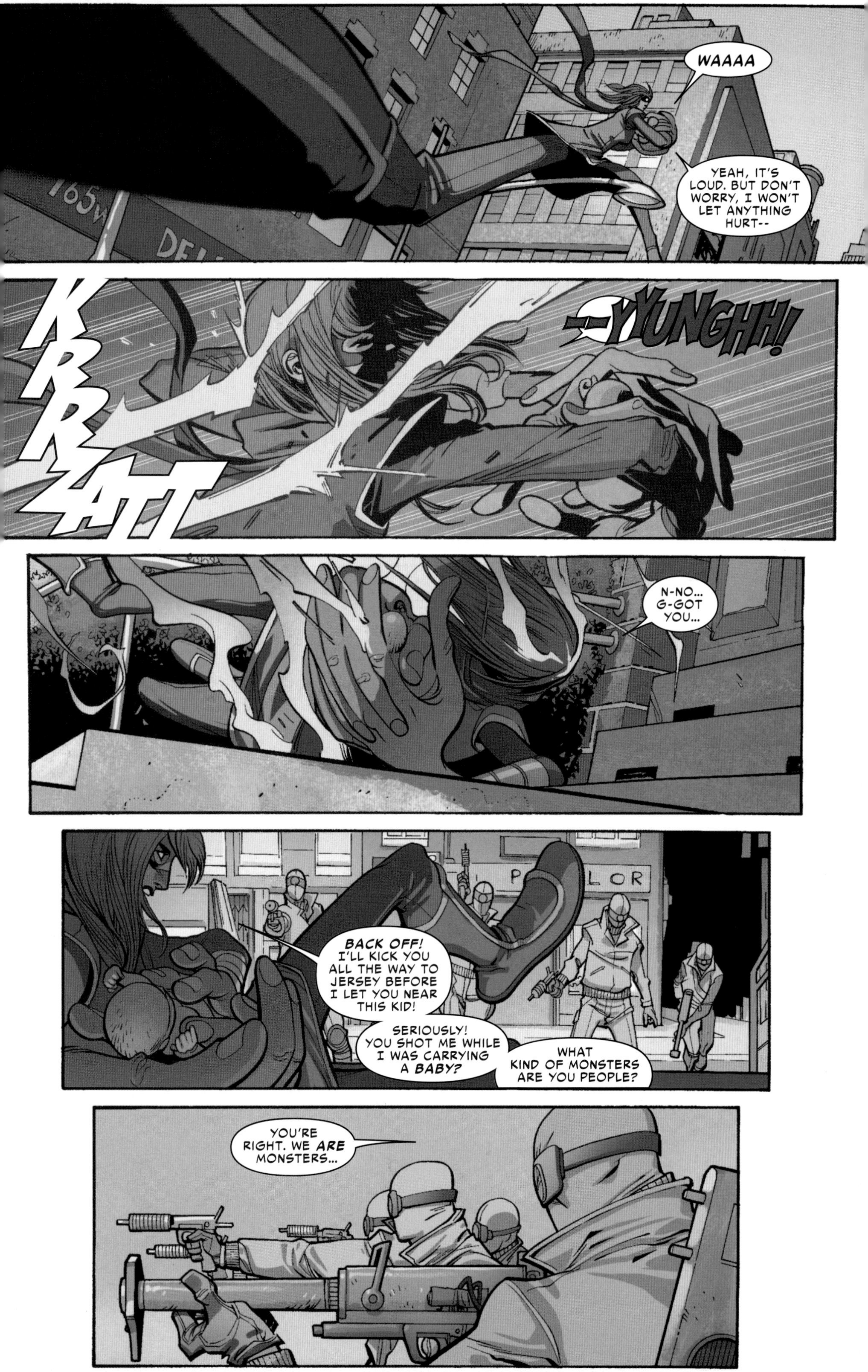
WAAAA
YEAH, IT'S LOUD. BUT DON'T WORRY, I WON'T LET ANYTHING HURT--
KRRZATT
--YYUNGHH!
N-NO... G-GOT YOU...
BACK OFF! I'LL KICK YOU ALL THE WAY TO JERSEY BEFORE I LET YOU NEAR THIS KID!
SERIOUSLY! YOU SHOT ME WHILE I WAS CARRYING A BABY?
WHAT KIND OF MONSTERS ARE YOU PEOPLE?
YOU'RE RIGHT. WE ARE MONSTERS...

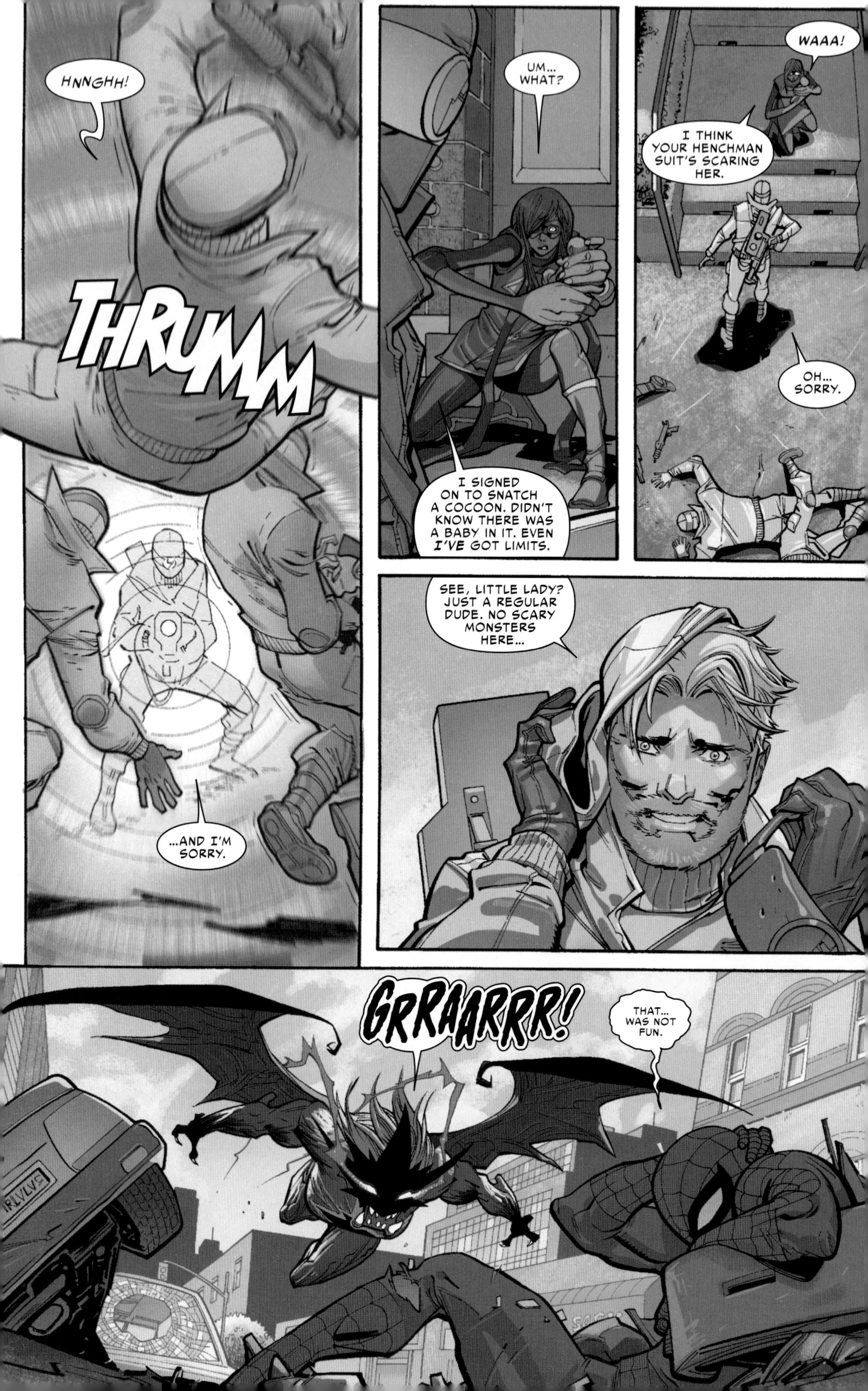
HNNGHH!
THRUMM
...AND I'M SORRY.
UM... WHAT?
I SIGNED ON TO SNATCH A COCOON. DIDN'T KNOW THERE WAS A BABY IN IT. EVEN *I'VE* GOT LIMITS.
WAAA!
I THINK YOUR HENCHMAN SUIT'S SCARING HER.
OH... SORRY.
SEE, LITTLE LADY? JUST A REGULAR DUDE. NO SCARY MONSTERS HERE...
GRRAARRR!
THAT... WAS NOT FUN.

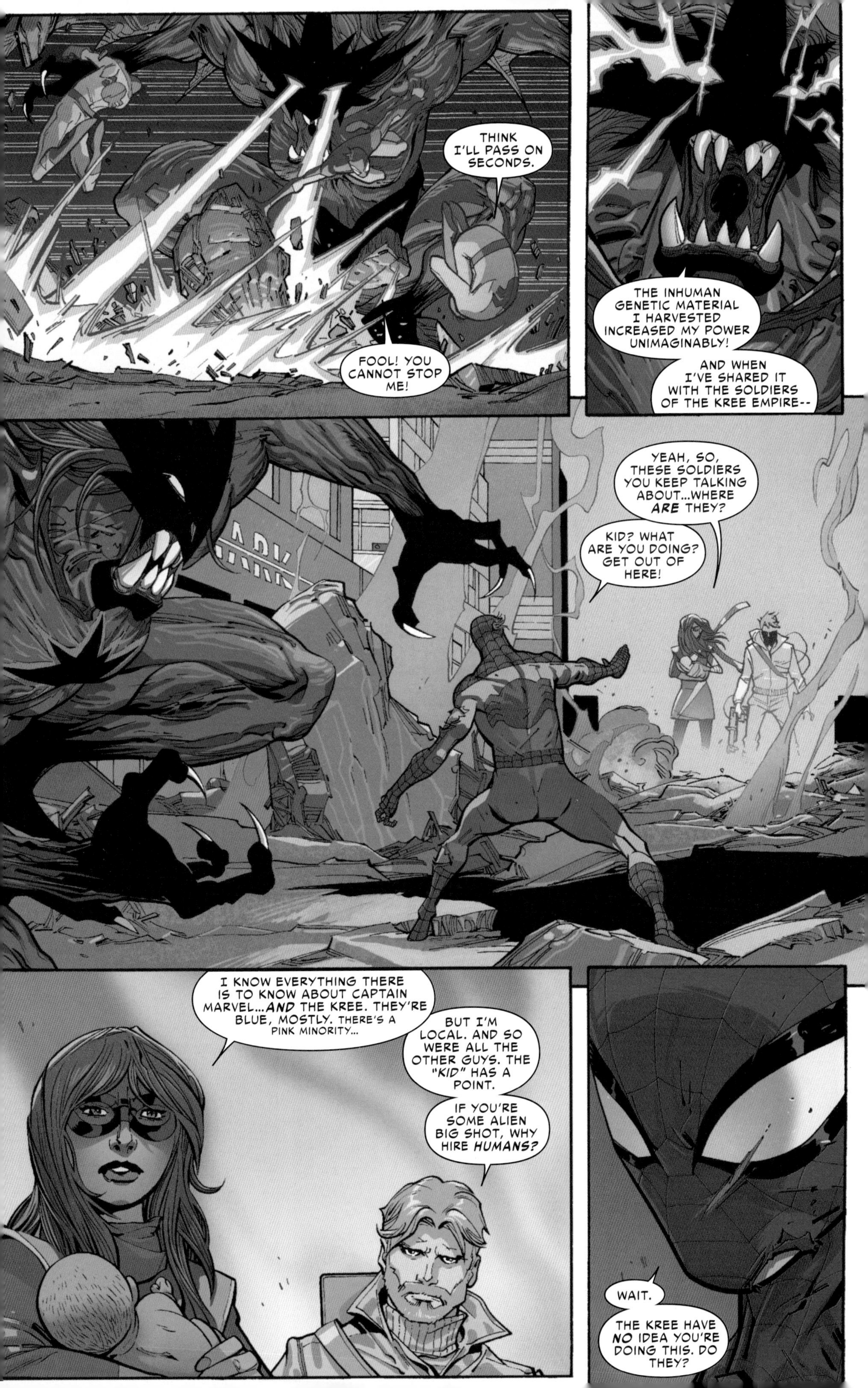

THINK I'LL PASS ON SECONDS.
FOOL! YOU CANNOT STOP ME!
THE INHUMAN GENETIC MATERIAL I HARVESTED INCREASED MY POWER UNIMAGINABLY!
AND WHEN I'VE SHARED IT WITH THE SOLDIERS OF THE KREE EMPIRE--
YEAH, SO, THESE SOLDIERS YOU KEEP TALKING ABOUT...WHERE *ARE* THEY?
KID? WHAT ARE YOU DOING? GET OUT OF HERE!
I KNOW EVERYTHING THERE IS TO KNOW ABOUT CAPTAIN MARVEL...*AND* THE KREE. THEY'RE BLUE, MOSTLY. THERE'S A PINK MINORITY...
BUT I'M LOCAL. AND SO WERE ALL THE OTHER GUYS. THE "*KID*" HAS A POINT.
IF YOU'RE SOME ALIEN BIG SHOT, WHY HIRE *HUMANS?*
WAIT.
THE KREE HAVE *NO* IDEA YOU'RE DOING THIS. DO THEY?

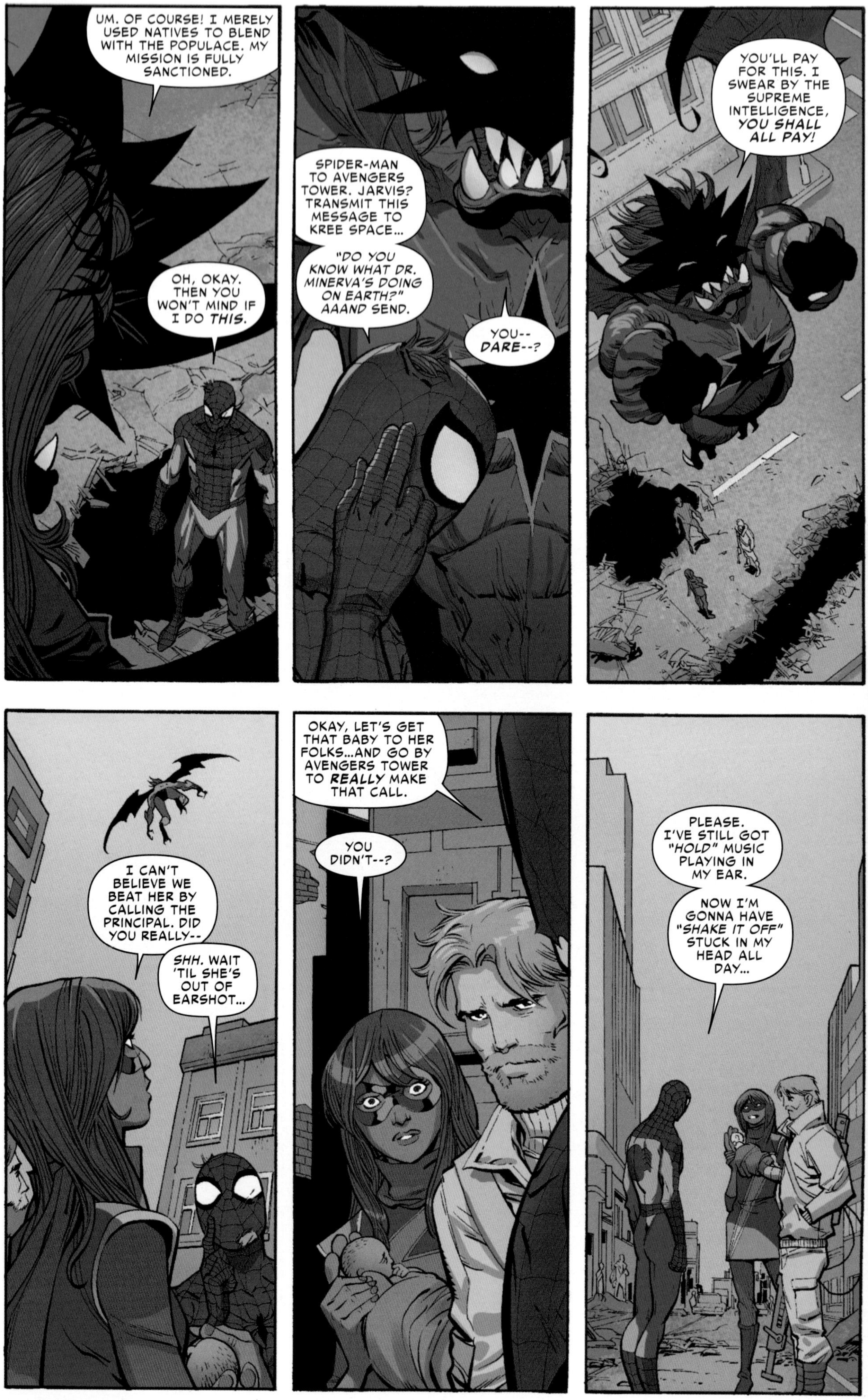
UM. OF COURSE! I MERELY USED NATIVES TO BLEND WITH THE POPULACE. MY MISSION IS FULLY SANCTIONED.
OH, OKAY. THEN YOU WON'T MIND IF I DO THIS.
SPIDER-MAN TO AVENGERS TOWER. JARVIS? TRANSMIT THIS MESSAGE TO KREE SPACE...
"DO YOU KNOW WHAT DR. MINERVA'S DOING ON EARTH?" AAAND SEND.
YOU-- DARE--?
YOU'LL PAY FOR THIS. I SWEAR BY THE SUPREME INTELLIGENCE, YOU SHALL ALL PAY!
I CAN'T BELIEVE WE BEAT HER BY CALLING THE PRINCIPAL. DID YOU REALLY--
SHH. WAIT 'TIL SHE'S OUT OF EARSHOT...
OKAY, LET'S GET THAT BABY TO HER FOLKS...AND GO BY AVENGERS TOWER TO REALLY MAKE THAT CALL.
YOU DIDN'T--?
PLEASE. I'VE STILL GOT "HOLD" MUSIC PLAYING IN MY EAR.
NOW I'M GONNA HAVE "SHAKE IT OFF" STUCK IN MY HEAD ALL DAY...

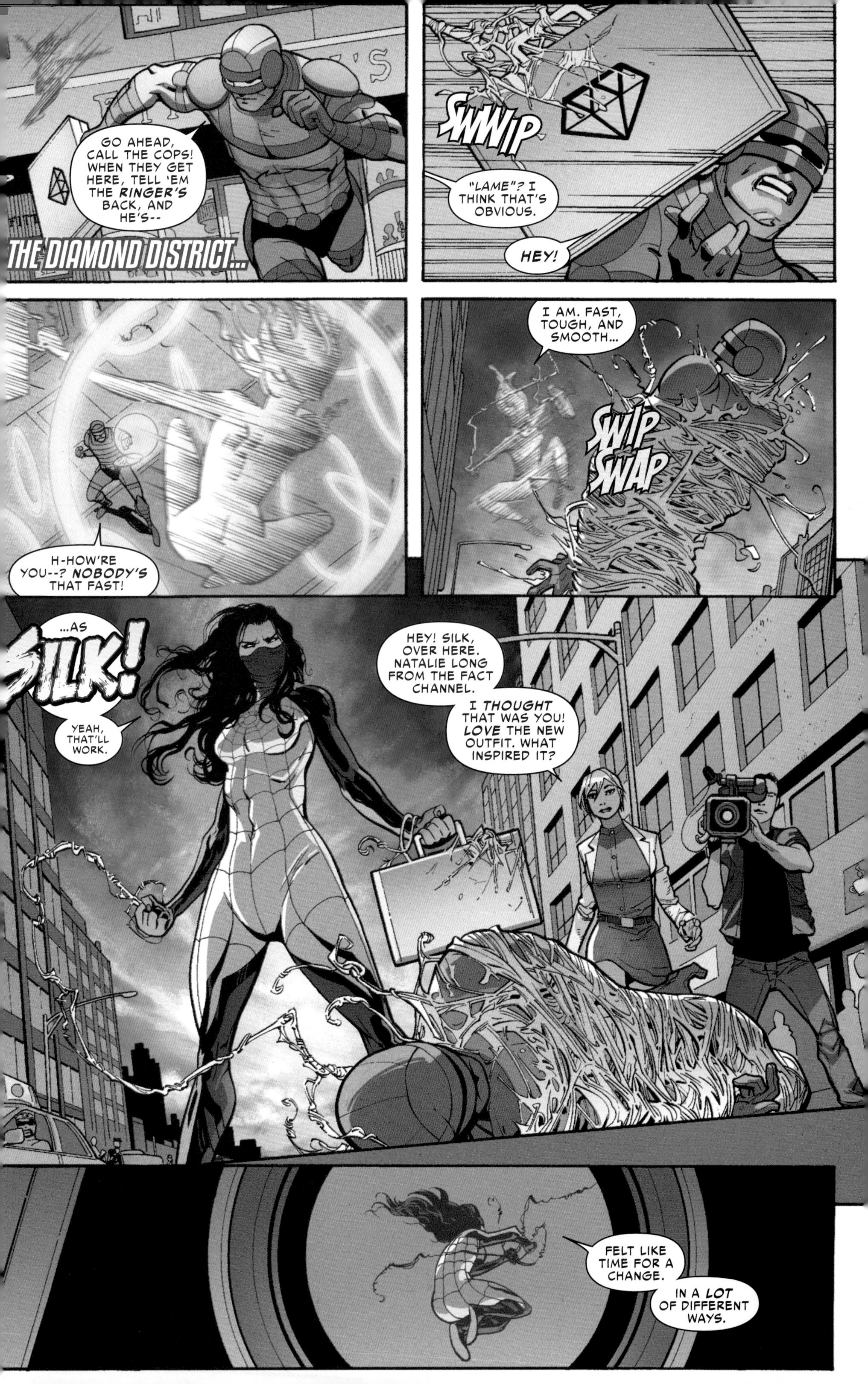

GO AHEAD, CALL THE COPS! WHEN THEY GET HERE, TELL 'EM THE RINGER'S BACK, AND HE'S--
THE DIAMOND DISTRICT...
SWWIP
"LAME"? I THINK THAT'S OBVIOUS.
HEY!
H-HOW'RE YOU--? NOBODY'S THAT FAST!
I AM. FAST, TOUGH, AND SMOOTH...
SWIP SWAP
...AS SILK!
YEAH, THAT'LL WORK.
HEY! SILK, OVER HERE. NATALIE LONG FROM THE FACT CHANNEL.
I THOUGHT THAT WAS YOU! LOVE THE NEW OUTFIT. WHAT INSPIRED IT?
FELT LIKE TIME FOR A CHANGE.
IN A LOT OF DIFFERENT WAYS.

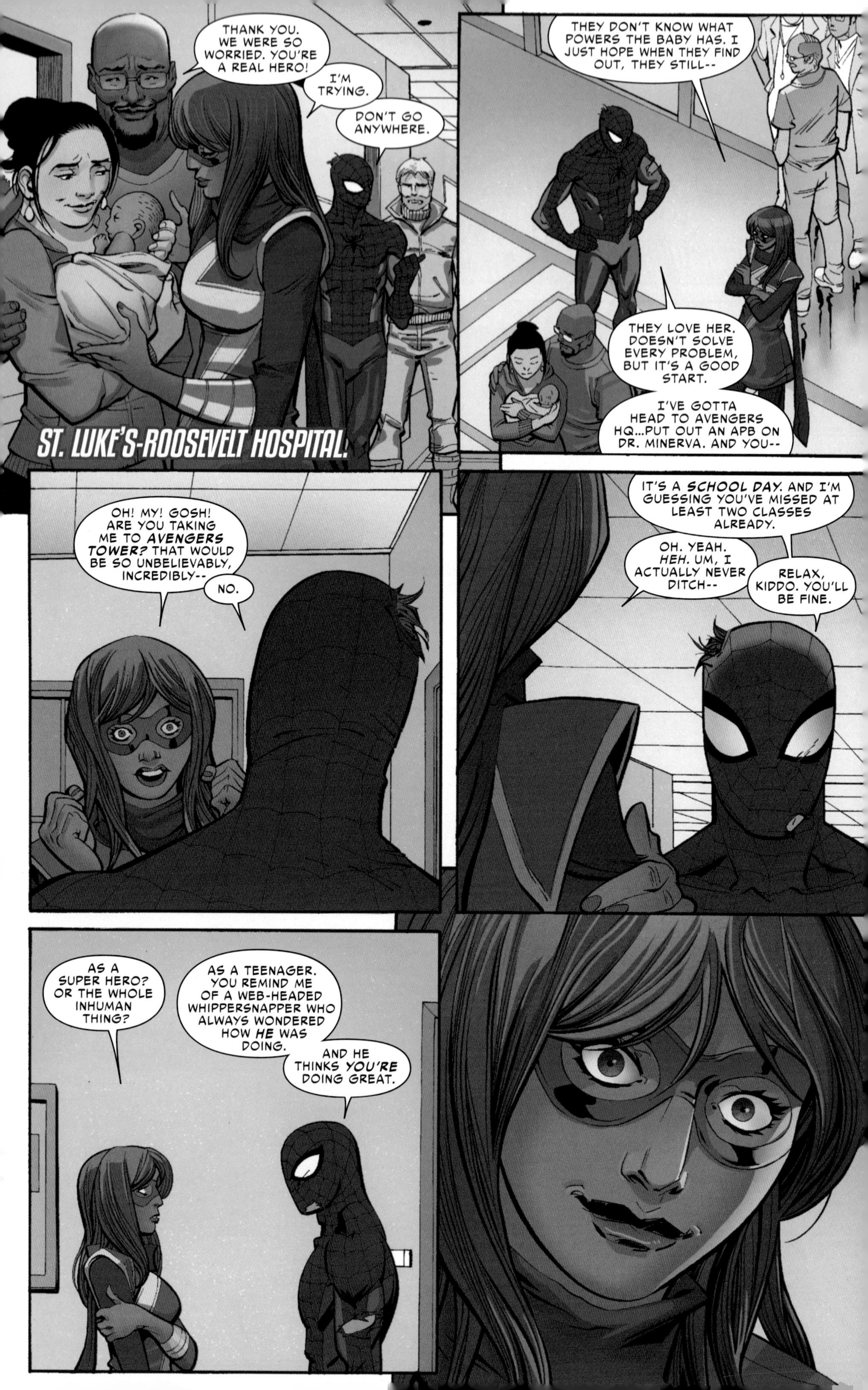
THANK YOU. WE WERE SO WORRIED. YOU'RE A REAL HERO!
I'M TRYING.
DON'T GO ANYWHERE.
ST. LUKE'S-ROOSEVELT HOSPITAL.
THEY DON'T KNOW WHAT POWERS THE BABY HAS. I JUST HOPE WHEN THEY FIND OUT, THEY STILL--
THEY LOVE HER. DOESN'T SOLVE EVERY PROBLEM, BUT IT'S A GOOD START.
I'VE GOTTA HEAD TO AVENGERS HQ...PUT OUT AN APB ON DR. MINERVA. AND YOU--
OH! MY! GOSH! ARE YOU TAKING ME TO AVENGERS TOWER? THAT WOULD BE SO UNBELIEVABLY, INCREDIBLY--
NO.
IT'S A SCHOOL DAY. AND I'M GUESSING YOU'VE MISSED AT LEAST TWO CLASSES ALREADY.
OH. YEAH. HEH. UM, I ACTUALLY NEVER DITCH--
RELAX, KIDDO. YOU'LL BE FINE.
AS A SUPER HERO? OR THE WHOLE INHUMAN THING?
AS A TEENAGER. YOU REMIND ME OF A WEB-HEADED WHIPPERSNAPPER WHO ALWAYS WONDERED HOW HE WAS DOING.
AND HE THINKS YOU'RE DOING GREAT.

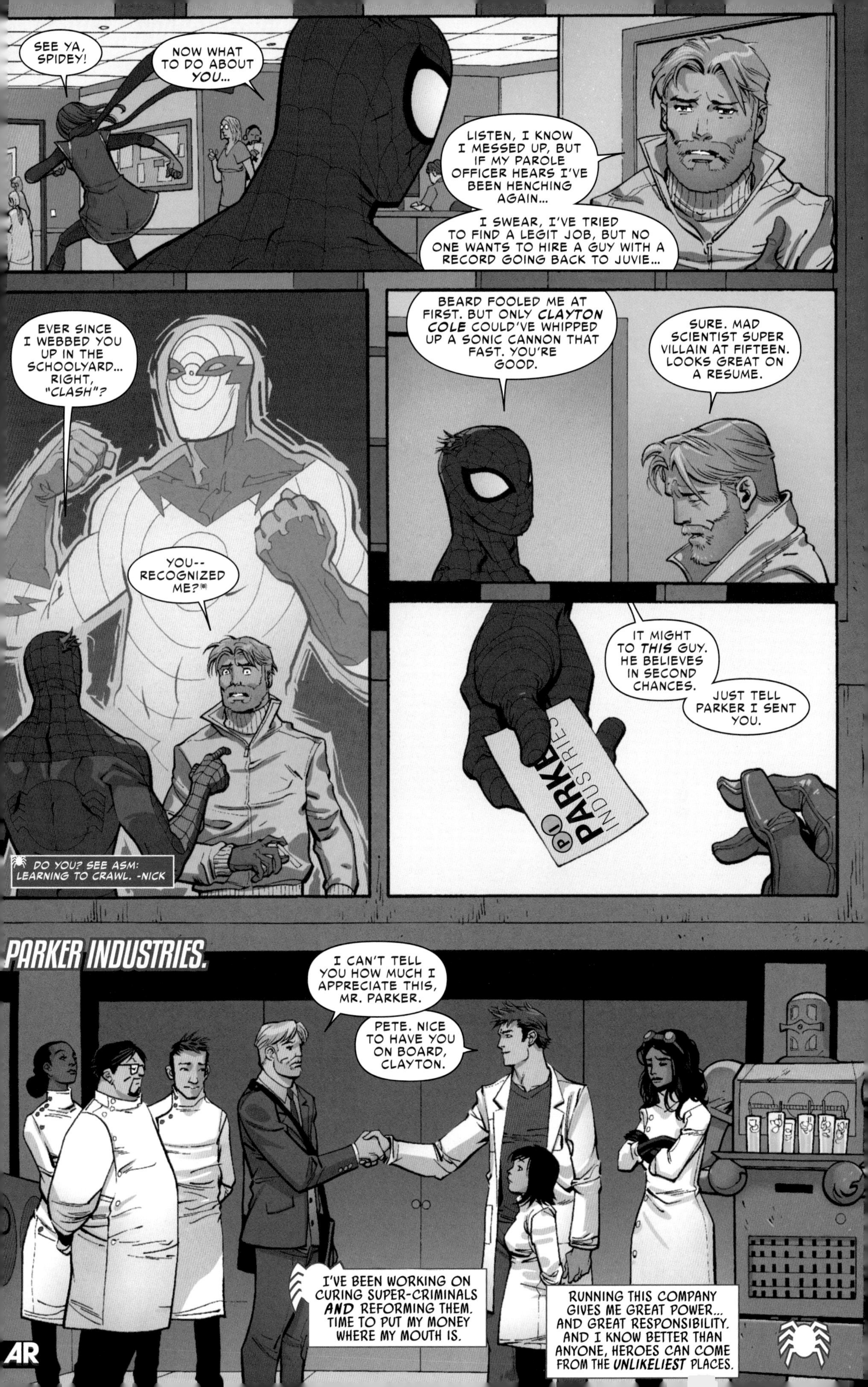
SEE YA, SPIDEY!
NOW WHAT TO DO ABOUT YOU...
LISTEN, I KNOW I MESSED UP, BUT IF MY PAROLE OFFICER HEARS I'VE BEEN HENCHING AGAIN...
I SWEAR, I'VE TRIED TO FIND A LEGIT JOB, BUT NO ONE WANTS TO HIRE A GUY WITH A RECORD GOING BACK TO JUVIE...
EVER SINCE I WEBBED YOU UP IN THE SCHOOLYARD... RIGHT, "CLASH"?
YOU-- RECOGNIZED ME?
DO YOU? SEE ASM: LEARNING TO CRAWL. -NICK
BEARD FOOLED ME AT FIRST. BUT ONLY CLAYTON COLE COULD'VE WHIPPED UP A SONIC CANNON THAT FAST. YOU'RE GOOD.
SURE. MAD SCIENTIST SUPER VILLAIN AT FIFTEEN. LOOKS GREAT ON A RESUME.
IT MIGHT TO THIS GUY. HE BELIEVES IN SECOND CHANCES.
JUST TELL PARKER I SENT YOU.
PI PARKER INDUSTRIES
PARKER INDUSTRIES.
I CAN'T TELL YOU HOW MUCH I APPRECIATE THIS, MR. PARKER.
PETE. NICE TO HAVE YOU ON BOARD, CLAYTON.
I'VE BEEN WORKING ON CURING SUPER-CRIMINALS AND REFORMING THEM. TIME TO PUT MY MONEY WHERE MY MOUTH IS.
RUNNING THIS COMPANY GIVES ME GREAT POWER... AND GREAT RESPONSIBILITY. AND I KNOW BETTER THAN ANYONE, HEROES CAN COME FROM THE UNLIKELIEST PLACES.
AR

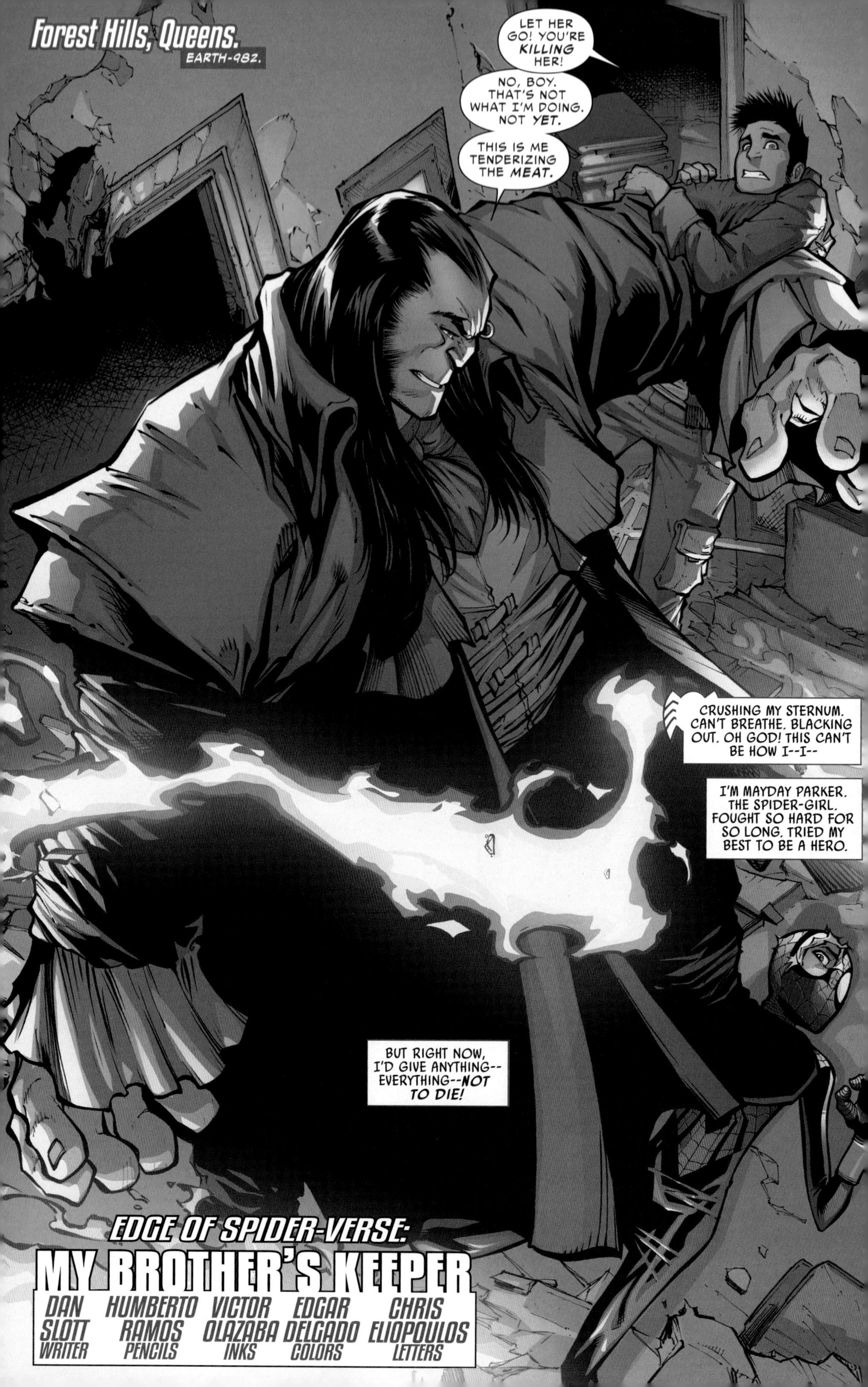

Forest Hills, Queens.
EARTH-982.
LET HER GO! YOU'RE KILLING HER!
NO, BOY. THAT'S NOT WHAT I'M DOING. NOT YET.
THIS IS ME TENDERIZING THE MEAT.
CRUSHING MY STERNUM. CAN'T BREATHE. BLACKING OUT. OH GOD! THIS CAN'T BE HOW I--I--
I'M MAYDAY PARKER. THE SPIDER-GIRL. FOUGHT SO HARD FOR SO LONG. TRIED MY BEST TO BE A HERO.
BUT RIGHT NOW, I'D GIVE ANYTHING-- EVERYTHING--NOT TO DIE!
EDGE OF SPIDER-VERSE:
MY BROTHER'S KEEPER
DAN SLOTT WRITER
HUMBERTO RAMOS PENCILS
VICTOR OLAZABA INKS
EDGAR DELGADO COLORS
CHRIS ELIOPOULOS LETTERS

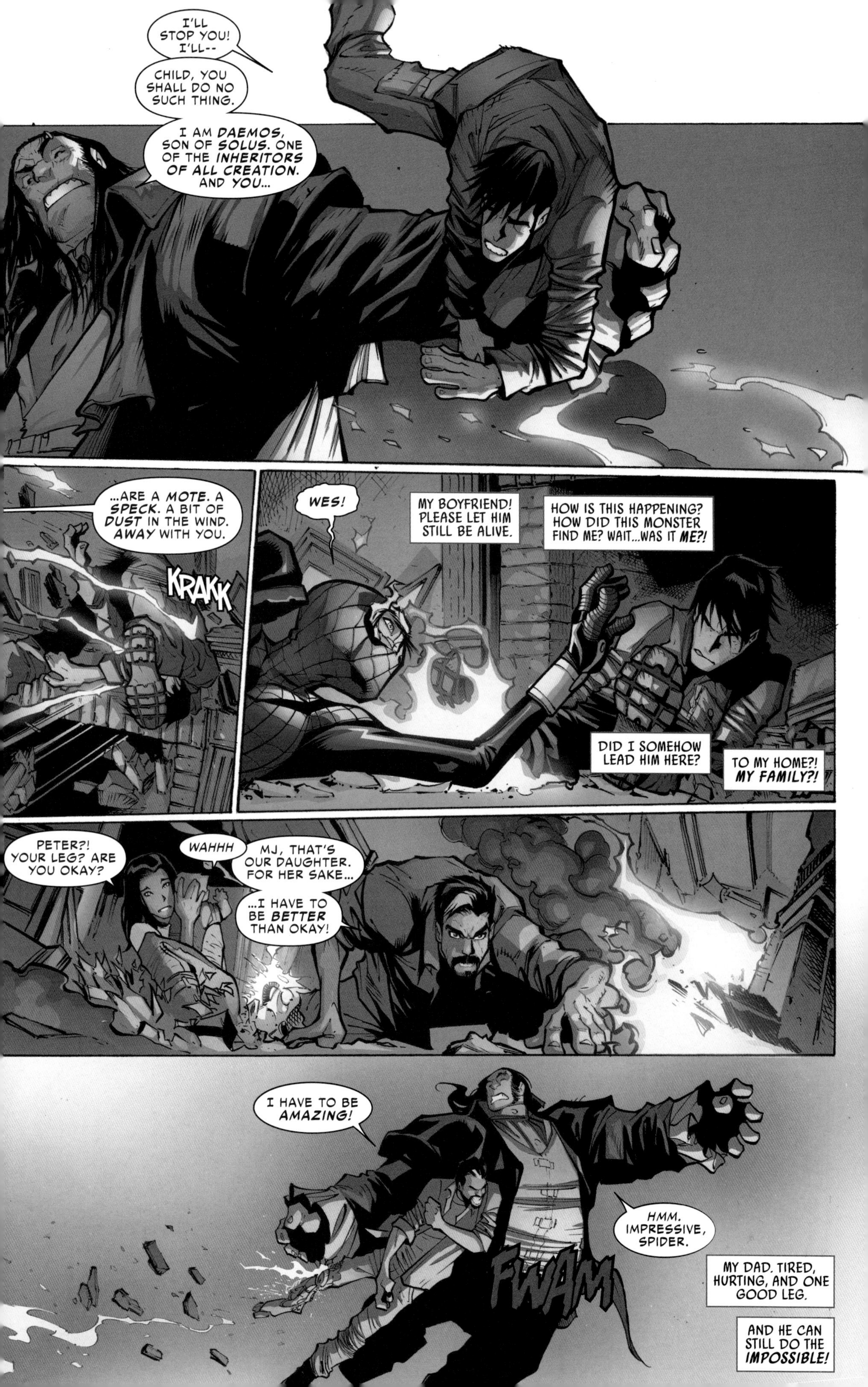
I'LL STOP YOU! I'LL--
CHILD, YOU SHALL DO NO SUCH THING.
I AM DAEMOS, SON OF SOLUS. ONE OF THE INHERITORS OF ALL CREATION. AND YOU...
...ARE A MOTE. A SPECK. A BIT OF DUST IN THE WIND. AWAY WITH YOU.
KRAKK
WES!
MY BOYFRIEND! PLEASE LET HIM STILL BE ALIVE.
HOW IS THIS HAPPENING? HOW DID THIS MONSTER FIND ME? WAIT...WAS IT ME?!
DID I SOMEHOW LEAD HIM HERE?
TO MY HOME?! MY FAMILY?!
PETER?! YOUR LEG? ARE YOU OKAY?
WAHHH
MJ, THAT'S OUR DAUGHTER. FOR HER SAKE...
...I HAVE TO BE BETTER THAN OKAY!
I HAVE TO BE AMAZING!
HMM. IMPRESSIVE, SPIDER.
FWAM
MY DAD. TIRED, HURTING, AND ONE GOOD LEG.
AND HE CAN STILL DO THE IMPOSSIBLE!

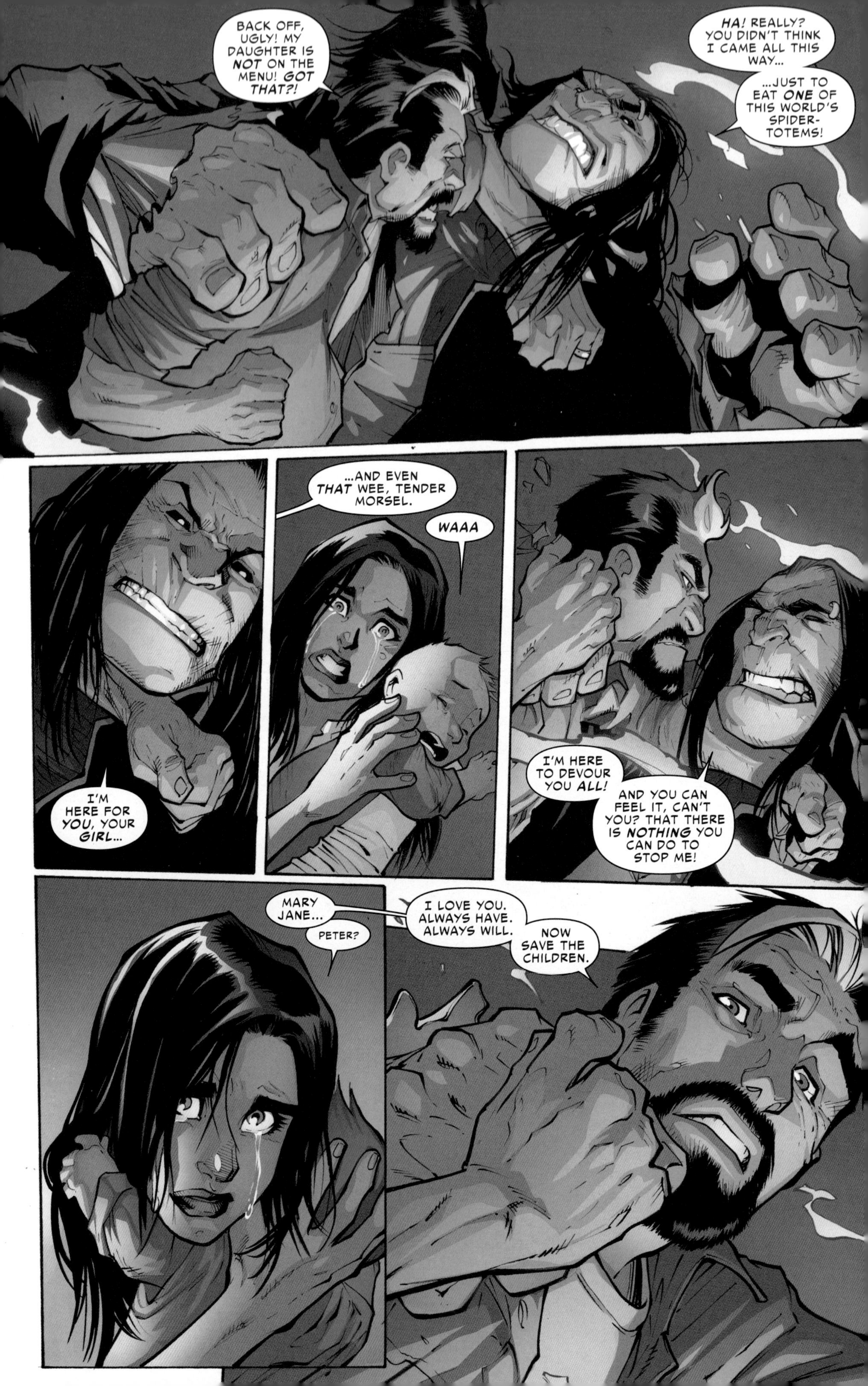
BACK OFF, UGLY! MY DAUGHTER IS NOT ON THE MENU! GOT THAT?!
HA! REALLY? YOU DIDN'T THINK I CAME ALL THIS WAY...
...JUST TO EAT ONE OF THIS WORLD'S SPIDER-TOTEMS!
I'M HERE FOR YOU, YOUR GIRL...
...AND EVEN THAT WEE, TENDER MORSEL.
WAAA
I'M HERE TO DEVOUR YOU ALL!
AND YOU CAN FEEL IT, CAN'T YOU? THAT THERE IS NOTHING YOU CAN DO TO STOP ME!
MARY JANE...
PETER?
I LOVE YOU. ALWAYS HAVE. ALWAYS WILL.
NOW SAVE THE CHILDREN.

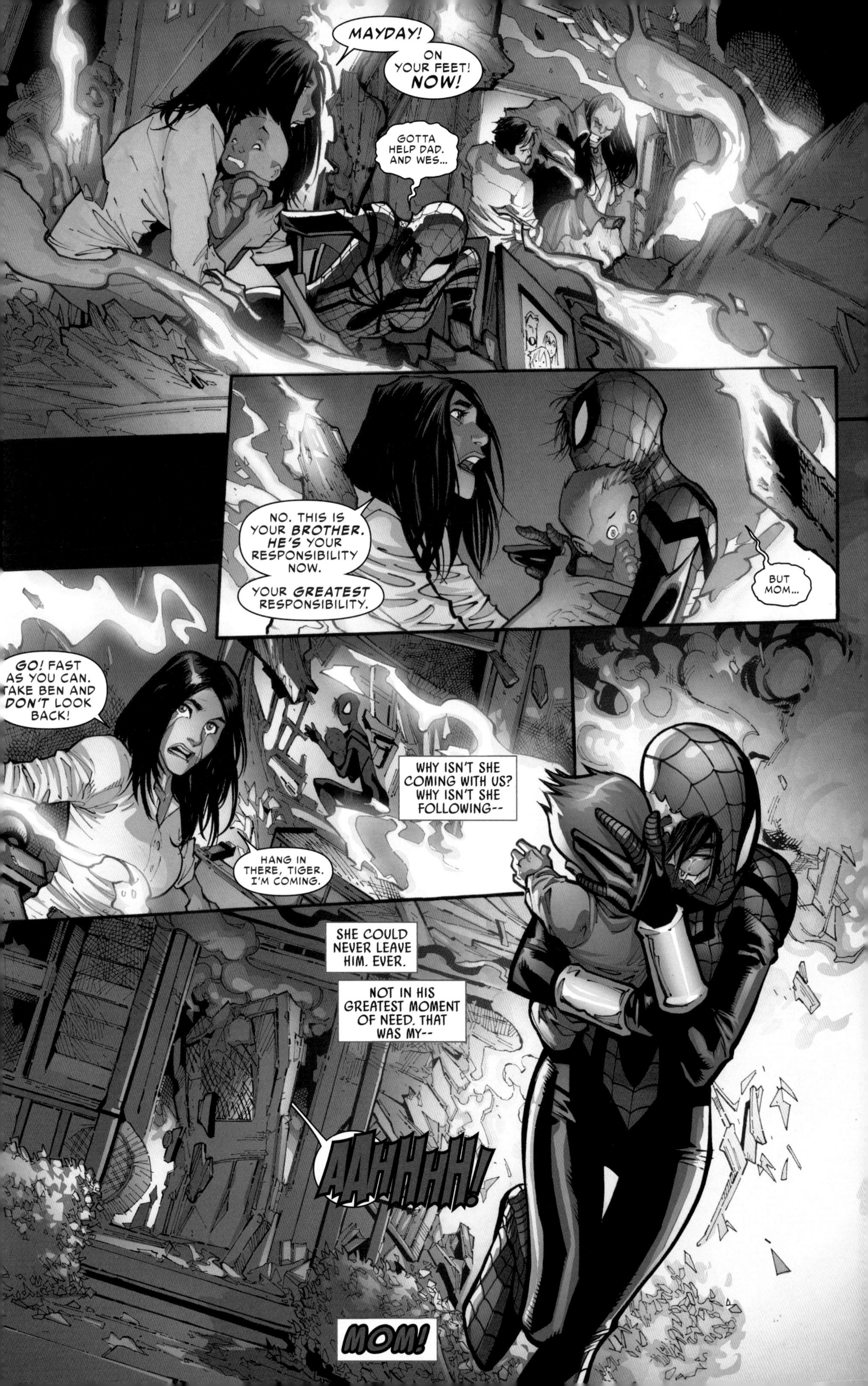
MAYDAY!
ON YOUR FEET! NOW!
GOTTA HELP DAD. AND WES...
NO. THIS IS YOUR BROTHER. HE'S YOUR RESPONSIBILITY NOW.
YOUR GREATEST RESPONSIBILITY.
BUT MOM...
GO! FAST AS YOU CAN. TAKE BEN AND DON'T LOOK BACK!
WHY ISN'T SHE COMING WITH US? WHY ISN'T SHE FOLLOWING--
HANG IN THERE, TIGER. I'M COMING.
SHE COULD NEVER LEAVE HIM. EVER.
NOT IN HIS GREATEST MOMENT OF NEED. THAT WAS MY--
AAHHHH!
MOM!

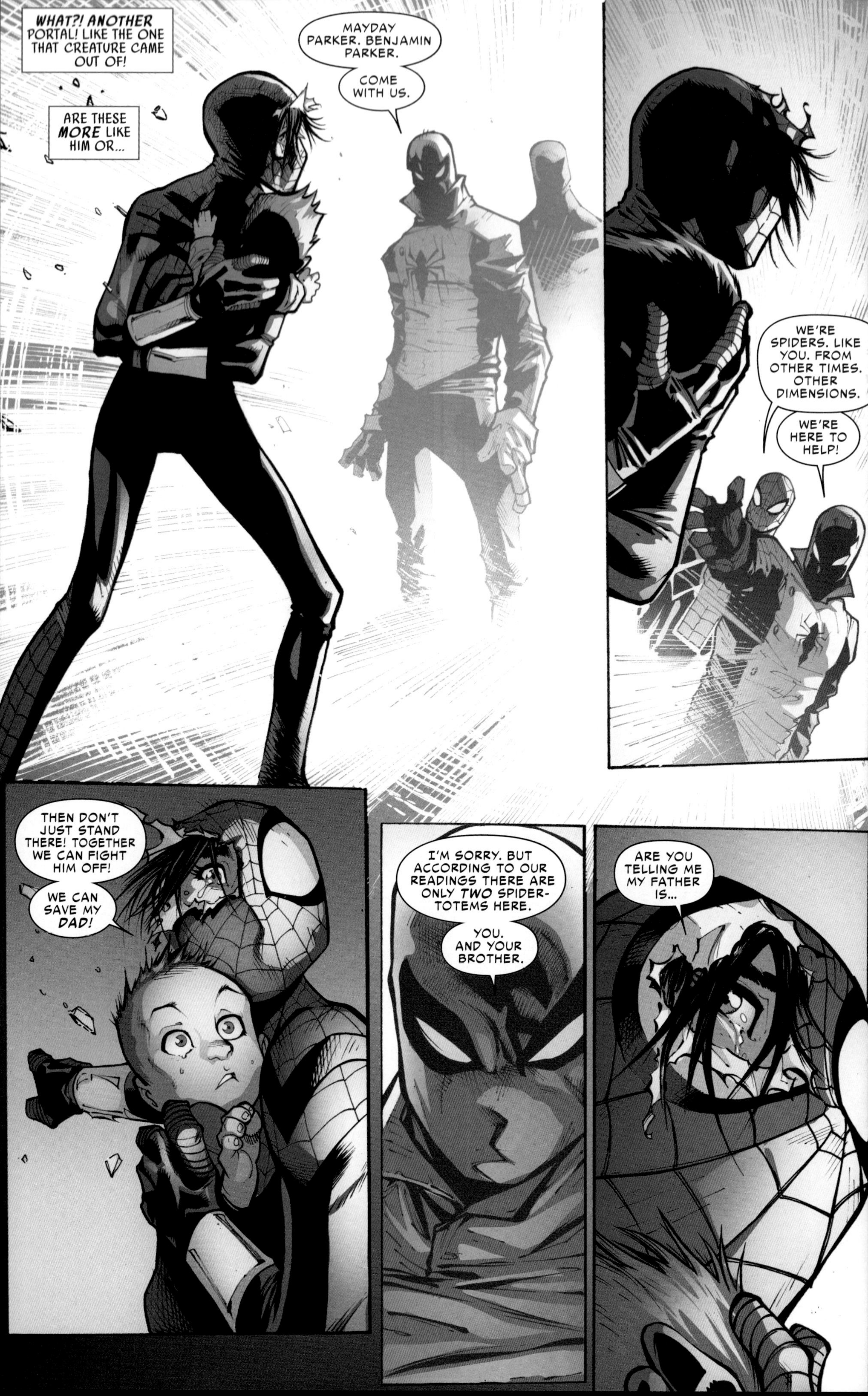
WHAT?! ANOTHER PORTAL! LIKE THE ONE THAT CREATURE CAME OUT OF!
ARE THESE MORE LIKE HIM OR...
MAYDAY PARKER. BENJAMIN PARKER.
COME WITH US.
WE'RE SPIDERS. LIKE YOU. FROM OTHER TIMES. OTHER DIMENSIONS.
WE'RE HERE TO HELP!
THEN DON'T JUST STAND THERE! TOGETHER WE CAN FIGHT HIM OFF!
WE CAN SAVE MY DAD!
I'M SORRY. BUT ACCORDING TO OUR READINGS THERE ARE ONLY TWO SPIDER-TOTEMS HERE.
YOU. AND YOUR BROTHER.
ARE YOU TELLING ME MY FATHER IS...

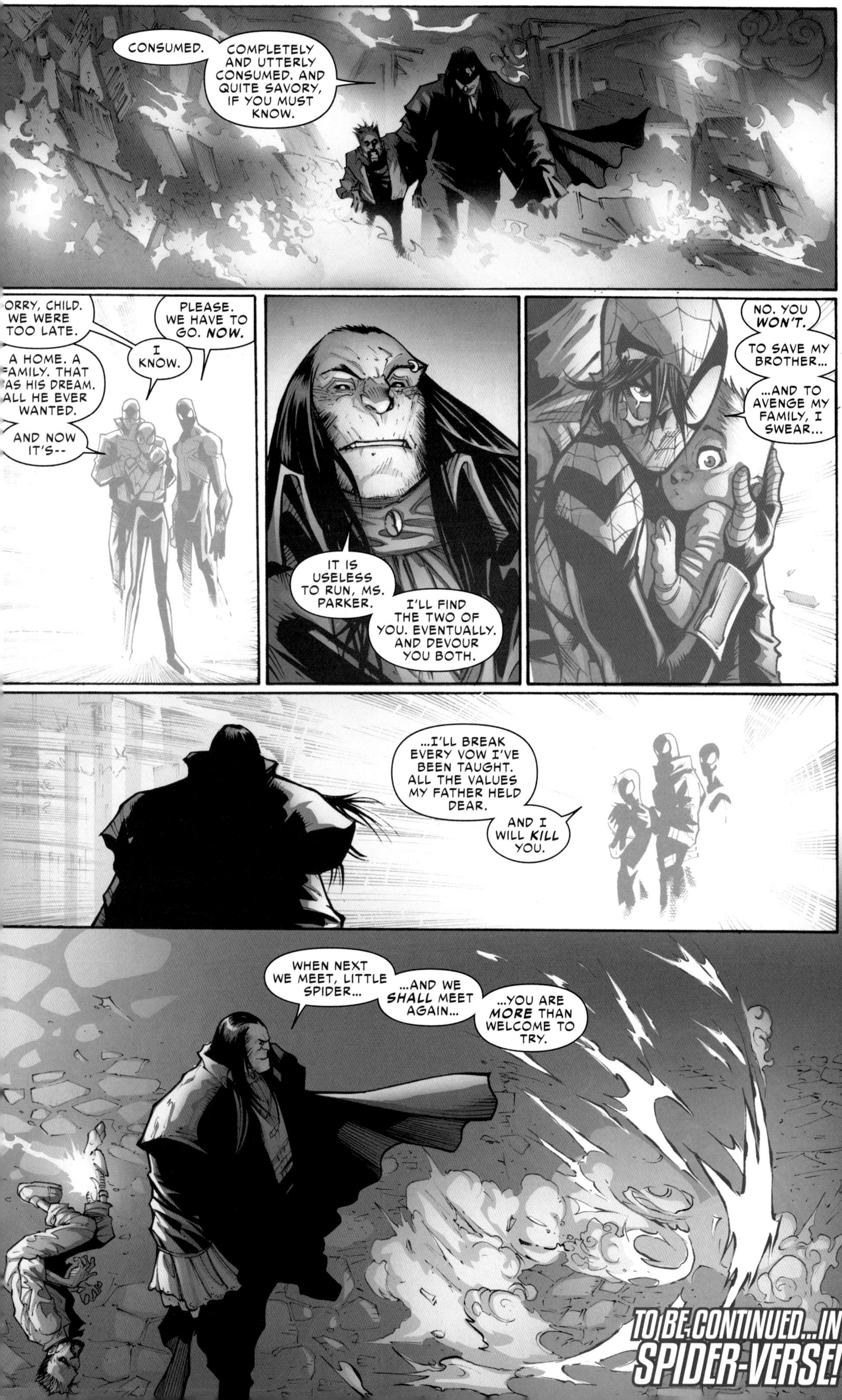
CONSUMED.
COMPLETELY AND UTTERLY CONSUMED. AND QUITE SAVORY, IF YOU MUST KNOW.
ORRY, CHILD. WE WERE TOO LATE.
A HOME. A FAMILY. THAT AS HIS DREAM. ALL HE EVER WANTED.
AND NOW IT'S--
I KNOW.
PLEASE. WE HAVE TO GO. NOW.
IT IS USELESS TO RUN, MS. PARKER.
I'LL FIND THE TWO OF YOU. EVENTUALLY. AND DEVOUR YOU BOTH.
NO. YOU WON'T.
TO SAVE MY BROTHER...
...AND TO AVENGE MY FAMILY, I SWEAR...
...I'LL BREAK EVERY VOW I'VE BEEN TAUGHT. ALL THE VALUES MY FATHER HELD DEAR.
AND I WILL KILL YOU.
WHEN NEXT WE MEET, LITTLE SPIDER...
...AND WE SHALL MEET AGAIN...
...YOU ARE MORE THAN WELCOME TO TRY.
TO BE CONTINUED...IN SPIDER-VERSE!

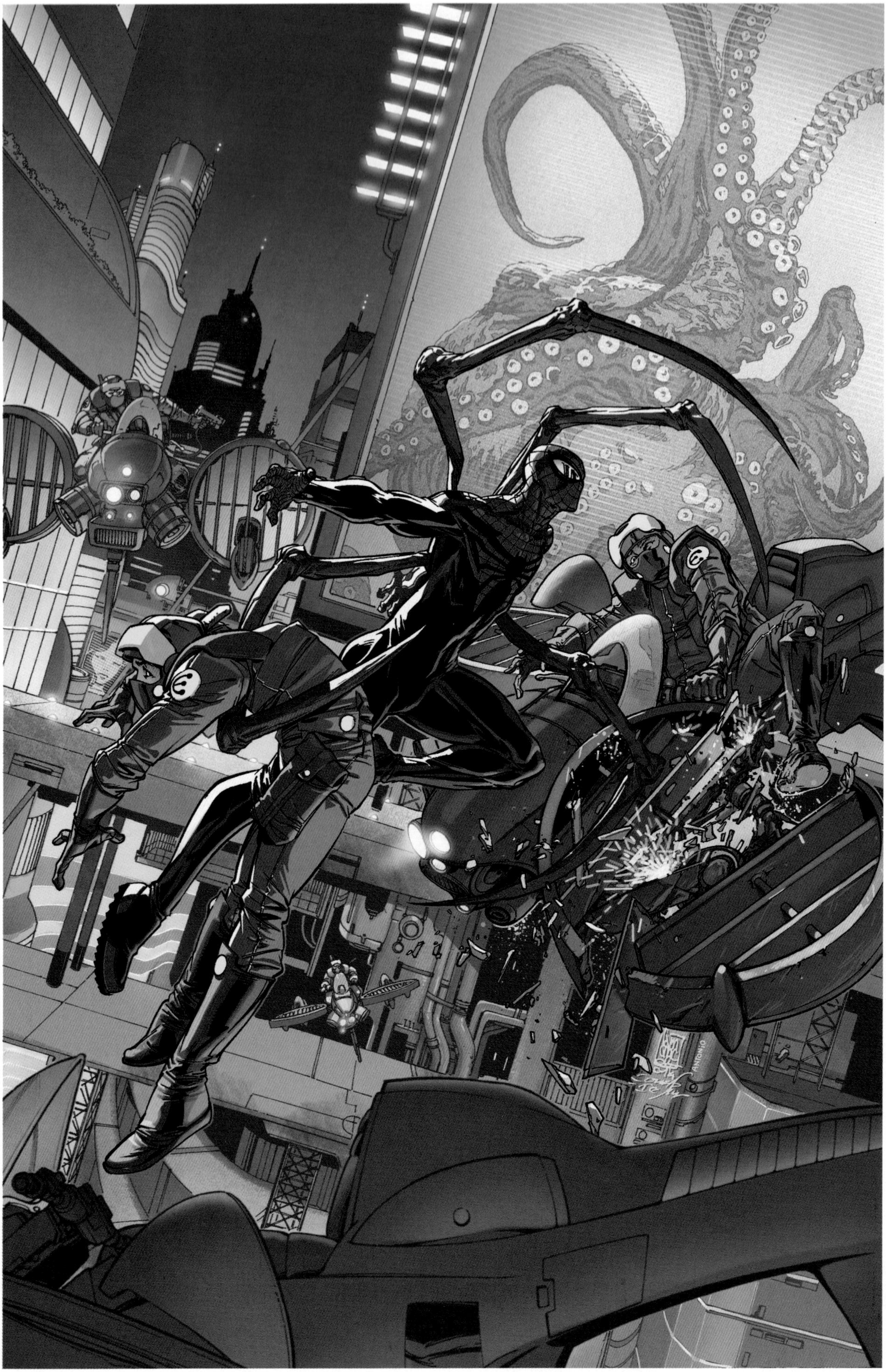

SUPERIOR SPIDER-MAN 32

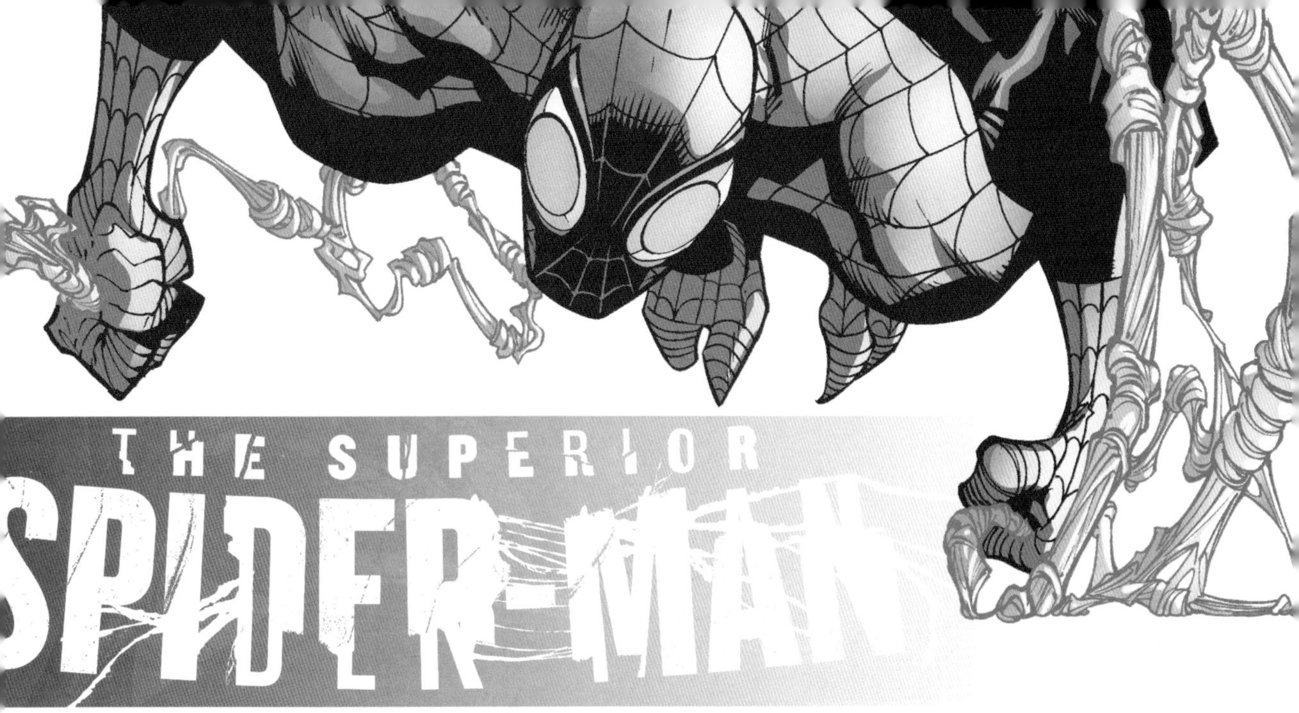
THE SUPERIOR
SPIDER-MAN

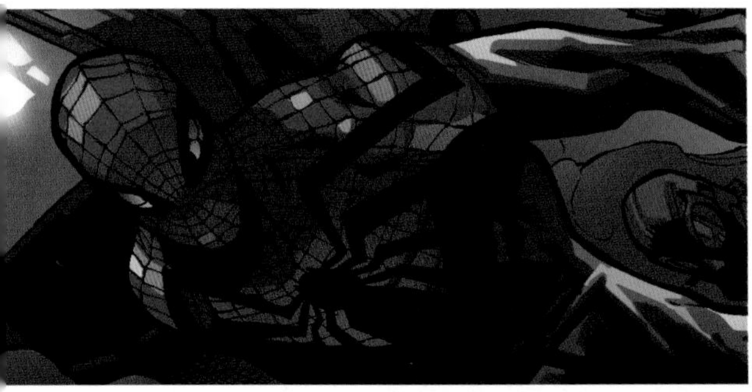

IN A LAST-DITCH EFFORT TO SAVE HIMSELF FROM DEATH, **OTTO OCTAVIUS** SWAPPED MINDS WITH SPIDER-MAN, LEAVING **PETER PARKER** TO DIE IN HIS PLACE. TAKING ON PETER'S SENSE OF RESPONSIBILITY, OTTO CARRIED ON HIS MISSION AS THE SUPERIOR SPIDER-MAN.

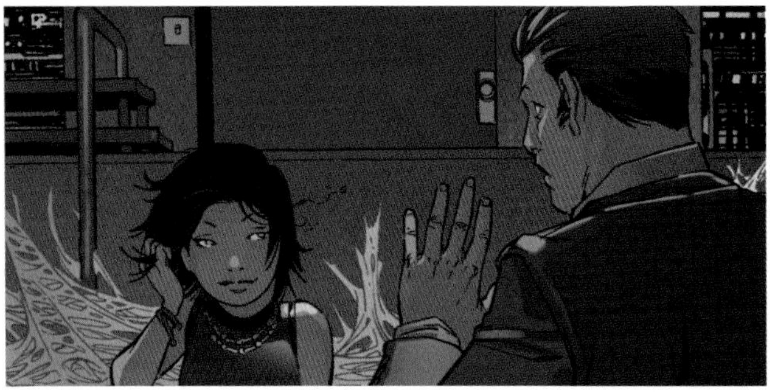

OTTO SET ABOUT IMPROVING PETER'S LIFE AND EVEN FELL IN LOVE WITH A WOMAN NAMED **ANNA MARIA MARCONI.**

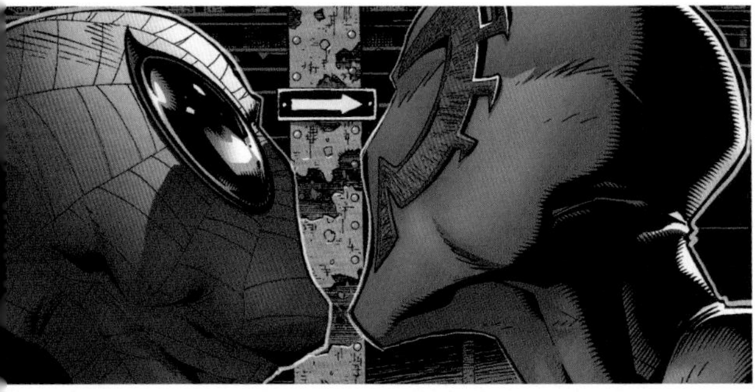

RECENTLY, WHEN A **TEMPORAL DISTORTION** THREATENED THE LIFE OF TYLER STONE, HEAD OF ALCHEMAX IN THE YEAR 2099, SPIDER-MAN 2099 TRAVELED BACK IN TIME TO HORIZON LABS BEFORE IT BECAME ALCHEMAX TO SAVE THE LIFE OF TIBERIUS STONE.

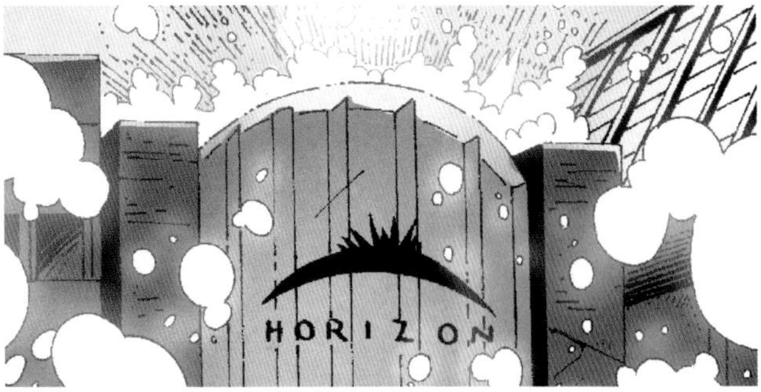
HORIZON

WHEN HORIZON LABS WAS LOST IN A TEMPORAL IMPLOSION, THE SUPERIOR SPIDER-MAN DISAPPEARED FOR 24 HOURS.* THIS IS WHERE HE WENT.

THIS STORY TAKES PLACE DURING* ***SUPERIOR SPIDER-MAN #19.*

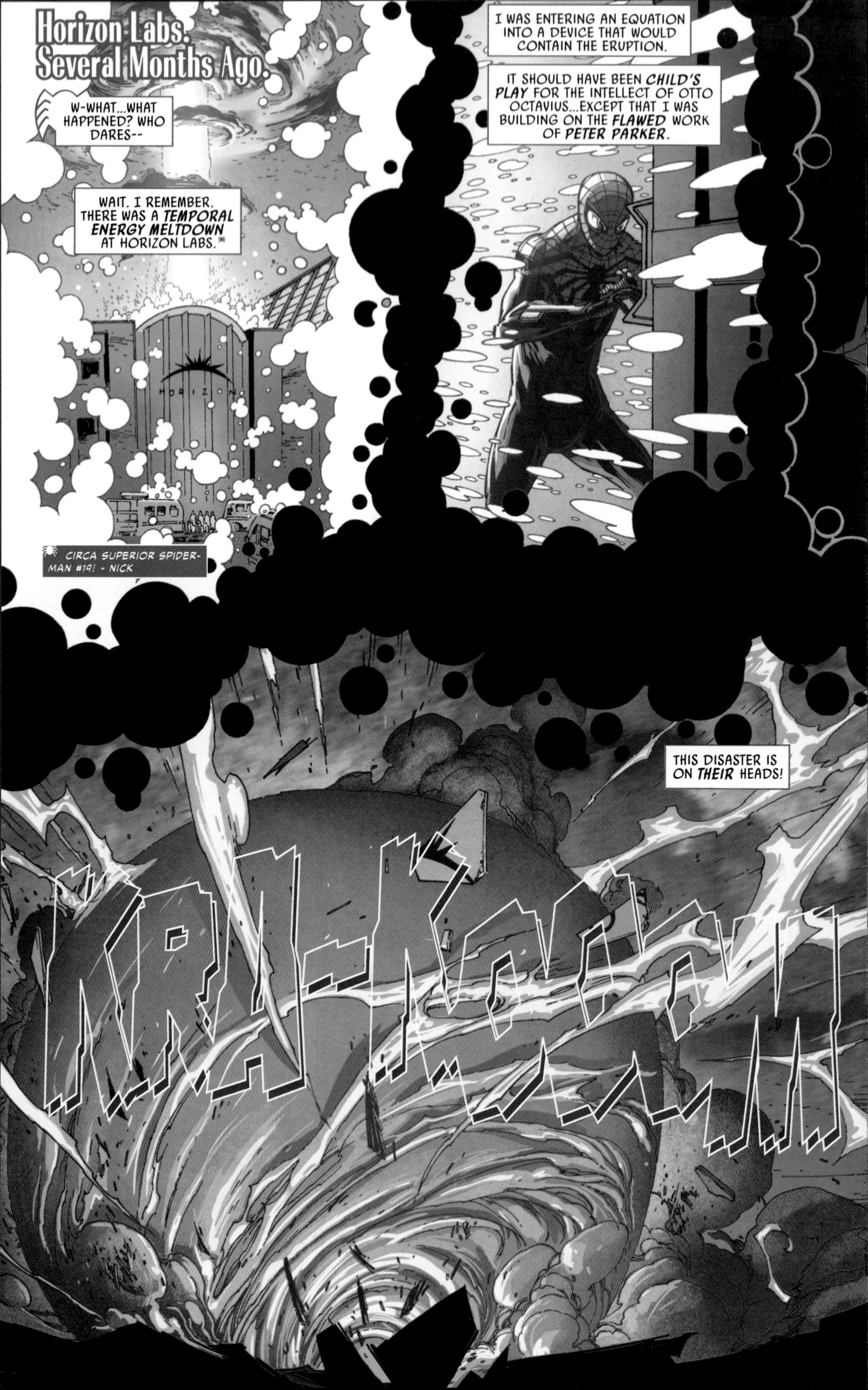
Horizon Labs. Several Months Ago.
W-WHAT...WHAT HAPPENED? WHO DARES--
WAIT. I REMEMBER. THERE WAS A TEMPORAL ENERGY MELTDOWN AT HORIZON LABS.*
*CIRCA SUPERIOR SPIDER-MAN #19! - NICK
I WAS ENTERING AN EQUATION INTO A DEVICE THAT WOULD CONTAIN THE ERUPTION.
IT SHOULD HAVE BEEN CHILD'S PLAY FOR THE INTELLECT OF OTTO OCTAVIUS...EXCEPT THAT I WAS BUILDING ON THE FLAWED WORK OF PETER PARKER.
THIS DISASTER IS ON THEIR HEADS!
KRA-KOOOOM

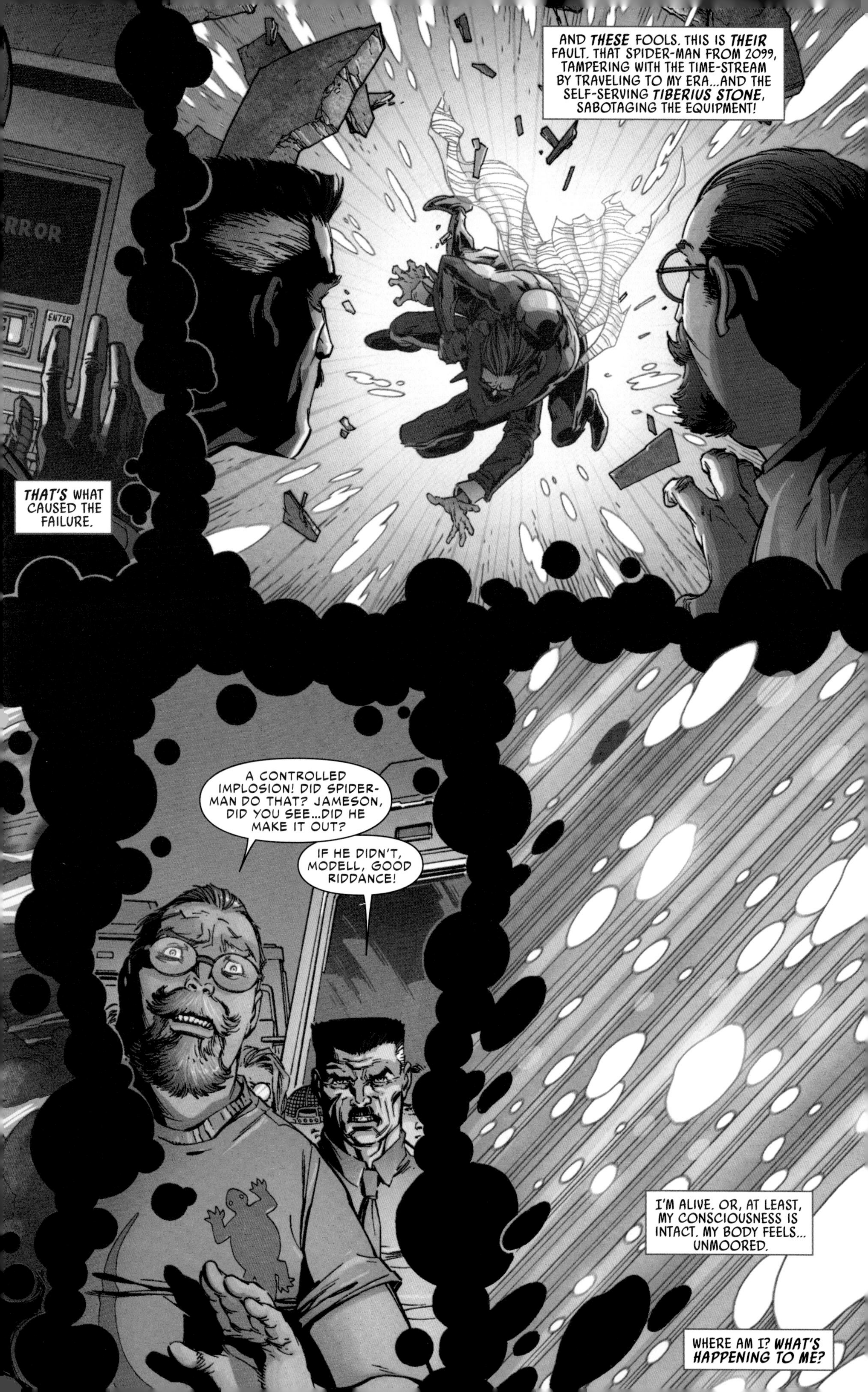
AND THESE FOOLS. THIS IS THEIR FAULT. THAT SPIDER-MAN FROM 2099, TAMPERING WITH THE TIME-STREAM BY TRAVELING TO MY ERA...AND THE SELF-SERVING TIBERIUS STONE, SABOTAGING THE EQUIPMENT!
RROR
ENTER
THAT'S WHAT CAUSED THE FAILURE.
A CONTROLLED IMPLOSION! DID SPIDER-MAN DO THAT? JAMESON, DID YOU SEE...DID HE MAKE IT OUT?
IF HE DIDN'T, MODELL, GOOD RIDDANCE!
I'M ALIVE. OR, AT LEAST, MY CONSCIOUSNESS IS INTACT. MY BODY FEELS... UNMOORED.
WHERE AM I? WHAT'S HAPPENING TO ME?

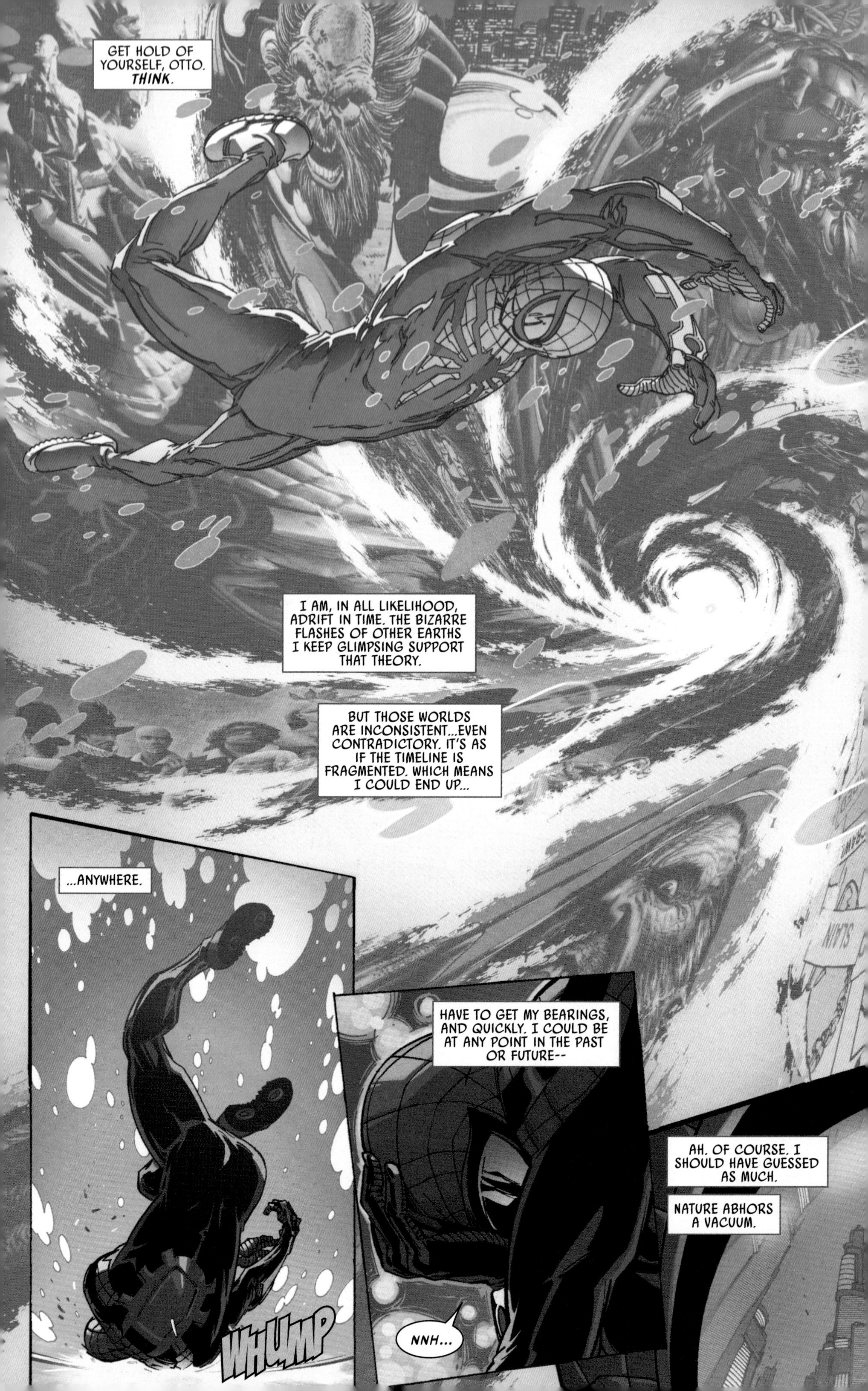
GET HOLD OF YOURSELF, OTTO. *THINK.*
I AM, IN ALL LIKELIHOOD, ADRIFT IN TIME. THE BIZARRE FLASHES OF OTHER EARTHS I KEEP GLIMPSING SUPPORT THAT THEORY.
BUT THOSE WORLDS ARE INCONSISTENT...EVEN CONTRADICTORY. IT'S AS IF THE TIMELINE IS FRAGMENTED. WHICH MEANS I COULD END UP...
...ANYWHERE.
WHUMP
HAVE TO GET MY BEARINGS, AND QUICKLY. I COULD BE AT ANY POINT IN THE PAST OR FUTURE--
NNH...
AH. OF COURSE. I SHOULD HAVE GUESSED AS MUCH.
NATURE ABHORS A VACUUM.

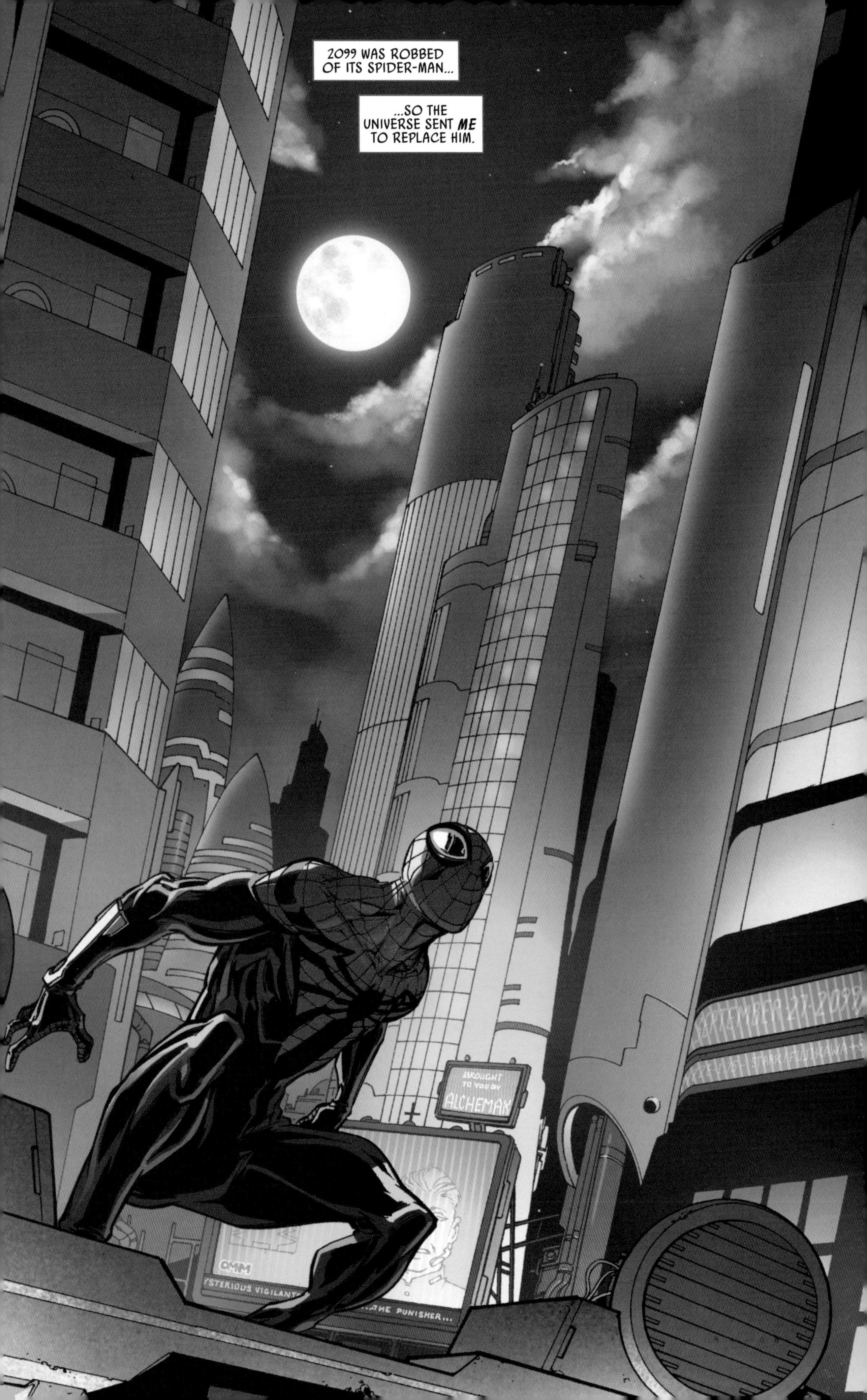
2099 WAS ROBBED OF ITS SPIDER-MAN...
...SO THE UNIVERSE SENT *ME* TO REPLACE HIM.
EPTEMBER 27-209
BROUGHT TO YOU BY ALCHEMAX
OMM
YSTERIOUS VIGILANT
...THE PUNISHER...

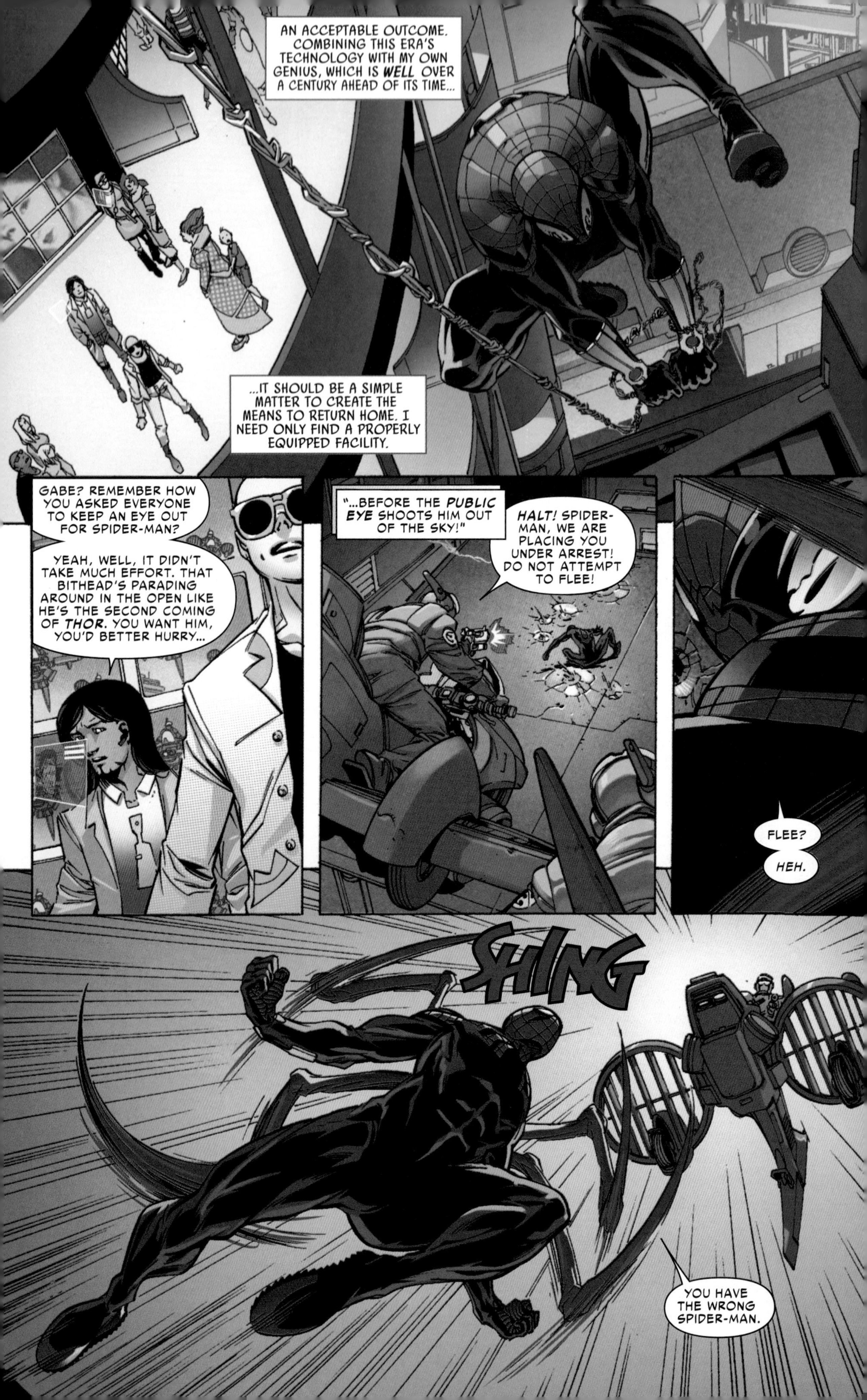
AN ACCEPTABLE OUTCOME. COMBINING THIS ERA'S TECHNOLOGY WITH MY OWN GENIUS, WHICH IS WELL OVER A CENTURY AHEAD OF ITS TIME...
...IT SHOULD BE A SIMPLE MATTER TO CREATE THE MEANS TO RETURN HOME. I NEED ONLY FIND A PROPERLY EQUIPPED FACILITY.
GABE? REMEMBER HOW YOU ASKED EVERYONE TO KEEP AN EYE OUT FOR SPIDER-MAN?
YEAH, WELL, IT DIDN'T TAKE MUCH EFFORT. THAT BITHEAD'S PARADING AROUND IN THE OPEN LIKE HE'S THE SECOND COMING OF THOR. YOU WANT HIM, YOU'D BETTER HURRY...
"...BEFORE THE PUBLIC EYE SHOOTS HIM OUT OF THE SKY!"
HALT! SPIDER-MAN, WE ARE PLACING YOU UNDER ARREST! DO NOT ATTEMPT TO FLEE!
FLEE?
HEH.
SHING
YOU HAVE THE WRONG SPIDER-MAN.

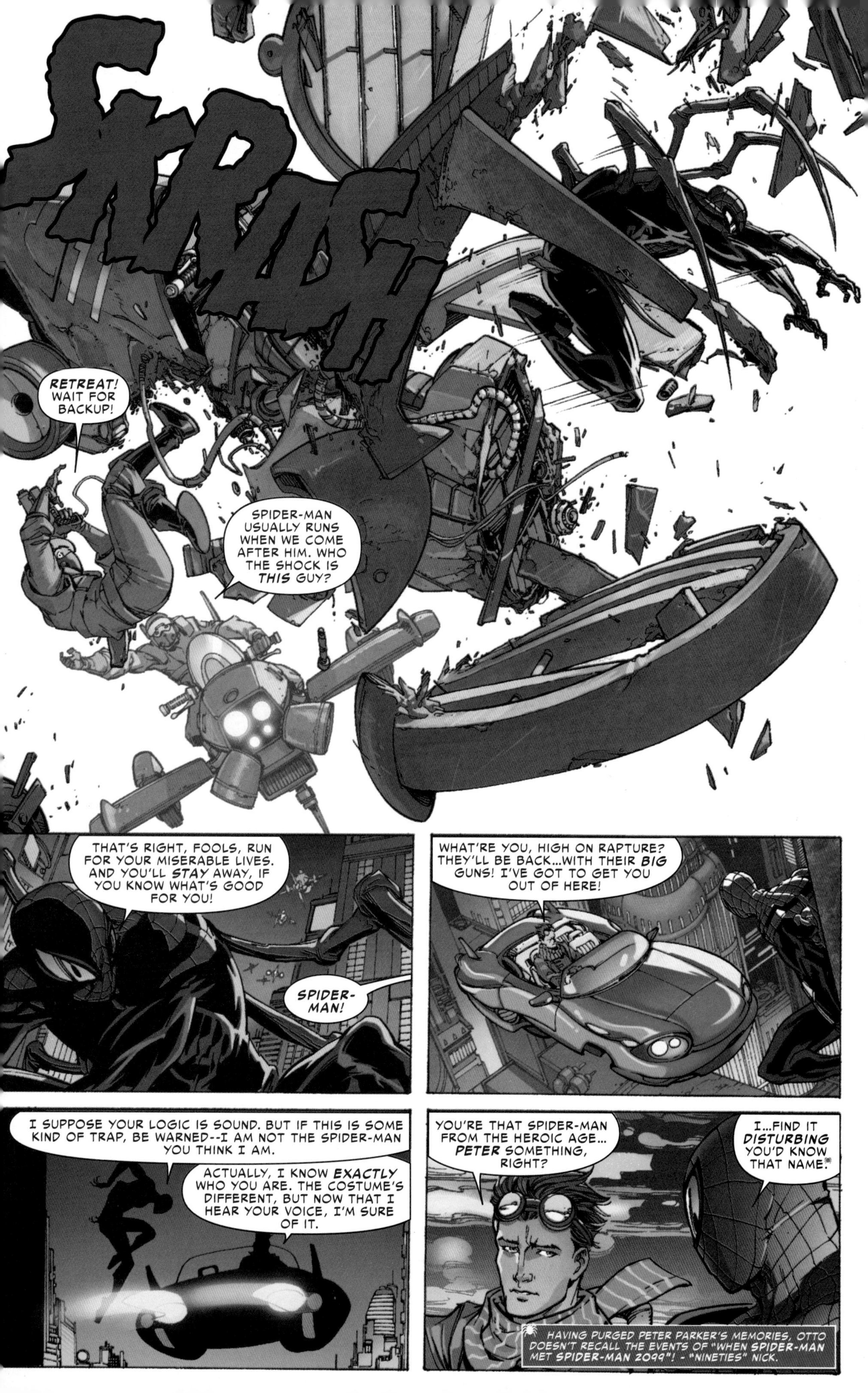

SKRASH
RETREAT! WAIT FOR BACKUP!
SPIDER-MAN USUALLY RUNS WHEN WE COME AFTER HIM. WHO THE SHOCK IS *THIS* GUY?
THAT'S RIGHT, FOOLS, RUN FOR YOUR MISERABLE LIVES. AND YOU'LL *STAY* AWAY, IF YOU KNOW WHAT'S GOOD FOR YOU!
SPIDER-MAN!
WHAT'RE YOU, HIGH ON RAPTURE? THEY'LL BE BACK...WITH THEIR *BIG* GUNS! I'VE GOT TO GET YOU OUT OF HERE!
I SUPPOSE YOUR LOGIC IS SOUND. BUT IF THIS IS SOME KIND OF TRAP, BE WARNED--I AM NOT THE SPIDER-MAN YOU THINK I AM.
ACTUALLY, I KNOW *EXACTLY* WHO YOU ARE. THE COSTUME'S DIFFERENT, BUT NOW THAT I HEAR YOUR VOICE, I'M SURE OF IT.
YOU'RE THAT SPIDER-MAN FROM THE HEROIC AGE... *PETER* SOMETHING, RIGHT?
I...FIND IT *DISTURBING* YOU'D KNOW THAT NAME.
HAVING PURGED PETER PARKER'S MEMORIES, OTTO DOESN'T RECALL THE EVENTS OF "WHEN SPIDER-MAN MET SPIDER-MAN 2099"! - "NINETIES" NICK.

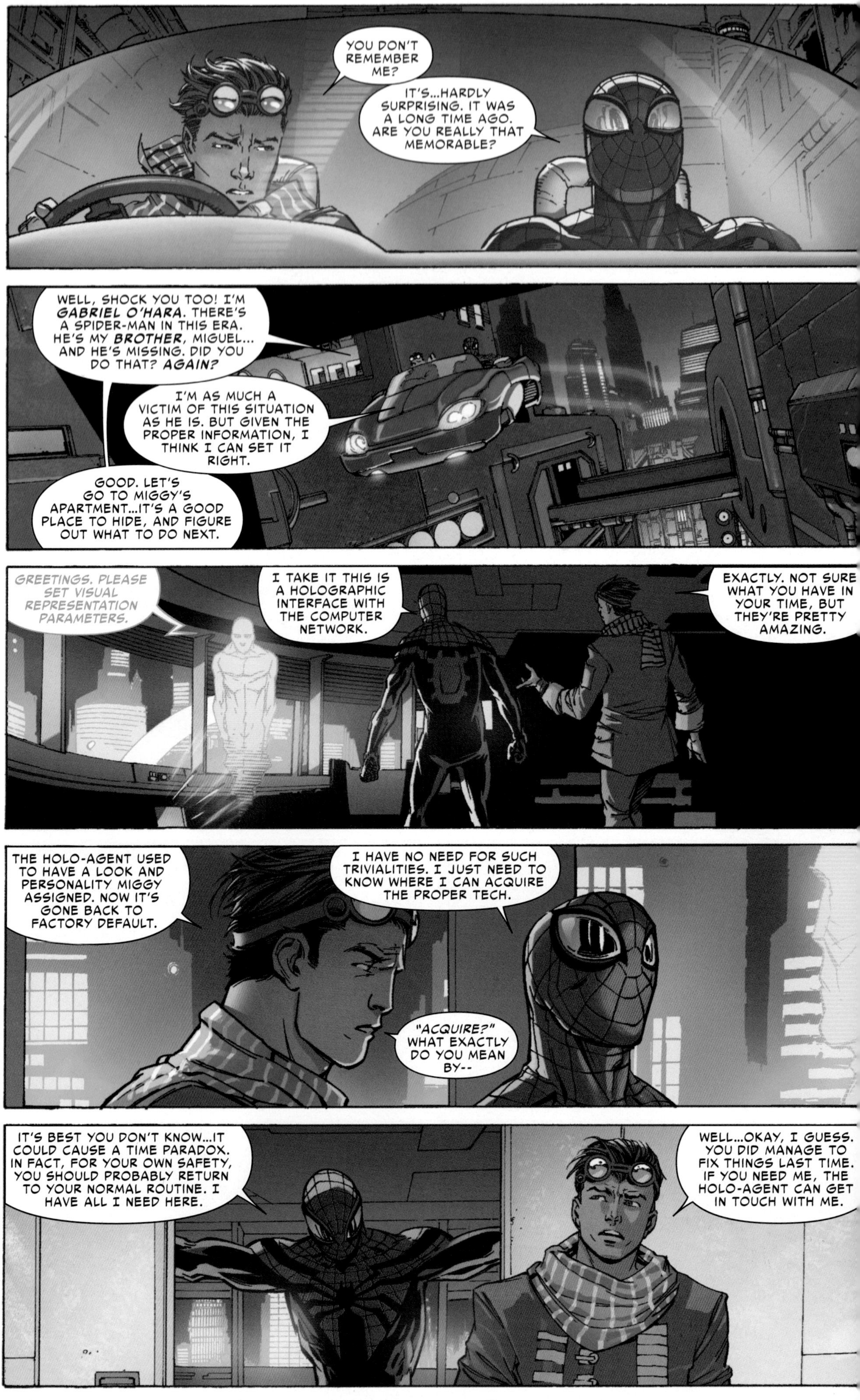
YOU DON'T REMEMBER ME?
IT'S...HARDLY SURPRISING. IT WAS A LONG TIME AGO. ARE YOU REALLY THAT MEMORABLE?
WELL, SHOCK YOU TOO! I'M *GABRIEL O'HARA*. THERE'S A SPIDER-MAN IN THIS ERA. HE'S MY *BROTHER*, MIGUEL... AND HE'S MISSING. DID YOU DO THAT? *AGAIN?*
I'M AS MUCH A VICTIM OF THIS SITUATION AS HE IS. BUT GIVEN THE PROPER INFORMATION, I THINK I CAN SET IT RIGHT.
GOOD. LET'S GO TO MIGGY'S APARTMENT...IT'S A GOOD PLACE TO HIDE, AND FIGURE OUT WHAT TO DO NEXT.
GREETINGS. PLEASE SET VISUAL REPRESENTATION PARAMETERS.
I TAKE IT THIS IS A HOLOGRAPHIC INTERFACE WITH THE COMPUTER NETWORK.
EXACTLY. NOT SURE WHAT YOU HAVE IN YOUR TIME, BUT THEY'RE PRETTY AMAZING.
THE HOLO-AGENT USED TO HAVE A LOOK AND PERSONALITY MIGGY ASSIGNED. NOW IT'S GONE BACK TO FACTORY DEFAULT.
I HAVE NO NEED FOR SUCH TRIVIALITIES. I JUST NEED TO KNOW WHERE I CAN ACQUIRE THE PROPER TECH.
"ACQUIRE?" WHAT EXACTLY DO YOU MEAN BY--
IT'S BEST YOU DON'T KNOW...IT COULD CAUSE A TIME PARADOX. IN FACT, FOR YOUR OWN SAFETY, YOU SHOULD PROBABLY RETURN TO YOUR NORMAL ROUTINE. I HAVE ALL I NEED HERE.
WELL...OKAY, I GUESS. YOU DID MANAGE TO FIX THINGS LAST TIME. IF YOU NEED ME, THE HOLO-AGENT CAN GET IN TOUCH WITH ME.

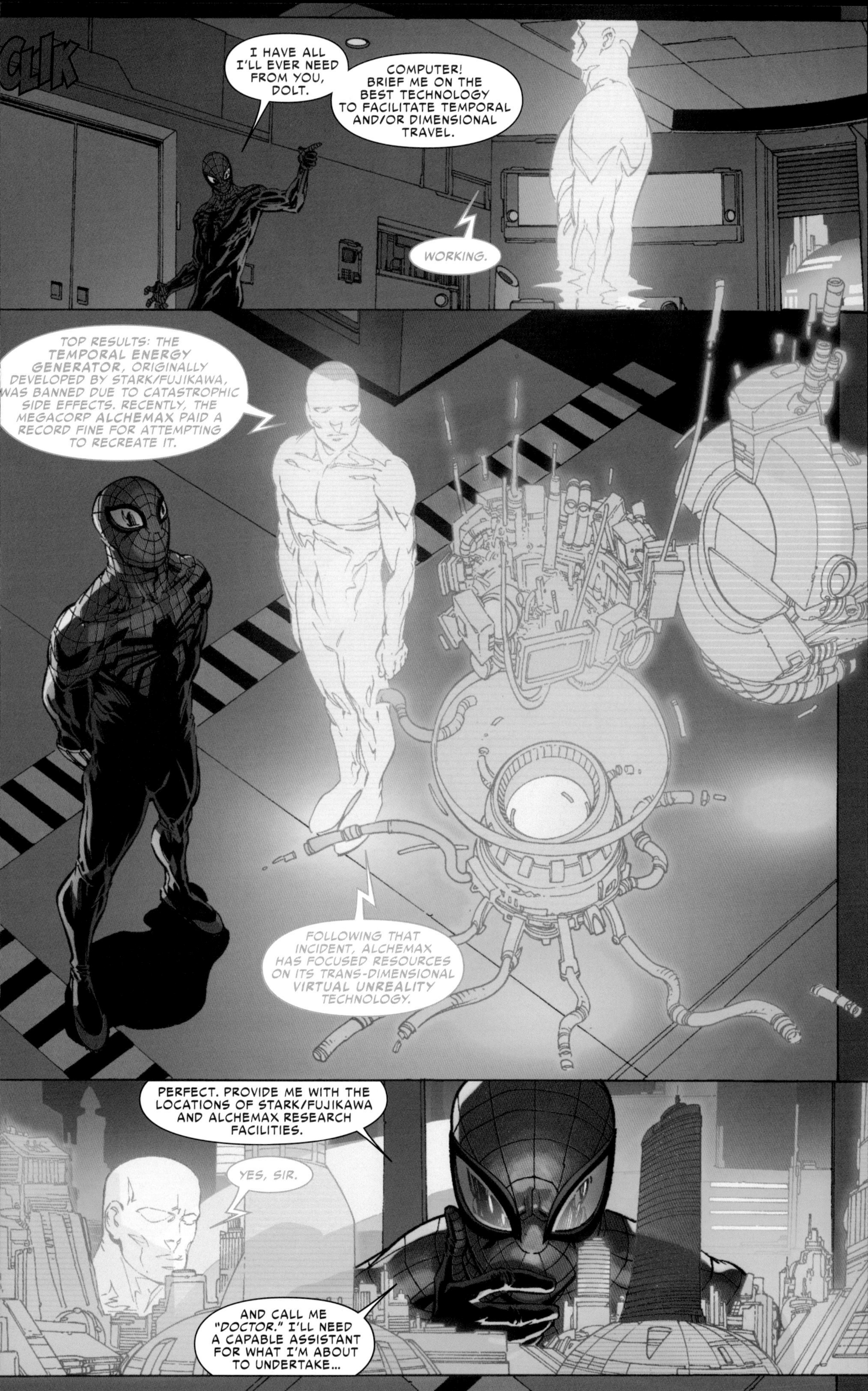

CLIK
I HAVE ALL I'LL EVER NEED FROM YOU, DOLT.
COMPUTER! BRIEF ME ON THE BEST TECHNOLOGY TO FACILITATE TEMPORAL AND/OR DIMENSIONAL TRAVEL.
WORKING.
TOP RESULTS: THE TEMPORAL ENERGY GENERATOR, ORIGINALLY DEVELOPED BY STARK/FUJIKAWA, WAS BANNED DUE TO CATASTROPHIC SIDE EFFECTS. RECENTLY, THE MEGACORP ALCHEMAX PAID A RECORD FINE FOR ATTEMPTING TO RECREATE IT.
FOLLOWING THAT INCIDENT, ALCHEMAX HAS FOCUSED RESOURCES ON ITS TRANS-DIMENSIONAL VIRTUAL UNREALITY TECHNOLOGY.
PERFECT. PROVIDE ME WITH THE LOCATIONS OF STARK/FUJIKAWA AND ALCHEMAX RESEARCH FACILITIES.
YES, SIR.
AND CALL ME "DOCTOR." I'LL NEED A CAPABLE ASSISTANT FOR WHAT I'M ABOUT TO UNDERTAKE...

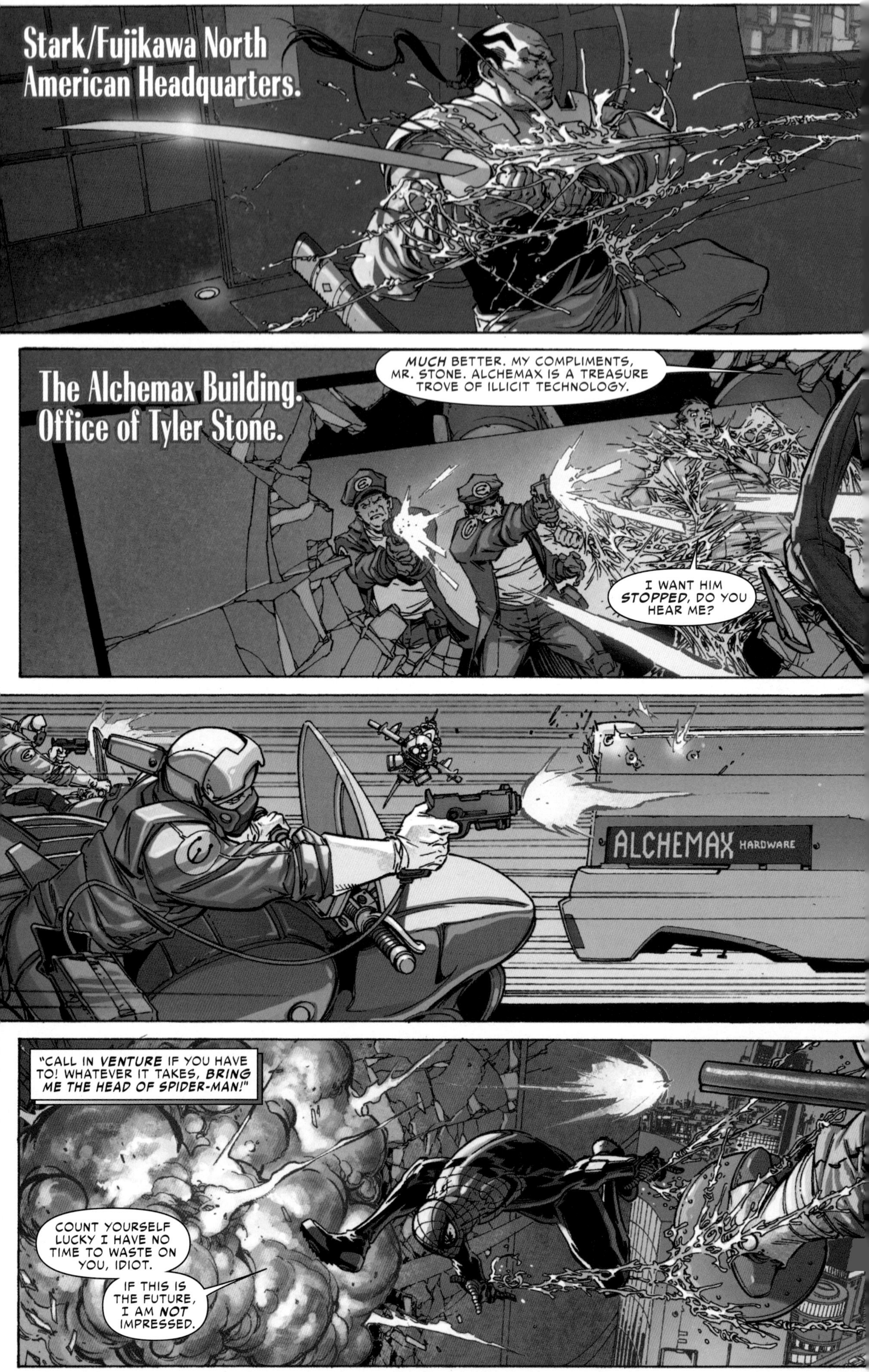
Stark/Fujikawa North American Headquarters.
The Alchemax Building. Office of Tyler Stone.
MUCH BETTER. MY COMPLIMENTS, MR. STONE. ALCHEMAX IS A TREASURE TROVE OF ILLICIT TECHNOLOGY.
I WANT HIM STOPPED, DO YOU HEAR ME?
ALCHEMAX HARDWARE
"CALL IN VENTURE IF YOU HAVE TO! WHATEVER IT TAKES, BRING ME THE HEAD OF SPIDER-MAN!"
COUNT YOURSELF LUCKY I HAVE NO TIME TO WASTE ON YOU, IDIOT.
IF THIS IS THE FUTURE, I AM NOT IMPRESSED.

DISAPPOINTING. YOUR COMPANY IS ACTUALLY ABIDING BY THE LAW, SPECIALIST. SLIM PICKINGS INDEED.

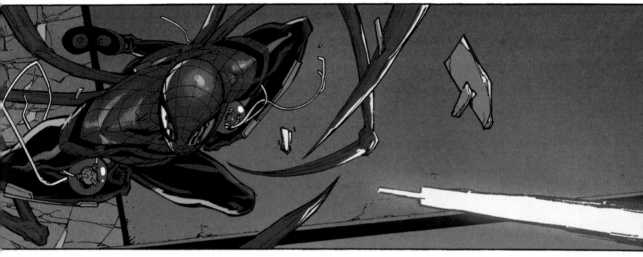

"BRING ALL THE RESOURCES OF THE PUBLIC EYE DOWN ON HIM!

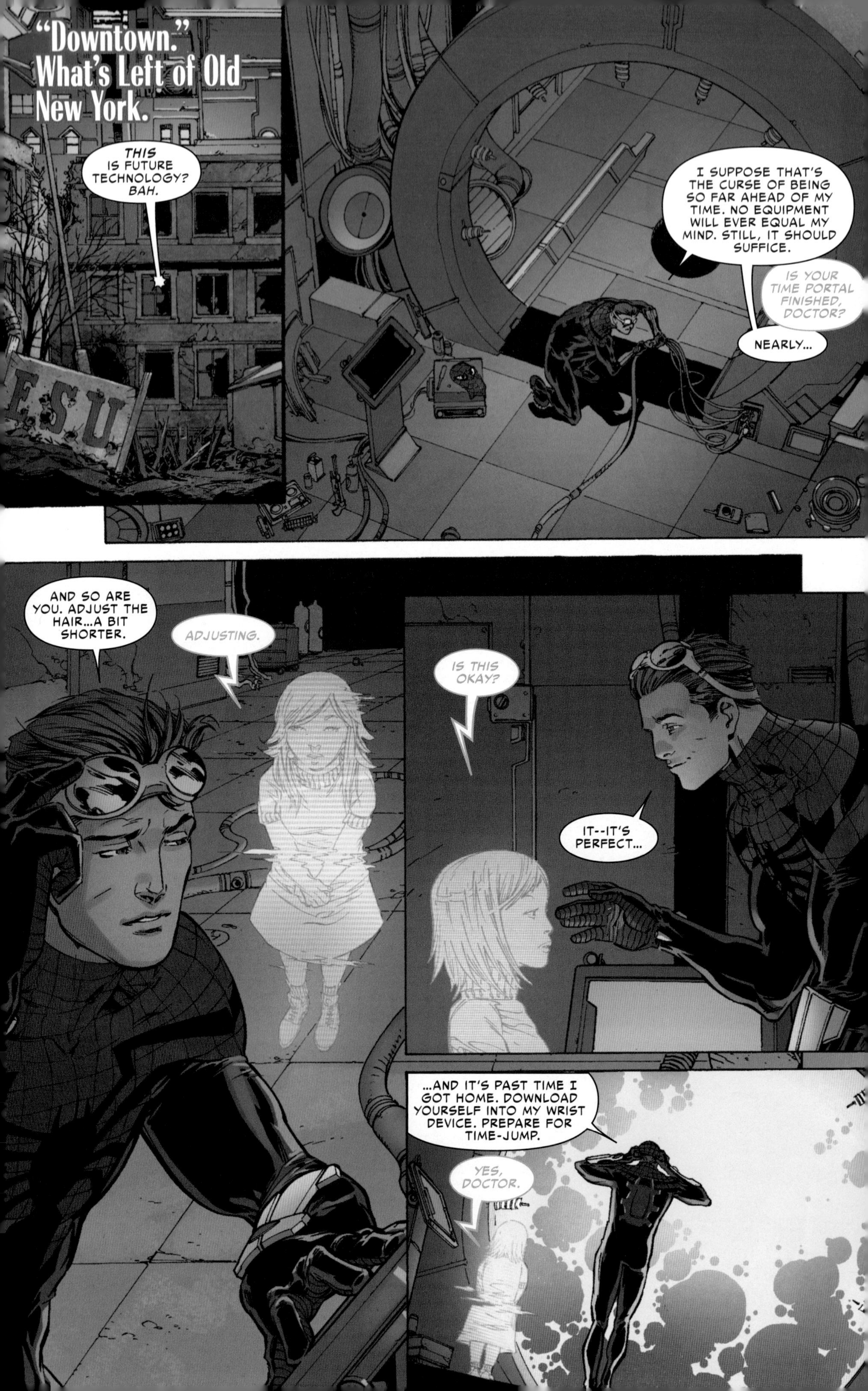

"Downtown." What's Left of Old New York.
THIS IS FUTURE TECHNOLOGY? BAH.
I SUPPOSE THAT'S THE CURSE OF BEING SO FAR AHEAD OF MY TIME. NO EQUIPMENT WILL EVER EQUAL MY MIND. STILL, IT SHOULD SUFFICE.
IS YOUR TIME PORTAL FINISHED, DOCTOR?
NEARLY...
AND SO ARE YOU. ADJUST THE HAIR...A BIT SHORTER.
ADJUSTING.
IS THIS OKAY?
IT--IT'S PERFECT...
...AND IT'S PAST TIME I GOT HOME. DOWNLOAD YOURSELF INTO MY WRIST DEVICE. PREPARE FOR TIME-JUMP.
YES, DOCTOR.

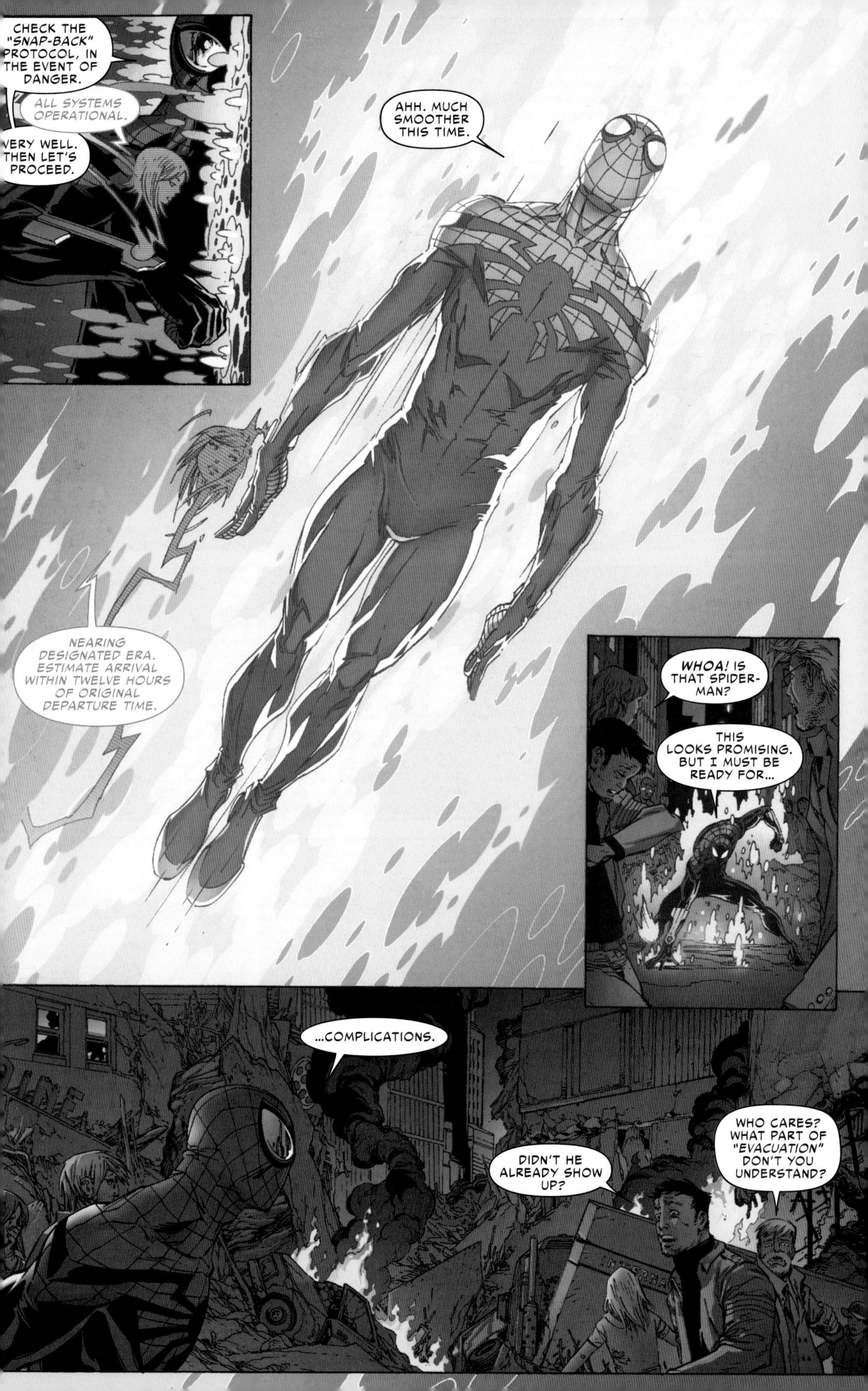
CHECK THE "SNAP-BACK" PROTOCOL, IN THE EVENT OF DANGER.
ALL SYSTEMS OPERATIONAL.
VERY WELL. THEN LET'S PROCEED.
AHH. MUCH SMOOTHER THIS TIME.
NEARING DESIGNATED ERA. ESTIMATE ARRIVAL WITHIN TWELVE HOURS OF ORIGINAL DEPARTURE TIME.
WHOA! IS THAT SPIDER-MAN?
THIS LOOKS PROMISING. BUT I MUST BE READY FOR...
...COMPLICATIONS.
DIDN'T HE ALREADY SHOW UP?
WHO CARES? WHAT PART OF "EVACUATION" DON'T YOU UNDERSTAND?

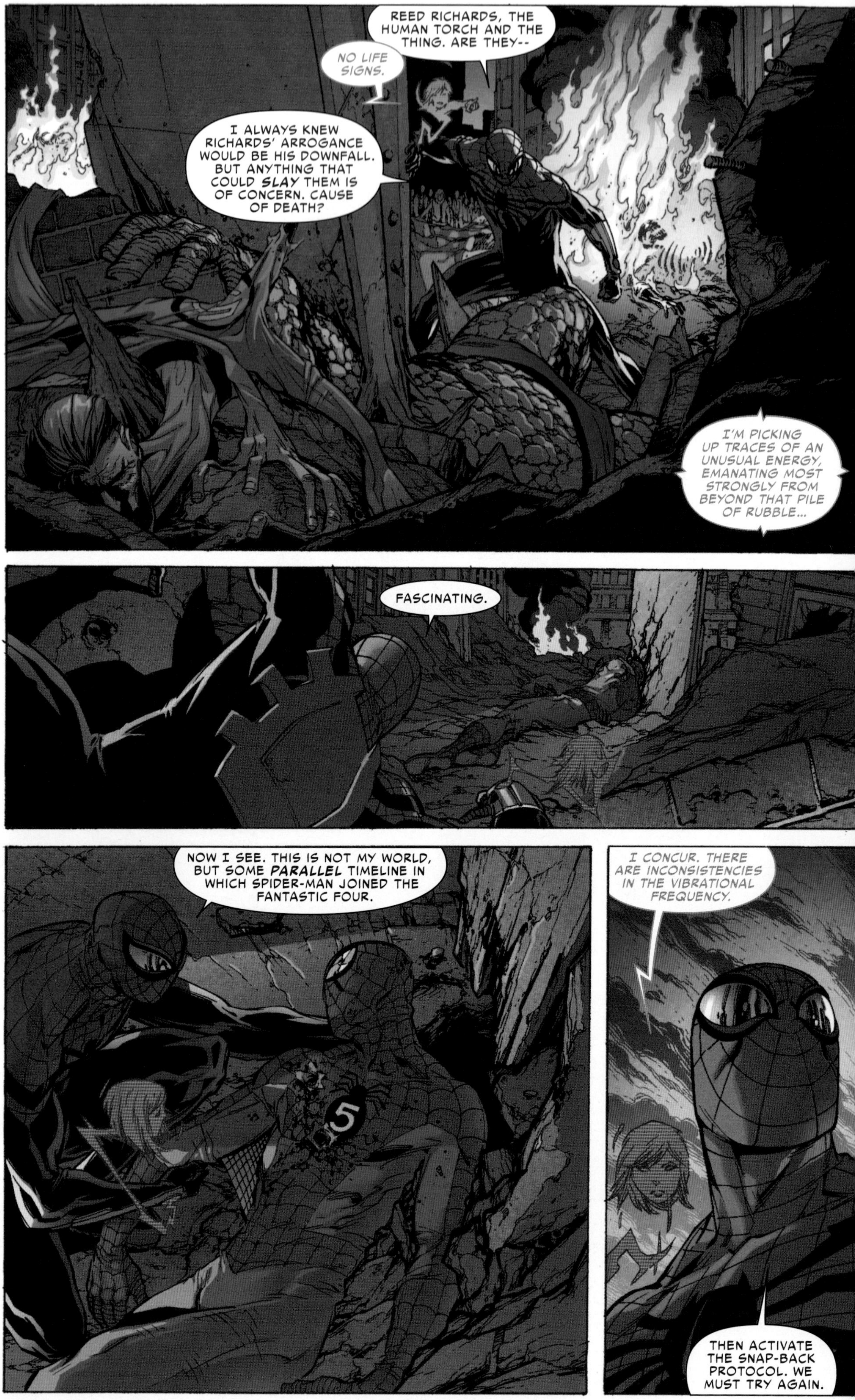
REED RICHARDS, THE HUMAN TORCH AND THE THING. ARE THEY--
NO LIFE SIGNS.
I ALWAYS KNEW RICHARDS' ARROGANCE WOULD BE HIS DOWNFALL. BUT ANYTHING THAT COULD SLAY THEM IS OF CONCERN. CAUSE OF DEATH?
I'M PICKING UP TRACES OF AN UNUSUAL ENERGY, EMANATING MOST STRONGLY FROM BEYOND THAT PILE OF RUBBLE...
FASCINATING.
NOW I SEE. THIS IS NOT MY WORLD, BUT SOME PARALLEL TIMELINE IN WHICH SPIDER-MAN JOINED THE FANTASTIC FOUR.
I CONCUR. THERE ARE INCONSISTENCIES IN THE VIBRATIONAL FREQUENCY.
THEN ACTIVATE THE SNAP-BACK PROTOCOL. WE MUST TRY AGAIN.

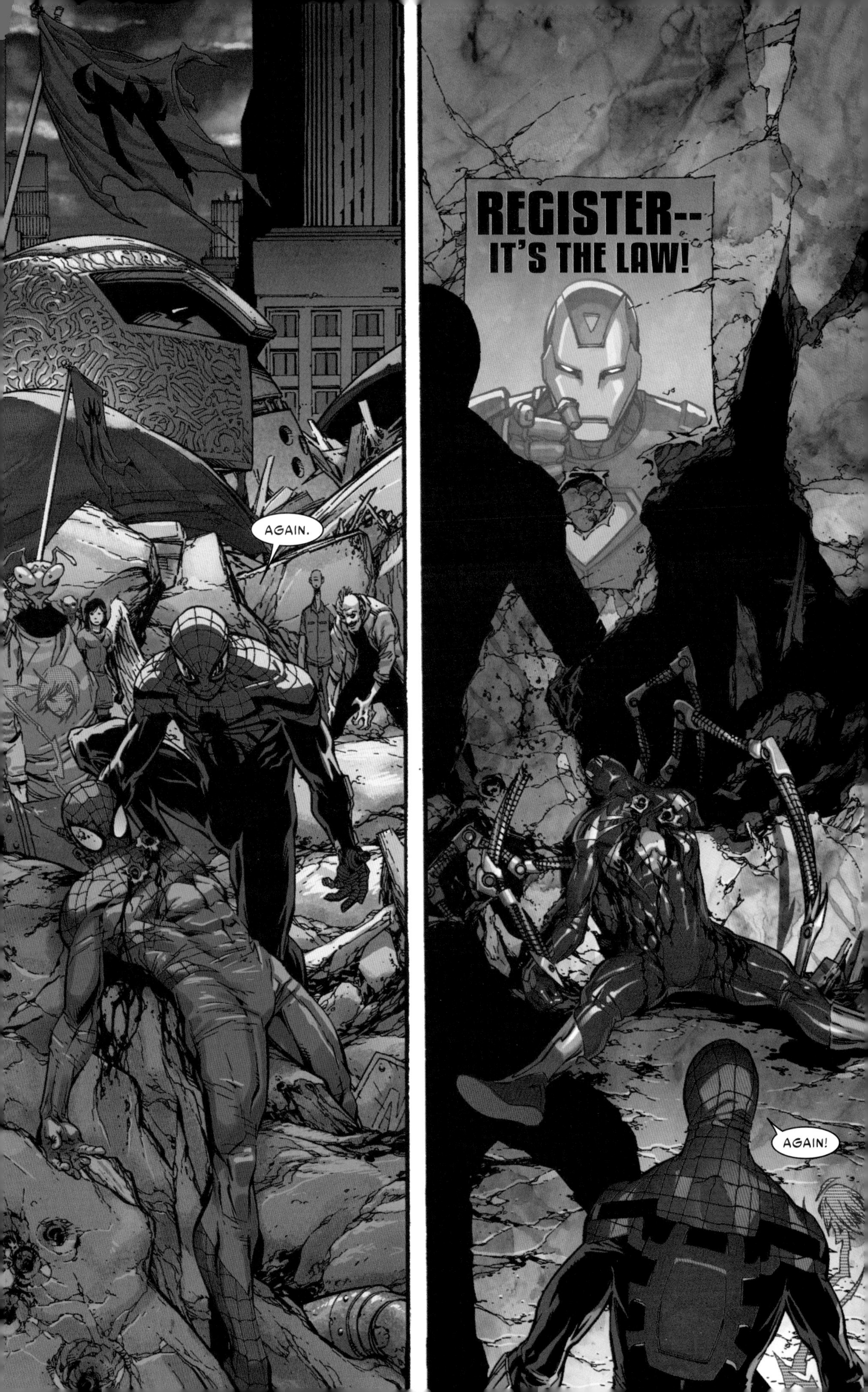
AGAIN.
REGISTER--
IT'S THE LAW!
AGAIN!

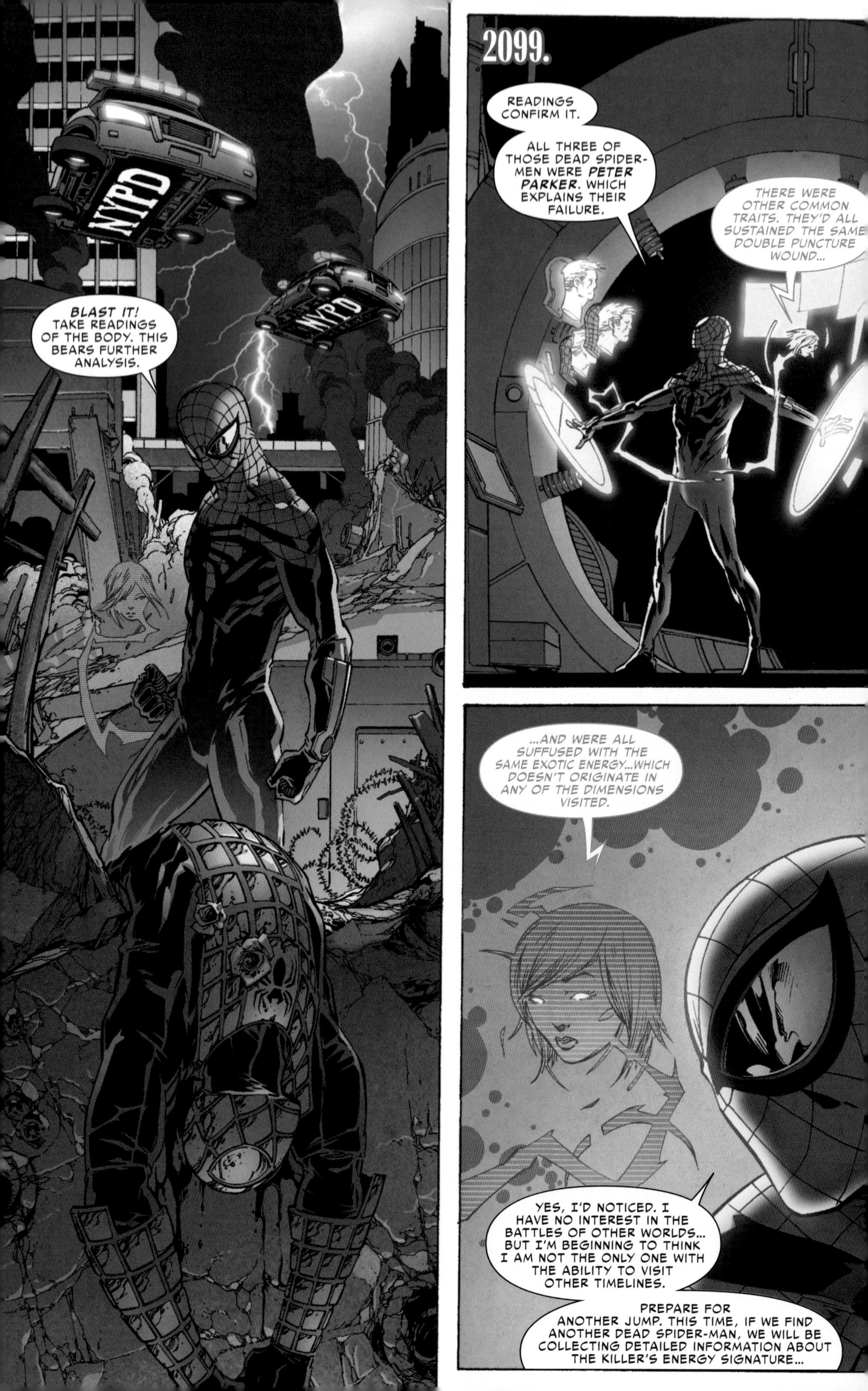
NYPD
NYPD
BLAST IT! TAKE READINGS OF THE BODY. THIS BEARS FURTHER ANALYSIS.
2099.
READINGS CONFIRM IT.
ALL THREE OF THOSE DEAD SPIDER-MEN WERE PETER PARKER. WHICH EXPLAINS THEIR FAILURE.
THERE WERE OTHER COMMON TRAITS. THEY'D ALL SUSTAINED THE SAME DOUBLE PUNCTURE WOUND...
...AND WERE ALL SUFFUSED WITH THE SAME EXOTIC ENERGY...WHICH DOESN'T ORIGINATE IN ANY OF THE DIMENSIONS VISITED.
YES, I'D NOTICED. I HAVE NO INTEREST IN THE BATTLES OF OTHER WORLDS... BUT I'M BEGINNING TO THINK I AM NOT THE ONLY ONE WITH THE ABILITY TO VISIT OTHER TIMELINES.
PREPARE FOR ANOTHER JUMP. THIS TIME, IF WE FIND ANOTHER DEAD SPIDER-MAN, WE WILL BE COLLECTING DETAILED INFORMATION ABOUT THE KILLER'S ENERGY SIGNATURE...

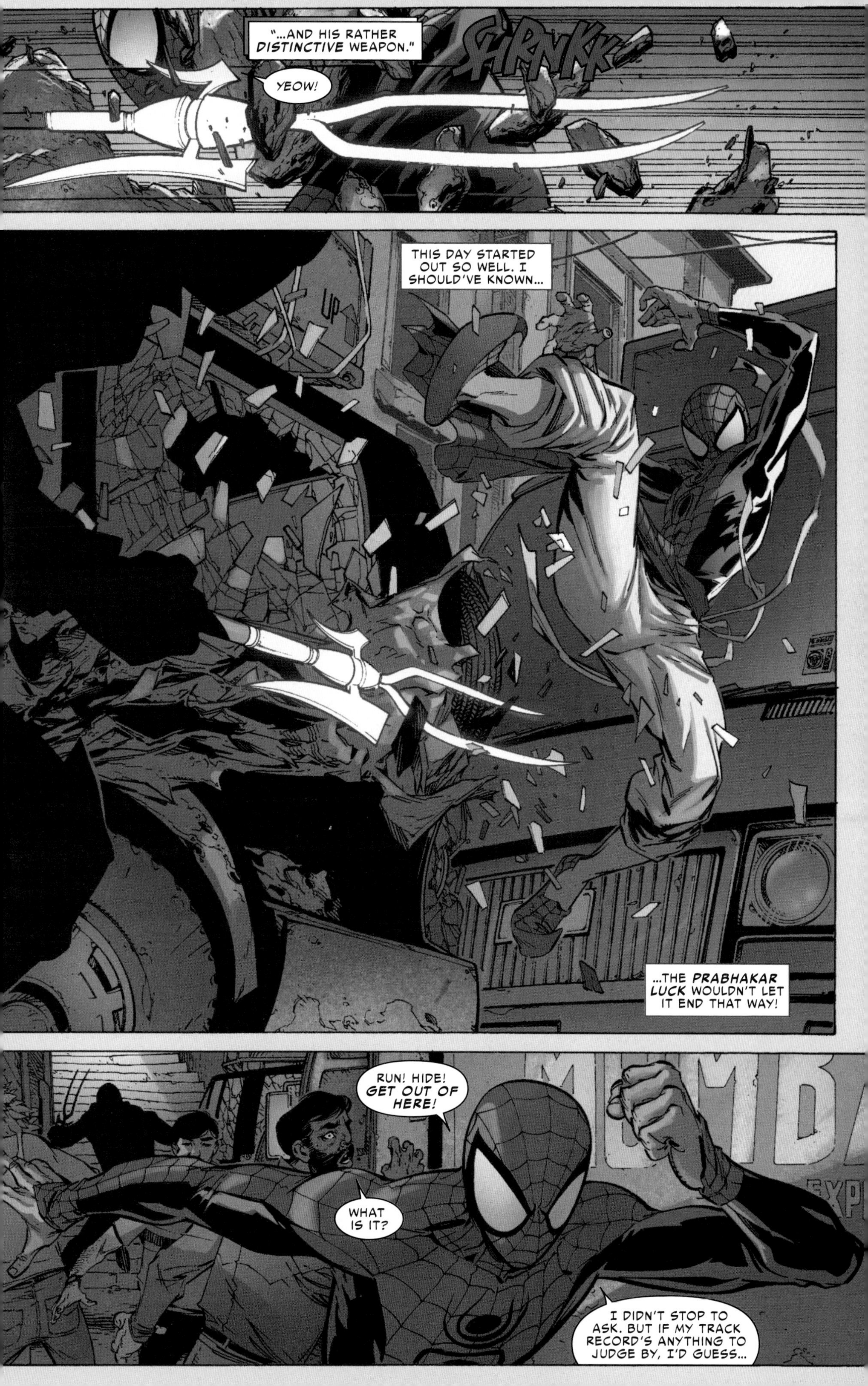
"...AND HIS RATHER *DISTINCTIVE* WEAPON."
SHRNKK
YEOW!
THIS DAY STARTED OUT SO WELL. I SHOULD'VE KNOWN...
...THE *PRABHAKAR LUCK* WOULDN'T LET IT END THAT WAY!
RUN! HIDE! *GET OUT OF HERE!*
WHAT IS IT?
I DIDN'T STOP TO ASK. BUT IF MY TRACK RECORD'S ANYTHING TO JUDGE BY, I'D GUESS...

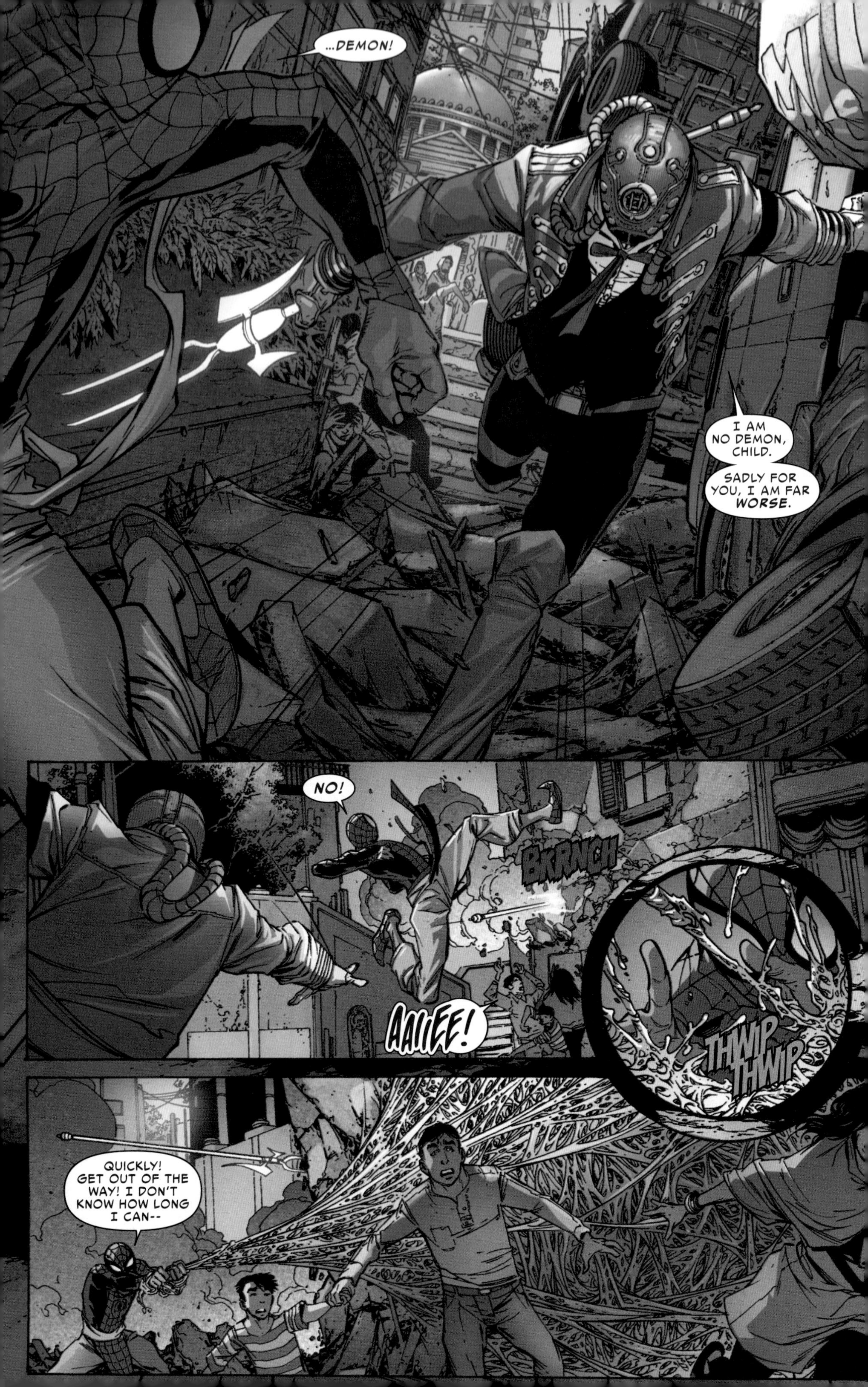
...DEMON!
I AM NO DEMON, CHILD.
SADLY FOR YOU, I AM FAR WORSE.
NO!
BKRNCH
AAIIEE!
THWIP THWIP
QUICKLY! GET OUT OF THE WAY! I DON'T KNOW HOW LONG I CAN--

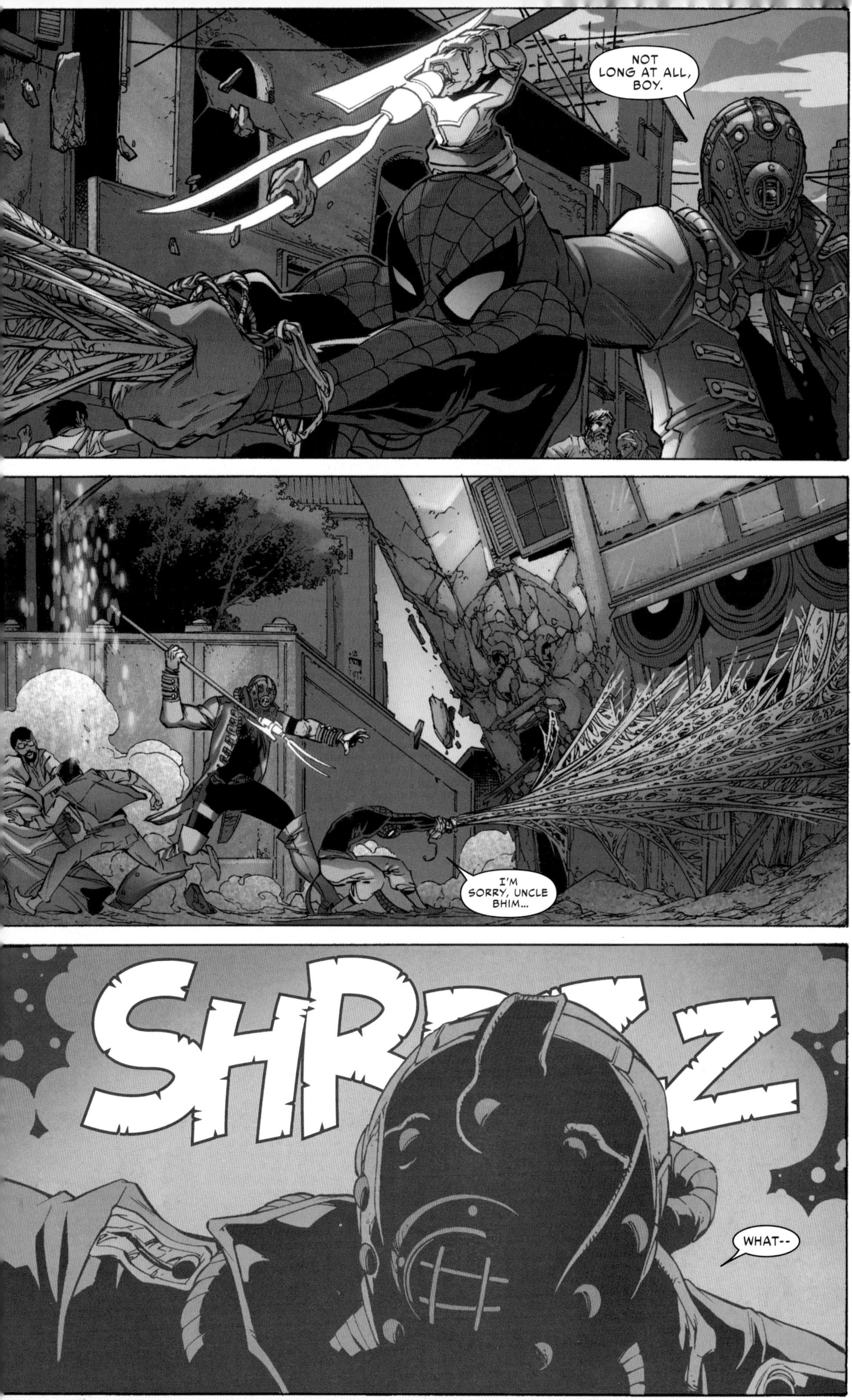
NOT LONG AT ALL, BOY.
I'M SORRY, UNCLE BHIM...
WHAT--

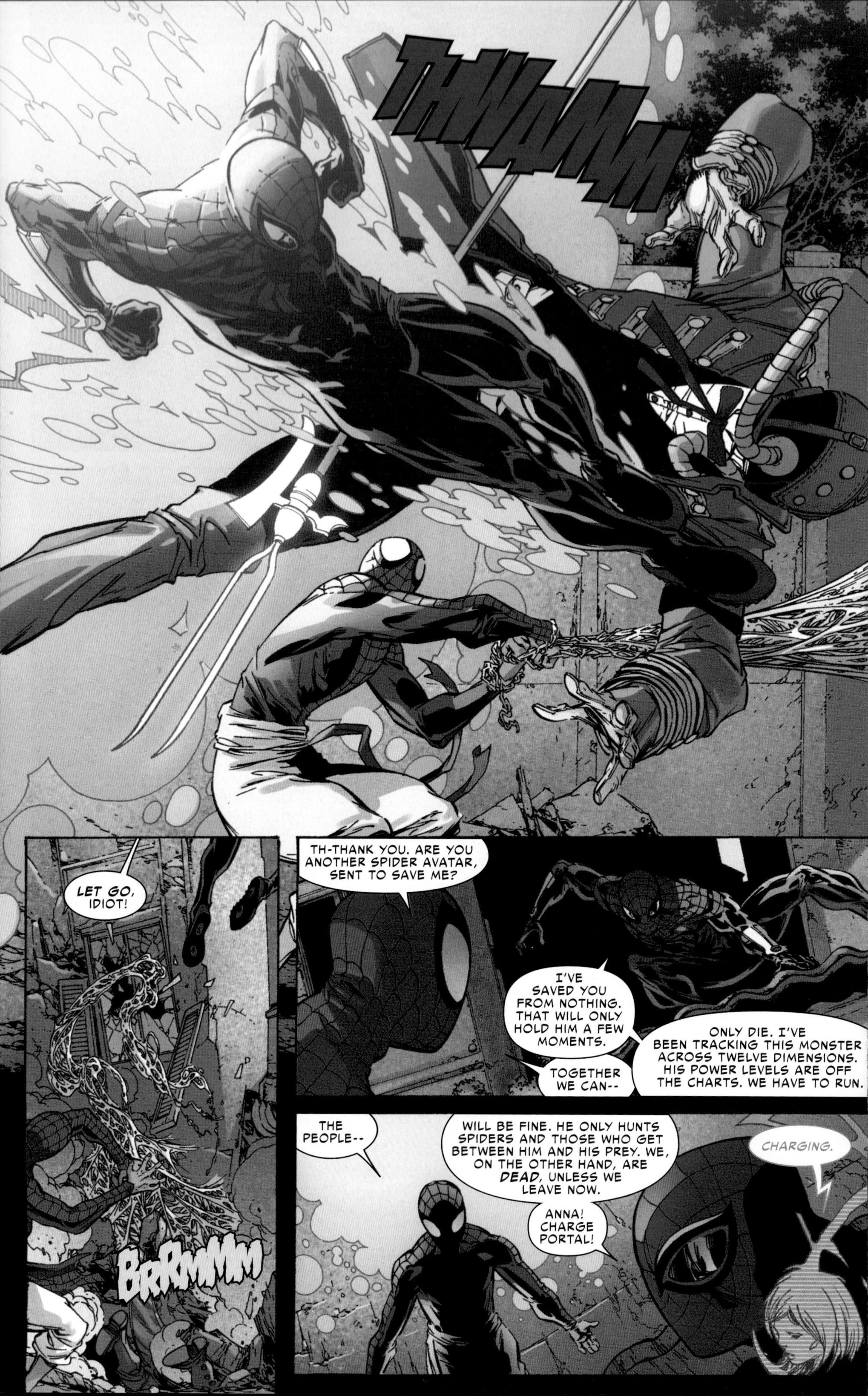
THWAMMM
LET GO, IDIOT!
BRRMMMM
TH-THANK YOU. ARE YOU ANOTHER SPIDER AVATAR, SENT TO SAVE ME?
I'VE SAVED YOU FROM NOTHING. THAT WILL ONLY HOLD HIM A FEW MOMENTS.
TOGETHER WE CAN--
ONLY DIE. I'VE BEEN TRACKING THIS MONSTER ACROSS TWELVE DIMENSIONS. HIS POWER LEVELS ARE OFF THE CHARTS. WE HAVE TO RUN.
THE PEOPLE--
WILL BE FINE. HE ONLY HUNTS SPIDERS AND THOSE WHO GET BETWEEN HIM AND HIS PREY. WE, ON THE OTHER HAND, ARE DEAD, UNLESS WE LEAVE NOW.
ANNA! CHARGE PORTAL!
CHARGING.

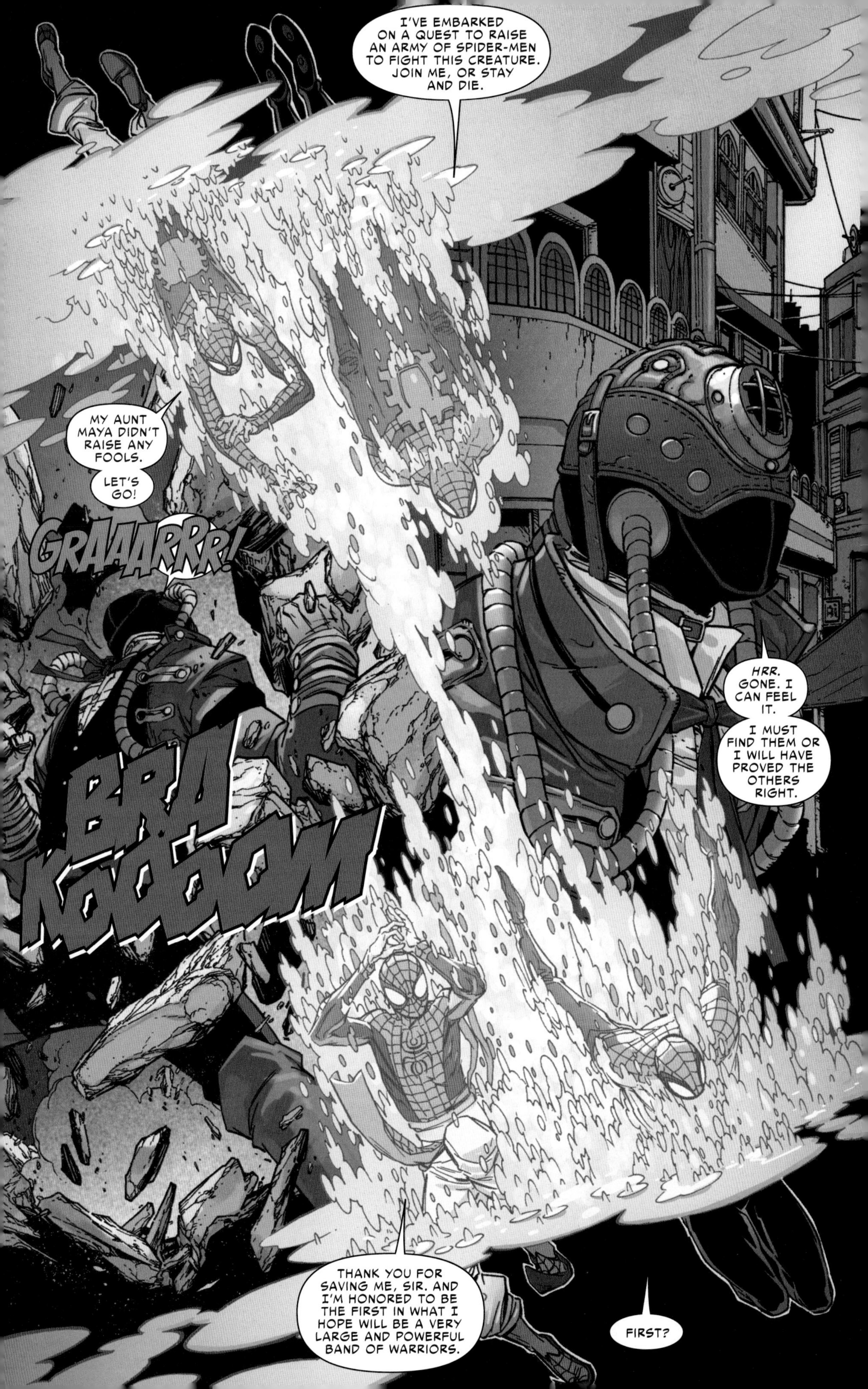
I'VE EMBARKED ON A QUEST TO RAISE AN ARMY OF SPIDER-MEN TO FIGHT THIS CREATURE. JOIN ME, OR STAY AND DIE.
MY AUNT MAYA DIDN'T RAISE ANY FOOLS.
LET'S GO!
GRAAARRR!
HRR. GONE. I CAN FEEL IT.
I MUST FIND THEM OR I WILL HAVE PROVED THE OTHERS RIGHT.
THANK YOU FOR SAVING ME, SIR. AND I'M HONORED TO BE THE FIRST IN WHAT I HOPE WILL BE A VERY LARGE AND POWERFUL BAND OF WARRIORS.
FIRST?

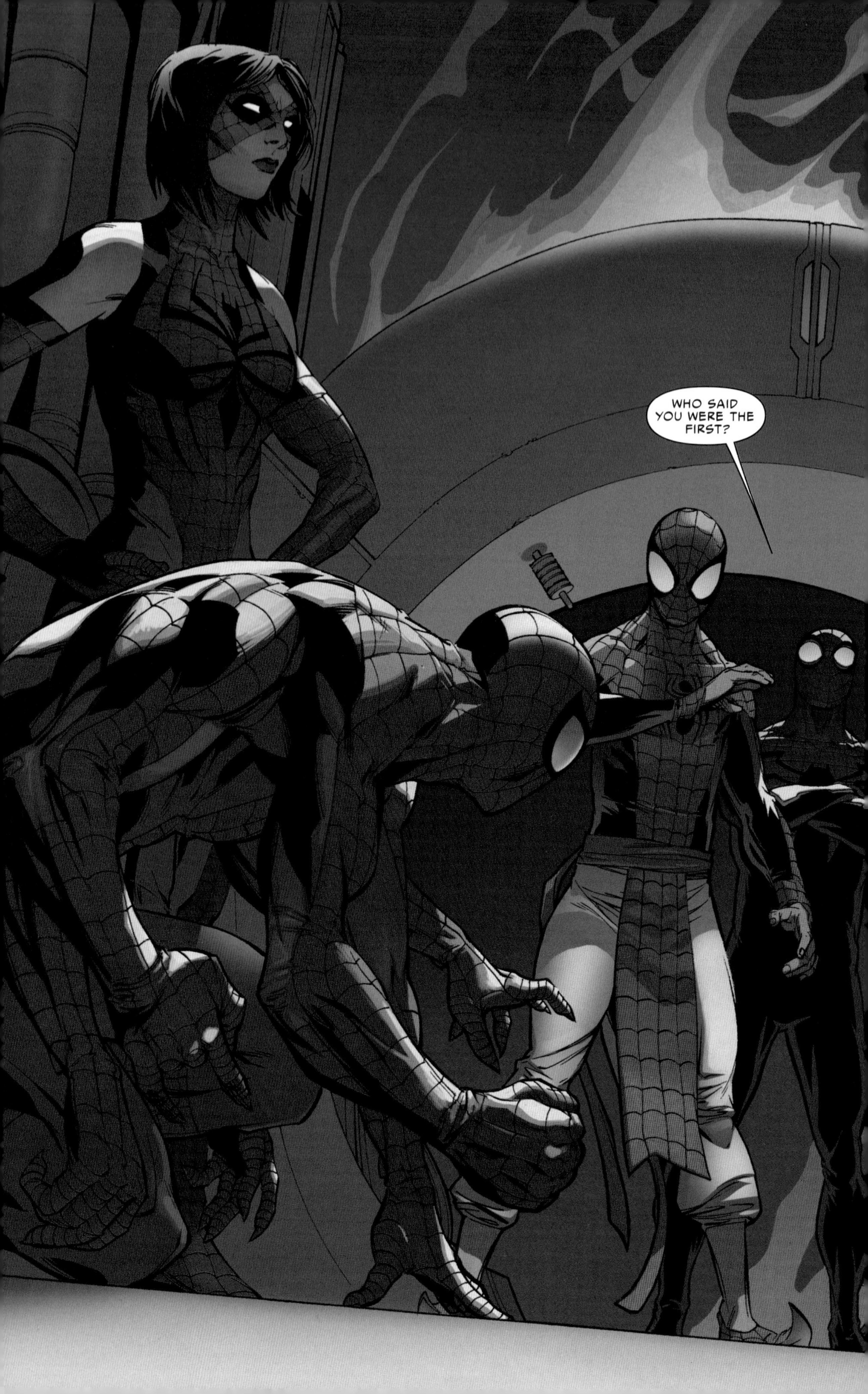
WHO SAID YOU WERE THE FIRST?

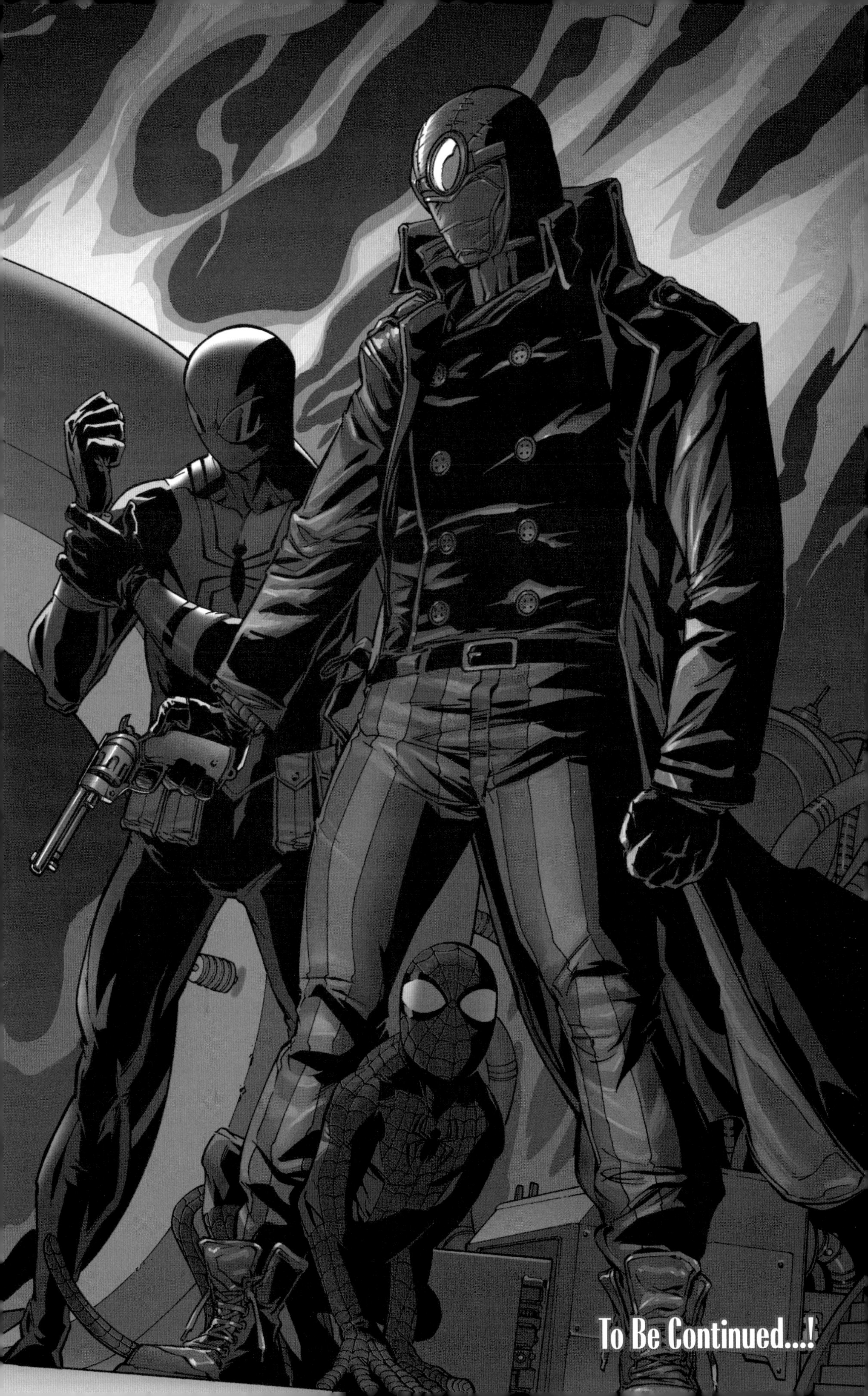
To Be Continued...!

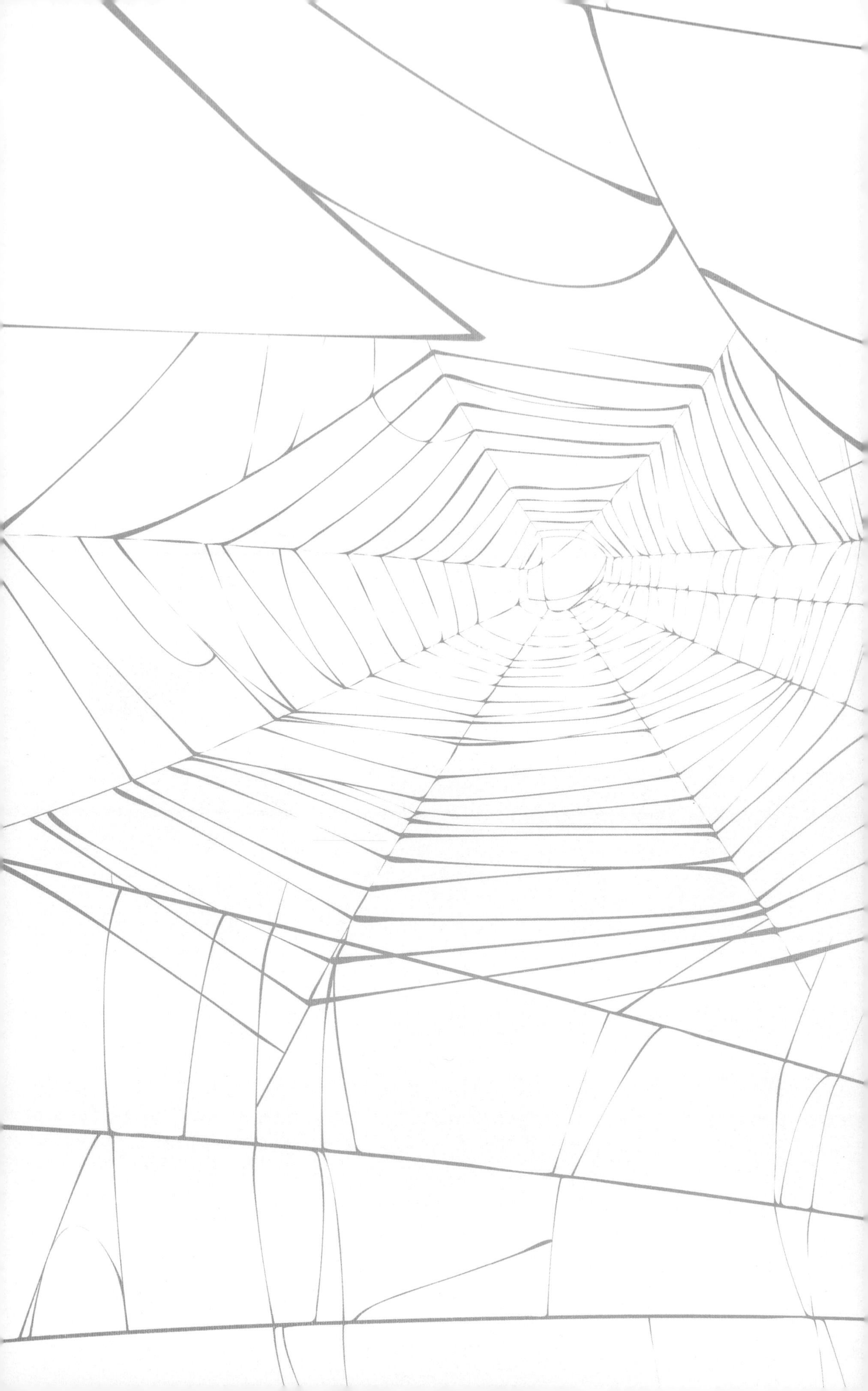

THE HARDEST THING I EVER DID WAS LEAVE MY OLD LIFE BEHIND. THAT LIFE, AND EVERYONE IN IT.

MARY JANE, AUNT MAY... AND, FOR ALL INTENTS AND PURPOSES, *PETER PARKER*.

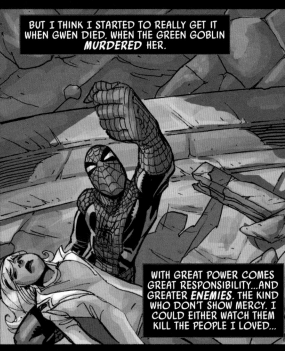

BUT I THINK I STARTED TO REALLY GET IT WHEN GWEN DIED. WHEN THE GREEN GOBLIN *MURDERED* HER.

WITH GREAT POWER COMES GREAT RESPONSIBILITY...AND GREATER *ENEMIES*. THE KIND WHO DON'T SHOW MERCY. I COULD EITHER WATCH THEM KILL THE PEOPLE I LOVED...

...OR ADMIT I'M AT *WAR*. AND START *ACTING* LIKE IT.

BLAM

WOLVERINE TRAINED ME. INTRODUCED ME TO LIFE OUT IN THE COLD. AND IT'S A DAMN GOOD THING HE DID.

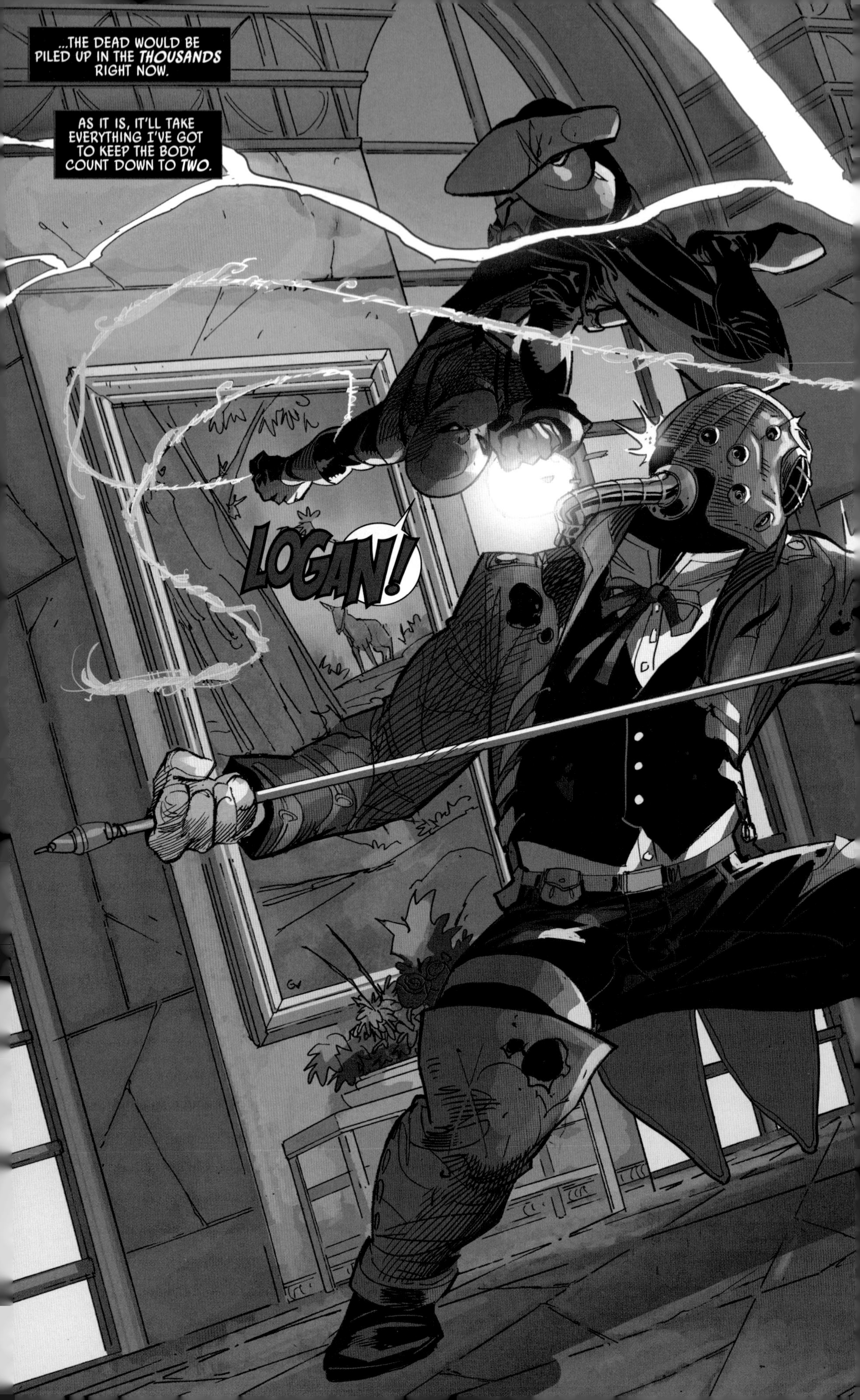
...THE DEAD WOULD BE PILED UP IN THE *THOUSANDS* RIGHT NOW.
AS IT IS, IT'LL TAKE EVERYTHING I'VE GOT TO KEEP THE BODY COUNT DOWN TO *TWO*.
LOGAN!

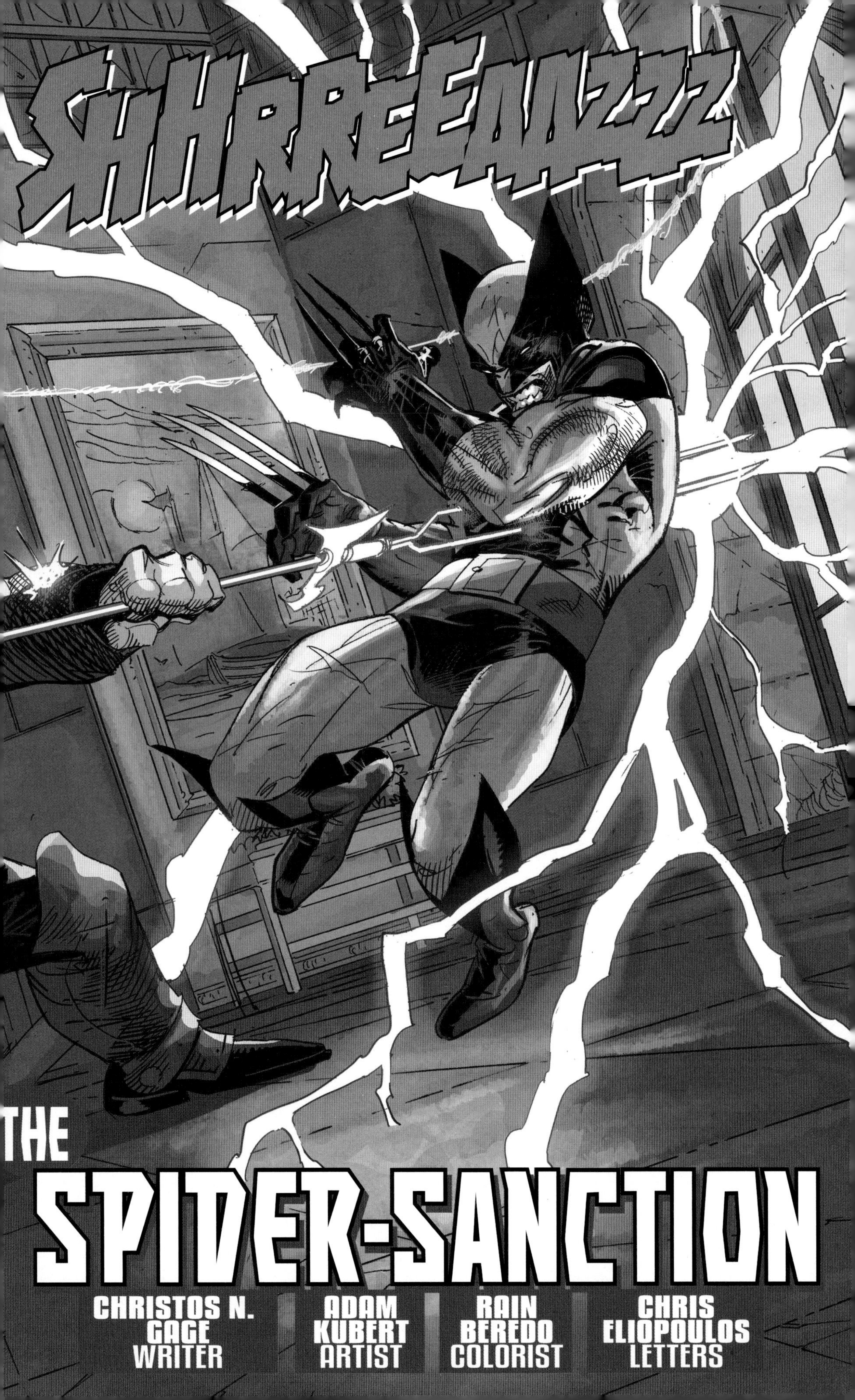
SHHRREEAAZZZ
THE
SPIDER-SANCTION
CHRISTOS N. GAGE WRITER
ADAM KUBERT ARTIST
RAIN BEREDO COLORIST
CHRIS ELIOPOULOS LETTERS

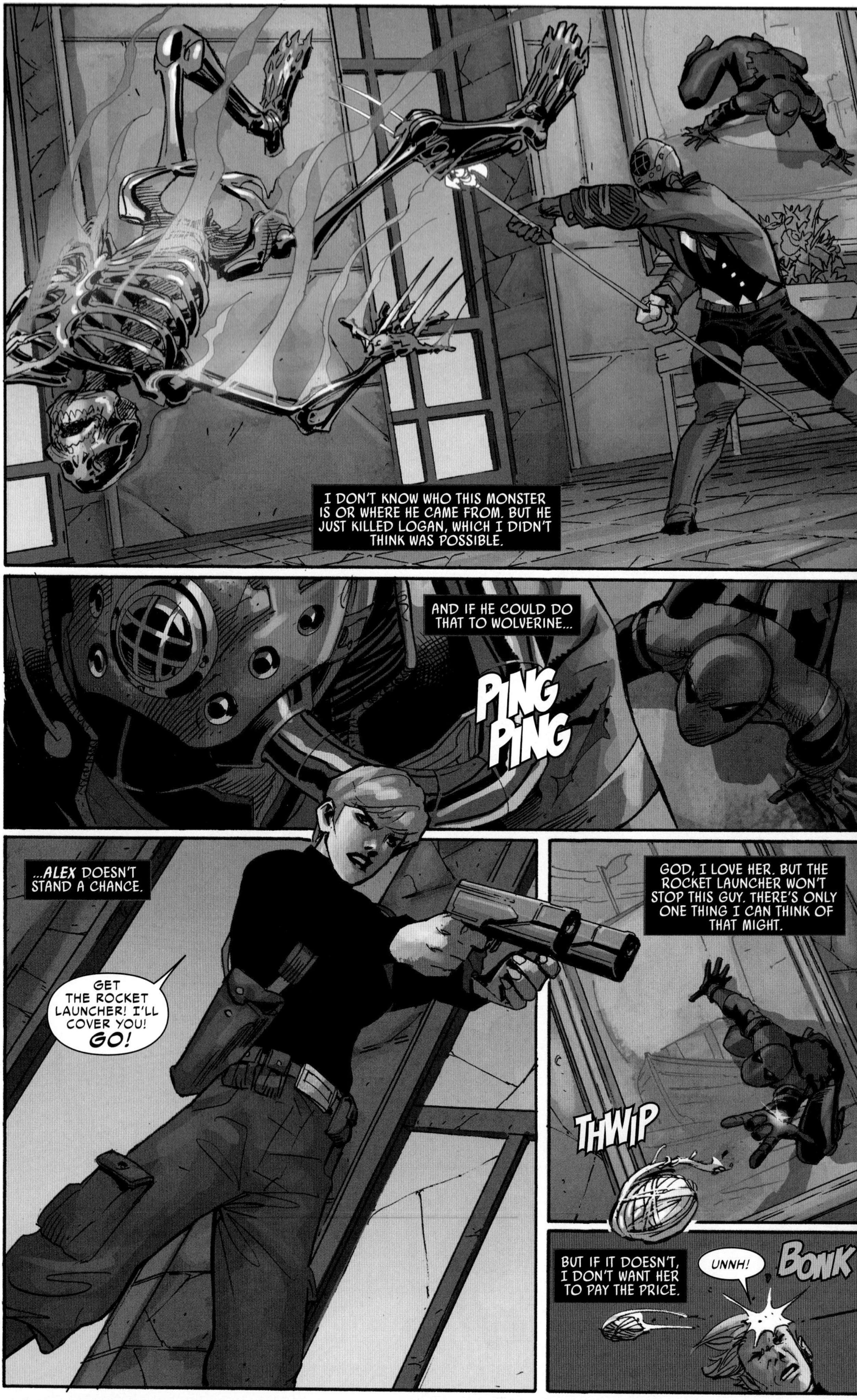
I DON'T KNOW WHO THIS MONSTER IS OR WHERE HE CAME FROM. BUT HE JUST KILLED LOGAN, WHICH I DIDN'T THINK WAS POSSIBLE.
AND IF HE COULD DO THAT TO WOLVERINE...
PING PING
...ALEX DOESN'T STAND A CHANCE.
GET THE ROCKET LAUNCHER! I'LL COVER YOU! GO!
GOD, I LOVE HER. BUT THE ROCKET LAUNCHER WON'T STOP THIS GUY. THERE'S ONLY ONE THING I CAN THINK OF THAT MIGHT.
THWIP
BUT IF IT DOESN'T, I DON'T WANT HER TO PAY THE PRICE.
UNNH!
BONK

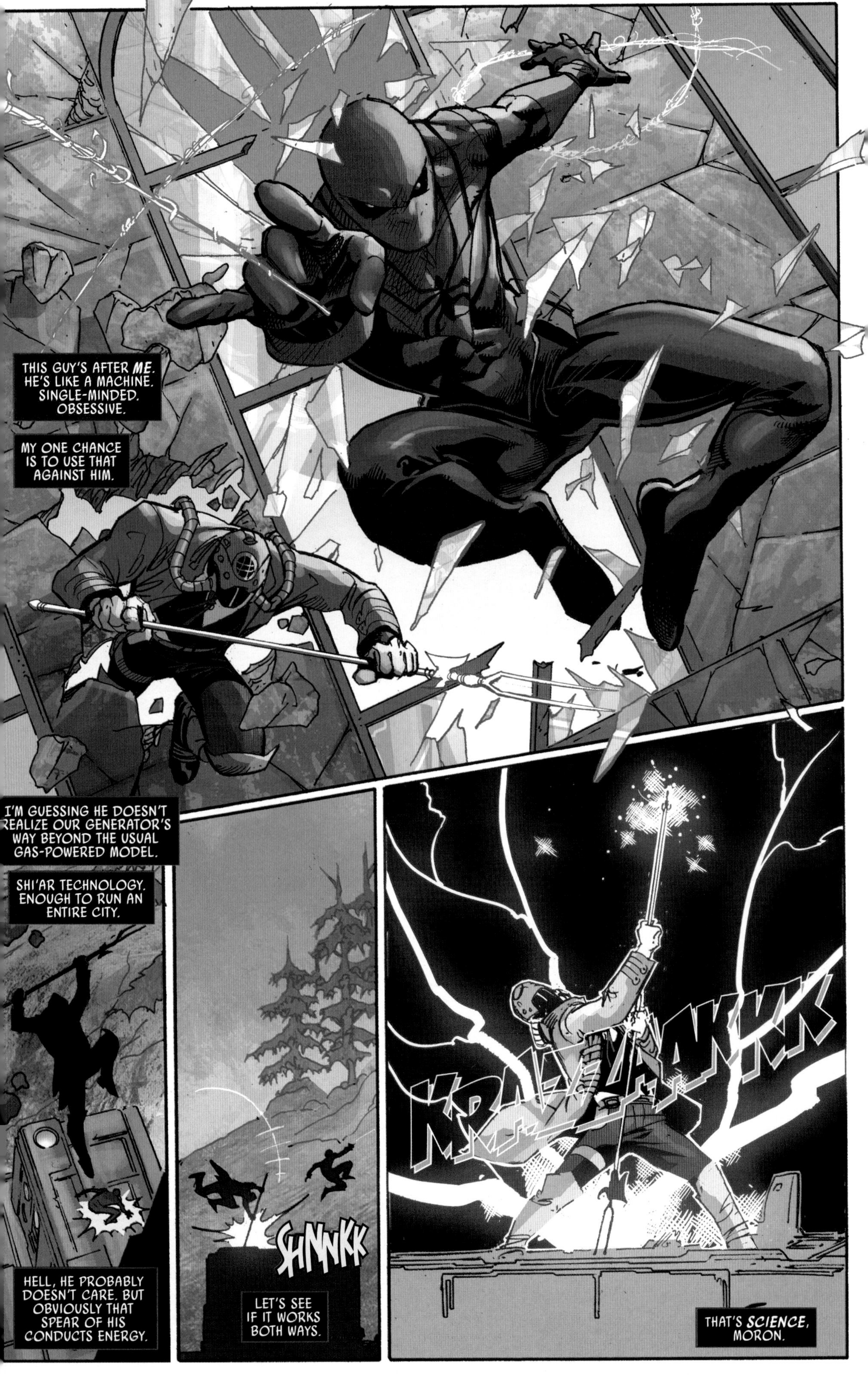
THIS GUY'S AFTER ME. HE'S LIKE A MACHINE. SINGLE-MINDED. OBSESSIVE.
MY ONE CHANCE IS TO USE THAT AGAINST HIM.
I'M GUESSING HE DOESN'T REALIZE OUR GENERATOR'S WAY BEYOND THE USUAL GAS-POWERED MODEL.
SHI'AR TECHNOLOGY. ENOUGH TO RUN AN ENTIRE CITY.
HELL, HE PROBABLY DOESN'T CARE. BUT OBVIOUSLY THAT SPEAR OF HIS CONDUCTS ENERGY.
SHNNKK
LET'S SEE IF IT WORKS BOTH WAYS.
KRAKLAKKK
THAT'S SCIENCE, MORON.

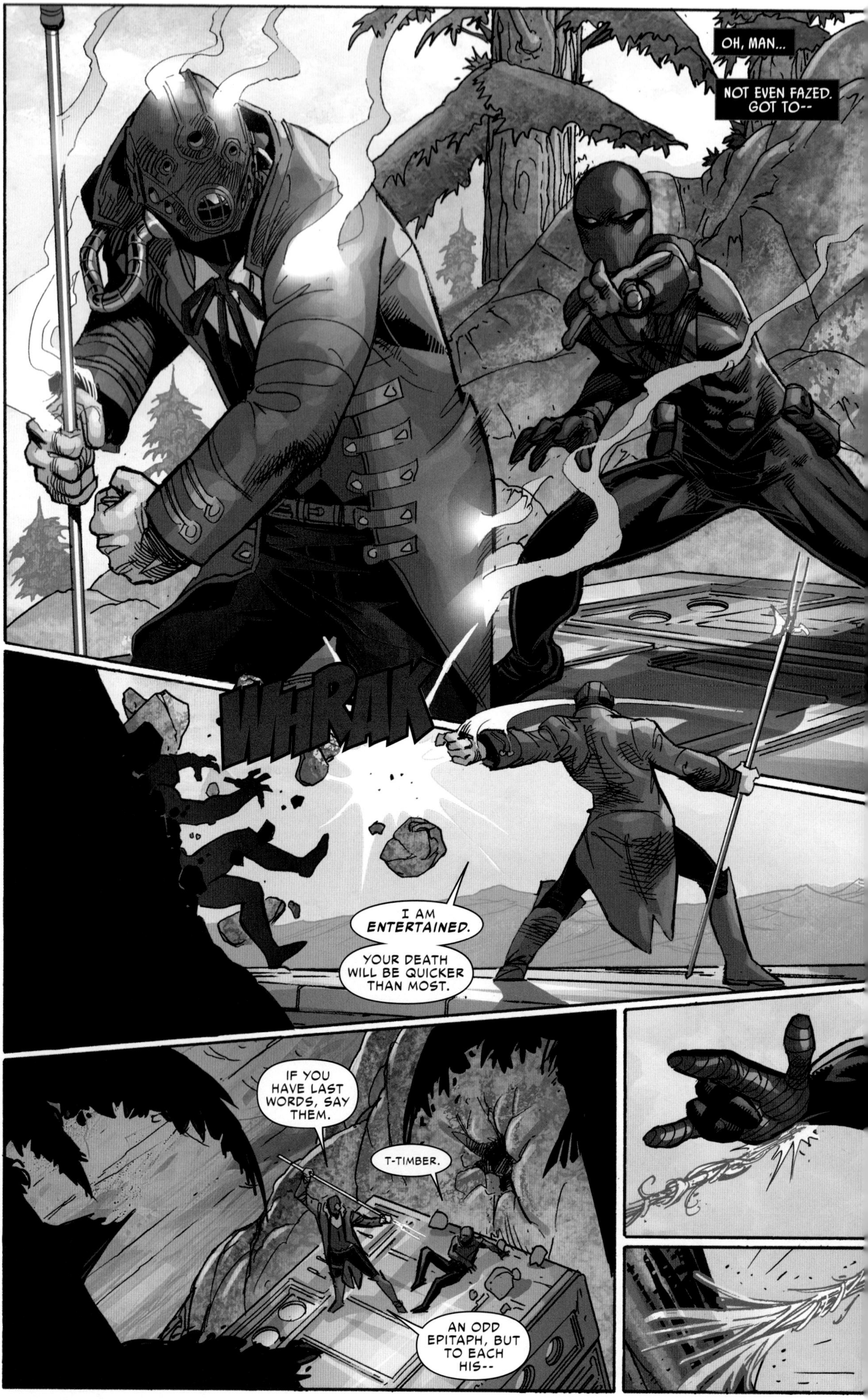
OH, MAN...
NOT EVEN FAZED. GOT TO--
WHRAK
I AM ENTERTAINED.
YOUR DEATH WILL BE QUICKER THAN MOST.
IF YOU HAVE LAST WORDS, SAY THEM.
T-TIMBER.
AN ODD EPITAPH, BUT TO EACH HIS--

BTHOOOM

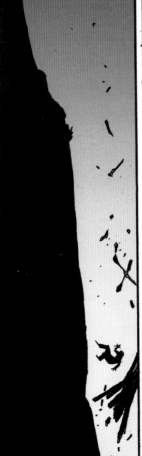

YOU'RE WELCOME, BY THE WAY.

THAT WON'T FINISH HIM. GONNA SEE IF I CAN.

WAIT, YOU FOOL!

LISTEN. I DON'T KNOW IF YOU REPLACED ME BACK IN THE STATES, OR IF YOU'RE FROM ANOTHER DIMENSION, OR WHAT. AND I DON'T CARE.

YOU *SHOULD* CARE, DOLT. AND YOU SHOULD SLOW DOWN.

NEWSFLASH: I'M NOT THE "*FRIENDLY NEIGHBORHOOD SPIDER-MAN*" ANYMORE. SOME FOLKS NEED KILLING, AND THIS MONSTER'S A PRIME EXAMPLE.

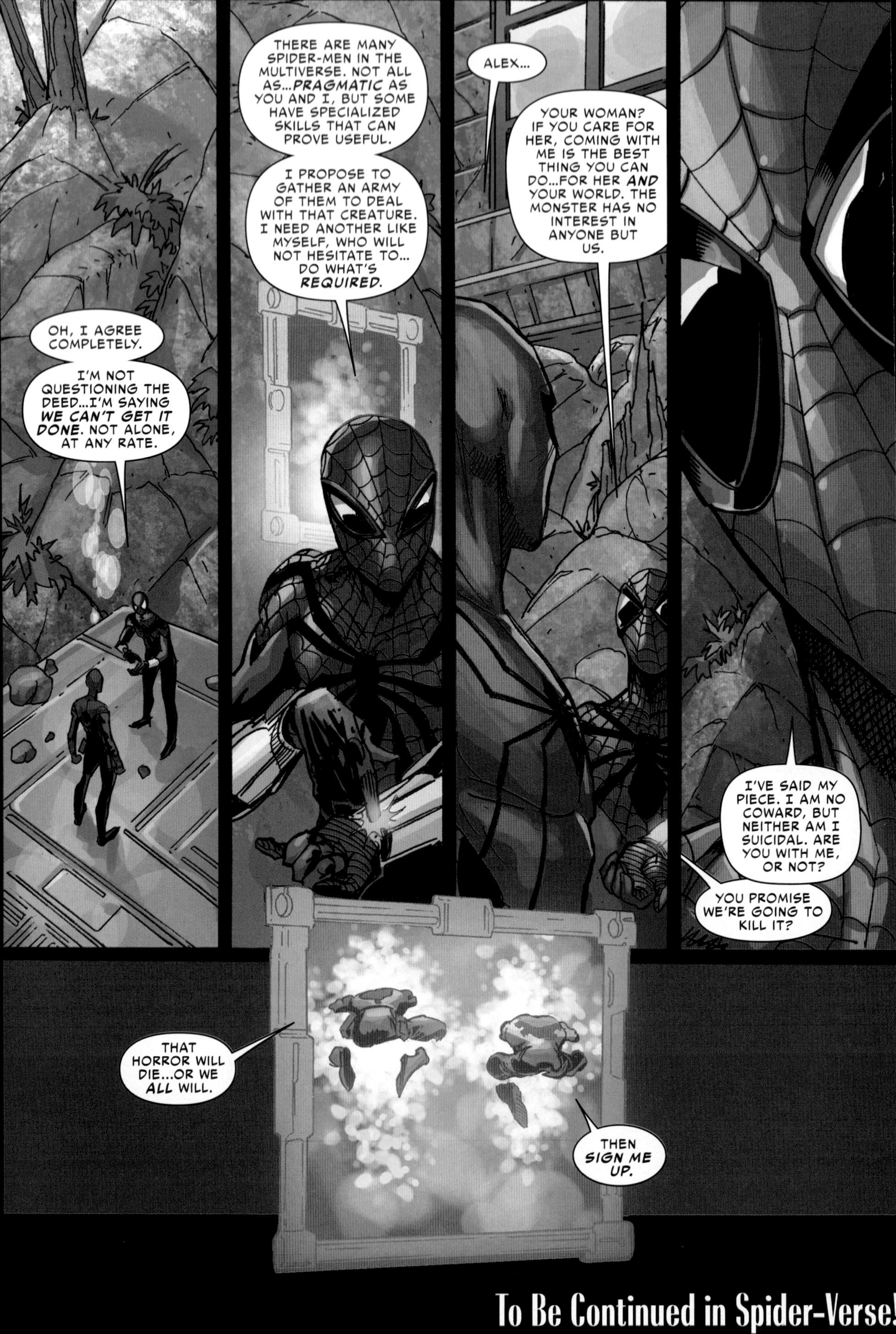
OH, I AGREE COMPLETELY.
I'M NOT QUESTIONING THE DEED...I'M SAYING *WE CAN'T GET IT DONE*. NOT ALONE, AT ANY RATE.
THERE ARE MANY SPIDER-MEN IN THE MULTIVERSE. NOT ALL AS...*PRAGMATIC* AS YOU AND I, BUT SOME HAVE SPECIALIZED SKILLS THAT CAN PROVE USEFUL.
I PROPOSE TO GATHER AN ARMY OF THEM TO DEAL WITH THAT CREATURE. I NEED ANOTHER LIKE MYSELF, WHO WILL NOT HESITATE TO... DO WHAT'S *REQUIRED*.
ALEX...
YOUR WOMAN? IF YOU CARE FOR HER, COMING WITH ME IS THE BEST THING YOU CAN DO...FOR HER *AND* YOUR WORLD. THE MONSTER HAS NO INTEREST IN ANYONE BUT US.
I'VE SAID MY PIECE. I AM NO COWARD, BUT NEITHER AM I SUICIDAL. ARE YOU WITH ME, OR NOT?
YOU PROMISE WE'RE GOING TO KILL IT?
THAT HORROR WILL DIE...OR WE *ALL* WILL.
THEN *SIGN ME UP*.
To Be Continued in Spider-Verse!

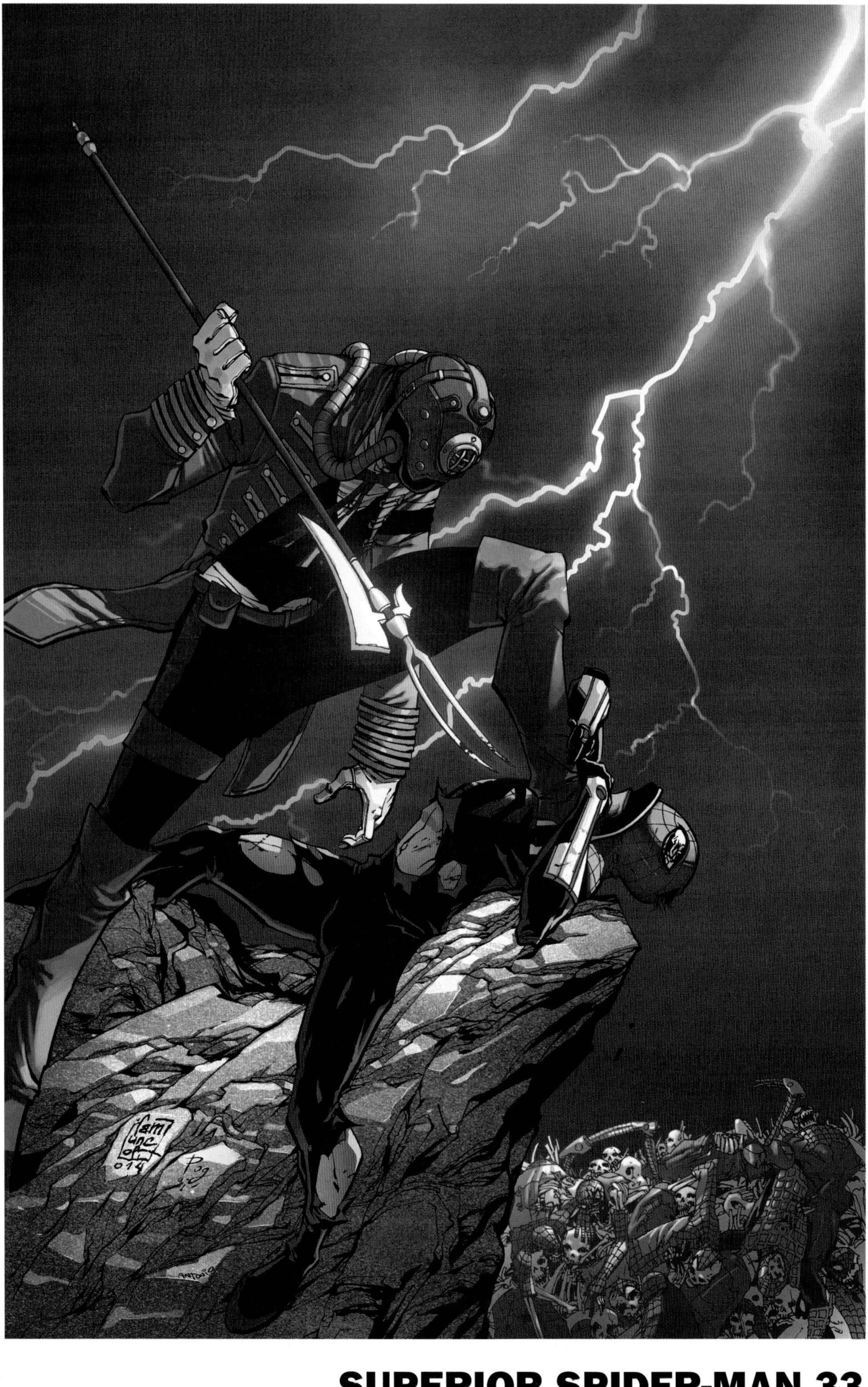

SUPERIOR SPIDER-MAN 33

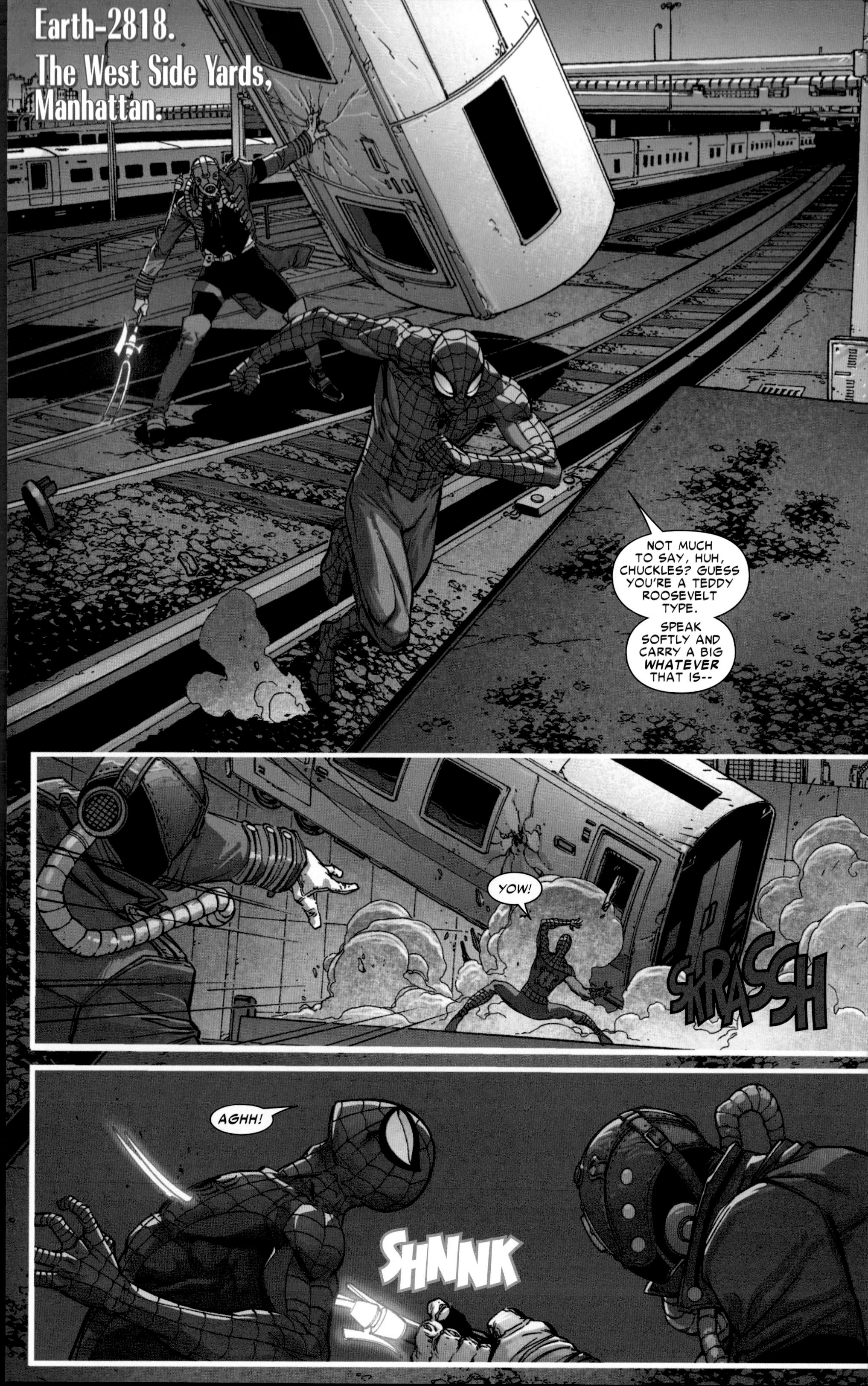
Earth-2818.
The West Side Yards, Manhattan.
NOT MUCH TO SAY, HUH, CHUCKLES? GUESS YOU'RE A TEDDY ROOSEVELT TYPE.
SPEAK SOFTLY AND CARRY A BIG *WHATEVER* THAT IS--
YOW!
SKRASSH
AGHH!
SHNNK

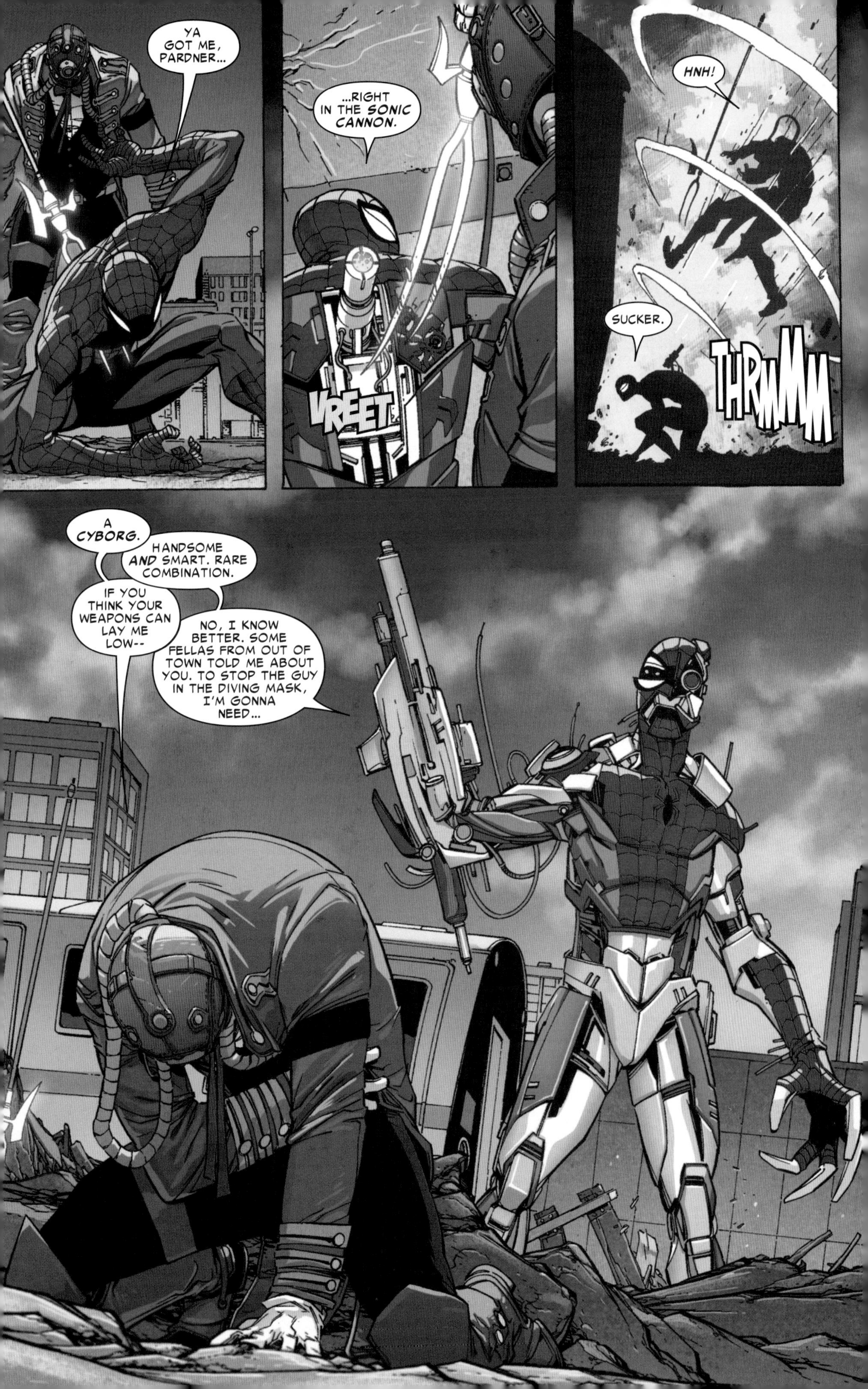
YA GOT ME, PARDNER...
...RIGHT IN THE SONIC CANNON.
VREET
HNH!
SUCKER.
THRMMM
A CYBORG.
HANDSOME AND SMART. RARE COMBINATION.
IF YOU THINK YOUR WEAPONS CAN LAY ME LOW--
NO, I KNOW BETTER. SOME FELLAS FROM OUT OF TOWN TOLD ME ABOUT YOU. TO STOP THE GUY IN THE DIVING MASK, I'M GONNA NEED...

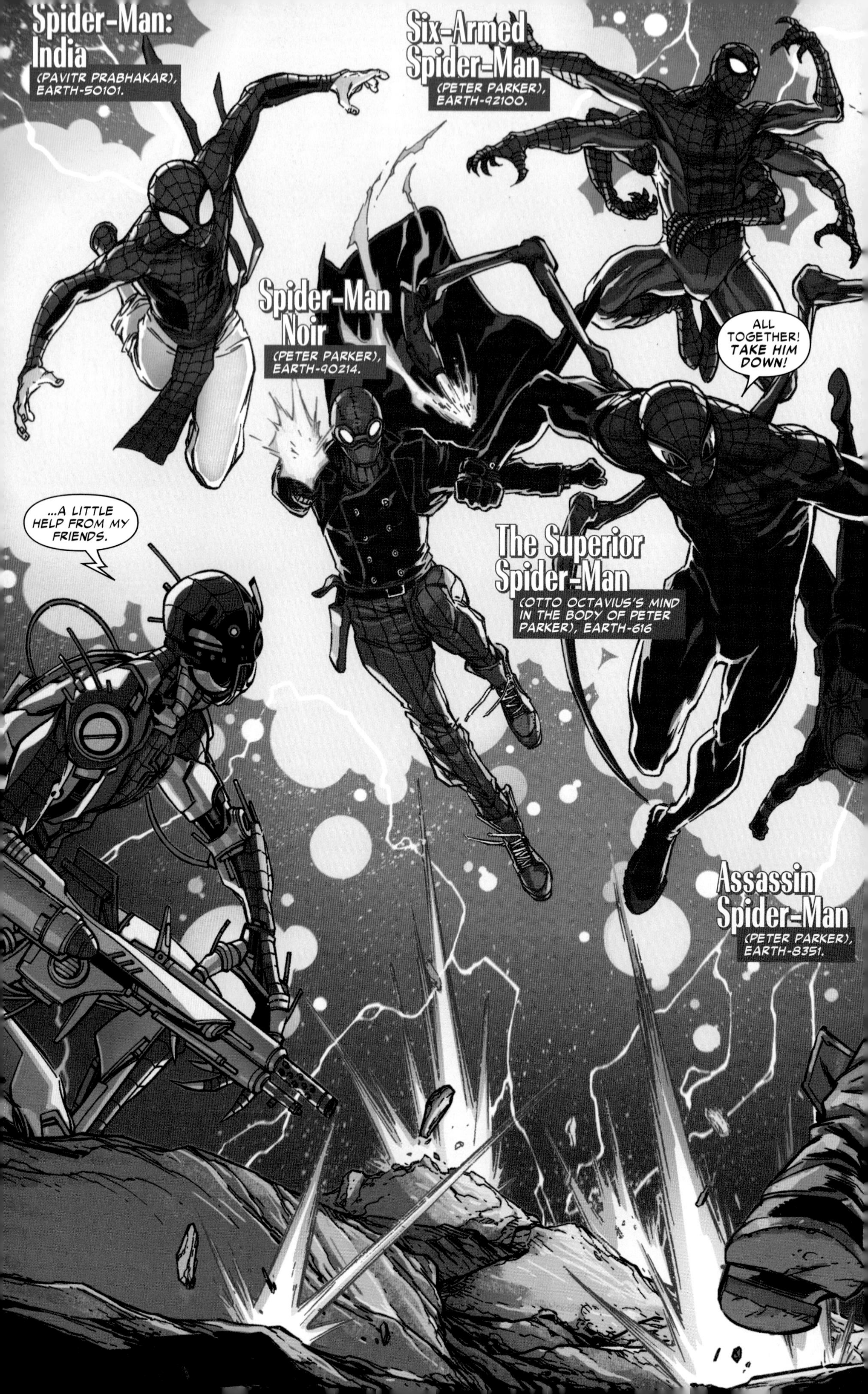
Spider-Man: India
(PAVITR PRABHAKAR), EARTH-50101.
Six-Armed Spider-Man
(PETER PARKER), EARTH-92100.
Spider-Man Noir
(PETER PARKER), EARTH-90214.
ALL TOGETHER! TAKE HIM DOWN!
...A LITTLE HELP FROM MY FRIENDS.
The Superior Spider-Man
(OTTO OCTAVIUS'S MIND IN THE BODY OF PETER PARKER), EARTH-616
Assassin Spider-Man
(PETER PARKER), EARTH-8351.

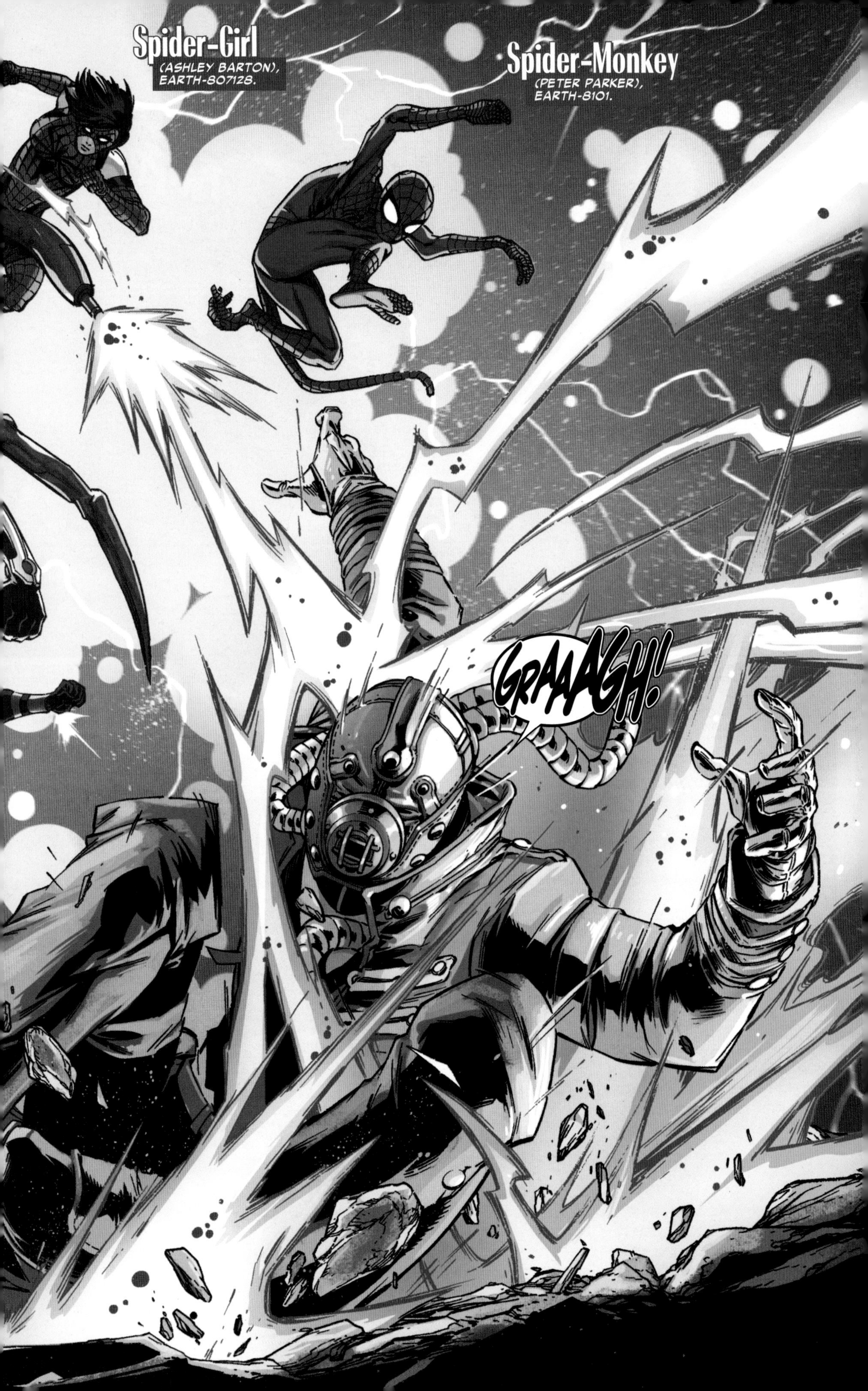
Spider-Girl
(ASHLEY BARTON), EARTH-807128.
Spider-Monkey
(PETER PARKER), EARTH-8101.
GRAAAGH!

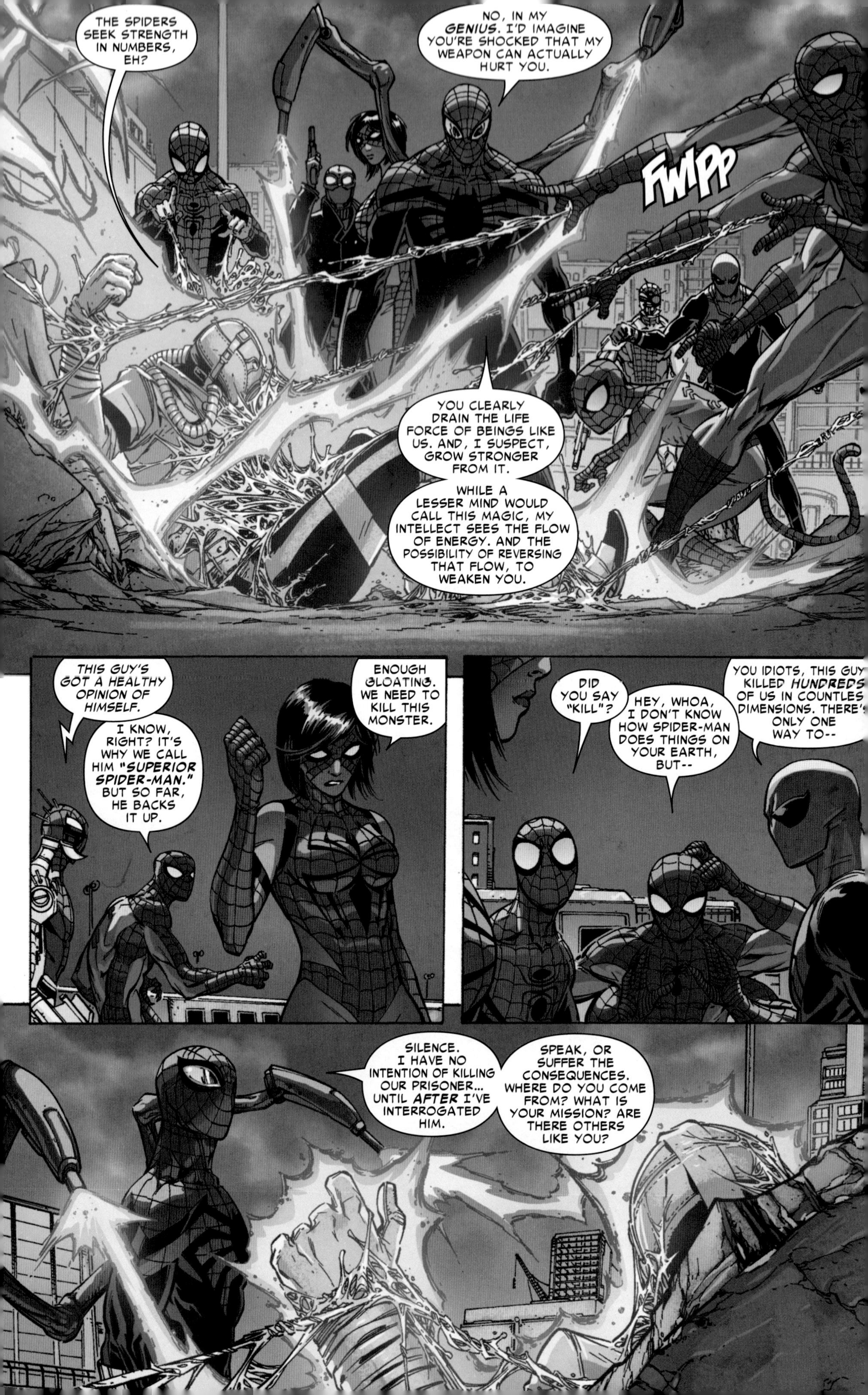
THE SPIDERS SEEK STRENGTH IN NUMBERS, EH?
NO, IN MY GENIUS. I'D IMAGINE YOU'RE SHOCKED THAT MY WEAPON CAN ACTUALLY HURT YOU.
FWIPP
YOU CLEARLY DRAIN THE LIFE FORCE OF BEINGS LIKE US. AND, I SUSPECT, GROW STRONGER FROM IT.
WHILE A LESSER MIND WOULD CALL THIS MAGIC, MY INTELLECT SEES THE FLOW OF ENERGY. AND THE POSSIBILITY OF REVERSING THAT FLOW, TO WEAKEN YOU.
THIS GUY'S GOT A HEALTHY OPINION OF HIMSELF.
I KNOW, RIGHT? IT'S WHY WE CALL HIM "SUPERIOR SPIDER-MAN." BUT SO FAR, HE BACKS IT UP.
ENOUGH GLOATING. WE NEED TO KILL THIS MONSTER.
DID YOU SAY "KILL"?
HEY, WHOA, I DON'T KNOW HOW SPIDER-MAN DOES THINGS ON YOUR EARTH, BUT--
YOU IDIOTS, THIS GUY KILLED HUNDREDS OF US IN COUNTLES DIMENSIONS. THERE'S ONLY ONE WAY TO--
SILENCE. I HAVE NO INTENTION OF KILLING OUR PRISONER... UNTIL AFTER I'VE INTERROGATED HIM.
SPEAK, OR SUFFER THE CONSEQUENCES. WHERE DO YOU COME FROM? WHAT IS YOUR MISSION? ARE THERE OTHERS LIKE YOU?

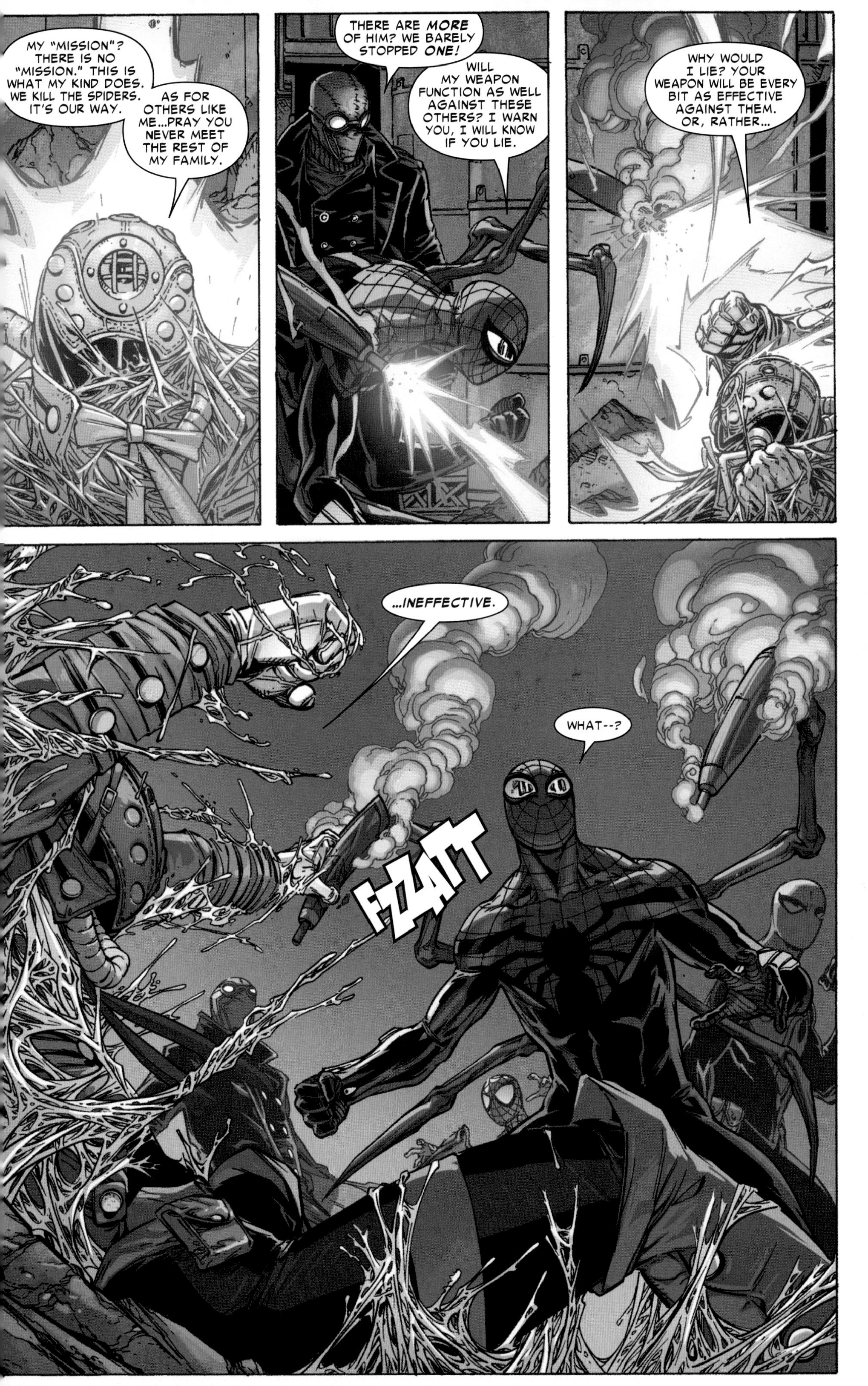
MY "MISSION"? THERE IS NO "MISSION." THIS IS WHAT MY KIND DOES. WE KILL THE SPIDERS. IT'S OUR WAY.
AS FOR OTHERS LIKE ME...PRAY YOU NEVER MEET THE REST OF MY FAMILY.
THERE ARE MORE OF HIM? WE BARELY STOPPED ONE!
WILL MY WEAPON FUNCTION AS WELL AGAINST THESE OTHERS? I WARN YOU, I WILL KNOW IF YOU LIE.
WHY WOULD I LIE? YOUR WEAPON WILL BE EVERY BIT AS EFFECTIVE AGAINST THEM. OR, RATHER...
...INEFFECTIVE.
WHAT--?
FZZATT

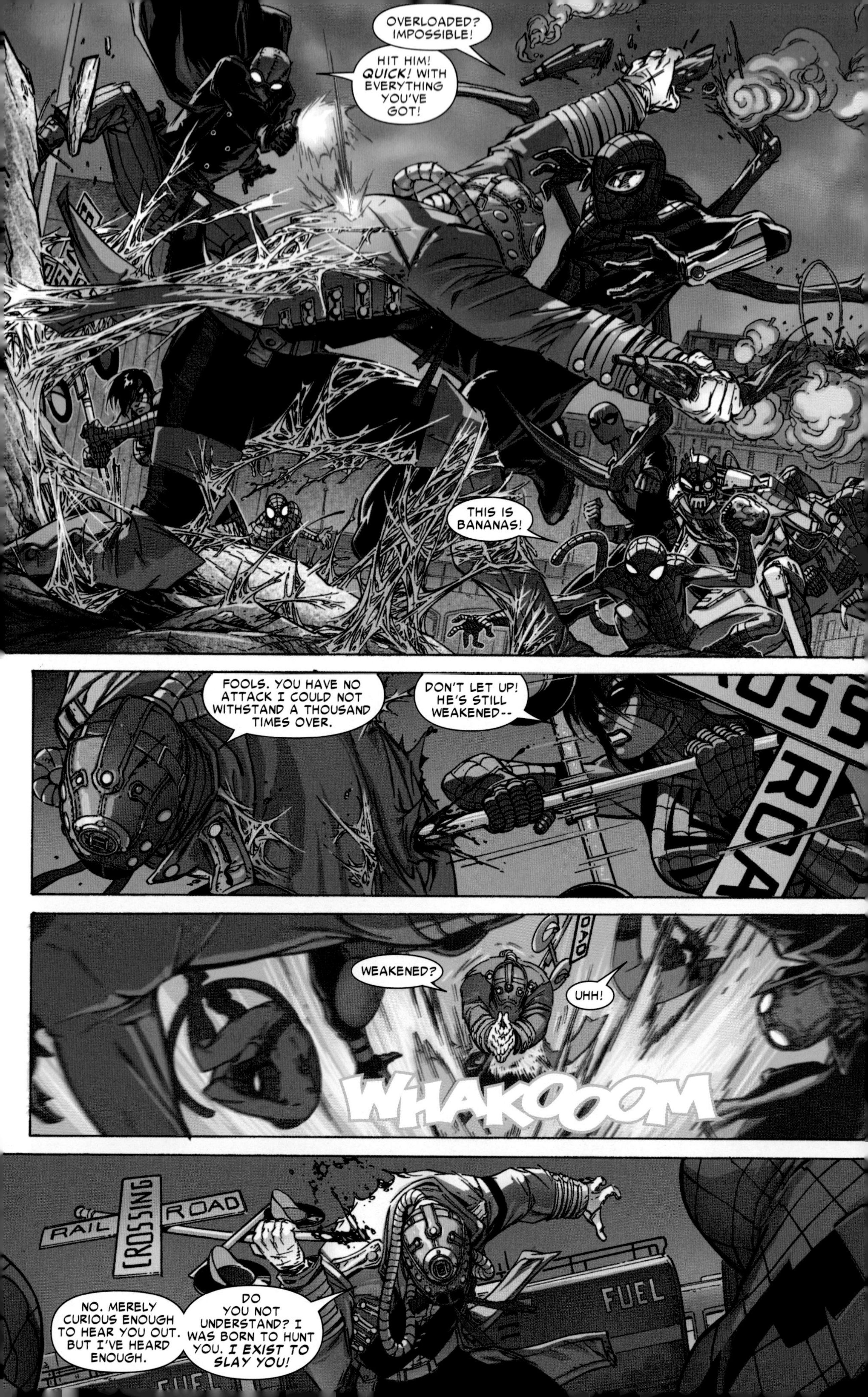
OVERLOADED? IMPOSSIBLE!
HIT HIM! QUICK! WITH EVERYTHING YOU'VE GOT!
THIS IS BANANAS!
FOOLS. YOU HAVE NO ATTACK I COULD NOT WITHSTAND A THOUSAND TIMES OVER.
DON'T LET UP! HE'S STILL WEAKENED--
WEAKENED?
UHH!
WHAKOOOM
RAIL CROSSING ROAD
FUEL
NO. MERELY CURIOUS ENOUGH TO HEAR YOU OUT. BUT I'VE HEARD ENOUGH.
DO YOU NOT UNDERSTAND? I WAS BORN TO HUNT YOU. I EXIST TO SLAY YOU!

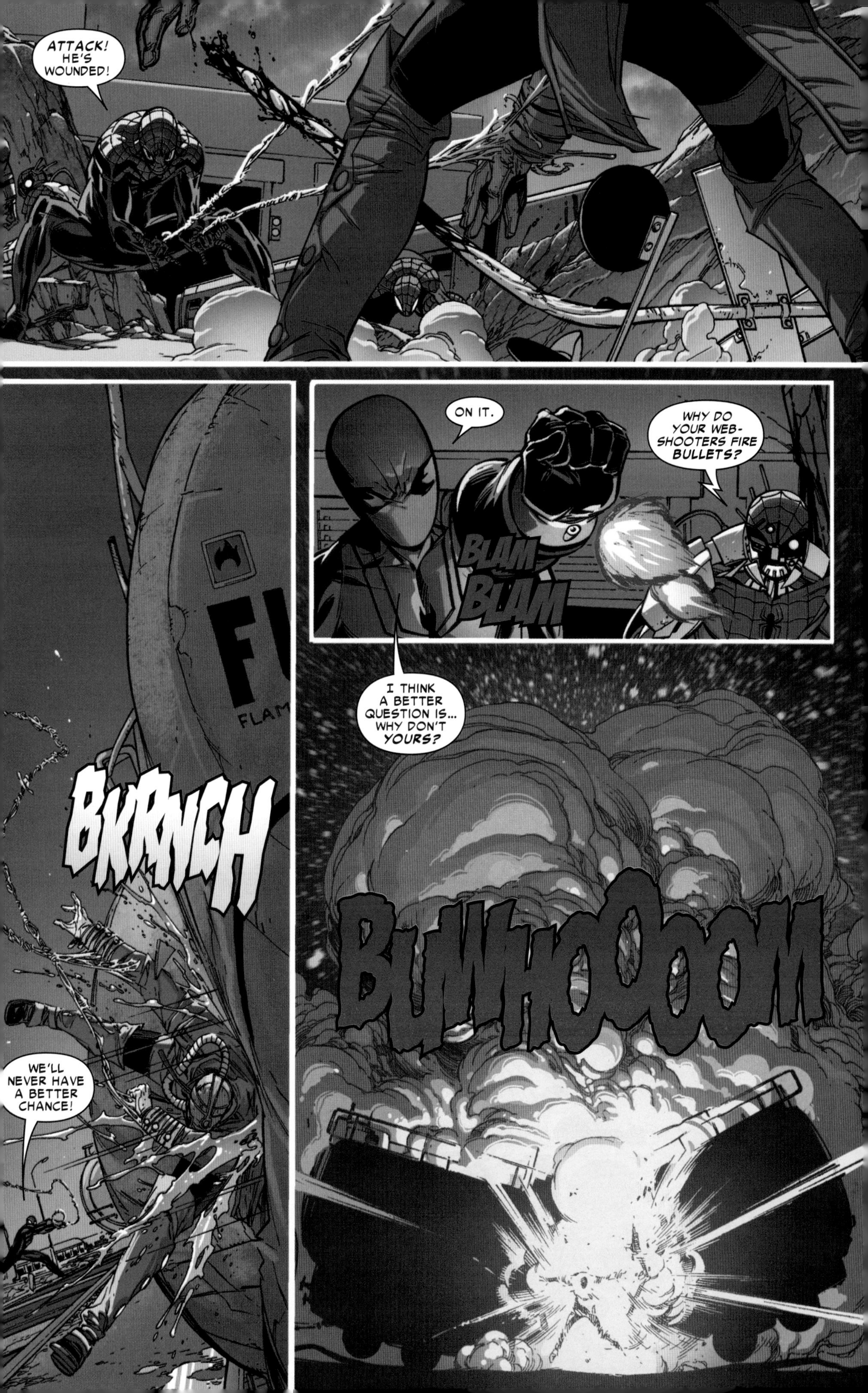
ATTACK! HE'S WOUNDED!
BKRNCH
WE'LL NEVER HAVE A BETTER CHANCE!
ON IT.
WHY DO YOUR WEB-SHOOTERS FIRE BULLETS?
BLAM BLAM
I THINK A BETTER QUESTION IS... WHY DON'T YOURS?
BUMHOOOOM

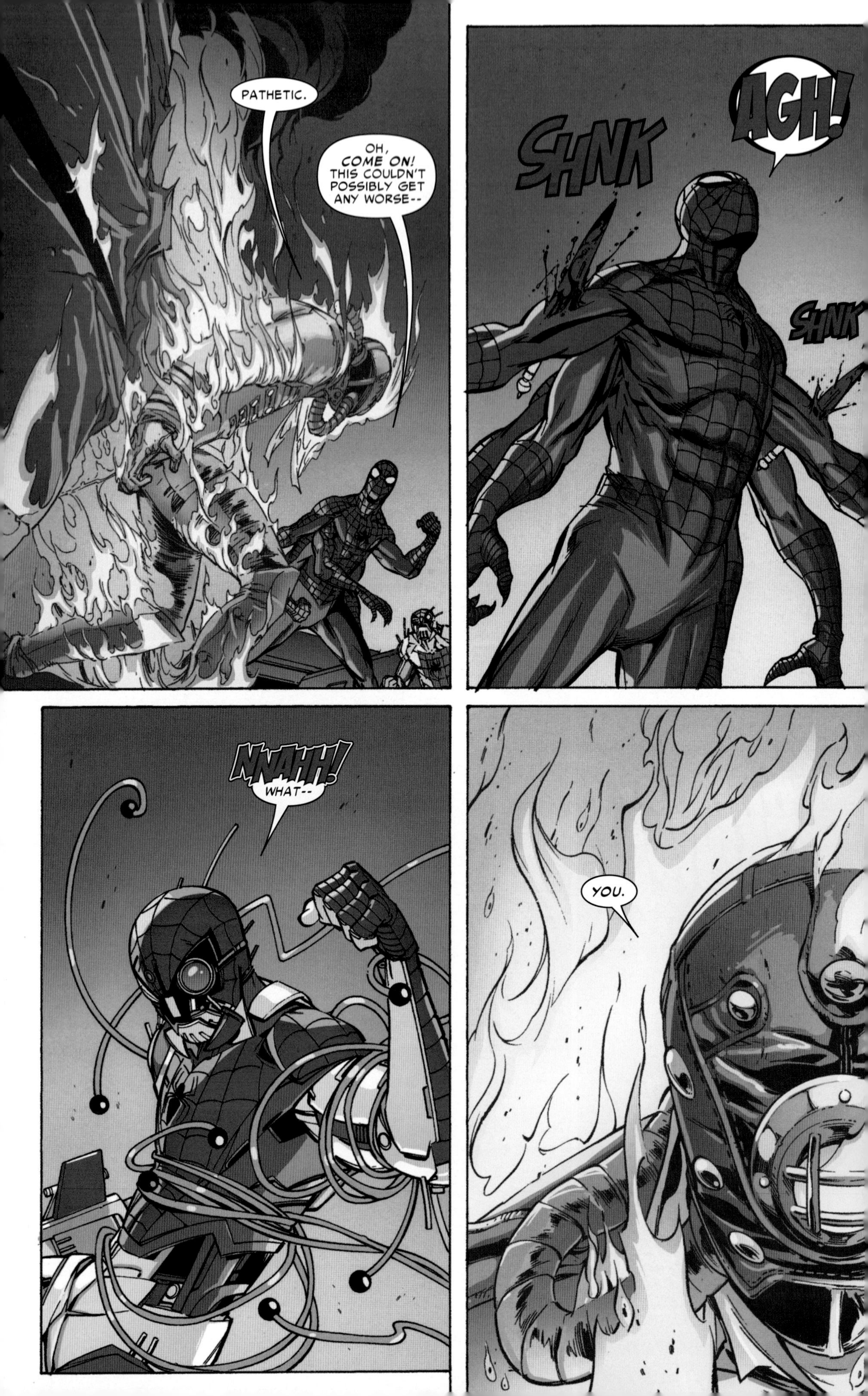
PATHETIC.
OH, COME ON! THIS COULDN'T POSSIBLY GET ANY WORSE--
SHNK
AGH!
SHNK
NNAHH!
WHAT--
YOU.

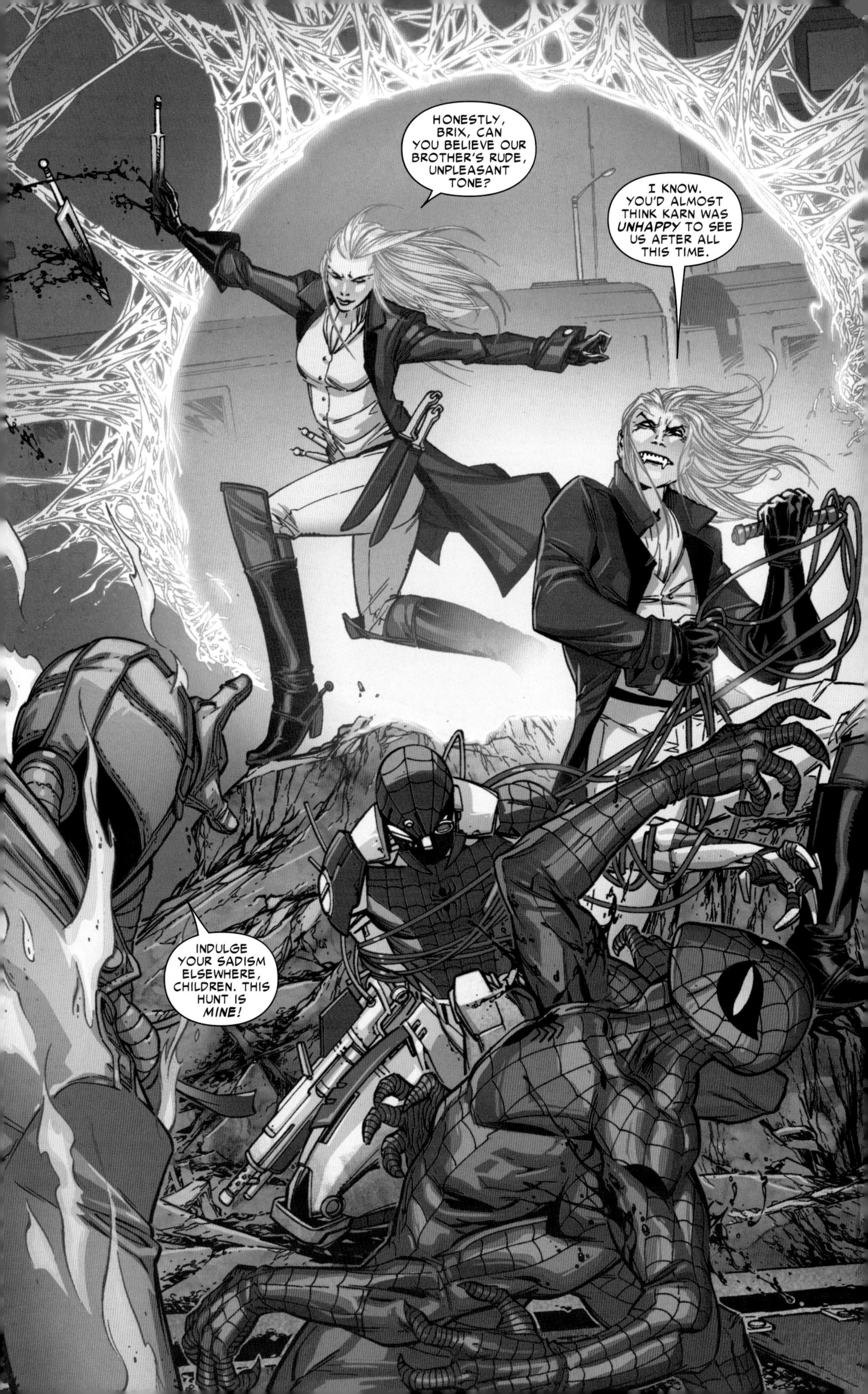
HONESTLY, BRIX, CAN YOU BELIEVE OUR BROTHER'S RUDE, UNPLEASANT TONE?
I KNOW. YOU'D ALMOST THINK KARN WAS *UNHAPPY* TO SEE US AFTER ALL THIS TIME.
INDULGE YOUR SADISM ELSEWHERE, CHILDREN. THIS HUNT IS *MINE!*

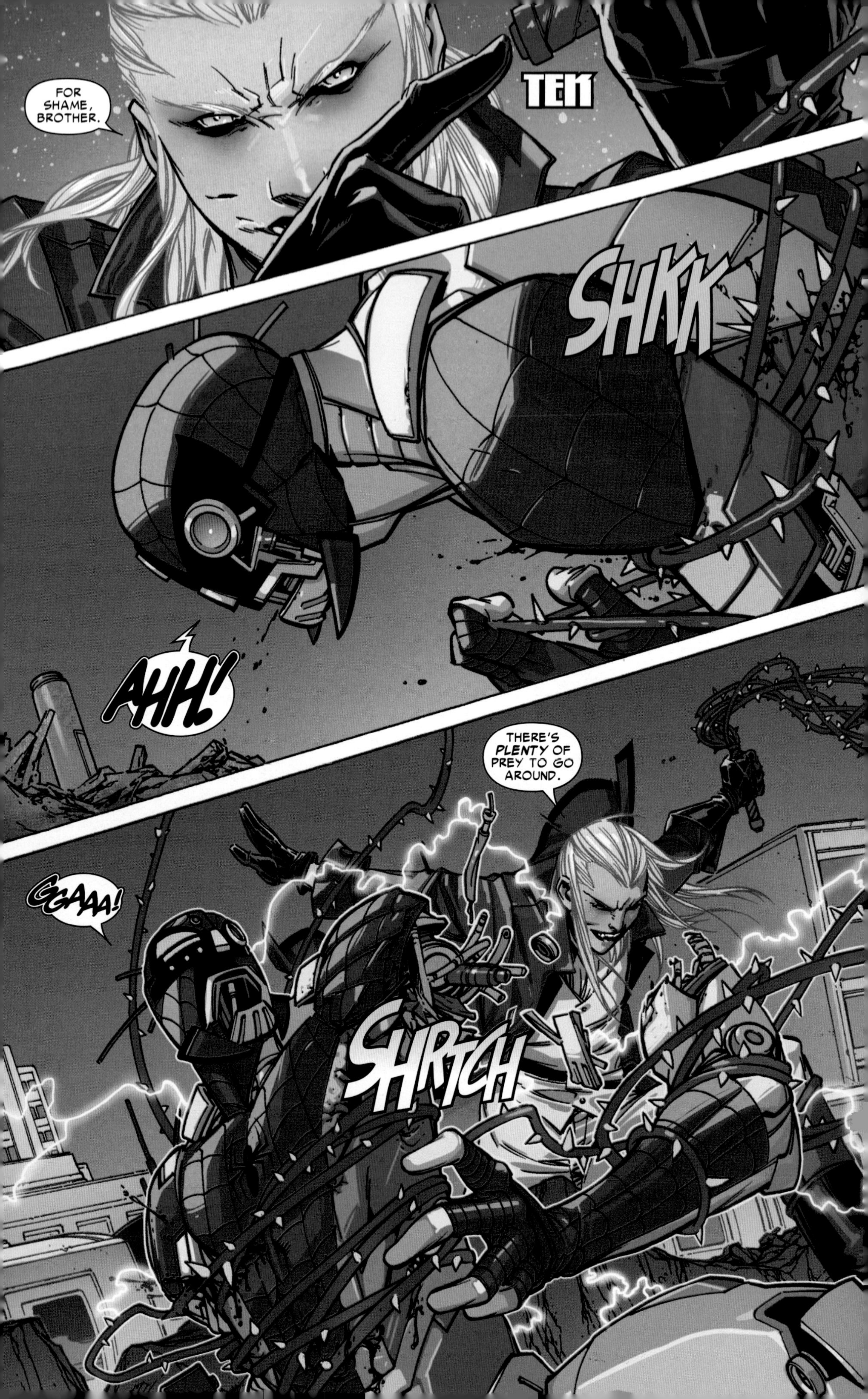
FOR SHAME, BROTHER.
TEK
SHKK
AHH!
THERE'S PLENTY OF PREY TO GO AROUND.
GGAAA!
SHRTCH

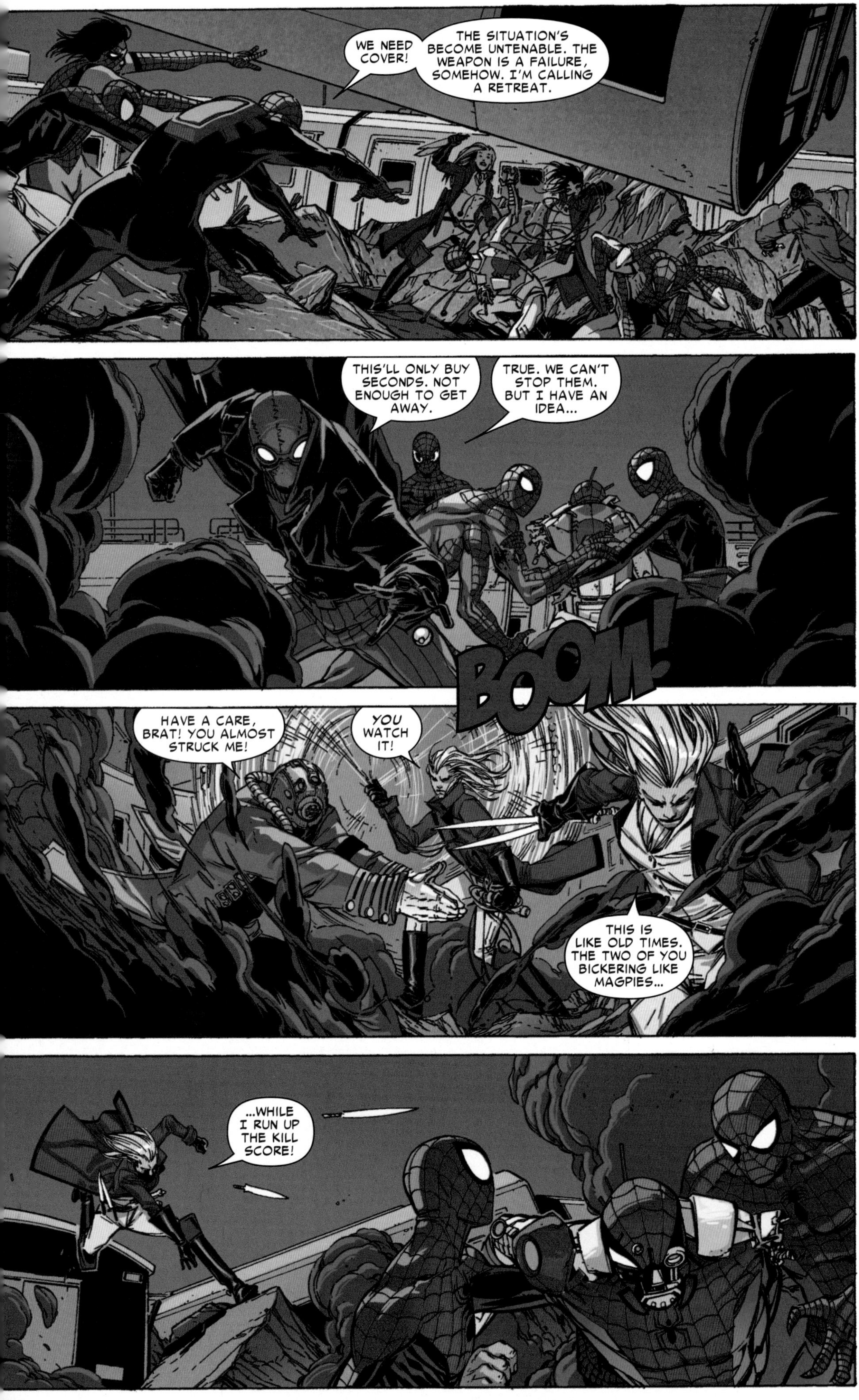
WE NEED COVER!
THE SITUATION'S BECOME UNTENABLE. THE WEAPON IS A FAILURE, SOMEHOW. I'M CALLING A RETREAT.
THIS'LL ONLY BUY SECONDS. NOT ENOUGH TO GET AWAY.
TRUE. WE CAN'T STOP THEM. BUT I HAVE AN IDEA...
BOOM!
HAVE A CARE, BRAT! YOU ALMOST STRUCK ME!
YOU WATCH IT!
THIS IS LIKE OLD TIMES. THE TWO OF YOU BICKERING LIKE MAGPIES...
...WHILE I RUN UP THE KILL SCORE!

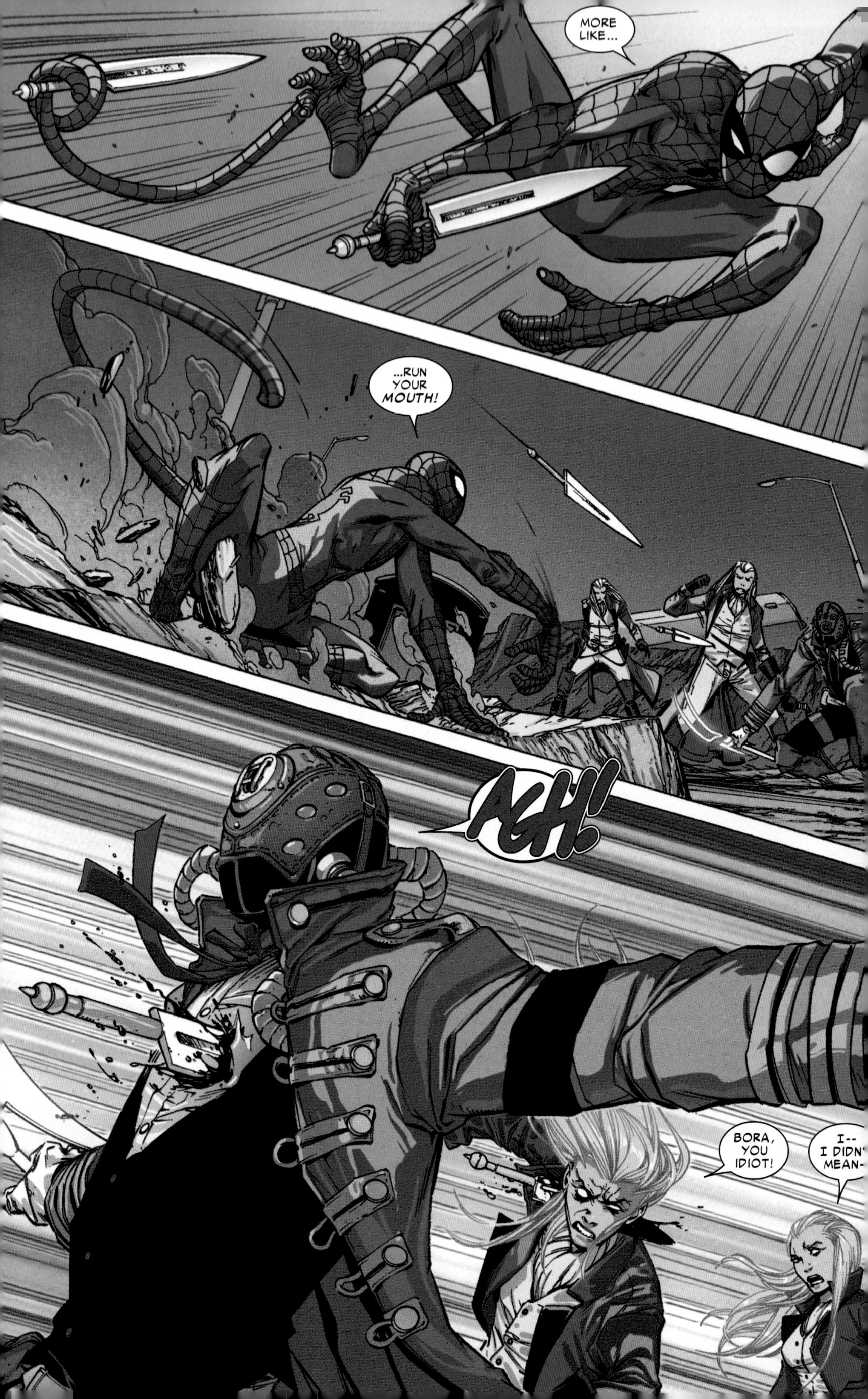
MORE LIKE...
...RUN YOUR MOUTH!
AGH!
BORA, YOU IDIOT!
I-- I DIDN' MEAN-

I'LL BROOK NO MORE HUMILIATION FROM YOU!

GFF!

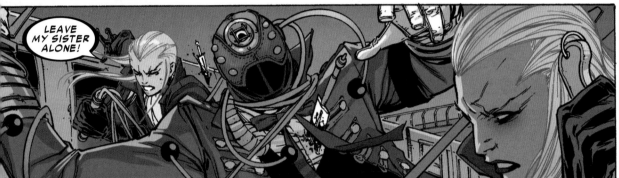

LEAVE MY SISTER ALONE!

YOU BROUGHT THIS ON YOURSELVES WHEN YOU CAME HERE TO SHAME ME!

WE CAME AFTER A TREASURE TROVE OF SPIDER-TOTEMS. YOUR SHAME IS YOUR OWN DOING, OUTCAST!

GRRAAA!

THAT ESCALATED QUICKLY.

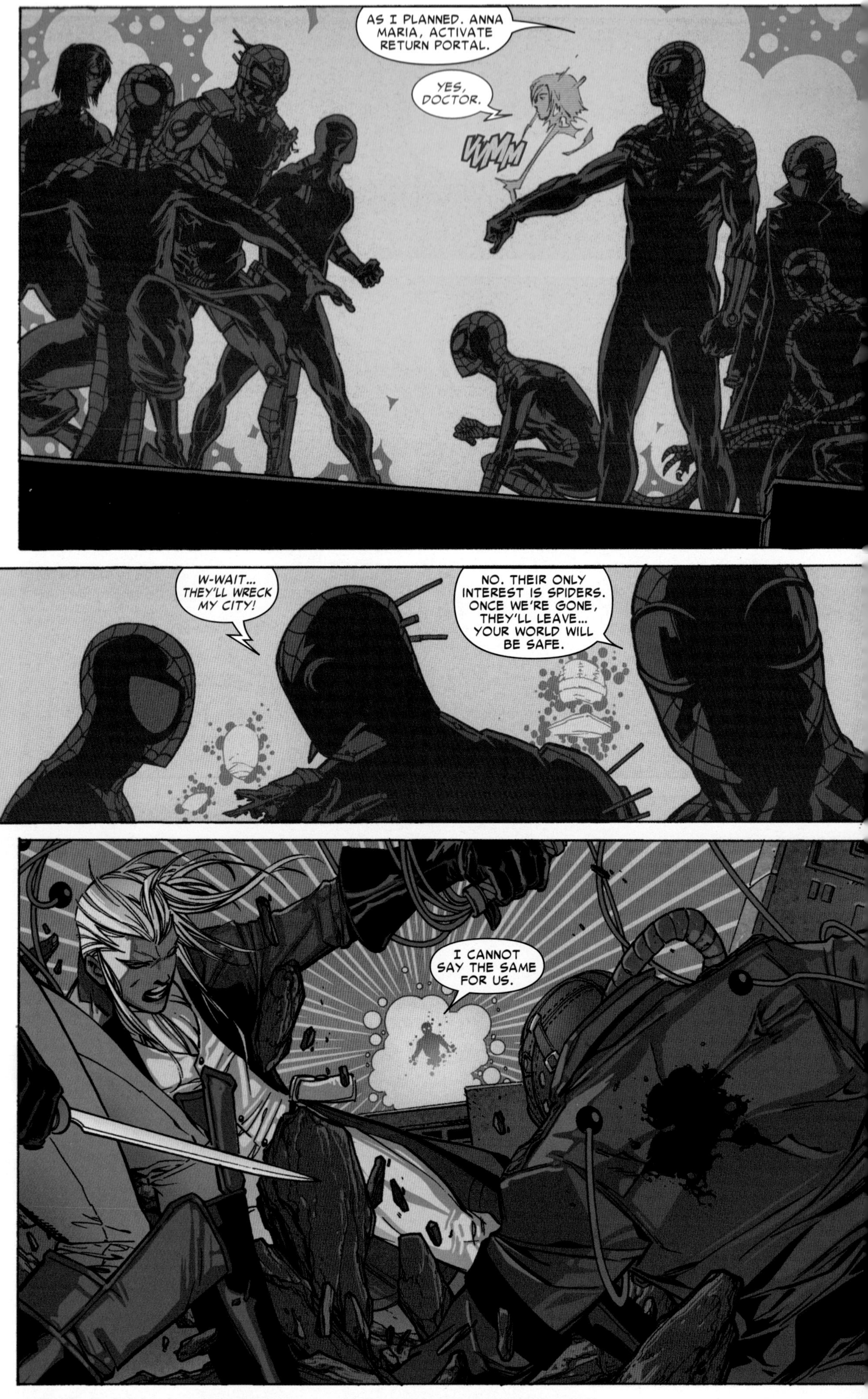
AS I PLANNED. ANNA MARIA, ACTIVATE RETURN PORTAL.
YES, DOCTOR.
VVMM
W-WAIT... THEY'LL WRECK MY CITY!
NO. THEIR ONLY INTEREST IS SPIDERS. ONCE WE'RE GONE, THEY'LL LEAVE... YOUR WORLD WILL BE SAFE.
I CANNOT SAY THE SAME FOR US.

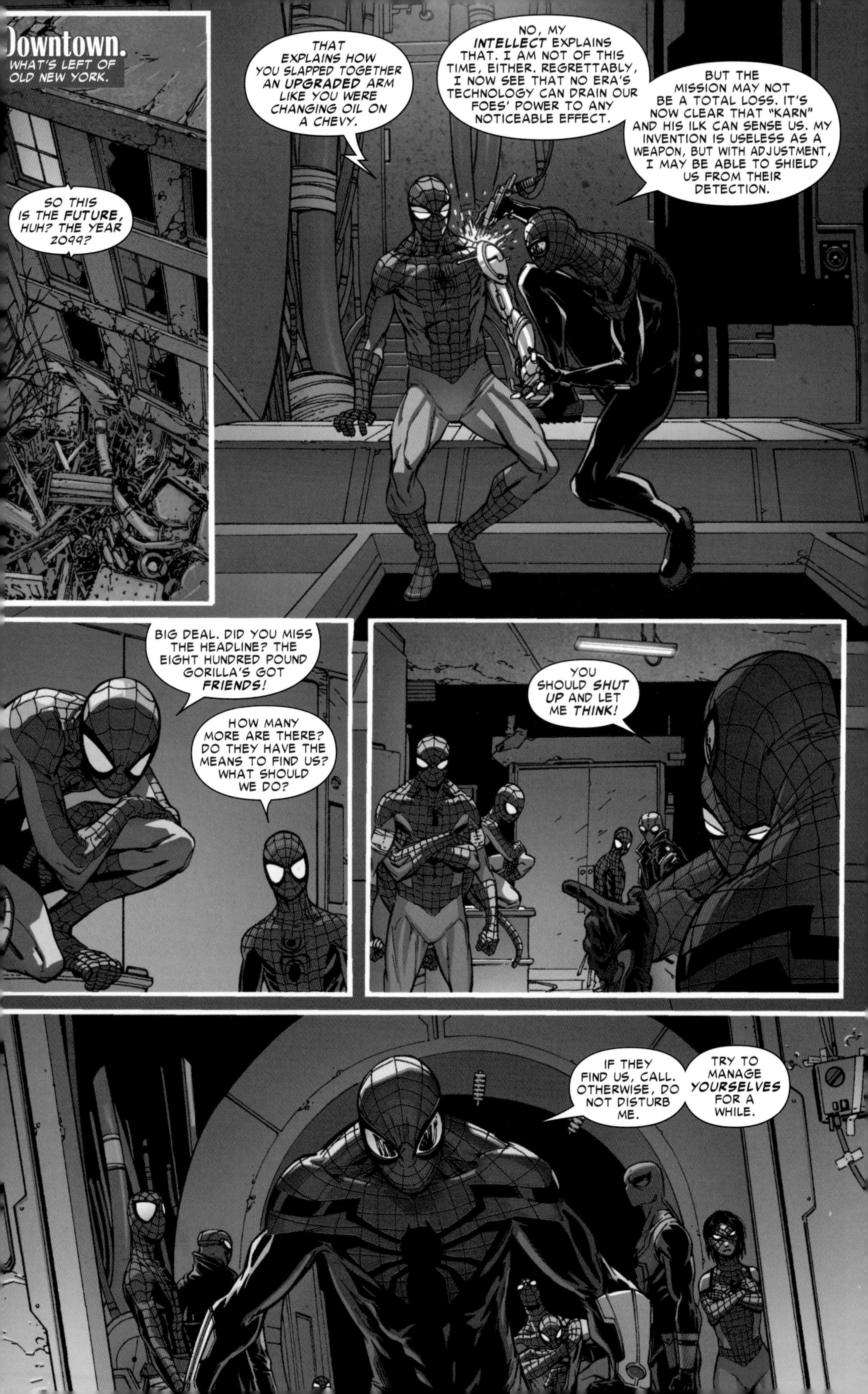
Downtown.
WHAT'S LEFT OF OLD NEW YORK.
SO THIS IS THE FUTURE, HUH? THE YEAR 2099?
THAT EXPLAINS HOW YOU SLAPPED TOGETHER AN UPGRADED ARM LIKE YOU WERE CHANGING OIL ON A CHEVY.
NO, MY INTELLECT EXPLAINS THAT. I AM NOT OF THIS TIME, EITHER. REGRETTABLY, I NOW SEE THAT NO ERA'S TECHNOLOGY CAN DRAIN OUR FOES' POWER TO ANY NOTICEABLE EFFECT.
BUT THE MISSION MAY NOT BE A TOTAL LOSS. IT'S NOW CLEAR THAT "KARN" AND HIS ILK CAN SENSE US. MY INVENTION IS USELESS AS A WEAPON, BUT WITH ADJUSTMENT, I MAY BE ABLE TO SHIELD US FROM THEIR DETECTION.
BIG DEAL. DID YOU MISS THE HEADLINE? THE EIGHT HUNDRED POUND GORILLA'S GOT FRIENDS!
HOW MANY MORE ARE THERE? DO THEY HAVE THE MEANS TO FIND US? WHAT SHOULD WE DO?
YOU SHOULD SHUT UP AND LET ME THINK!
IF THEY FIND US, CALL. OTHERWISE, DO NOT DISTURB ME.
TRY TO MANAGE YOURSELVES FOR A WHILE.

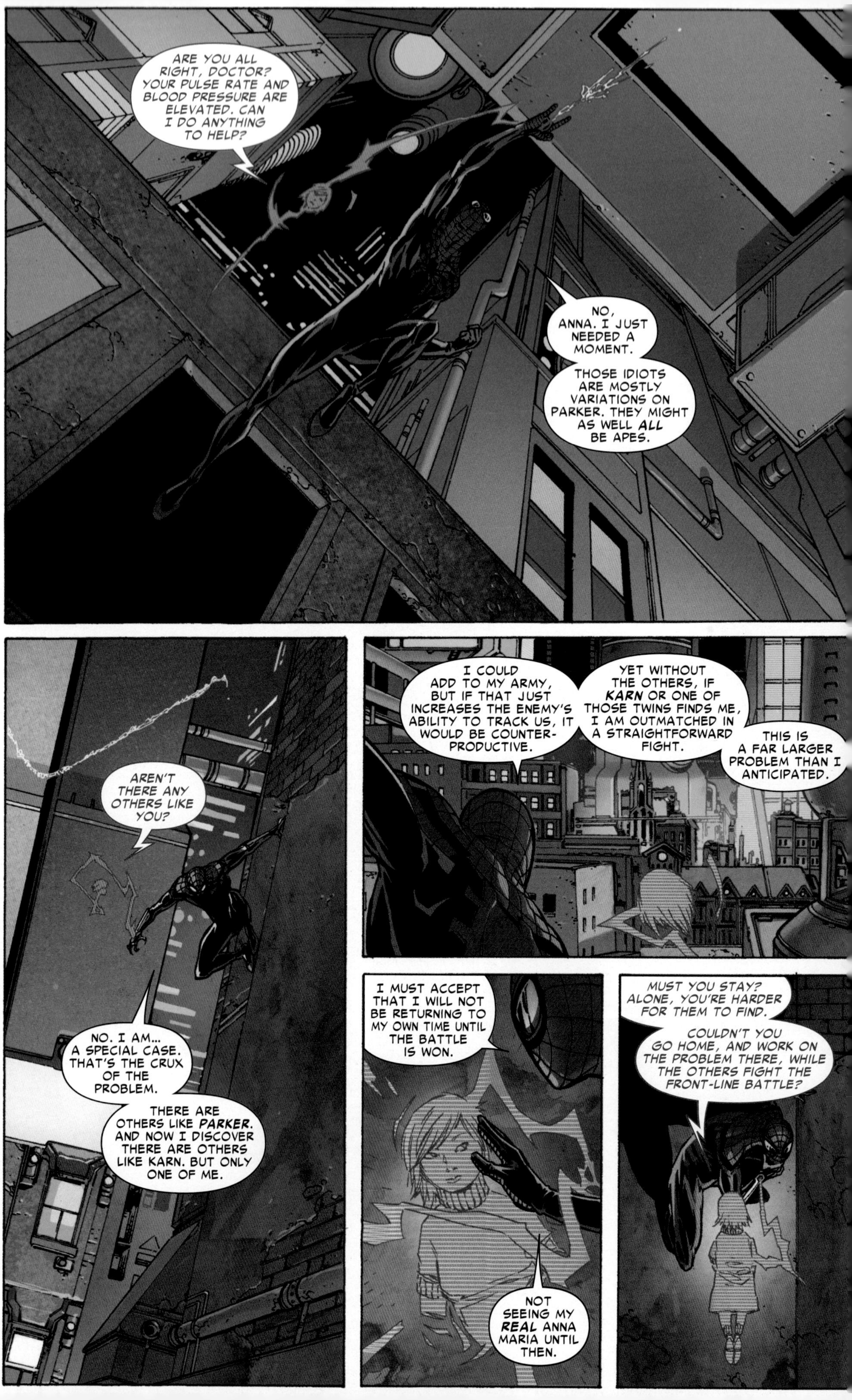

ARE YOU ALL RIGHT, DOCTOR? YOUR PULSE RATE AND BLOOD PRESSURE ARE ELEVATED. CAN I DO ANYTHING TO HELP?
NO, ANNA. I JUST NEEDED A MOMENT.
THOSE IDIOTS ARE MOSTLY VARIATIONS ON PARKER. THEY MIGHT AS WELL ***ALL*** BE APES.
AREN'T THERE ANY OTHERS LIKE YOU?
NO. I AM... A SPECIAL CASE. THAT'S THE CRUX OF THE PROBLEM.
THERE ARE OTHERS LIKE ***PARKER***. AND NOW I DISCOVER THERE ARE OTHERS LIKE KARN. BUT ONLY ONE OF ME.
I COULD ADD TO MY ARMY, BUT IF THAT JUST INCREASES THE ENEMY'S ABILITY TO TRACK US, IT WOULD BE COUNTER-PRODUCTIVE.
YET WITHOUT THE OTHERS, IF ***KARN*** OR ONE OF THOSE TWINS FINDS ME, I AM OUTMATCHED IN A STRAIGHTFORWARD FIGHT.
THIS IS A FAR LARGER PROBLEM THAN I ANTICIPATED.
I MUST ACCEPT THAT I WILL NOT BE RETURNING TO MY OWN TIME UNTIL THE BATTLE IS WON.
NOT SEEING MY ***REAL*** ANNA MARIA UNTIL THEN.
MUST YOU STAY? ALONE, YOU'RE HARDER FOR THEM TO FIND.
COULDN'T YOU GO HOME, AND WORK ON THE PROBLEM THERE, WHILE THE OTHERS FIGHT THE FRONT-LINE BATTLE?

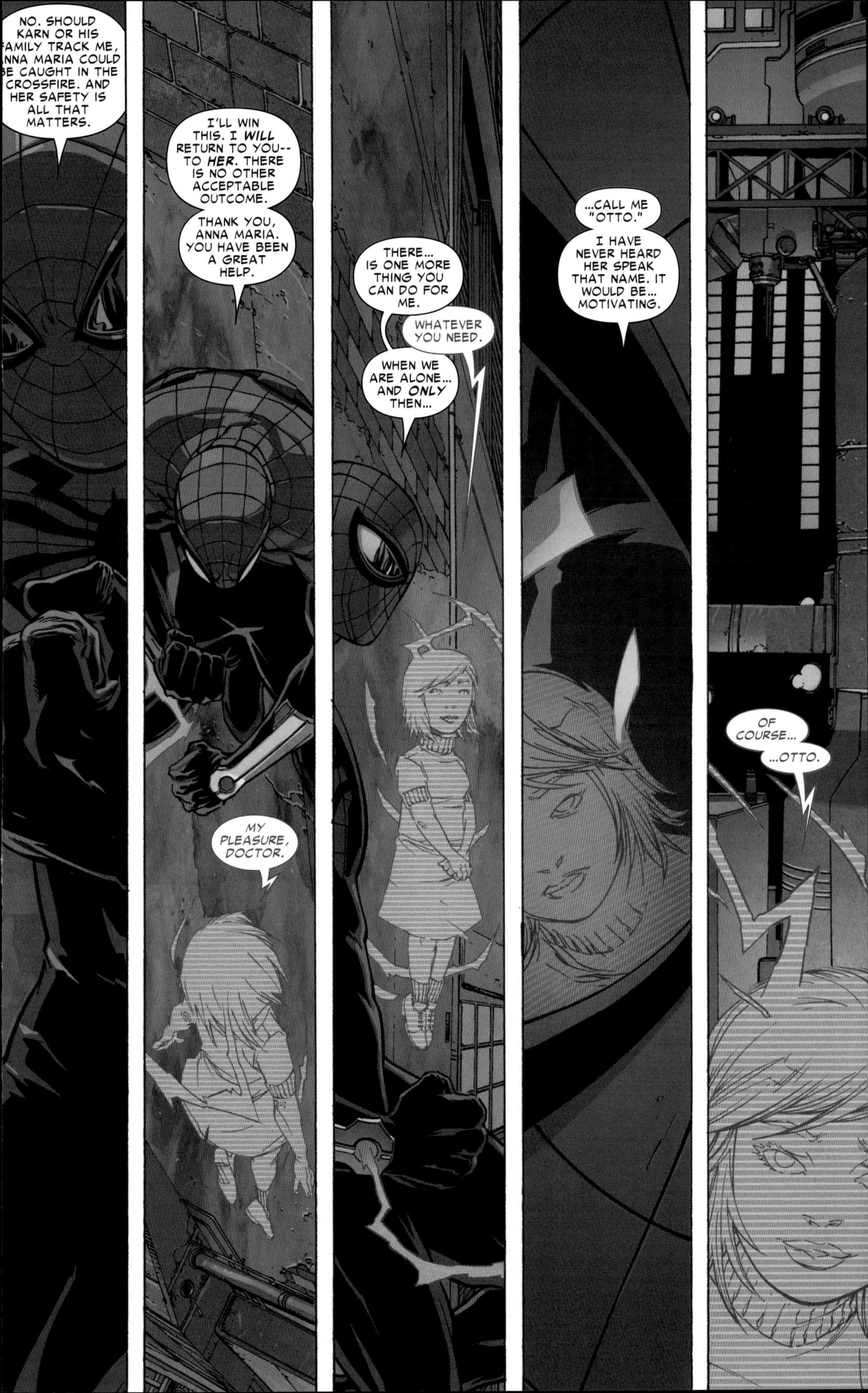
NO. SHOULD KARN OR HIS FAMILY TRACK ME, ANNA MARIA COULD BE CAUGHT IN THE CROSSFIRE. AND HER SAFETY IS ALL THAT MATTERS.
I'LL WIN THIS. I *WILL* RETURN TO YOU-- TO *HER*. THERE IS NO OTHER ACCEPTABLE OUTCOME.
THANK YOU, ANNA MARIA. YOU HAVE BEEN A GREAT HELP.
MY PLEASURE, DOCTOR.
THERE... IS ONE MORE THING YOU CAN DO FOR ME.
WHATEVER YOU NEED.
WHEN WE ARE ALONE... AND *ONLY* THEN...
...CALL ME "OTTO."
I HAVE NEVER HEARD HER SPEAK THAT NAME. IT WOULD BE... MOTIVATING.
OF COURSE...
...OTTO.

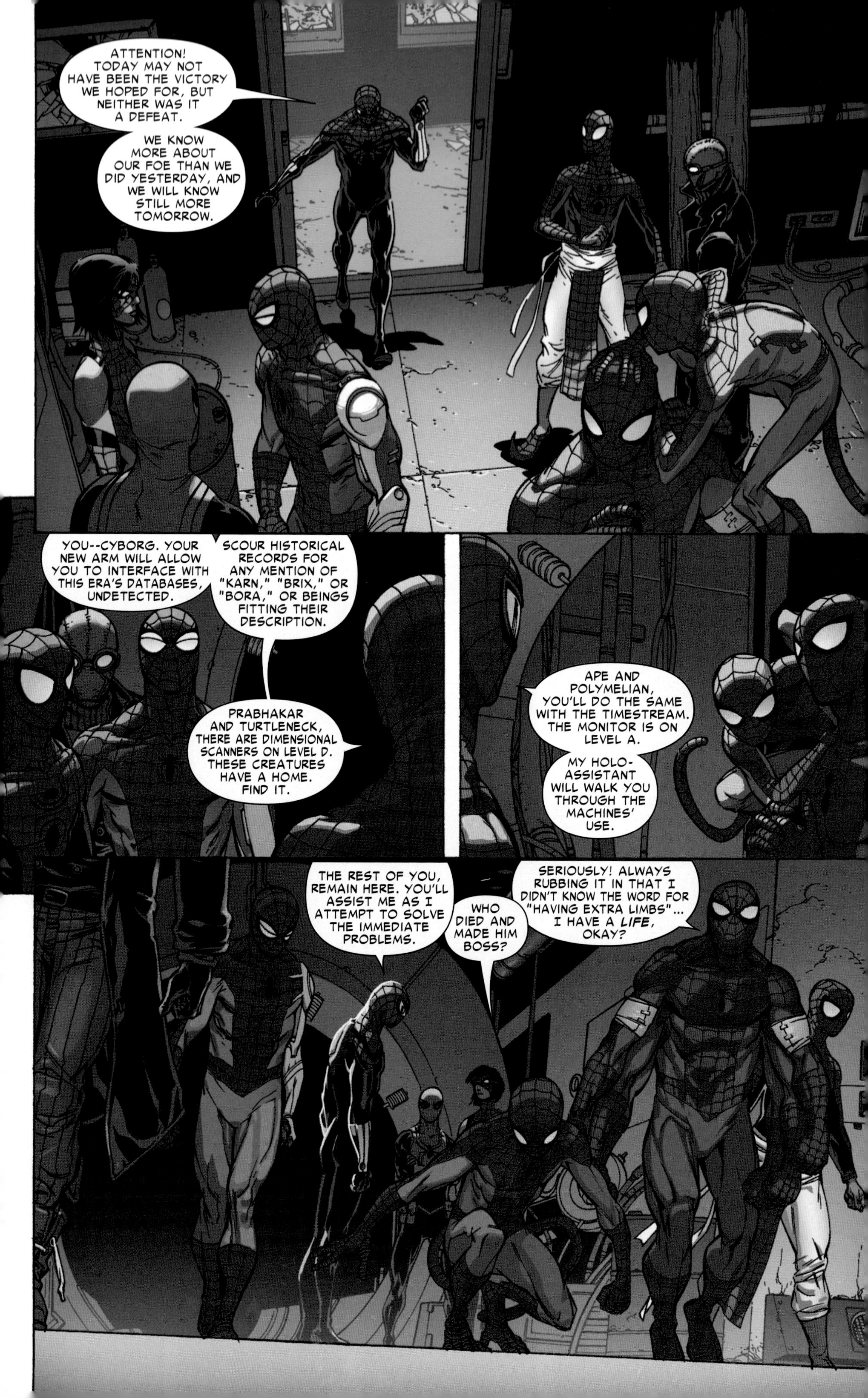
ATTENTION! TODAY MAY NOT HAVE BEEN THE VICTORY WE HOPED FOR, BUT NEITHER WAS IT A DEFEAT.
WE KNOW MORE ABOUT OUR FOE THAN WE DID YESTERDAY, AND WE WILL KNOW STILL MORE TOMORROW.
YOU--CYBORG. YOUR NEW ARM WILL ALLOW YOU TO INTERFACE WITH THIS ERA'S DATABASES, UNDETECTED.
SCOUR HISTORICAL RECORDS FOR ANY MENTION OF "KARN," "BRIX," OR "BORA," OR BEINGS FITTING THEIR DESCRIPTION.
PRABHAKAR AND TURTLENECK, THERE ARE DIMENSIONAL SCANNERS ON LEVEL D. THESE CREATURES HAVE A HOME. FIND IT.
APE AND POLYMELIAN, YOU'LL DO THE SAME WITH THE TIMESTREAM. THE MONITOR IS ON LEVEL A.
MY HOLO-ASSISTANT WILL WALK YOU THROUGH THE MACHINES' USE.
THE REST OF YOU, REMAIN HERE. YOU'LL ASSIST ME AS I ATTEMPT TO SOLVE THE IMMEDIATE PROBLEMS.
WHO DIED AND MADE HIM BOSS?
SERIOUSLY! ALWAYS RUBBING IT IN THAT I DIDN'T KNOW THE WORD FOR "HAVING EXTRA LIMBS"... I HAVE A *LIFE*, OKAY?

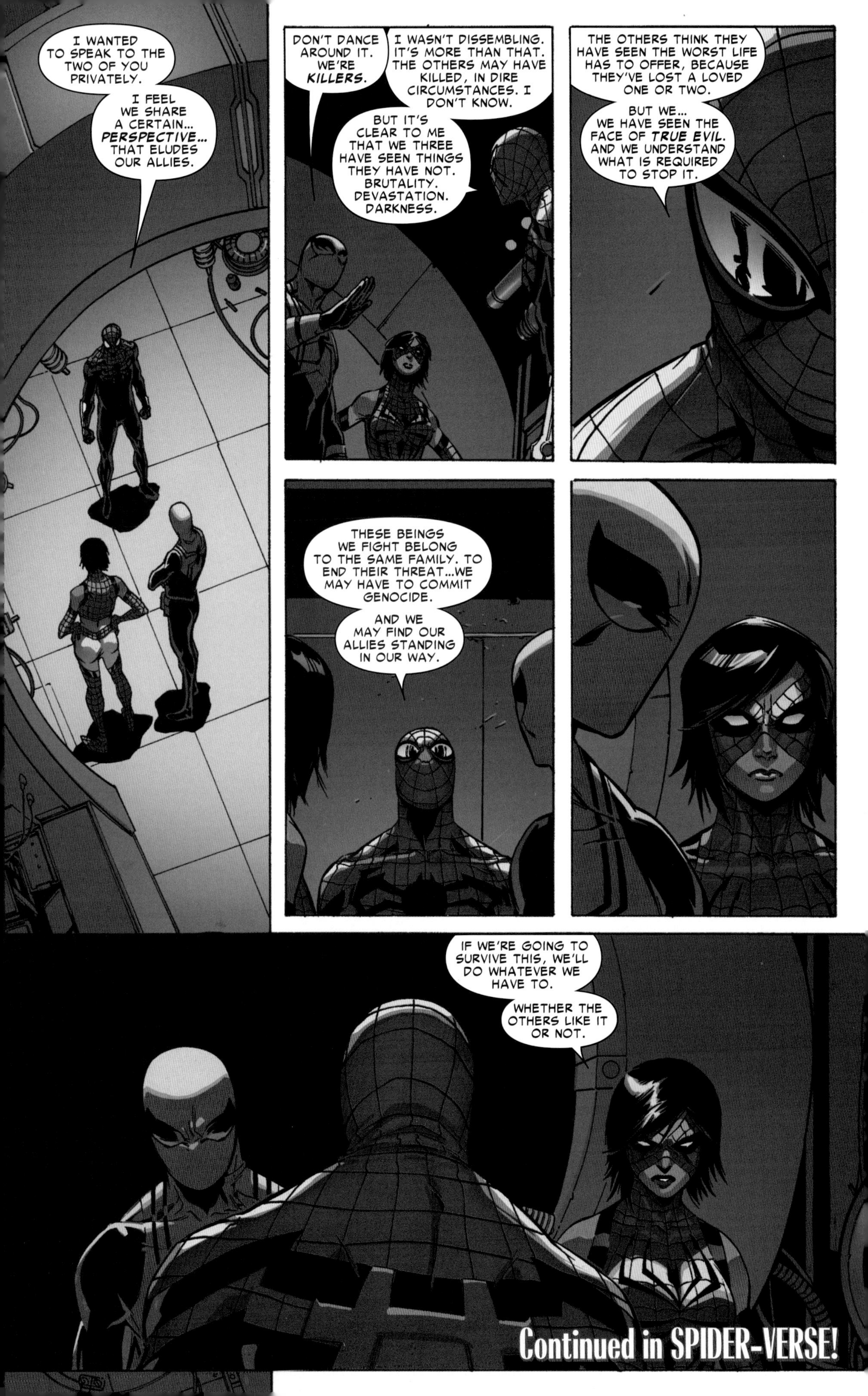
I WANTED TO SPEAK TO THE TWO OF YOU PRIVATELY.
I FEEL WE SHARE A CERTAIN... *PERSPECTIVE*... THAT ELUDES OUR ALLIES.
DON'T DANCE AROUND IT. WE'RE *KILLERS*.
I WASN'T DISSEMBLING. IT'S MORE THAN THAT. THE OTHERS MAY HAVE KILLED, IN DIRE CIRCUMSTANCES. I DON'T KNOW.
BUT IT'S CLEAR TO ME THAT WE THREE HAVE SEEN THINGS THEY HAVE NOT. BRUTALITY. DEVASTATION. DARKNESS.
THE OTHERS THINK THEY HAVE SEEN THE WORST LIFE HAS TO OFFER, BECAUSE THEY'VE LOST A LOVED ONE OR TWO.
BUT WE... WE HAVE SEEN THE FACE OF *TRUE EVIL*. AND WE UNDERSTAND WHAT IS REQUIRED TO STOP IT.
THESE BEINGS WE FIGHT BELONG TO THE SAME FAMILY. TO END THEIR THREAT...WE MAY HAVE TO COMMIT GENOCIDE.
AND WE MAY FIND OUR ALLIES STANDING IN OUR WAY.
IF WE'RE GOING TO SURVIVE THIS, WE'LL DO WHATEVER WE HAVE TO.
WHETHER THE OTHERS LIKE IT OR NOT.
Continued in SPIDER-VERSE!

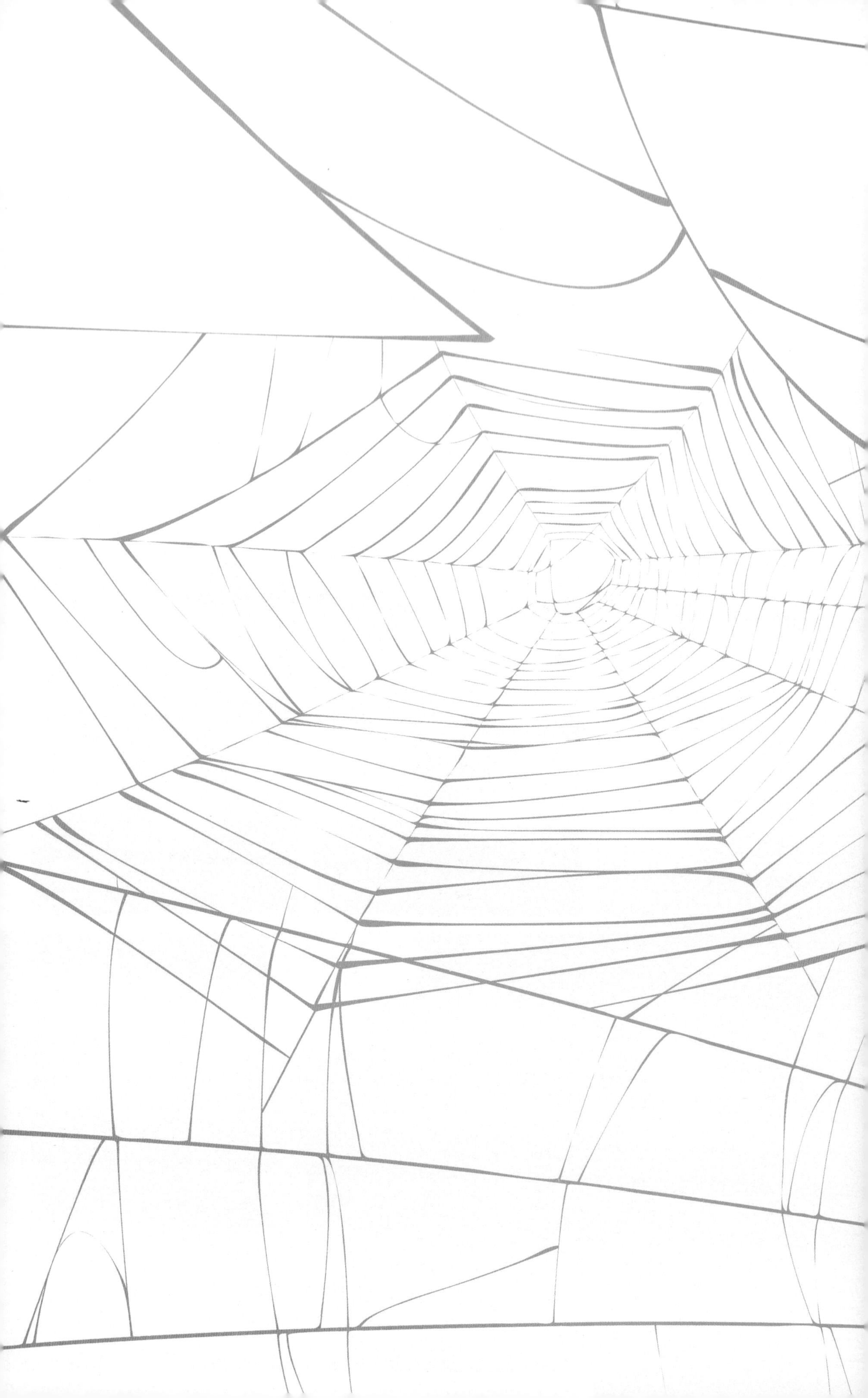

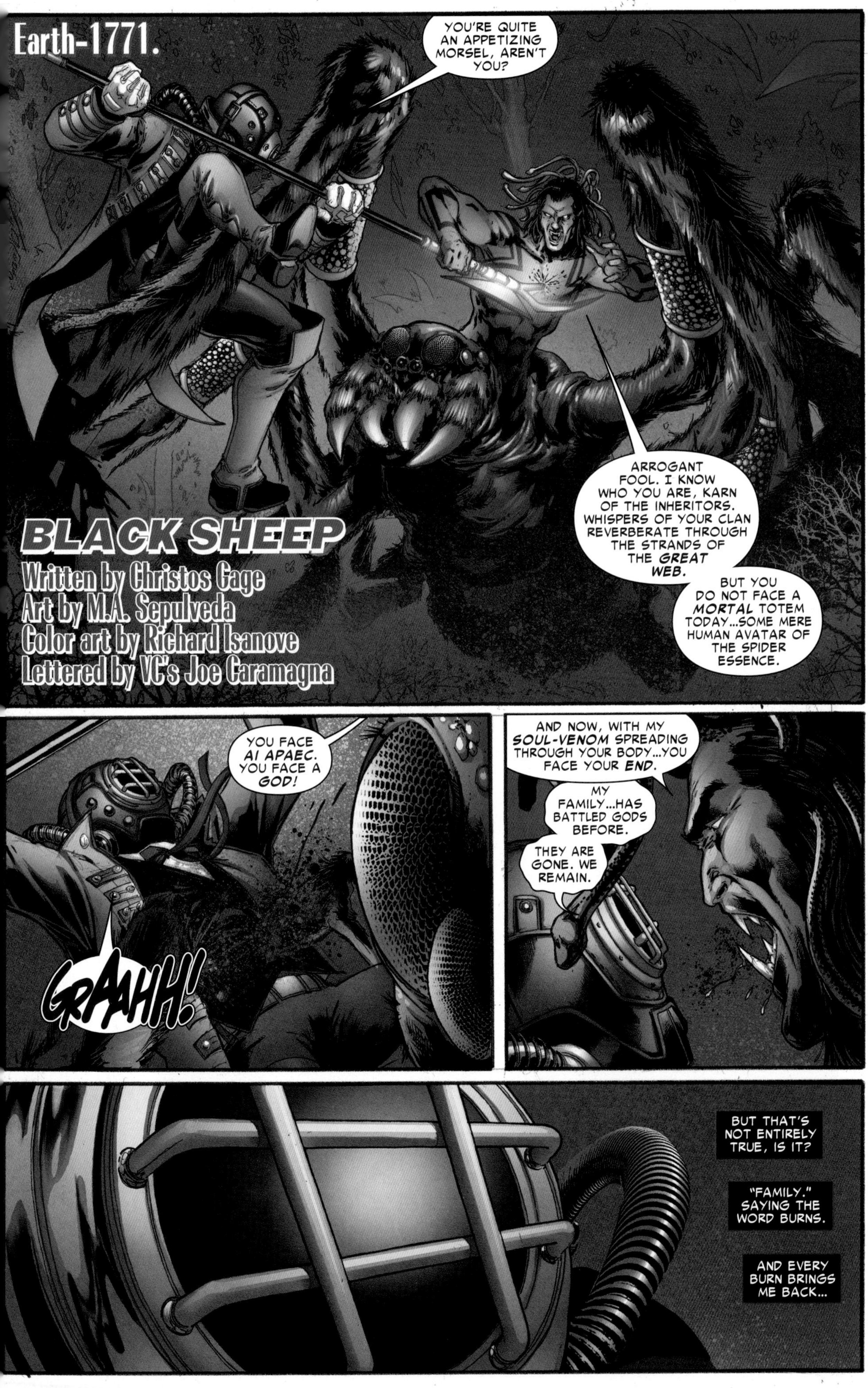
Earth-1771.
YOU'RE QUITE AN APPETIZING MORSEL, AREN'T YOU?
ARROGANT FOOL. I KNOW WHO YOU ARE, KARN OF THE INHERITORS. WHISPERS OF YOUR CLAN REVERBERATE THROUGH THE STRANDS OF THE GREAT WEB.
BUT YOU DO NOT FACE A MORTAL TOTEM TODAY...SOME MERE HUMAN AVATAR OF THE SPIDER ESSENCE.
BLACK SHEEP
Written by Christos Gage
Art by M.A. Sepulveda
Color art by Richard Isanove
Lettered by VC's Joe Caramagna
YOU FACE AI APAEC. YOU FACE A GOD!
GRAAHH!
AND NOW, WITH MY SOUL-VENOM SPREADING THROUGH YOUR BODY...YOU FACE YOUR END.
MY FAMILY...HAS BATTLED GODS BEFORE.
THEY ARE GONE. WE REMAIN.
BUT THAT'S NOT ENTIRELY TRUE, IS IT?
"FAMILY." SAYING THE WORD BURNS.
AND EVERY BURN BRINGS ME BACK...

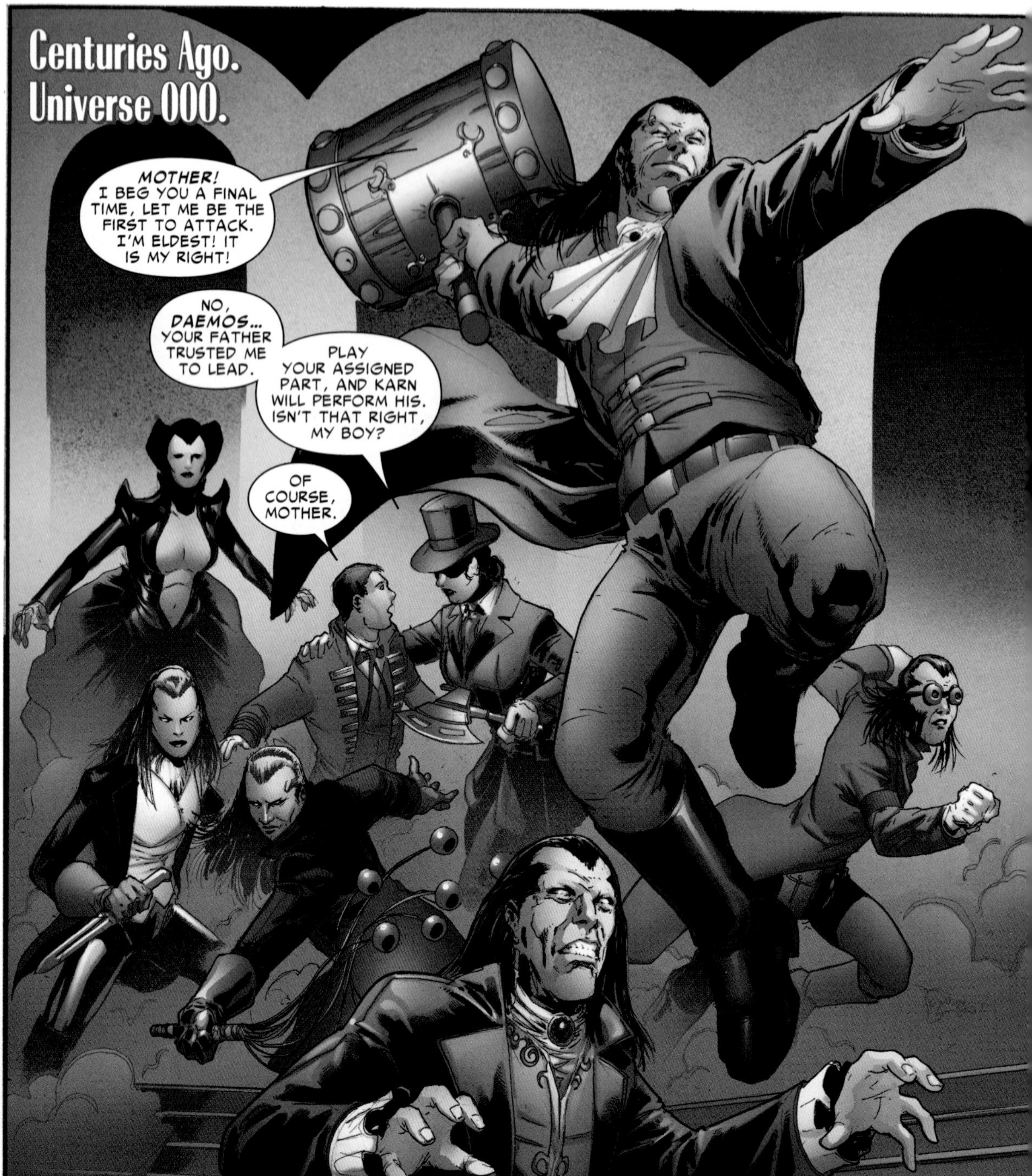
Centuries Ago.
Universe 000.
MOTHER! I BEG YOU A FINAL TIME, LET ME BE THE FIRST TO ATTACK. I'M ELDEST! IT IS MY RIGHT!
NO, DAEMOS... YOUR FATHER TRUSTED ME TO LEAD.
PLAY YOUR ASSIGNED PART, AND KARN WILL PERFORM HIS. ISN'T THAT RIGHT, MY BOY?
OF COURSE, MOTHER.

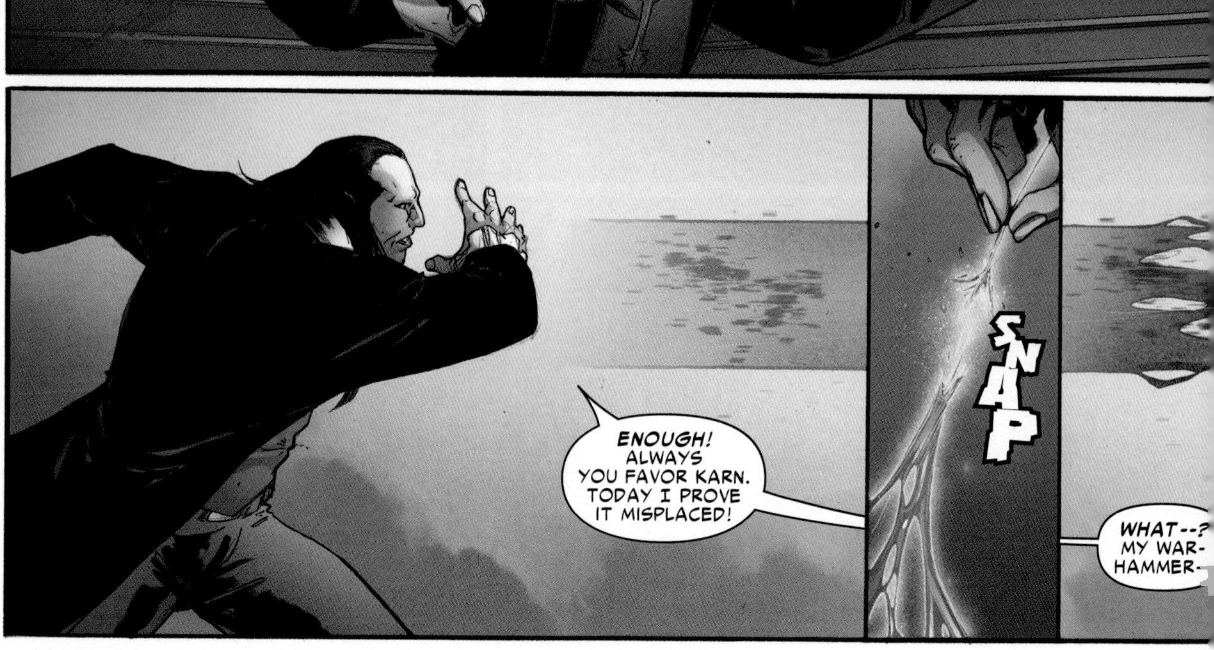
ENOUGH! ALWAYS YOU FAVOR KARN. TODAY I PROVE IT MISPLACED!
SNAP
WHAT--? MY WAR-HAMMER-

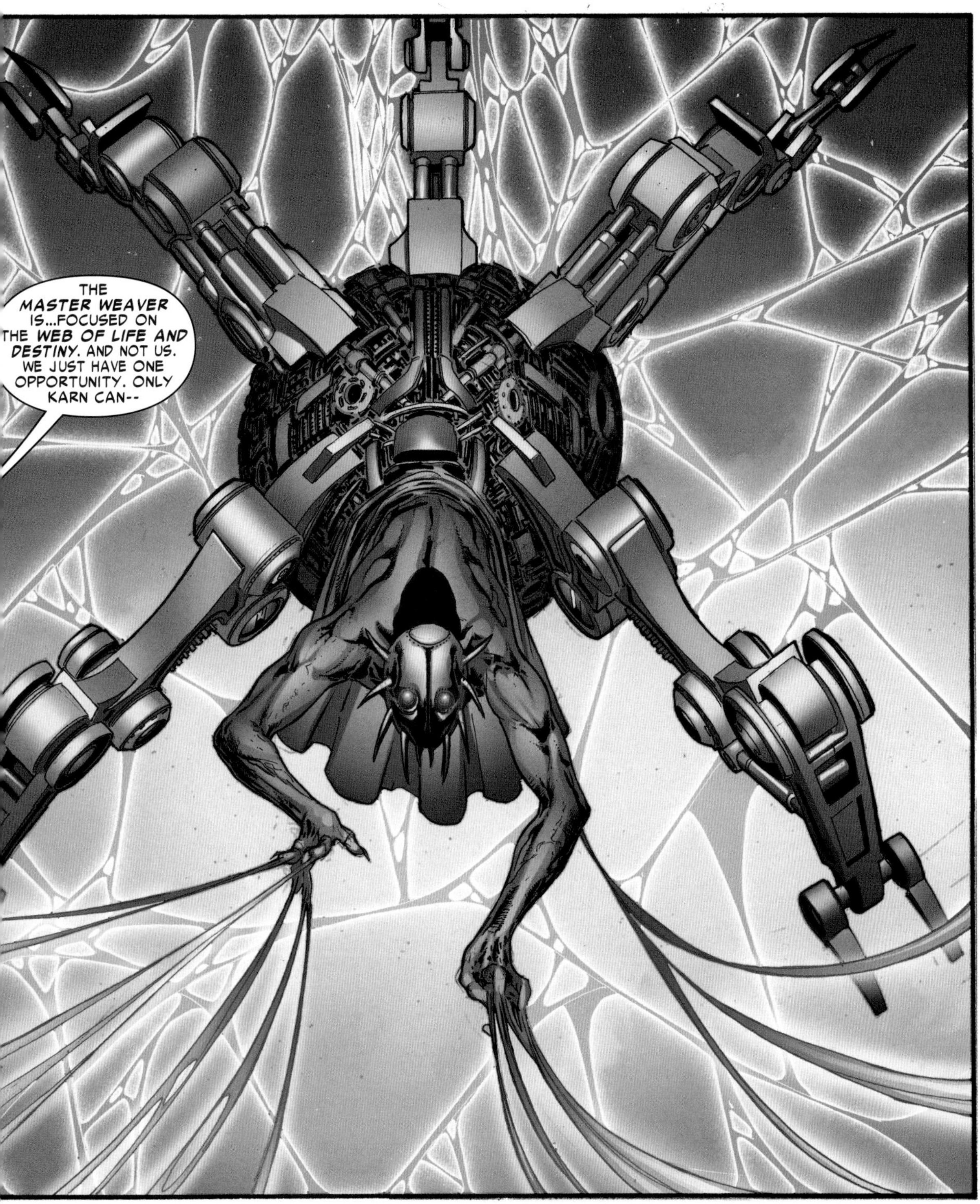
THE *MASTER WEAVER* IS...FOCUSED ON THE *WEB OF LIFE AND DESTINY*. AND NOT US. WE JUST HAVE ONE OPPORTUNITY. ONLY KARN CAN--

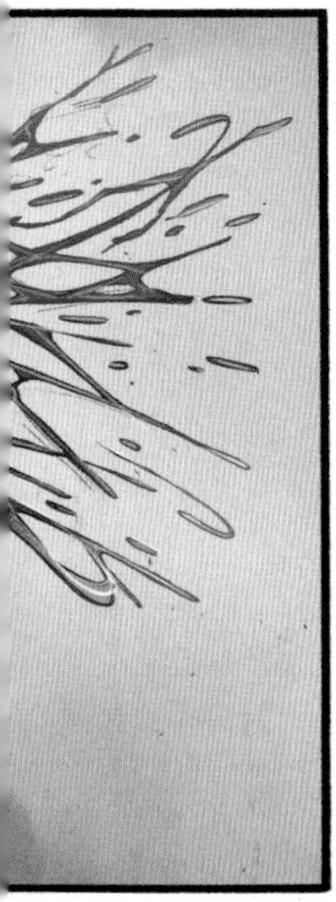

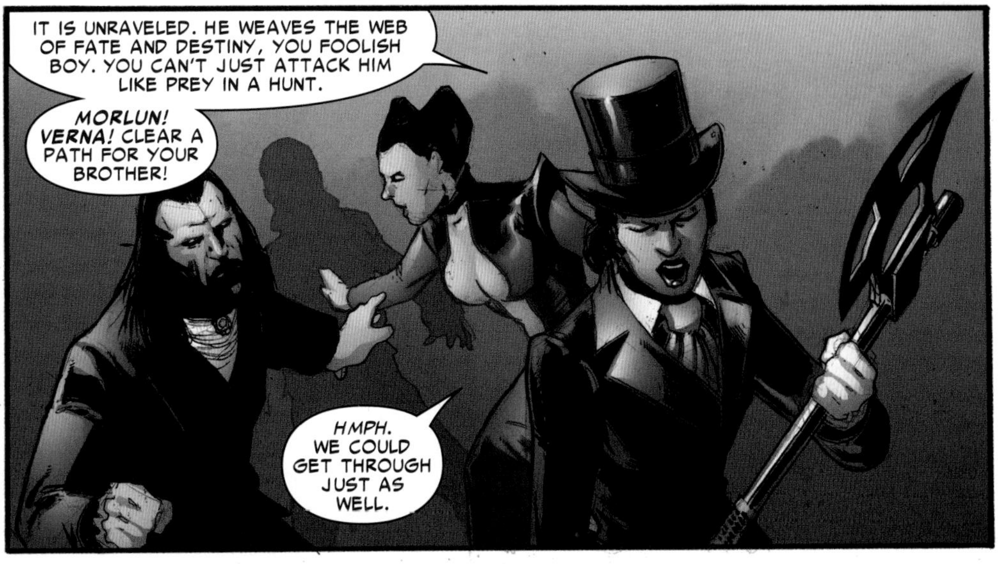
IT IS UNRAVELED. HE WEAVES THE WEB OF FATE AND DESTINY, YOU FOOLISH BOY. YOU CAN'T JUST ATTACK HIM LIKE PREY IN A HUNT.
MORLUN! VERNA! CLEAR A PATH FOR YOUR BROTHER!
HMPH. WE COULD GET THROUGH JUST AS WELL.

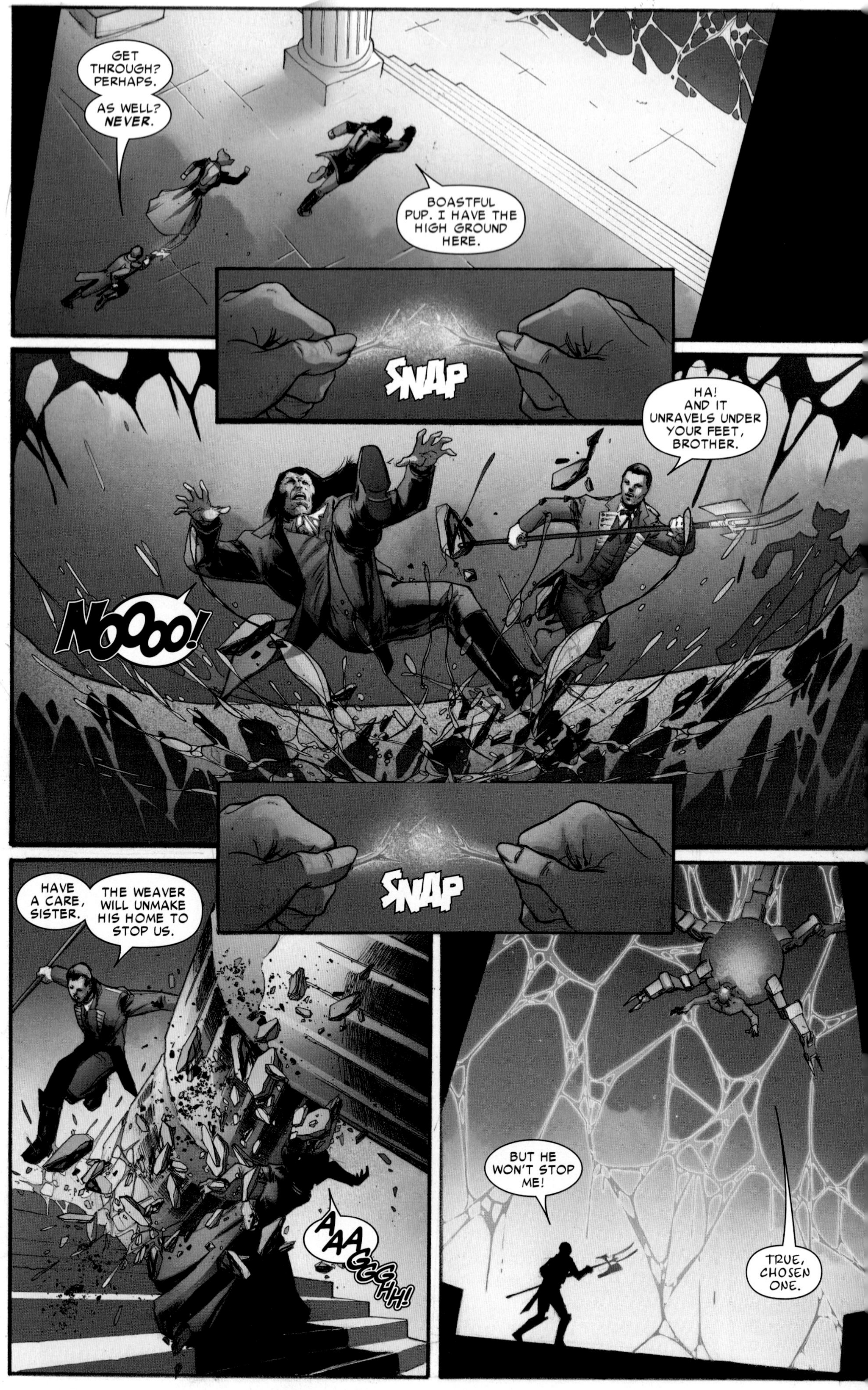
GET THROUGH? PERHAPS.
AS WELL? NEVER.
BOASTFUL PUP. I HAVE THE HIGH GROUND HERE.
SNAP
HA! AND IT UNRAVELS UNDER YOUR FEET, BROTHER.
NOOOO!
SNAP
HAVE A CARE, SISTER.
THE WEAVER WILL UNMAKE HIS HOME TO STOP US.
AAAGGGHH!
BUT HE WON'T STOP ME!
TRUE, CHOSEN ONE.

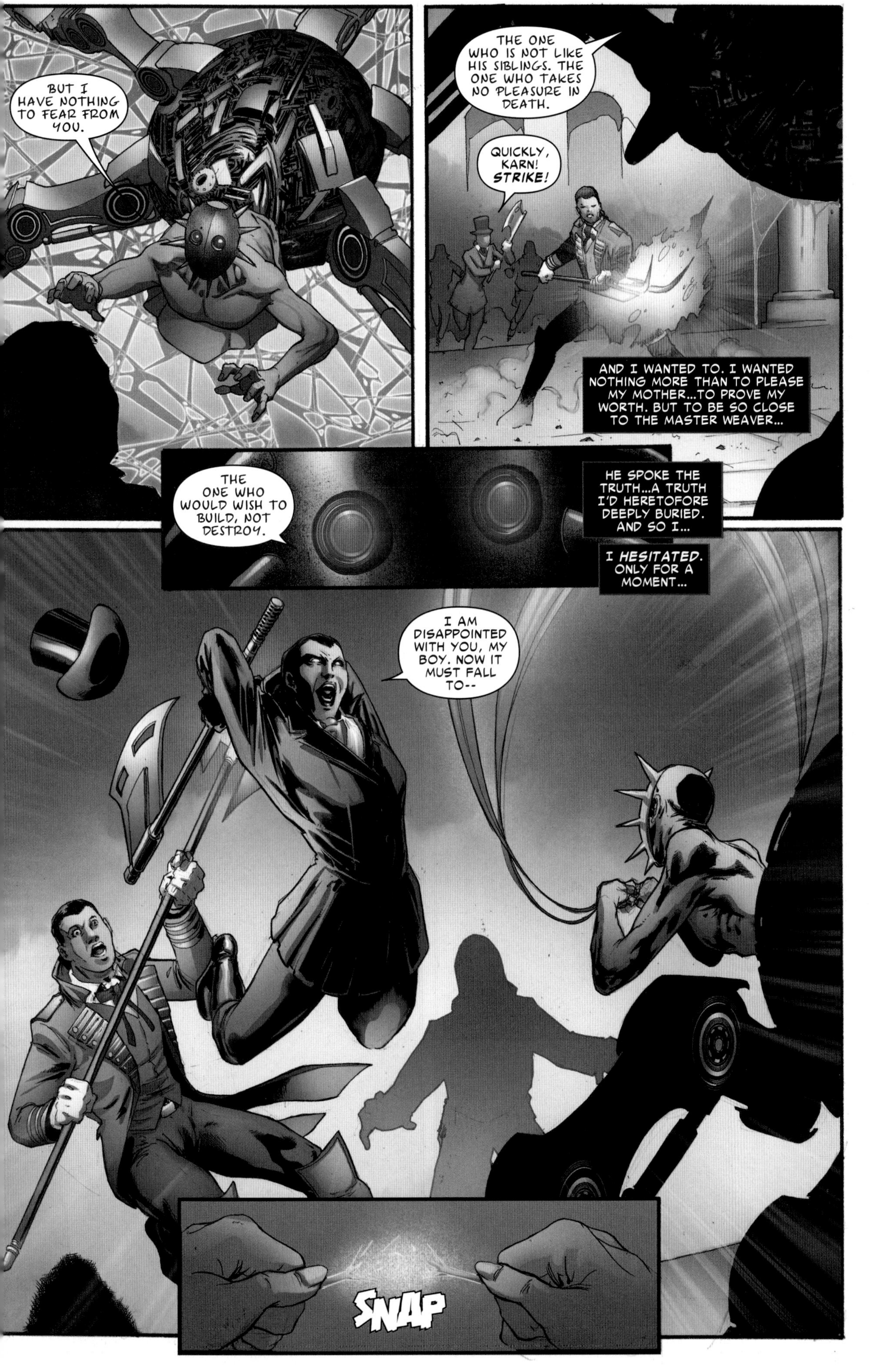
BUT I HAVE NOTHING TO FEAR FROM YOU.
THE ONE WHO IS NOT LIKE HIS SIBLINGS. THE ONE WHO TAKES NO PLEASURE IN DEATH.
QUICKLY, KARN! STRIKE!
AND I WANTED TO. I WANTED NOTHING MORE THAN TO PLEASE MY MOTHER...TO PROVE MY WORTH. BUT TO BE SO CLOSE TO THE MASTER WEAVER...
THE ONE WHO WOULD WISH TO BUILD, NOT DESTROY.
HE SPOKE THE TRUTH...A TRUTH I'D HERETOFORE DEEPLY BURIED. AND SO I...
I HESITATED. ONLY FOR A MOMENT...
I AM DISAPPOINTED WITH YOU, MY BOY. NOW IT MUST FALL TO--
SNAP

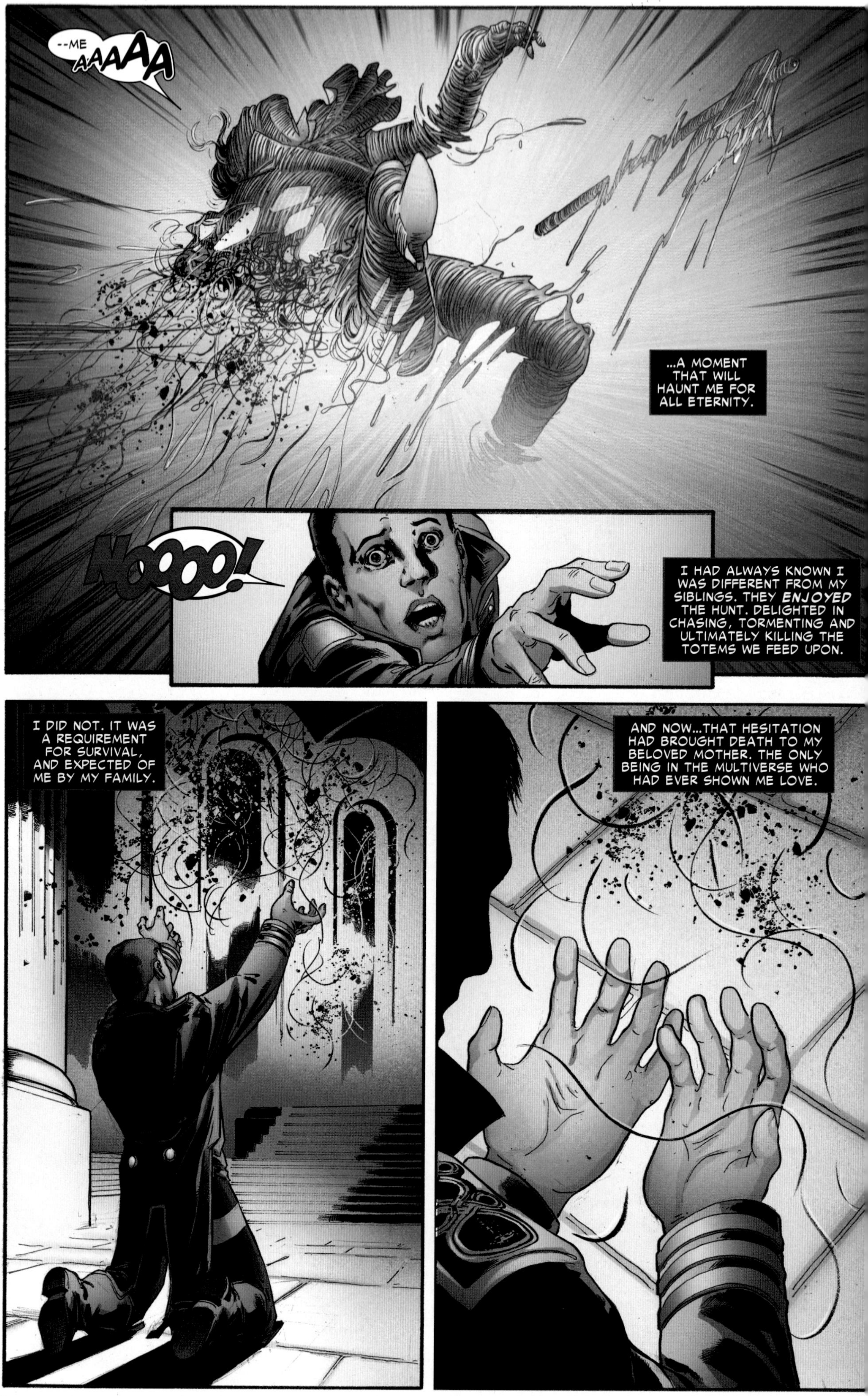
--ME AAAAA
...A MOMENT THAT WILL HAUNT ME FOR ALL ETERNITY.
NOOOO!
I HAD ALWAYS KNOWN I WAS DIFFERENT FROM MY SIBLINGS. THEY ENJOYED THE HUNT. DELIGHTED IN CHASING, TORMENTING AND ULTIMATELY KILLING THE TOTEMS WE FEED UPON.
I DID NOT. IT WAS A REQUIREMENT FOR SURVIVAL, AND EXPECTED OF ME BY MY FAMILY.
AND NOW...THAT HESITATION HAD BROUGHT DEATH TO MY BELOVED MOTHER. THE ONLY BEING IN THE MULTIVERSE WHO HAD EVER SHOWN ME LOVE.

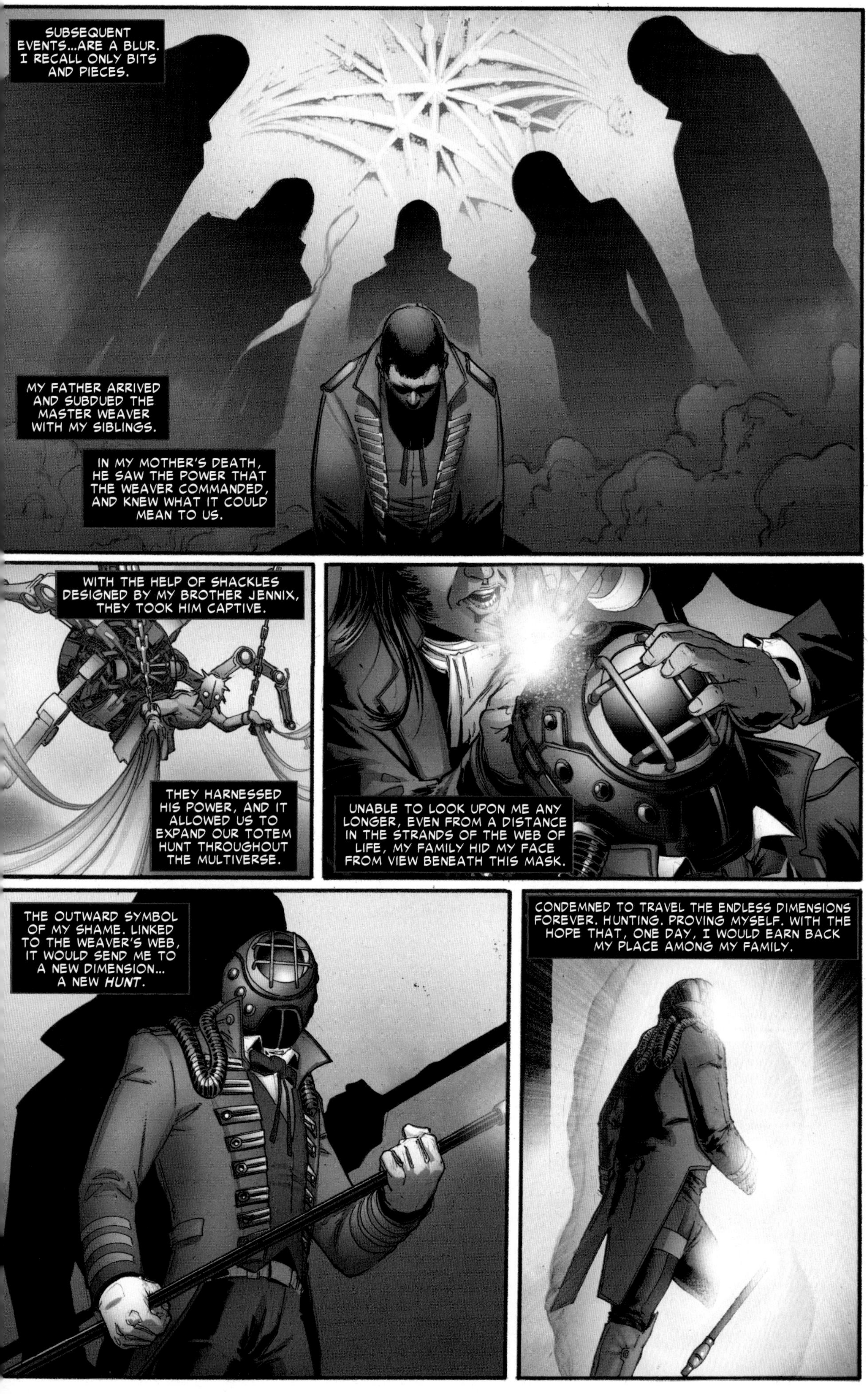
SUBSEQUENT EVENTS...ARE A BLUR. I RECALL ONLY BITS AND PIECES.
MY FATHER ARRIVED AND SUBDUED THE MASTER WEAVER WITH MY SIBLINGS.
IN MY MOTHER'S DEATH, HE SAW THE POWER THAT THE WEAVER COMMANDED, AND KNEW WHAT IT COULD MEAN TO US.
WITH THE HELP OF SHACKLES DESIGNED BY MY BROTHER JENNIX, THEY TOOK HIM CAPTIVE.
THEY HARNESSED HIS POWER, AND IT ALLOWED US TO EXPAND OUR TOTEM HUNT THROUGHOUT THE MULTIVERSE.
UNABLE TO LOOK UPON ME ANY LONGER, EVEN FROM A DISTANCE IN THE STRANDS OF THE WEB OF LIFE, MY FAMILY HID MY FACE FROM VIEW BENEATH THIS MASK.
THE OUTWARD SYMBOL OF MY SHAME. LINKED TO THE WEAVER'S WEB, IT WOULD SEND ME TO A NEW DIMENSION... A NEW *HUNT*.
CONDEMNED TO TRAVEL THE ENDLESS DIMENSIONS FOREVER. HUNTING. PROVING MYSELF. WITH THE HOPE THAT, ONE DAY, I WOULD EARN BACK MY PLACE AMONG MY FAMILY.

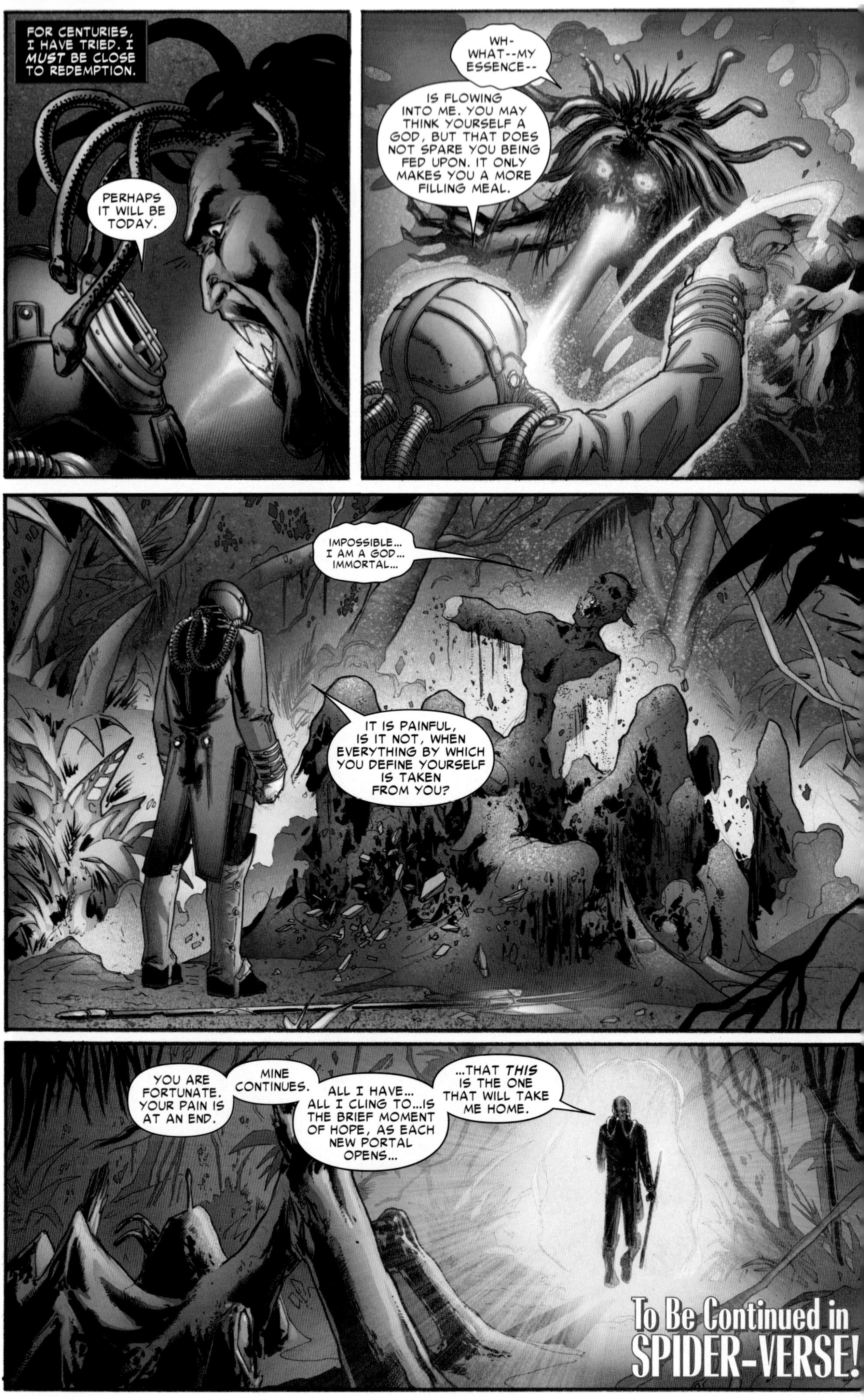
FOR CENTURIES, I HAVE TRIED. I *MUST* BE CLOSE TO REDEMPTION.
PERHAPS IT WILL BE TODAY.
WH-WHAT--MY ESSENCE--
IS FLOWING INTO ME. YOU MAY THINK YOURSELF A GOD, BUT THAT DOES NOT SPARE YOU BEING FED UPON. IT ONLY MAKES YOU A MORE FILLING MEAL.
IMPOSSIBLE... I AM A GOD... IMMORTAL...
IT IS PAINFUL, IS IT NOT, WHEN EVERYTHING BY WHICH YOU DEFINE YOURSELF IS TAKEN FROM YOU?
YOU ARE FORTUNATE. YOUR PAIN IS AT AN END.
MINE CONTINUES.
ALL I HAVE... ALL I CLING TO...IS THE BRIEF MOMENT OF HOPE, AS EACH NEW PORTAL OPENS...
...THAT *THIS* IS THE ONE THAT WILL TAKE ME HOME.
To Be Continued in SPIDER-VERSE!

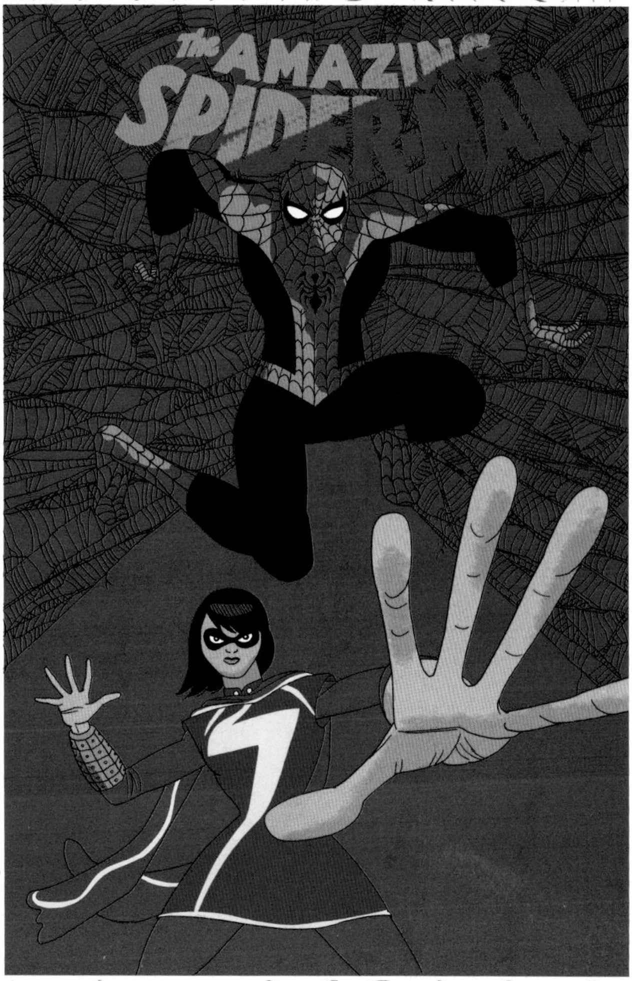
The AMAZING SPIDER-MAN

AMAZING SPIDER-MAN 7 VARIANT
BY JAVIER PULIDO

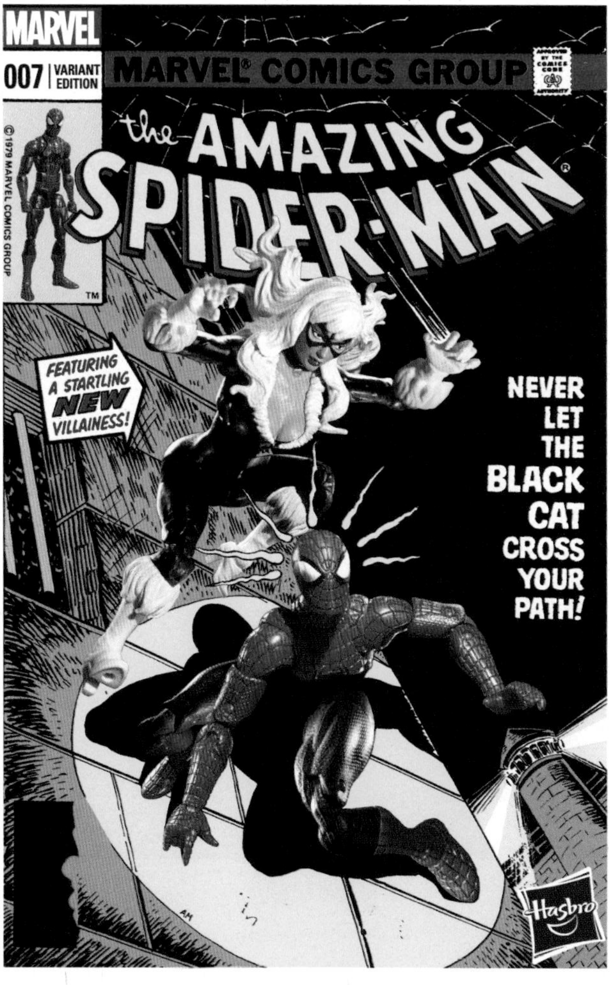
MARVEL
007 VARIANT EDITION
MARVEL COMICS GROUP
the AMAZING SPIDER-MAN
© 1979 MARVEL COMICS GROUP
TM
FEATURING A STARTLING NEW VILLAINESS!
NEVER LET THE BLACK CAT CROSS YOUR PATH!
Hasbro

AMAZING SPIDER-MAN 7
HASBRO VARIANT

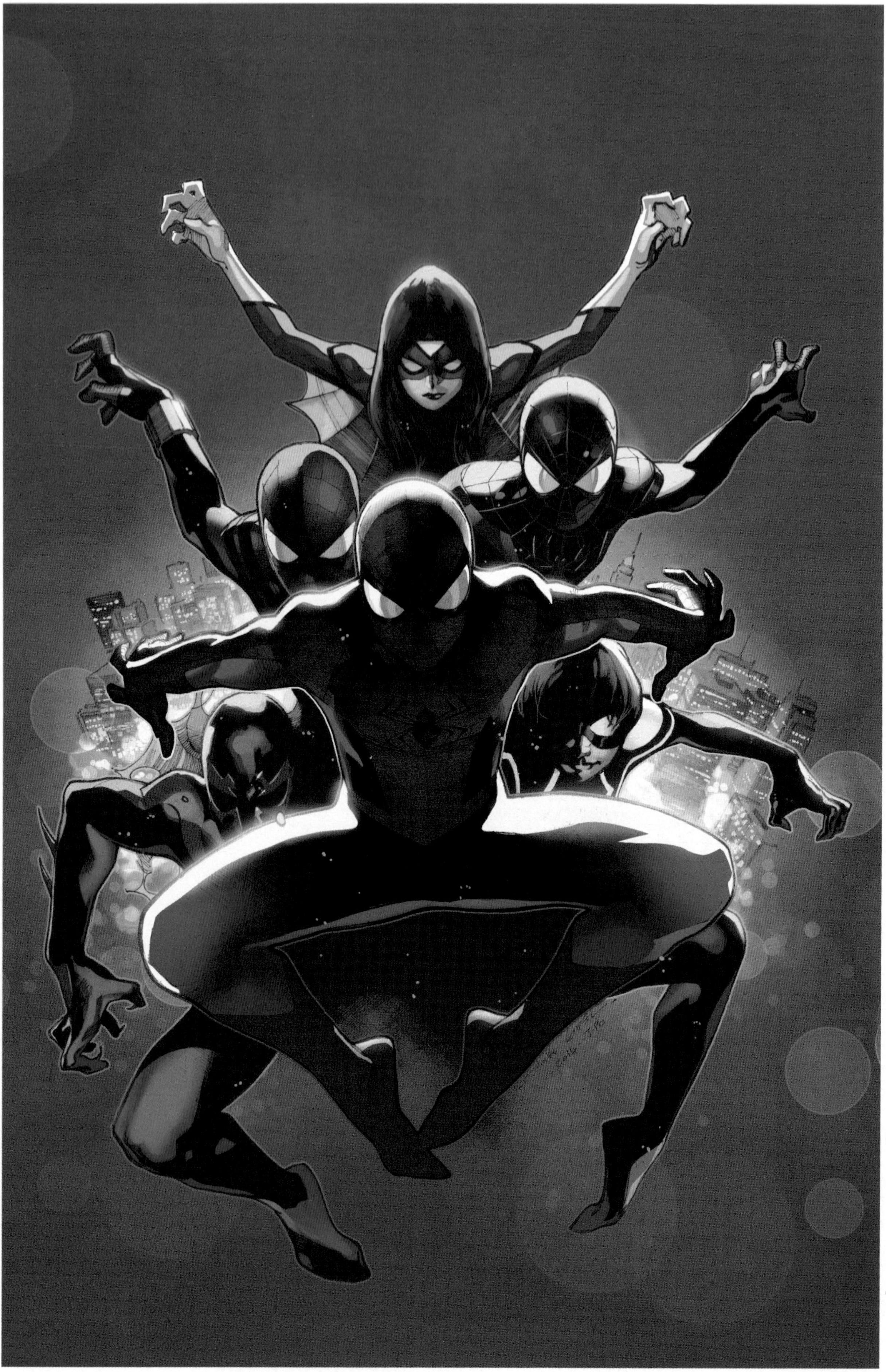

AMAZING SPIDER-MAN 9
SPIDER-VERSE, PART ONE: THE GATHERING

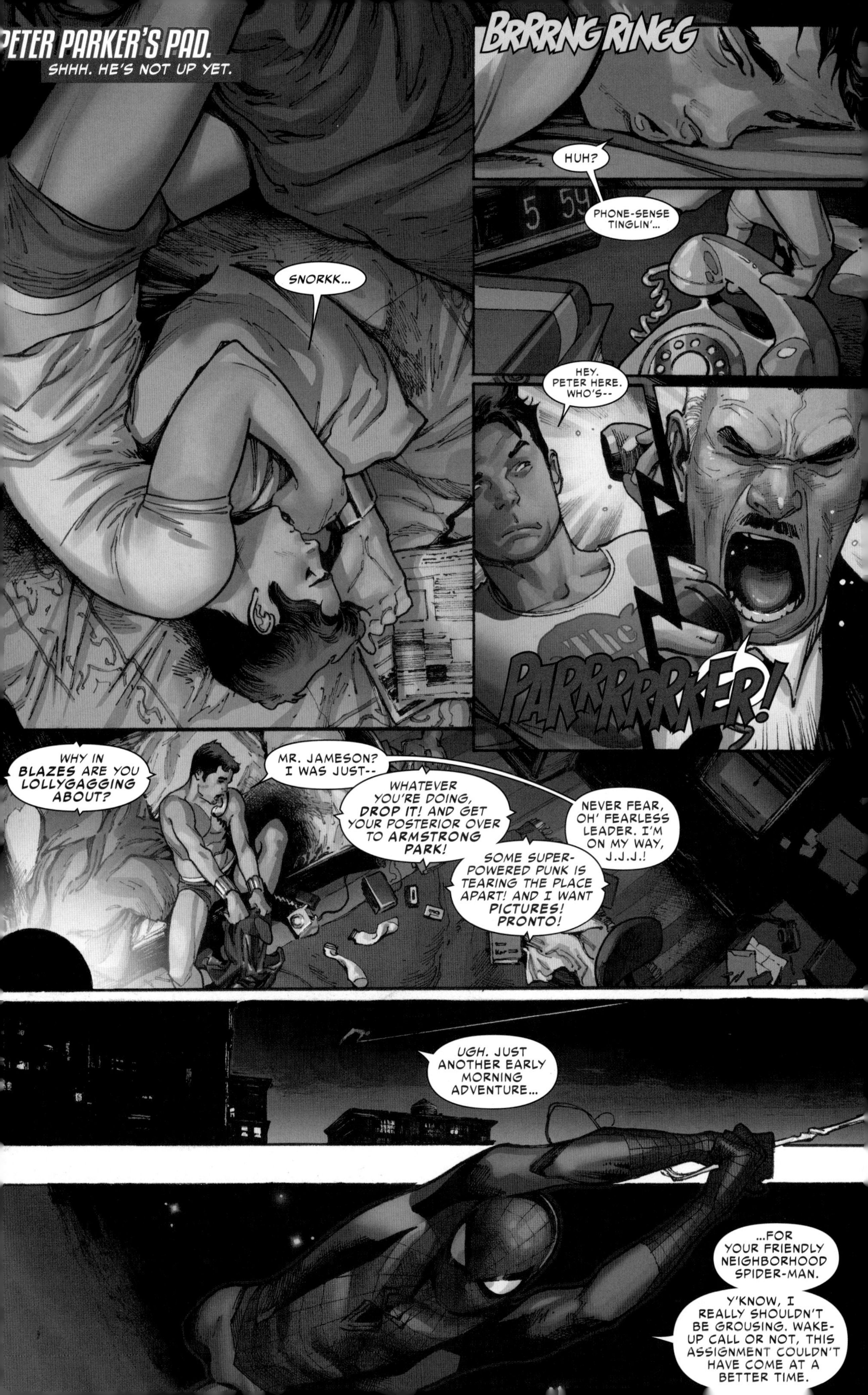
PETER PARKER'S PAD.
SHHH. HE'S NOT UP YET.
SNORKK...
BRRRNG RINGG
HUH?
PHONE-SENSE TINGLIN'...
HEY. PETER HERE. WHO'S--
PARRRRRRKER!
WHY IN BLAZES ARE YOU LOLLYGAGGING ABOUT?
MR. JAMESON? I WAS JUST--
WHATEVER YOU'RE DOING, DROP IT! AND GET YOUR POSTERIOR OVER TO ARMSTRONG PARK!
SOME SUPER-POWERED PUNK IS TEARING THE PLACE APART! AND I WANT PICTURES! PRONTO!
NEVER FEAR, OH' FEARLESS LEADER. I'M ON MY WAY, J.J.J.!
UGH. JUST ANOTHER EARLY MORNING ADVENTURE...
...FOR YOUR FRIENDLY NEIGHBORHOOD SPIDER-MAN.
Y'KNOW, I REALLY SHOULDN'T BE GROUSING. WAKE-UP CALL OR NOT, THIS ASSIGNMENT COULDN'T HAVE COME AT A BETTER TIME.

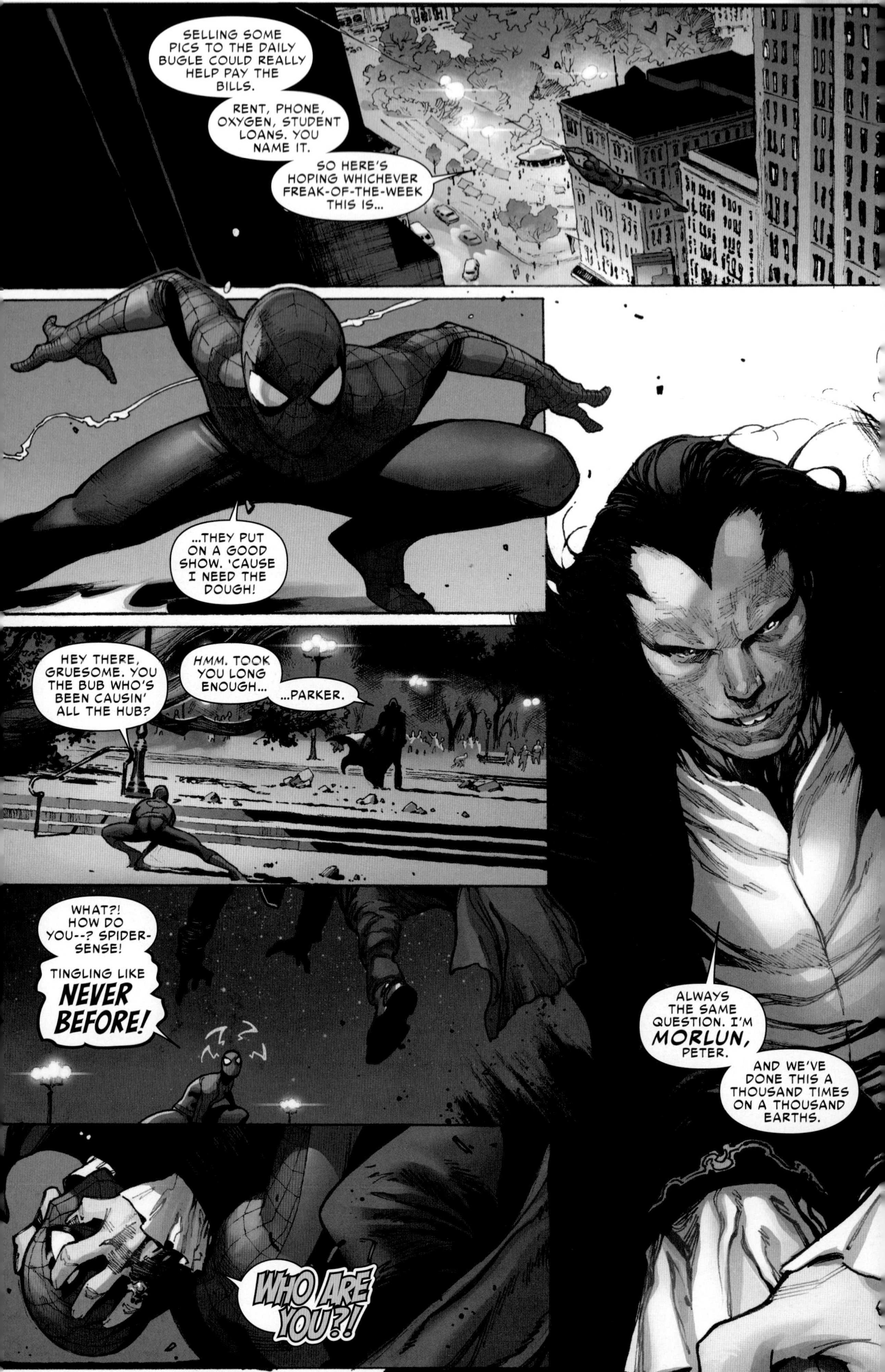
SELLING SOME PICS TO THE DAILY BUGLE COULD REALLY HELP PAY THE BILLS.
RENT, PHONE, OXYGEN, STUDENT LOANS. YOU NAME IT.
SO HERE'S HOPING WHICHEVER FREAK-OF-THE-WEEK THIS IS...
...THEY PUT ON A GOOD SHOW. 'CAUSE I NEED THE DOUGH!
HEY THERE, GRUESOME. YOU THE BUB WHO'S BEEN CAUSIN' ALL THE HUB?
HMM. TOOK YOU LONG ENOUGH...
...PARKER.
WHAT?! HOW DO YOU--? SPIDER-SENSE!
TINGLING LIKE NEVER BEFORE!
WHO ARE YOU?!
ALWAYS THE SAME QUESTION. I'M MORLUN, PETER.
AND WE'VE DONE THIS A THOUSAND TIMES ON A THOUSAND EARTHS.

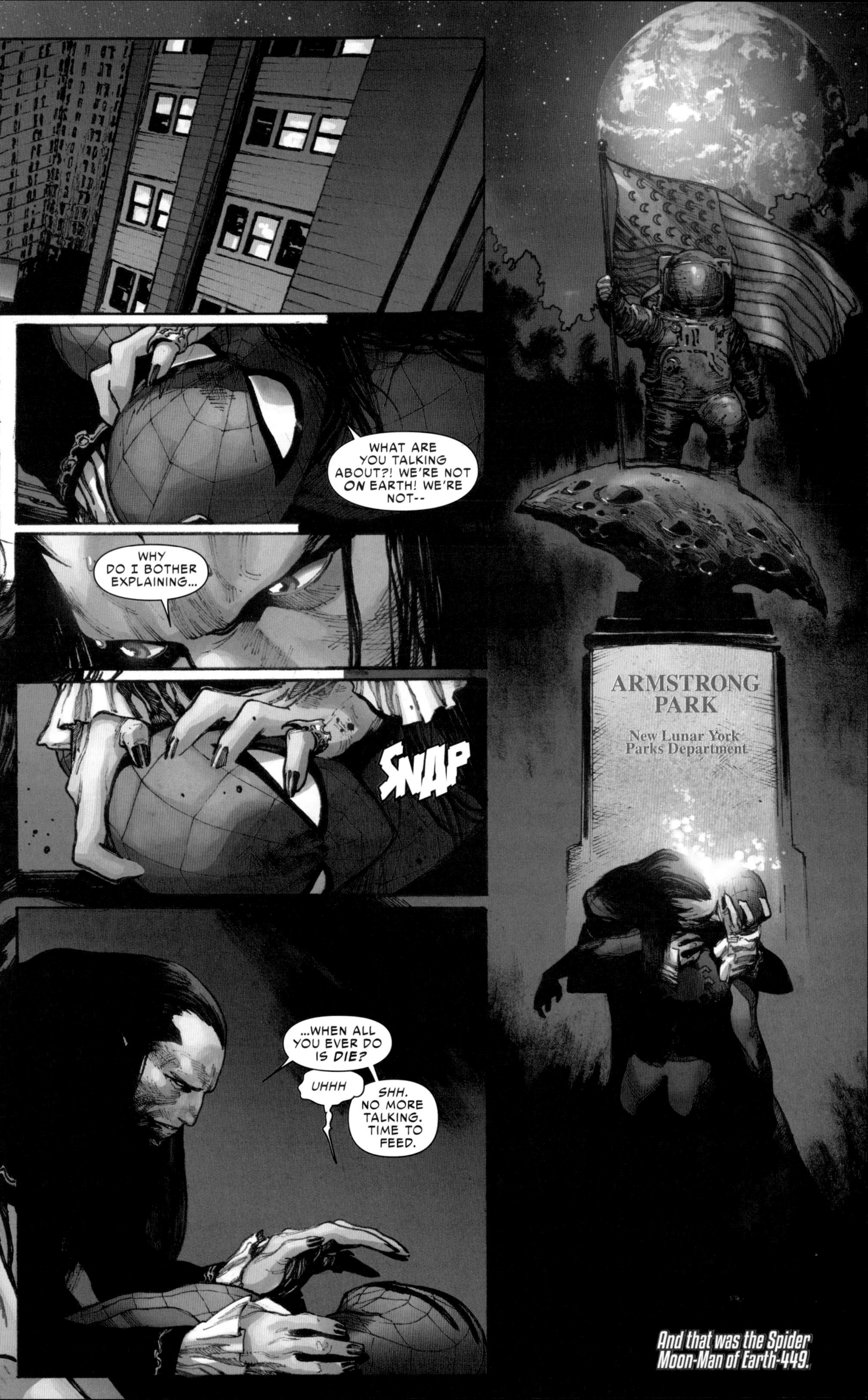

WHAT ARE YOU TALKING ABOUT?! WE'RE NOT ON EARTH! WE'RE NOT--
WHY DO I BOTHER EXPLAINING...
SNAP
...WHEN ALL YOU EVER DO IS DIE?
UHHH
SHH. NO MORE TALKING. TIME TO FEED.
ARMSTRONG PARK
New Lunar York Parks Department
And that was the Spider Moon-Man of Earth-449.

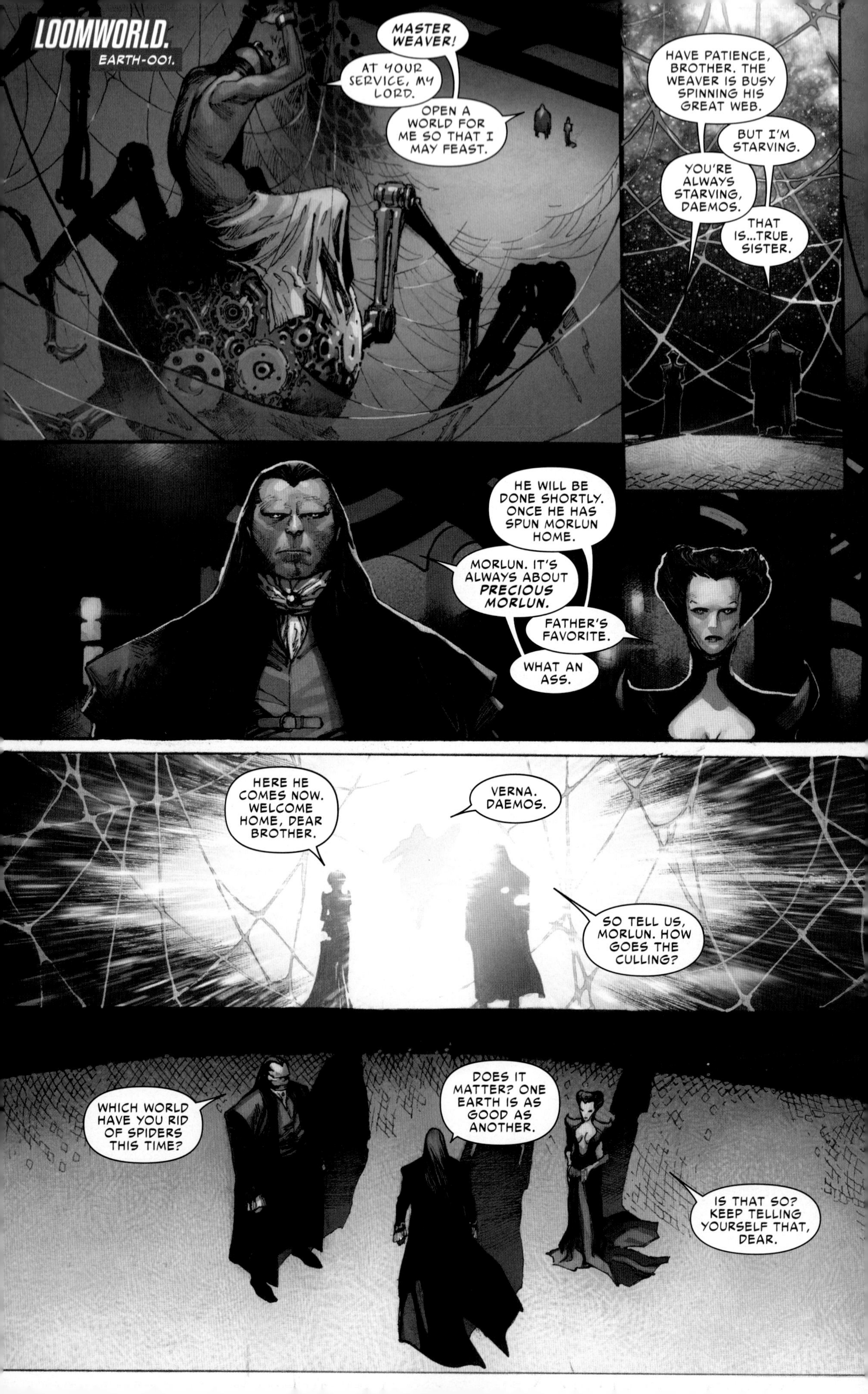

LOOMWORLD.
EARTH-001.
MASTER WEAVER!
AT YOUR SERVICE, MY LORD.
OPEN A WORLD FOR ME SO THAT I MAY FEAST.
HAVE PATIENCE, BROTHER. THE WEAVER IS BUSY SPINNING HIS GREAT WEB.
BUT I'M STARVING.
YOU'RE ALWAYS STARVING, DAEMOS.
THAT IS...TRUE, SISTER.
HE WILL BE DONE SHORTLY. ONCE HE HAS SPUN MORLUN HOME.
MORLUN. IT'S ALWAYS ABOUT *PRECIOUS MORLUN.*
FATHER'S FAVORITE.
WHAT AN ASS.
HERE HE COMES NOW. WELCOME HOME, DEAR BROTHER.
VERNA. DAEMOS.
SO TELL US, MORLUN. HOW GOES THE CULLING?
WHICH WORLD HAVE YOU RID OF SPIDERS THIS TIME?
DOES IT MATTER? ONE EARTH IS AS GOOD AS ANOTHER.
IS THAT SO? KEEP TELLING YOURSELF THAT, DEAR.

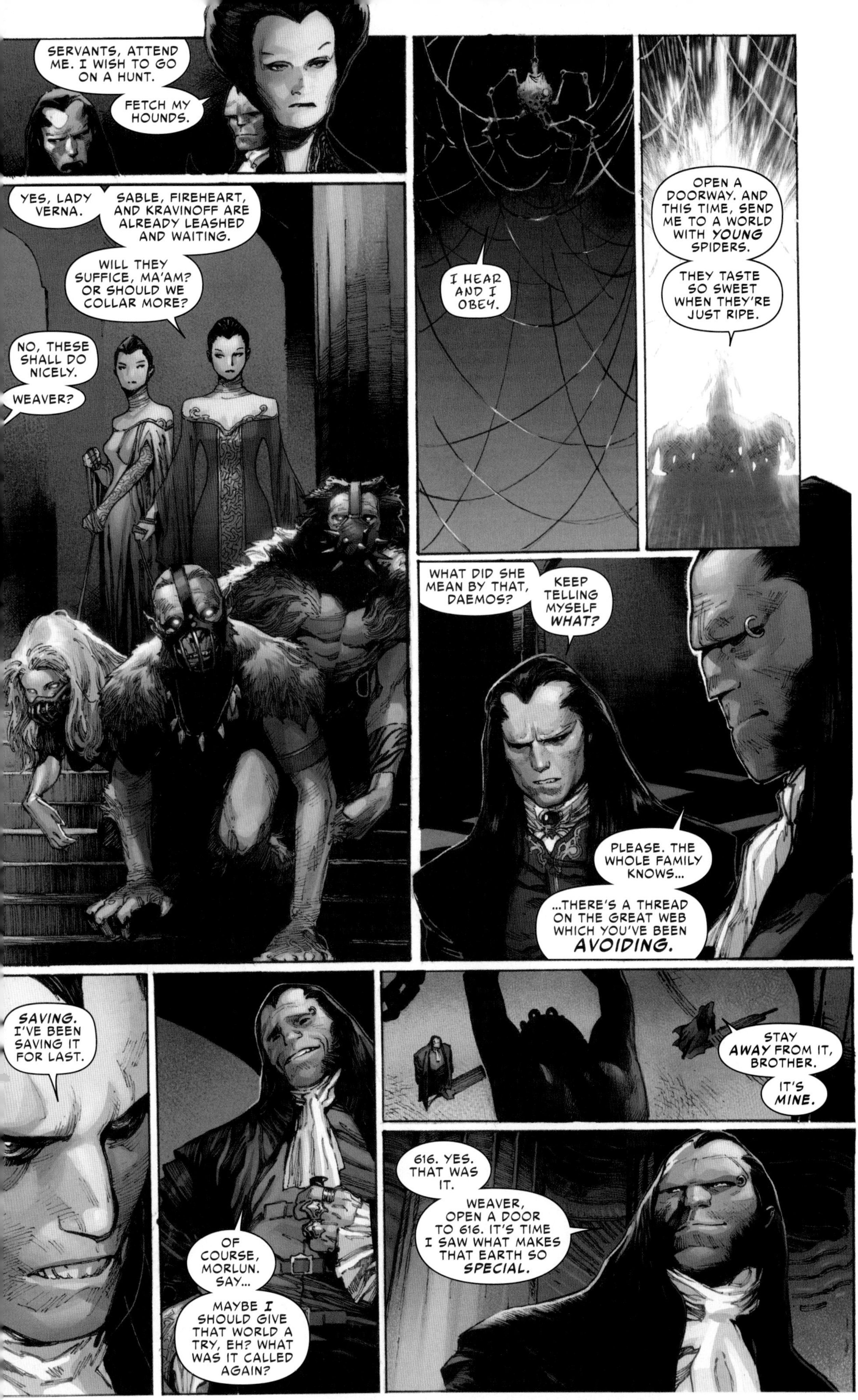
SERVANTS, ATTEND ME. I WISH TO GO ON A HUNT.
FETCH MY HOUNDS.
I HEAR AND I OBEY.
OPEN A DOORWAY. AND THIS TIME, SEND ME TO A WORLD WITH YOUNG SPIDERS.
THEY TASTE SO SWEET WHEN THEY'RE JUST RIPE.
YES, LADY VERNA.
SABLE, FIREHEART, AND KRAVINOFF ARE ALREADY LEASHED AND WAITING.
WILL THEY SUFFICE, MA'AM? OR SHOULD WE COLLAR MORE?
NO, THESE SHALL DO NICELY.
WEAVER?
WHAT DID SHE MEAN BY THAT, DAEMOS?
KEEP TELLING MYSELF WHAT?
PLEASE. THE WHOLE FAMILY KNOWS...
...THERE'S A THREAD ON THE GREAT WEB WHICH YOU'VE BEEN AVOIDING.
SAVING. I'VE BEEN SAVING IT FOR LAST.
OF COURSE, MORLUN. SAY...
MAYBE I SHOULD GIVE THAT WORLD A TRY, EH? WHAT WAS IT CALLED AGAIN?
STAY AWAY FROM IT, BROTHER.
IT'S MINE.
616. YES. THAT WAS IT.
WEAVER, OPEN A DOOR TO 616. IT'S TIME I SAW WHAT MAKES THAT EARTH SO SPECIAL.

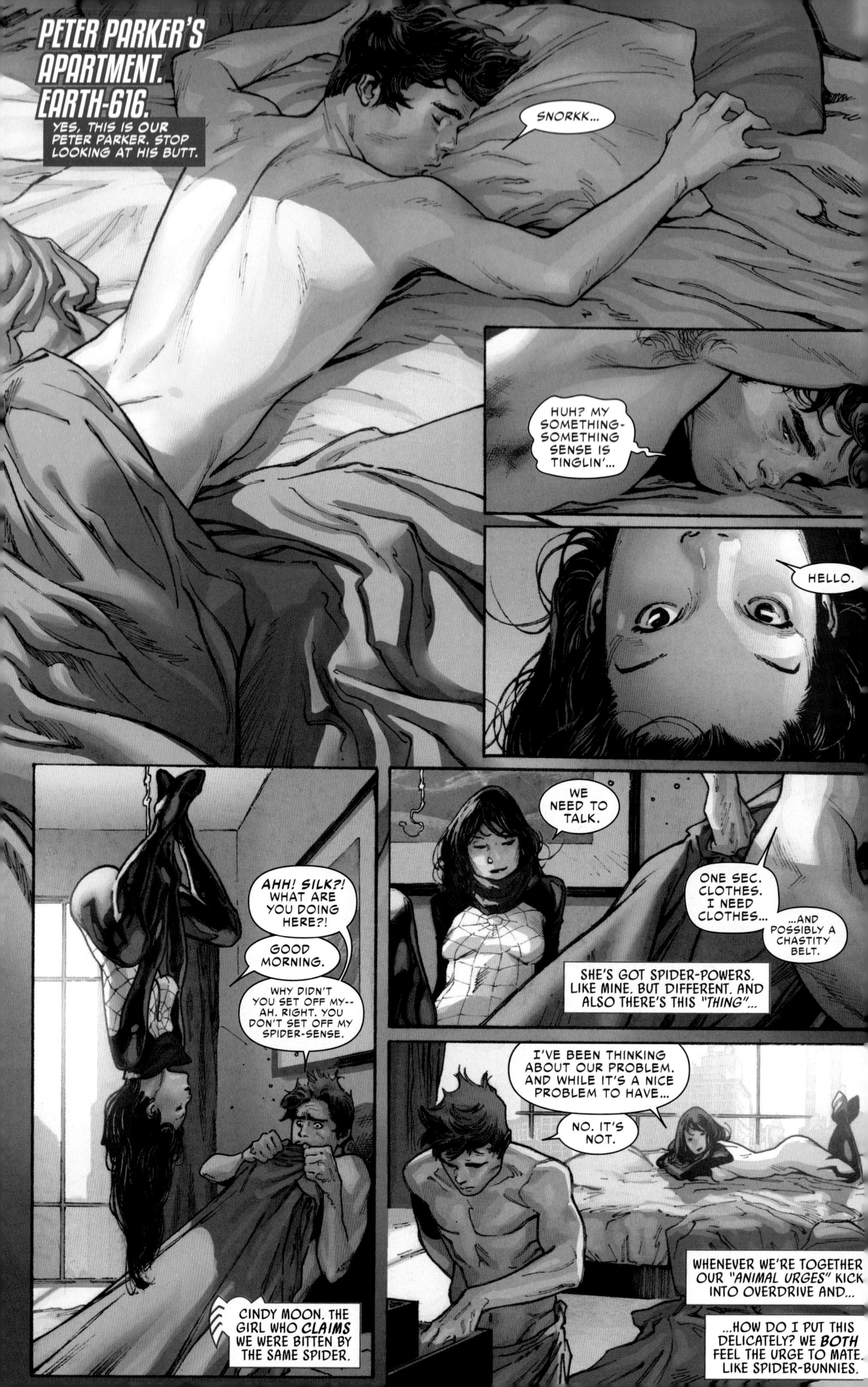

PETER PARKER'S APARTMENT. EARTH-616.
YES, THIS IS OUR PETER PARKER. STOP LOOKING AT HIS BUTT.
SNORKK...
HUH? MY SOMETHING-SOMETHING SENSE IS TINGLIN'...
HELLO.
AHH! SILK?! WHAT ARE YOU DOING HERE?!
GOOD MORNING.
WHY DIDN'T YOU SET OFF MY--AH. RIGHT. YOU DON'T SET OFF MY SPIDER-SENSE.
CINDY MOON. THE GIRL WHO CLAIMS WE WERE BITTEN BY THE SAME SPIDER.
WE NEED TO TALK.
ONE SEC. CLOTHES. I NEED CLOTHES...
...AND POSSIBLY A CHASTITY BELT.
SHE'S GOT SPIDER-POWERS. LIKE MINE. BUT DIFFERENT. AND ALSO THERE'S THIS "THING"...
I'VE BEEN THINKING ABOUT OUR PROBLEM. AND WHILE IT'S A NICE PROBLEM TO HAVE...
NO. IT'S NOT.
WHENEVER WE'RE TOGETHER OUR "ANIMAL URGES" KICK INTO OVERDRIVE AND...
...HOW DO I PUT THIS DELICATELY? WE BOTH FEEL THE URGE TO MATE. LIKE SPIDER-BUNNIES.

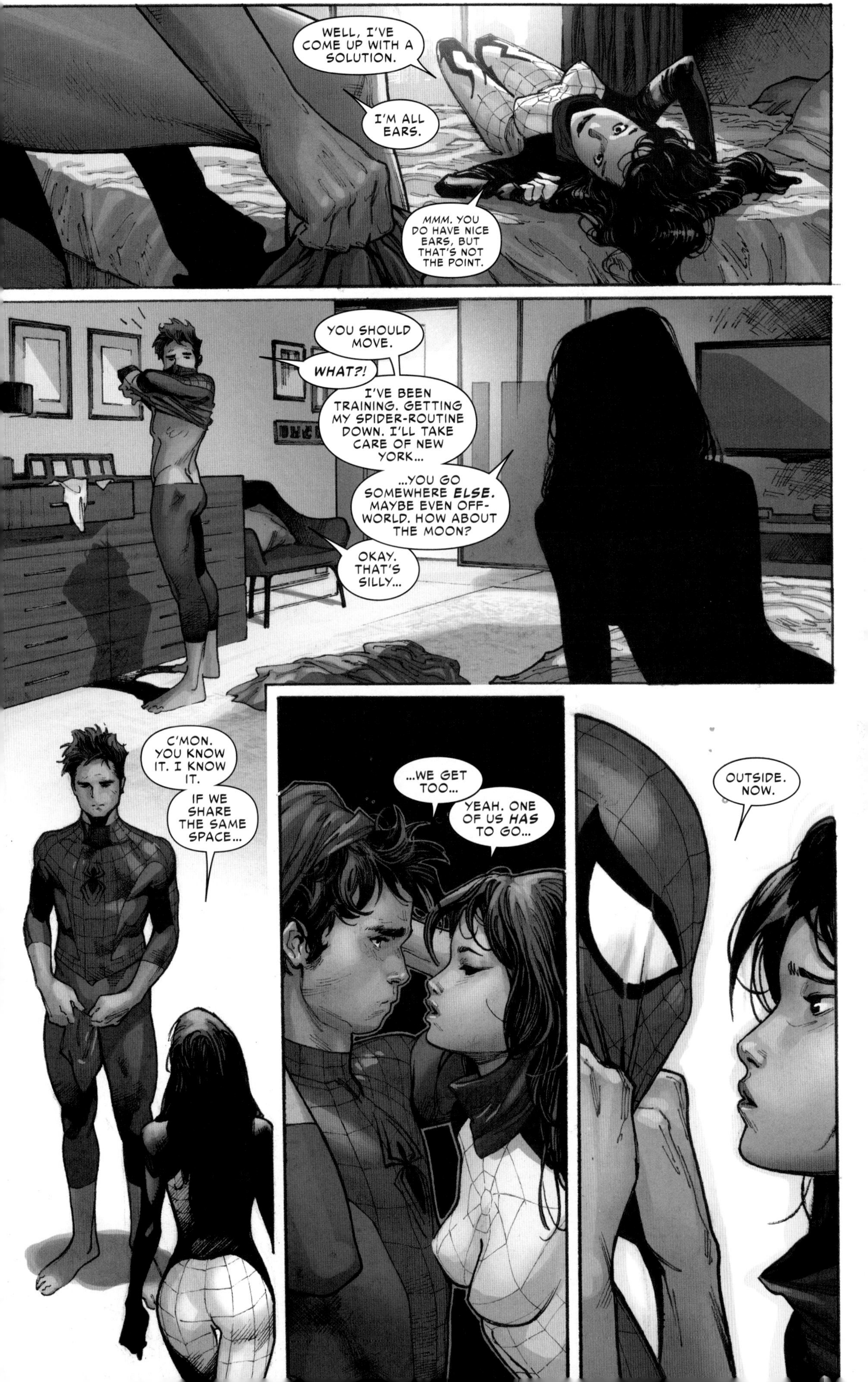
WELL, I'VE COME UP WITH A SOLUTION.
I'M ALL EARS.
MMM. YOU DO HAVE NICE EARS, BUT THAT'S NOT THE POINT.
YOU SHOULD MOVE.
WHAT?!
I'VE BEEN TRAINING. GETTING MY SPIDER-ROUTINE DOWN. I'LL TAKE CARE OF NEW YORK...
...YOU GO SOMEWHERE *ELSE.* MAYBE EVEN OFF-WORLD. HOW ABOUT THE MOON?
OKAY. THAT'S SILLY...
C'MON. YOU KNOW IT. I KNOW IT.
IF WE SHARE THE SAME SPACE...
...WE GET TOO...
YEAH. ONE OF US *HAS* TO GO...
OUTSIDE. NOW.

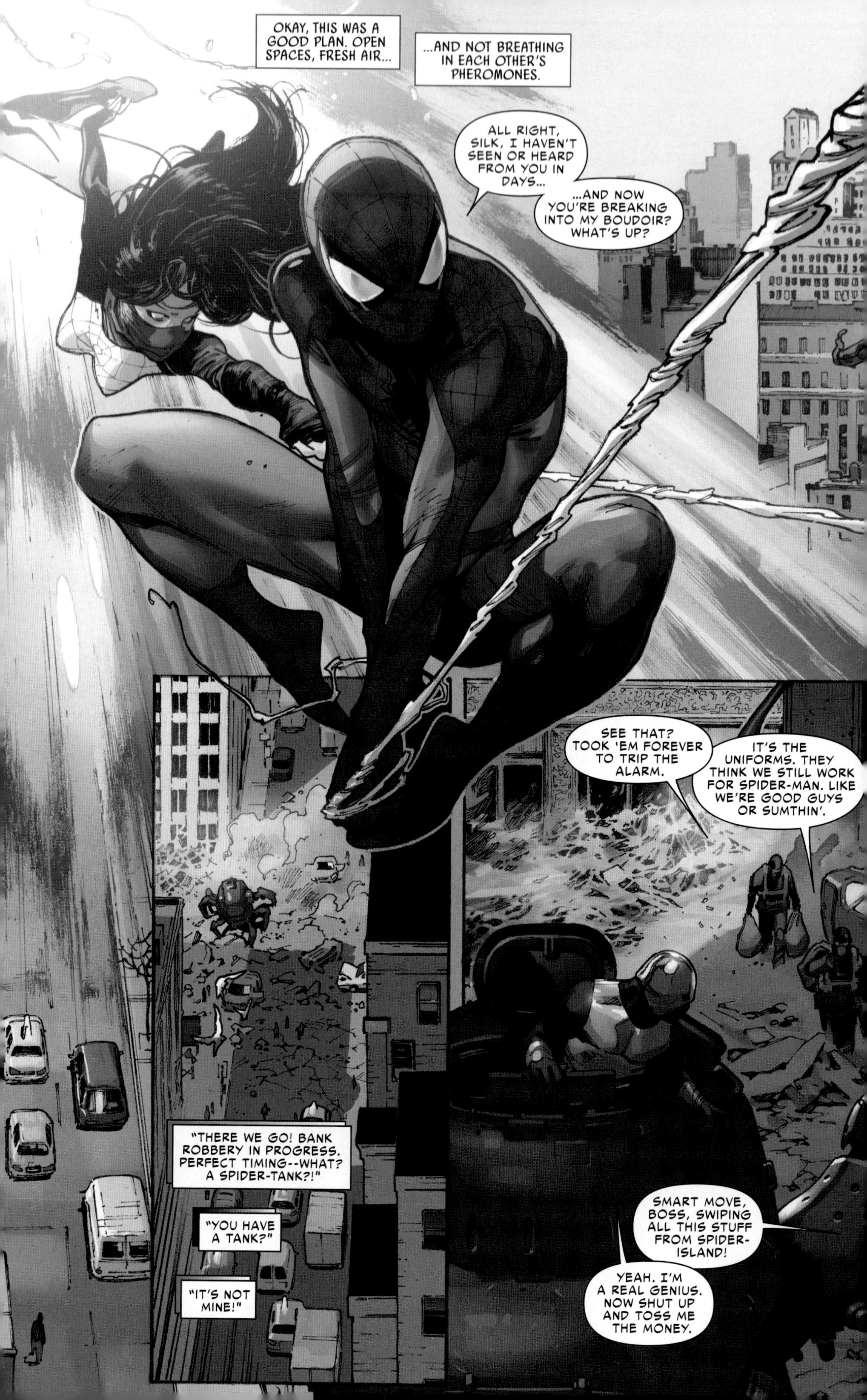
OKAY, THIS WAS A GOOD PLAN. OPEN SPACES, FRESH AIR...
...AND NOT BREATHING IN EACH OTHER'S PHEROMONES.
ALL RIGHT, SILK, I HAVEN'T SEEN OR HEARD FROM YOU IN DAYS...
...AND NOW YOU'RE BREAKING INTO MY BOUDOIR? WHAT'S UP?
SEE THAT? TOOK 'EM FOREVER TO TRIP THE ALARM.
IT'S THE UNIFORMS. THEY THINK WE STILL WORK FOR SPIDER-MAN. LIKE WE'RE GOOD GUYS OR SUMTHIN'.
"THERE WE GO! BANK ROBBERY IN PROGRESS. PERFECT TIMING--WHAT? A SPIDER-TANK?!"
"YOU HAVE A TANK?"
"IT'S NOT MINE!"
SMART MOVE, BOSS, SWIPING ALL THIS STUFF FROM SPIDER-ISLAND!
YEAH. I'M A REAL GENIUS. NOW SHUT UP AND TOSS ME THE MONEY.

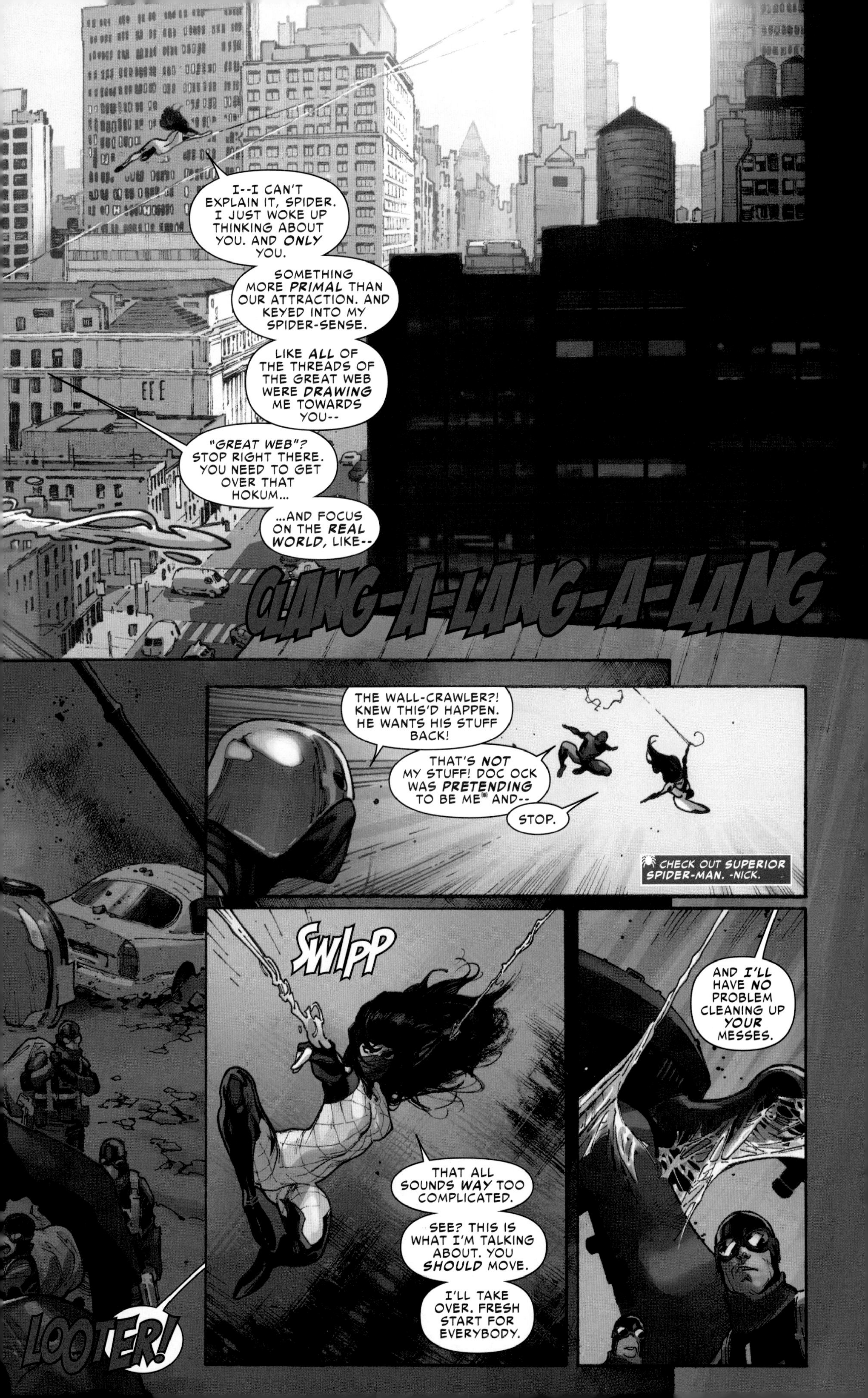
I--I CAN'T EXPLAIN IT, SPIDER. I JUST WOKE UP THINKING ABOUT YOU. AND ONLY YOU.
SOMETHING MORE PRIMAL THAN OUR ATTRACTION. AND KEYED INTO MY SPIDER-SENSE.
LIKE ALL OF THE THREADS OF THE GREAT WEB WERE DRAWING ME TOWARDS YOU--
"GREAT WEB"? STOP RIGHT THERE. YOU NEED TO GET OVER THAT HOKUM...
...AND FOCUS ON THE REAL WORLD, LIKE--
CLANG-A-LANG-A-LANG
THE WALL-CRAWLER?! KNEW THIS'D HAPPEN. HE WANTS HIS STUFF BACK!
THAT'S NOT MY STUFF! DOC OCK WAS PRETENDING TO BE ME* AND--
STOP.
*CHECK OUT SUPERIOR SPIDER-MAN. -NICK.
SWIPP
THAT ALL SOUNDS WAY TOO COMPLICATED.
SEE? THIS IS WHAT I'M TALKING ABOUT. YOU SHOULD MOVE.
I'LL TAKE OVER. FRESH START FOR EVERYBODY.
AND I'LL HAVE NO PROBLEM CLEANING UP YOUR MESSES.
LOOTER!

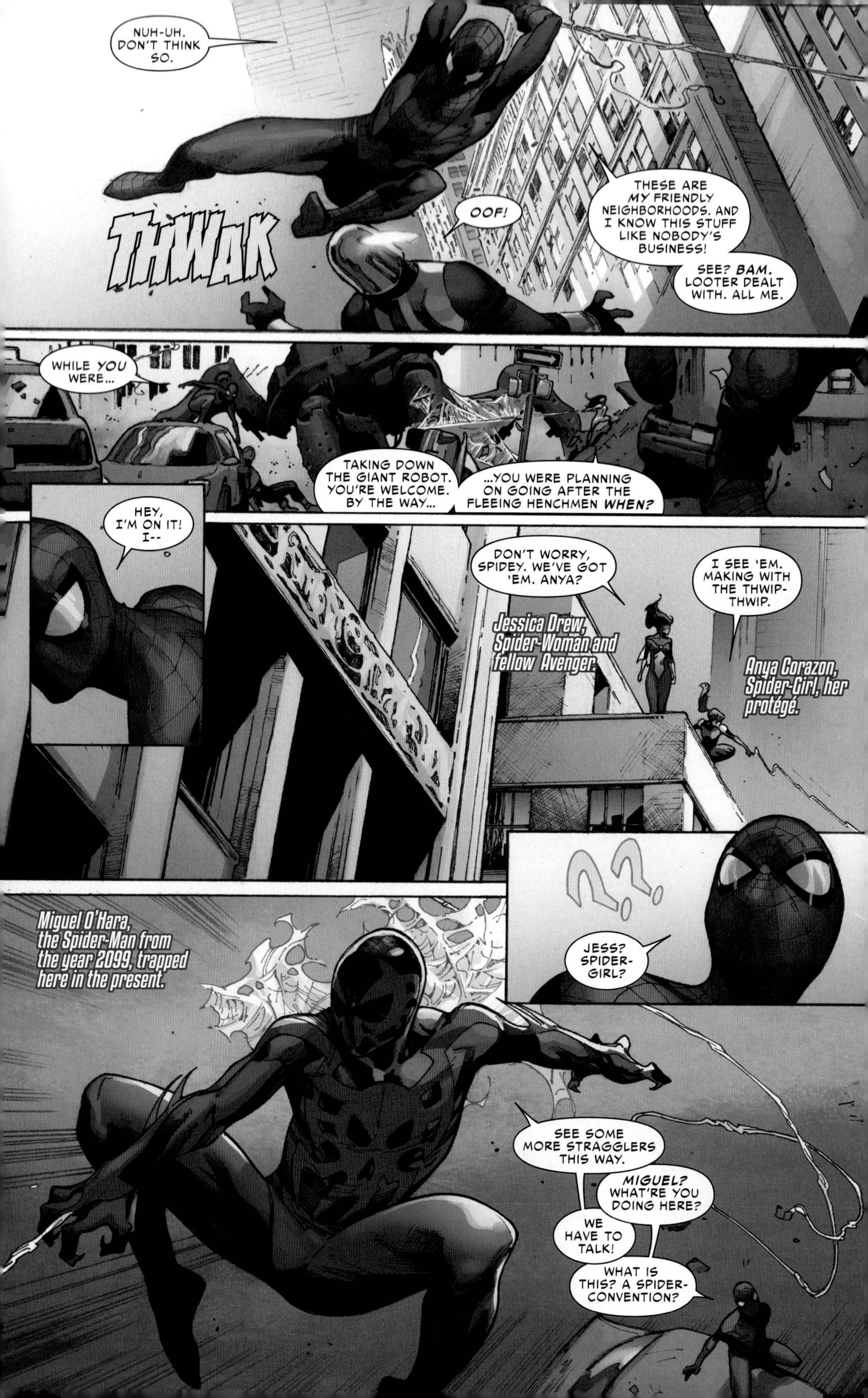
NUH-UH. DON'T THINK SO.
THWAK
OOF!
THESE ARE MY FRIENDLY NEIGHBORHOODS. AND I KNOW THIS STUFF LIKE NOBODY'S BUSINESS!
SEE? BAM. LOOTER DEALT WITH. ALL ME.
WHILE YOU WERE...
TAKING DOWN THE GIANT ROBOT. YOU'RE WELCOME. BY THE WAY...
...YOU WERE PLANNING ON GOING AFTER THE FLEEING HENCHMEN WHEN?
HEY, I'M ON IT! I--
DON'T WORRY, SPIDEY. WE'VE GOT 'EM. ANYA?
Jessica Drew, Spider-Woman and fellow Avenger.
I SEE 'EM. MAKING WITH THE THWIP-THWIP.
Anya Corazon, Spider-Girl, her protégé.
??
JESS? SPIDER-GIRL?
Miguel O'Hara, the Spider-Man from the year 2099, trapped here in the present.
SEE SOME MORE STRAGGLERS THIS WAY.
MIGUEL? WHAT'RE YOU DOING HERE?
WE HAVE TO TALK!
WHAT IS THIS? A SPIDER-CONVENTION?

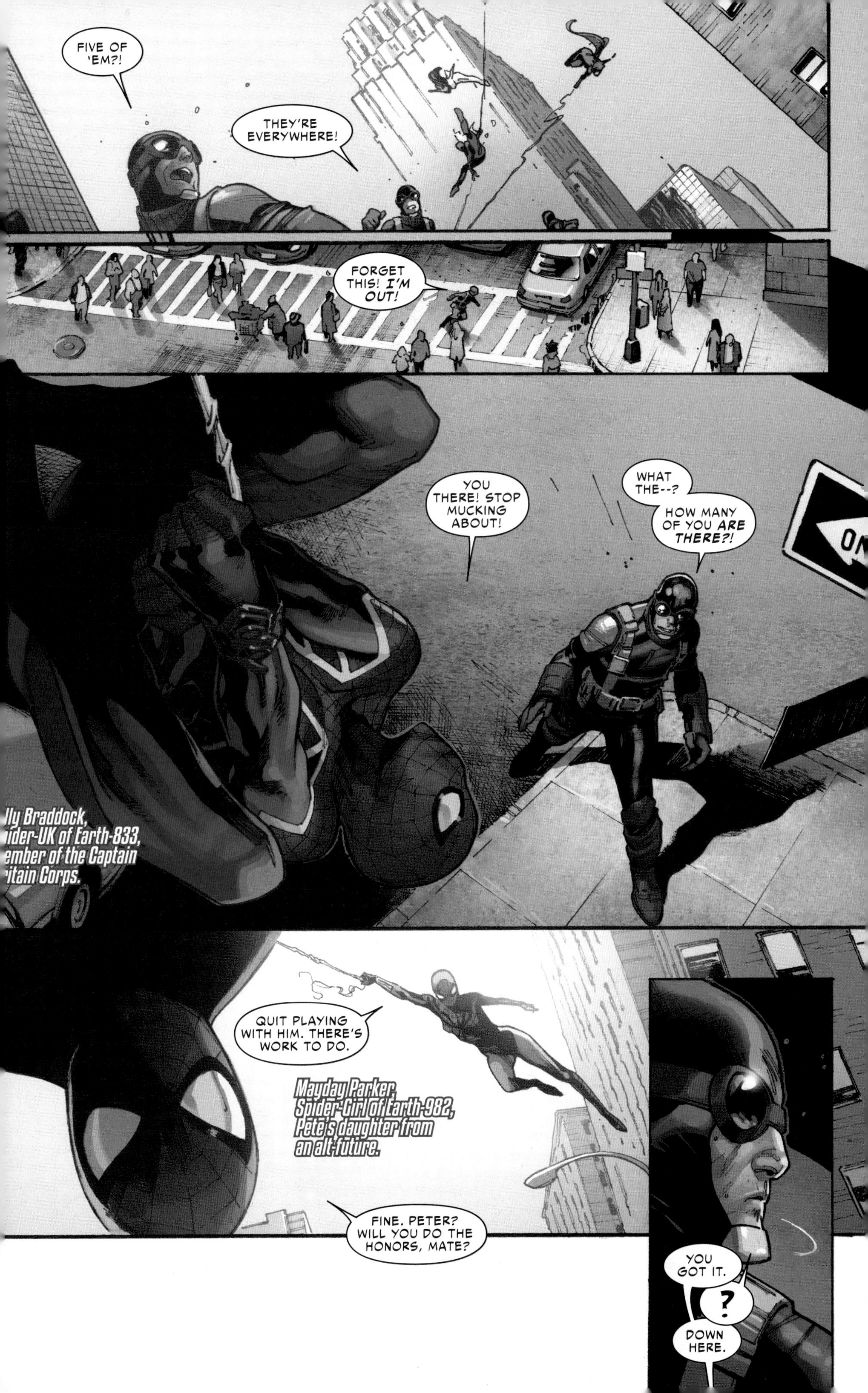

FIVE OF 'EM?!
THEY'RE EVERYWHERE!
FORGET THIS! I'M OUT!
YOU THERE! STOP MUCKING ABOUT!
WHAT THE--?
HOW MANY OF YOU ARE THERE?!
ON
lly Braddock, ider-UK of Earth-833, ember of the Captain itain Corps.
QUIT PLAYING WITH HIM. THERE'S WORK TO DO.
Mayday Parker, Spider-Girl of Earth-982, Pete's daughter from an alt-future.
FINE. PETER? WILL YOU DO THE HONORS, MATE?
YOU GOT IT.
?
DOWN HERE.

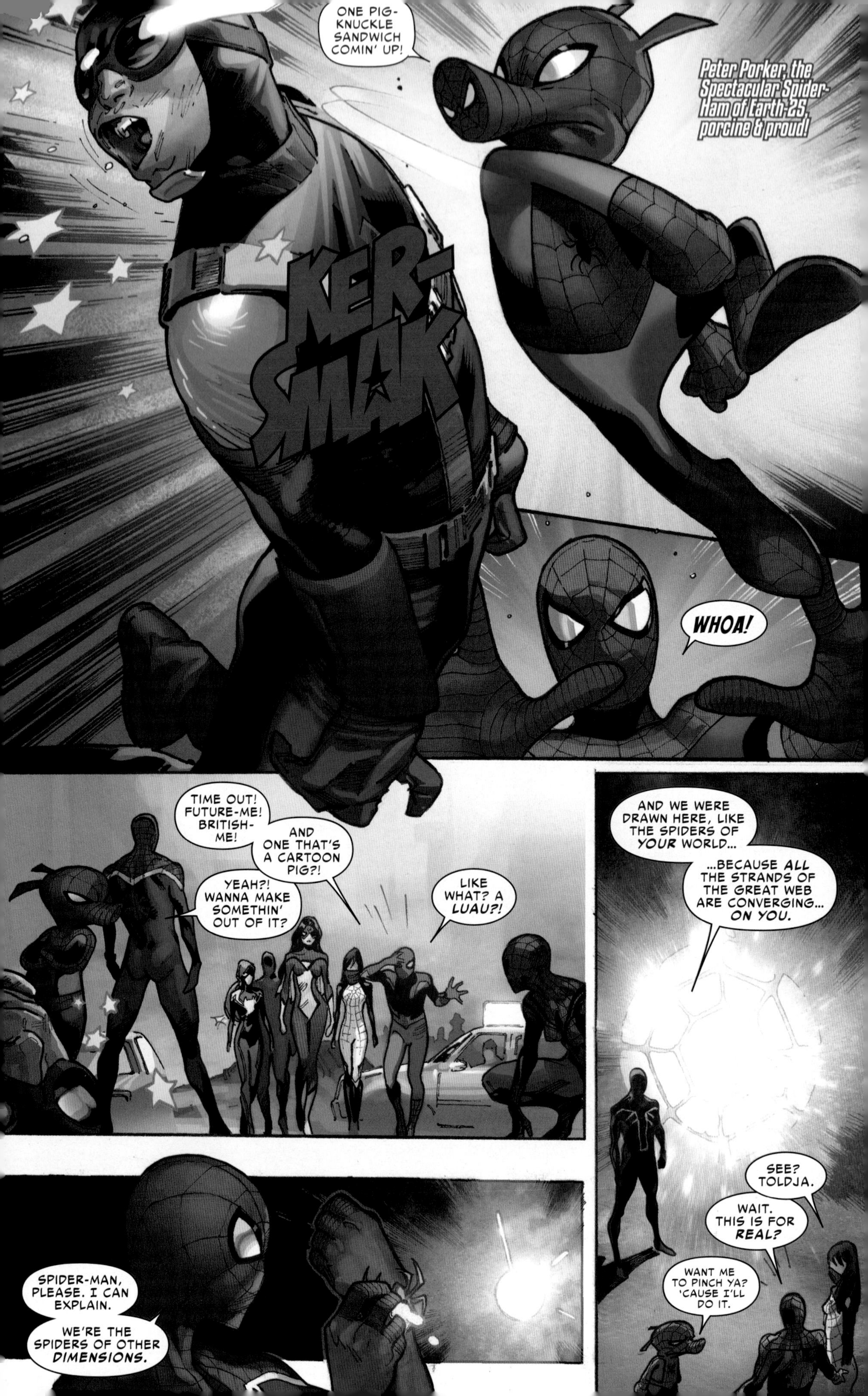
ONE PIG-KNUCKLE SANDWICH COMIN' UP!
Peter Porker, the Spectacular Spider-Ham of Earth-25, porcine & proud!
KER-SMAK
WHOA!
TIME OUT! FUTURE-ME! BRITISH-ME!
AND ONE THAT'S A CARTOON PIG?!
YEAH?! WANNA MAKE SOMETHIN' OUT OF IT?
LIKE WHAT? A LUAU?!
SPIDER-MAN, PLEASE. I CAN EXPLAIN.
WE'RE THE SPIDERS OF OTHER DIMENSIONS.
AND WE WERE DRAWN HERE, LIKE THE SPIDERS OF YOUR WORLD...
...BECAUSE ALL THE STRANDS OF THE GREAT WEB ARE CONVERGING... ON YOU.
SEE? TOLDJA.
WAIT. THIS IS FOR REAL?
WANT ME TO PINCH YA? 'CAUSE I'LL DO IT.

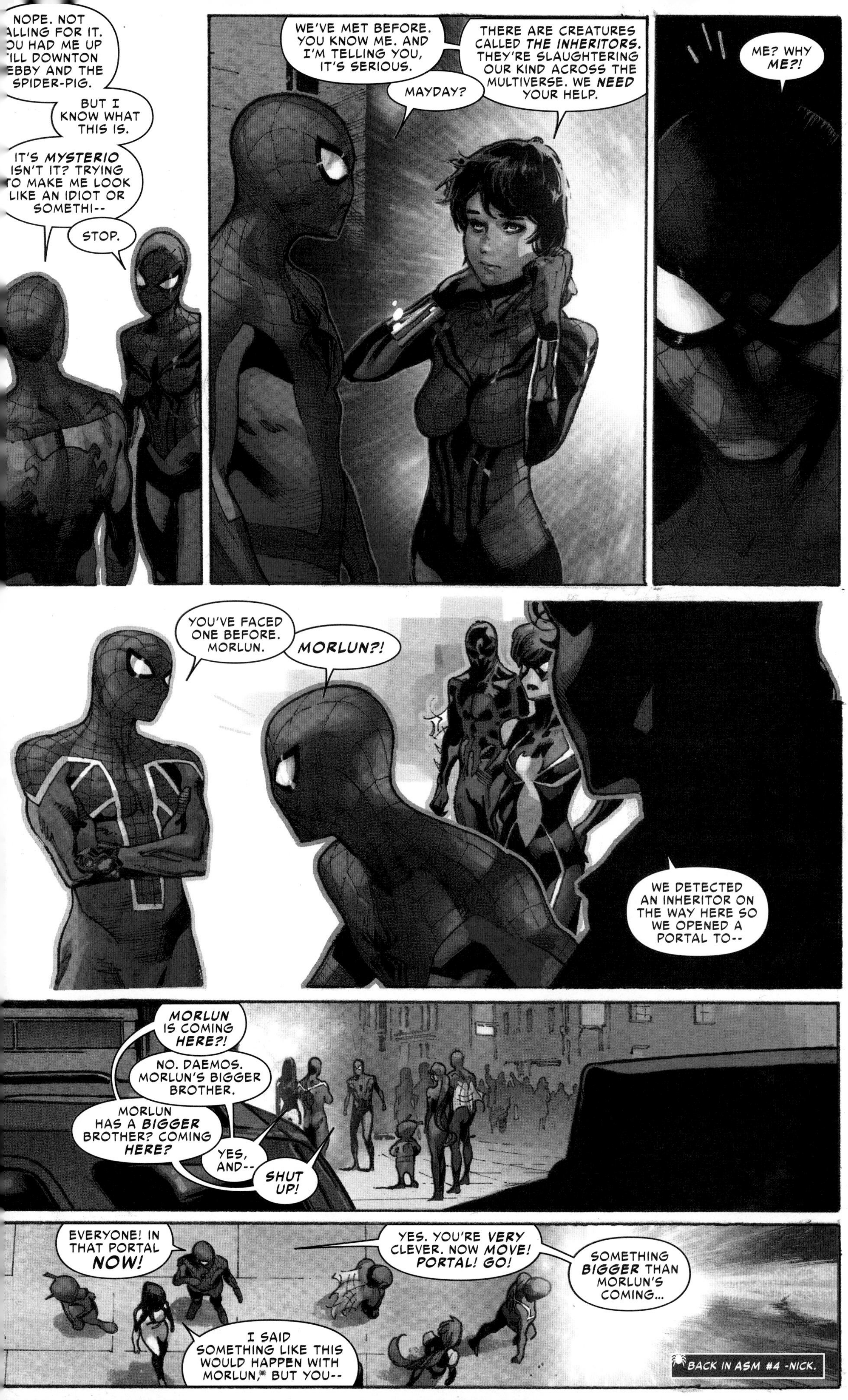
NOPE. NOT
FALLING FOR IT.
YOU HAD ME UP
TILL DOWNTON
ABBY AND THE
SPIDER-PIG.
BUT I
KNOW WHAT
THIS IS.
IT'S MYSTERIO
ISN'T IT? TRYING
TO MAKE ME LOOK
LIKE AN IDIOT OR
SOMETHI--
STOP.
WE'VE MET BEFORE. YOU KNOW ME. AND I'M TELLING YOU, IT'S SERIOUS.
MAYDAY?
THERE ARE CREATURES CALLED THE INHERITORS. THEY'RE SLAUGHTERING OUR KIND ACROSS THE MULTIVERSE. WE NEED YOUR HELP.
ME? WHY ME?!
YOU'VE FACED ONE BEFORE. MORLUN.
MORLUN?!
WE DETECTED AN INHERITOR ON THE WAY HERE SO WE OPENED A PORTAL TO--
MORLUN IS COMING HERE?!
NO. DAEMOS. MORLUN'S BIGGER BROTHER.
MORLUN HAS A BIGGER BROTHER? COMING HERE?
YES, AND--
SHUT UP!
EVERYONE! IN THAT PORTAL NOW!
YES. YOU'RE VERY CLEVER. NOW MOVE! PORTAL! GO!
SOMETHING BIGGER THAN MORLUN'S COMING...
I SAID SOMETHING LIKE THIS WOULD HAPPEN WITH MORLUN,* BUT YOU--
*BACK IN ASM #4 -NICK.

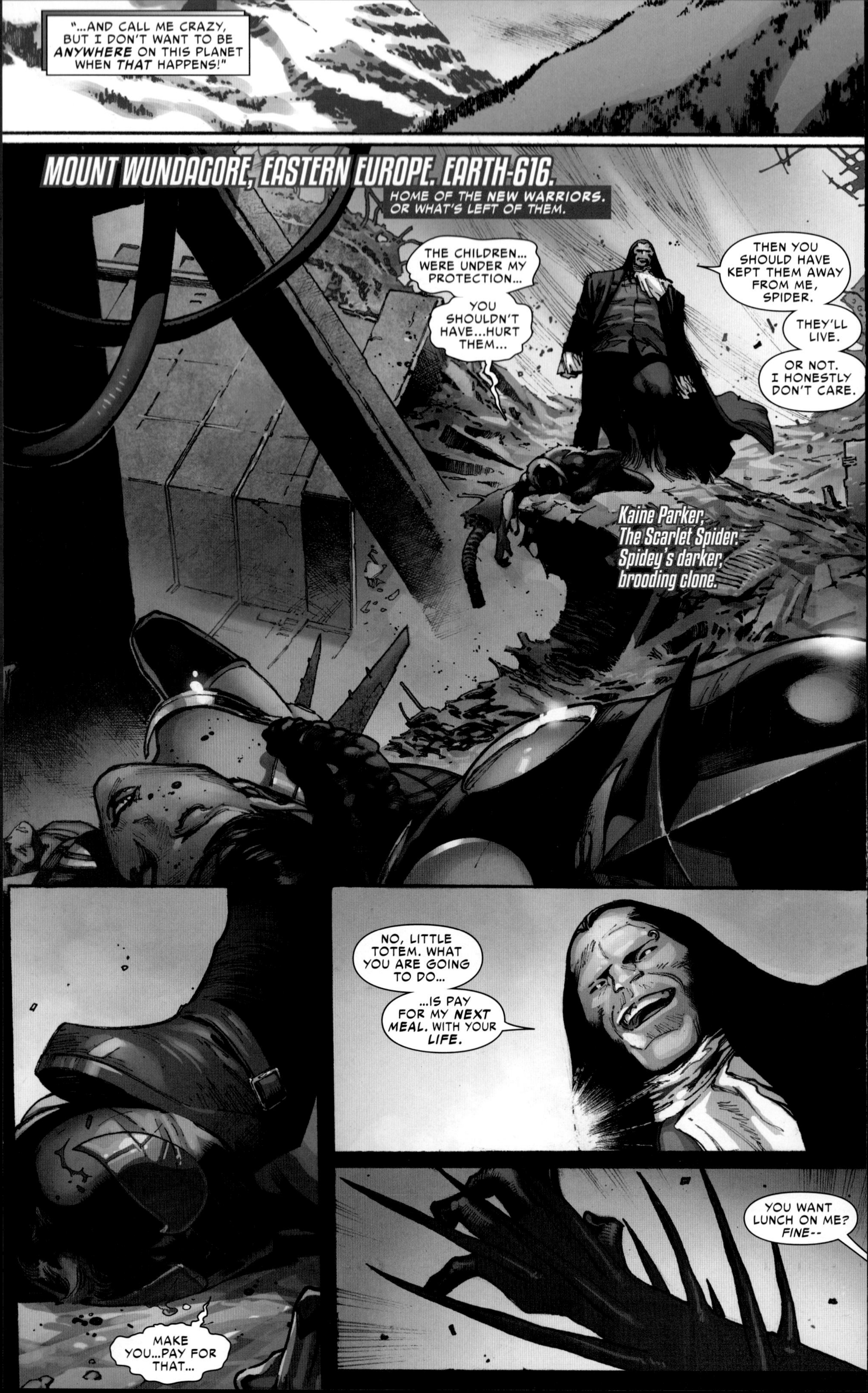
"...AND CALL ME CRAZY, BUT I DON'T WANT TO BE ANYWHERE ON THIS PLANET WHEN THAT HAPPENS!"
MOUNT WUNDAGORE, EASTERN EUROPE. EARTH-616.
HOME OF THE NEW WARRIORS. OR WHAT'S LEFT OF THEM.
THE CHILDREN... WERE UNDER MY PROTECTION...
YOU SHOULDN'T HAVE...HURT THEM...
THEN YOU SHOULD HAVE KEPT THEM AWAY FROM ME, SPIDER.
THEY'LL LIVE.
OR NOT. I HONESTLY DON'T CARE.
Kaine Parker, The Scarlet Spider. Spidey's darker, brooding clone.
MAKE YOU...PAY FOR THAT...
NO, LITTLE TOTEM. WHAT YOU ARE GOING TO DO...
...IS PAY FOR MY NEXT MEAL. WITH YOUR LIFE.
YOU WANT LUNCH ON ME? FINE--

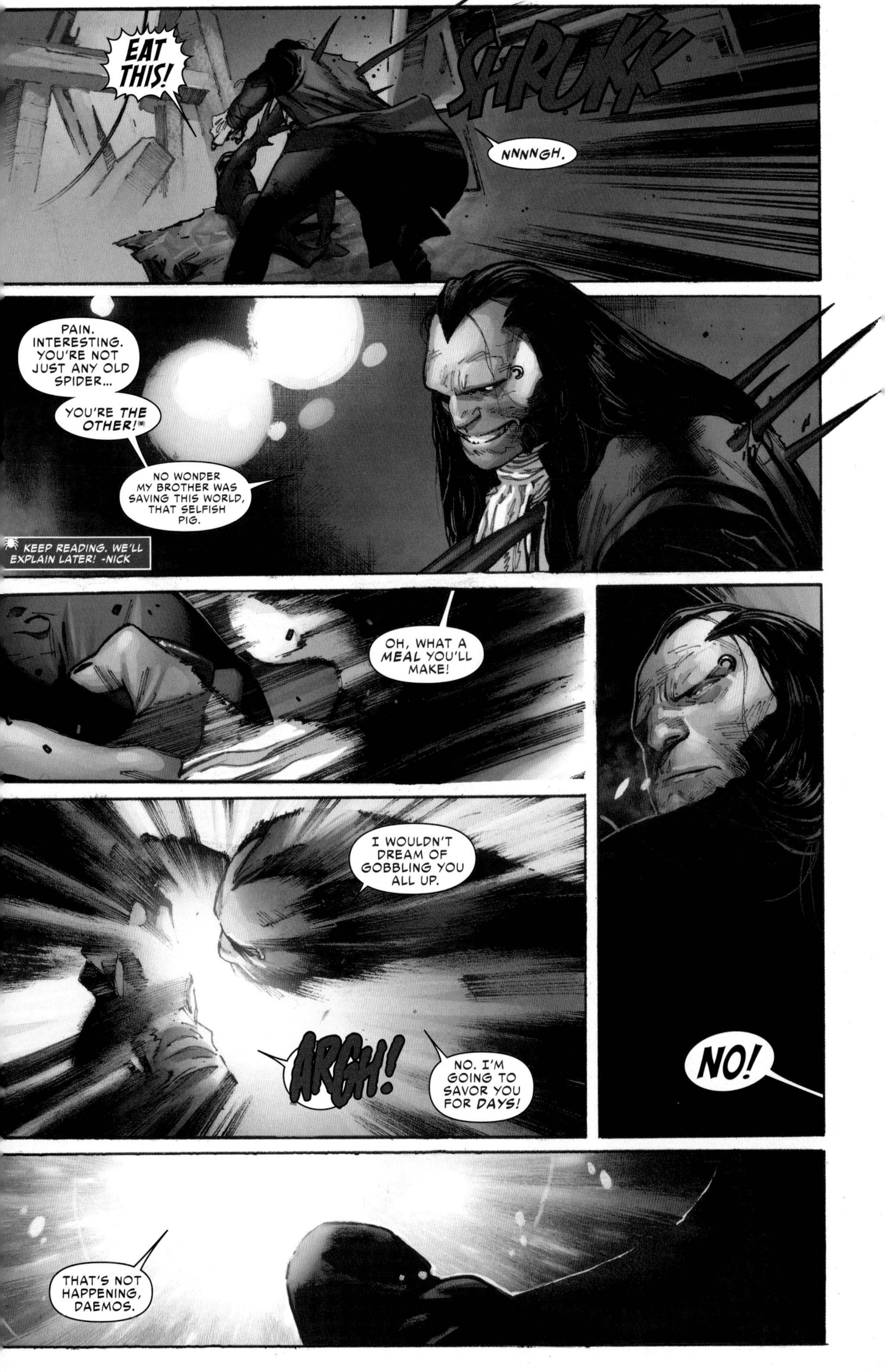
EAT THIS!
SHRUKK
NNNNGH.
PAIN. INTERESTING. YOU'RE NOT JUST ANY OLD SPIDER...
YOU'RE THE OTHER!
NO WONDER MY BROTHER WAS SAVING THIS WORLD, THAT SELFISH PIG.
KEEP READING. WE'LL EXPLAIN LATER! -NICK
OH, WHAT A MEAL YOU'LL MAKE!
I WOULDN'T DREAM OF GOBBLING YOU ALL UP.
ARGH!
NO. I'M GOING TO SAVOR YOU FOR DAYS!
NO!
THAT'S NOT HAPPENING, DAEMOS.

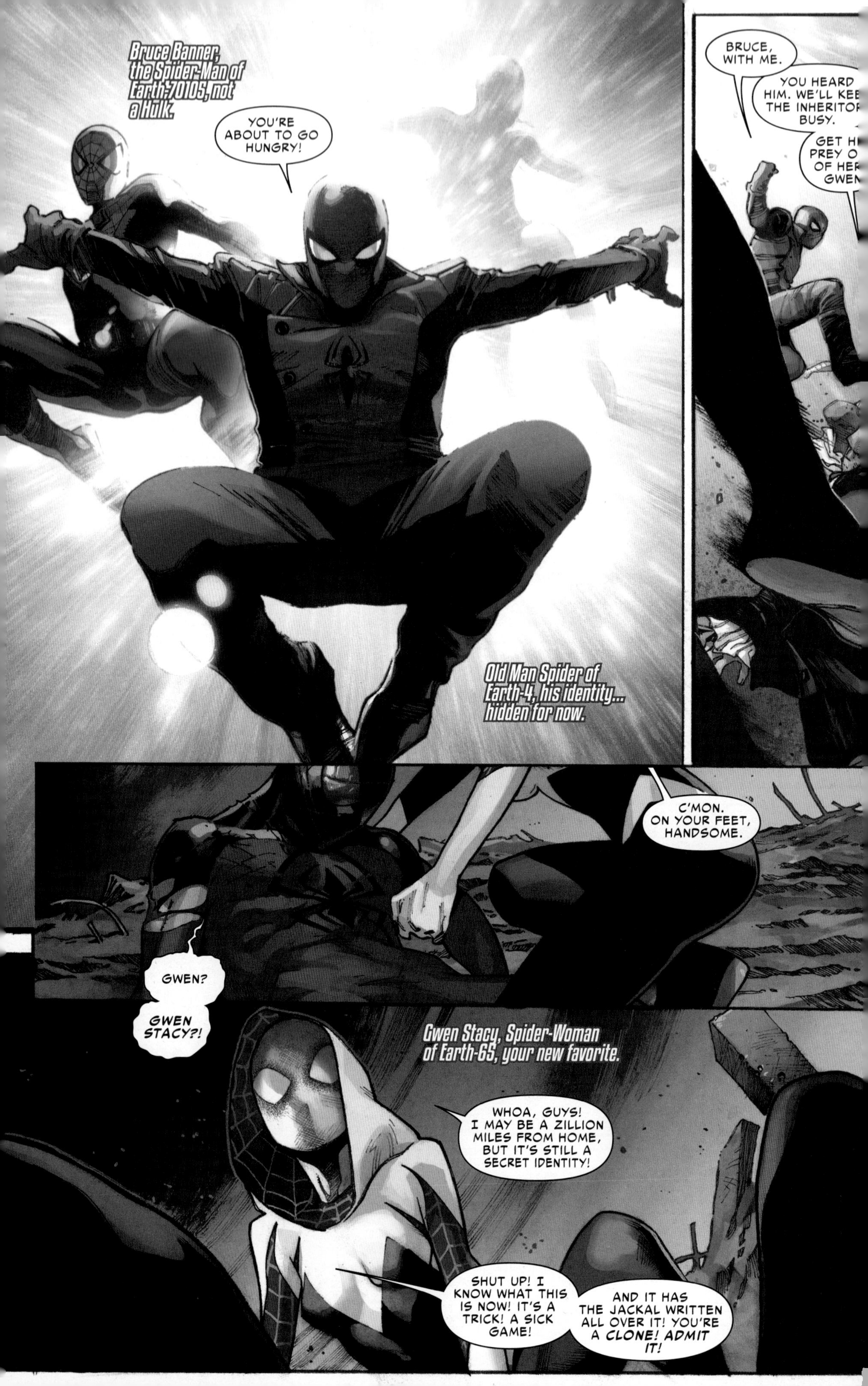
Bruce Banner, the Spider-Man of Earth-70105, not a Hulk.
YOU'RE ABOUT TO GO HUNGRY!
Old Man Spider of Earth-4, his identity... hidden for now.
BRUCE, WITH ME.
YOU HEARD HIM. WE'LL KEE THE INHERITOR BUSY.
GET H PREY O OF HER GWEN
C'MON. ON YOUR FEET, HANDSOME.
GWEN?
GWEN STACY?!
Gwen Stacy, Spider-Woman of Earth-65, your new favorite.
WHOA, GUYS! I MAY BE A ZILLION MILES FROM HOME, BUT IT'S STILL A SECRET IDENTITY!
SHUT UP! I KNOW WHAT THIS IS NOW! IT'S A TRICK! A SICK GAME!
AND IT HAS THE JACKAL WRITTEN ALL OVER IT! YOU'RE A CLONE! ADMIT IT!

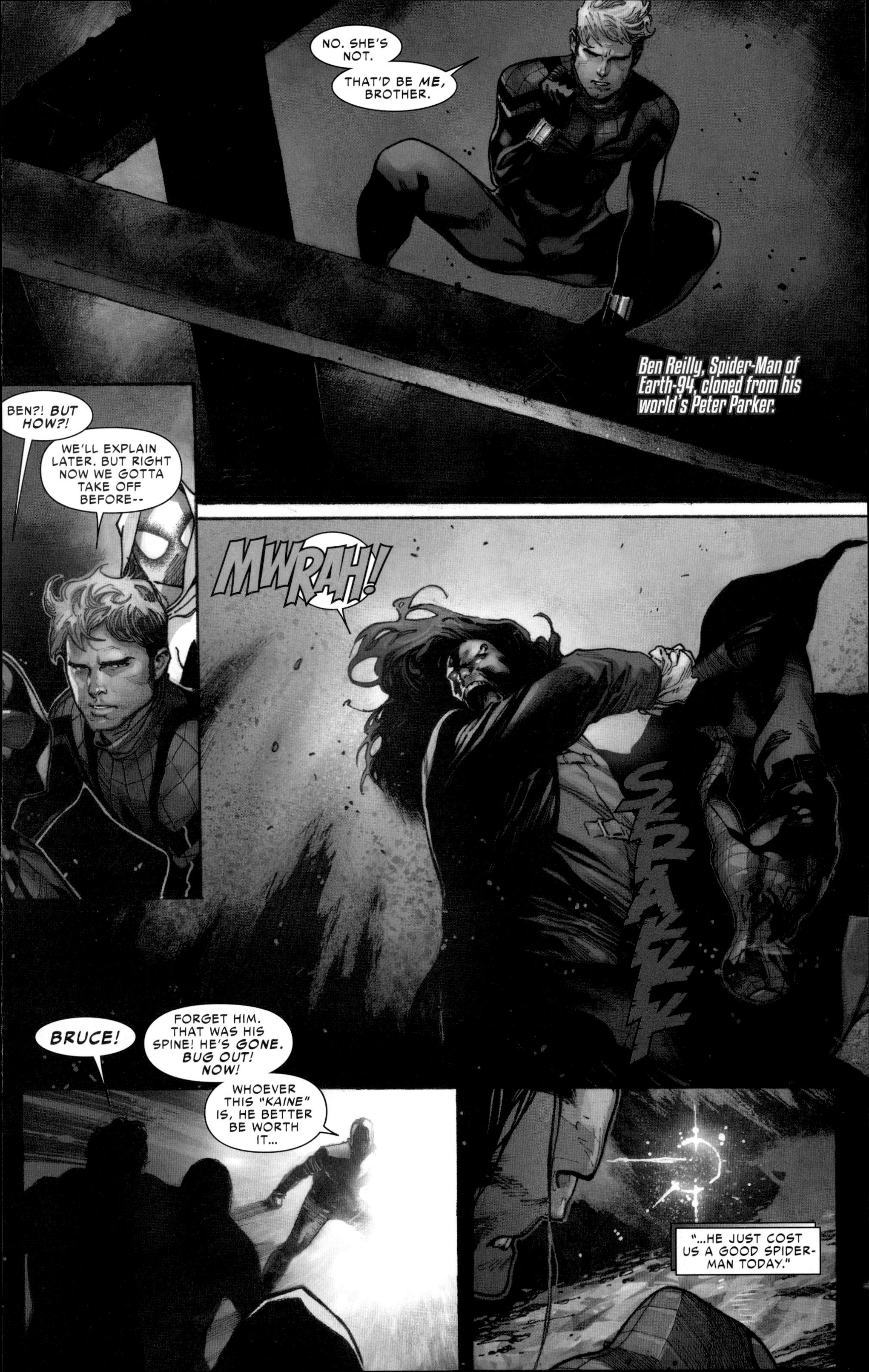
NO. SHE'S NOT.
THAT'D BE *ME*, BROTHER.
Ben Reilly, Spider-Man of Earth-94, cloned from his world's Peter Parker.
BEN?! *BUT HOW?!*
WE'LL EXPLAIN LATER. BUT RIGHT NOW WE GOTTA TAKE OFF BEFORE--
MWRAH!
SKRAKK
BRUCE!
FORGET HIM. THAT WAS HIS SPINE! HE'S *GONE*. *BUG OUT! NOW!*
WHOEVER THIS "*KAINE*" IS, HE BETTER BE WORTH IT...
"...HE JUST COST US A GOOD SPIDER-MAN TODAY."

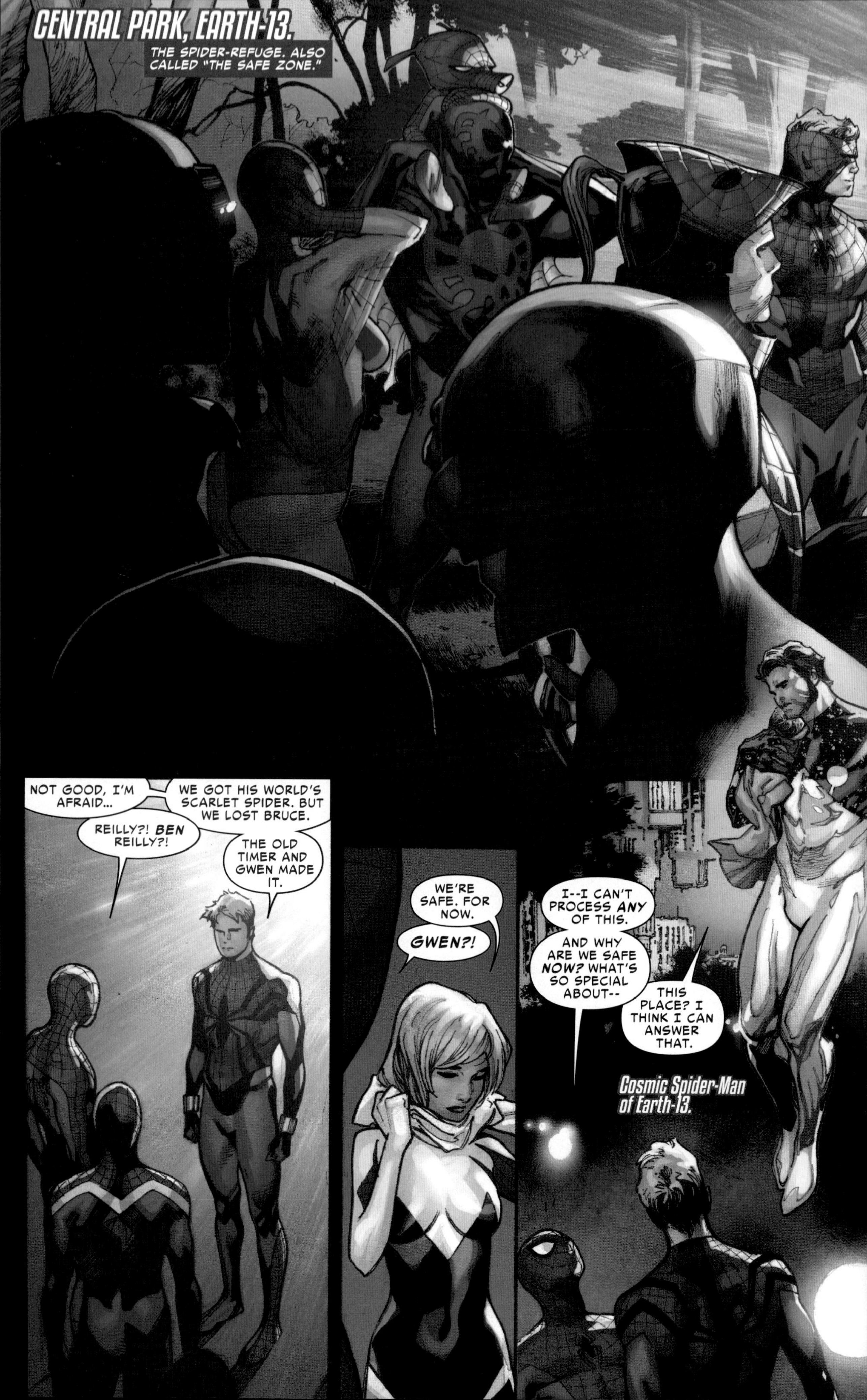

CENTRAL PARK, EARTH-13.
THE SPIDER-REFUGE. ALSO CALLED "THE SAFE ZONE."
NOT GOOD, I'M AFRAID...
WE GOT HIS WORLD'S SCARLET SPIDER. BUT WE LOST BRUCE.
REILLY?! BEN REILLY?!
THE OLD TIMER AND GWEN MADE IT.
WE'RE SAFE. FOR NOW.
GWEN?!
I--I CAN'T PROCESS ANY OF THIS.
AND WHY ARE WE SAFE NOW? WHAT'S SO SPECIAL ABOUT--
THIS PLACE? I THINK I CAN ANSWER THAT.
Cosmic Spider-Man of Earth-13.

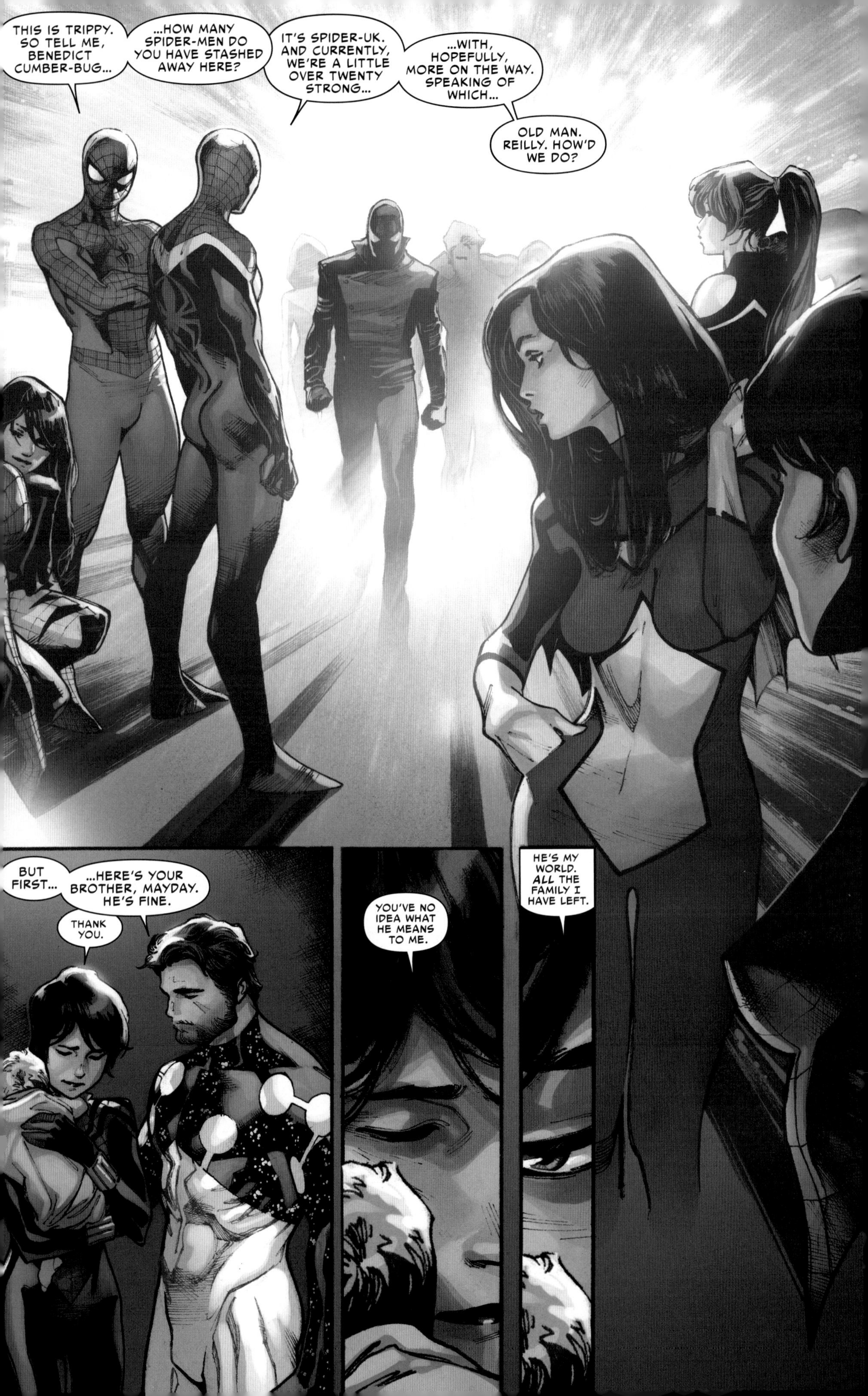
THIS IS TRIPPY. SO TELL ME, BENEDICT CUMBER-BUG...
...HOW MANY SPIDER-MEN DO YOU HAVE STASHED AWAY HERE?
IT'S SPIDER-UK. AND CURRENTLY, WE'RE A LITTLE OVER TWENTY STRONG...
...WITH, HOPEFULLY, MORE ON THE WAY. SPEAKING OF WHICH...
OLD MAN. REILLY. HOW'D WE DO?
BUT FIRST...
...HERE'S YOUR BROTHER, MAYDAY. HE'S FINE.
THANK YOU.
YOU'VE NO IDEA WHAT HE MEANS TO ME.
HE'S MY WORLD. ALL THE FAMILY I HAVE LEFT.

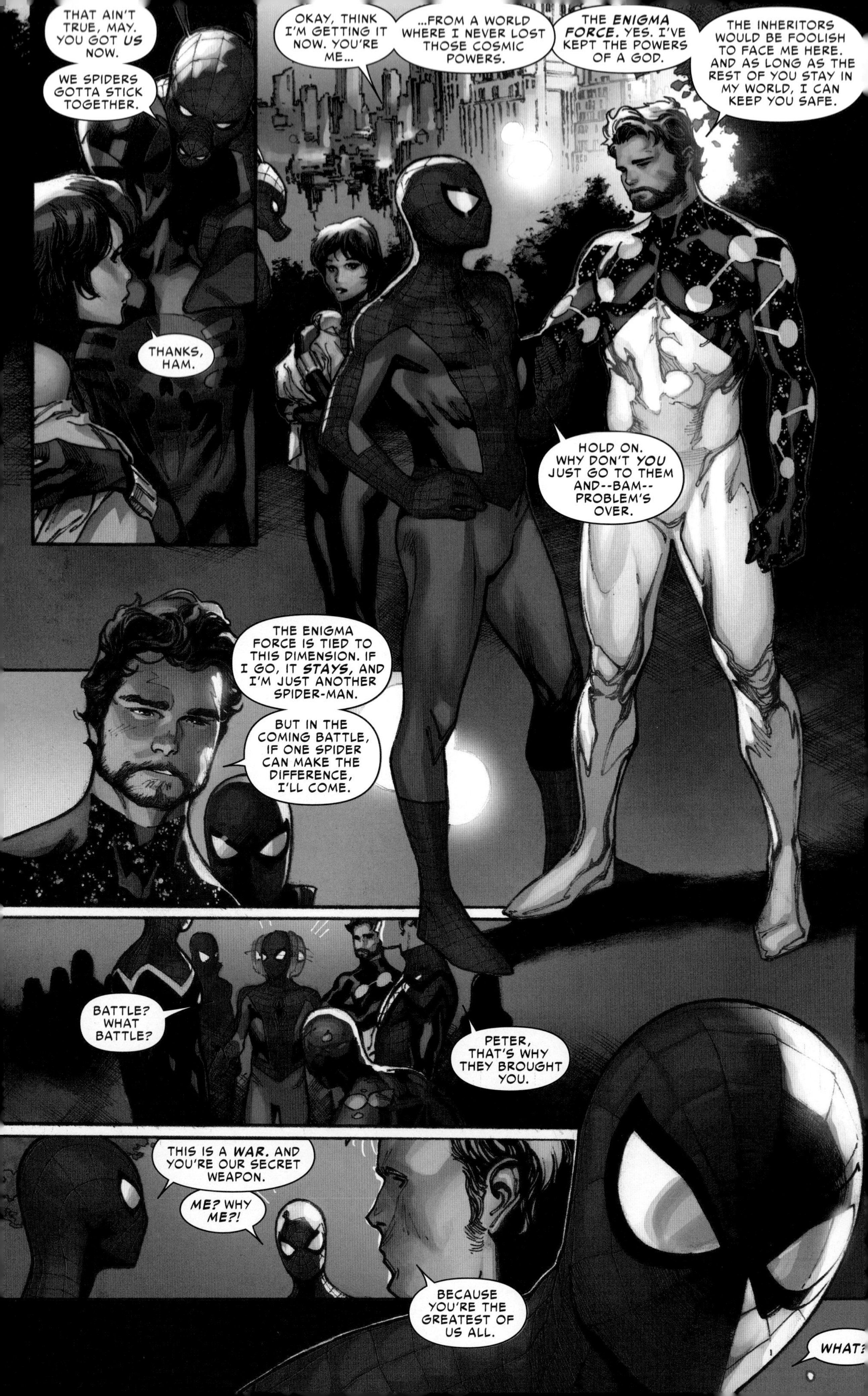
THAT AIN'T TRUE, MAY. YOU GOT US NOW.
WE SPIDERS GOTTA STICK TOGETHER.
THANKS, HAM.
OKAY, THINK I'M GETTING IT NOW. YOU'RE ME...
...FROM A WORLD WHERE I NEVER LOST THOSE COSMIC POWERS.
THE ENIGMA FORCE. YES. I'VE KEPT THE POWERS OF A GOD.
THE INHERITORS WOULD BE FOOLISH TO FACE ME HERE. AND AS LONG AS THE REST OF YOU STAY IN MY WORLD, I CAN KEEP YOU SAFE.
HOLD ON. WHY DON'T YOU JUST GO TO THEM AND--BAM--PROBLEM'S OVER.
THE ENIGMA FORCE IS TIED TO THIS DIMENSION. IF I GO, IT STAYS, AND I'M JUST ANOTHER SPIDER-MAN.
BUT IN THE COMING BATTLE, IF ONE SPIDER CAN MAKE THE DIFFERENCE, I'LL COME.
BATTLE? WHAT BATTLE?
PETER, THAT'S WHY THEY BROUGHT YOU.
THIS IS A WAR. AND YOU'RE OUR SECRET WEAPON.
ME? WHY ME?!
BECAUSE YOU'RE THE GREATEST OF US ALL.
WHAT?

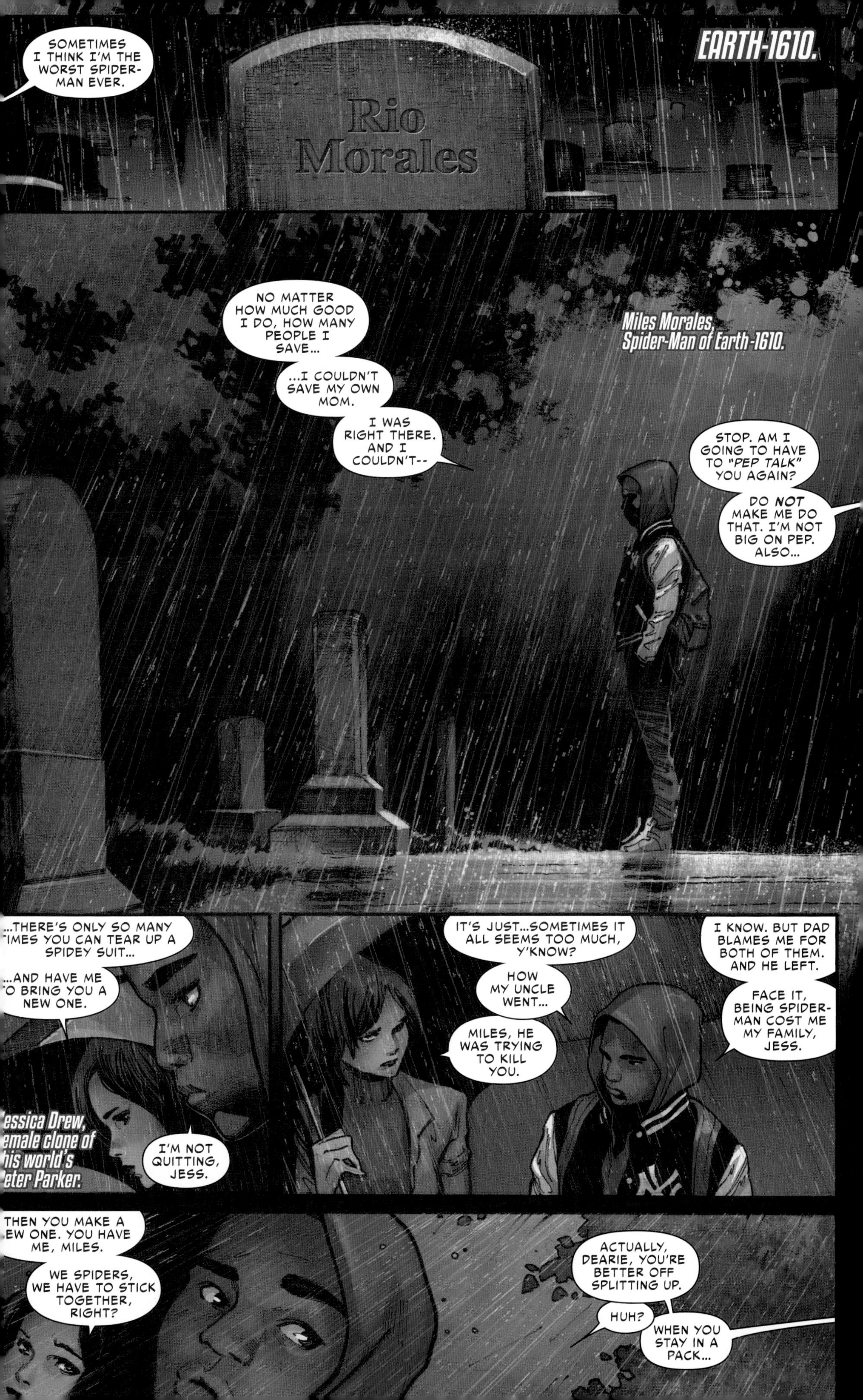
EARTH-1610.
SOMETIMES I THINK I'M THE WORST SPIDER-MAN EVER.
Rio Morales
NO MATTER HOW MUCH GOOD I DO, HOW MANY PEOPLE I SAVE...
...I COULDN'T SAVE MY OWN MOM.
I WAS RIGHT THERE. AND I COULDN'T--
Miles Morales, Spider-Man of Earth-1610.
STOP. AM I GOING TO HAVE TO "PEP TALK" YOU AGAIN?
DO NOT MAKE ME DO THAT. I'M NOT BIG ON PEP. ALSO...
...THERE'S ONLY SO MANY TIMES YOU CAN TEAR UP A SPIDEY SUIT...
...AND HAVE ME TO BRING YOU A NEW ONE.
Jessica Drew, female clone of this world's Peter Parker.
I'M NOT QUITTING, JESS.
IT'S JUST...SOMETIMES IT ALL SEEMS TOO MUCH, Y'KNOW?
HOW MY UNCLE WENT...
MILES, HE WAS TRYING TO KILL YOU.
I KNOW. BUT DAD BLAMES ME FOR BOTH OF THEM. AND HE LEFT.
FACE IT, BEING SPIDER-MAN COST ME MY FAMILY, JESS.
THEN YOU MAKE A NEW ONE. YOU HAVE ME, MILES.
WE SPIDERS, WE HAVE TO STICK TOGETHER, RIGHT?
ACTUALLY, DEARIE, YOU'RE BETTER OFF SPLITTING UP.
HUH?
WHEN YOU STAY IN A PACK...

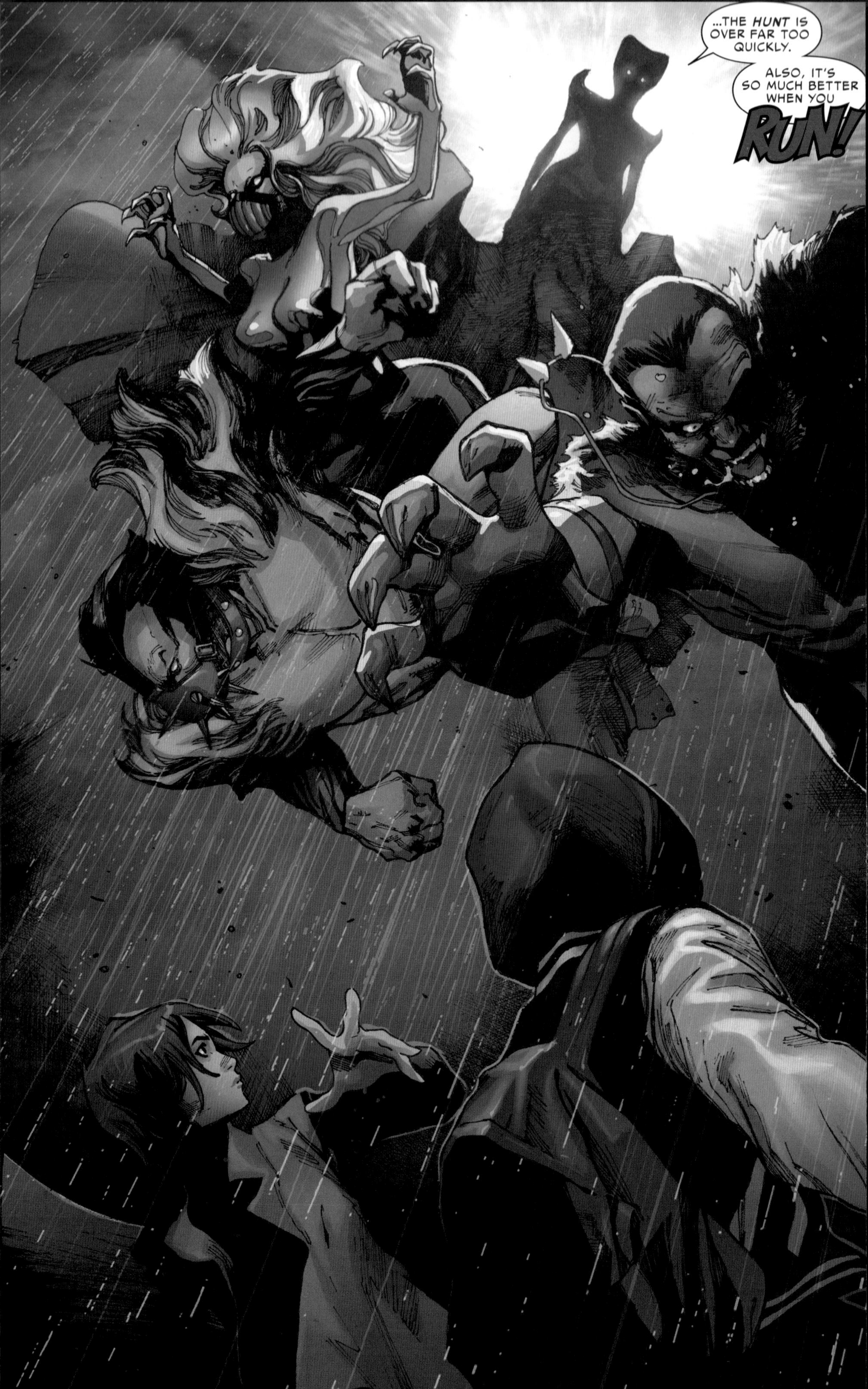
...THE *HUNT* IS OVER FAR TOO QUICKLY.
ALSO, IT'S SO MUCH BETTER WHEN YOU
RUN!

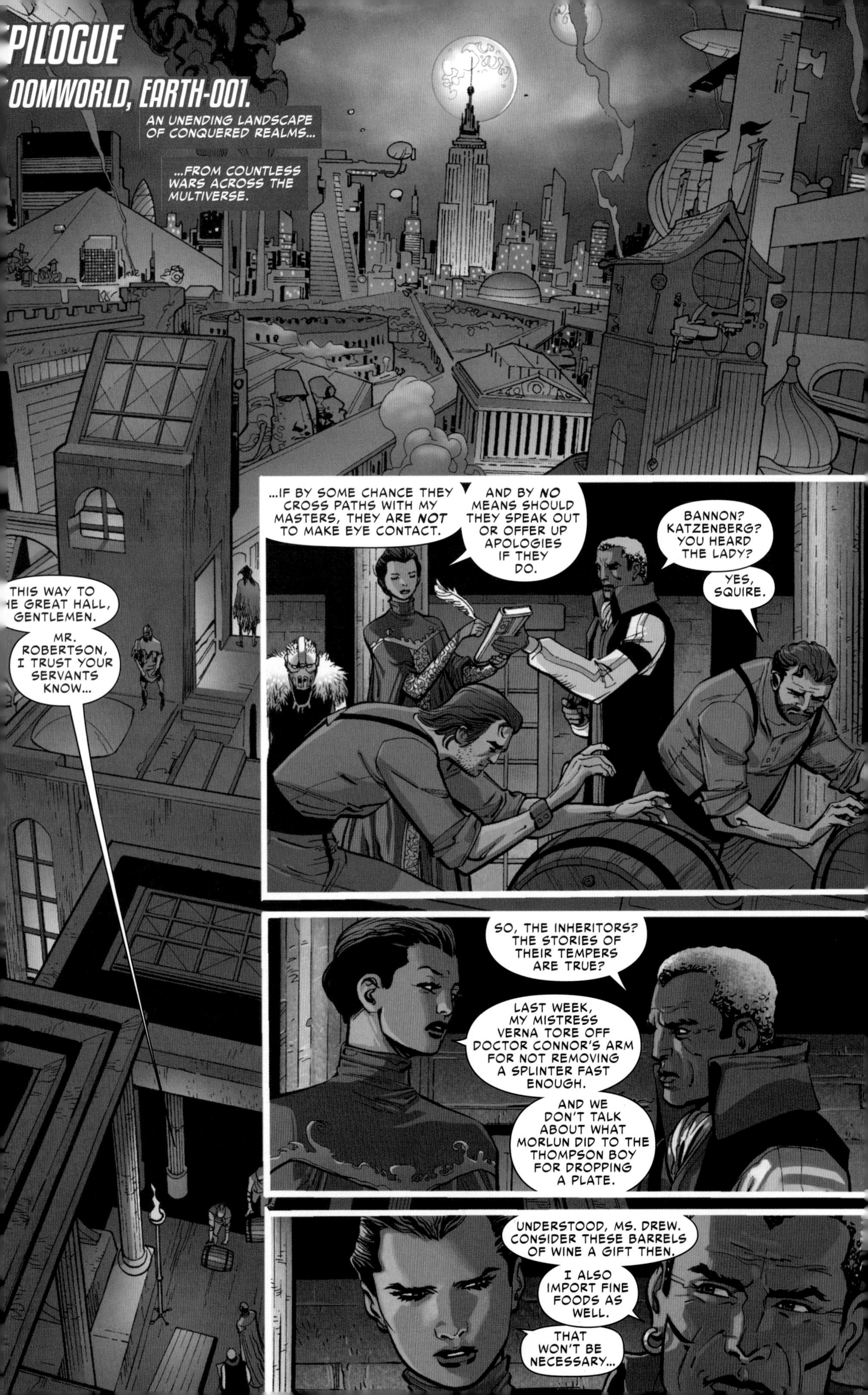
PILOGUE
OOMWORLD, EARTH-001.
AN UNENDING LANDSCAPE OF CONQUERED REALMS...
...FROM COUNTLESS WARS ACROSS THE MULTIVERSE.
THIS WAY TO HE GREAT HALL, GENTLEMEN.
MR. ROBERTSON, I TRUST YOUR SERVANTS KNOW...
...IF BY SOME CHANCE THEY CROSS PATHS WITH MY MASTERS, THEY ARE NOT TO MAKE EYE CONTACT.
AND BY NO MEANS SHOULD THEY SPEAK OUT OR OFFER UP APOLOGIES IF THEY DO.
BANNON? KATZENBERG? YOU HEARD THE LADY?
YES, SQUIRE.
SO, THE INHERITORS? THE STORIES OF THEIR TEMPERS ARE TRUE?
LAST WEEK, MY MISTRESS VERNA TORE OFF DOCTOR CONNOR'S ARM FOR NOT REMOVING A SPLINTER FAST ENOUGH.
AND WE DON'T TALK ABOUT WHAT MORLUN DID TO THE THOMPSON BOY FOR DROPPING A PLATE.
UNDERSTOOD, MS. DREW. CONSIDER THESE BARRELS OF WINE A GIFT THEN.
I ALSO IMPORT FINE FOODS AS WELL.
THAT WON'T BE NECESSARY...

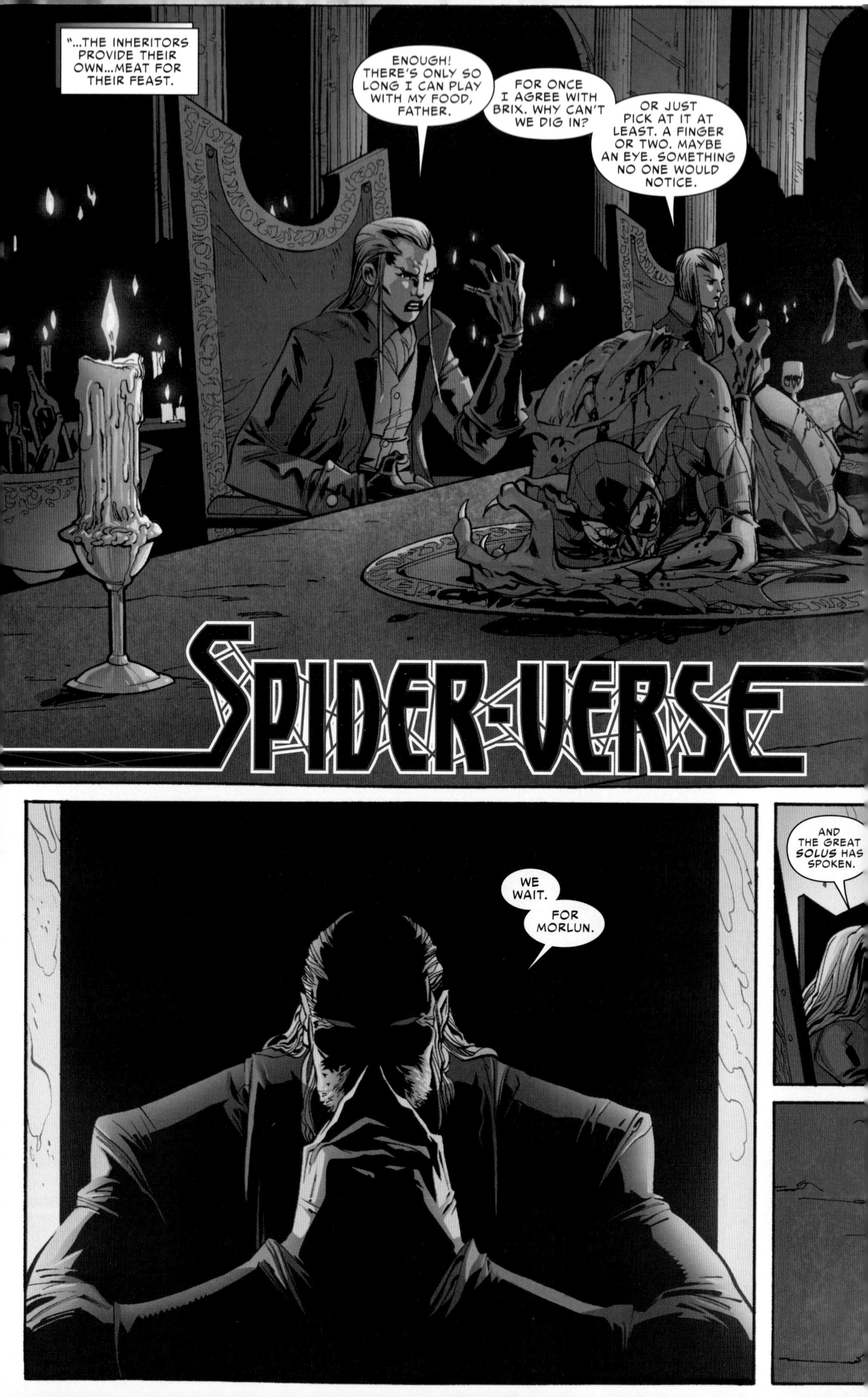
"...THE INHERITORS PROVIDE THEIR OWN...MEAT FOR THEIR FEAST.
ENOUGH! THERE'S ONLY SO LONG I CAN PLAY WITH MY FOOD, FATHER.
FOR ONCE I AGREE WITH BRIX. WHY CAN'T WE DIG IN?
OR JUST PICK AT IT AT LEAST. A FINGER OR TWO. MAYBE AN EYE. SOMETHING NO ONE WOULD NOTICE.
SPIDER-VERSE
WE WAIT.
FOR MORLUN.
AND THE GREAT SOLUS HAS SPOKEN.

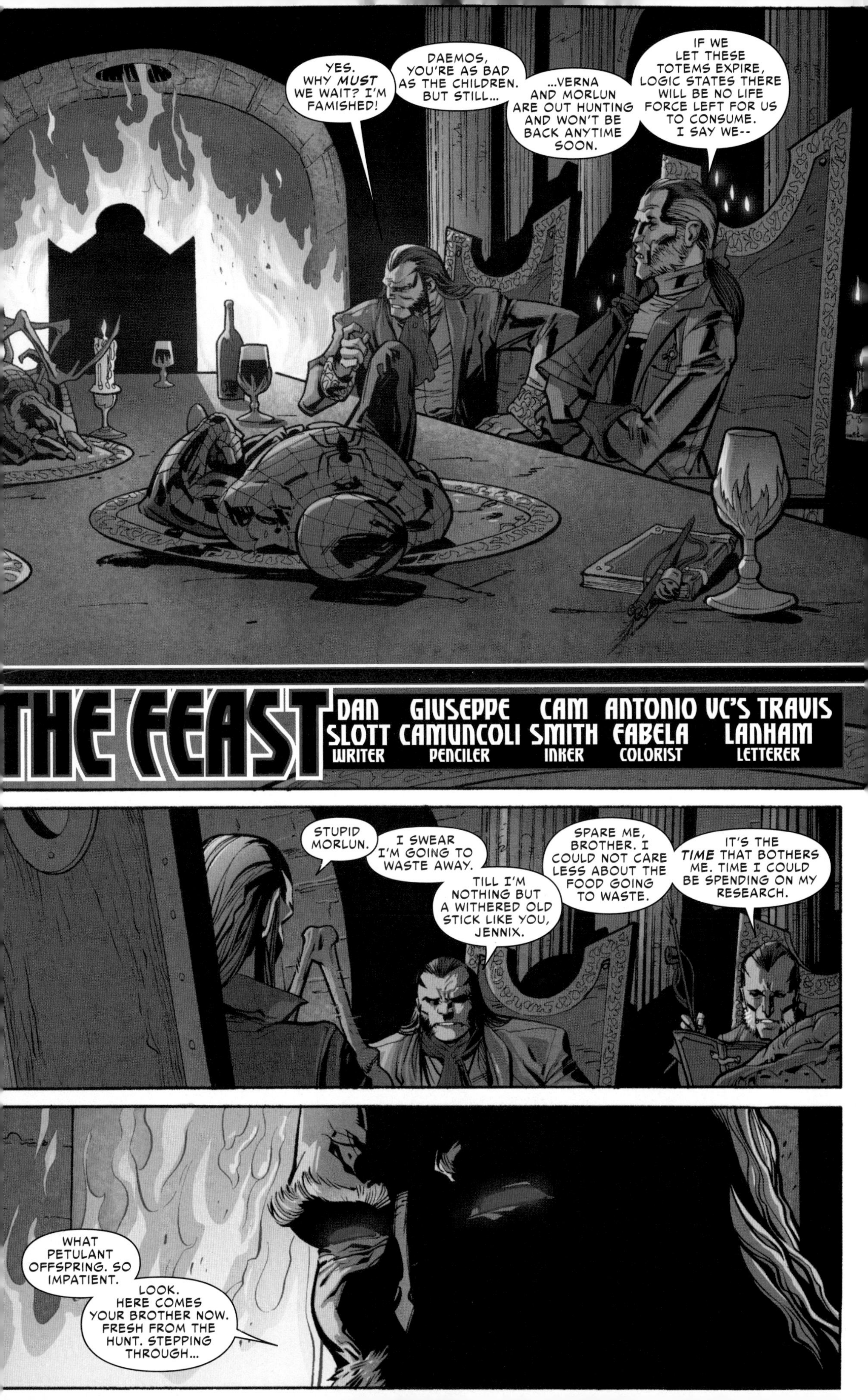
YES. WHY MUST WE WAIT? I'M FAMISHED!
DAEMOS, YOU'RE AS BAD AS THE CHILDREN. BUT STILL...
...VERNA AND MORLUN ARE OUT HUNTING AND WON'T BE BACK ANYTIME SOON.
IF WE LET THESE TOTEMS EXPIRE, LOGIC STATES THERE WILL BE NO LIFE FORCE LEFT FOR US TO CONSUME. I SAY WE--
THE FEAST
DAN SLOTT WRITER
GIUSEPPE CAMUNCOLI PENCILER
CAM SMITH INKER
ANTONIO FABELA COLORIST
VC'S TRAVIS LANHAM LETTERER
STUPID MORLUN.
I SWEAR I'M GOING TO WASTE AWAY.
TILL I'M NOTHING BUT A WITHERED OLD STICK LIKE YOU, JENNIX.
SPARE ME, BROTHER. I COULD NOT CARE LESS ABOUT THE FOOD GOING TO WASTE.
IT'S THE TIME THAT BOTHERS ME. TIME I COULD BE SPENDING ON MY RESEARCH.
WHAT PETULANT OFFSPRING. SO IMPATIENT.
LOOK. HERE COMES YOUR BROTHER NOW. FRESH FROM THE HUNT. STEPPING THROUGH...

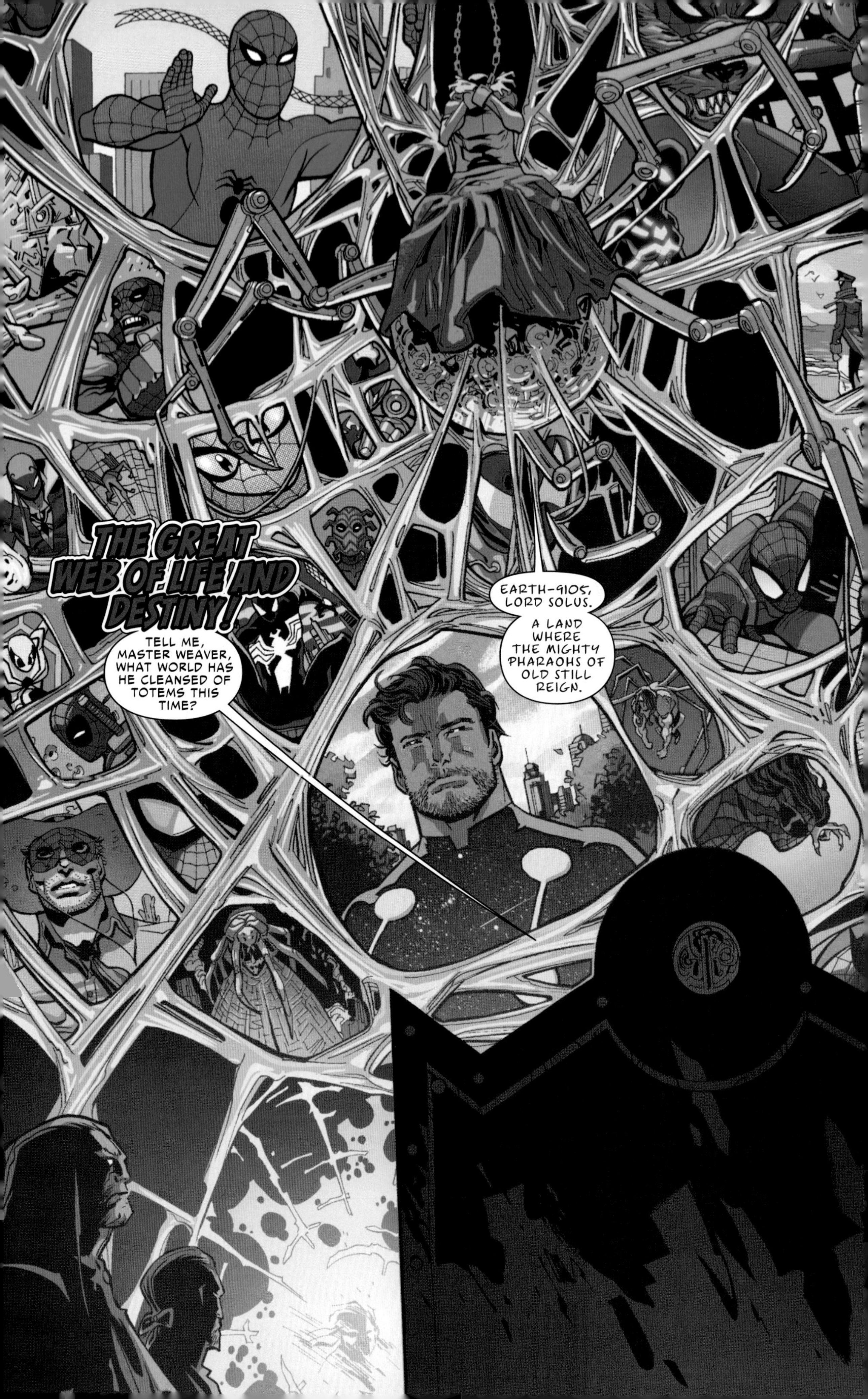

THE GREAT WEB OF LIFE AND DESTINY!
TELL ME, MASTER WEAVER, WHAT WORLD HAS HE CLEANSED OF TOTEMS THIS TIME?
EARTH-9105, LORD SOLUS.
A LAND WHERE THE MIGHTY PHARAOHS OF OLD STILL REIGN.

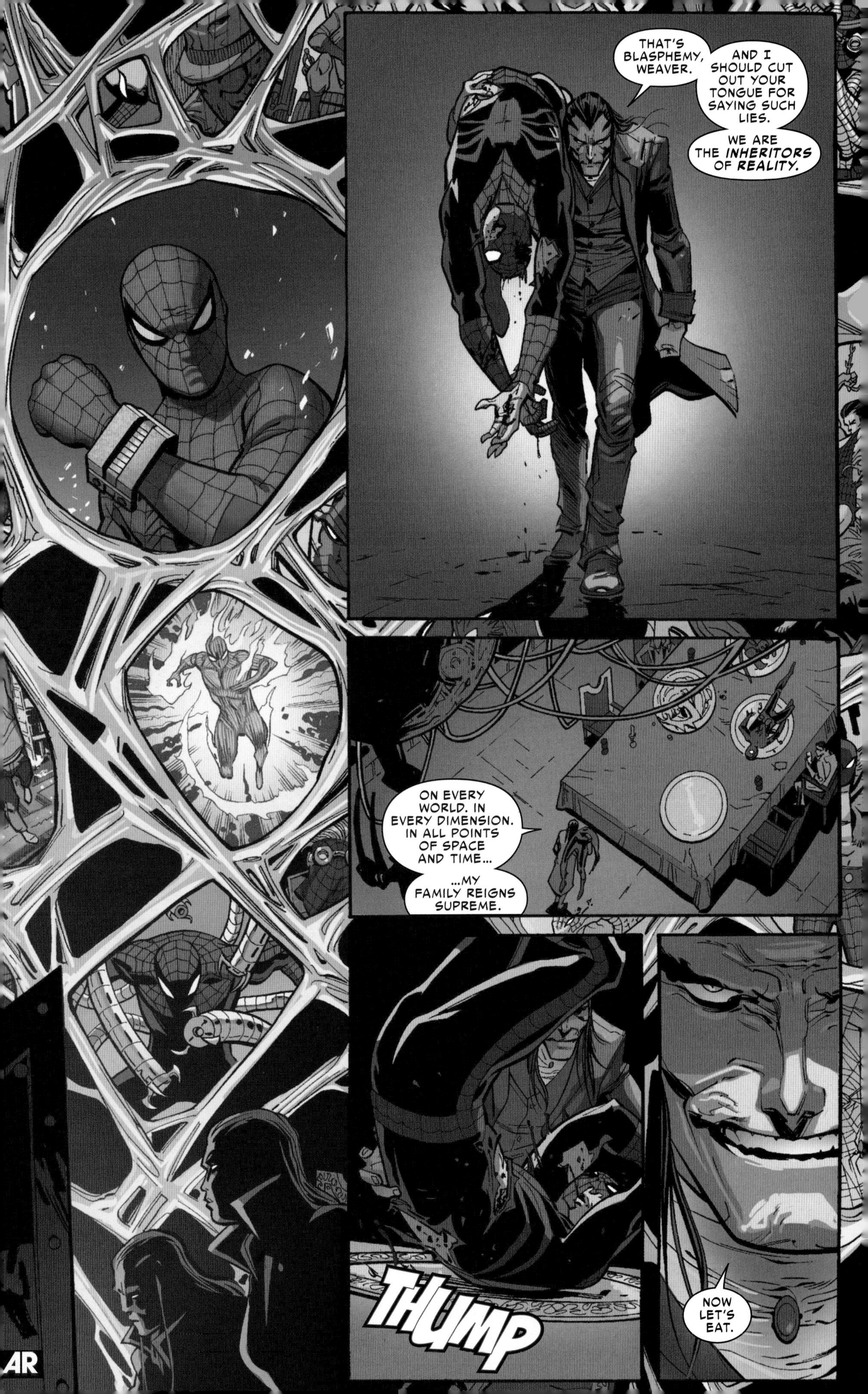
THAT'S BLASPHEMY, WEAVER.
AND I SHOULD CUT OUT YOUR TONGUE FOR SAYING SUCH LIES.
WE ARE THE INHERITORS OF REALITY.
ON EVERY WORLD. IN EVERY DIMENSION. IN ALL POINTS OF SPACE AND TIME...
...MY FAMILY REIGNS SUPREME.
THUMP
NOW LET'S EAT.
AR

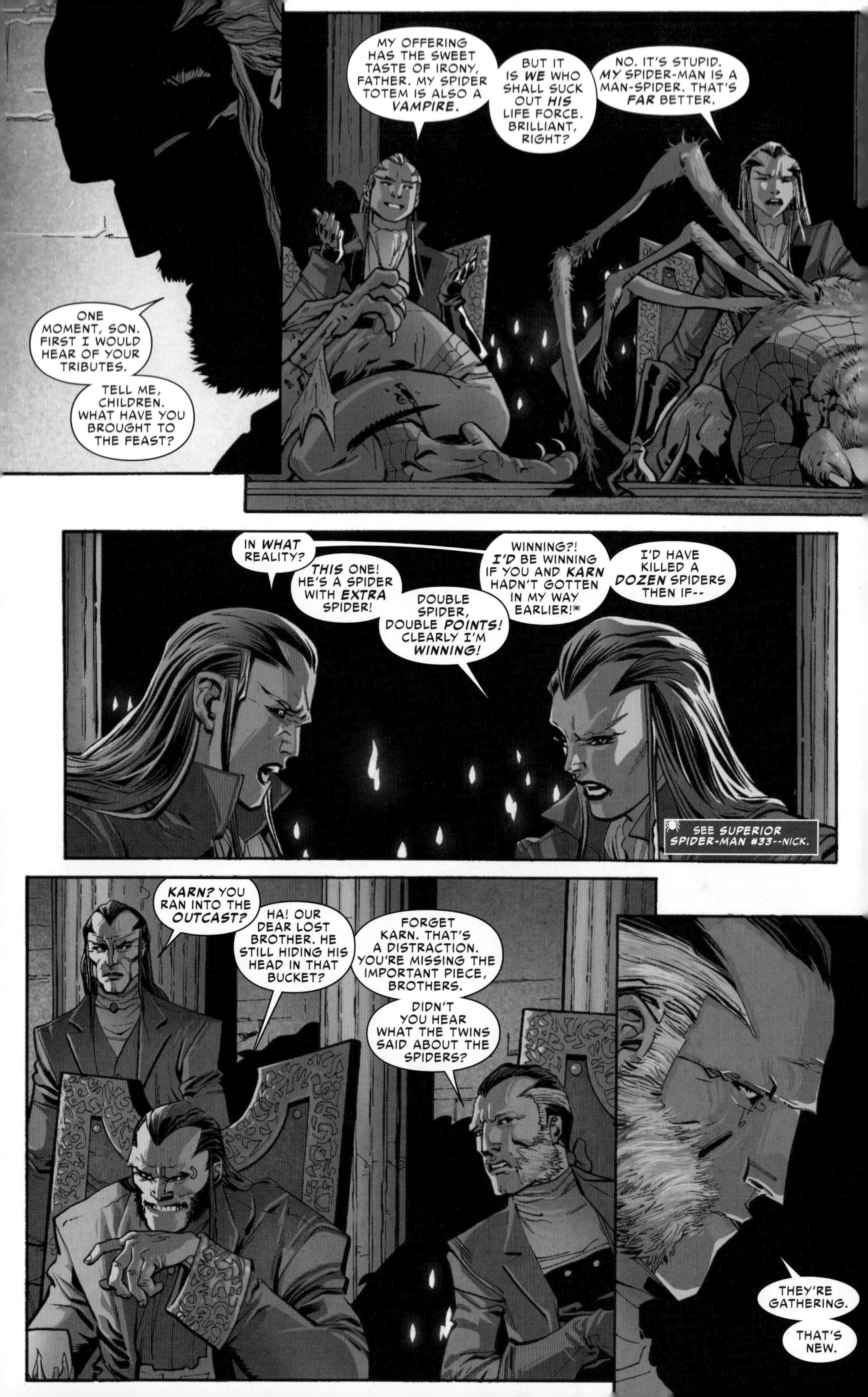
ONE MOMENT, SON. FIRST I WOULD HEAR OF YOUR TRIBUTES.
TELL ME, CHILDREN. WHAT HAVE YOU BROUGHT TO THE FEAST?
MY OFFERING HAS THE SWEET TASTE OF IRONY, FATHER. MY SPIDER TOTEM IS ALSO A VAMPIRE.
BUT IT IS WE WHO SHALL SUCK OUT HIS LIFE FORCE. BRILLIANT, RIGHT?
NO. IT'S STUPID. MY SPIDER-MAN IS A MAN-SPIDER. THAT'S FAR BETTER.
IN WHAT REALITY?
THIS ONE! HE'S A SPIDER WITH EXTRA SPIDER!
DOUBLE SPIDER, DOUBLE POINTS! CLEARLY I'M WINNING!
WINNING?! I'D BE WINNING IF YOU AND KARN HADN'T GOTTEN IN MY WAY EARLIER!
I'D HAVE KILLED A DOZEN SPIDERS THEN IF--
SEE SUPERIOR SPIDER-MAN #33--NICK.
KARN? YOU RAN INTO THE OUTCAST?
HA! OUR DEAR LOST BROTHER. HE STILL HIDING HIS HEAD IN THAT BUCKET?
FORGET KARN. THAT'S A DISTRACTION. YOU'RE MISSING THE IMPORTANT PIECE, BROTHERS.
DIDN'T YOU HEAR WHAT THE TWINS SAID ABOUT THE SPIDERS?
THEY'RE GATHERING.
THAT'S NEW.

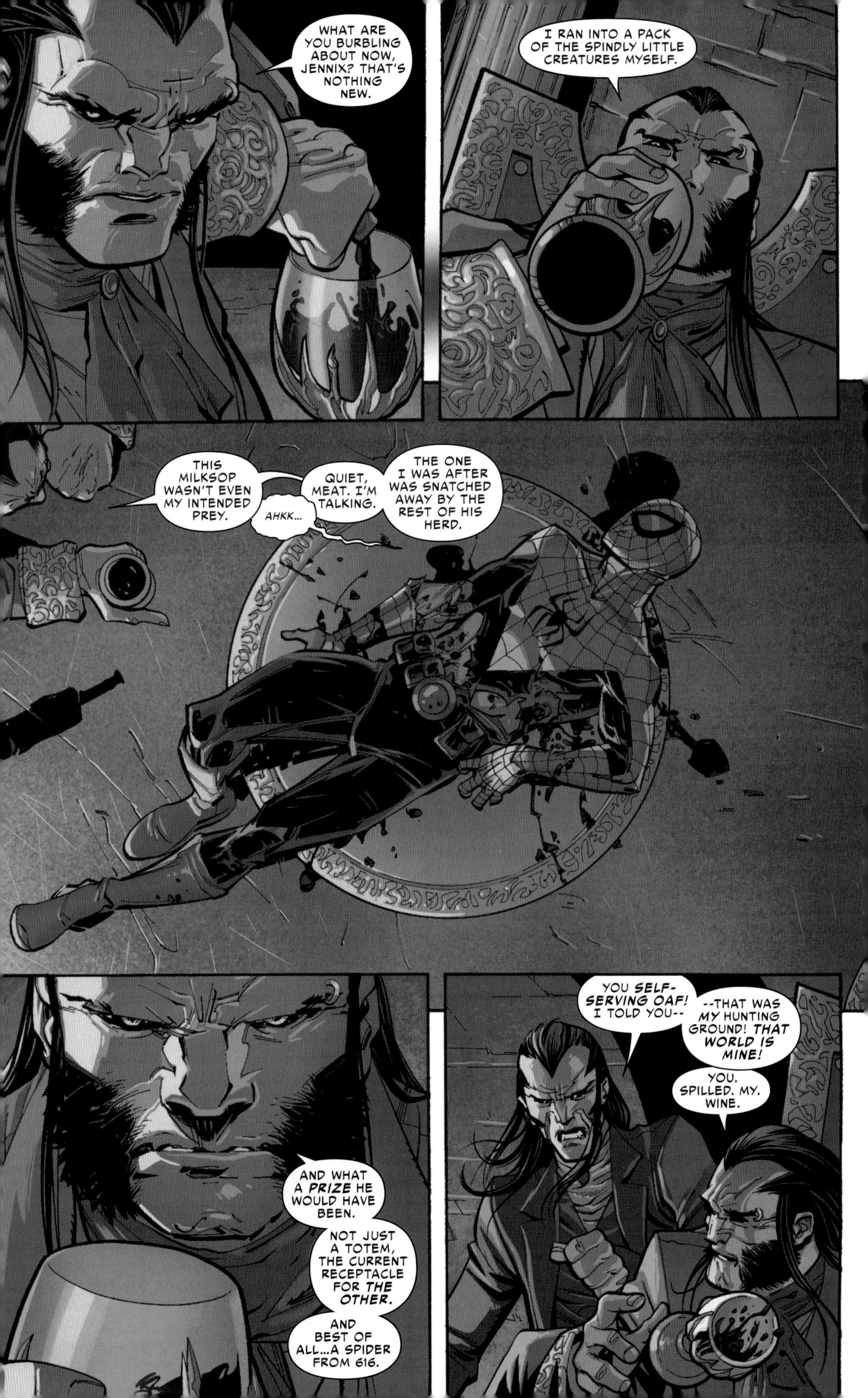

WHAT ARE YOU BURBLING ABOUT NOW, JENNIX? THAT'S NOTHING NEW.
I RAN INTO A PACK OF THE SPINDLY LITTLE CREATURES MYSELF.
THIS MILKSOP WASN'T EVEN MY INTENDED PREY.
AHKK...
QUIET, MEAT. I'M TALKING.
THE ONE I WAS AFTER WAS SNATCHED AWAY BY THE REST OF HIS HERD.
AND WHAT A PRIZE HE WOULD HAVE BEEN.
NOT JUST A TOTEM, THE CURRENT RECEPTACLE FOR THE OTHER.
AND BEST OF ALL...A SPIDER FROM 616.
YOU SELF-SERVING OAF! I TOLD YOU--
--THAT WAS MY HUNTING GROUND! THAT WORLD IS MINE!
YOU. SPILLED. MY. WINE.

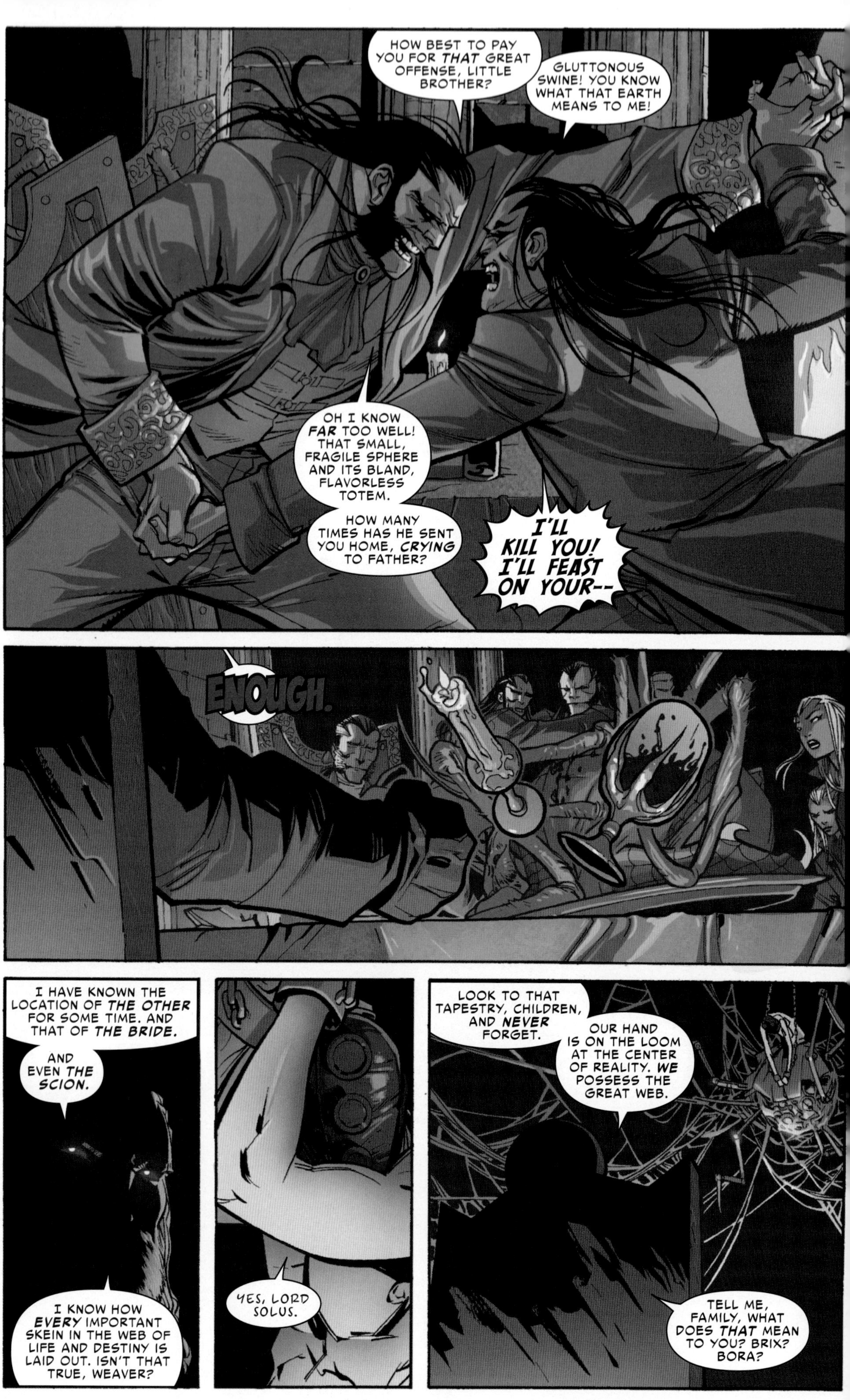
HOW BEST TO PAY YOU FOR THAT GREAT OFFENSE, LITTLE BROTHER?
GLUTTONOUS SWINE! YOU KNOW WHAT THAT EARTH MEANS TO ME!
OH I KNOW FAR TOO WELL! THAT SMALL, FRAGILE SPHERE AND ITS BLAND, FLAVORLESS TOTEM.
HOW MANY TIMES HAS HE SENT YOU HOME, CRYING TO FATHER?
I'LL KILL YOU! I'LL FEAST ON YOUR--
ENOUGH.
I HAVE KNOWN THE LOCATION OF THE OTHER FOR SOME TIME. AND THAT OF THE BRIDE.
AND EVEN THE SCION.
I KNOW HOW EVERY IMPORTANT SKEIN IN THE WEB OF LIFE AND DESTINY IS LAID OUT. ISN'T THAT TRUE, WEAVER?
YES, LORD SOLUS.
LOOK TO THAT TAPESTRY, CHILDREN, AND NEVER FORGET.
OUR HAND IS ON THE LOOM AT THE CENTER OF REALITY. WE POSSESS THE GREAT WEB.
TELL ME, FAMILY, WHAT DOES THAT MEAN TO YOU? BRIX? BORA?

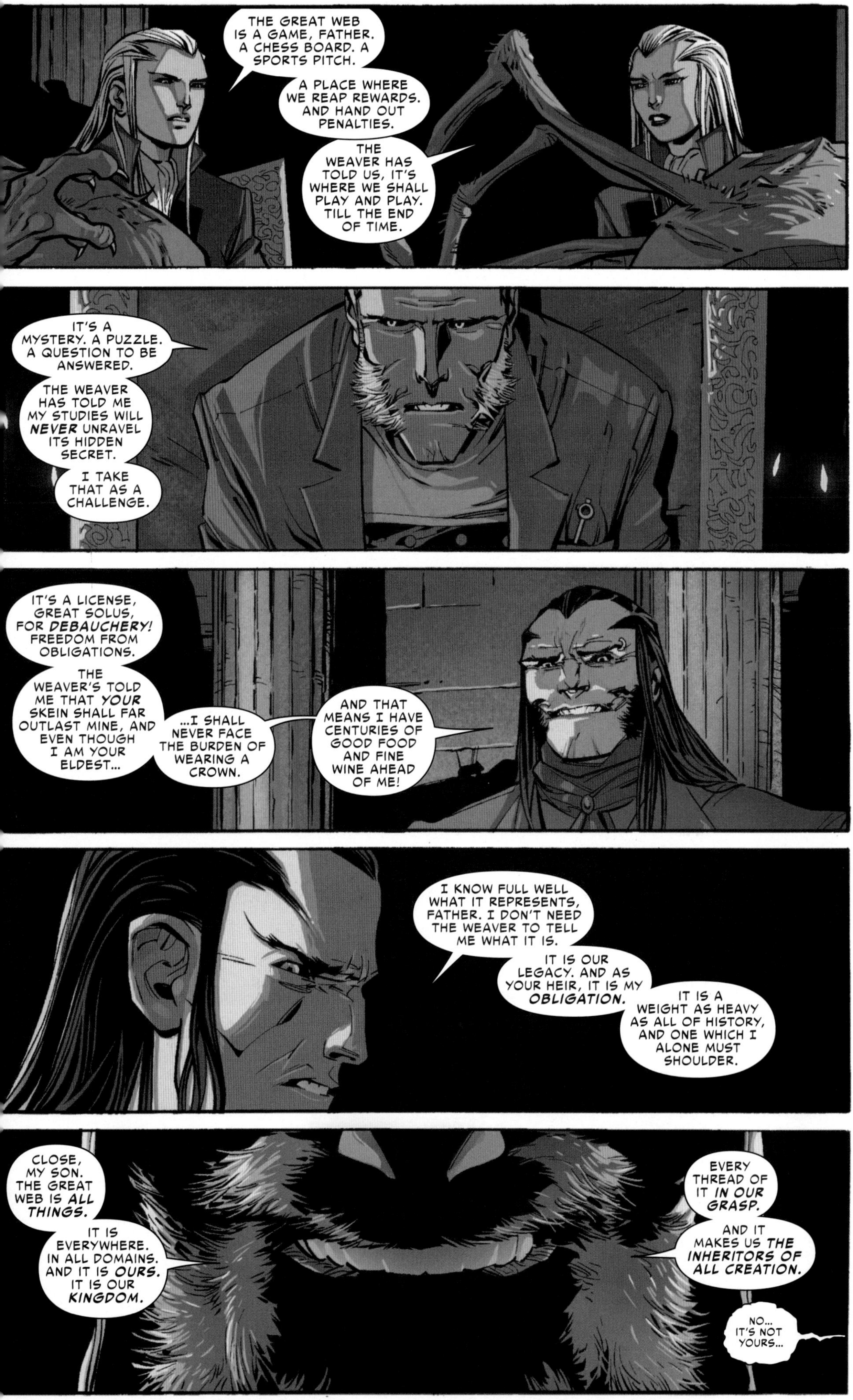
THE GREAT WEB IS A GAME, FATHER. A CHESS BOARD. A SPORTS PITCH.
A PLACE WHERE WE REAP REWARDS. AND HAND OUT PENALTIES.
THE WEAVER HAS TOLD US, IT'S WHERE WE SHALL PLAY AND PLAY. TILL THE END OF TIME.
IT'S A MYSTERY. A PUZZLE. A QUESTION TO BE ANSWERED.
THE WEAVER HAS TOLD ME MY STUDIES WILL NEVER UNRAVEL ITS HIDDEN SECRET.
I TAKE THAT AS A CHALLENGE.
IT'S A LICENSE, GREAT SOLUS, FOR DEBAUCHERY! FREEDOM FROM OBLIGATIONS.
THE WEAVER'S TOLD ME THAT YOUR SKEIN SHALL FAR OUTLAST MINE, AND EVEN THOUGH I AM YOUR ELDEST...
...I SHALL NEVER FACE THE BURDEN OF WEARING A CROWN.
AND THAT MEANS I HAVE CENTURIES OF GOOD FOOD AND FINE WINE AHEAD OF ME!
I KNOW FULL WELL WHAT IT REPRESENTS, FATHER. I DON'T NEED THE WEAVER TO TELL ME WHAT IT IS.
IT IS OUR LEGACY. AND AS YOUR HEIR, IT IS MY OBLIGATION.
IT IS A WEIGHT AS HEAVY AS ALL OF HISTORY, AND ONE WHICH I ALONE MUST SHOULDER.
CLOSE, MY SON. THE GREAT WEB IS ALL THINGS.
IT IS EVERYWHERE. IN ALL DOMAINS. AND IT IS OURS. IT IS OUR KINGDOM.
EVERY THREAD OF IT IN OUR GRASP.
AND IT MAKES US THE INHERITORS OF ALL CREATION.
NO... IT'S NOT YOURS...

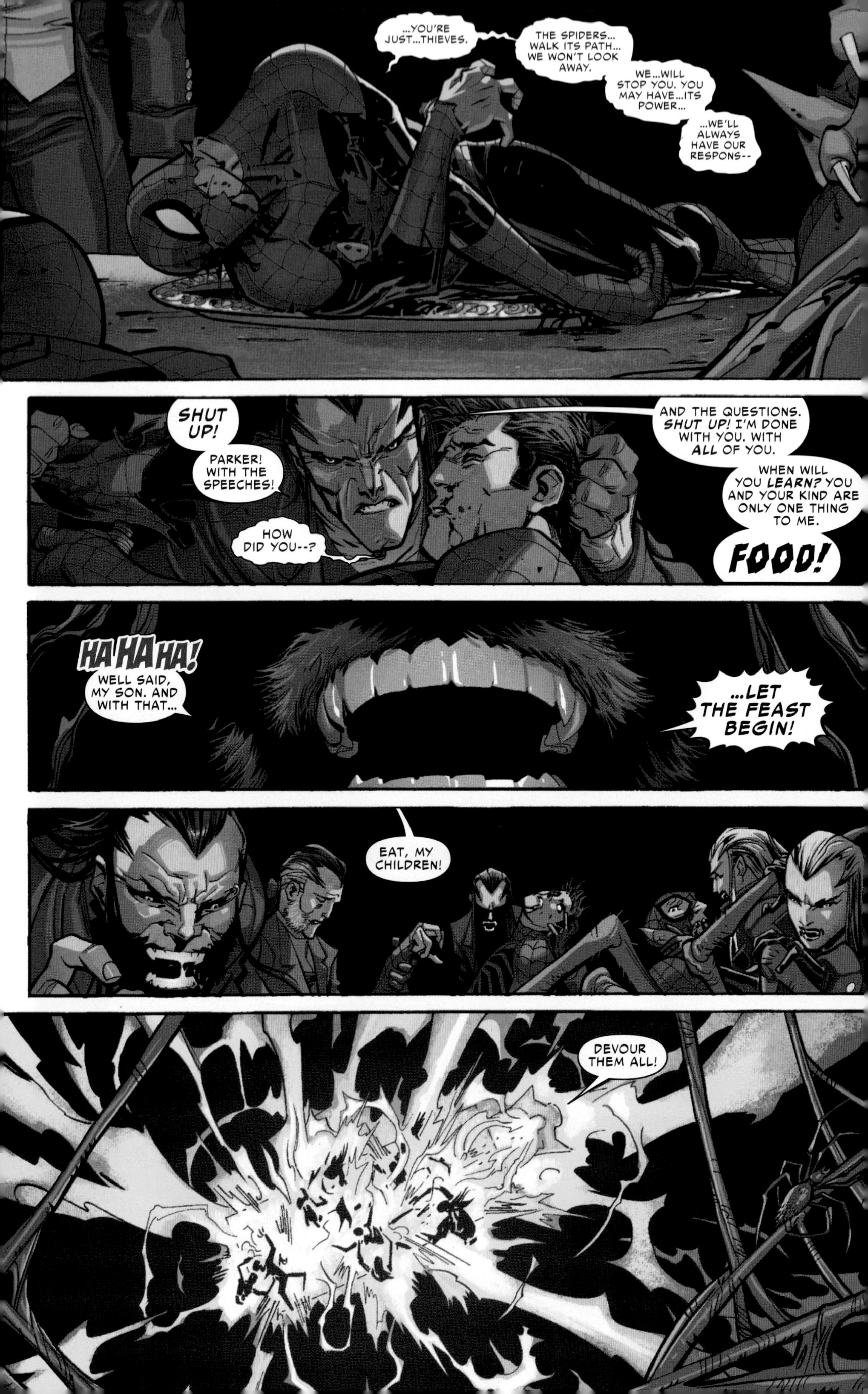
...YOU'RE JUST...THIEVES.
THE SPIDERS... WALK ITS PATH... WE WON'T LOOK AWAY.
WE...WILL STOP YOU. YOU MAY HAVE...ITS POWER...
...WE'LL ALWAYS HAVE OUR RESPONS--
SHUT UP!
PARKER! WITH THE SPEECHES!
HOW DID YOU--?
AND THE QUESTIONS. SHUT UP! I'M DONE WITH YOU. WITH ALL OF YOU.
WHEN WILL YOU LEARN? YOU AND YOUR KIND ARE ONLY ONE THING TO ME.
FOOD!
HA HA HA!
WELL SAID, MY SON. AND WITH THAT...
...LET THE FEAST BEGIN!
EAT, MY CHILDREN!
DEVOUR THEM ALL!

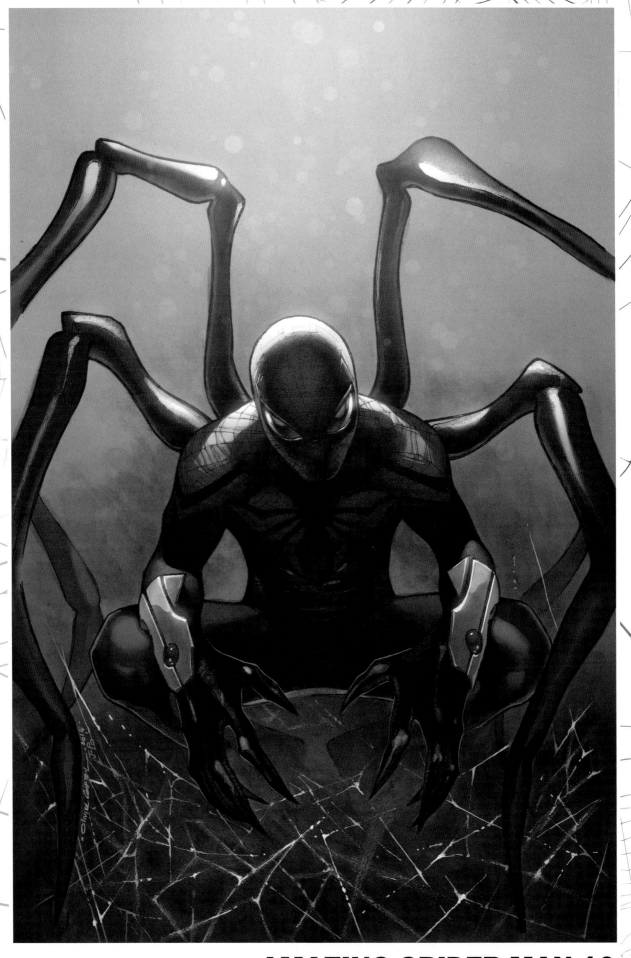

AMAZING SPIDER-MAN 10
SPIDER-VERSE, PART TWO: SUPERIOR FORCE

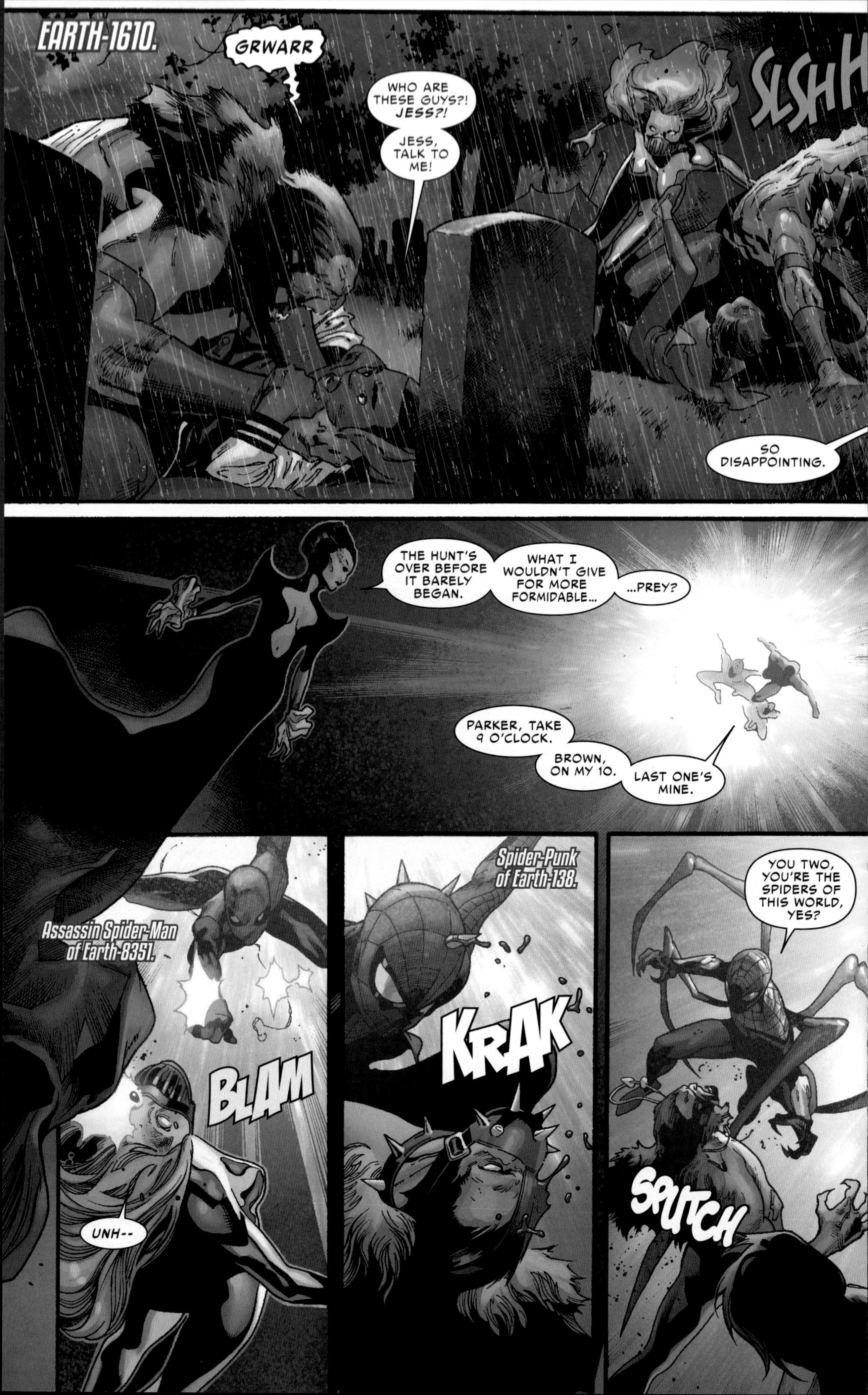
EARTH-1610.
GRWARR
WHO ARE THESE GUYS?! JESS?!
JESS, TALK TO ME!
SLSHH
SO DISAPPOINTING.
THE HUNT'S OVER BEFORE IT BARELY BEGAN.
WHAT I WOULDN'T GIVE FOR MORE FORMIDABLE...
...PREY?
PARKER, TAKE 9 O'CLOCK.
BROWN, ON MY 10.
LAST ONE'S MINE.
Assassin Spider-Man of Earth-8351.
BLAM
UNH--
Spider-Punk of Earth-138.
KRAK
YOU TWO, YOU'RE THE SPIDERS OF THIS WORLD, YES?
SPLUTCH

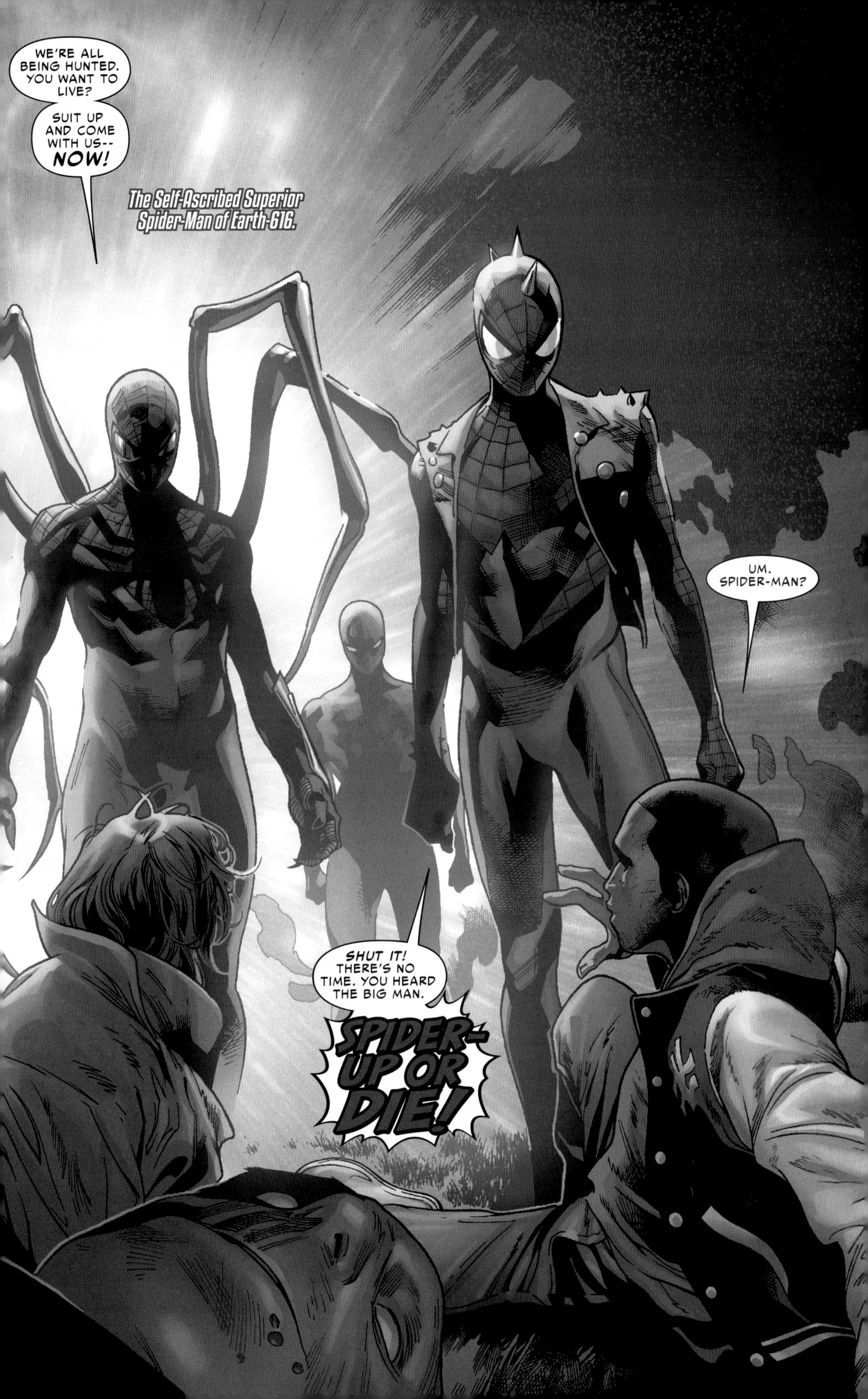
WE'RE ALL BEING HUNTED. YOU WANT TO LIVE?
SUIT UP AND COME WITH US-- NOW!
The Self-Ascribed Superior Spider-Man of Earth-616.
UM. SPIDER-MAN?
SHUT IT! THERE'S NO TIME. YOU HEARD THE BIG MAN.
SPIDER-UP OR DIE!

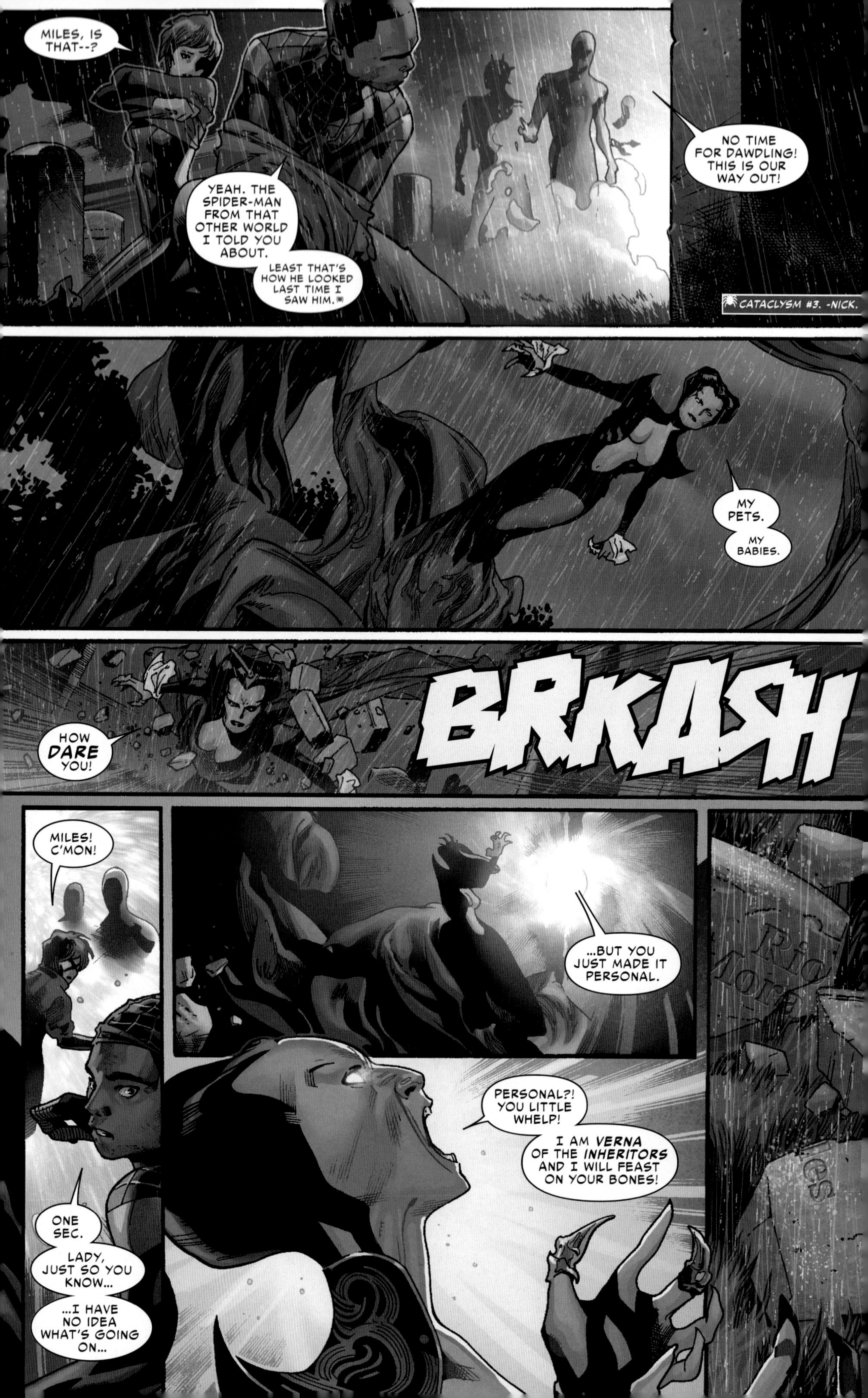
MILES, IS THAT--?
YEAH. THE SPIDER-MAN FROM THAT OTHER WORLD I TOLD YOU ABOUT.
LEAST THAT'S HOW HE LOOKED LAST TIME I SAW HIM.
NO TIME FOR DAWDLING! THIS IS OUR WAY OUT!
CATACLYSM #3. -NICK.
MY PETS.
MY BABIES.
HOW DARE YOU!
BRKASH
MILES! C'MON!
...BUT YOU JUST MADE IT PERSONAL.
PERSONAL?! YOU LITTLE WHELP!
I AM VERNA OF THE INHERITORS AND I WILL FEAST ON YOUR BONES!
ONE SEC.
LADY, JUST SO YOU KNOW...
...I HAVE NO IDEA WHAT'S GOING ON...

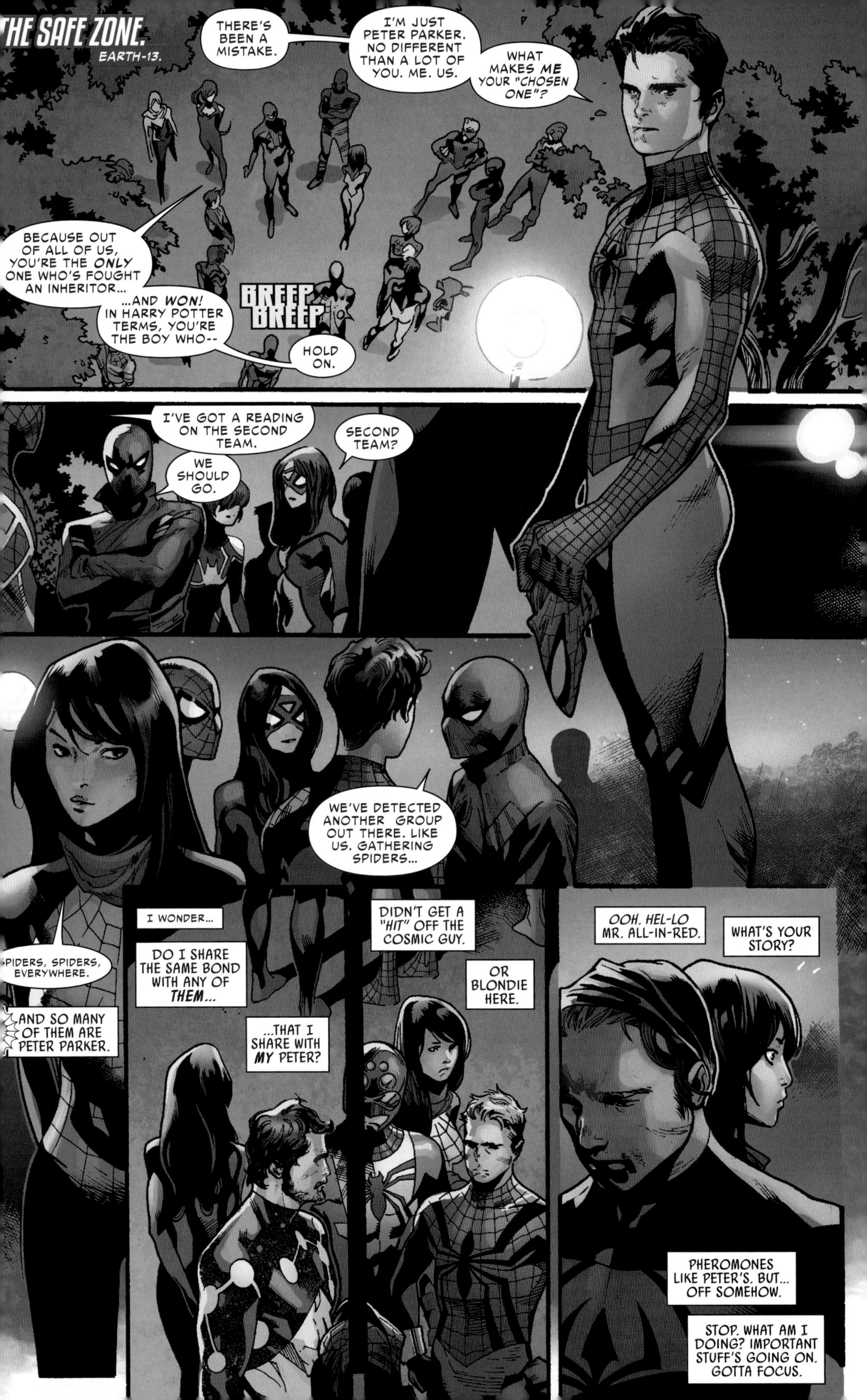
THE SAFE ZONE.
EARTH-13.
THERE'S BEEN A MISTAKE.
I'M JUST PETER PARKER. NO DIFFERENT THAN A LOT OF YOU. ME. US.
WHAT MAKES ME YOUR "CHOSEN ONE"?
BECAUSE OUT OF ALL OF US, YOU'RE THE ONLY ONE WHO'S FOUGHT AN INHERITOR...
...AND WON! IN HARRY POTTER TERMS, YOU'RE THE BOY WHO--
BREEP BREEP
HOLD ON.
I'VE GOT A READING ON THE SECOND TEAM.
WE SHOULD GO.
SECOND TEAM?
WE'VE DETECTED ANOTHER GROUP OUT THERE. LIKE US. GATHERING SPIDERS...
SPIDERS, SPIDERS, EVERYWHERE.
AND SO MANY OF THEM ARE PETER PARKER.
I WONDER...
DO I SHARE THE SAME BOND WITH ANY OF THEM...
...THAT I SHARE WITH MY PETER?
DIDN'T GET A "HIT" OFF THE COSMIC GUY.
OR BLONDIE HERE.
OOH. HEL-LO MR. ALL-IN-RED.
WHAT'S YOUR STORY?
PHEROMONES LIKE PETER'S. BUT... OFF SOMEHOW.
STOP. WHAT AM I DOING? IMPORTANT STUFF'S GOING ON. GOTTA FOCUS.

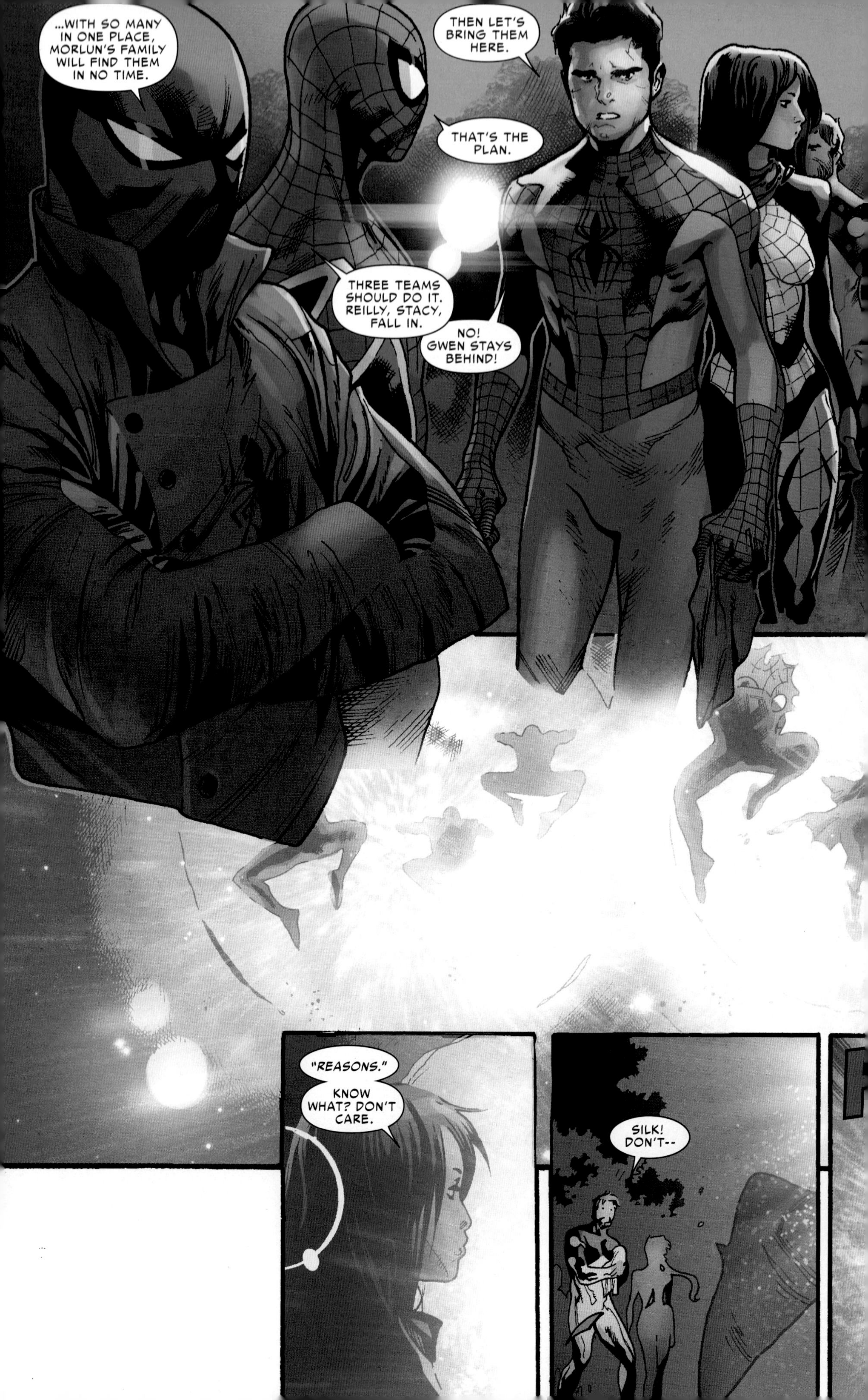
...WITH SO MANY IN ONE PLACE, MORLUN'S FAMILY WILL FIND THEM IN NO TIME.
THEN LET'S BRING THEM HERE.
THAT'S THE PLAN.
THREE TEAMS SHOULD DO IT. REILLY, STACY, FALL IN.
NO! GWEN STAYS BEHIND!
"REASONS."
KNOW WHAT? DON'T CARE.
SILK! DON'T--

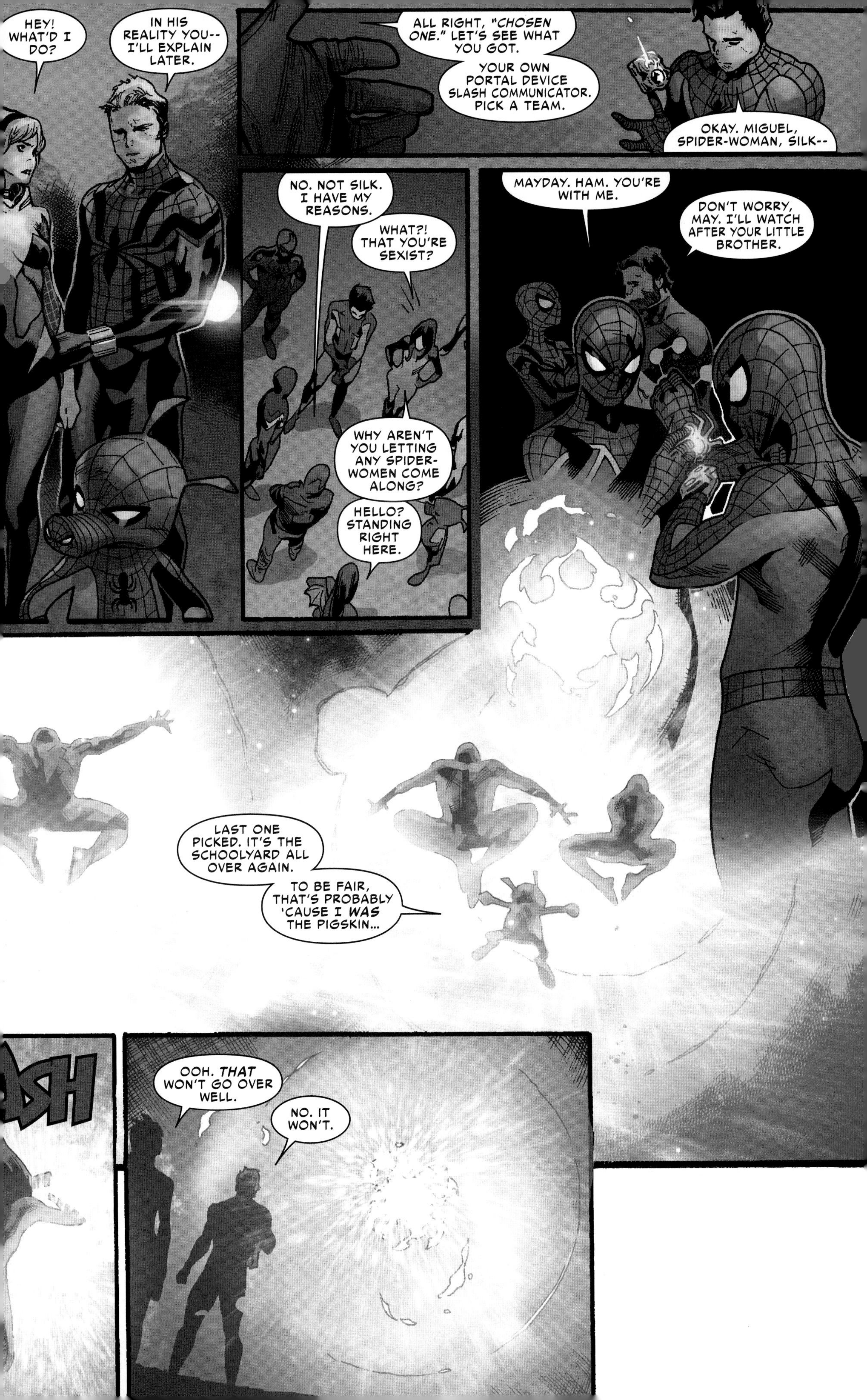
HEY! WHAT'D I DO?
IN HIS REALITY YOU-- I'LL EXPLAIN LATER.
ALL RIGHT, "CHOSEN ONE." LET'S SEE WHAT YOU GOT.
YOUR OWN PORTAL DEVICE SLASH COMMUNICATOR. PICK A TEAM.
OKAY. MIGUEL, SPIDER-WOMAN, SILK--
NO. NOT SILK. I HAVE MY REASONS.
WHAT?! THAT YOU'RE SEXIST?
WHY AREN'T YOU LETTING ANY SPIDER-WOMEN COME ALONG?
HELLO? STANDING RIGHT HERE.
MAYDAY. HAM. YOU'RE WITH ME.
DON'T WORRY, MAY. I'LL WATCH AFTER YOUR LITTLE BROTHER.
LAST ONE PICKED. IT'S THE SCHOOLYARD ALL OVER AGAIN.
TO BE FAIR, THAT'S PROBABLY 'CAUSE I *WAS* THE PIGSKIN...
OOH. *THAT* WON'T GO OVER WELL.
NO. IT WON'T.

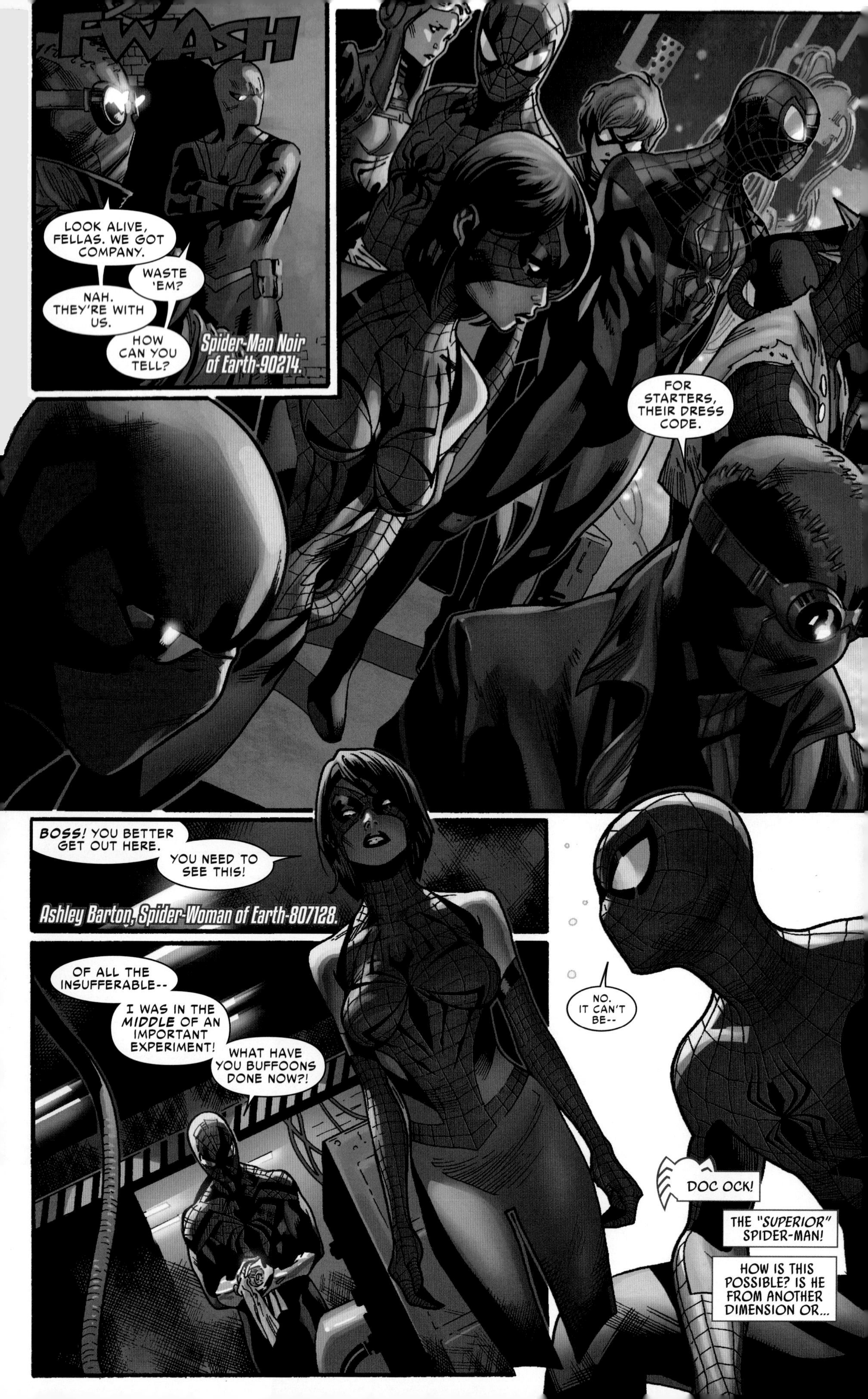
FWASH
LOOK ALIVE, FELLAS. WE GOT COMPANY.
WASTE 'EM?
NAH. THEY'RE WITH US.
HOW CAN YOU TELL?
Spider-Man Noir of Earth-90214.
FOR STARTERS, THEIR DRESS CODE.
BOSS! YOU BETTER GET OUT HERE.
YOU NEED TO SEE THIS!
Ashley Barton, Spider-Woman of Earth-807128.
OF ALL THE INSUFFERABLE--
I WAS IN THE MIDDLE OF AN IMPORTANT EXPERIMENT!
WHAT HAVE YOU BUFFOONS DONE NOW?!
NO. IT CAN'T BE--
DOC OCK!
THE "SUPERIOR" SPIDER-MAN!
HOW IS THIS POSSIBLE? IS HE FROM ANOTHER DIMENSION OR...

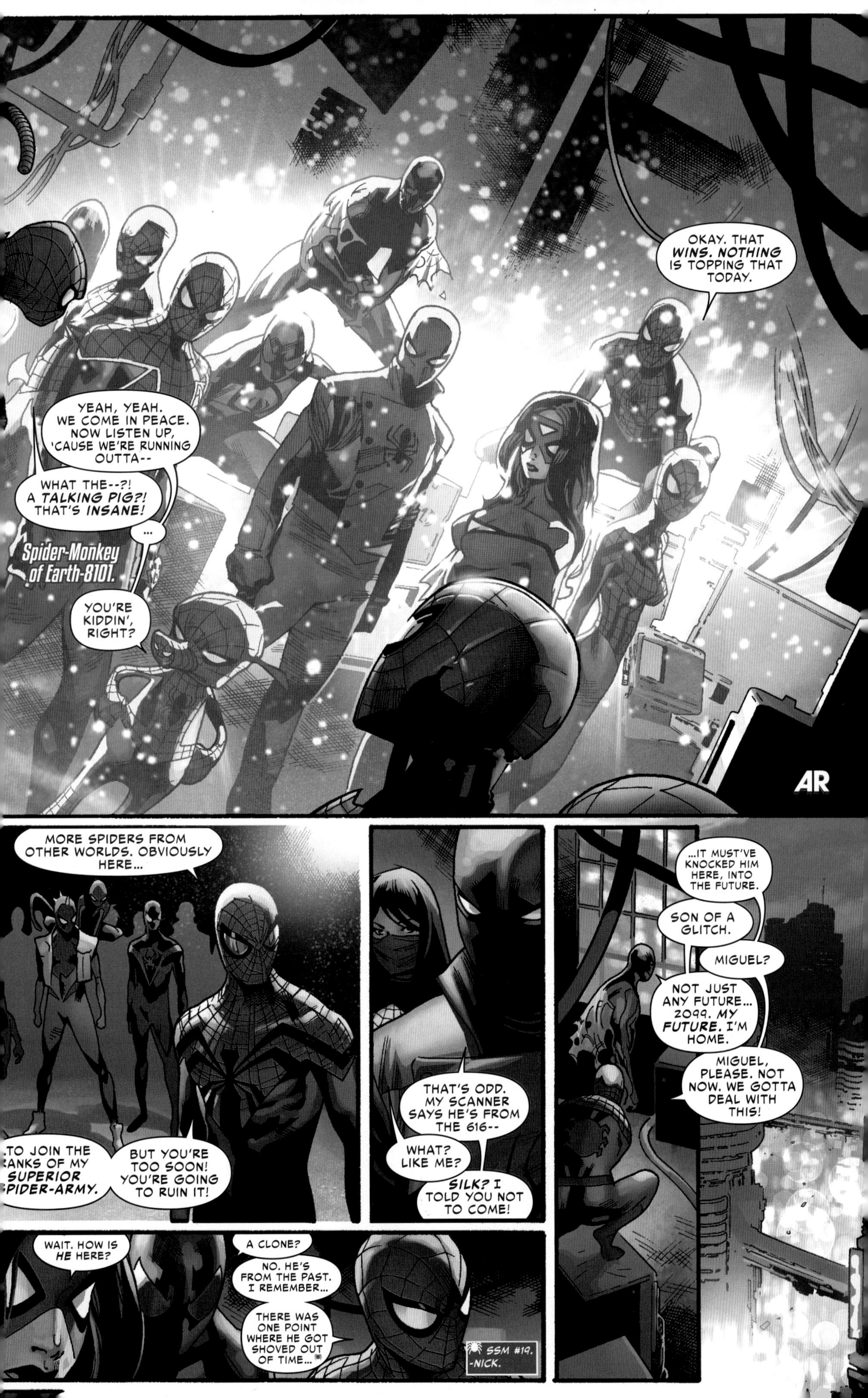
OKAY. THAT WINS. NOTHING IS TOPPING THAT TODAY.
YEAH, YEAH. WE COME IN PEACE. NOW LISTEN UP, 'CAUSE WE'RE RUNNING OUTTA--
WHAT THE--?! A TALKING PIG?! THAT'S INSANE!
...
Spider-Monkey of Earth-8101.
YOU'RE KIDDIN', RIGHT?
AR
MORE SPIDERS FROM OTHER WORLDS. OBVIOUSLY HERE...
...TO JOIN THE RANKS OF MY SUPERIOR SPIDER-ARMY.
BUT YOU'RE TOO SOON! YOU'RE GOING TO RUIN IT!
THAT'S ODD. MY SCANNER SAYS HE'S FROM THE 616--
WHAT? LIKE ME?
SILK? I TOLD YOU NOT TO COME!
...IT MUST'VE KNOCKED HIM HERE, INTO THE FUTURE.
SON OF A GLITCH.
MIGUEL?
NOT JUST ANY FUTURE... 2099. MY FUTURE. I'M HOME.
MIGUEL, PLEASE. NOT NOW. WE GOTTA DEAL WITH THIS!
WAIT. HOW IS HE HERE?
A CLONE?
NO. HE'S FROM THE PAST. I REMEMBER...
THERE WAS ONE POINT WHERE HE GOT SHOVED OUT OF TIME...
SSM #19. -NICK.

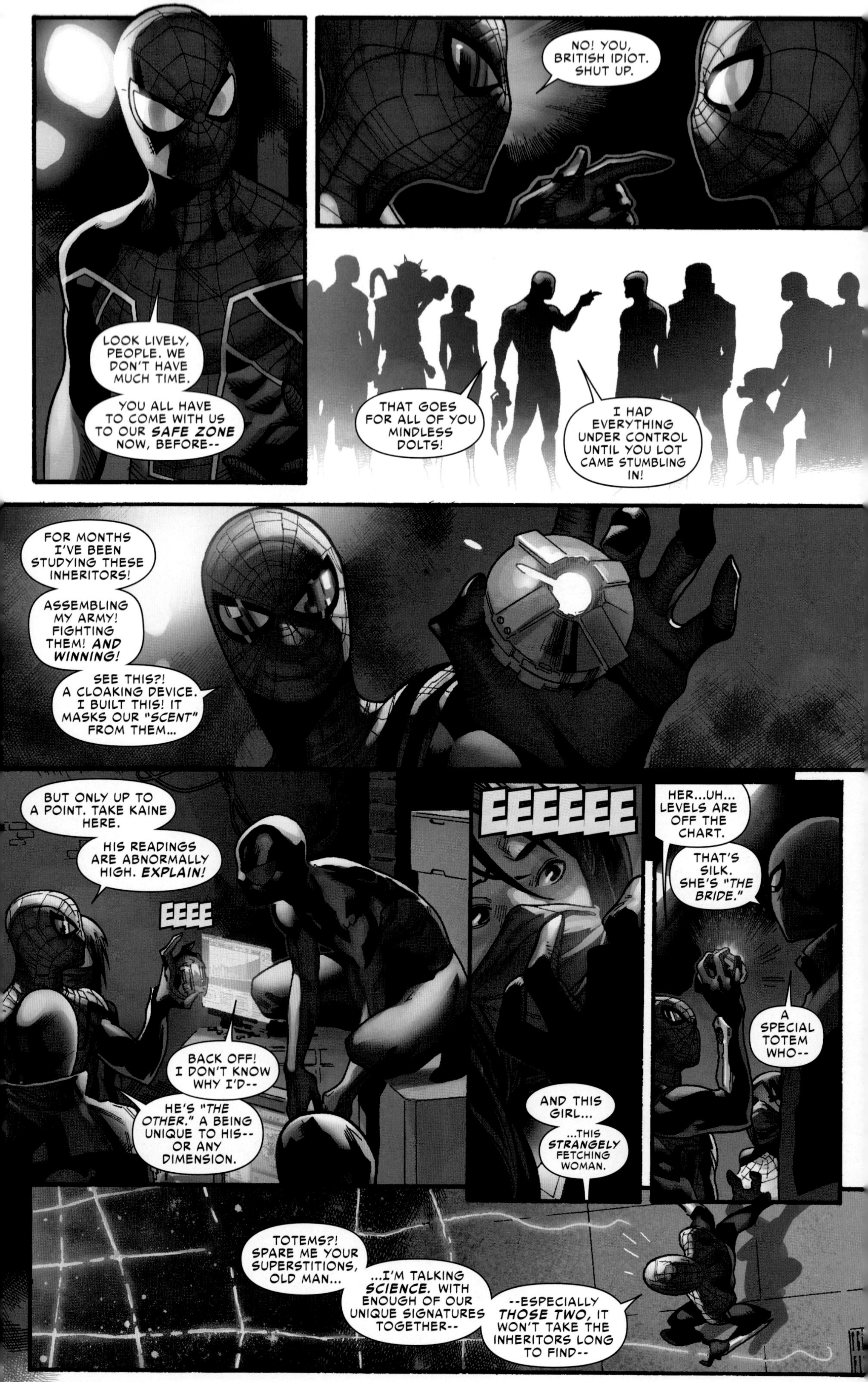

LOOK LIVELY, PEOPLE. WE DON'T HAVE MUCH TIME.
YOU ALL HAVE TO COME WITH US TO OUR SAFE ZONE NOW, BEFORE--
NO! YOU, BRITISH IDIOT. SHUT UP.
THAT GOES FOR ALL OF YOU MINDLESS DOLTS!
I HAD EVERYTHING UNDER CONTROL UNTIL YOU LOT CAME STUMBLING IN!
FOR MONTHS I'VE BEEN STUDYING THESE INHERITORS!
ASSEMBLING MY ARMY! FIGHTING THEM! AND WINNING!
SEE THIS?! A CLOAKING DEVICE. I BUILT THIS! IT MASKS OUR "SCENT" FROM THEM...
BUT ONLY UP TO A POINT. TAKE KAINE HERE.
HIS READINGS ARE ABNORMALLY HIGH. EXPLAIN!
EEEE
BACK OFF! I DON'T KNOW WHY I'D--
HE'S "THE OTHER." A BEING UNIQUE TO HIS-- OR ANY DIMENSION.
EEEEEE
AND THIS GIRL...
...THIS STRANGELY FETCHING WOMAN.
HER...UH... LEVELS ARE OFF THE CHART.
THAT'S SILK. SHE'S "THE BRIDE."
A SPECIAL TOTEM WHO--
TOTEMS?! SPARE ME YOUR SUPERSTITIONS, OLD MAN...
...I'M TALKING SCIENCE. WITH ENOUGH OF OUR UNIQUE SIGNATURES TOGETHER--
--ESPECIALLY THOSE TWO, IT WON'T TAKE THE INHERITORS LONG TO FIND--

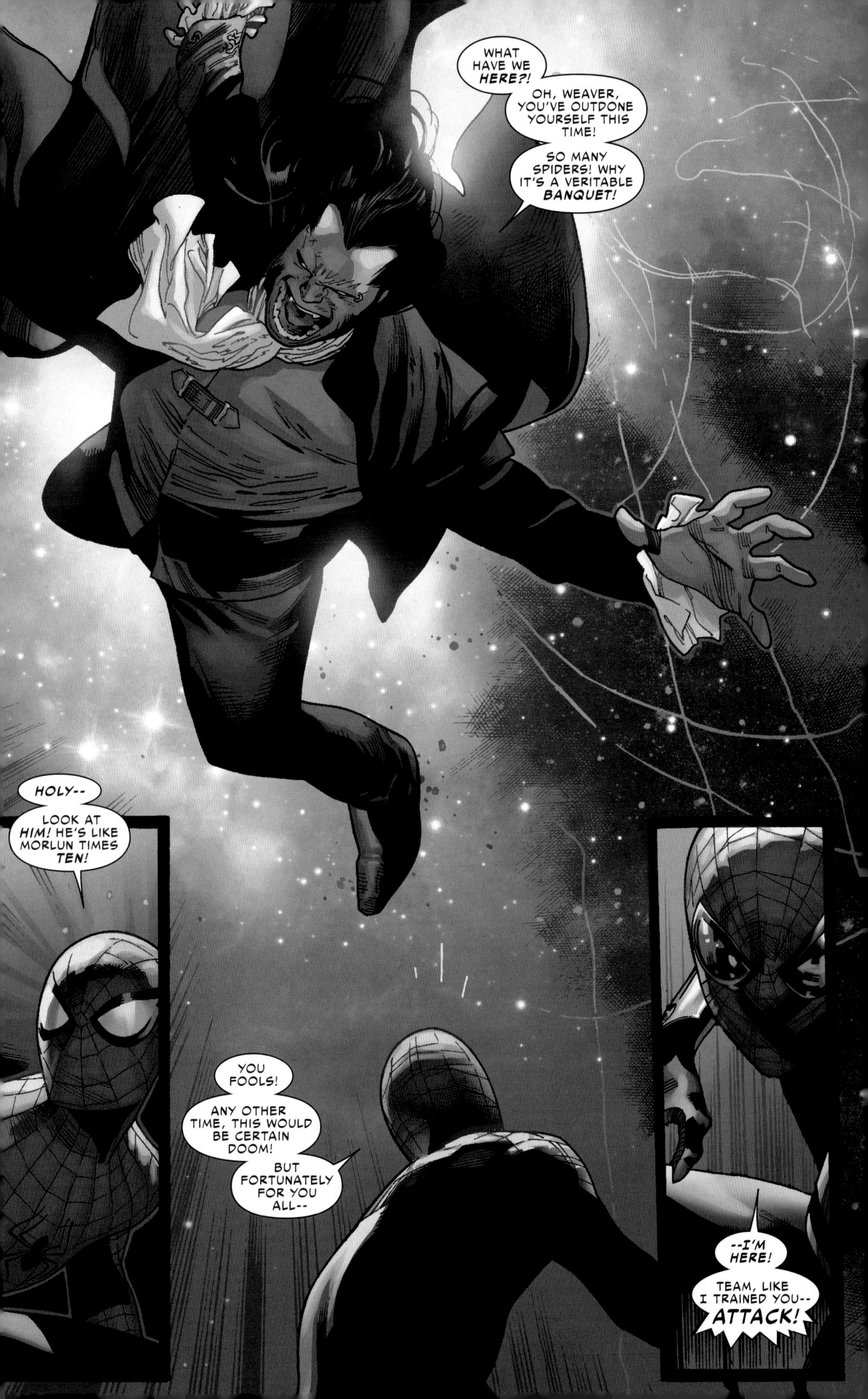
WHAT HAVE WE HERE?!
OH, WEAVER, YOU'VE OUTDONE YOURSELF THIS TIME!
SO MANY SPIDERS! WHY IT'S A VERITABLE BANQUET!
HOLY--
LOOK AT HIM! HE'S LIKE MORLUN TIMES TEN!
YOU FOOLS!
ANY OTHER TIME, THIS WOULD BE CERTAIN DOOM!
BUT FORTUNATELY FOR YOU ALL--
--I'M HERE!
TEAM, LIKE I TRAINED YOU-- ATTACK!

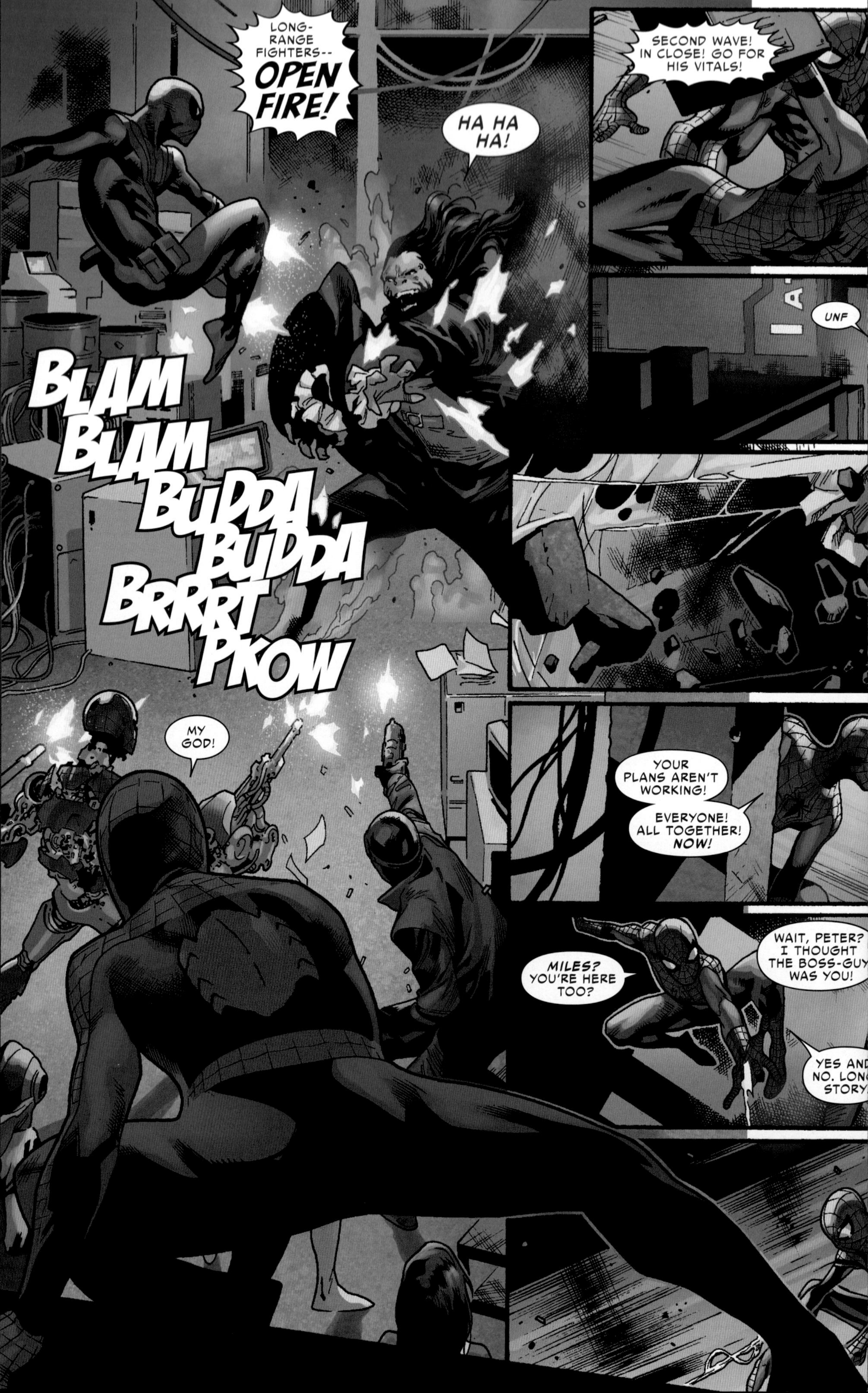
LONG-RANGE FIGHTERS-- OPEN FIRE!
HA HA HA!
BLAM BLAM BUDDA BUDDA BRRRT PKOW
MY GOD!
SECOND WAVE! IN CLOSE! GO FOR HIS VITALS!
UNF
YOUR PLANS AREN'T WORKING!
EVERYONE! ALL TOGETHER! NOW!
MILES? YOU'RE HERE TOO?
WAIT, PETER? I THOUGHT THE BOSS-GUY WAS YOU!
YES AND NO. LONG STORY

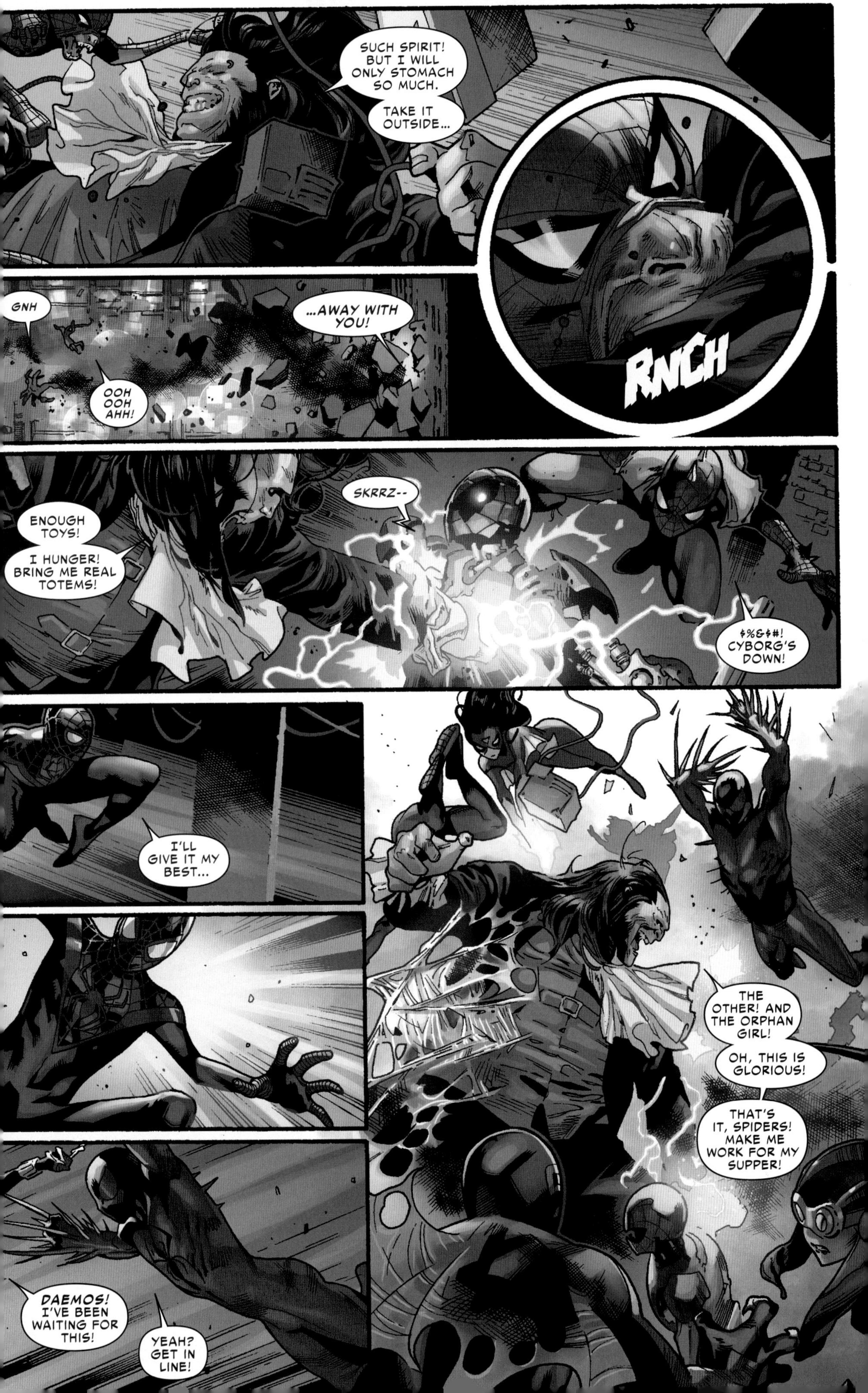
SUCH SPIRIT! BUT I WILL ONLY STOMACH SO MUCH.
TAKE IT OUTSIDE...
RNCH
GNH
...AWAY WITH YOU!
OOH OOH AHH!
ENOUGH TOYS!
I HUNGER! BRING ME REAL TOTEMS!
SKRRZ--
$%&$#! CYBORG'S DOWN!
I'LL GIVE IT MY BEST...
THE OTHER! AND THE ORPHAN GIRL!
OH, THIS IS GLORIOUS!
THAT'S IT, SPIDERS! MAKE ME WORK FOR MY SUPPER!
DAEMOS! I'VE BEEN WAITING FOR THIS!
YEAH? GET IN LINE!

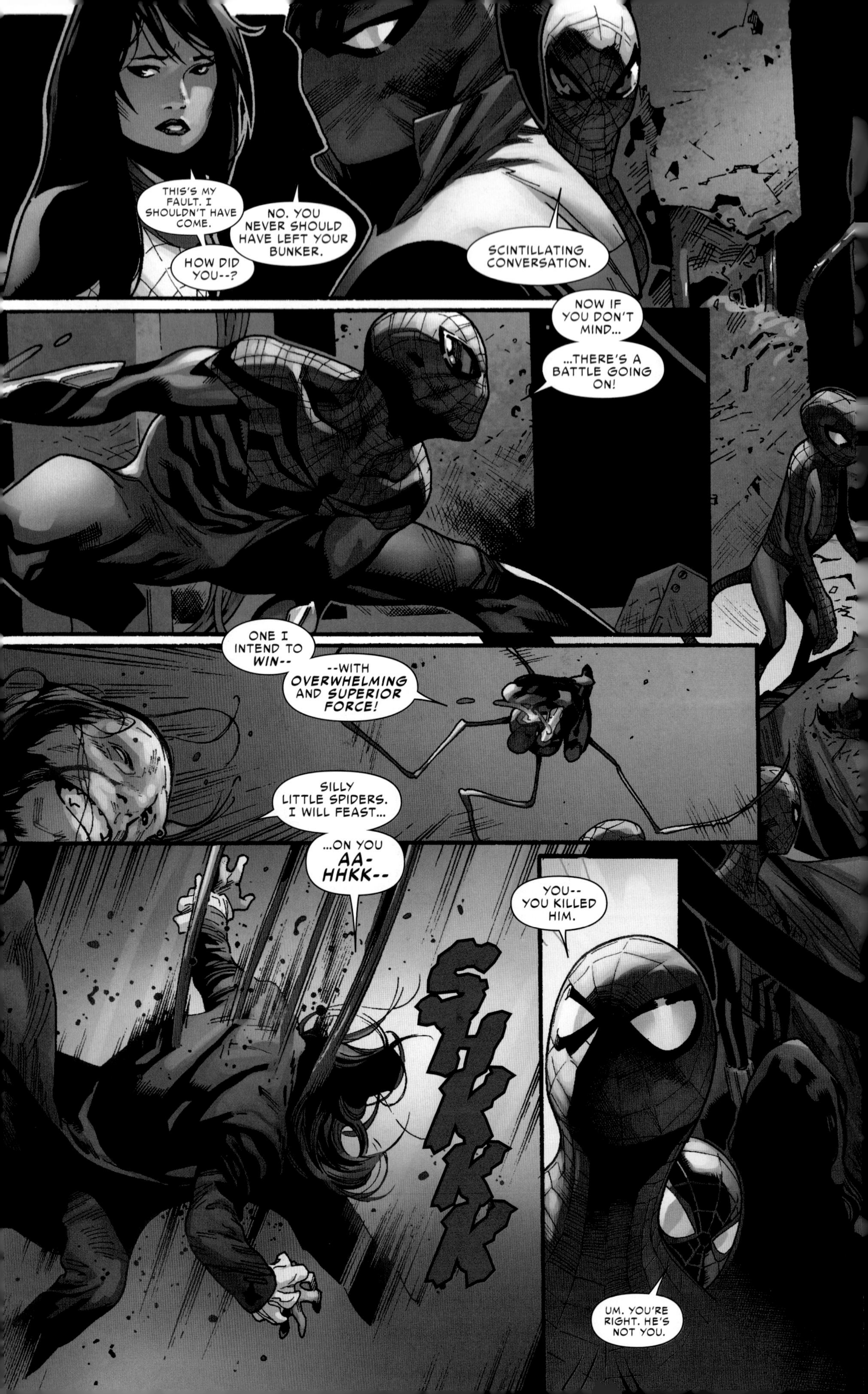
THIS'S MY FAULT. I SHOULDN'T HAVE COME.
NO. YOU NEVER SHOULD HAVE LEFT YOUR BUNKER.
HOW DID YOU--?
SCINTILLATING CONVERSATION.
NOW IF YOU DON'T MIND...
...THERE'S A BATTLE GOING ON!
ONE I INTEND TO WIN--
--WITH OVERWHELMING AND SUPERIOR FORCE!
SILLY LITTLE SPIDERS. I WILL FEAST...
...ON YOU AA-HHKK--
SHKK
YOU-- YOU KILLED HIM.
UM. YOU'RE RIGHT. HE'S NOT YOU.

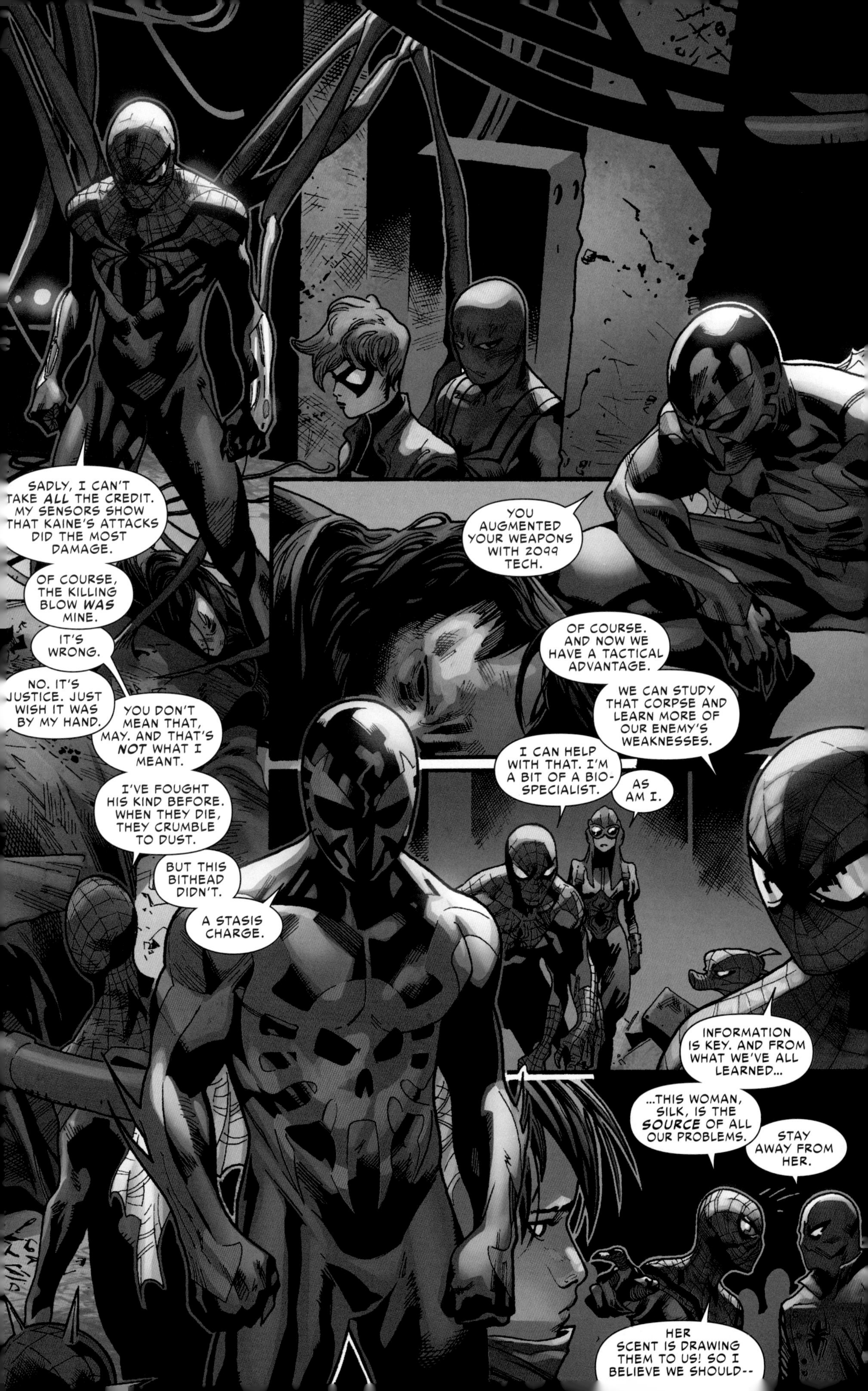
SADLY, I CAN'T TAKE ALL THE CREDIT. MY SENSORS SHOW THAT KAINE'S ATTACKS DID THE MOST DAMAGE.
OF COURSE, THE KILLING BLOW WAS MINE.
YOU AUGMENTED YOUR WEAPONS WITH 2099 TECH.
OF COURSE. AND NOW WE HAVE A TACTICAL ADVANTAGE.
WE CAN STUDY THAT CORPSE AND LEARN MORE OF OUR ENEMY'S WEAKNESSES.
IT'S WRONG.
NO. IT'S JUSTICE. JUST WISH IT WAS BY MY HAND.
YOU DON'T MEAN THAT, MAY. AND THAT'S NOT WHAT I MEANT.
I CAN HELP WITH THAT. I'M A BIT OF A BIO-SPECIALIST.
AS AM I.
I'VE FOUGHT HIS KIND BEFORE. WHEN THEY DIE, THEY CRUMBLE TO DUST.
BUT THIS BITHEAD DIDN'T.
A STASIS CHARGE.
INFORMATION IS KEY. AND FROM WHAT WE'VE ALL LEARNED...
...THIS WOMAN, SILK, IS THE SOURCE OF ALL OUR PROBLEMS.
STAY AWAY FROM HER.
HER SCENT IS DRAWING THEM TO US! SO I BELIEVE WE SHOULD--

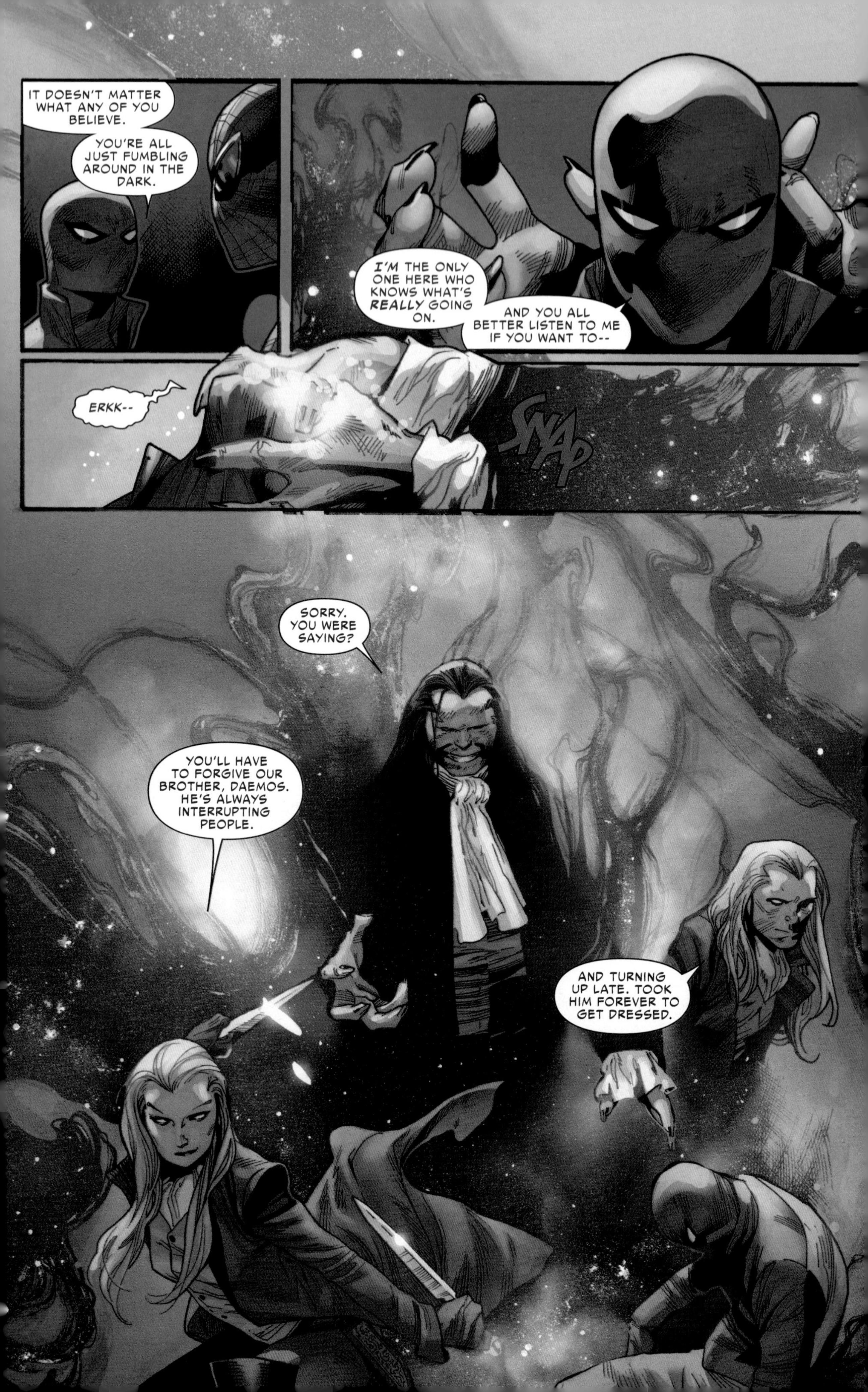
IT DOESN'T MATTER WHAT ANY OF YOU BELIEVE.
YOU'RE ALL JUST FUMBLING AROUND IN THE DARK.
I'M THE ONLY ONE HERE WHO KNOWS WHAT'S REALLY GOING ON.
AND YOU ALL BETTER LISTEN TO ME IF YOU WANT TO--
ERKK--
SNAP
SORRY. YOU WERE SAYING?
YOU'LL HAVE TO FORGIVE OUR BROTHER, DAEMOS. HE'S ALWAYS INTERRUPTING PEOPLE.
AND TURNING UP LATE. TOOK HIM FOREVER TO GET DRESSED.

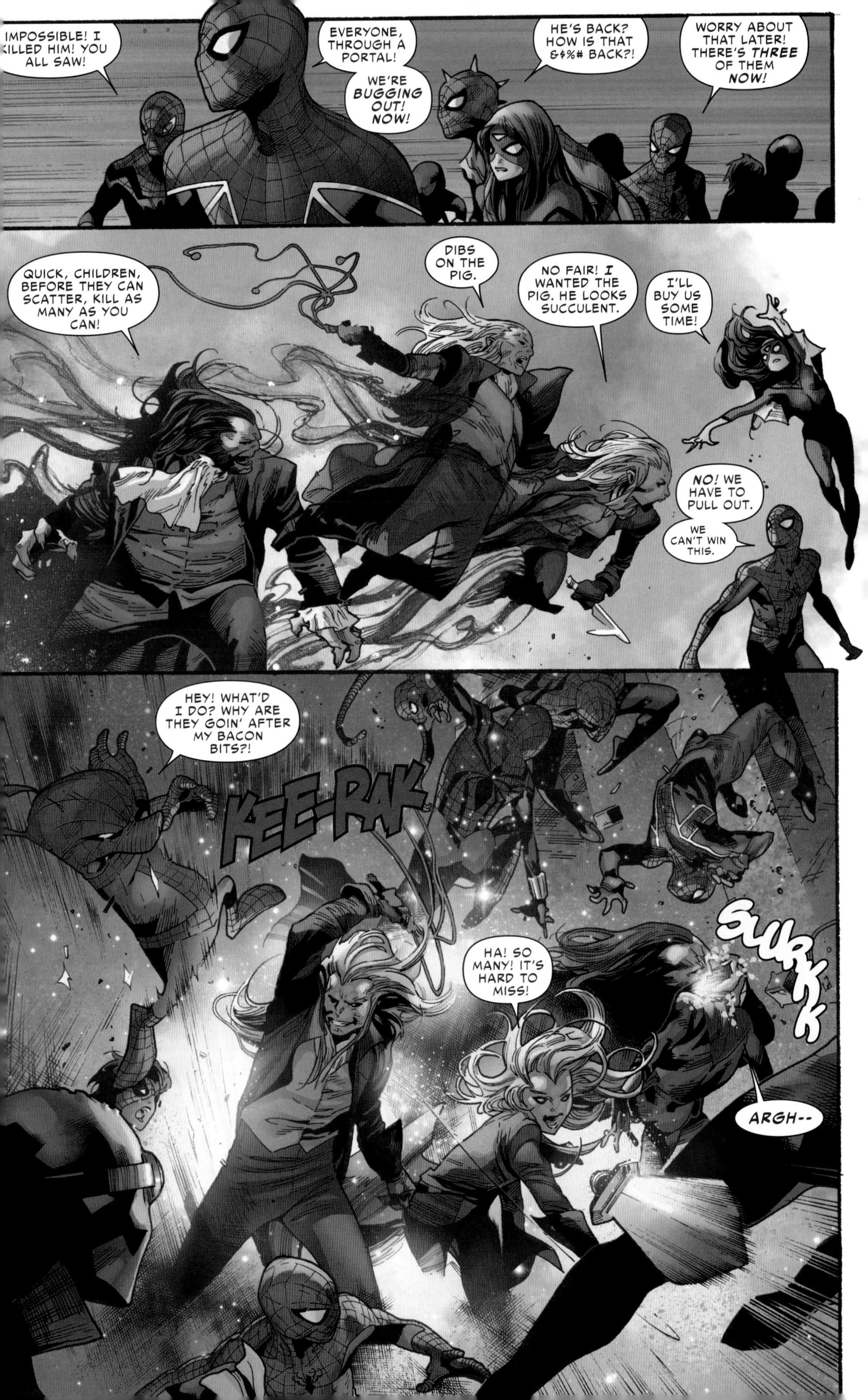

IMPOSSIBLE! I KILLED HIM! YOU ALL SAW!
EVERYONE, THROUGH A PORTAL!
WE'RE BUGGING OUT! NOW!
HE'S BACK? HOW IS THAT &$%# BACK?!
WORRY ABOUT THAT LATER! THERE'S THREE OF THEM NOW!
QUICK, CHILDREN, BEFORE THEY CAN SCATTER, KILL AS MANY AS YOU CAN!
DIBS ON THE PIG.
NO FAIR! I WANTED THE PIG. HE LOOKS SUCCULENT.
I'LL BUY US SOME TIME!
NO! WE HAVE TO PULL OUT.
WE CAN'T WIN THIS.
HEY! WHAT'D I DO? WHY ARE THEY GOIN' AFTER MY BACON BITS?!
KEE-RAK
HA! SO MANY! IT'S HARD TO MISS!
SLURKK
ARGH--

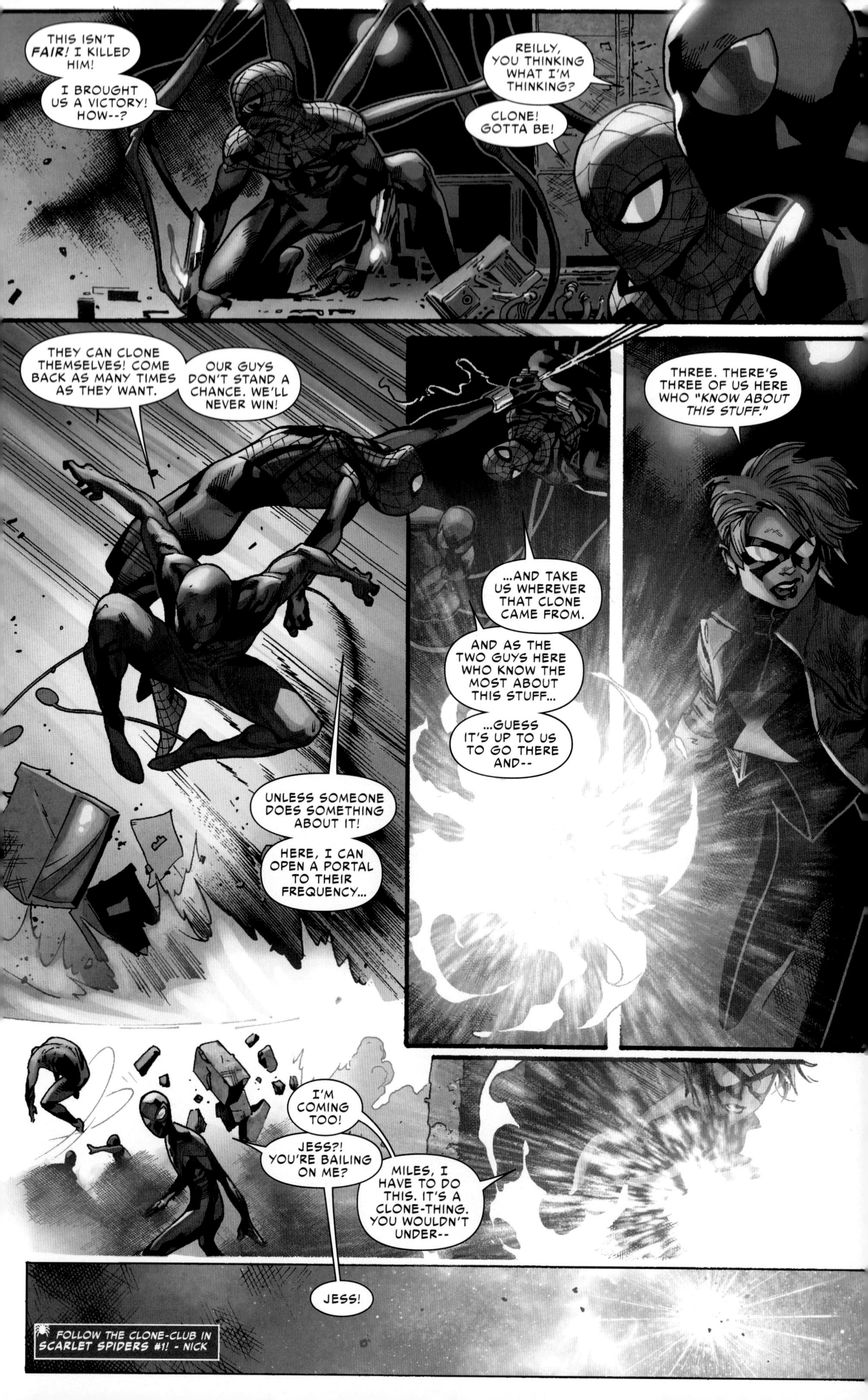
THIS ISN'T FAIR! I KILLED HIM!
I BROUGHT US A VICTORY! HOW--?
REILLY, YOU THINKING WHAT I'M THINKING?
CLONE! GOTTA BE!
THEY CAN CLONE THEMSELVES! COME BACK AS MANY TIMES AS THEY WANT.
OUR GUYS DON'T STAND A CHANCE. WE'LL NEVER WIN!
UNLESS SOMEONE DOES SOMETHING ABOUT IT!
HERE, I CAN OPEN A PORTAL TO THEIR FREQUENCY...
...AND TAKE US WHEREVER THAT CLONE CAME FROM.
AND AS THE TWO GUYS HERE WHO KNOW THE MOST ABOUT THIS STUFF...
...GUESS IT'S UP TO US TO GO THERE AND--
THREE. THERE'S THREE OF US HERE WHO "KNOW ABOUT THIS STUFF."
I'M COMING TOO!
JESS?! YOU'RE BAILING ON ME?
MILES, I HAVE TO DO THIS. IT'S A CLONE-THING. YOU WOULDN'T UNDER--
JESS!
FOLLOW THE CLONE-CLUB IN SCARLET SPIDERS #1! - NICK

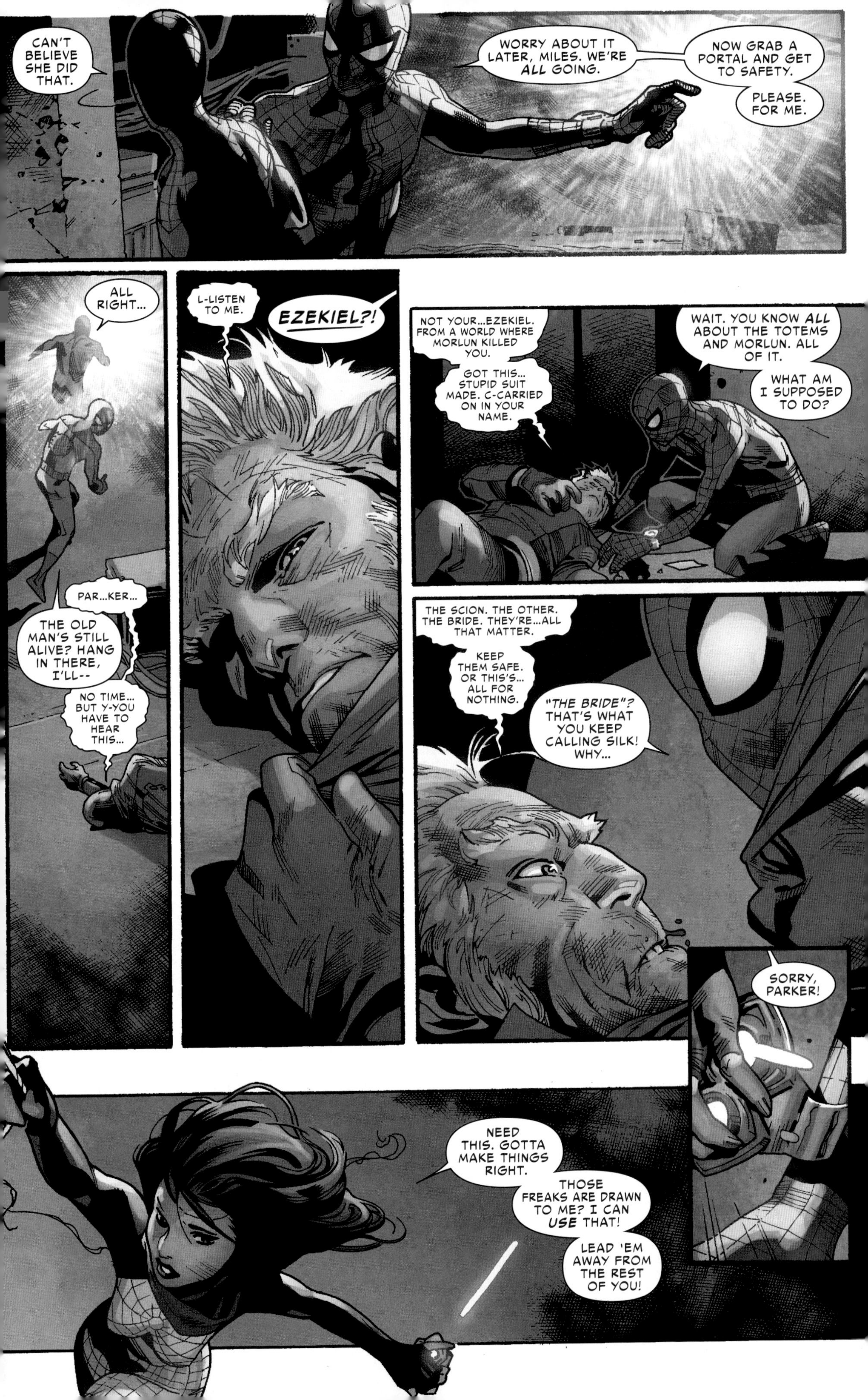
CAN'T BELIEVE SHE DID THAT.
WORRY ABOUT IT LATER, MILES. WE'RE ALL GOING.
NOW GRAB A PORTAL AND GET TO SAFETY.
PLEASE. FOR ME.
ALL RIGHT...
PAR...KER...
THE OLD MAN'S STILL ALIVE? HANG IN THERE, I'LL--
NO TIME... BUT Y-YOU HAVE TO HEAR THIS...
L-LISTEN TO ME.
EZEKIEL?!
NOT YOUR...EZEKIEL. FROM A WORLD WHERE MORLUN KILLED YOU.
GOT THIS... STUPID SUIT MADE. C-CARRIED ON IN YOUR NAME.
WAIT. YOU KNOW ALL ABOUT THE TOTEMS AND MORLUN. ALL OF IT.
WHAT AM I SUPPOSED TO DO?
THE SCION. THE OTHER. THE BRIDE. THEY'RE...ALL THAT MATTER.
KEEP THEM SAFE. OR THIS'S... ALL FOR NOTHING.
"THE BRIDE"? THAT'S WHAT YOU KEEP CALLING SILK! WHY...
SORRY, PARKER!
NEED THIS. GOTTA MAKE THINGS RIGHT.
THOSE FREAKS ARE DRAWN TO ME? I CAN USE THAT!
LEAD 'EM AWAY FROM THE REST OF YOU!

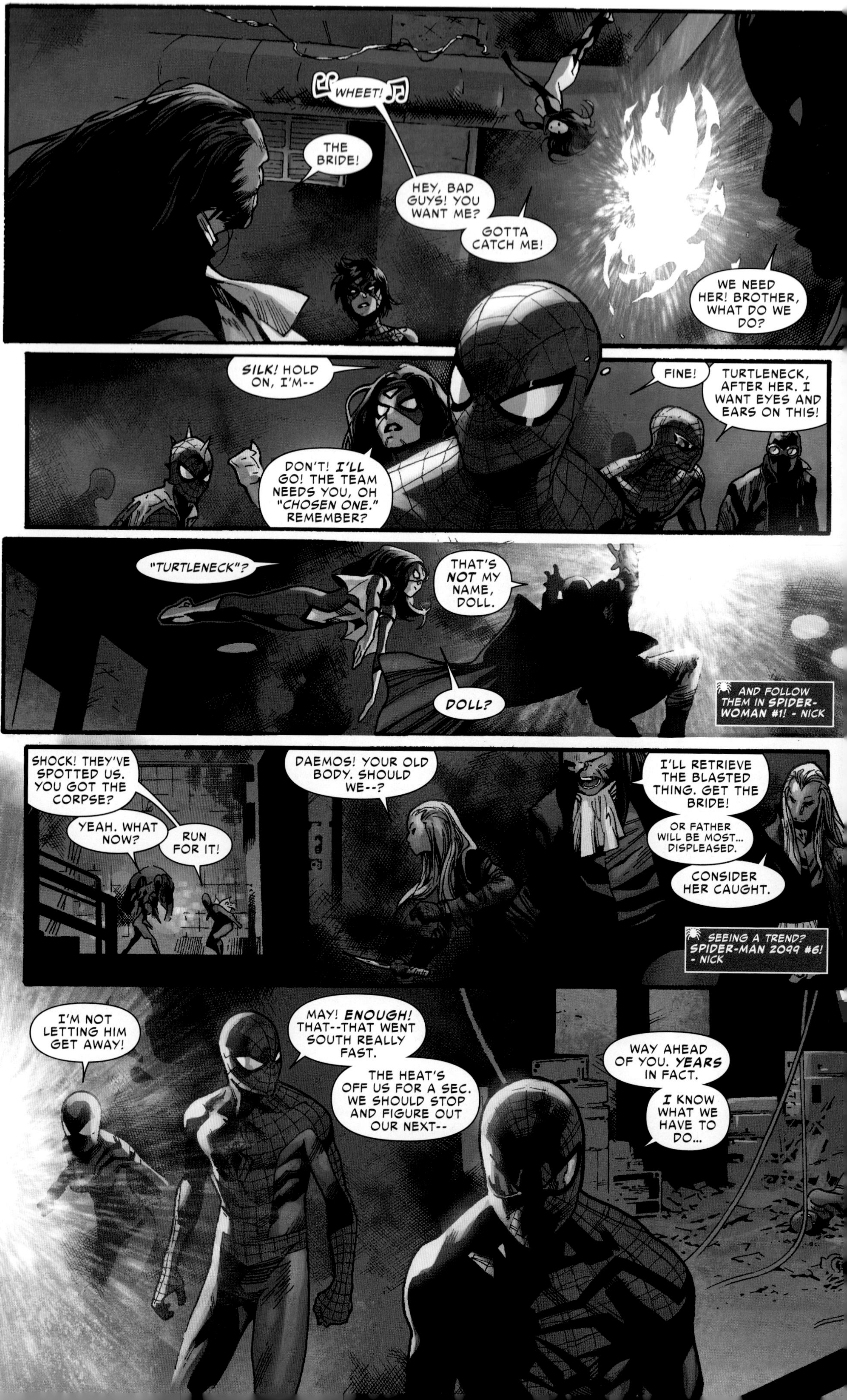

WHEET!
THE BRIDE!
HEY, BAD GUYS! YOU WANT ME?
GOTTA CATCH ME!
WE NEED HER! BROTHER, WHAT DO WE DO?
SILK! HOLD ON, I'M--
DON'T! I'LL GO! THE TEAM NEEDS YOU, OH "CHOSEN ONE." REMEMBER?
FINE!
TURTLENECK, AFTER HER. I WANT EYES AND EARS ON THIS!
"TURTLENECK"?
THAT'S NOT MY NAME, DOLL.
DOLL?
AND FOLLOW THEM IN SPIDER-WOMAN #1! - NICK
SHOCK! THEY'VE SPOTTED US. YOU GOT THE CORPSE?
YEAH. WHAT NOW?
RUN FOR IT!
DAEMOS! YOUR OLD BODY. SHOULD WE--?
I'LL RETRIEVE THE BLASTED THING. GET THE BRIDE!
OR FATHER WILL BE MOST... DISPLEASED.
CONSIDER HER CAUGHT.
SEEING A TREND? SPIDER-MAN 2099 #6! - NICK
I'M NOT LETTING HIM GET AWAY!
MAY! ENOUGH! THAT--THAT WENT SOUTH REALLY FAST.
THE HEAT'S OFF US FOR A SEC. WE SHOULD STOP AND FIGURE OUT OUR NEXT--
WAY AHEAD OF YOU. YEARS IN FACT.
I KNOW WHAT WE HAVE TO DO...

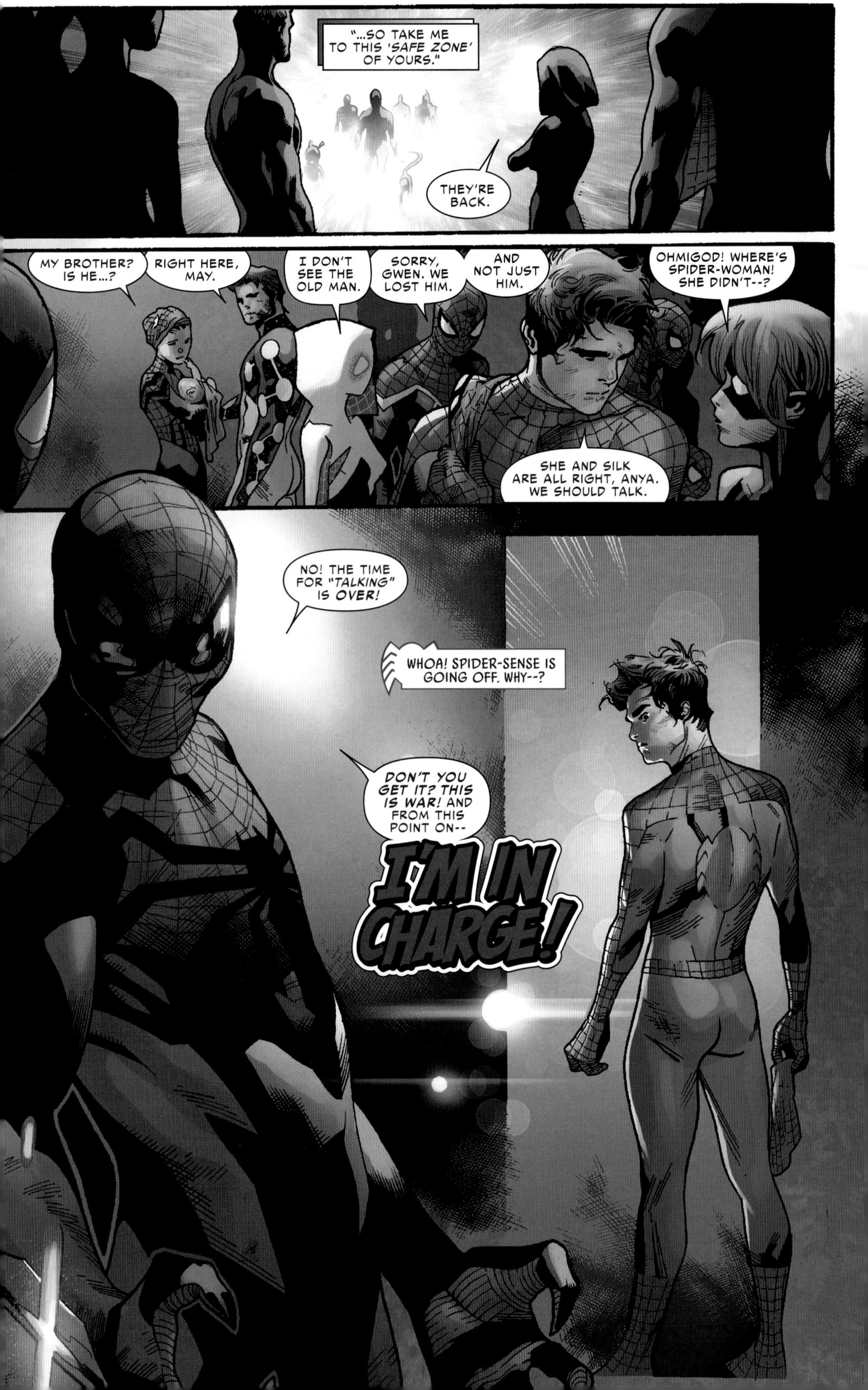
"...SO TAKE ME TO THIS 'SAFE ZONE' OF YOURS."
THEY'RE BACK.
MY BROTHER? IS HE...?
RIGHT HERE, MAY.
I DON'T SEE THE OLD MAN.
SORRY, GWEN. WE LOST HIM.
AND NOT JUST HIM.
OHMIGOD! WHERE'S SPIDER-WOMAN! SHE DIDN'T--?
SHE AND SILK ARE ALL RIGHT, ANYA. WE SHOULD TALK.
NO! THE TIME FOR "TALKING" IS OVER!
WHOA! SPIDER-SENSE IS GOING OFF. WHY--?
DON'T YOU GET IT? THIS IS WAR! AND FROM THIS POINT ON--
I'M IN CHARGE!

AMAZING SPIDER-MAN 7 DEADPOOL 75TH ANNIVERSARY VARIANT
BY MICHAEL GOLDEN

AMAZING SPIDER-MAN 7 VARIANT
BY CHOO YIHANG GARY

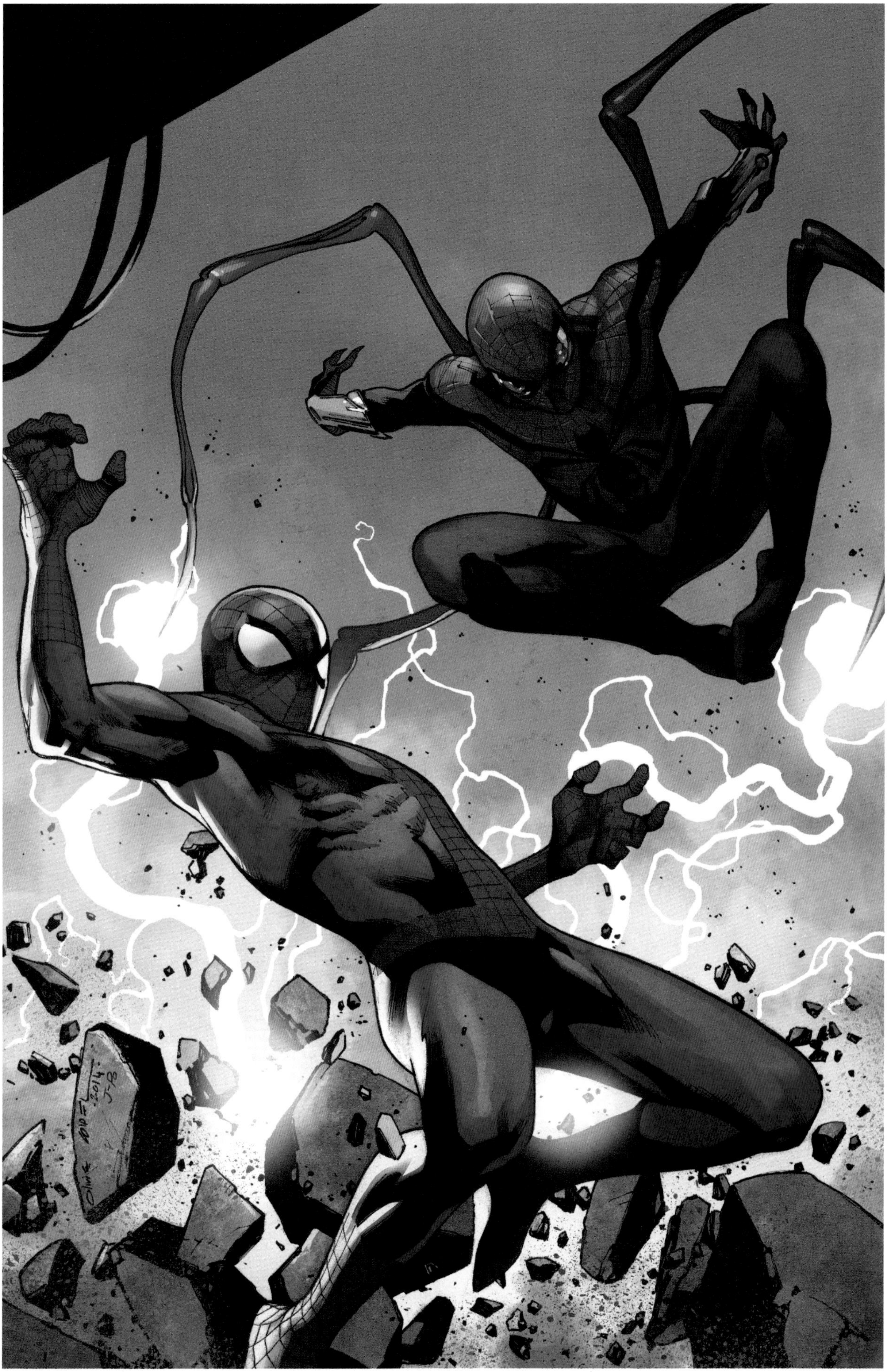

AMAZING SPIDER-MAN 11
SPIDER-VERSE, PART THREE: HIGHER GROUND

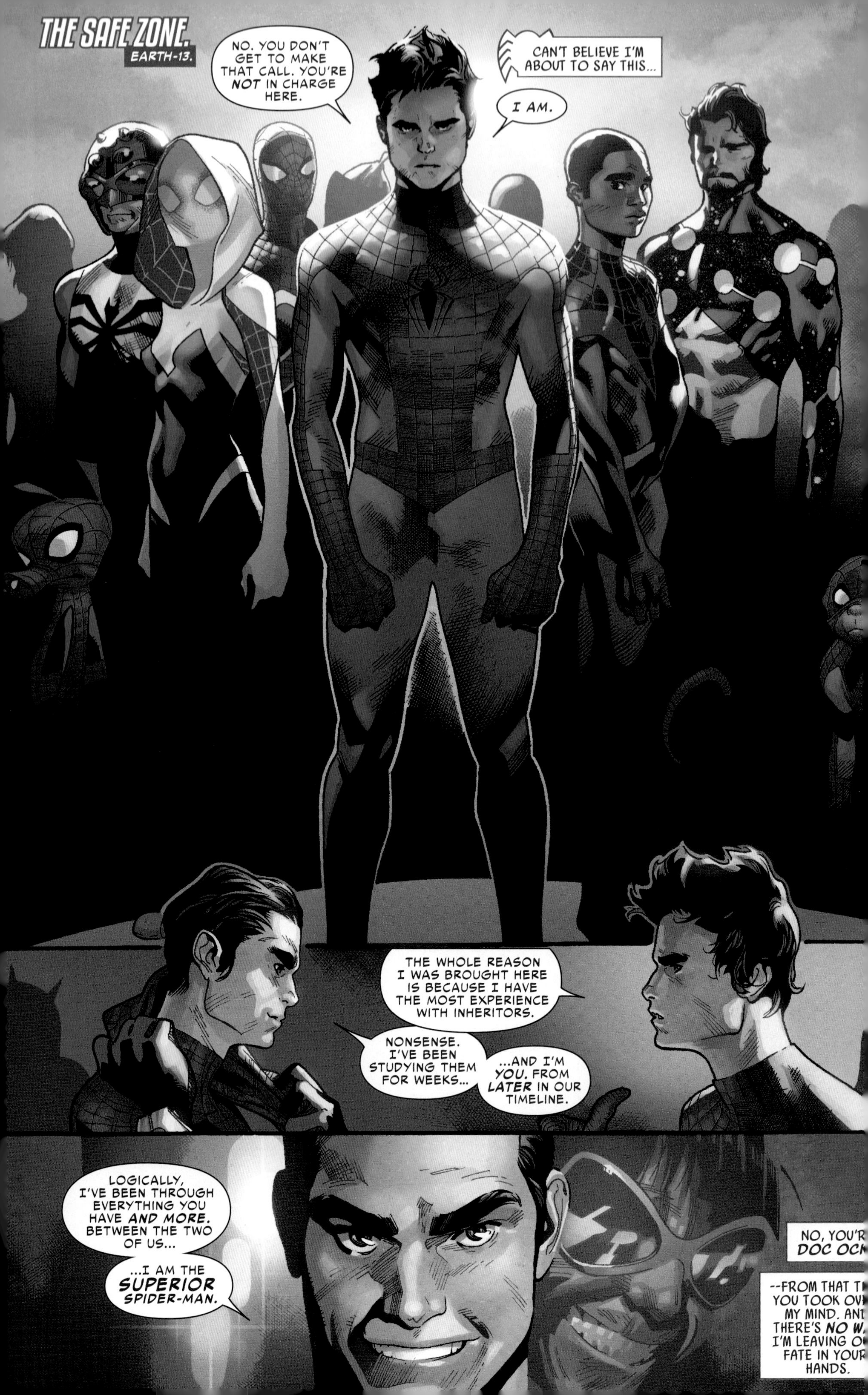

THE SAFE ZONE.
EARTH-13.
NO. YOU DON'T GET TO MAKE THAT CALL. YOU'RE NOT IN CHARGE HERE.
CAN'T BELIEVE I'M ABOUT TO SAY THIS...
I AM.
THE WHOLE REASON I WAS BROUGHT HERE IS BECAUSE I HAVE THE MOST EXPERIENCE WITH INHERITORS.
NONSENSE. I'VE BEEN STUDYING THEM FOR WEEKS...
...AND I'M YOU. FROM LATER IN OUR TIMELINE.
LOGICALLY, I'VE BEEN THROUGH EVERYTHING YOU HAVE AND MORE. BETWEEN THE TWO OF US...
...I AM THE SUPERIOR SPIDER-MAN.

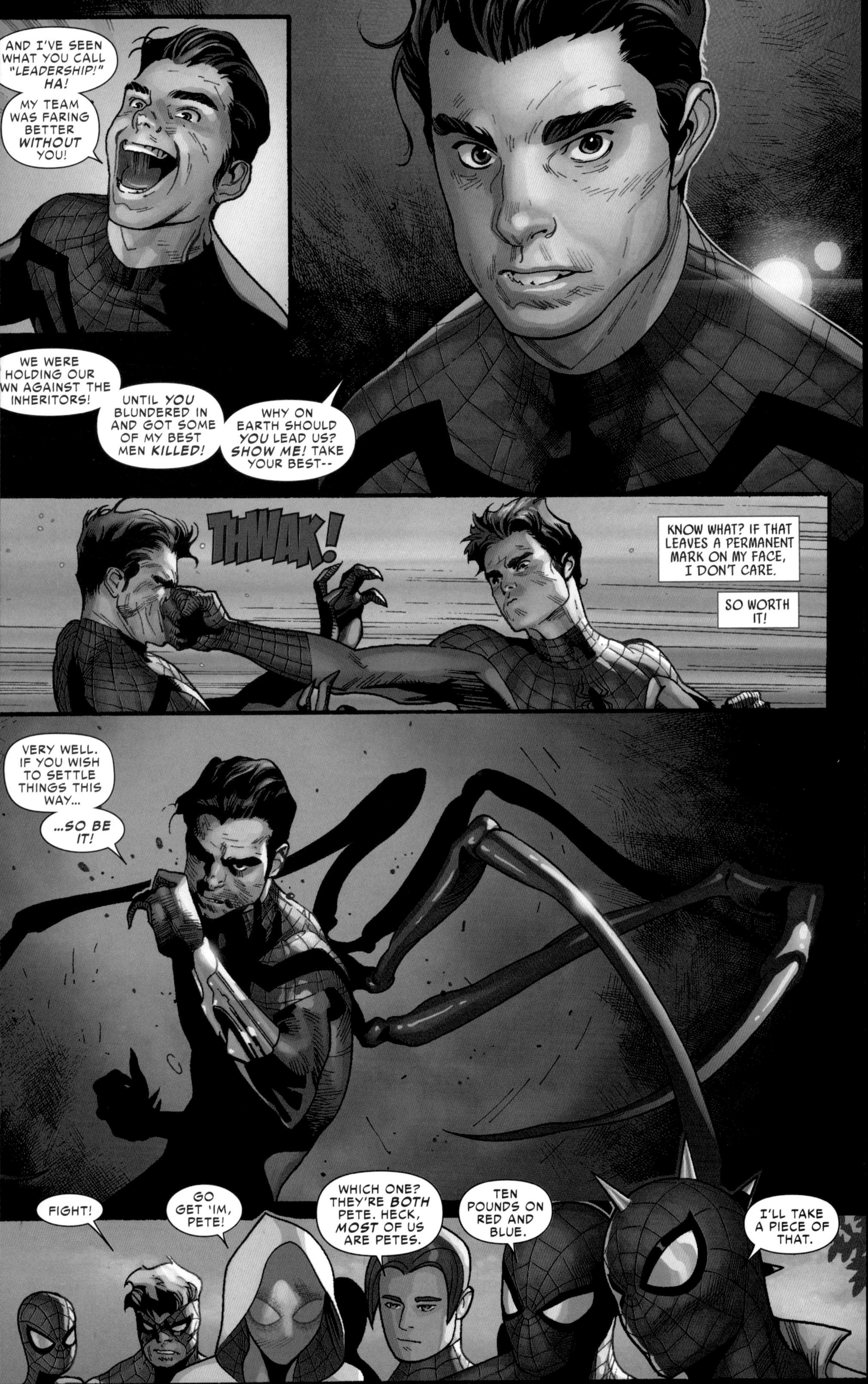
AND I'VE SEEN WHAT YOU CALL "LEADERSHIP!" HA!
MY TEAM WAS FARING BETTER WITHOUT YOU!
WE WERE HOLDING OUR WN AGAINST THE INHERITORS!
UNTIL YOU BLUNDERED IN AND GOT SOME OF MY BEST MEN KILLED!
WHY ON EARTH SHOULD YOU LEAD US? SHOW ME! TAKE YOUR BEST--
THWAK!
KNOW WHAT? IF THAT LEAVES A PERMANENT MARK ON MY FACE, I DON'T CARE.
SO WORTH IT!
VERY WELL. IF YOU WISH TO SETTLE THINGS THIS WAY...
...SO BE IT!
FIGHT!
GO GET 'IM, PETE!
WHICH ONE? THEY'RE BOTH PETE. HECK, MOST OF US ARE PETES.
TEN POUNDS ON RED AND BLUE.
I'LL TAKE A PIECE OF THAT.

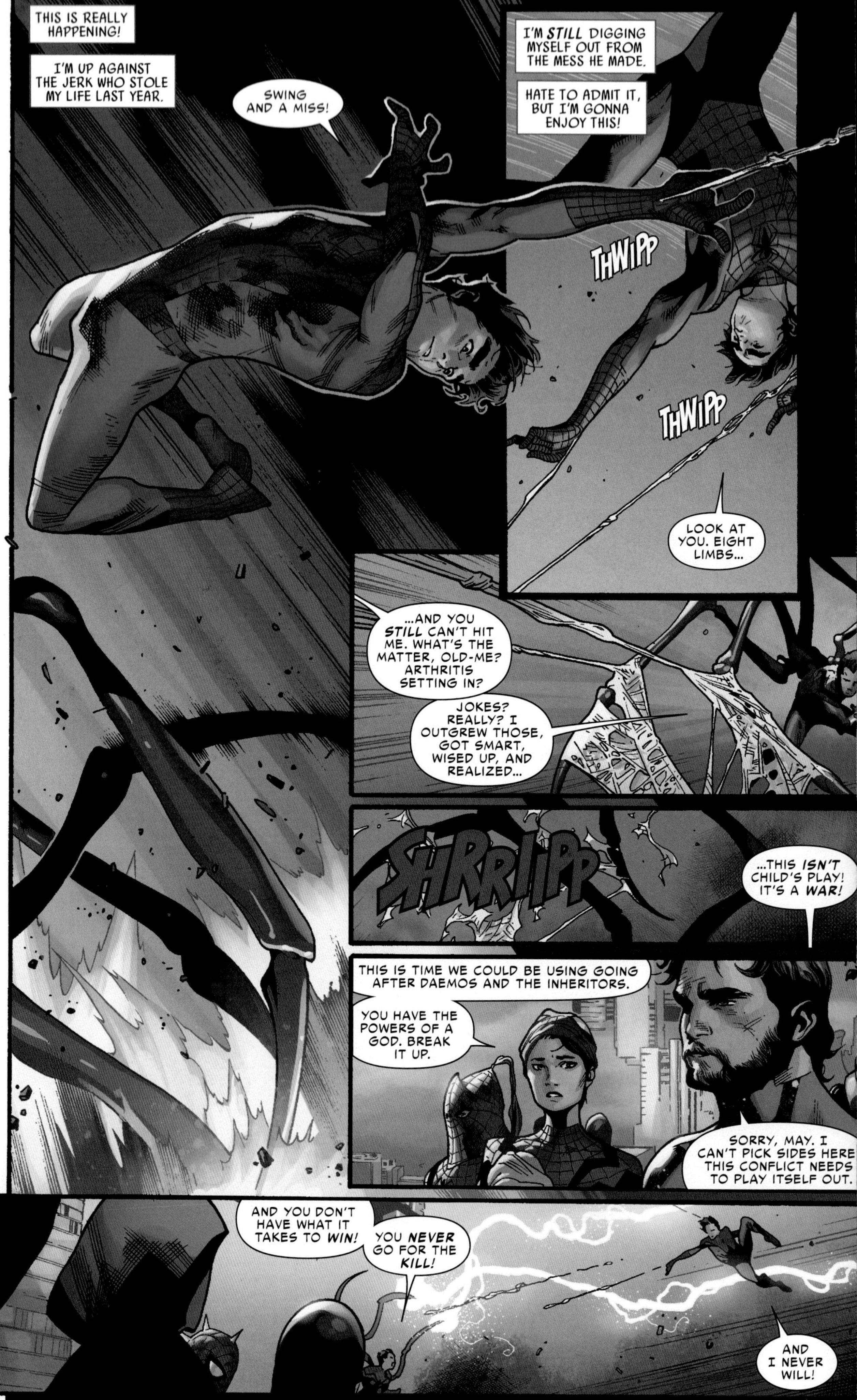
THIS IS REALLY HAPPENING!
I'M UP AGAINST THE JERK WHO STOLE MY LIFE LAST YEAR.
SWING AND A MISS!
I'M STILL DIGGING MYSELF OUT FROM THE MESS HE MADE.
HATE TO ADMIT IT, BUT I'M GONNA ENJOY THIS!
THWIPP
THWIPP
LOOK AT YOU. EIGHT LIMBS...
...AND YOU STILL CAN'T HIT ME. WHAT'S THE MATTER, OLD-ME? ARTHRITIS SETTING IN?
JOKES? REALLY? I OUTGREW THOSE, GOT SMART, WISED UP, AND REALIZED...
SHRRIIPP
...THIS ISN'T CHILD'S PLAY! IT'S A WAR!
THIS IS TIME WE COULD BE USING GOING AFTER DAEMOS AND THE INHERITORS.
YOU HAVE THE POWERS OF A GOD. BREAK IT UP.
SORRY, MAY. I CAN'T PICK SIDES HERE. THIS CONFLICT NEEDS TO PLAY ITSELF OUT.
AND YOU DON'T HAVE WHAT IT TAKES TO WIN!
YOU NEVER GO FOR THE KILL!
AND I NEVER WILL!

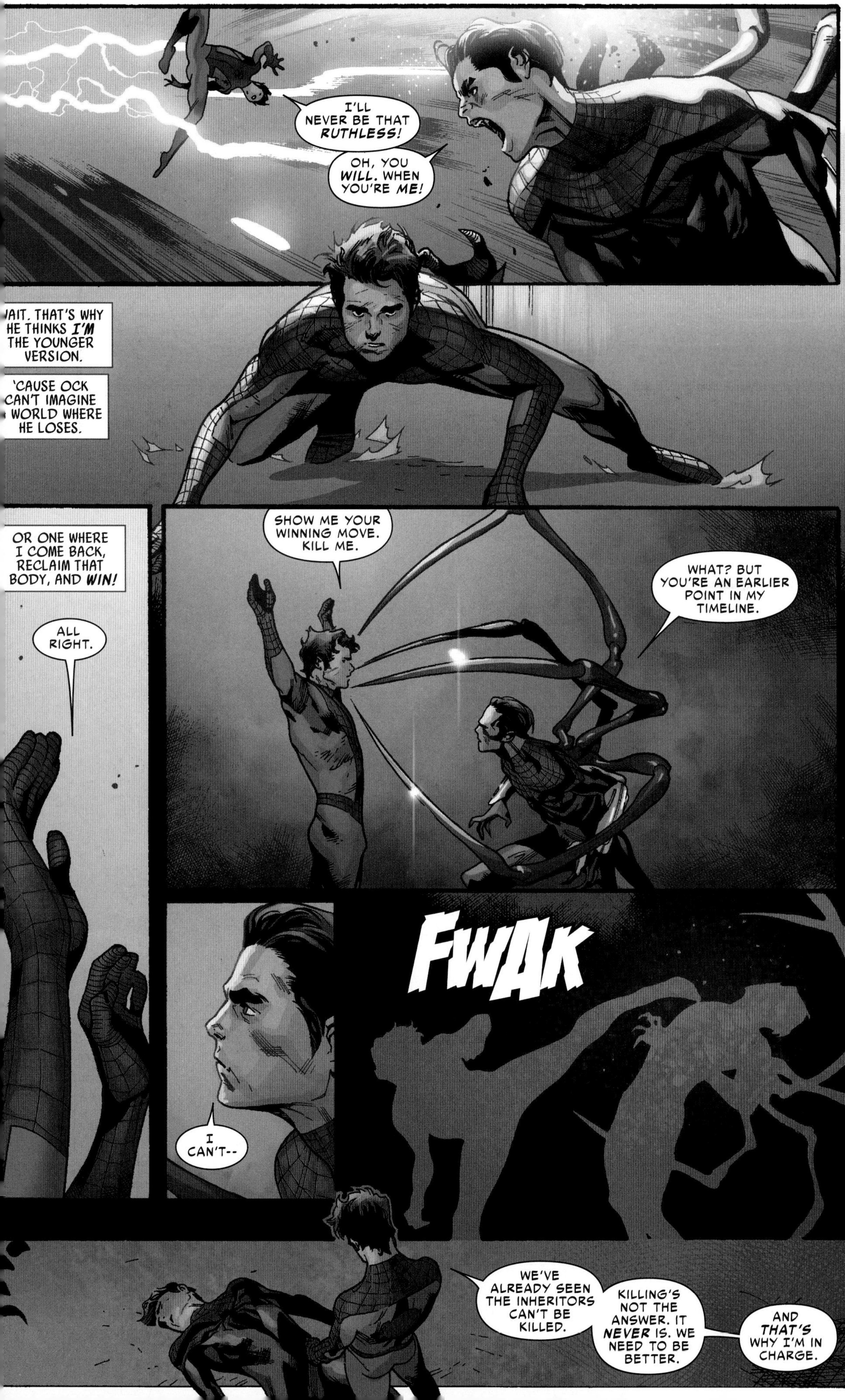
I'LL NEVER BE THAT RUTHLESS!
OH, YOU WILL. WHEN YOU'RE ME!
AIT. THAT'S WHY HE THINKS I'M THE YOUNGER VERSION.
'CAUSE OCK CAN'T IMAGINE WORLD WHERE HE LOSES.
OR ONE WHERE I COME BACK, RECLAIM THAT BODY, AND WIN!
ALL RIGHT.
SHOW ME YOUR WINNING MOVE. KILL ME.
WHAT? BUT YOU'RE AN EARLIER POINT IN MY TIMELINE.
I CAN'T--
FWAK
WE'VE ALREADY SEEN THE INHERITORS CAN'T BE KILLED.
KILLING'S NOT THE ANSWER. IT NEVER IS. WE NEED TO BE BETTER.
AND THAT'S WHY I'M IN CHARGE.

EARTH-13989.
ARE YOU WATCHING, FATHER? CAN YOU SEE MY LATEST KILL?
THE GREAT SPIDER-WOLF OF THE LYCANSPHERE!
AWROOO
IS THIS TRIBUTE ENOUGH, LORD SOLUS?!
IS MY HUNT AT LONG LAST OVER?! MAY I FINALLY COME HOME?!

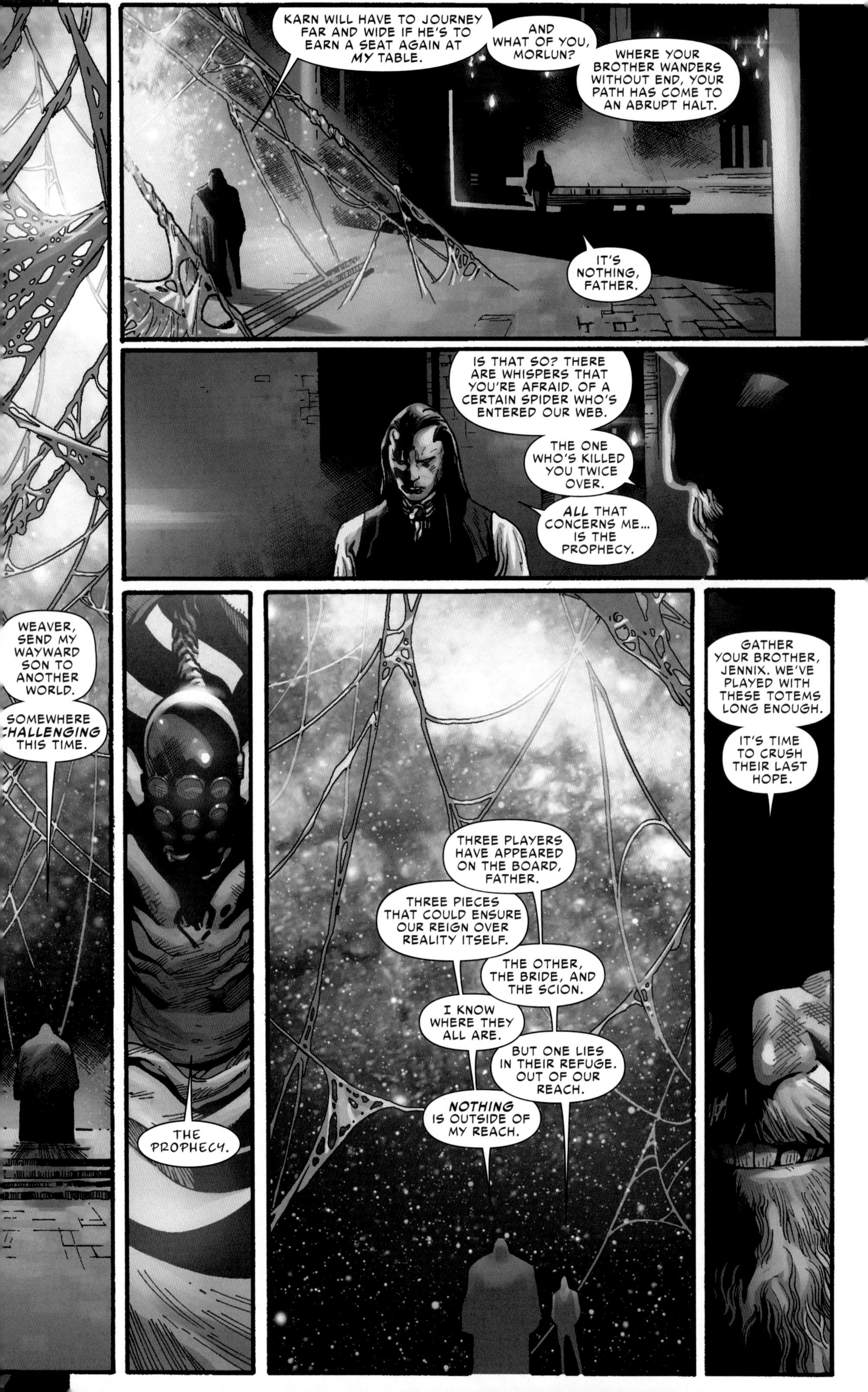
KARN WILL HAVE TO JOURNEY FAR AND WIDE IF HE'S TO EARN A SEAT AGAIN AT *MY* TABLE.
AND WHAT OF YOU, MORLUN?
WHERE YOUR BROTHER WANDERS WITHOUT END, YOUR PATH HAS COME TO AN ABRUPT HALT.
IT'S NOTHING, FATHER.
IS THAT SO? THERE ARE WHISPERS THAT YOU'RE AFRAID. OF A CERTAIN SPIDER WHO'S ENTERED OUR WEB.
THE ONE WHO'S KILLED YOU TWICE OVER.
ALL THAT CONCERNS ME... IS THE PROPHECY.
WEAVER, SEND MY WAYWARD SON TO ANOTHER WORLD.
SOMEWHERE *CHALLENGING* THIS TIME.
THE PROPHECY.
THREE PLAYERS HAVE APPEARED ON THE BOARD, FATHER.
THREE PIECES THAT COULD ENSURE OUR REIGN OVER REALITY ITSELF.
THE OTHER, THE BRIDE, AND THE SCION.
I KNOW WHERE THEY ALL ARE.
BUT ONE LIES IN THEIR REFUGE. OUT OF OUR REACH.
NOTHING IS OUTSIDE OF MY REACH.
GATHER YOUR BROTHER, JENNIX. WE'VE PLAYED WITH THESE TOTEMS LONG ENOUGH.
IT'S TIME TO CRUSH THEIR LAST HOPE.

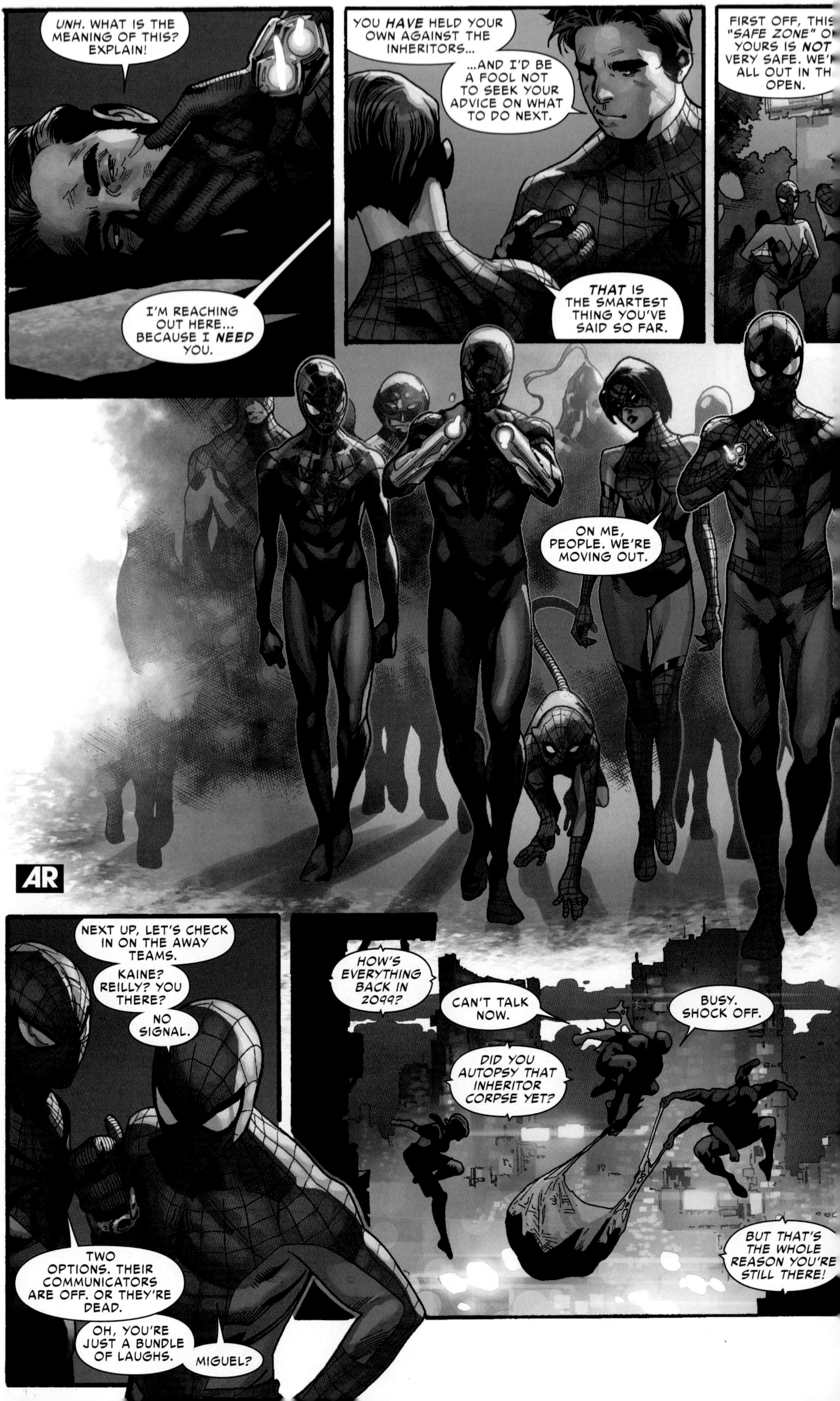

UNH. WHAT IS THE MEANING OF THIS? EXPLAIN!
I'M REACHING OUT HERE... BECAUSE I NEED YOU.
YOU HAVE HELD YOUR OWN AGAINST THE INHERITORS...
...AND I'D BE A FOOL NOT TO SEEK YOUR ADVICE ON WHAT TO DO NEXT.
THAT IS THE SMARTEST THING YOU'VE SAID SO FAR.
FIRST OFF, THIS "SAFE ZONE" OF YOURS IS NOT VERY SAFE. WE'RE ALL OUT IN THE OPEN.
ON ME, PEOPLE. WE'RE MOVING OUT.
NEXT UP, LET'S CHECK IN ON THE AWAY TEAMS.
KAINE? REILLY? YOU THERE?
NO SIGNAL.
TWO OPTIONS. THEIR COMMUNICATORS ARE OFF. OR THEY'RE DEAD.
OH, YOU'RE JUST A BUNDLE OF LAUGHS.
MIGUEL?
HOW'S EVERYTHING BACK IN 2099?
CAN'T TALK NOW.
BUSY. SHOCK OFF.
DID YOU AUTOPSY THAT INHERITOR CORPSE YET?
BUT THAT'S THE WHOLE REASON YOU'RE STILL THERE!

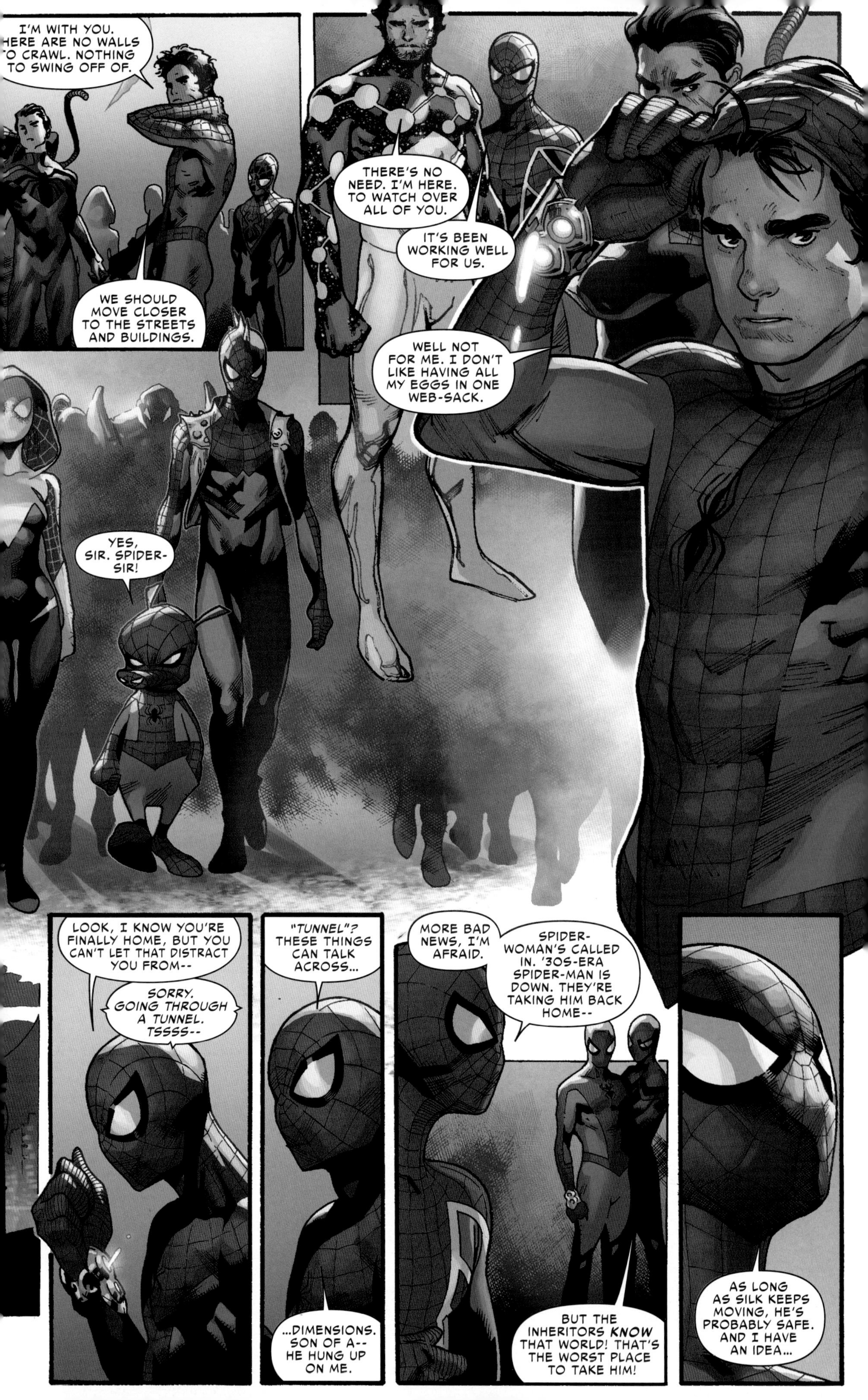

I'M WITH YOU. HERE ARE NO WALLS TO CRAWL. NOTHING TO SWING OFF OF.
WE SHOULD MOVE CLOSER TO THE STREETS AND BUILDINGS.
THERE'S NO NEED. I'M HERE. TO WATCH OVER ALL OF YOU.
IT'S BEEN WORKING WELL FOR US.
WELL NOT FOR ME. I DON'T LIKE HAVING ALL MY EGGS IN ONE WEB-SACK.
YES, SIR. SPIDER-SIR!
LOOK, I KNOW YOU'RE FINALLY HOME, BUT YOU CAN'T LET THAT DISTRACT YOU FROM--
SORRY. GOING THROUGH A TUNNEL. TSSSS--
"TUNNEL"? THESE THINGS CAN TALK ACROSS...
...DIMENSIONS. SON OF A-- HE HUNG UP ON ME.
MORE BAD NEWS, I'M AFRAID.
SPIDER-WOMAN'S CALLED IN. '30S-ERA SPIDER-MAN IS DOWN. THEY'RE TAKING HIM BACK HOME--
BUT THE INHERITORS KNOW THAT WORLD! THAT'S THE WORST PLACE TO TAKE HIM!
AS LONG AS SILK KEEPS MOVING, HE'S PROBABLY SAFE. AND I HAVE AN IDEA...

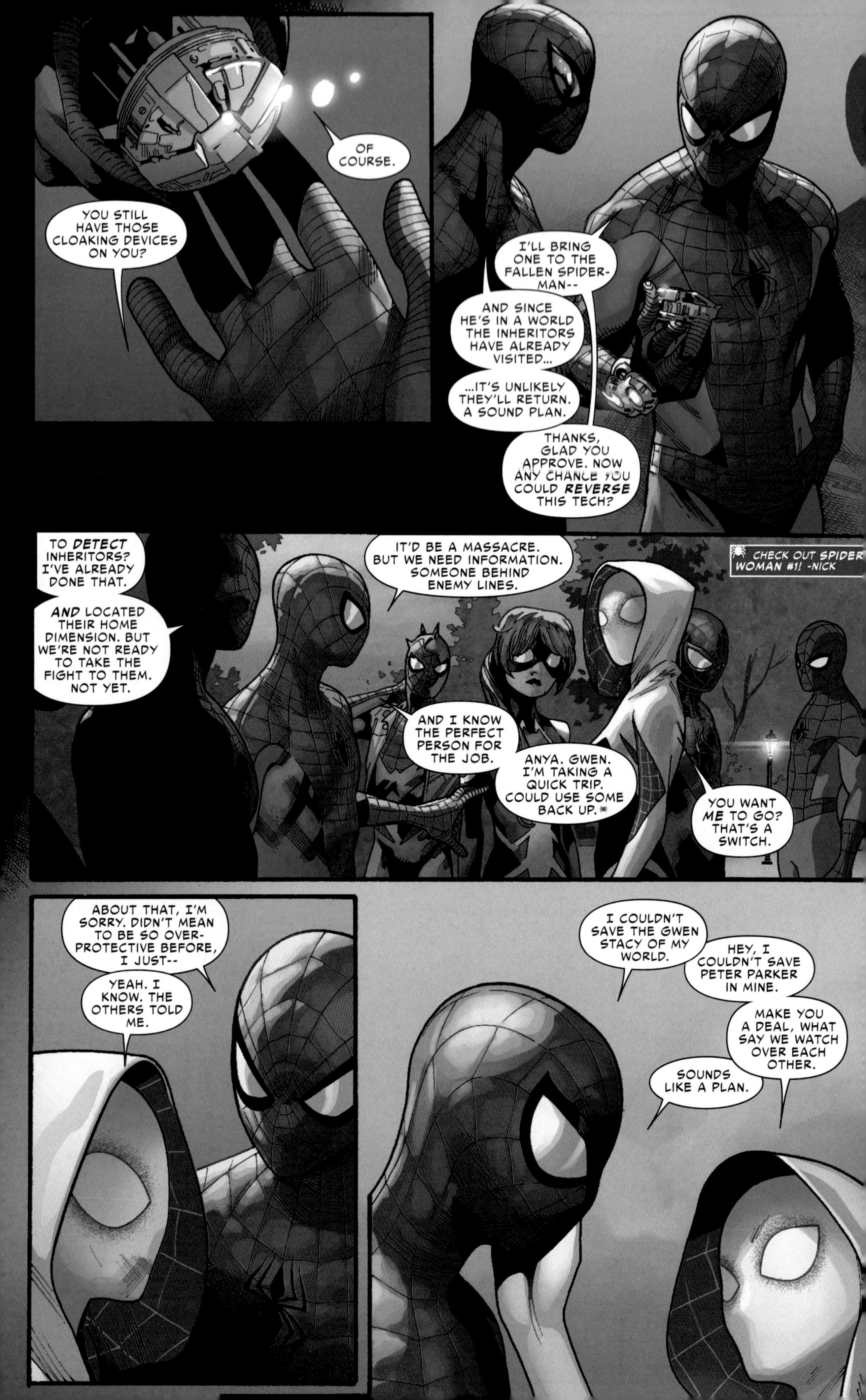

YOU STILL HAVE THOSE CLOAKING DEVICES ON YOU?
OF COURSE.
I'LL BRING ONE TO THE FALLEN SPIDER-MAN--
AND SINCE HE'S IN A WORLD THE INHERITORS HAVE ALREADY VISITED...
...IT'S UNLIKELY THEY'LL RETURN. A SOUND PLAN.
THANKS, GLAD YOU APPROVE. NOW ANY CHANCE YOU COULD *REVERSE* THIS TECH?
TO *DETECT* INHERITORS? I'VE ALREADY DONE THAT.
AND LOCATED THEIR HOME DIMENSION. BUT WE'RE NOT READY TO TAKE THE FIGHT TO THEM. NOT YET.
IT'D BE A MASSACRE. BUT WE NEED INFORMATION. SOMEONE BEHIND ENEMY LINES.
CHECK OUT *SPIDER WOMAN #1!* -NICK
AND I KNOW THE PERFECT PERSON FOR THE JOB.
ANYA. GWEN. I'M TAKING A QUICK TRIP. COULD USE SOME BACK UP.
YOU WANT *ME* TO GO? THAT'S A SWITCH.
ABOUT THAT, I'M SORRY. DIDN'T MEAN TO BE SO OVER-PROTECTIVE BEFORE, I JUST--
YEAH. I KNOW. THE OTHERS TOLD ME.
I COULDN'T SAVE THE GWEN STACY OF MY WORLD.
HEY, I COULDN'T SAVE PETER PARKER IN MINE.
MAKE YOU A DEAL, WHAT SAY WE WATCH OVER EACH OTHER.
SOUNDS LIKE A PLAN.

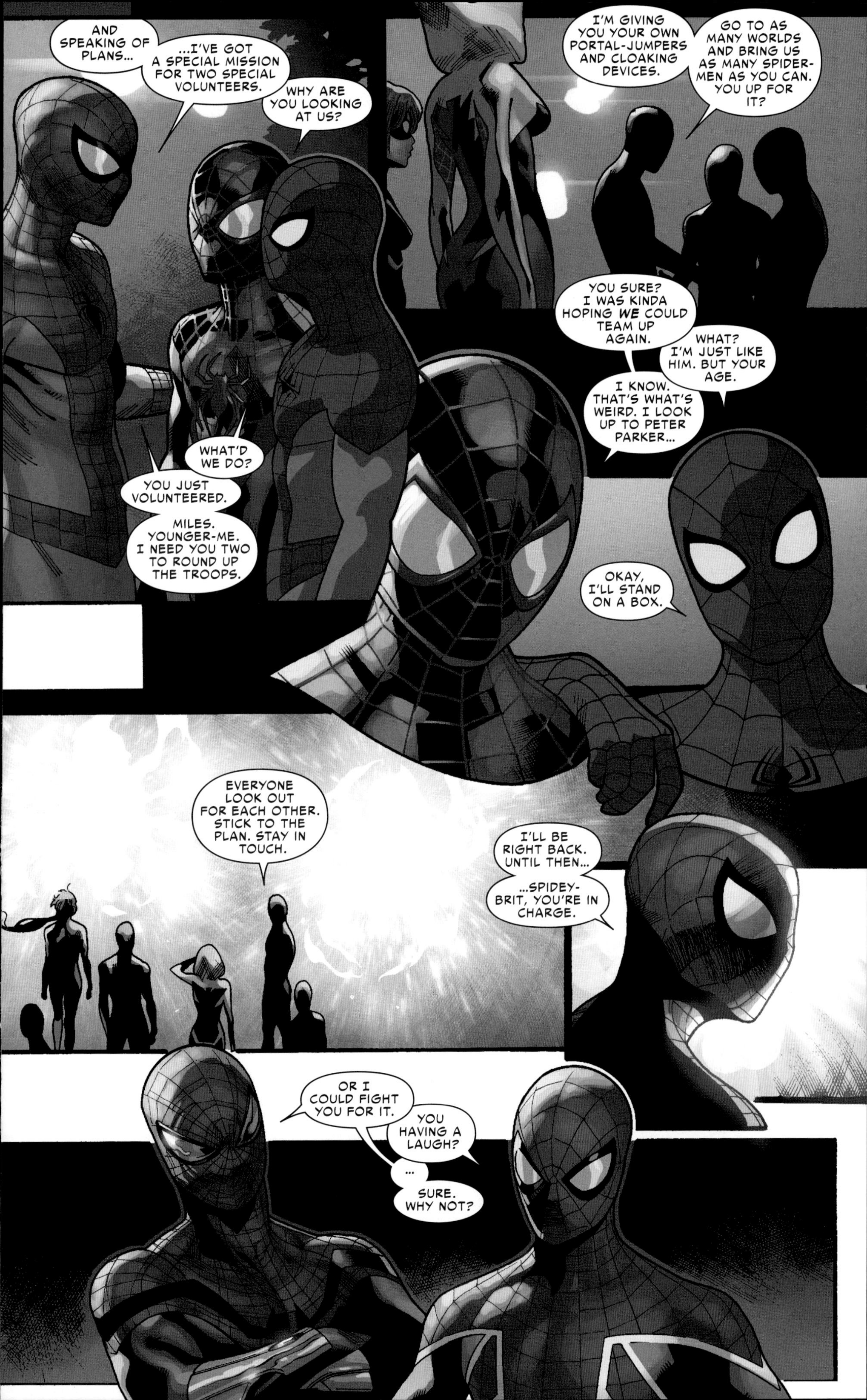
AND SPEAKING OF PLANS...
...I'VE GOT A SPECIAL MISSION FOR TWO SPECIAL VOLUNTEERS.
WHY ARE YOU LOOKING AT US?
WHAT'D WE DO?
YOU JUST VOLUNTEERED.
MILES. YOUNGER-ME. I NEED YOU TWO TO ROUND UP THE TROOPS.
I'M GIVING YOU YOUR OWN PORTAL-JUMPERS AND CLOAKING DEVICES.
GO TO AS MANY WORLDS AND BRING US AS MANY SPIDER-MEN AS YOU CAN. YOU UP FOR IT?
YOU SURE? I WAS KINDA HOPING WE COULD TEAM UP AGAIN.
WHAT? I'M JUST LIKE HIM. BUT YOUR AGE.
I KNOW. THAT'S WHAT'S WEIRD. I LOOK UP TO PETER PARKER...
OKAY, I'LL STAND ON A BOX.
EVERYONE LOOK OUT FOR EACH OTHER. STICK TO THE PLAN. STAY IN TOUCH.
I'LL BE RIGHT BACK. UNTIL THEN...
...SPIDEY-BRIT, YOU'RE IN CHARGE.
OR I COULD FIGHT YOU FOR IT.
YOU HAVING A LAUGH?
...
SURE. WHY NOT?

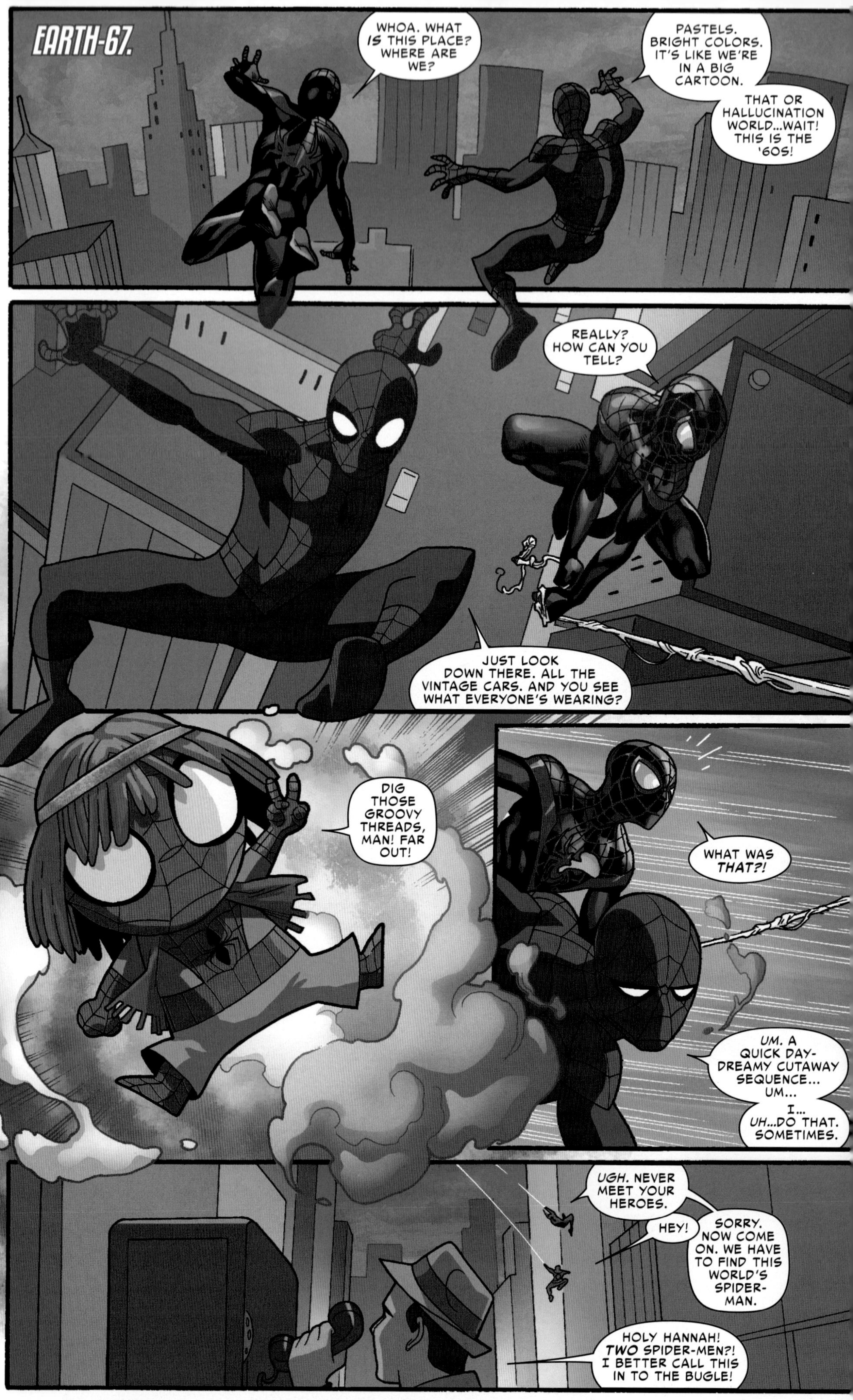
EARTH-67.
WHOA. WHAT IS THIS PLACE? WHERE ARE WE?
PASTELS. BRIGHT COLORS. IT'S LIKE WE'RE IN A BIG CARTOON.
THAT OR HALLUCINATION WORLD...WAIT! THIS IS THE '60S!
REALLY? HOW CAN YOU TELL?
JUST LOOK DOWN THERE. ALL THE VINTAGE CARS. AND YOU SEE WHAT EVERYONE'S WEARING?
DIG THOSE GROOVY THREADS, MAN! FAR OUT!
WHAT WAS THAT?!
UM. A QUICK DAY-DREAMY CUTAWAY SEQUENCE... UM...
I... UH...DO THAT. SOMETIMES.
UGH. NEVER MEET YOUR HEROES.
HEY!
SORRY. NOW COME ON. WE HAVE TO FIND THIS WORLD'S SPIDER-MAN.
HOLY HANNAH! TWO SPIDER-MEN?! I BETTER CALL THIS IN TO THE BUGLE!

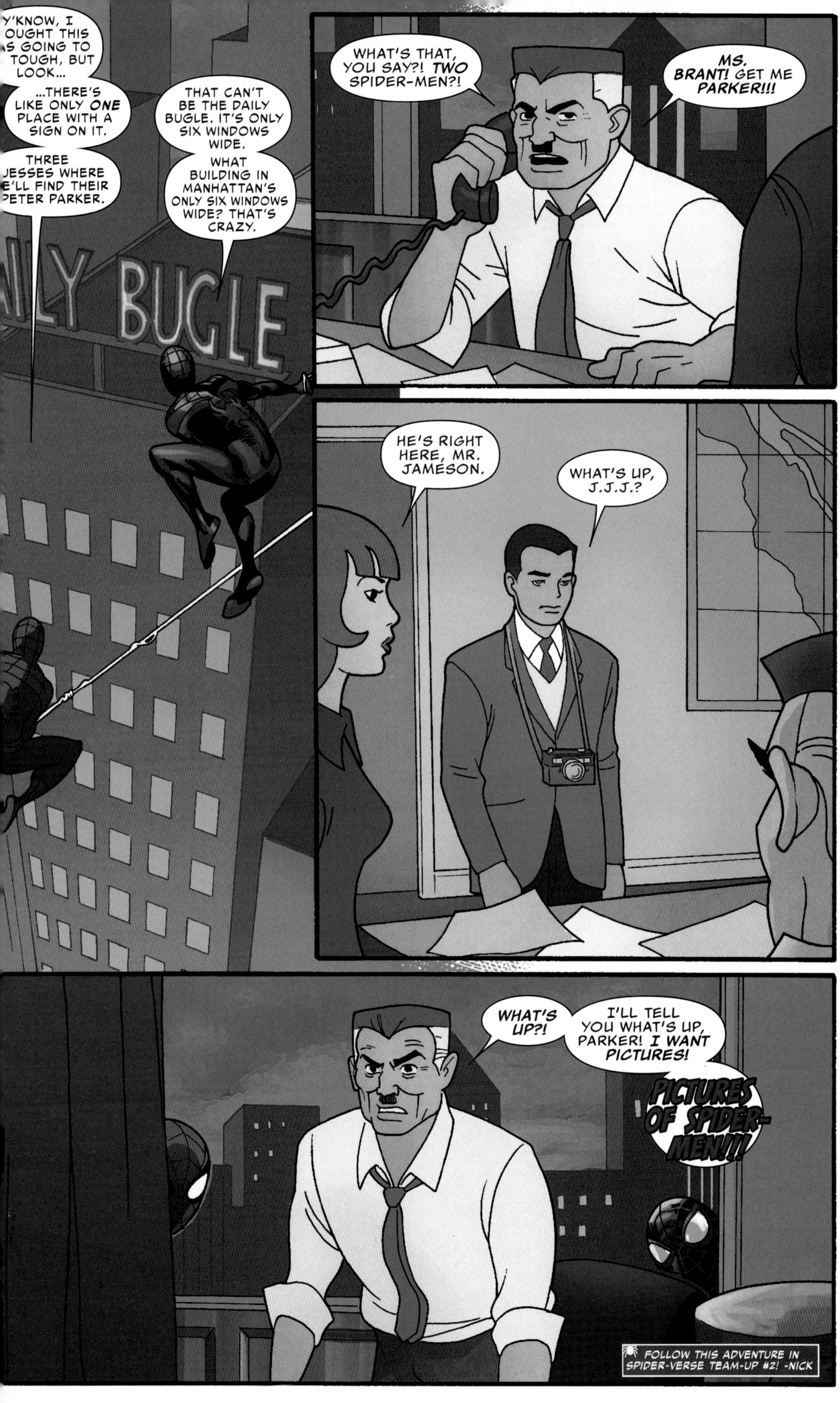
Y'KNOW, I
OUGHT THIS
S GOING TO
TOUGH, BUT
LOOK...
...THERE'S LIKE ONLY ONE PLACE WITH A SIGN ON IT.
THREE
ESSES WHERE
E'LL FIND THEIR
PETER PARKER.
THAT CAN'T BE THE DAILY BUGLE. IT'S ONLY SIX WINDOWS WIDE.
WHAT BUILDING IN MANHATTAN'S ONLY SIX WINDOWS WIDE? THAT'S CRAZY.
LY BUGLE
WHAT'S THAT, YOU SAY?! TWO SPIDER-MEN?!
MS. BRANT! GET ME PARKER!!!
HE'S RIGHT HERE, MR. JAMESON.
WHAT'S UP, J.J.J.?
WHAT'S UP?!
I'LL TELL YOU WHAT'S UP, PARKER! I WANT PICTURES!
PICTURES OF SPIDER-MEN!!!
FOLLOW THIS ADVENTURE IN SPIDER-VERSE TEAM-UP #2! -NICK

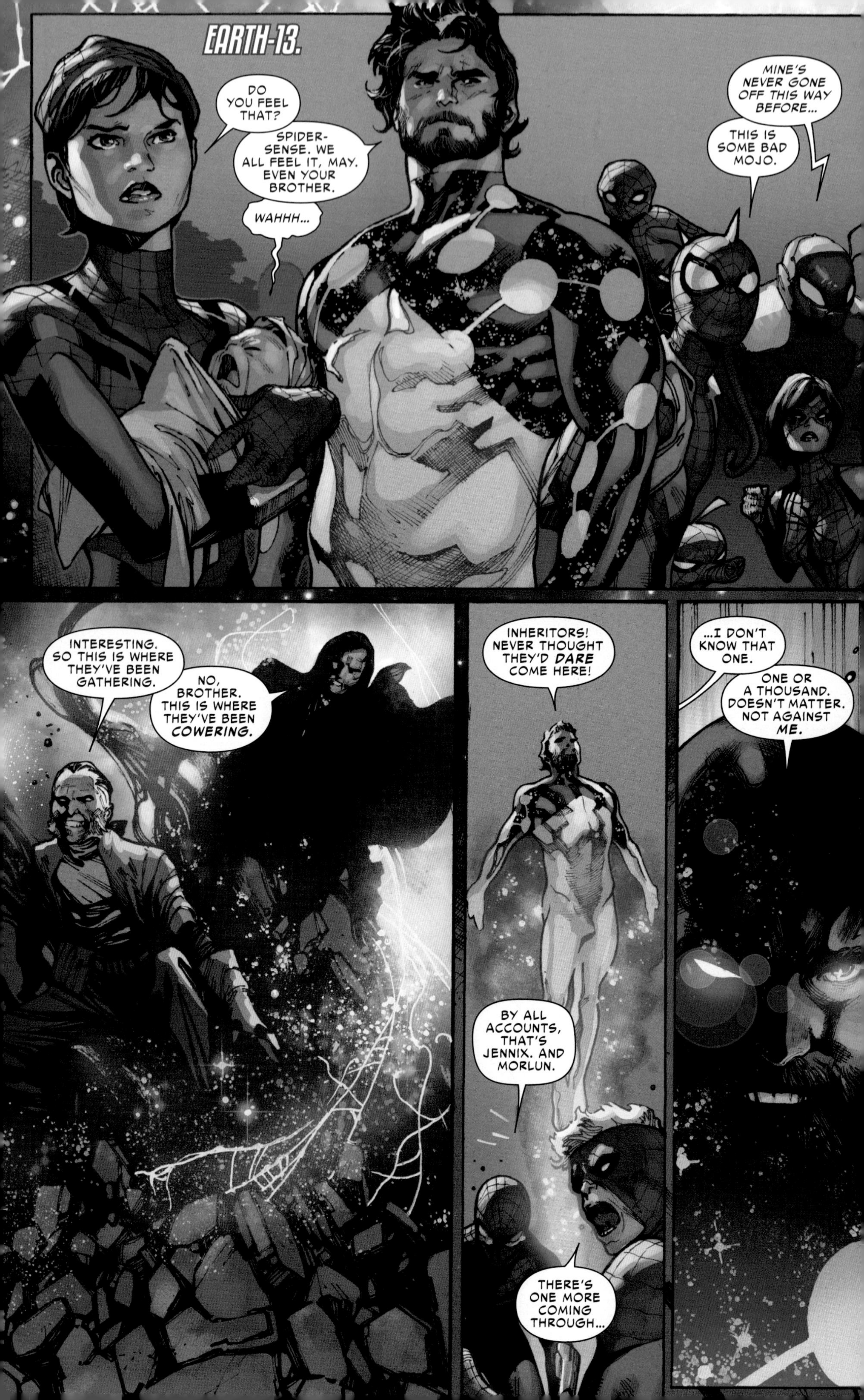
EARTH-13.
DO YOU FEEL THAT?
SPIDER-SENSE. WE ALL FEEL IT, MAY. EVEN YOUR BROTHER.
WAHHH...
MINE'S NEVER GONE OFF THIS WAY BEFORE...
THIS IS SOME BAD MOJO.
INTERESTING. SO THIS IS WHERE THEY'VE BEEN GATHERING.
NO, BROTHER. THIS IS WHERE THEY'VE BEEN COWERING.
INHERITORS! NEVER THOUGHT THEY'D DARE COME HERE!
BY ALL ACCOUNTS, THAT'S JENNIX. AND MORLUN.
THERE'S ONE MORE COMING THROUGH...
...I DON'T KNOW THAT ONE.
ONE OR A THOUSAND. DOESN'T MATTER. NOT AGAINST ME.

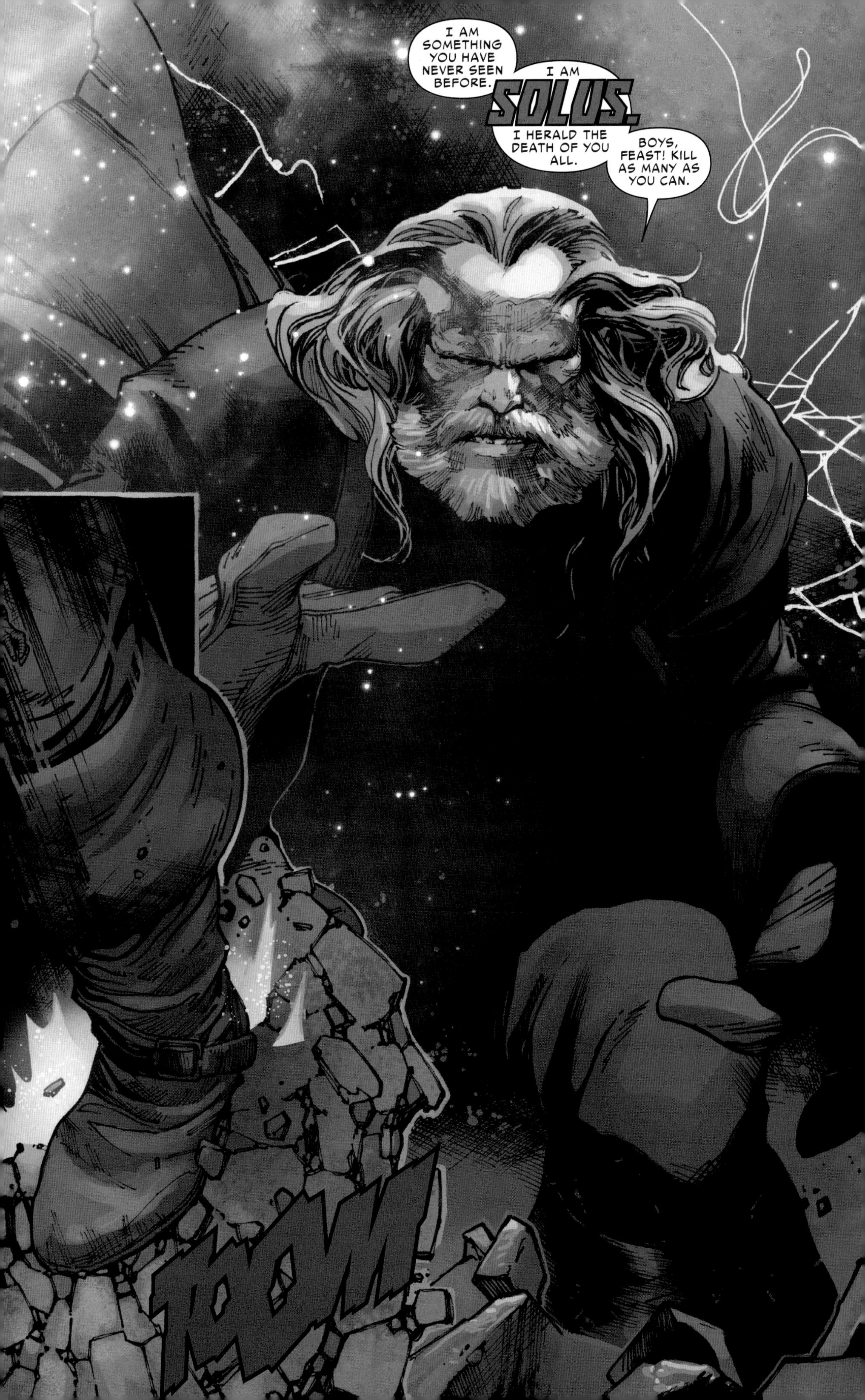
I AM SOMETHING YOU HAVE NEVER SEEN BEFORE.
I AM SOLUS.
I HERALD THE DEATH OF YOU ALL.
BOYS, FEAST! KILL AS MANY AS YOU CAN.

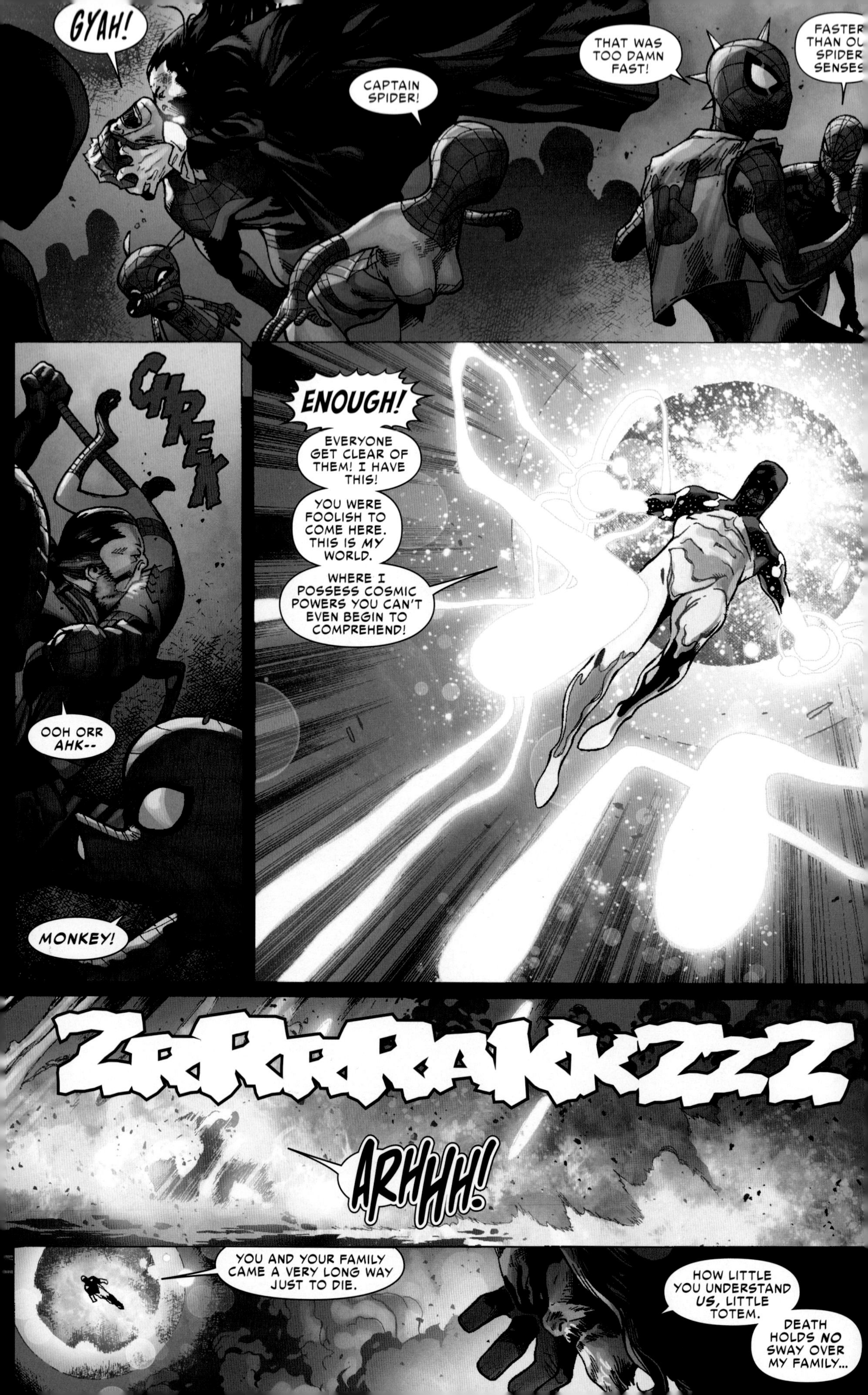
GYAH!
CAPTAIN SPIDER!
THAT WAS TOO DAMN FAST!
FASTER THAN OU SPIDER SENSES
CHREK
ENOUGH!
EVERYONE GET CLEAR OF THEM! I HAVE THIS!
YOU WERE FOOLISH TO COME HERE. THIS IS MY WORLD.
WHERE I POSSESS COSMIC POWERS YOU CAN'T EVEN BEGIN TO COMPREHEND!
OOH ORR AHK--
MONKEY!
ZRRRRAKKZZZ
ARHHH!
YOU AND YOUR FAMILY CAME A VERY LONG WAY JUST TO DIE.
HOW LITTLE YOU UNDERSTAND US, LITTLE TOTEM.
DEATH HOLDS NO SWAY OVER MY FAMILY...

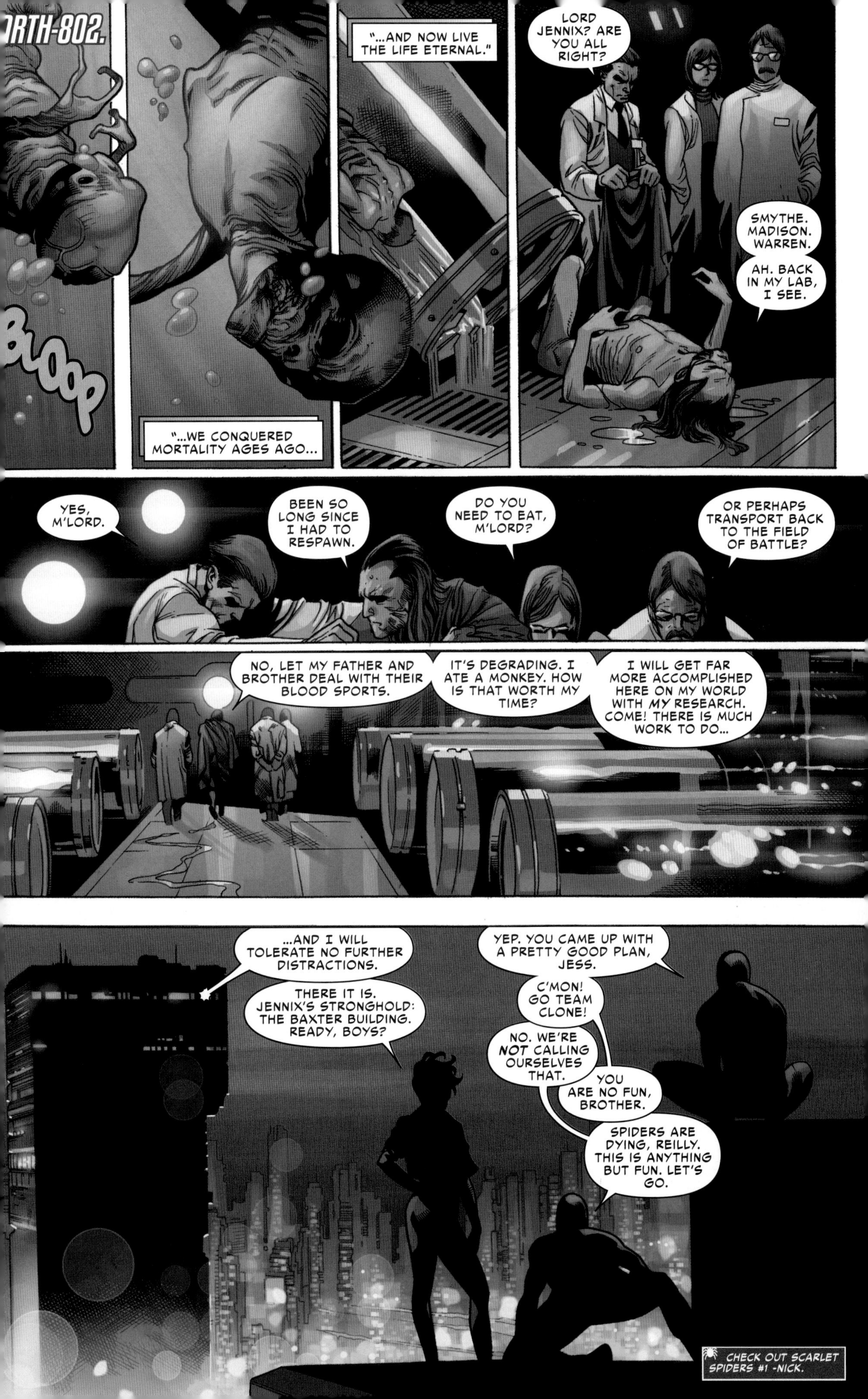

RTH-802.
BLOOP
"...WE CONQUERED MORTALITY AGES AGO...
"...AND NOW LIVE THE LIFE ETERNAL."
LORD JENNIX? ARE YOU ALL RIGHT?
SMYTHE. MADISON. WARREN.
AH. BACK IN MY LAB, I SEE.
YES, M'LORD.
BEEN SO LONG SINCE I HAD TO RESPAWN.
DO YOU NEED TO EAT, M'LORD?
OR PERHAPS TRANSPORT BACK TO THE FIELD OF BATTLE?
NO, LET MY FATHER AND BROTHER DEAL WITH THEIR BLOOD SPORTS.
IT'S DEGRADING. I ATE A MONKEY. HOW IS THAT WORTH MY TIME?
I WILL GET FAR MORE ACCOMPLISHED HERE ON MY WORLD WITH *MY* RESEARCH. COME! THERE IS MUCH WORK TO DO...
...AND I WILL TOLERATE NO FURTHER DISTRACTIONS.
THERE IT IS. JENNIX'S STRONGHOLD: THE BAXTER BUILDING. READY, BOYS?
YEP. YOU CAME UP WITH A PRETTY GOOD PLAN, JESS.
C'MON! GO TEAM CLONE!
NO. WE'RE *NOT* CALLING OURSELVES THAT.
YOU ARE NO FUN, BROTHER.
SPIDERS ARE DYING, REILLY. THIS IS ANYTHING BUT FUN. LET'S GO.
CHECK OUT SCARLET SPIDERS #1 -NICK.

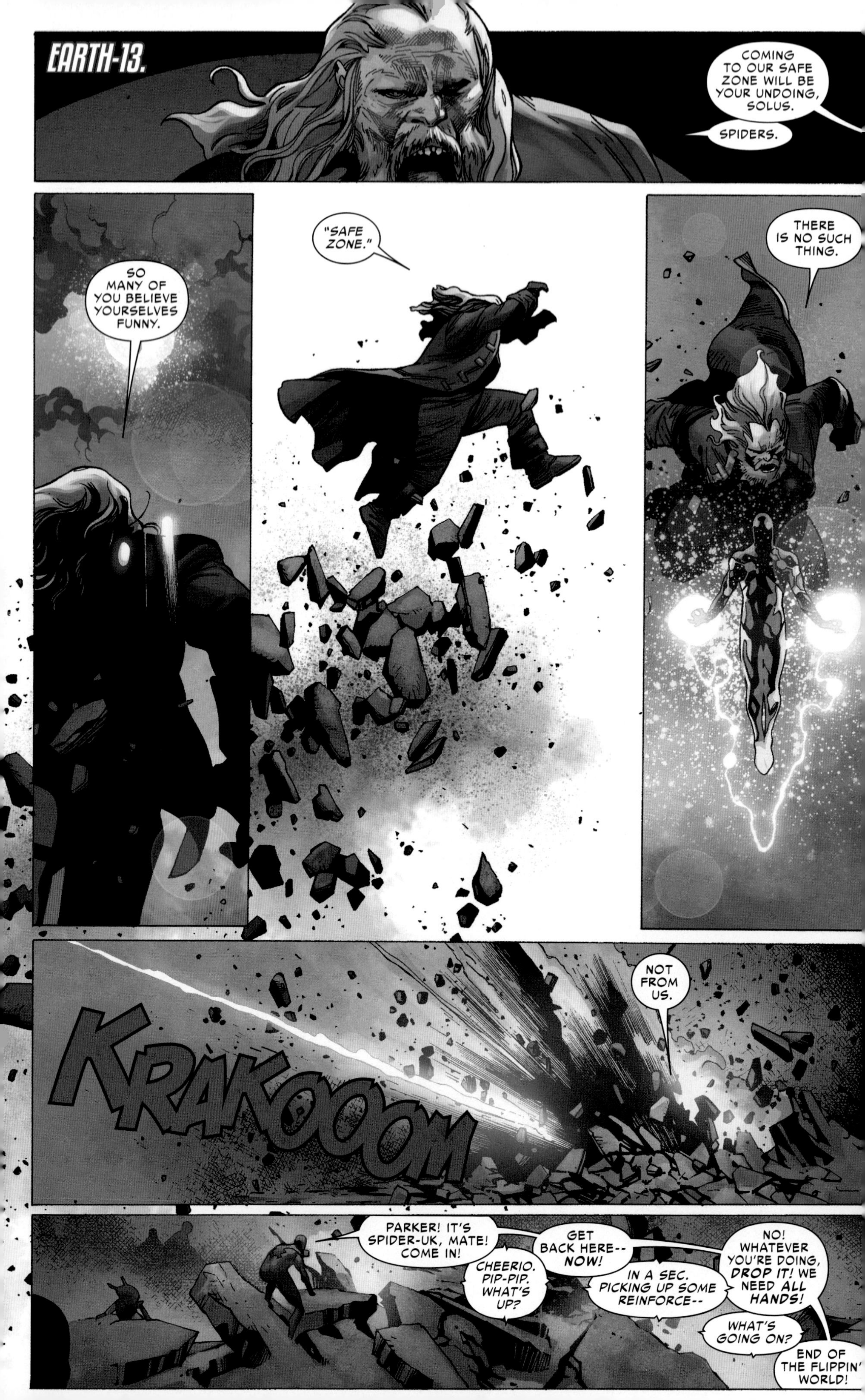
EARTH-13.
COMING TO OUR SAFE ZONE WILL BE YOUR UNDOING, SOLUS.
SPIDERS.
SO MANY OF YOU BELIEVE YOURSELVES FUNNY.
"SAFE ZONE."
THERE IS NO SUCH THING.
KRAKOOOM
NOT FROM US.
PARKER! IT'S SPIDER-UK, MATE! COME IN!
CHEERIO. PIP-PIP. WHAT'S UP?
GET BACK HERE-- NOW!
IN A SEC. PICKING UP SOME REINFORCE--
NO! WHATEVER YOU'RE DOING, DROP IT! WE NEED ALL HANDS!
WHAT'S GOING ON?
END OF THE FLIPPIN' WORLD!

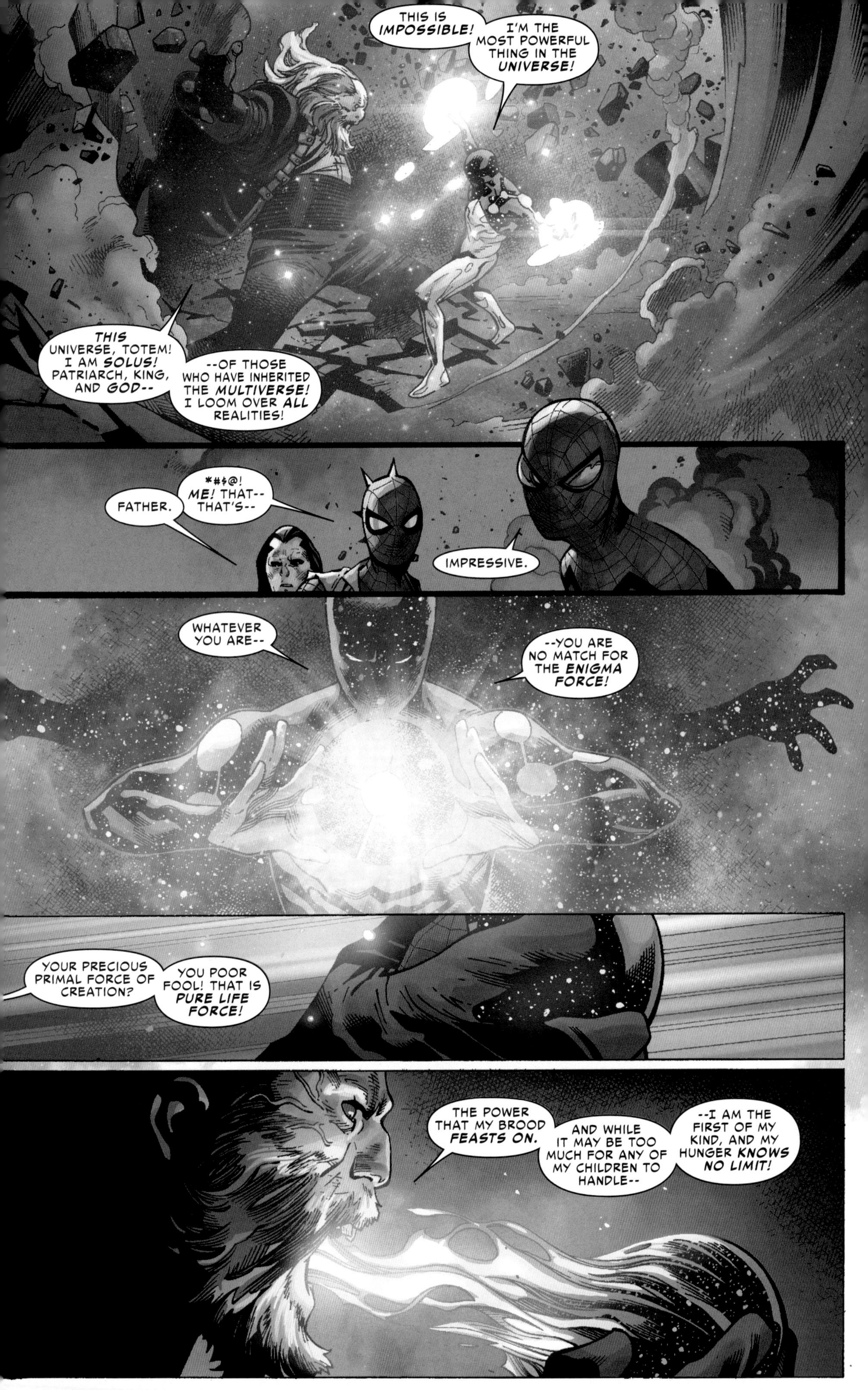
THIS IS IMPOSSIBLE!
I'M THE MOST POWERFUL THING IN THE UNIVERSE!
THIS UNIVERSE, TOTEM! I AM SOLUS! PATRIARCH, KING, AND GOD--
--OF THOSE WHO HAVE INHERITED THE MULTIVERSE! I LOOM OVER ALL REALITIES!
FATHER.
*#$@! ME! THAT--THAT'S--
IMPRESSIVE.
WHATEVER YOU ARE--
--YOU ARE NO MATCH FOR THE ENIGMA FORCE!
YOUR PRECIOUS PRIMAL FORCE OF CREATION?
YOU POOR FOOL! THAT IS PURE LIFE FORCE!
THE POWER THAT MY BROOD FEASTS ON.
AND WHILE IT MAY BE TOO MUCH FOR ANY OF MY CHILDREN TO HANDLE--
--I AM THE FIRST OF MY KIND, AND MY HUNGER KNOWS NO LIMIT!

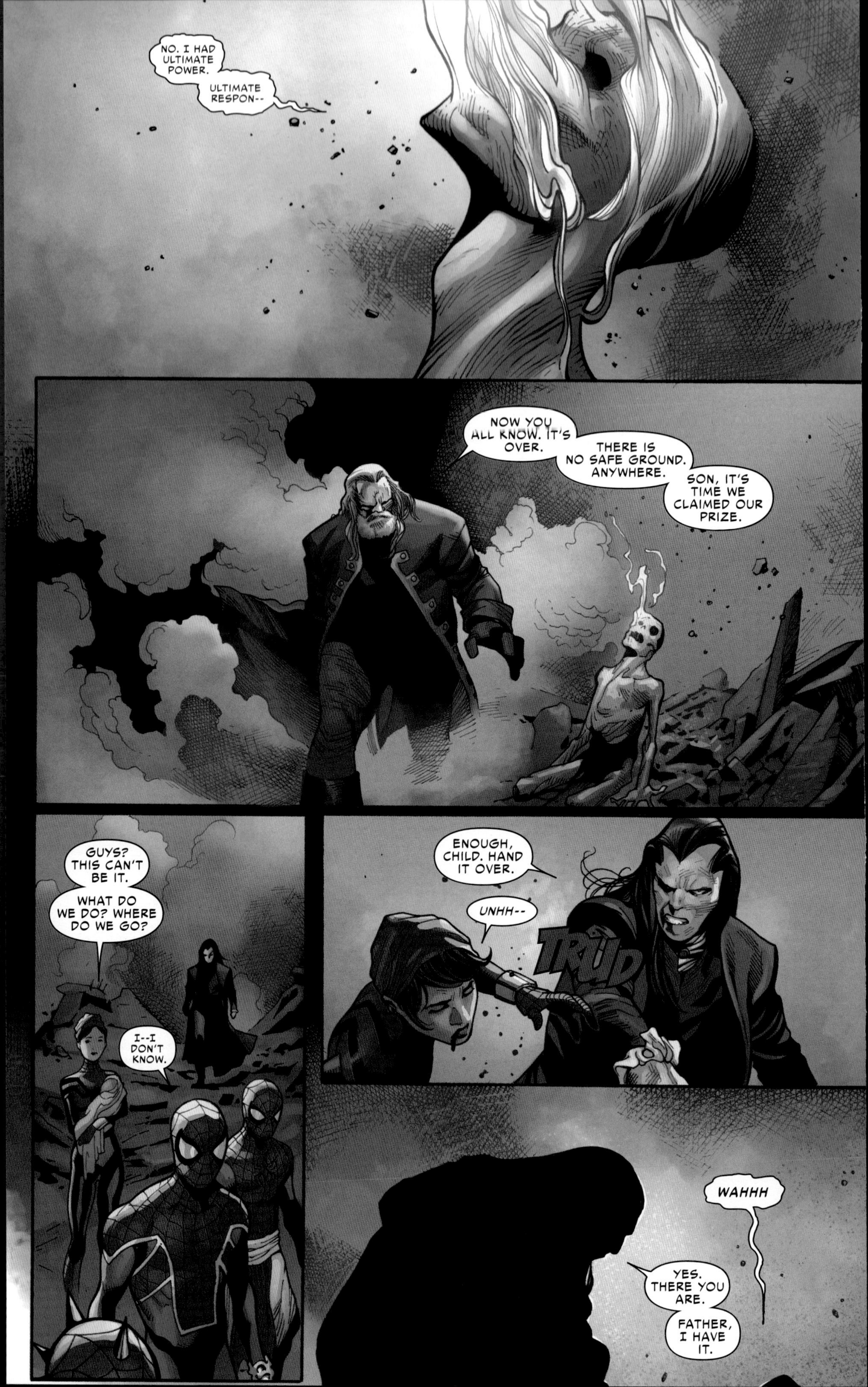
NO. I HAD ULTIMATE POWER.
ULTIMATE RESPON--
NOW YOU ALL KNOW. IT'S OVER.
THERE IS NO SAFE GROUND. ANYWHERE.
SON, IT'S TIME WE CLAIMED OUR PRIZE.
GUYS? THIS CAN'T BE IT.
WHAT DO WE DO? WHERE DO WE GO?
I--I DON'T KNOW.
ENOUGH, CHILD. HAND IT OVER.
UNHH--
TRUD
WAHHH
YES. THERE YOU ARE.
FATHER, I HAVE IT.

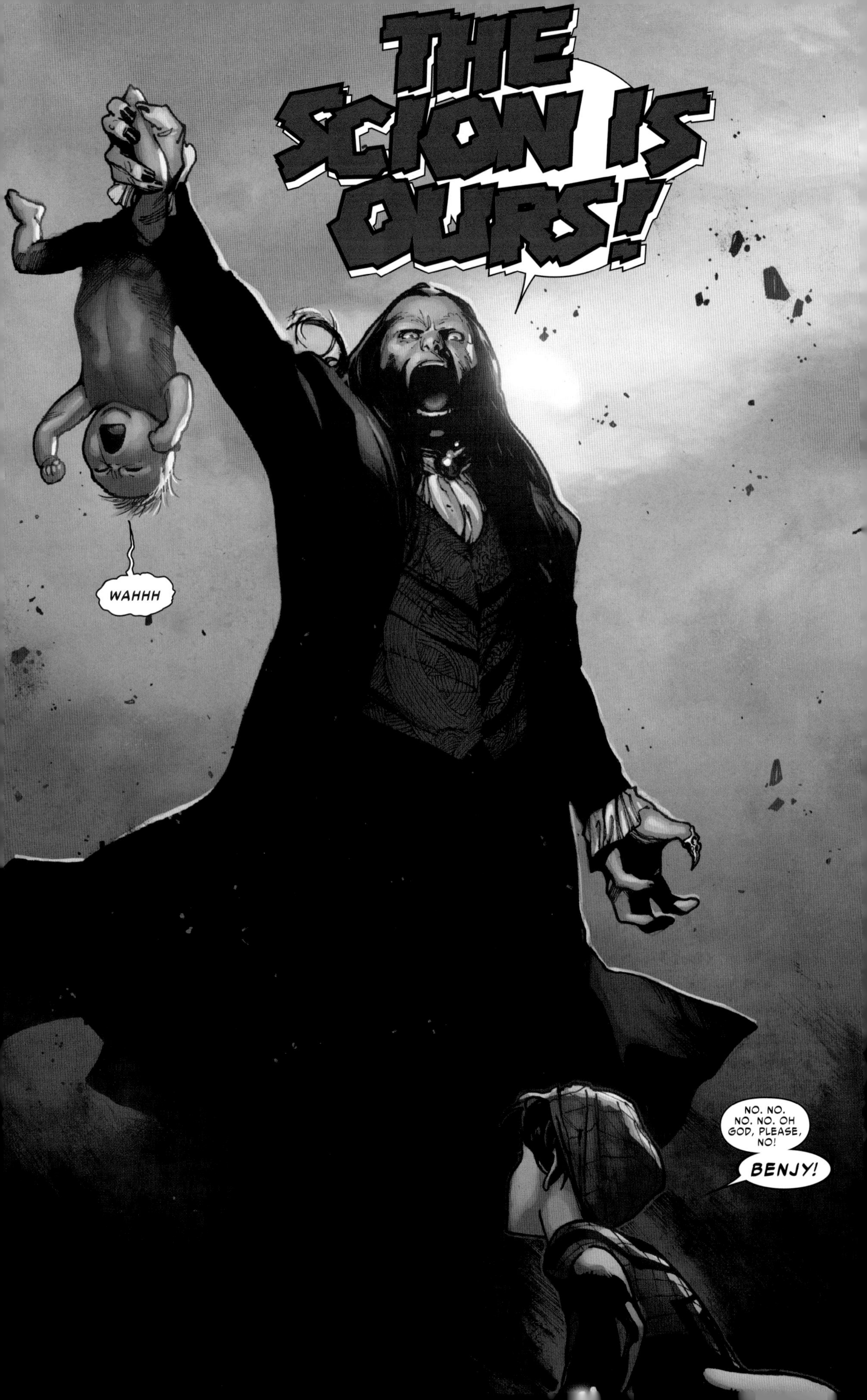
THE SCION IS OURS!
WAHHH
NO. NO. NO. NO. OH GOD, PLEASE, NO!
BENJY!

AMAZING SPIDER-MAN 7 VARIANT
BY BILL SIENKIEWICZ

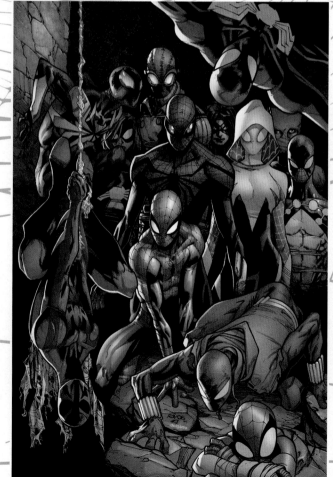

AMAZING SPIDER-MAN 7 VARIANT
BY HUMBERTO RAMOS
& EDGAR DELGADO

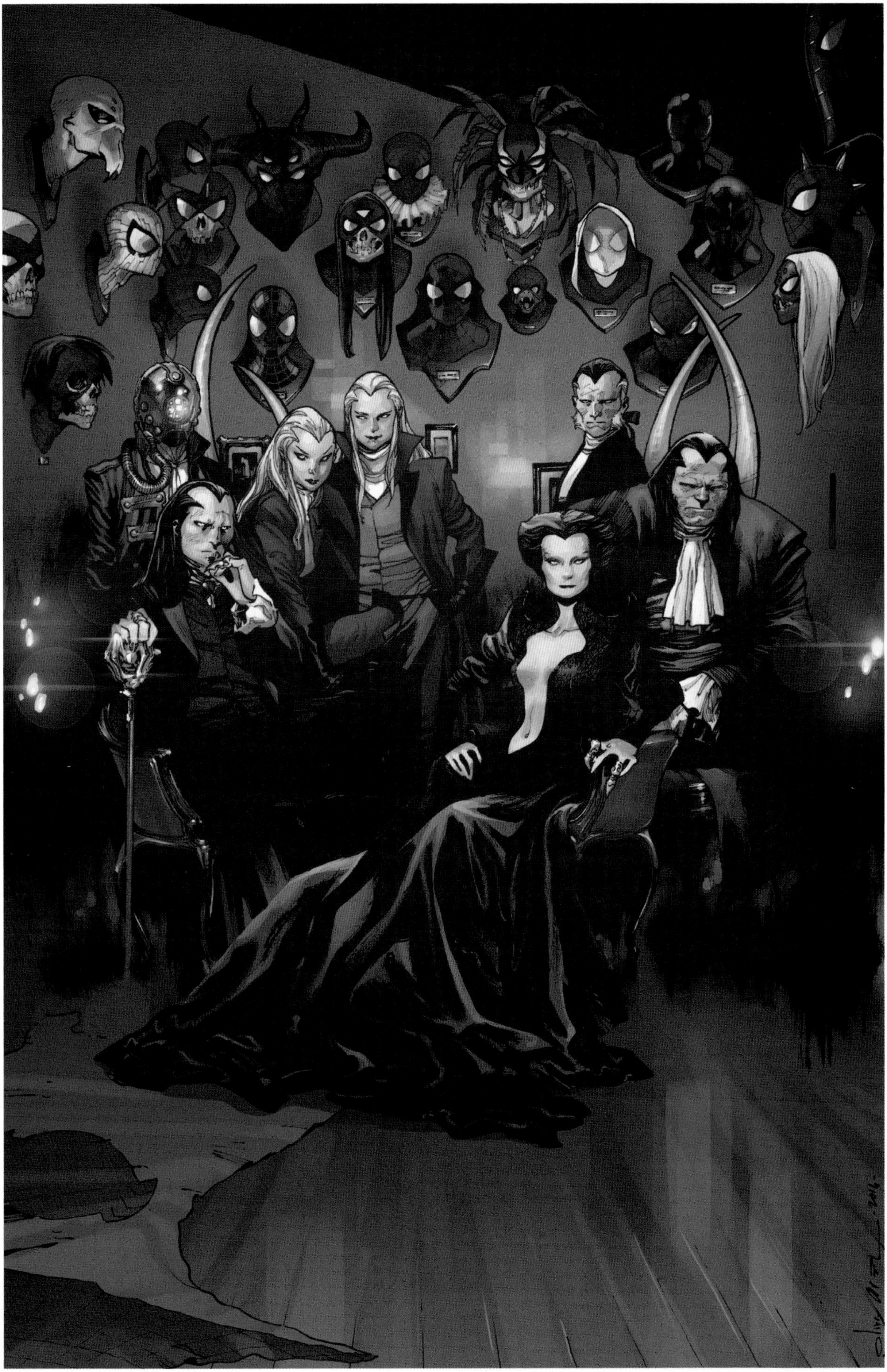

AMAZING SPIDER-MAN 12

SPIDER-VERSE, PART FOUR: ANYWHERE BUT HERE

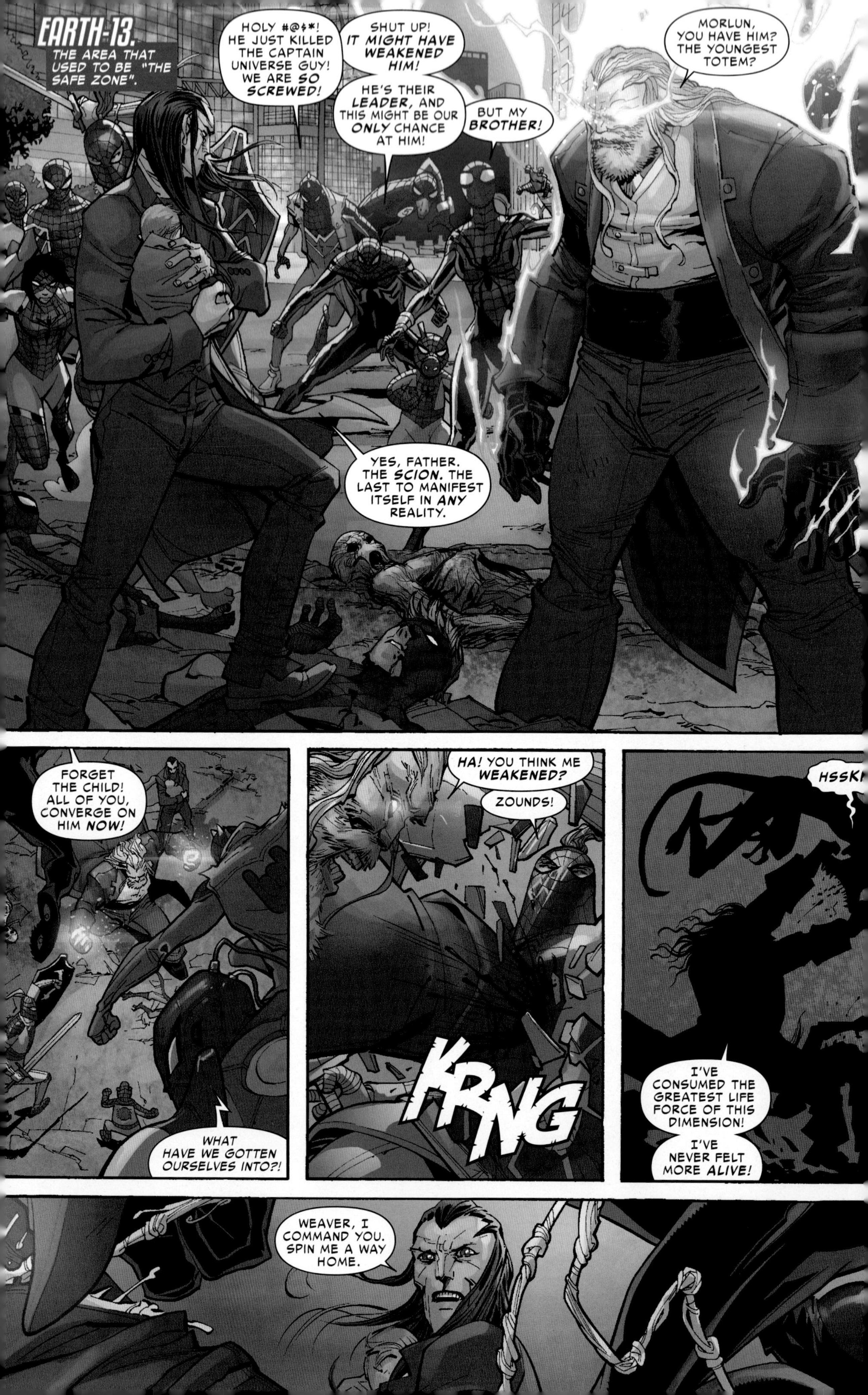
EARTH-13.
THE AREA THAT USED TO BE "THE SAFE ZONE".
HOLY #@$*! HE JUST KILLED THE CAPTAIN UNIVERSE GUY! WE ARE SO SCREWED!
SHUT UP! IT MIGHT HAVE WEAKENED HIM!
HE'S THEIR LEADER, AND THIS MIGHT BE OUR ONLY CHANCE AT HIM!
BUT MY BROTHER!
MORLUN, YOU HAVE HIM? THE YOUNGEST TOTEM?
YES, FATHER. THE SCION. THE LAST TO MANIFEST ITSELF IN ANY REALITY.
FORGET THE CHILD! ALL OF YOU, CONVERGE ON HIM NOW!
WHAT HAVE WE GOTTEN OURSELVES INTO?!
HA! YOU THINK ME WEAKENED?
ZOUNDS!
KRNG
HSSK
I'VE CONSUMED THE GREATEST LIFE FORCE OF THIS DIMENSION!
I'VE NEVER FELT MORE ALIVE!
WEAVER, I COMMAND YOU. SPIN ME A WAY HOME.

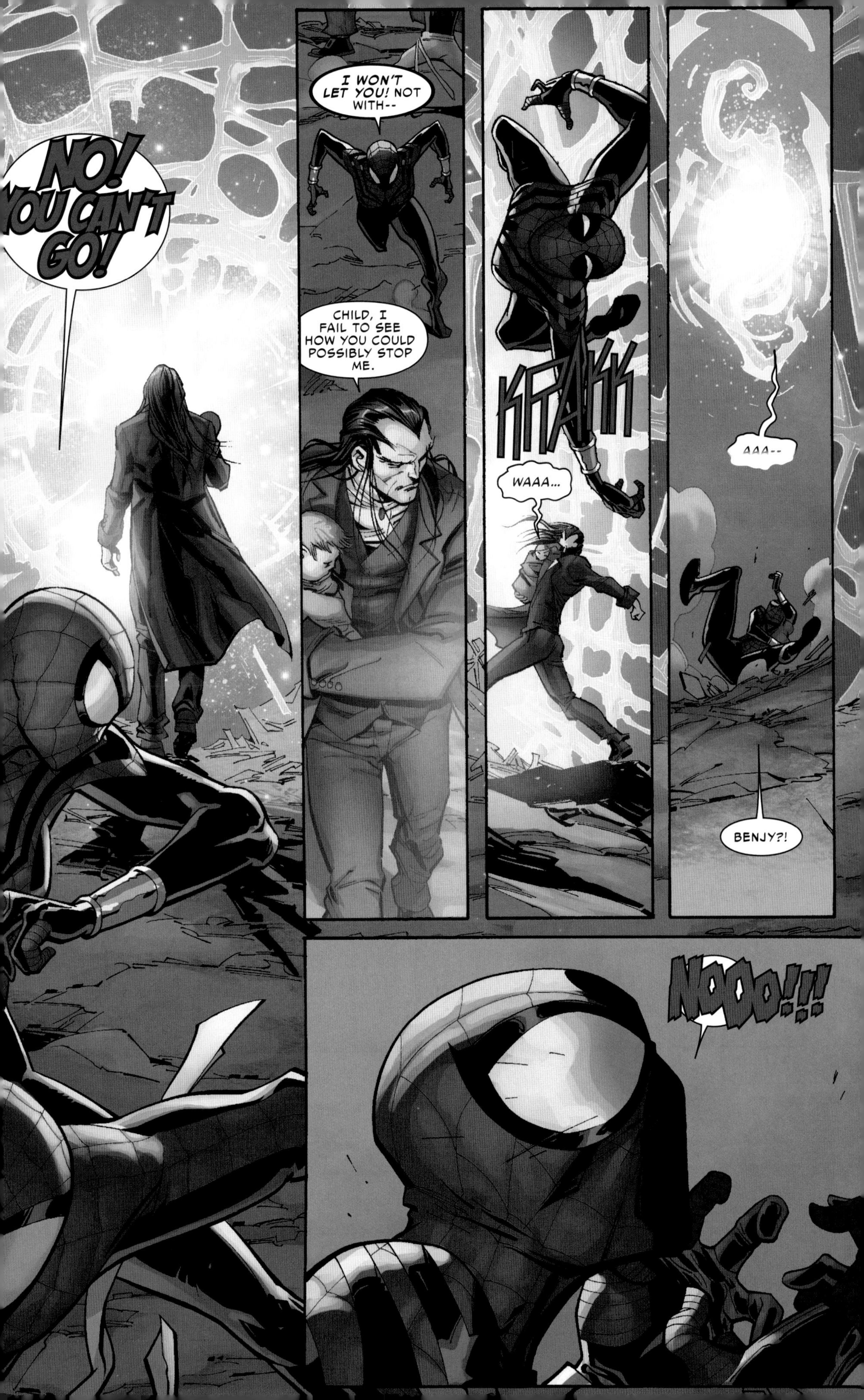
NO! YOU CAN'T GO!
I WON'T LET YOU! NOT WITH--
CHILD, I FAIL TO SEE HOW YOU COULD POSSIBLY STOP ME.
KRAKK
WAAA...
AAA--
BENJY?!
NOOO!!!

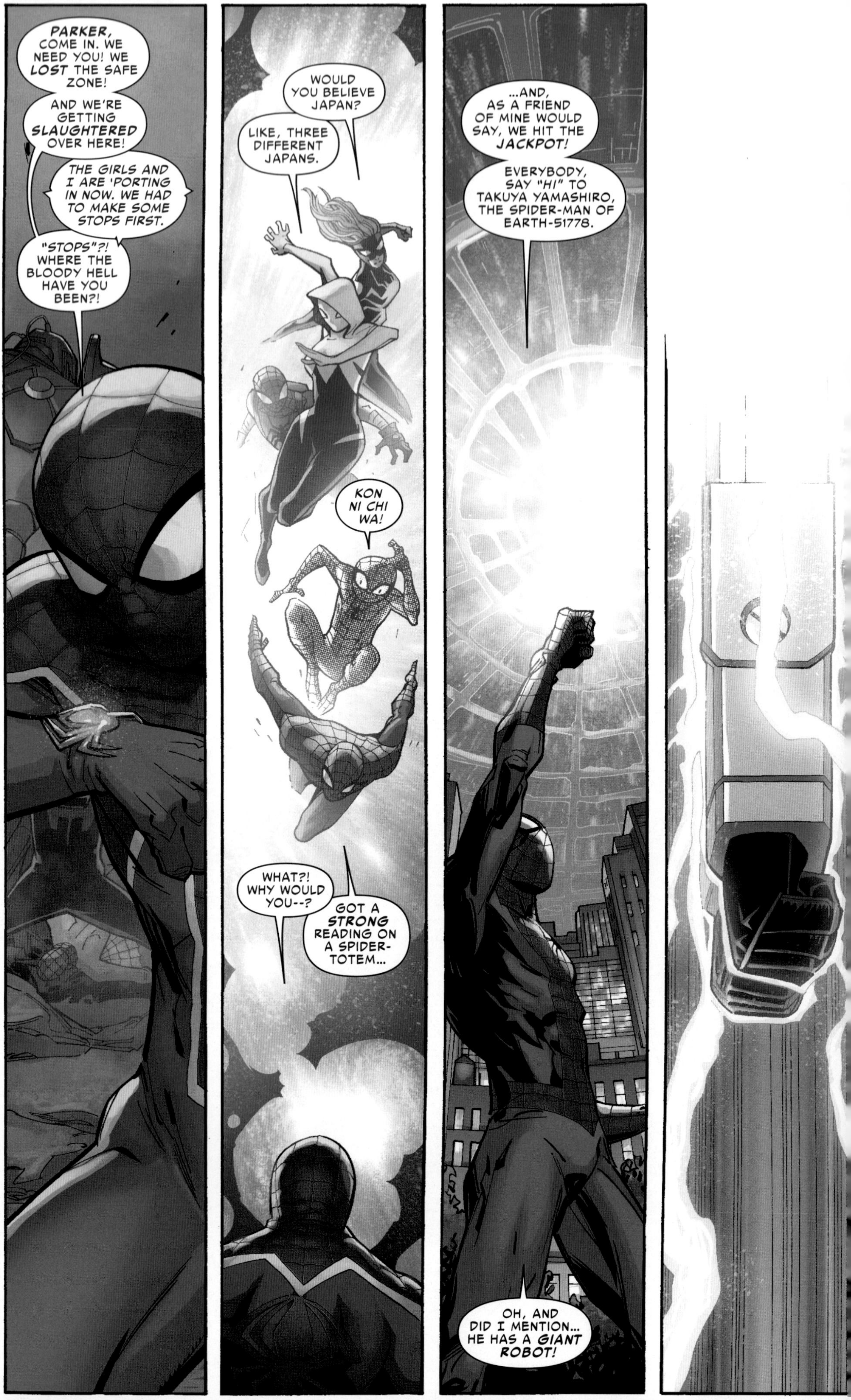
PARKER, COME IN. WE NEED YOU! WE LOST THE SAFE ZONE!
AND WE'RE GETTING SLAUGHTERED OVER HERE!
THE GIRLS AND I ARE 'PORTING IN NOW. WE HAD TO MAKE SOME STOPS FIRST.
"STOPS"?! WHERE THE BLOODY HELL HAVE YOU BEEN?!
WOULD YOU BELIEVE JAPAN?
LIKE, THREE DIFFERENT JAPANS.
KON NI CHI WA!
WHAT?! WHY WOULD YOU--?
GOT A STRONG READING ON A SPIDER-TOTEM...
...AND, AS A FRIEND OF MINE WOULD SAY, WE HIT THE JACKPOT!
EVERYBODY, SAY "HI" TO TAKUYA YAMASHIRO, THE SPIDER-MAN OF EARTH-51778.
OH, AND DID I MENTION... HE HAS A GIANT ROBOT!

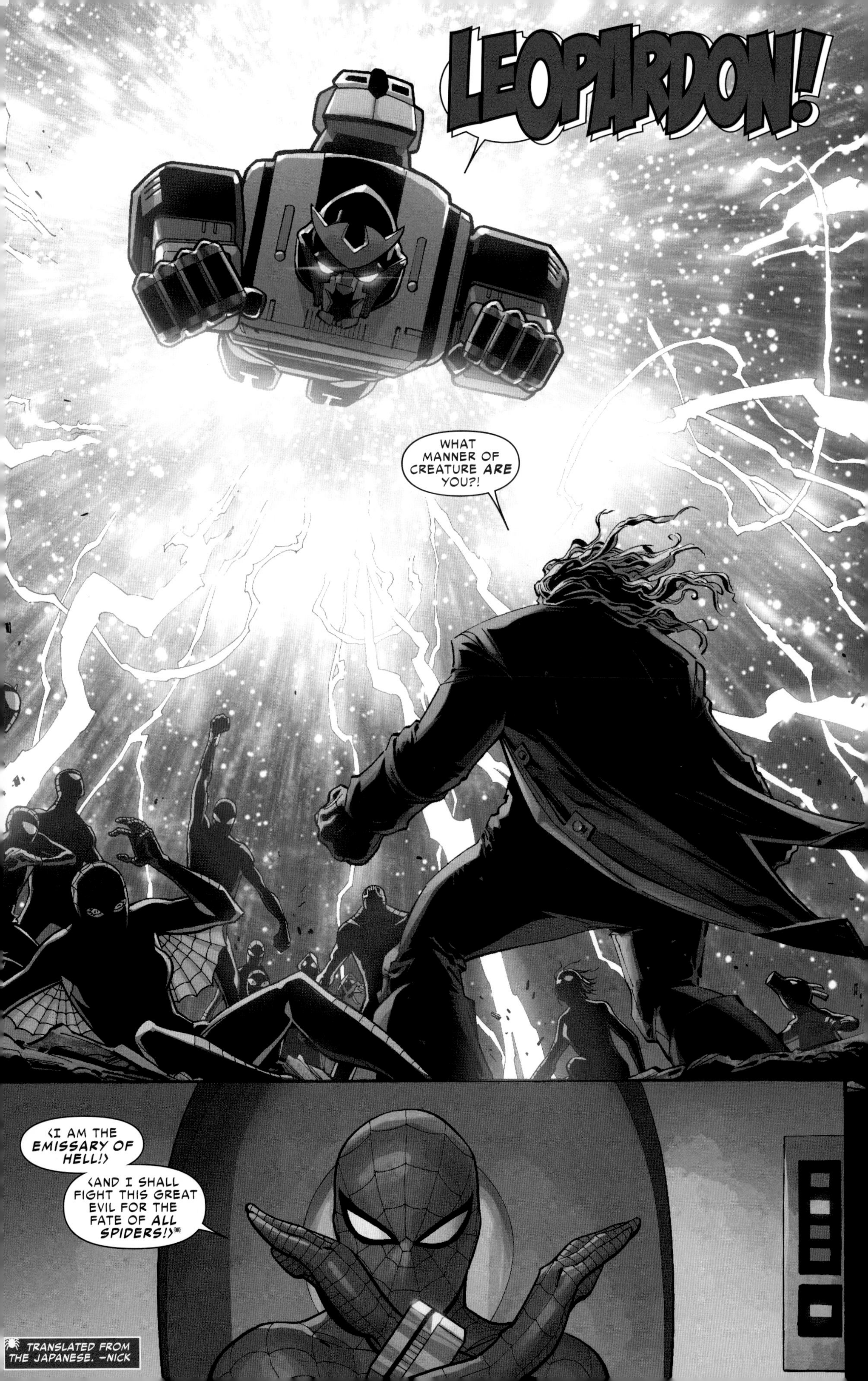
LEOPARDON!
WHAT MANNER OF CREATURE ARE YOU?!
‹I AM THE EMISSARY OF HELL!›
‹AND I SHALL FIGHT THIS GREAT EVIL FOR THE FATE OF ALL SPIDERS!›*
TRANSLATED FROM THE JAPANESE. –NICK

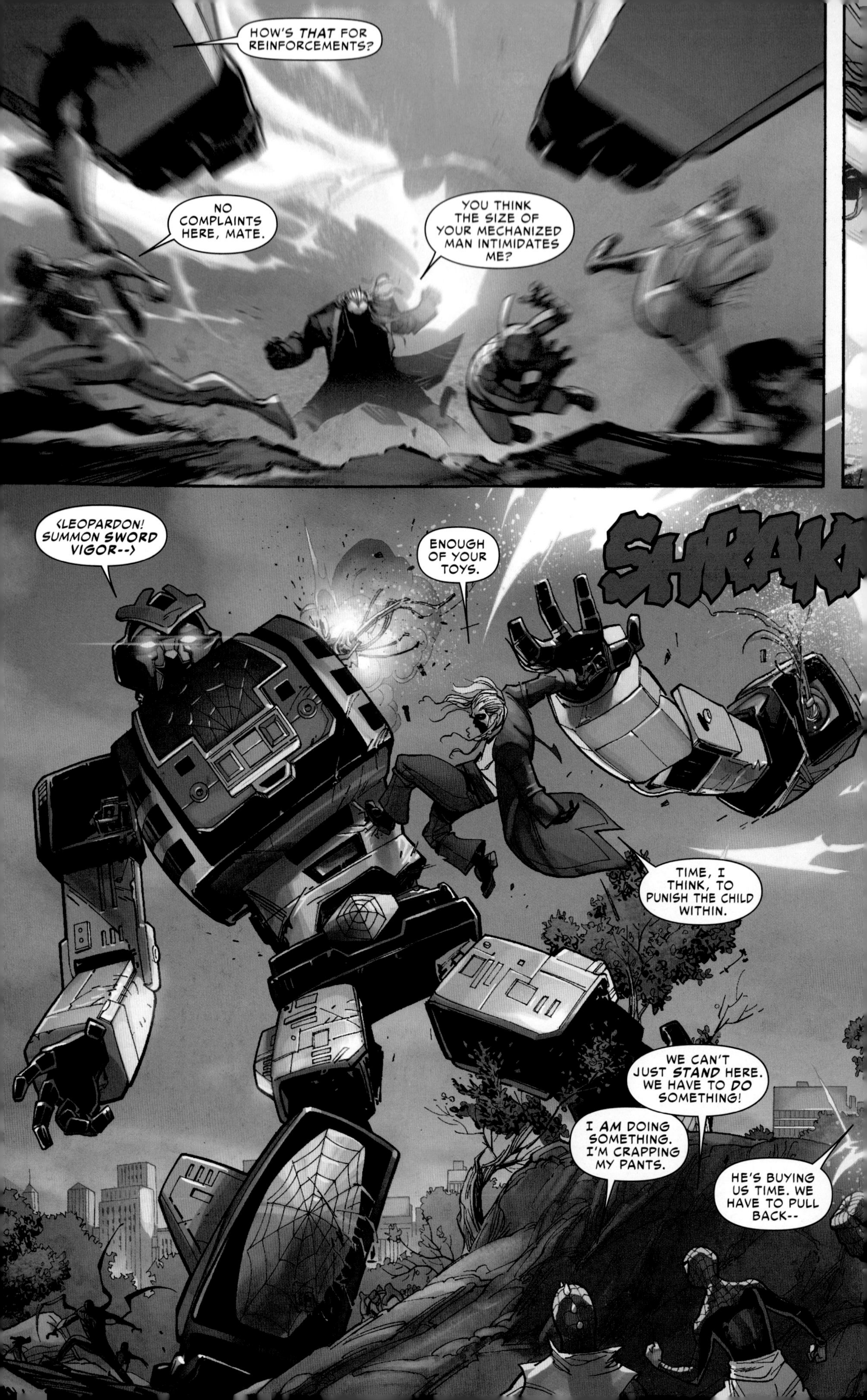
HOW'S THAT FOR REINFORCEMENTS?
NO COMPLAINTS HERE, MATE.
YOU THINK THE SIZE OF YOUR MECHANIZED MAN INTIMIDATES ME?
<LEOPARDON! SUMMON SWORD VIGOR-->
ENOUGH OF YOUR TOYS.
SHRAK
TIME, I THINK, TO PUNISH THE CHILD WITHIN.
WE CAN'T JUST STAND HERE. WE HAVE TO DO SOMETHING!
I AM DOING SOMETHING. I'M CRAPPING MY PANTS.
HE'S BUYING US TIME. WE HAVE TO PULL BACK--

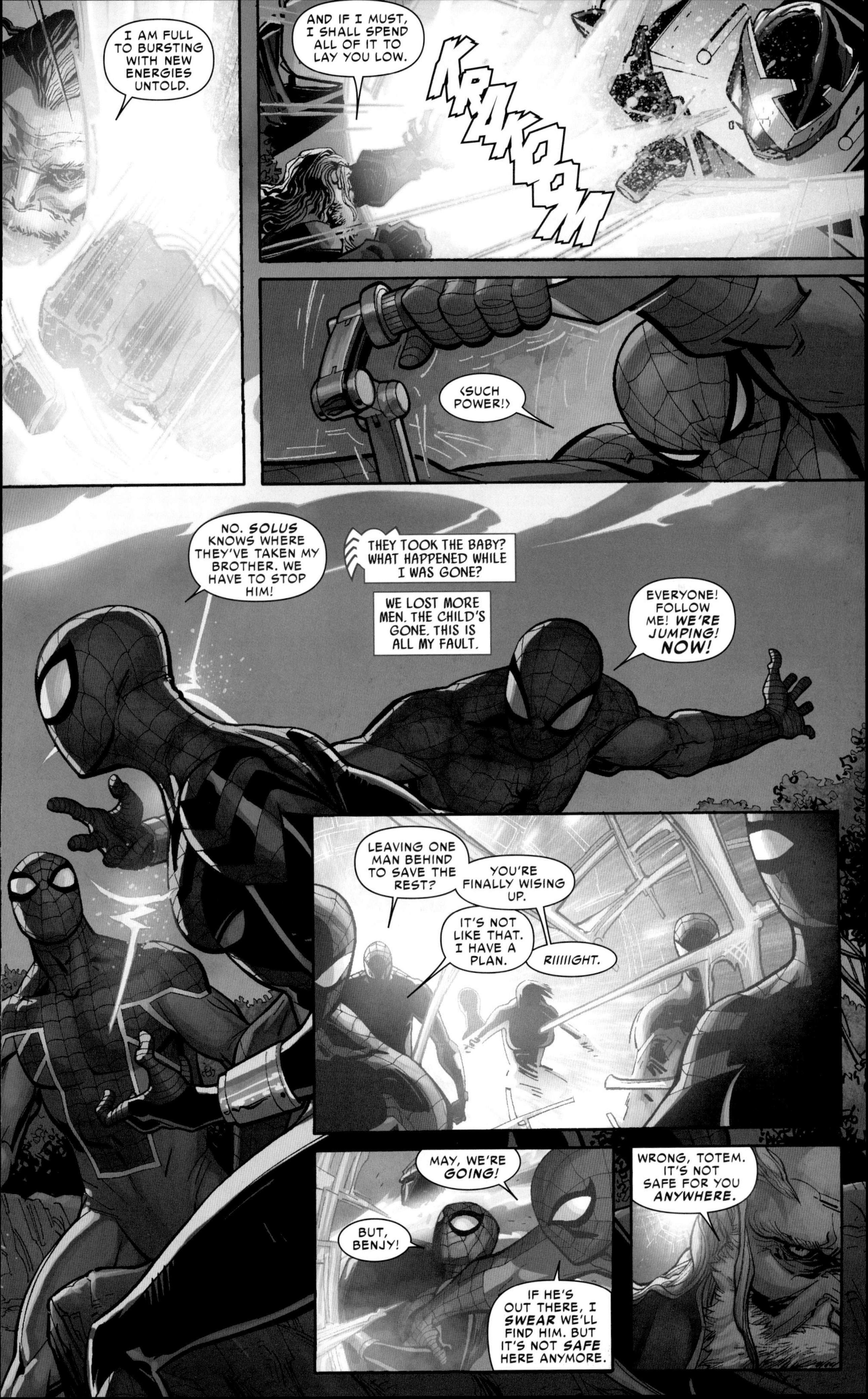
I AM FULL TO BURSTING WITH NEW ENERGIES UNTOLD.
AND IF I MUST, I SHALL SPEND ALL OF IT TO LAY YOU LOW.
KRAKOOM
‹SUCH POWER!›
NO. SOLUS KNOWS WHERE THEY'VE TAKEN MY BROTHER. WE HAVE TO STOP HIM!
THEY TOOK THE BABY? WHAT HAPPENED WHILE I WAS GONE?
WE LOST MORE MEN. THE CHILD'S GONE. THIS IS ALL MY FAULT.
EVERYONE! FOLLOW ME! WE'RE JUMPING! NOW!
LEAVING ONE MAN BEHIND TO SAVE THE REST?
YOU'RE FINALLY WISING UP.
IT'S NOT LIKE THAT. I HAVE A PLAN.
RIIIIIGHT.
MAY, WE'RE GOING!
BUT, BENJY!
IF HE'S OUT THERE, I SWEAR WE'LL FIND HIM. BUT IT'S NOT SAFE HERE ANYMORE.
WRONG, TOTEM. IT'S NOT SAFE FOR YOU ANYWHERE.

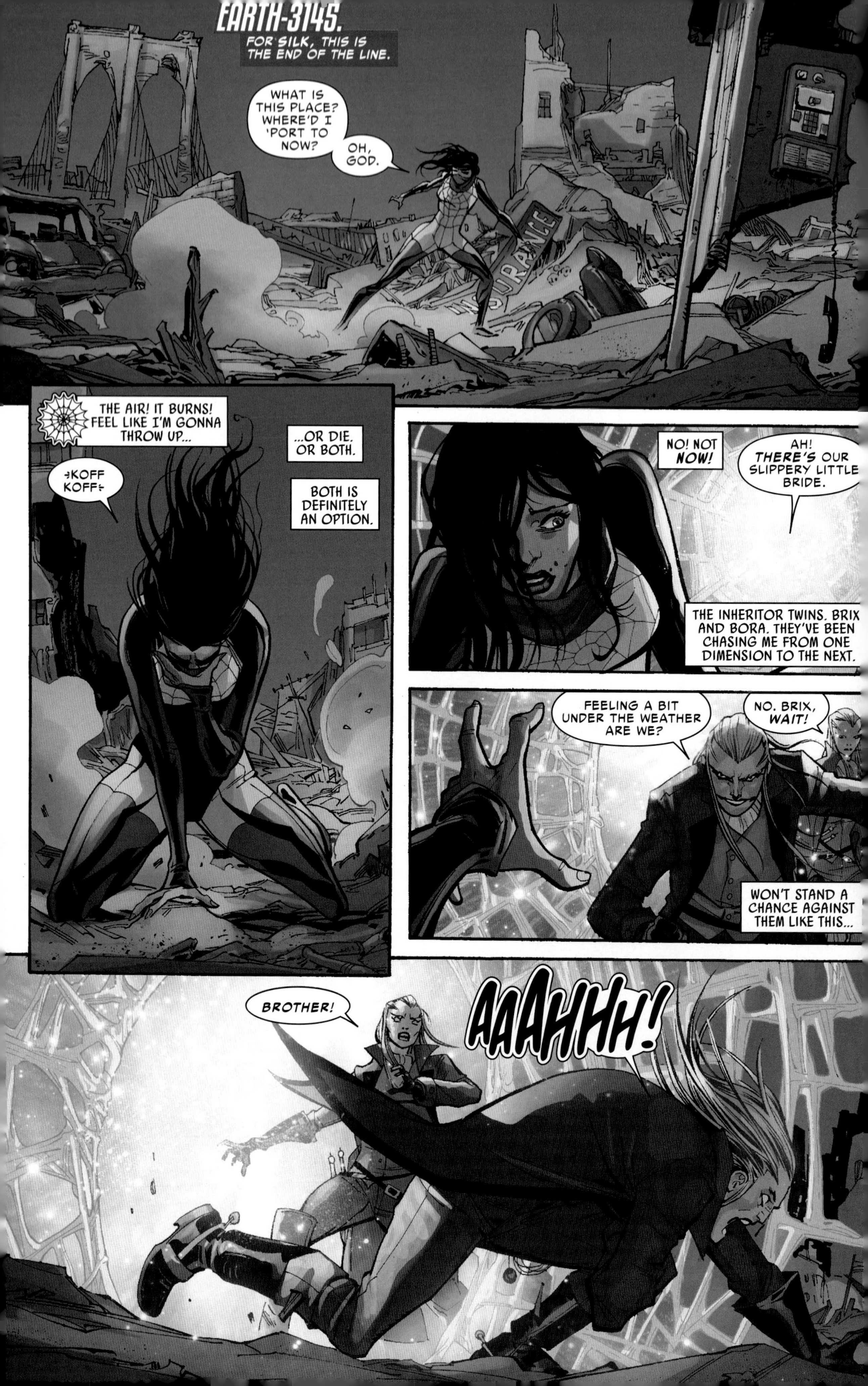
EARTH-3145.
FOR SILK, THIS IS THE END OF THE LINE.
WHAT IS THIS PLACE? WHERE'D I 'PORT TO NOW?
OH, GOD.
INSURANCE
THE AIR! IT BURNS! FEEL LIKE I'M GONNA THROW UP...
...OR DIE. OR BOTH.
BOTH IS DEFINITELY AN OPTION.
KOFF KOFF
NO! NOT NOW!
AH! THERE'S OUR SLIPPERY LITTLE BRIDE.
THE INHERITOR TWINS, BRIX AND BORA. THEY'VE BEEN CHASING ME FROM ONE DIMENSION TO THE NEXT.
FEELING A BIT UNDER THE WEATHER ARE WE?
NO. BRIX, WAIT!
WON'T STAND A CHANCE AGAINST THEM LIKE THIS...
BROTHER!
AAAHHH!

GET... **GAHH!** ...BACK HERE!

WHAT WAS THAT?

EXACTLY WHAT IT LOOKED LIKE. EARTH-3145. POST-THERMO--

--NUCLEAR-WAR.

HUH?

THIS WHOLE WORLD'S *IRRADIATED.*

IT HURTS LIKE HELL, BUT IT LOOKS LIKE IT HURTS THEM A *LOT* MORE THAN IT HURTS ME.

Y'KNOW WHAT? I'LL TAKE IT.

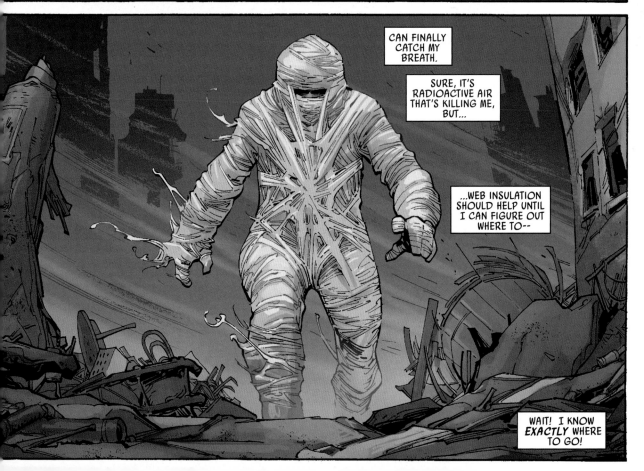

CAN FINALLY CATCH MY BREATH.

SURE, IT'S RADIOACTIVE AIR THAT'S KILLING ME, BUT...

...WEB INSULATION SHOULD HELP UNTIL I CAN FIGURE OUT WHERE TO--

WAIT! I KNOW *EXACTLY* WHERE TO GO!

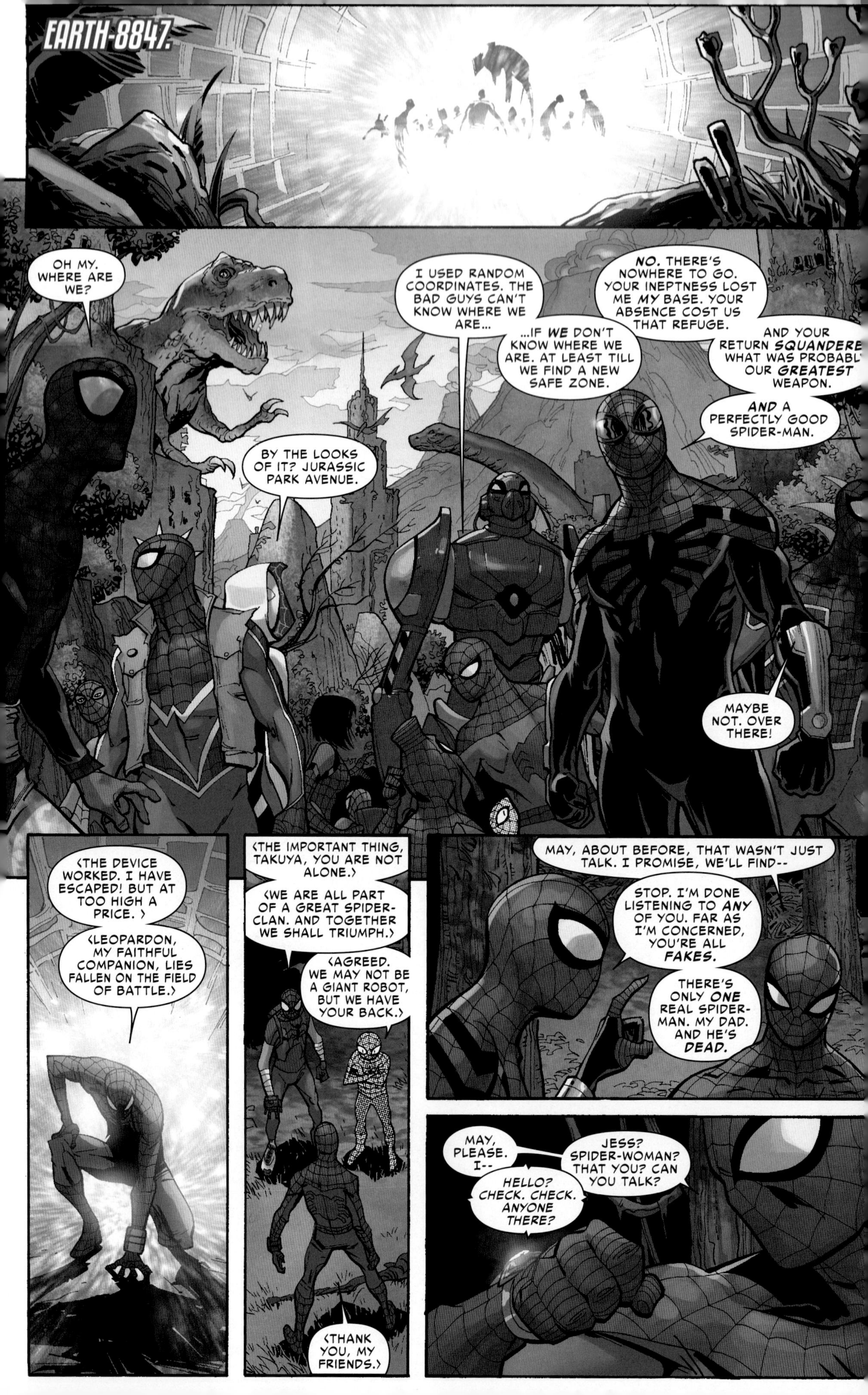
EARTH-8847.
OH MY. WHERE ARE WE?
BY THE LOOKS OF IT? JURASSIC PARK AVENUE.
I USED RANDOM COORDINATES. THE BAD GUYS CAN'T KNOW WHERE WE ARE...
...IF WE DON'T KNOW WHERE WE ARE. AT LEAST TILL WE FIND A NEW SAFE ZONE.
NO. THERE'S NOWHERE TO GO. YOUR INEPTNESS LOST ME MY BASE. YOUR ABSENCE COST US THAT REFUGE.
AND YOUR RETURN SQUANDERE WHAT WAS PROBABL OUR GREATEST WEAPON.
AND A PERFECTLY GOOD SPIDER-MAN.
MAYBE NOT. OVER THERE!
‹THE DEVICE WORKED. I HAVE ESCAPED! BUT AT TOO HIGH A PRICE.›
‹LEOPARDON, MY FAITHFUL COMPANION, LIES FALLEN ON THE FIELD OF BATTLE.›
‹THE IMPORTANT THING, TAKUYA, YOU ARE NOT ALONE.›
‹WE ARE ALL PART OF A GREAT SPIDER-CLAN. AND TOGETHER WE SHALL TRIUMPH.›
‹AGREED. WE MAY NOT BE A GIANT ROBOT, BUT WE HAVE YOUR BACK.›
‹THANK YOU, MY FRIENDS.›
MAY, ABOUT BEFORE, THAT WASN'T JUST TALK. I PROMISE, WE'LL FIND--
STOP. I'M DONE LISTENING TO ANY OF YOU. FAR AS I'M CONCERNED, YOU'RE ALL FAKES.
THERE'S ONLY ONE REAL SPIDER-MAN. MY DAD. AND HE'S DEAD.
MAY, PLEASE. I--
JESS? SPIDER-WOMAN? THAT YOU? CAN YOU TALK?
HELLO? CHECK. CHECK. ANYONE THERE?

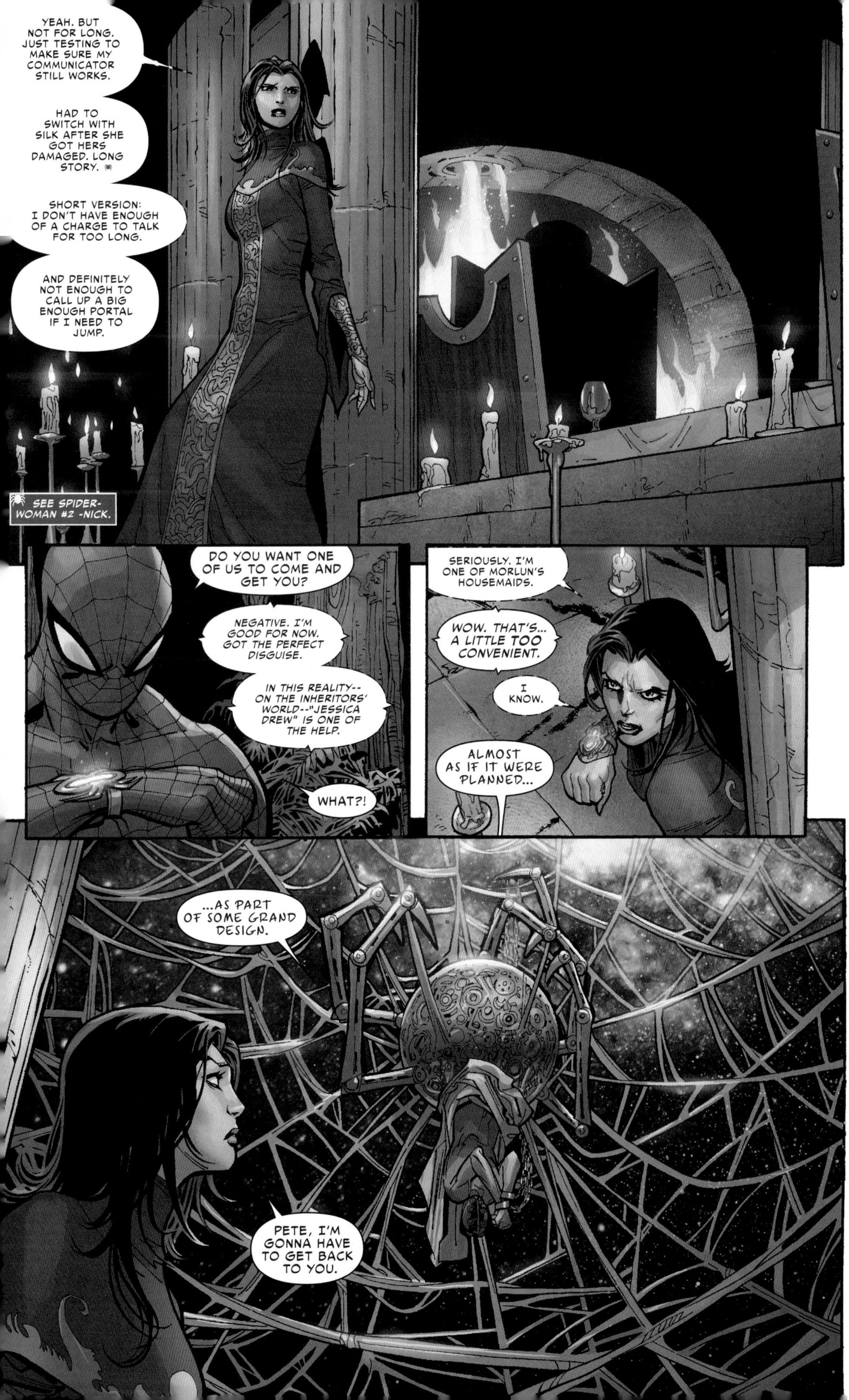
YEAH. BUT NOT FOR LONG. JUST TESTING TO MAKE SURE MY COMMUNICATOR STILL WORKS.
HAD TO SWITCH WITH SILK AFTER SHE GOT HERS DAMAGED. LONG STORY.
SHORT VERSION: I DON'T HAVE ENOUGH OF A CHARGE TO TALK FOR TOO LONG.
AND DEFINITELY NOT ENOUGH TO CALL UP A BIG ENOUGH PORTAL IF I NEED TO JUMP.
SEE SPIDER-WOMAN #2 -NICK.
DO YOU WANT ONE OF US TO COME AND GET YOU?
NEGATIVE. I'M GOOD FOR NOW. GOT THE PERFECT DISGUISE.
IN THIS REALITY-- ON THE INHERITORS' WORLD--"JESSICA DREW" IS ONE OF THE HELP.
WHAT?!
SERIOUSLY. I'M ONE OF MORLUN'S HOUSEMAIDS.
WOW. THAT'S... A LITTLE TOO CONVENIENT.
I KNOW.
ALMOST AS IF IT WERE PLANNED...
...AS PART OF SOME GRAND DESIGN.
PETE, I'M GONNA HAVE TO GET BACK TO YOU.

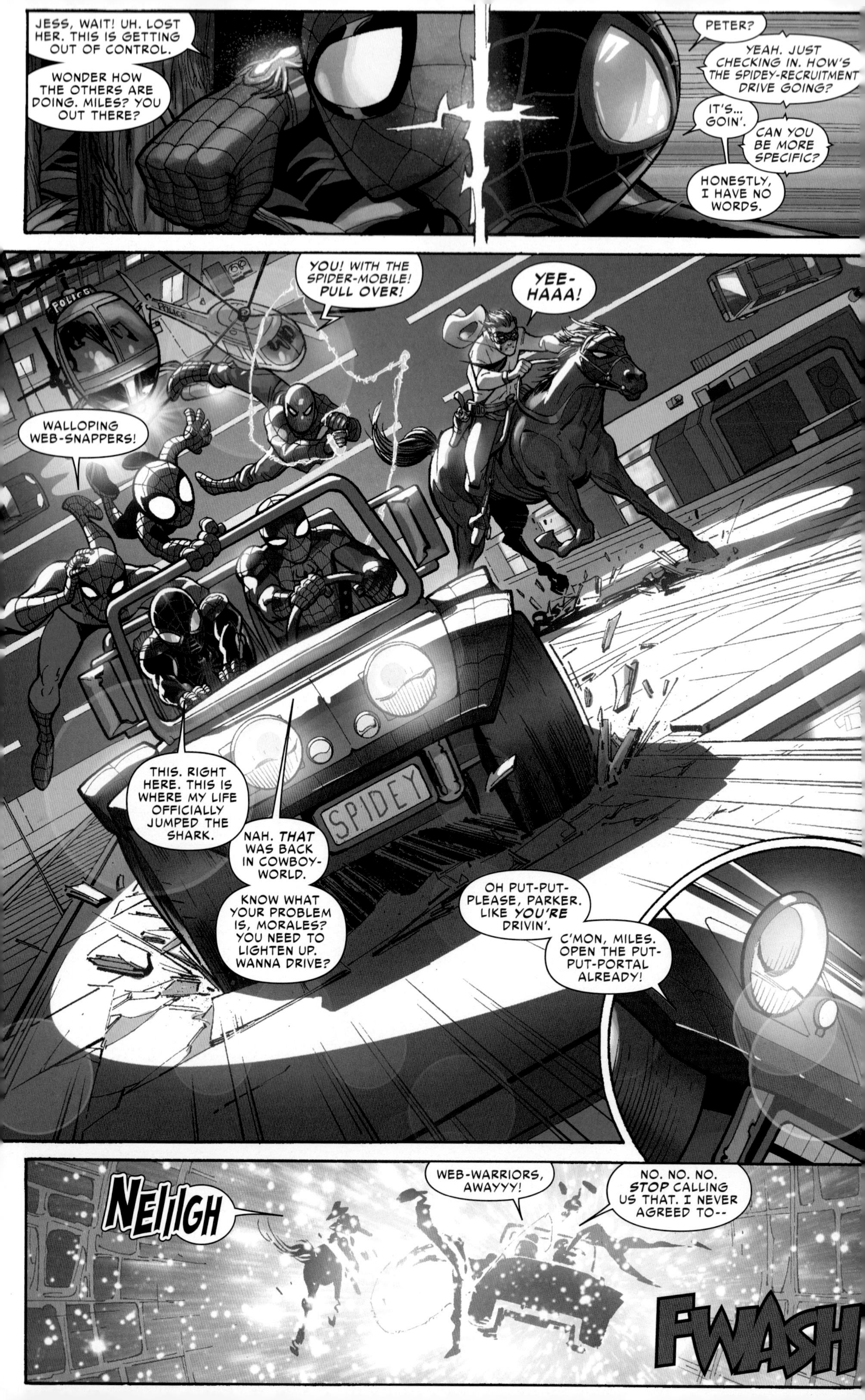

JESS, WAIT! UH. LOST HER. THIS IS GETTING OUT OF CONTROL.
WONDER HOW THE OTHERS ARE DOING. MILES? YOU OUT THERE?
PETER?
YEAH. JUST CHECKING IN. HOW'S THE SPIDEY-RECRUITMENT DRIVE GOING?
IT'S... GOIN'.
CAN YOU BE MORE SPECIFIC?
HONESTLY, I HAVE NO WORDS.
YOU! WITH THE SPIDER-MOBILE! PULL OVER!
YEE-HAAA!
POLICE
WALLOPING WEB-SNAPPERS!
SPIDEY
THIS. RIGHT HERE. THIS IS WHERE MY LIFE OFFICIALLY JUMPED THE SHARK.
NAH. THAT WAS BACK IN COWBOY-WORLD.
KNOW WHAT YOUR PROBLEM IS, MORALES? YOU NEED TO LIGHTEN UP. WANNA DRIVE?
OH PUT-PUT-PLEASE, PARKER. LIKE YOU'RE DRIVIN'.
C'MON, MILES. OPEN THE PUT-PUT-PORTAL ALREADY!
NEIIIGH
WEB-WARRIORS, AWAYYY!
NO. NO. NO. STOP CALLING US THAT. I NEVER AGREED TO--
FWASH

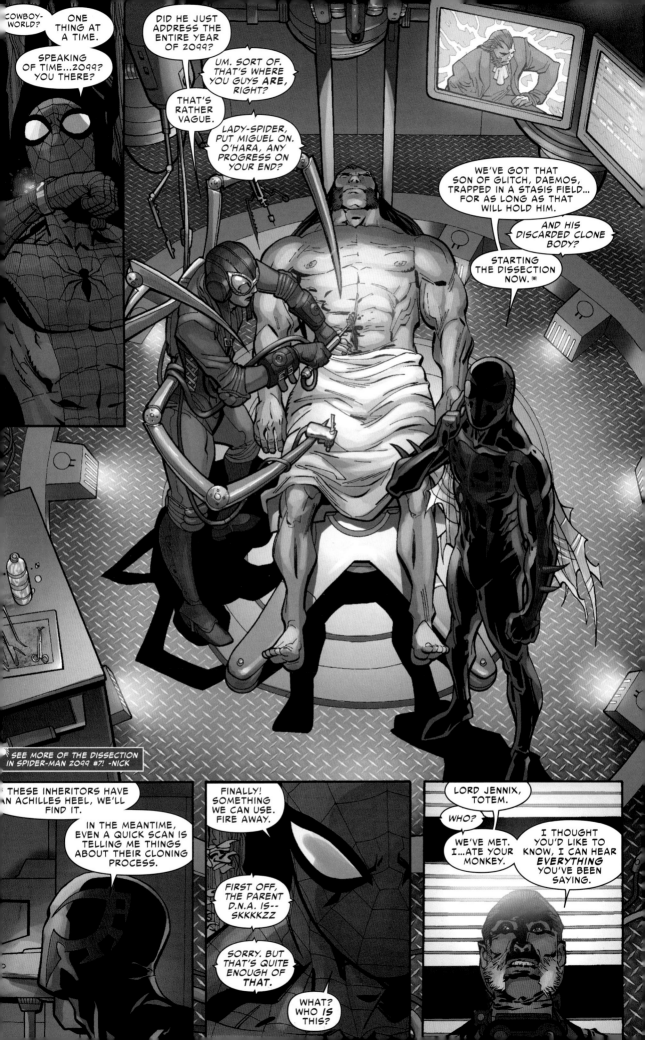

COWBOY-WORLD?

ONE THING AT A TIME.

SPEAKING OF TIME...2099? YOU THERE?

DID HE JUST ADDRESS THE ENTIRE YEAR OF 2099?

UM. SORT OF. THAT'S WHERE YOU GUYS ARE, RIGHT?

THAT'S RATHER VAGUE.

LADY-SPIDER, PUT MIGUEL ON. O'HARA, ANY PROGRESS ON YOUR END?

WE'VE GOT THAT SON OF GLITCH, DAEMOS, TRAPPED IN A STASIS FIELD... FOR AS LONG AS THAT WILL HOLD HIM.

AND HIS DISCARDED CLONE BODY?

STARTING THE DISSECTION NOW. ※

※ SEE MORE OF THE DISSECTION IN SPIDER-MAN 2099 #7! -NICK

THESE INHERITORS HAVE AN ACHILLES HEEL, WE'LL FIND IT.

IN THE MEANTIME, EVEN A QUICK SCAN IS TELLING ME THINGS ABOUT THEIR CLONING PROCESS.

FINALLY! SOMETHING WE CAN USE. FIRE AWAY.

FIRST OFF, THE PARENT D.N.A. IS-- SKKKKZZ

SORRY. BUT THAT'S QUITE ENOUGH OF THAT.

WHAT? WHO IS THIS?

LORD JENNIX, TOTEM.

WHO?

WE'VE MET. I...ATE YOUR MONKEY.

I THOUGHT YOU'D LIKE TO KNOW, I CAN HEAR EVERYTHING YOU'VE BEEN SAYING.

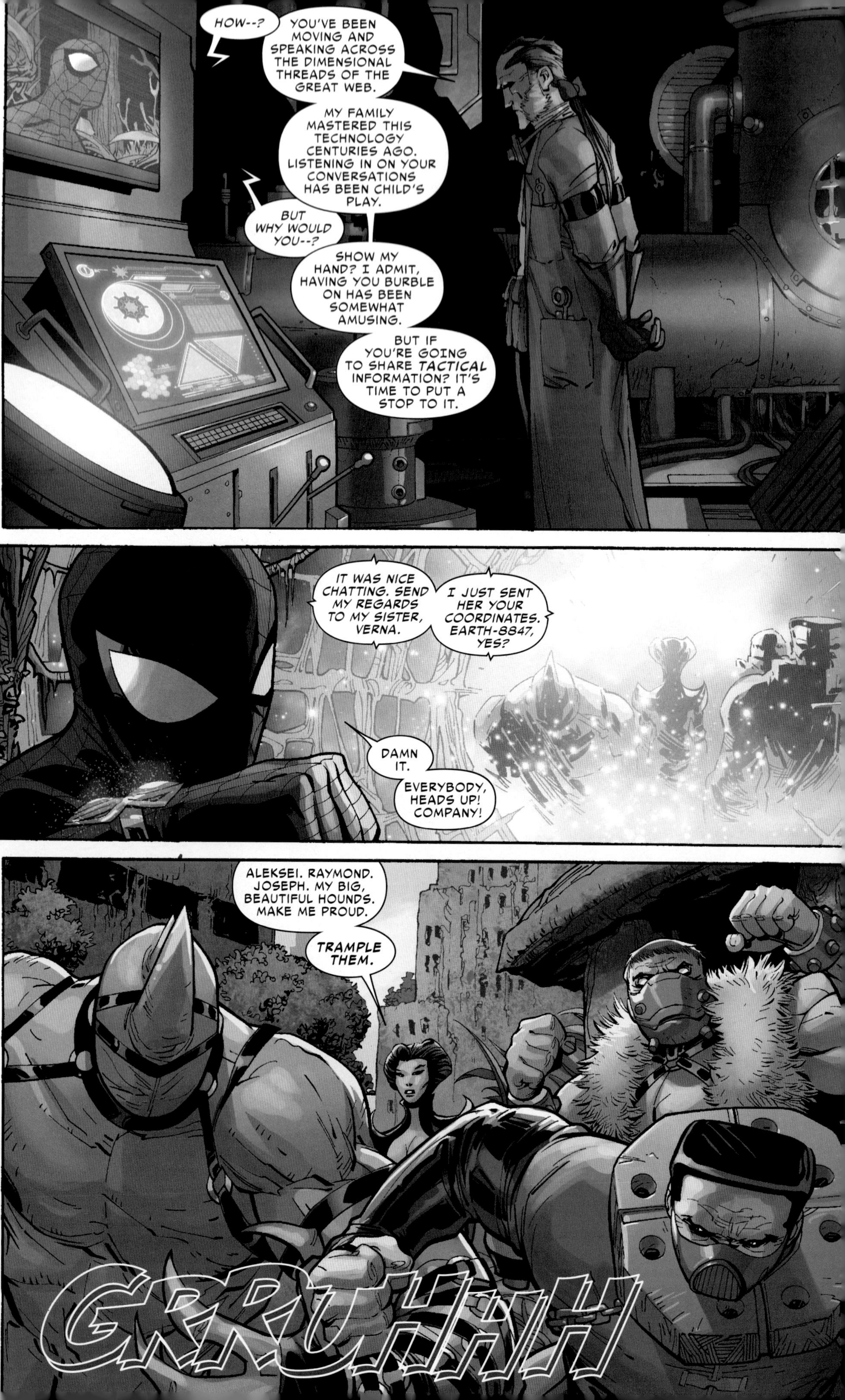
HOW--?
YOU'VE BEEN MOVING AND SPEAKING ACROSS THE DIMENSIONAL THREADS OF THE GREAT WEB.
MY FAMILY MASTERED THIS TECHNOLOGY CENTURIES AGO. LISTENING IN ON YOUR CONVERSATIONS HAS BEEN CHILD'S PLAY.
BUT WHY WOULD YOU--?
SHOW MY HAND? I ADMIT, HAVING YOU BURBLE ON HAS BEEN SOMEWHAT AMUSING.
BUT IF YOU'RE GOING TO SHARE TACTICAL INFORMATION? IT'S TIME TO PUT A STOP TO IT.
IT WAS NICE CHATTING. SEND MY REGARDS TO MY SISTER, VERNA.
I JUST SENT HER YOUR COORDINATES. EARTH-8847, YES?
DAMN IT.
EVERYBODY, HEADS UP! COMPANY!
ALEKSEI. RAYMOND. JOSEPH. MY BIG, BEAUTIFUL HOUNDS. MAKE ME PROUD.
TRAMPLE THEM.
GRRUHHH

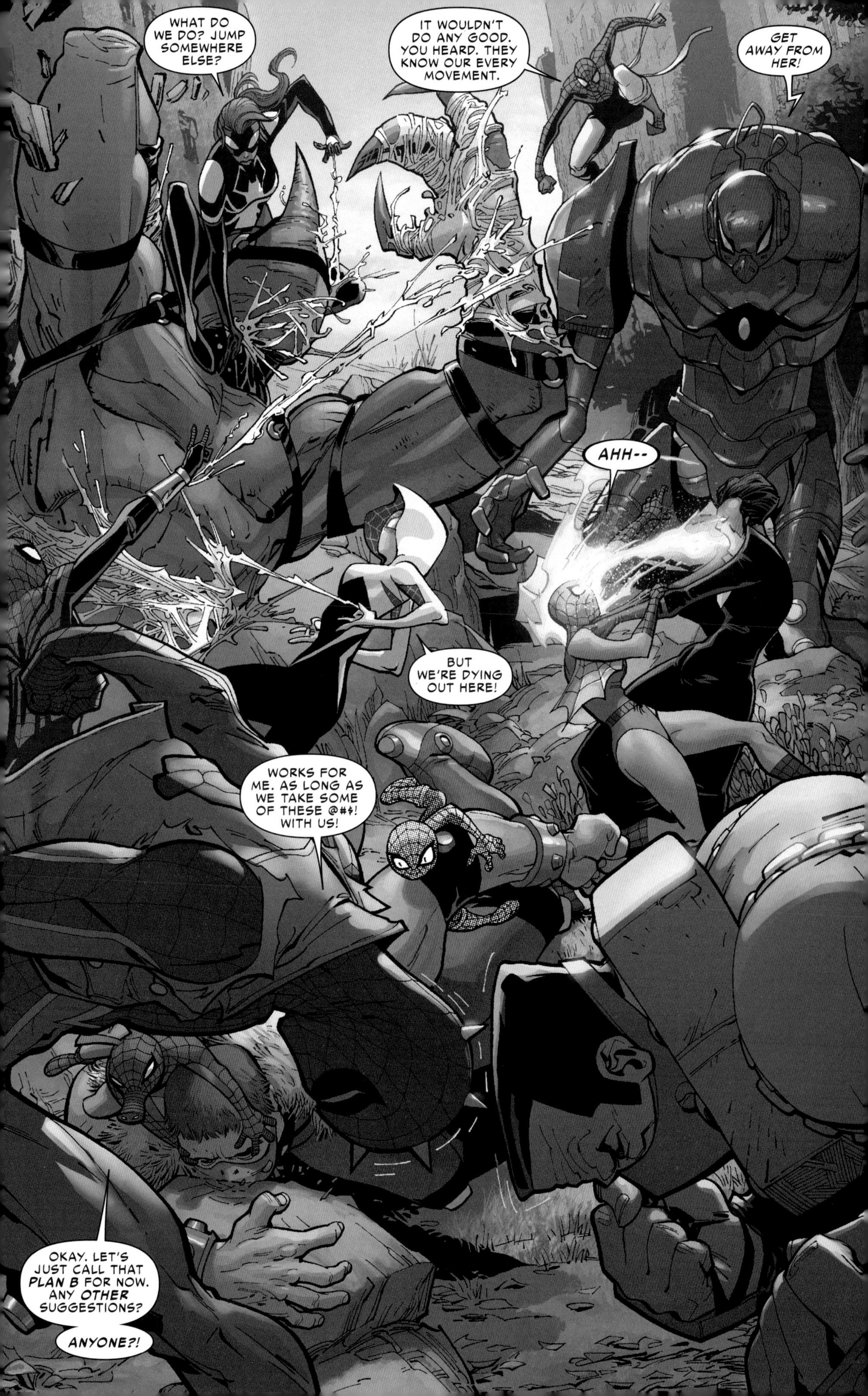

WHAT DO WE DO? JUMP SOMEWHERE ELSE?
IT WOULDN'T DO ANY GOOD. YOU HEARD. THEY KNOW OUR EVERY MOVEMENT.
GET AWAY FROM HER!
AHH--
BUT WE'RE DYING OUT HERE!
WORKS FOR ME. AS LONG AS WE TAKE SOME OF THESE @#$! WITH US!
OKAY. LET'S JUST CALL THAT PLAN B FOR NOW. ANY OTHER SUGGESTIONS?
ANYONE?!

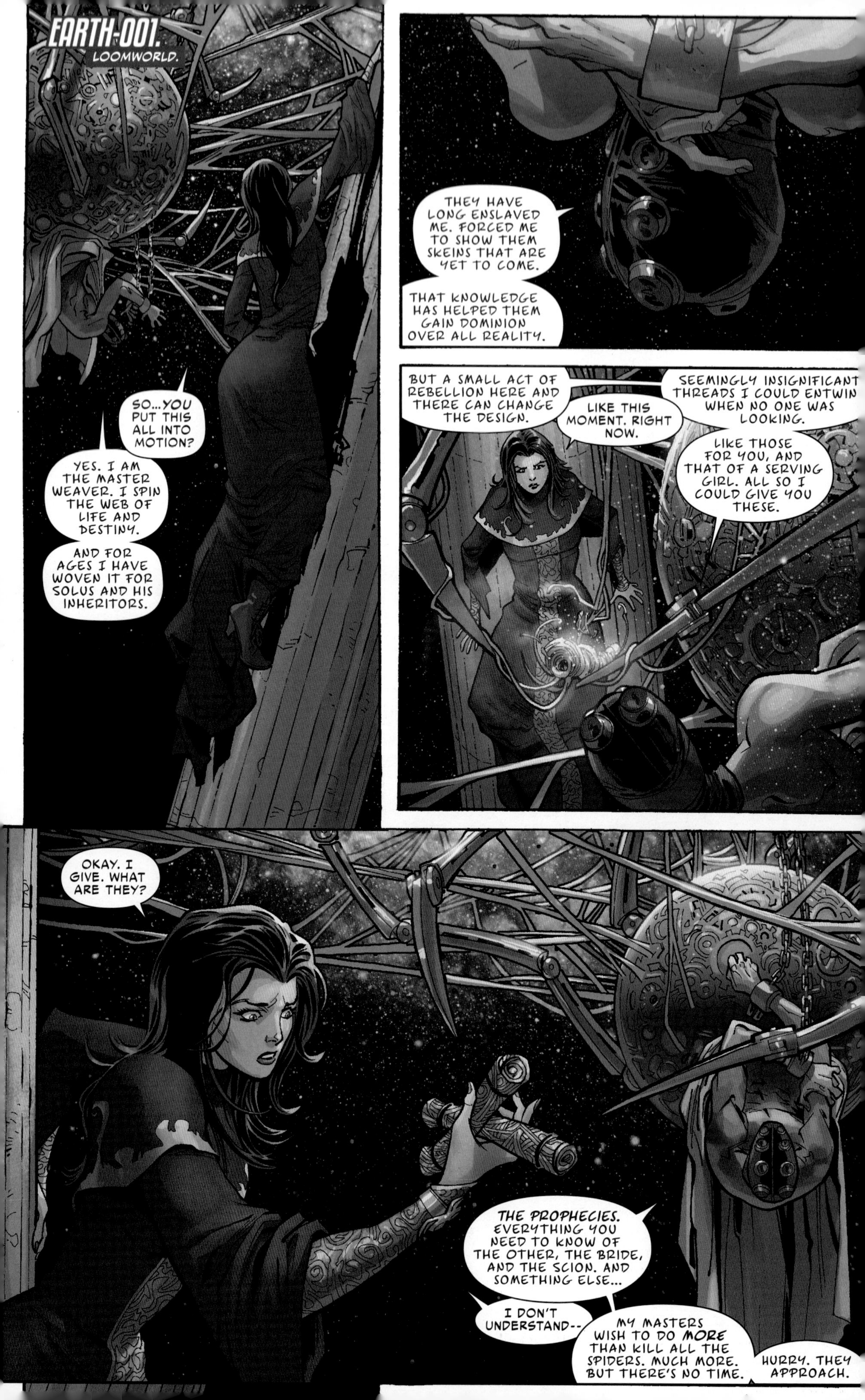
EARTH-001.
LOOMWORLD.
SO...YOU PUT THIS ALL INTO MOTION?
YES. I AM THE MASTER WEAVER. I SPIN THE WEB OF LIFE AND DESTINY.
AND FOR AGES I HAVE WOVEN IT FOR SOLUS AND HIS INHERITORS.
THEY HAVE LONG ENSLAVED ME. FORCED ME TO SHOW THEM SKEINS THAT ARE YET TO COME.
THAT KNOWLEDGE HAS HELPED THEM GAIN DOMINION OVER ALL REALITY.
BUT A SMALL ACT OF REBELLION HERE AND THERE CAN CHANGE THE DESIGN.
LIKE THIS MOMENT. RIGHT NOW.
SEEMINGLY INSIGNIFICANT THREADS I COULD ENTWIN WHEN NO ONE WAS LOOKING.
LIKE THOSE FOR YOU, AND THAT OF A SERVING GIRL. ALL SO I COULD GIVE YOU THESE.
OKAY. I GIVE. WHAT ARE THEY?
THE PROPHECIES. EVERYTHING YOU NEED TO KNOW OF THE OTHER, THE BRIDE, AND THE SCION. AND SOMETHING ELSE...
I DON'T UNDERSTAND--
MY MASTERS WISH TO DO MORE THAN KILL ALL THE SPIDERS. MUCH MORE. BUT THERE'S NO TIME.
HURRY. THEY APPROACH.

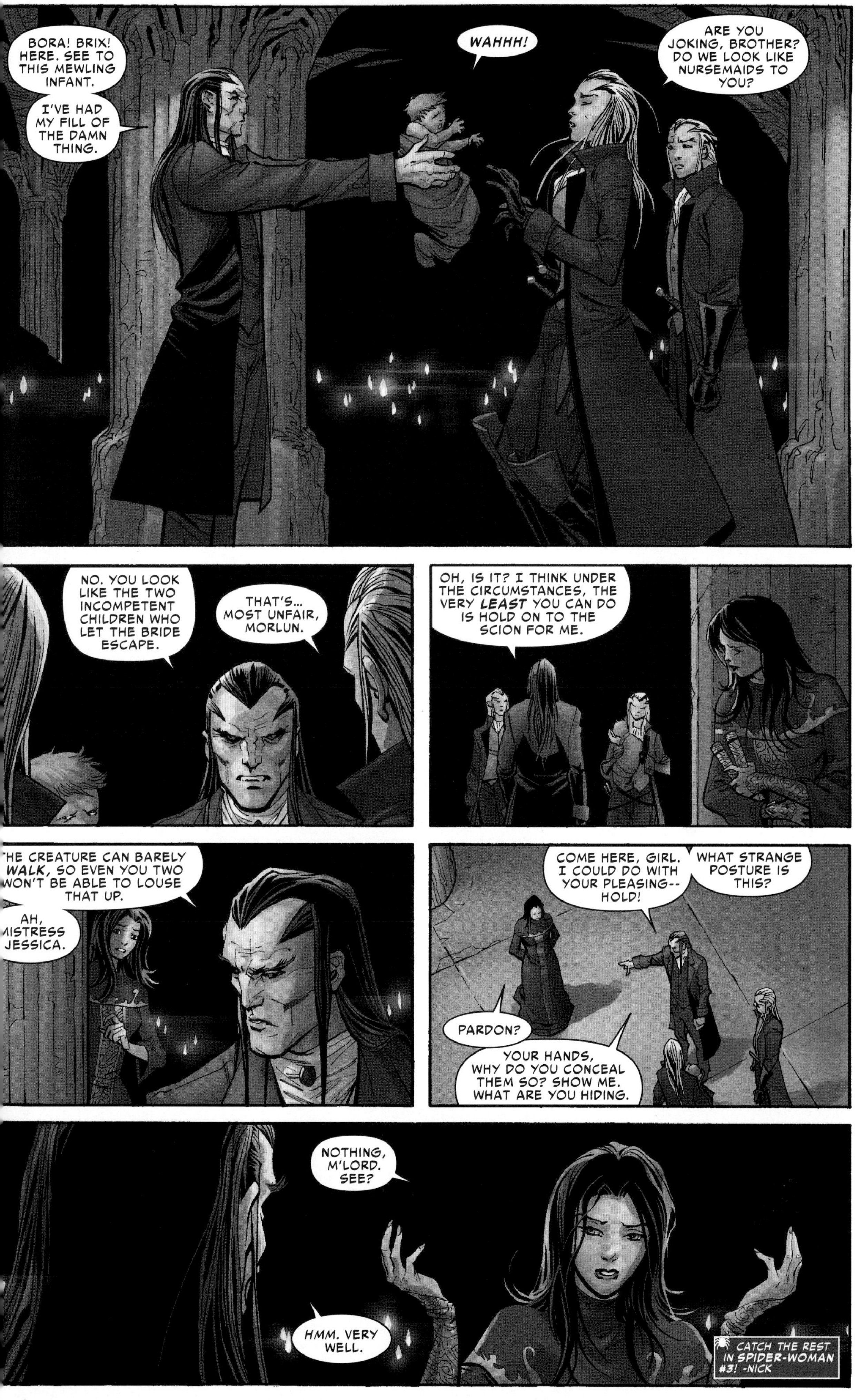
BORA! BRIX! HERE. SEE TO THIS MEWLING INFANT.
I'VE HAD MY FILL OF THE DAMN THING.
WAHHH!
ARE YOU JOKING, BROTHER? DO WE LOOK LIKE NURSEMAIDS TO YOU?
NO. YOU LOOK LIKE THE TWO INCOMPETENT CHILDREN WHO LET THE BRIDE ESCAPE.
THAT'S... MOST UNFAIR, MORLUN.
OH, IS IT? I THINK UNDER THE CIRCUMSTANCES, THE VERY LEAST YOU CAN DO IS HOLD ON TO THE SCION FOR ME.
THE CREATURE CAN BARELY WALK, SO EVEN YOU TWO WON'T BE ABLE TO LOUSE THAT UP.
AH, MISTRESS JESSICA.
COME HERE, GIRL. I COULD DO WITH YOUR PLEASING-- HOLD!
WHAT STRANGE POSTURE IS THIS?
PARDON?
YOUR HANDS, WHY DO YOU CONCEAL THEM SO? SHOW ME. WHAT ARE YOU HIDING.
NOTHING, M'LORD. SEE?
HMM. VERY WELL.
CATCH THE REST IN SPIDER-WOMAN #3! -NICK

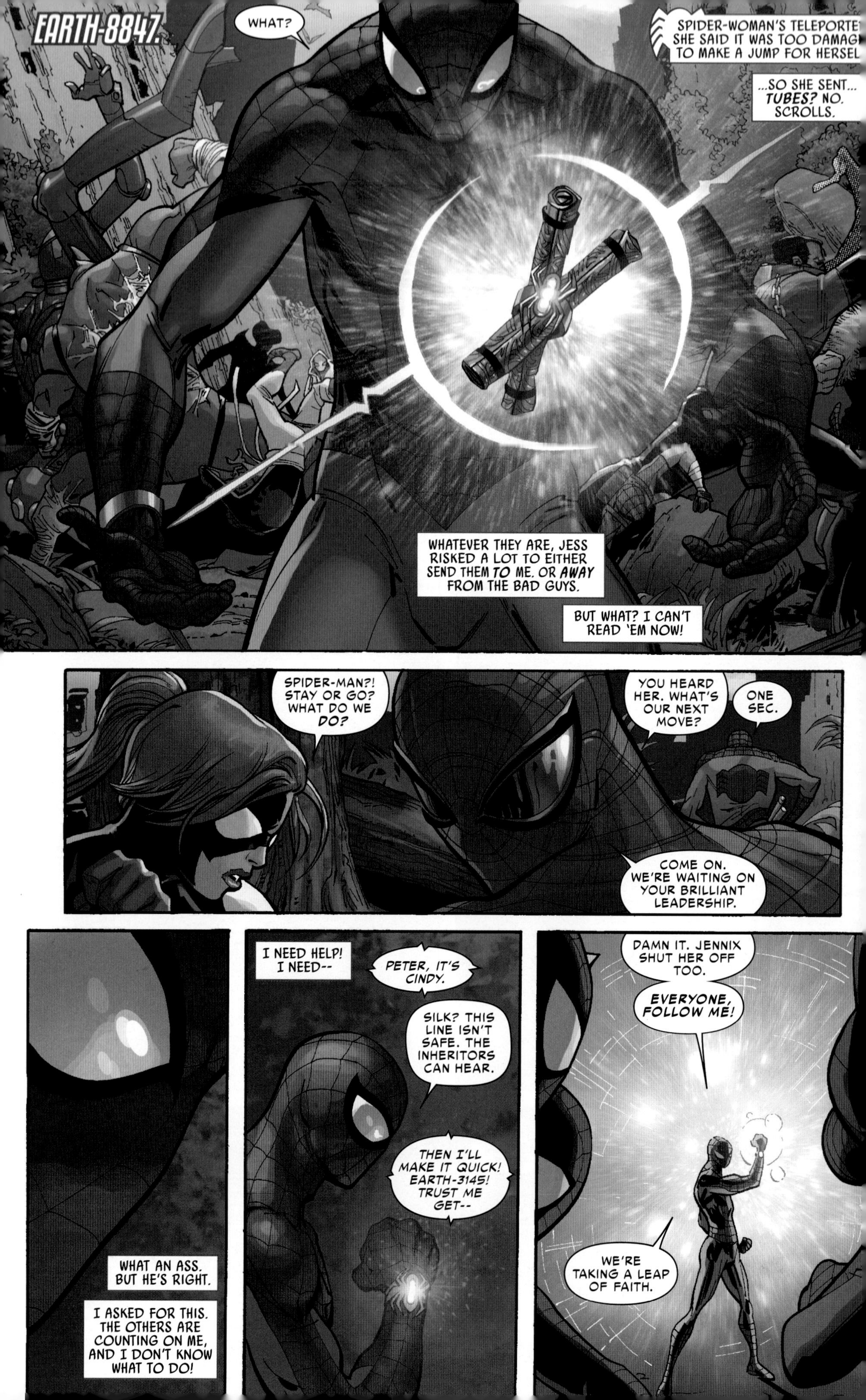
EARTH-8847.
WHAT?
SPIDER-WOMAN'S TELEPORTE
SHE SAID IT WAS TOO DAMAG
TO MAKE A JUMP FOR HERSEL
...SO SHE SENT... TUBES? NO. SCROLLS.
WHATEVER THEY ARE, JESS RISKED A LOT TO EITHER SEND THEM TO ME. OR AWAY FROM THE BAD GUYS.
BUT WHAT? I CAN'T READ 'EM NOW!
SPIDER-MAN?! STAY OR GO? WHAT DO WE DO?
YOU HEARD HER. WHAT'S OUR NEXT MOVE?
ONE SEC.
COME ON. WE'RE WAITING ON YOUR BRILLIANT LEADERSHIP.
WHAT AN ASS. BUT HE'S RIGHT.
I ASKED FOR THIS. THE OTHERS ARE COUNTING ON ME, AND I DON'T KNOW WHAT TO DO!
I NEED HELP! I NEED--
PETER, IT'S CINDY.
SILK? THIS LINE ISN'T SAFE. THE INHERITORS CAN HEAR.
THEN I'LL MAKE IT QUICK! EARTH-3145! TRUST ME GET--
DAMN IT. JENNIX SHUT HER OFF TOO.
EVERYONE, FOLLOW ME!
WE'RE TAKING A LEAP OF FAITH.

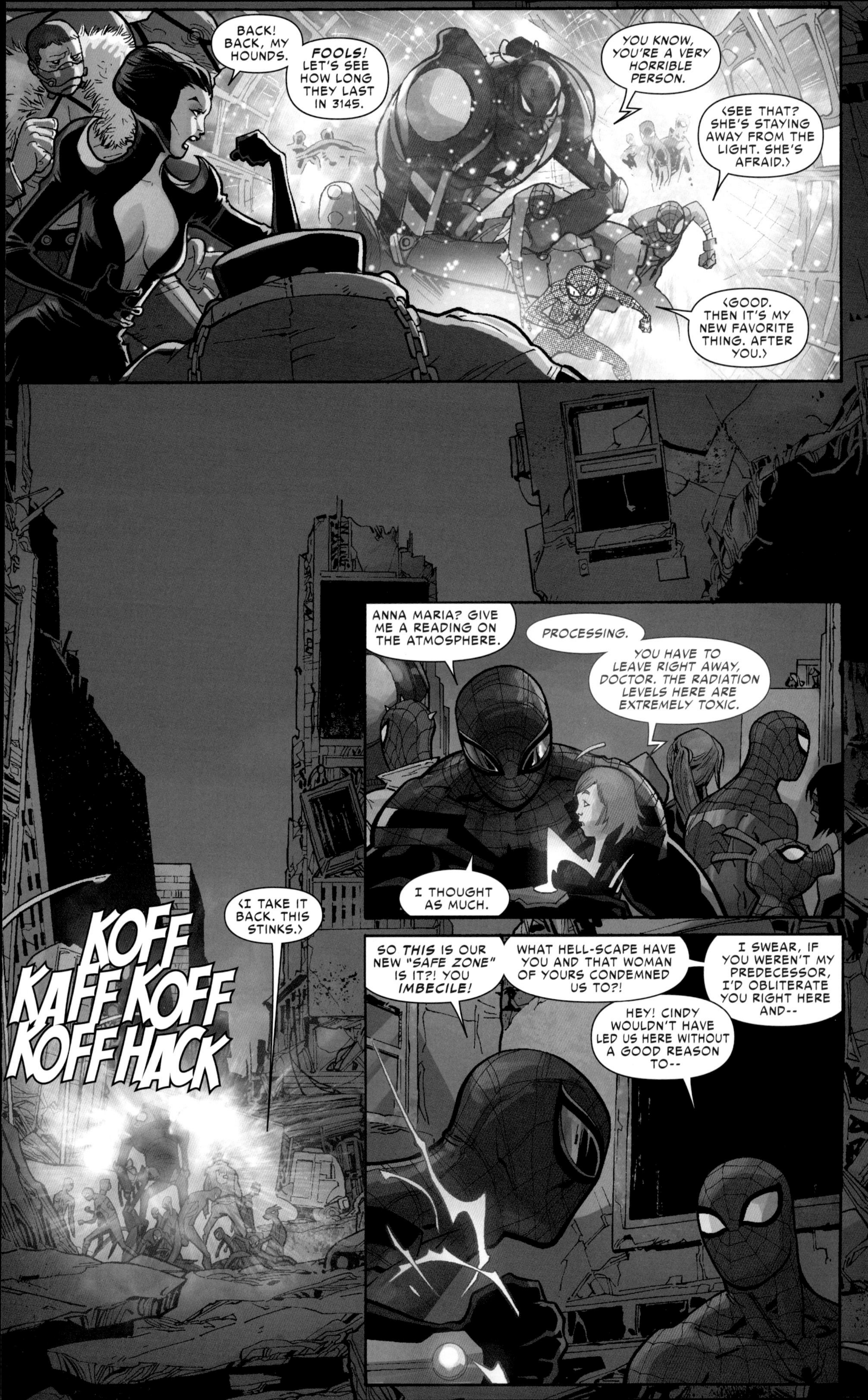
BACK! BACK, MY HOUNDS.
FOOLS! LET'S SEE HOW LONG THEY LAST IN 3145.
YOU KNOW, YOU'RE A VERY HORRIBLE PERSON.
‹SEE THAT? SHE'S STAYING AWAY FROM THE LIGHT. SHE'S AFRAID.›
‹GOOD. THEN IT'S MY NEW FAVORITE THING. AFTER YOU.›
ANNA MARIA? GIVE ME A READING ON THE ATMOSPHERE.
PROCESSING.
YOU HAVE TO LEAVE RIGHT AWAY, DOCTOR. THE RADIATION LEVELS HERE ARE EXTREMELY TOXIC.
I THOUGHT AS MUCH.
KOFF KAFF KOFF KOFF HACK
‹I TAKE IT BACK. THIS STINKS.›
SO THIS IS OUR NEW "SAFE ZONE" IS IT?! YOU IMBECILE!
WHAT HELL-SCAPE HAVE YOU AND THAT WOMAN OF YOURS CONDEMNED US TO?!
I SWEAR, IF YOU WEREN'T MY PREDECESSOR, I'D OBLITERATE YOU RIGHT HERE AND--
HEY! CINDY WOULDN'T HAVE LED US HERE WITHOUT A GOOD REASON TO--

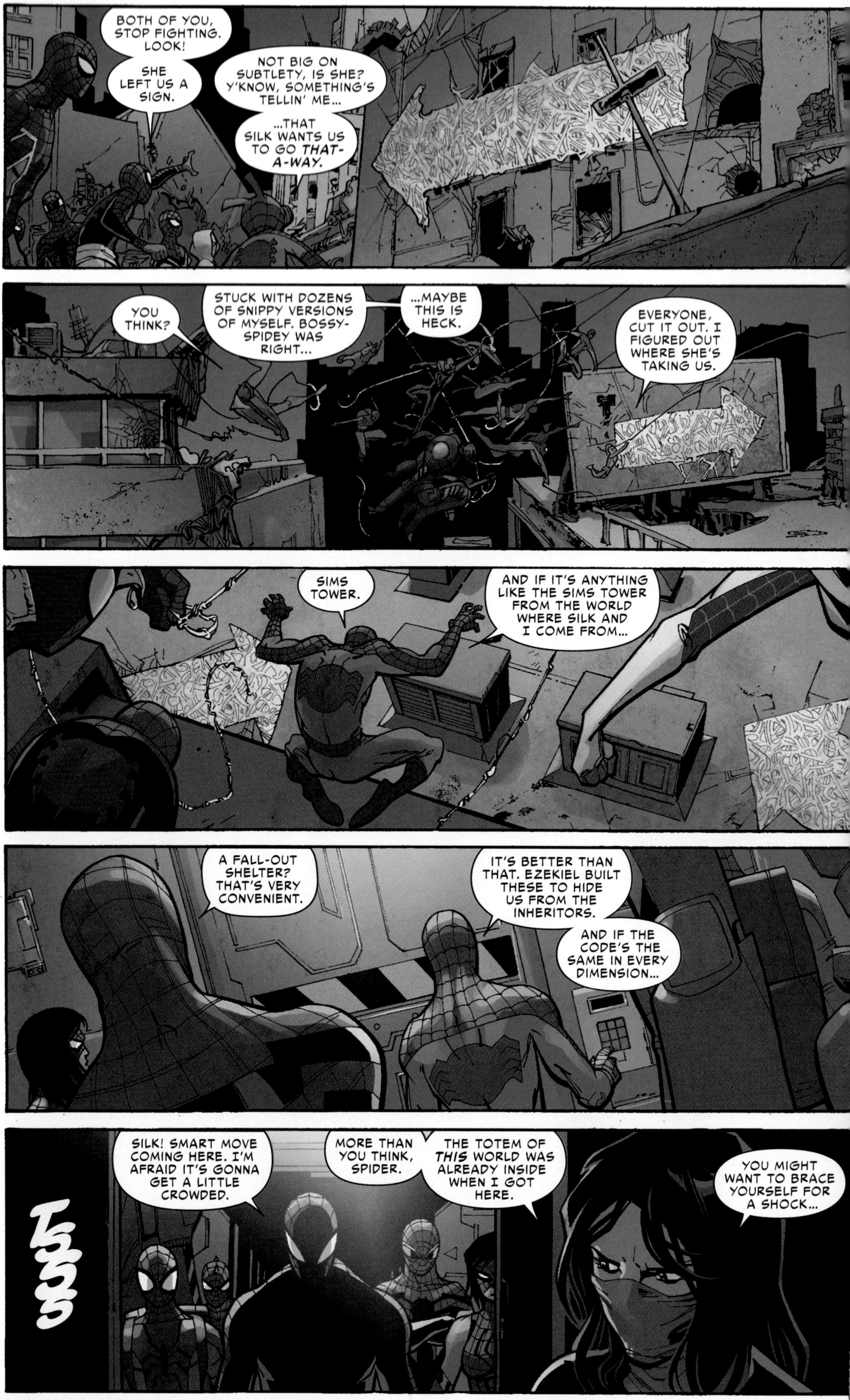
BOTH OF YOU, STOP FIGHTING. LOOK!
SHE LEFT US A SIGN.
NOT BIG ON SUBTLETY, IS SHE? Y'KNOW, SOMETHING'S TELLIN' ME...
...THAT SILK WANTS US TO GO *THAT-A-WAY.*
YOU THINK?
STUCK WITH DOZENS OF SNIPPY VERSIONS OF MYSELF. BOSSY-SPIDEY WAS RIGHT...
...MAYBE THIS IS HECK.
EVERYONE, CUT IT OUT. I FIGURED OUT WHERE SHE'S TAKING US.
SIMS TOWER.
AND IF IT'S ANYTHING LIKE THE SIMS TOWER FROM THE WORLD WHERE SILK AND I COME FROM...
A FALL-OUT SHELTER? THAT'S VERY CONVENIENT.
IT'S BETTER THAN THAT. EZEKIEL BUILT THESE TO HIDE US FROM THE INHERITORS.
AND IF THE CODE'S THE SAME IN EVERY DIMENSION...
TSSSS
SILK! SMART MOVE COMING HERE. I'M AFRAID IT'S GONNA GET A LITTLE CROWDED.
MORE THAN YOU THINK, SPIDER.
THE TOTEM OF *THIS* WORLD WAS ALREADY INSIDE WHEN I GOT HERE.
YOU MIGHT WANT TO BRACE YOURSELF FOR A SHOCK...

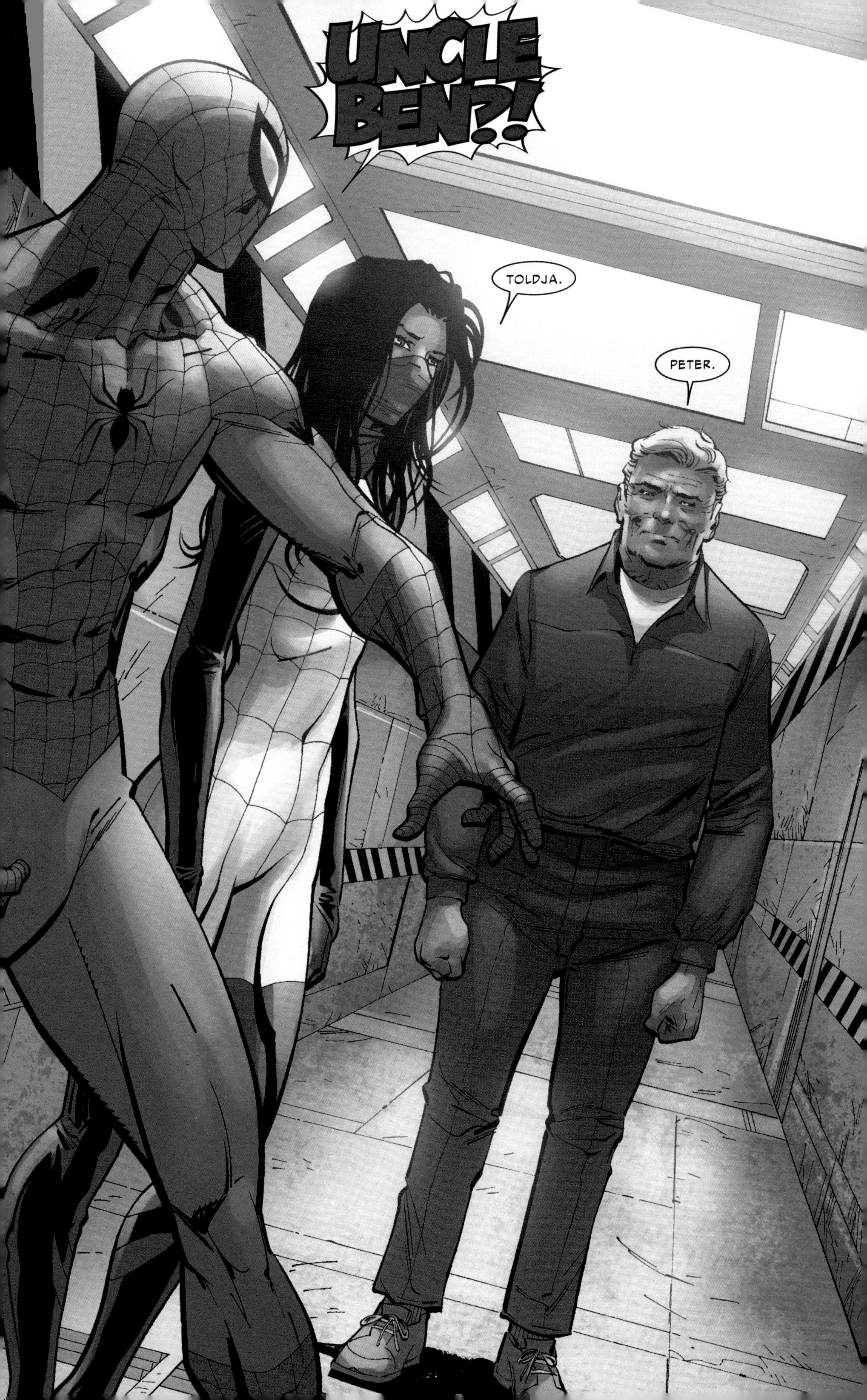
UNCLE BEN?!
TOLDJA.
PETER.

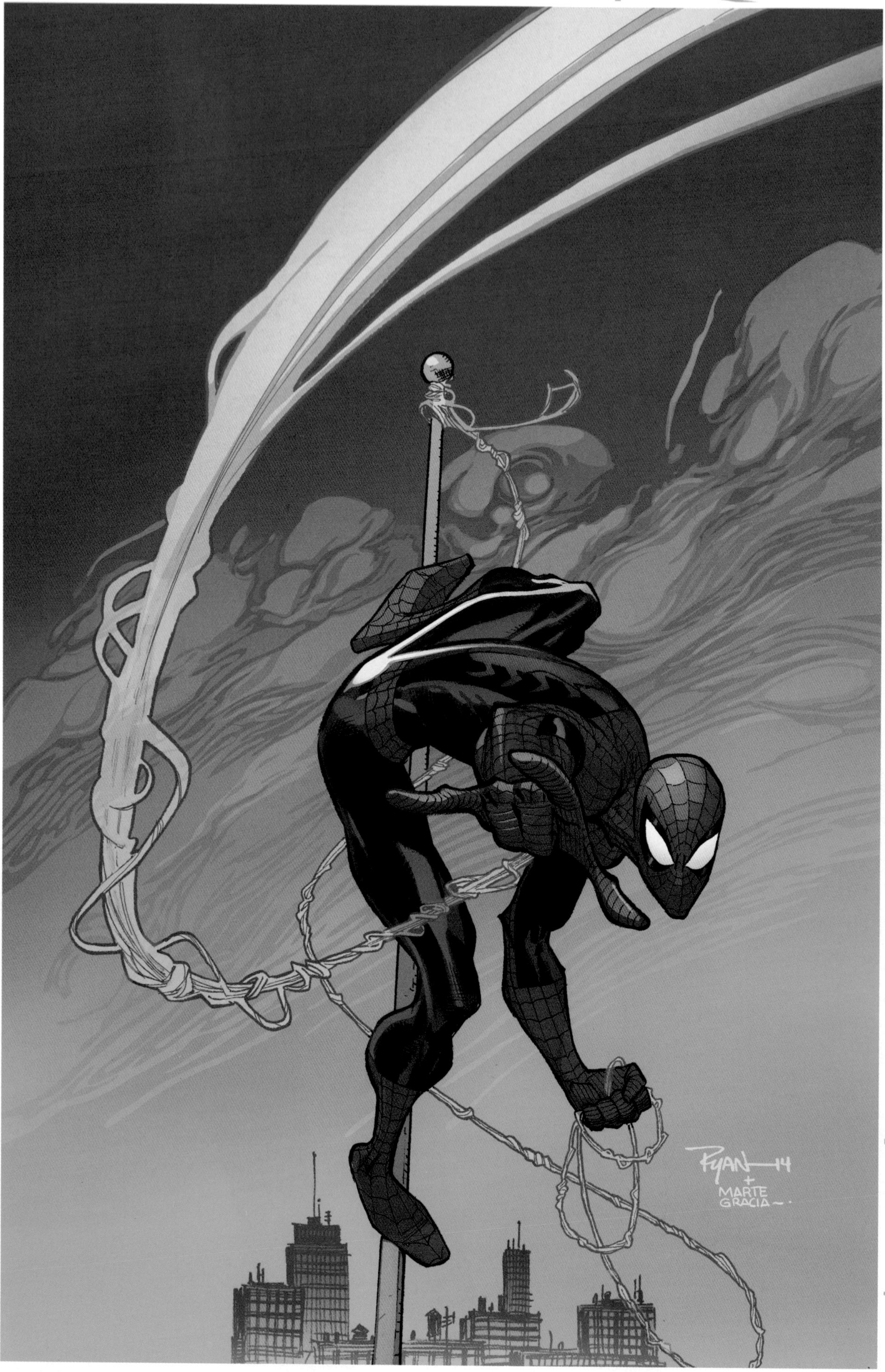
RYAN 14
+
MARTE
GRACIA

AMAZING SPIDER-MAN 8 VARIANT

BY RYAN OTTLEY & MARTE GRACIA

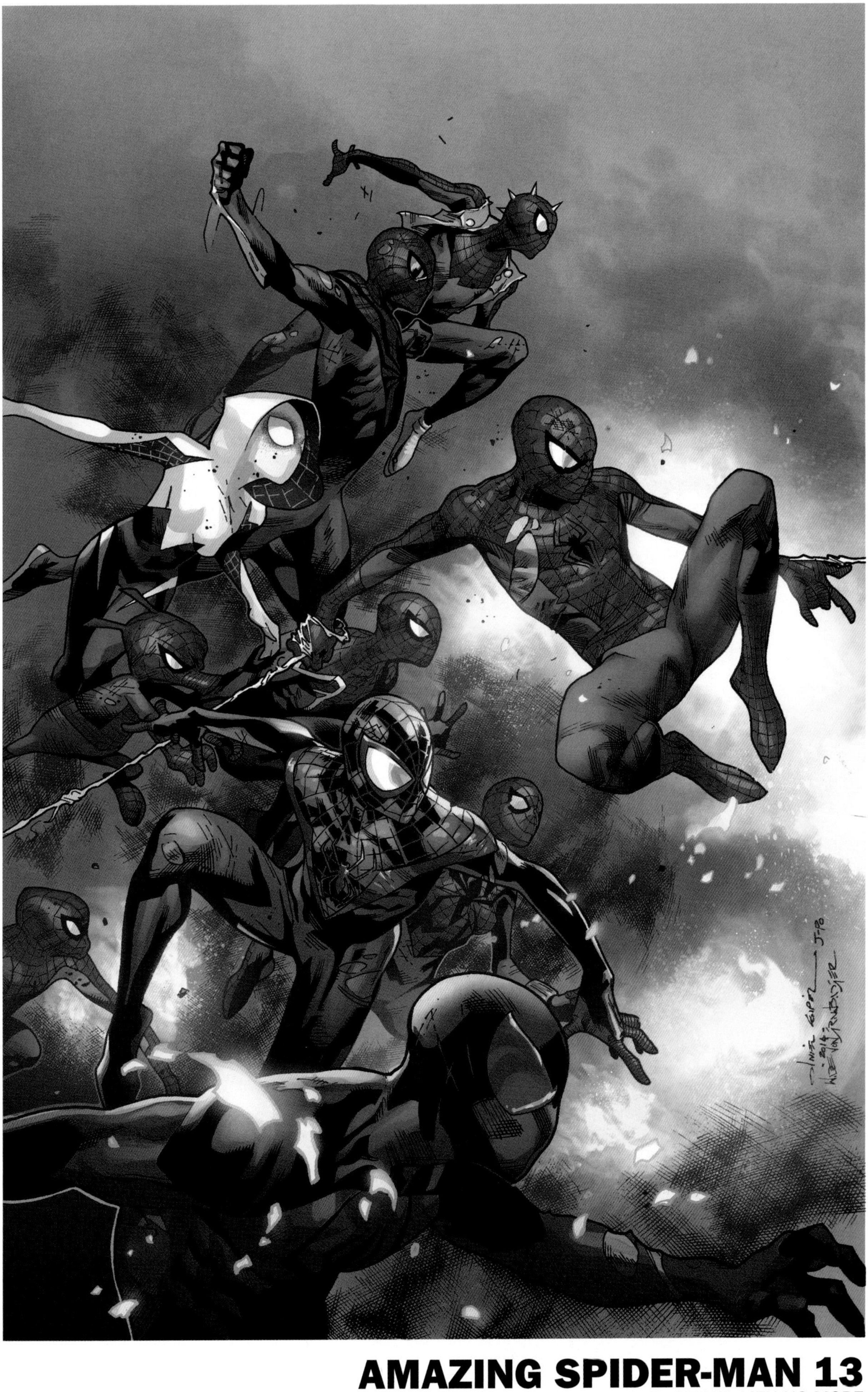

AMAZING SPIDER-MAN 13
SPIDER-VERSE, PART FIVE: SPIDER-MEN NO MORE

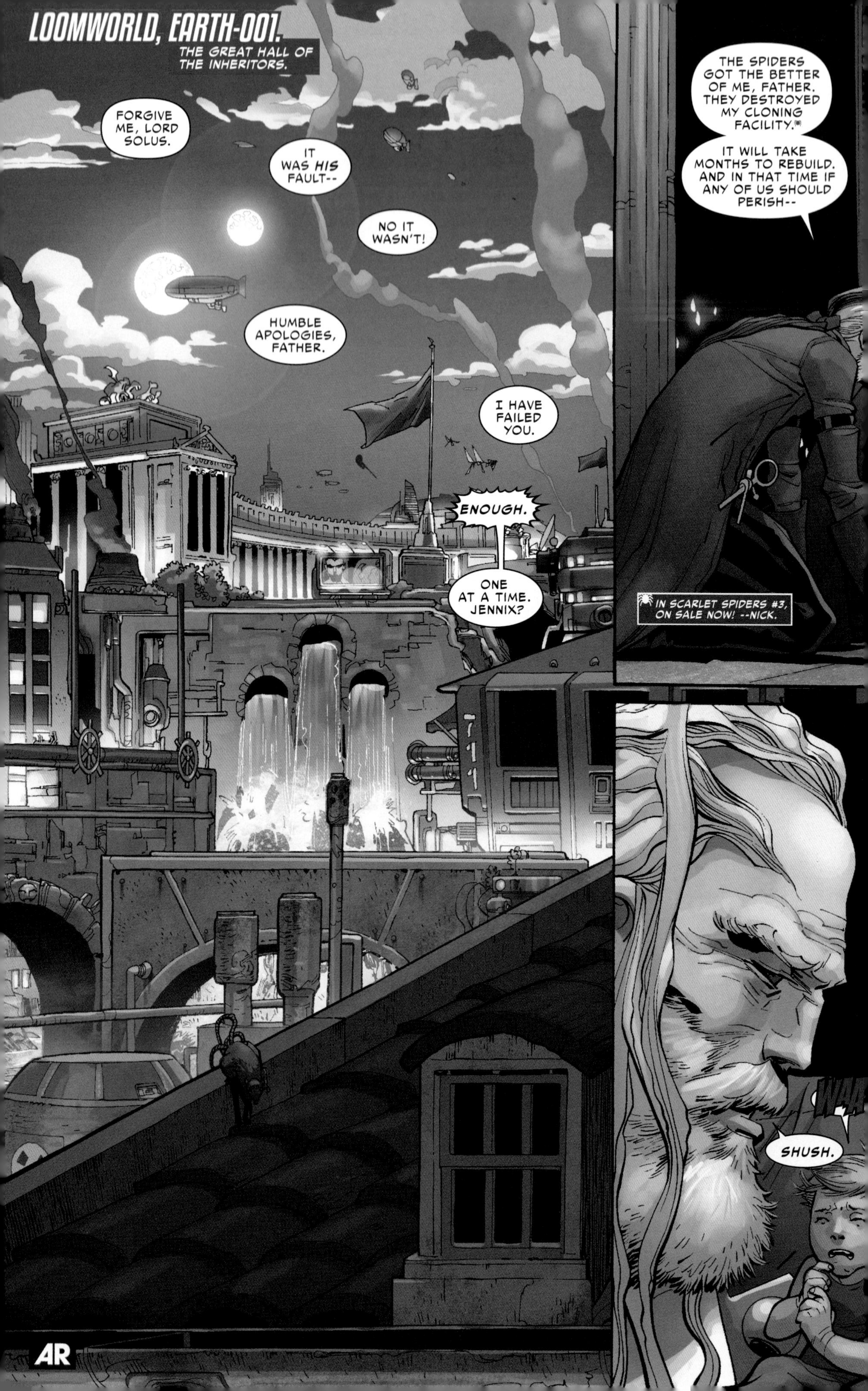
LOOMWORLD, EARTH-001.
THE GREAT HALL OF THE INHERITORS.
FORGIVE ME, LORD SOLUS.
IT WAS HIS FAULT--
NO IT WASN'T!
HUMBLE APOLOGIES, FATHER.
I HAVE FAILED YOU.
ENOUGH.
ONE AT A TIME. JENNIX?
THE SPIDERS GOT THE BETTER OF ME, FATHER. THEY DESTROYED MY CLONING FACILITY.*
IT WILL TAKE MONTHS TO REBUILD. AND IN THAT TIME IF ANY OF US SHOULD PERISH--
*IN SCARLET SPIDERS #3, ON SALE NOW! --NICK.
WAA
SHUSH.

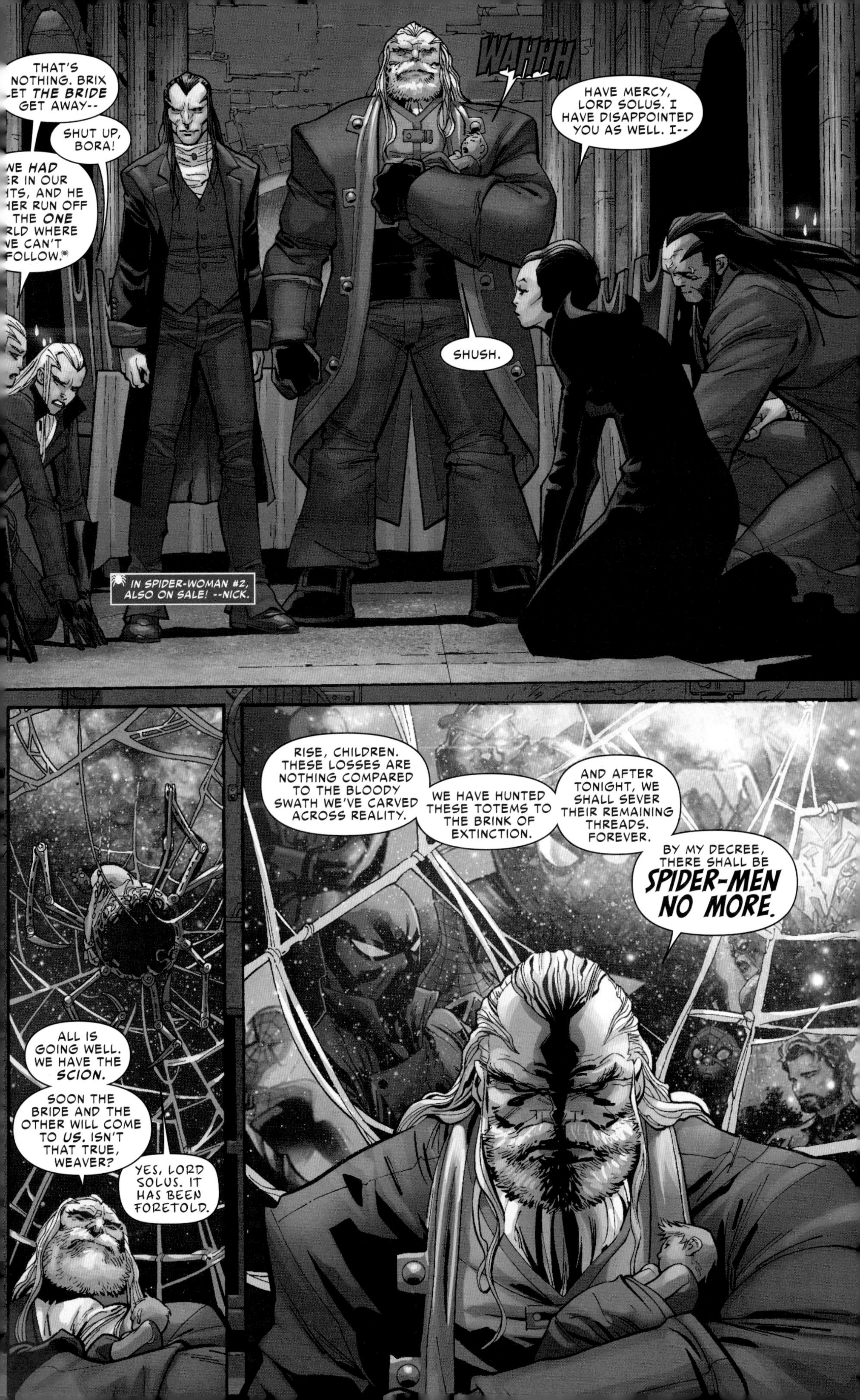
THAT'S NOTHING. BRIX LET THE BRIDE GET AWAY--
SHUT UP, BORA!
WE HAD ER IN OUR HTS, AND HE HER RUN OFF THE ONE RLD WHERE WE CAN'T FOLLOW.
WAHHH
HAVE MERCY, LORD SOLUS. I HAVE DISAPPOINTED YOU AS WELL. I--
SHUSH.
IN SPIDER-WOMAN #2, ALSO ON SALE! --NICK.
ALL IS GOING WELL. WE HAVE THE SCION.
SOON THE BRIDE AND THE OTHER WILL COME TO US. ISN'T THAT TRUE, WEAVER?
YES, LORD SOLUS. IT HAS BEEN FORETOLD.
RISE, CHILDREN. THESE LOSSES ARE NOTHING COMPARED TO THE BLOODY SWATH WE'VE CARVED ACROSS REALITY.
WE HAVE HUNTED THESE TOTEMS TO THE BRINK OF EXTINCTION.
AND AFTER TONIGHT, WE SHALL SEVER THEIR REMAINING THREADS. FOREVER.
BY MY DECREE, THERE SHALL BE SPIDER-MEN NO MORE.

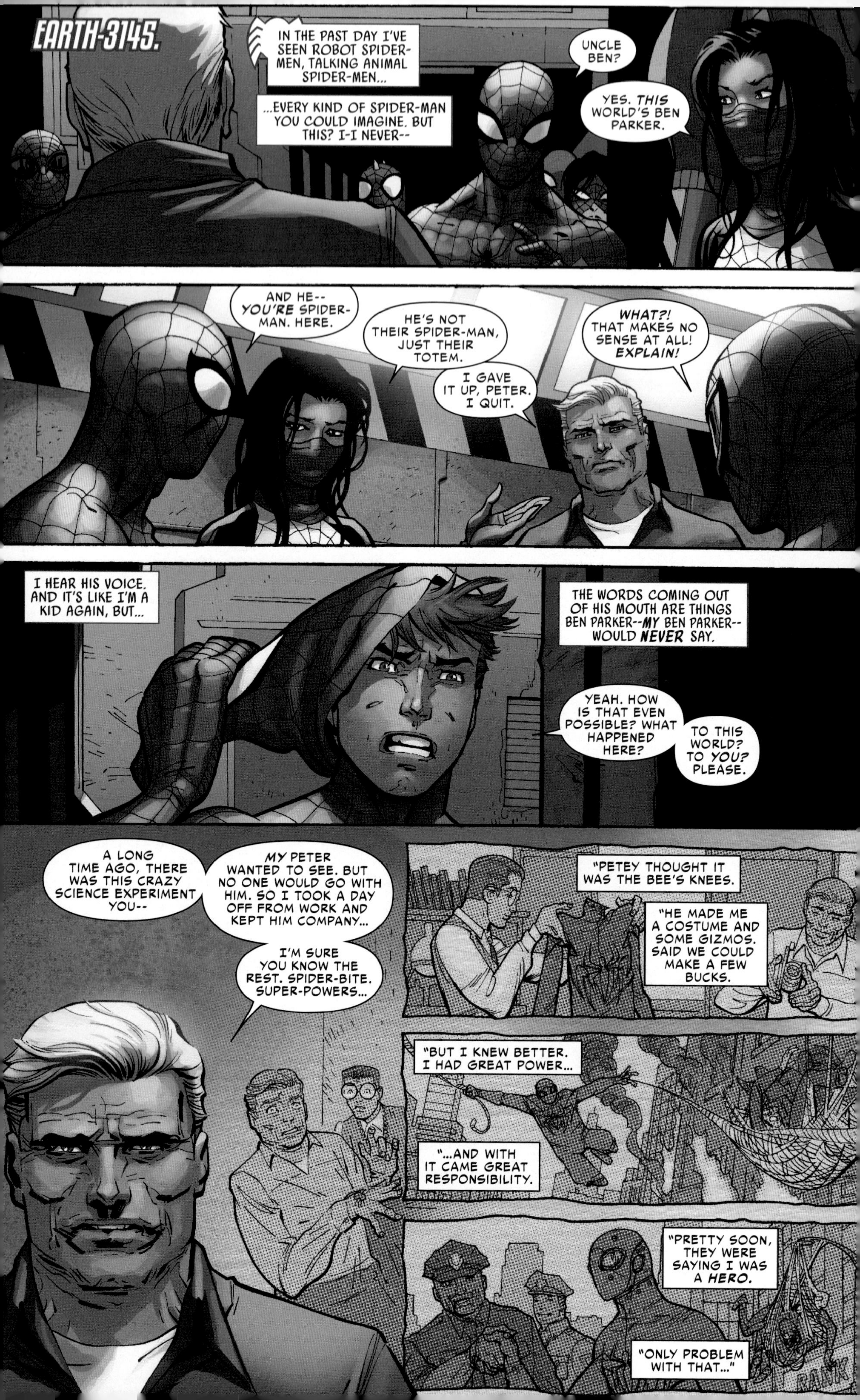
EARTH-3145.
IN THE PAST DAY I'VE SEEN ROBOT SPIDER-MEN, TALKING ANIMAL SPIDER-MEN...
...EVERY KIND OF SPIDER-MAN YOU COULD IMAGINE. BUT THIS? I-I NEVER--
UNCLE BEN?
YES. *THIS* WORLD'S BEN PARKER.
AND HE-- *YOU'RE* SPIDER-MAN. HERE.
HE'S NOT THEIR SPIDER-MAN, JUST THEIR TOTEM.
I GAVE IT UP, PETER. I QUIT.
WHAT?! THAT MAKES NO SENSE AT ALL! *EXPLAIN!*
I HEAR HIS VOICE. AND IT'S LIKE I'M A KID AGAIN, BUT...
THE WORDS COMING OUT OF HIS MOUTH ARE THINGS BEN PARKER--*MY* BEN PARKER--WOULD *NEVER* SAY.
YEAH. HOW IS THAT EVEN POSSIBLE? WHAT HAPPENED HERE?
TO THIS WORLD? TO *YOU?* PLEASE.
A LONG TIME AGO, THERE WAS THIS CRAZY SCIENCE EXPERIMENT YOU--
MY PETER WANTED TO SEE. BUT NO ONE WOULD GO WITH HIM. SO I TOOK A DAY OFF FROM WORK AND KEPT HIM COMPANY...
I'M SURE YOU KNOW THE REST. SPIDER-BITE. SUPER-POWERS...
"PETEY THOUGHT IT WAS THE BEE'S KNEES.
"HE MADE ME A COSTUME AND SOME GIZMOS. SAID WE COULD MAKE A FEW BUCKS.
"BUT I KNEW BETTER. I HAD GREAT POWER...
"...AND WITH IT CAME GREAT RESPONSIBILITY.
"PRETTY SOON, THEY WERE SAYING I WAS A *HERO.*
"ONLY PROBLEM WITH THAT..."

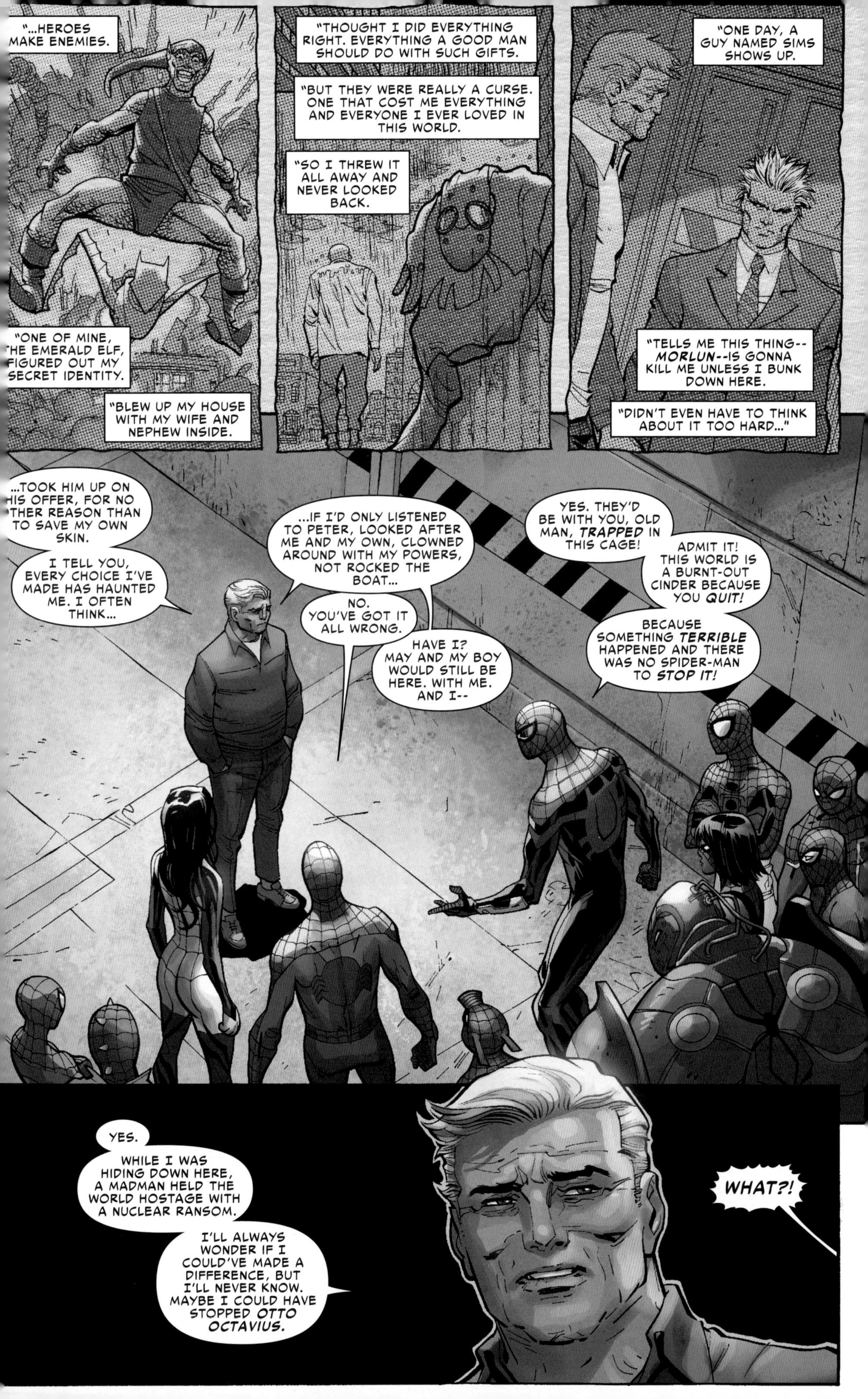
"...HEROES MAKE ENEMIES.
"ONE OF MINE, THE EMERALD ELF, FIGURED OUT MY SECRET IDENTITY.
"BLEW UP MY HOUSE WITH MY WIFE AND NEPHEW INSIDE.
"THOUGHT I DID EVERYTHING RIGHT. EVERYTHING A GOOD MAN SHOULD DO WITH SUCH GIFTS.
"BUT THEY WERE REALLY A CURSE. ONE THAT COST ME EVERYTHING AND EVERYONE I EVER LOVED IN THIS WORLD.
"SO I THREW IT ALL AWAY AND NEVER LOOKED BACK.
"ONE DAY, A GUY NAMED SIMS SHOWS UP.
"TELLS ME THIS THING--MORLUN--IS GONNA KILL ME UNLESS I BUNK DOWN HERE.
"DIDN'T EVEN HAVE TO THINK ABOUT IT TOO HARD..."
...TOOK HIM UP ON HIS OFFER, FOR NO OTHER REASON THAN TO SAVE MY OWN SKIN.
I TELL YOU, EVERY CHOICE I'VE MADE HAS HAUNTED ME. I OFTEN THINK...
...IF I'D ONLY LISTENED TO PETER, LOOKED AFTER ME AND MY OWN, CLOWNED AROUND WITH MY POWERS, NOT ROCKED THE BOAT...
NO. YOU'VE GOT IT ALL WRONG.
HAVE I? MAY AND MY BOY WOULD STILL BE HERE. WITH ME. AND I--
YES. THEY'D BE WITH YOU, OLD MAN, TRAPPED IN THIS CAGE!
ADMIT IT! THIS WORLD IS A BURNT-OUT CINDER BECAUSE YOU QUIT!
BECAUSE SOMETHING TERRIBLE HAPPENED AND THERE WAS NO SPIDER-MAN TO STOP IT!
YES.
WHILE I WAS HIDING DOWN HERE, A MADMAN HELD THE WORLD HOSTAGE WITH A NUCLEAR RANSOM.
I'LL ALWAYS WONDER IF I COULD'VE MADE A DIFFERENCE, BUT I'LL NEVER KNOW. MAYBE I COULD HAVE STOPPED OTTO OCTAVIUS.
WHAT?!

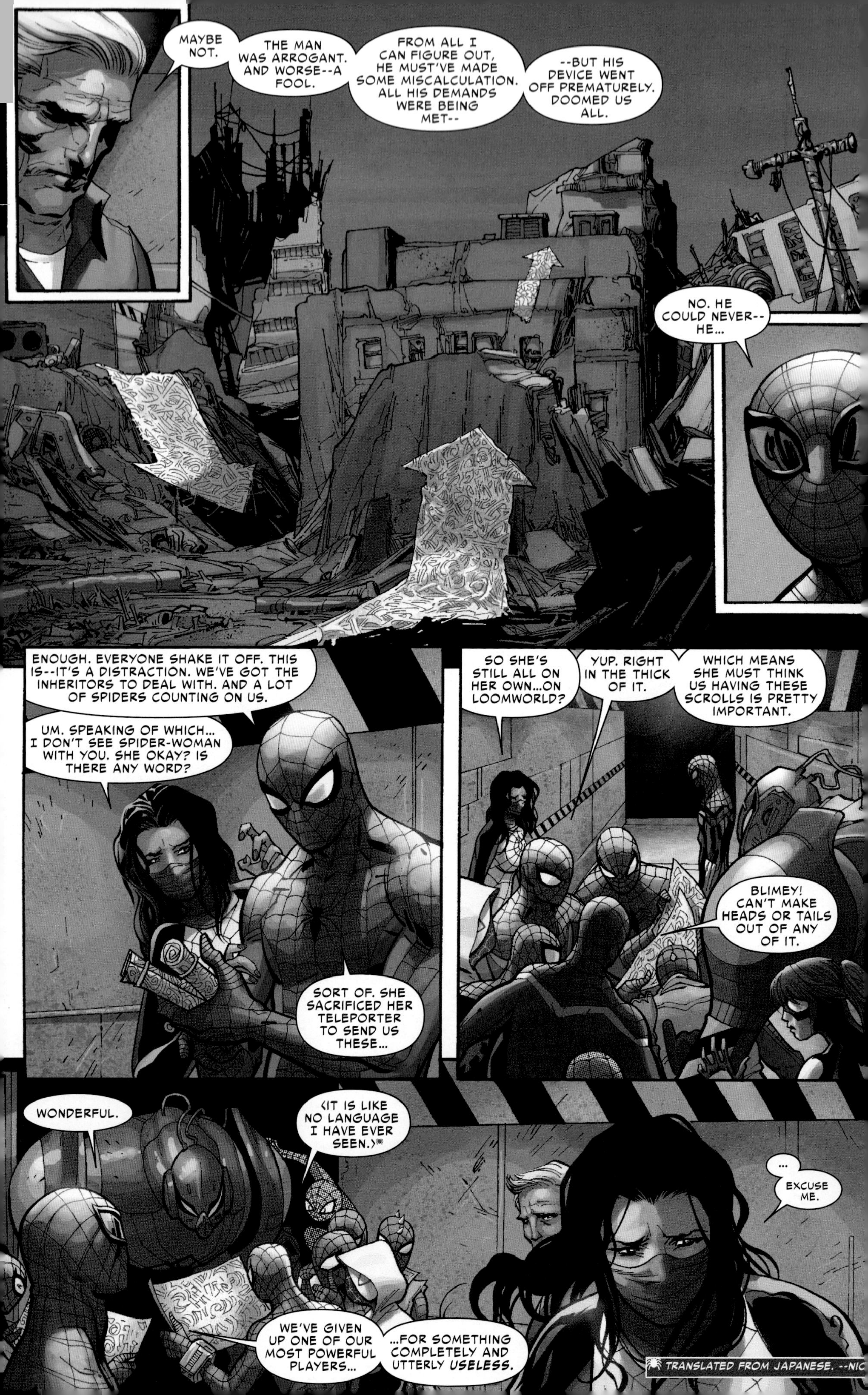
MAYBE NOT.
THE MAN WAS ARROGANT. AND WORSE--A FOOL.
FROM ALL I CAN FIGURE OUT, HE MUST'VE MADE SOME MISCALCULATION. ALL HIS DEMANDS WERE BEING MET--
--BUT HIS DEVICE WENT OFF PREMATURELY. DOOMED US ALL.
NO. HE COULD NEVER-- HE...
ENOUGH. EVERYONE SHAKE IT OFF. THIS IS--IT'S A DISTRACTION. WE'VE GOT THE INHERITORS TO DEAL WITH. AND A LOT OF SPIDERS COUNTING ON US.
UM. SPEAKING OF WHICH... I DON'T SEE SPIDER-WOMAN WITH YOU. SHE OKAY? IS THERE ANY WORD?
SORT OF. SHE SACRIFICED HER TELEPORTER TO SEND US THESE...
SO SHE'S STILL ALL ON HER OWN...ON LOOMWORLD?
YUP. RIGHT IN THE THICK OF IT.
WHICH MEANS SHE MUST THINK US HAVING THESE SCROLLS IS PRETTY IMPORTANT.
BLIMEY! CAN'T MAKE HEADS OR TAILS OUT OF ANY OF IT.
WONDERFUL.
‹IT IS LIKE NO LANGUAGE I HAVE EVER SEEN.›
...
EXCUSE ME.
WE'VE GIVEN UP ONE OF OUR MOST POWERFUL PLAYERS...
...FOR SOMETHING COMPLETELY AND UTTERLY *USELESS*.
TRANSLATED FROM JAPANESE. --NIC

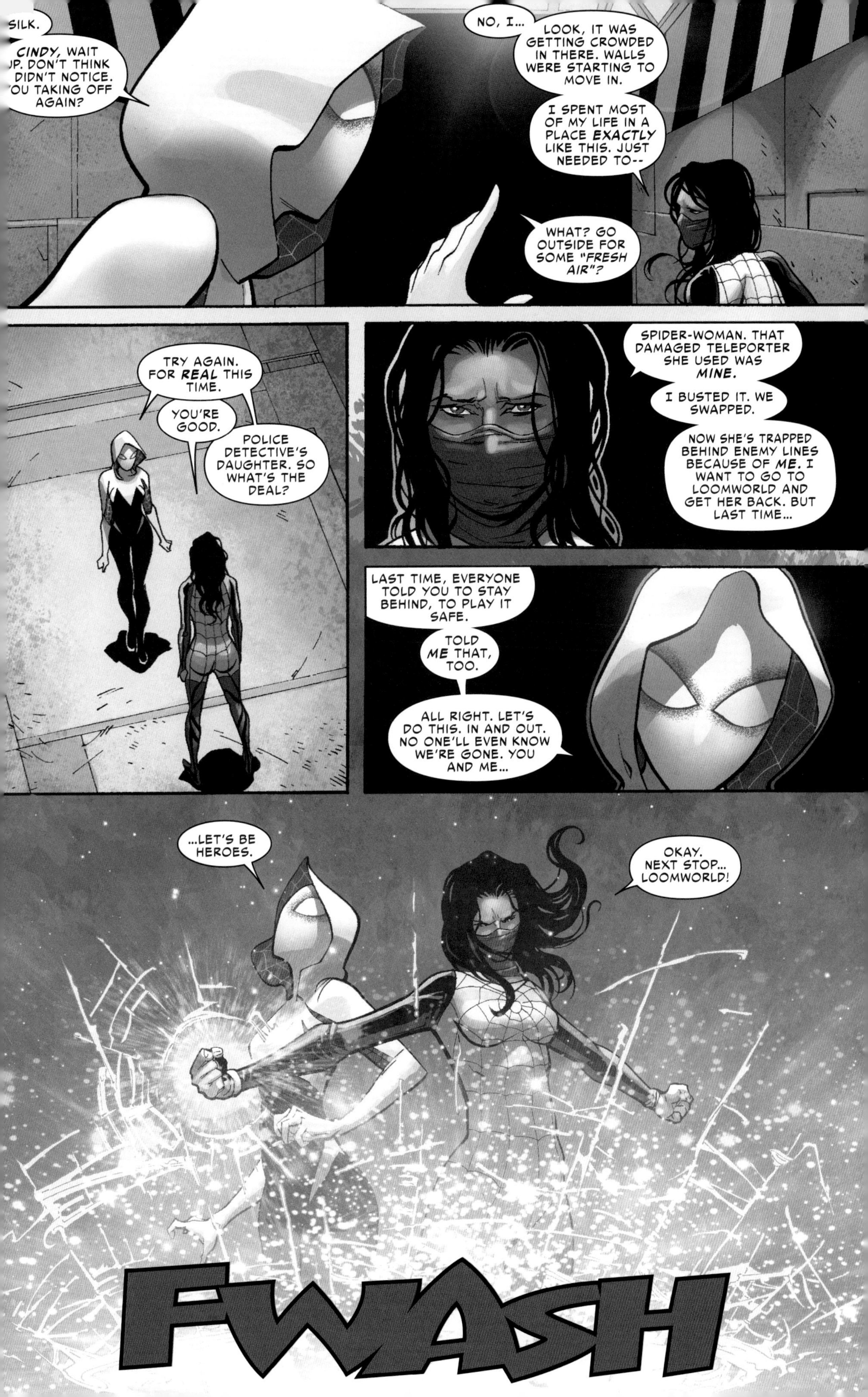
SILK.
CINDY, WAIT UP. DON'T THINK I DIDN'T NOTICE. YOU TAKING OFF AGAIN?
NO, I...
LOOK, IT WAS GETTING CROWDED IN THERE. WALLS WERE STARTING TO MOVE IN.
I SPENT MOST OF MY LIFE IN A PLACE EXACTLY LIKE THIS. JUST NEEDED TO--
WHAT? GO OUTSIDE FOR SOME "FRESH AIR"?
TRY AGAIN. FOR REAL THIS TIME.
YOU'RE GOOD.
POLICE DETECTIVE'S DAUGHTER. SO WHAT'S THE DEAL?
SPIDER-WOMAN. THAT DAMAGED TELEPORTER SHE USED WAS MINE.
I BUSTED IT. WE SWAPPED.
NOW SHE'S TRAPPED BEHIND ENEMY LINES BECAUSE OF ME. I WANT TO GO TO LOOMWORLD AND GET HER BACK. BUT LAST TIME...
LAST TIME, EVERYONE TOLD YOU TO STAY BEHIND, TO PLAY IT SAFE.
TOLD ME THAT, TOO.
ALL RIGHT. LET'S DO THIS. IN AND OUT. NO ONE'LL EVEN KNOW WE'RE GONE. YOU AND ME...
...LET'S BE HEROES.
OKAY. NEXT STOP... LOOMWORLD!
FWASH

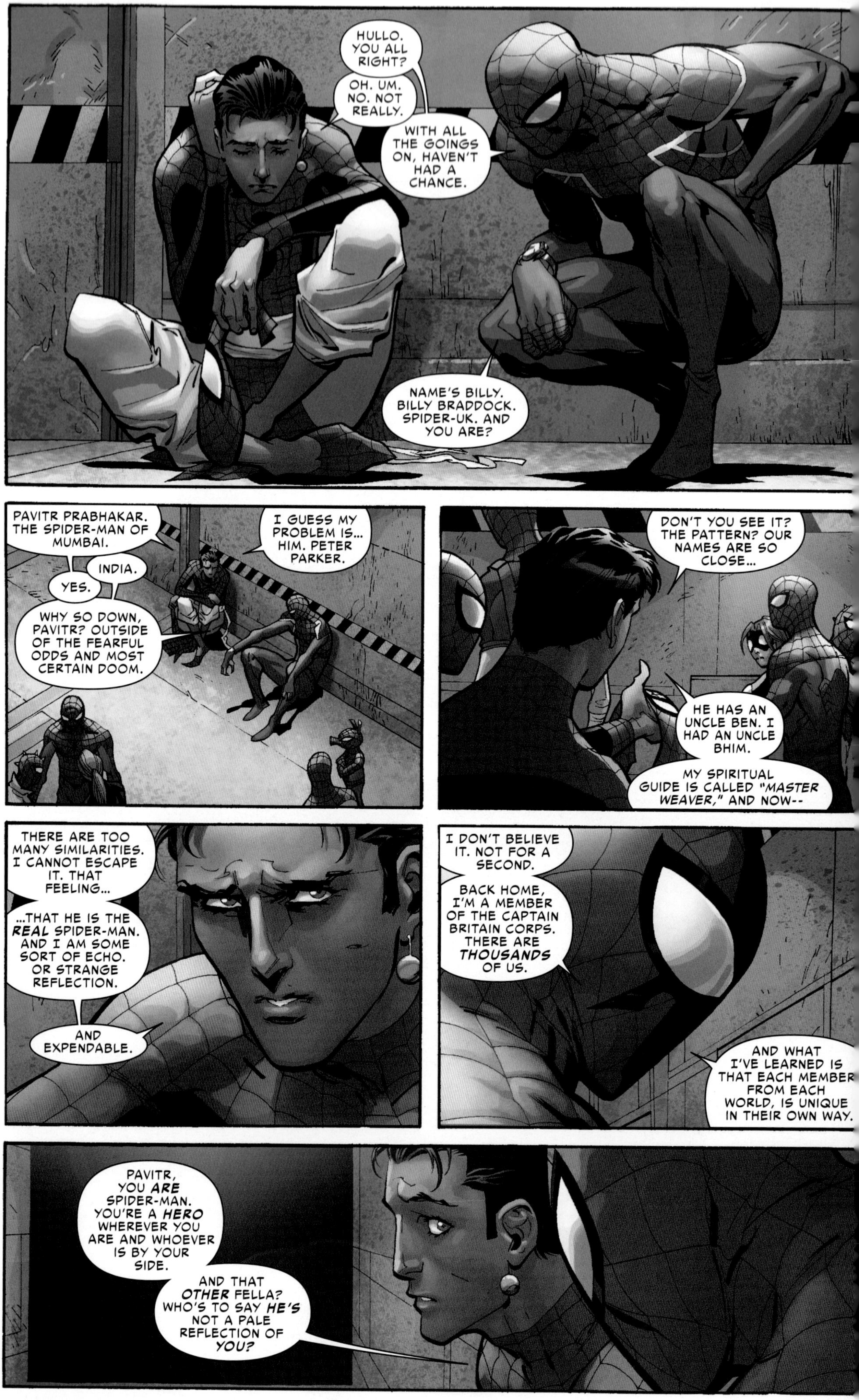
HULLO. YOU ALL RIGHT?
OH. UM. NO. NOT REALLY.
WITH ALL THE GOINGS ON, HAVEN'T HAD A CHANCE.
NAME'S BILLY. BILLY BRADDOCK. SPIDER-UK. AND YOU ARE?
PAVITR PRABHAKAR. THE SPIDER-MAN OF MUMBAI.
INDIA.
YES.
WHY SO DOWN, PAVITR? OUTSIDE OF THE FEARFUL ODDS AND MOST CERTAIN DOOM.
I GUESS MY PROBLEM IS... HIM. PETER PARKER.
DON'T YOU SEE IT? THE PATTERN? OUR NAMES ARE SO CLOSE...
HE HAS AN UNCLE BEN. I HAD AN UNCLE BHIM.
MY SPIRITUAL GUIDE IS CALLED "MASTER WEAVER," AND NOW--
THERE ARE TOO MANY SIMILARITIES. I CANNOT ESCAPE IT. THAT FEELING...
...THAT HE IS THE REAL SPIDER-MAN. AND I AM SOME SORT OF ECHO. OR STRANGE REFLECTION.
AND EXPENDABLE.
I DON'T BELIEVE IT. NOT FOR A SECOND.
BACK HOME, I'M A MEMBER OF THE CAPTAIN BRITAIN CORPS. THERE ARE THOUSANDS OF US.
AND WHAT I'VE LEARNED IS THAT EACH MEMBER FROM EACH WORLD, IS UNIQUE IN THEIR OWN WAY.
PAVITR, YOU ARE SPIDER-MAN. YOU'RE A HERO WHEREVER YOU ARE AND WHOEVER IS BY YOUR SIDE.
AND THAT OTHER FELLA? WHO'S TO SAY HE'S NOT A PALE REFLECTION OF YOU?

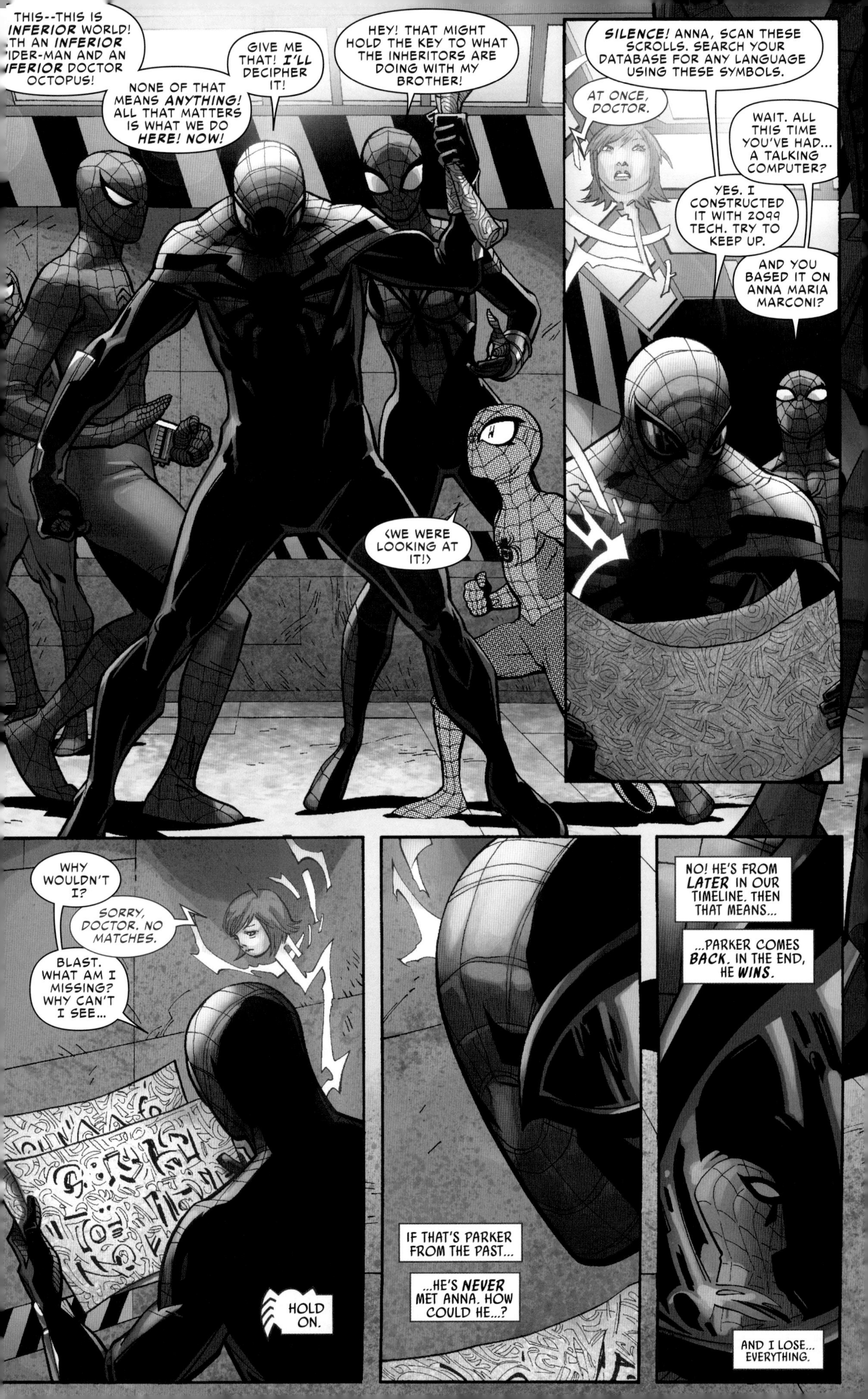
THIS--THIS IS INFERIOR WORLD! ...TH AN INFERIOR ...IDER-MAN AND AN ...FERIOR DOCTOR OCTOPUS!
NONE OF THAT MEANS ANYTHING! ALL THAT MATTERS IS WHAT WE DO HERE! NOW!
GIVE ME THAT! I'LL DECIPHER IT!
HEY! THAT MIGHT HOLD THE KEY TO WHAT THE INHERITORS ARE DOING WITH MY BROTHER!
‹WE WERE LOOKING AT IT!›
SILENCE! ANNA, SCAN THESE SCROLLS. SEARCH YOUR DATABASE FOR ANY LANGUAGE USING THESE SYMBOLS.
AT ONCE, DOCTOR.
WAIT. ALL THIS TIME YOU'VE HAD... A TALKING COMPUTER?
YES. I CONSTRUCTED IT WITH 2099 TECH. TRY TO KEEP UP.
AND YOU BASED IT ON ANNA MARIA MARCONI?
WHY WOULDN'T I?
SORRY, DOCTOR. NO MATCHES.
BLAST. WHAT AM I MISSING? WHY CAN'T I SEE...
HOLD ON.
IF THAT'S PARKER FROM THE PAST...
...HE'S NEVER MET ANNA. HOW COULD HE...?
NO! HE'S FROM LATER IN OUR TIMELINE. THEN THAT MEANS...
...PARKER COMES BACK. IN THE END, HE WINS.
AND I LOSE... EVERYTHING.

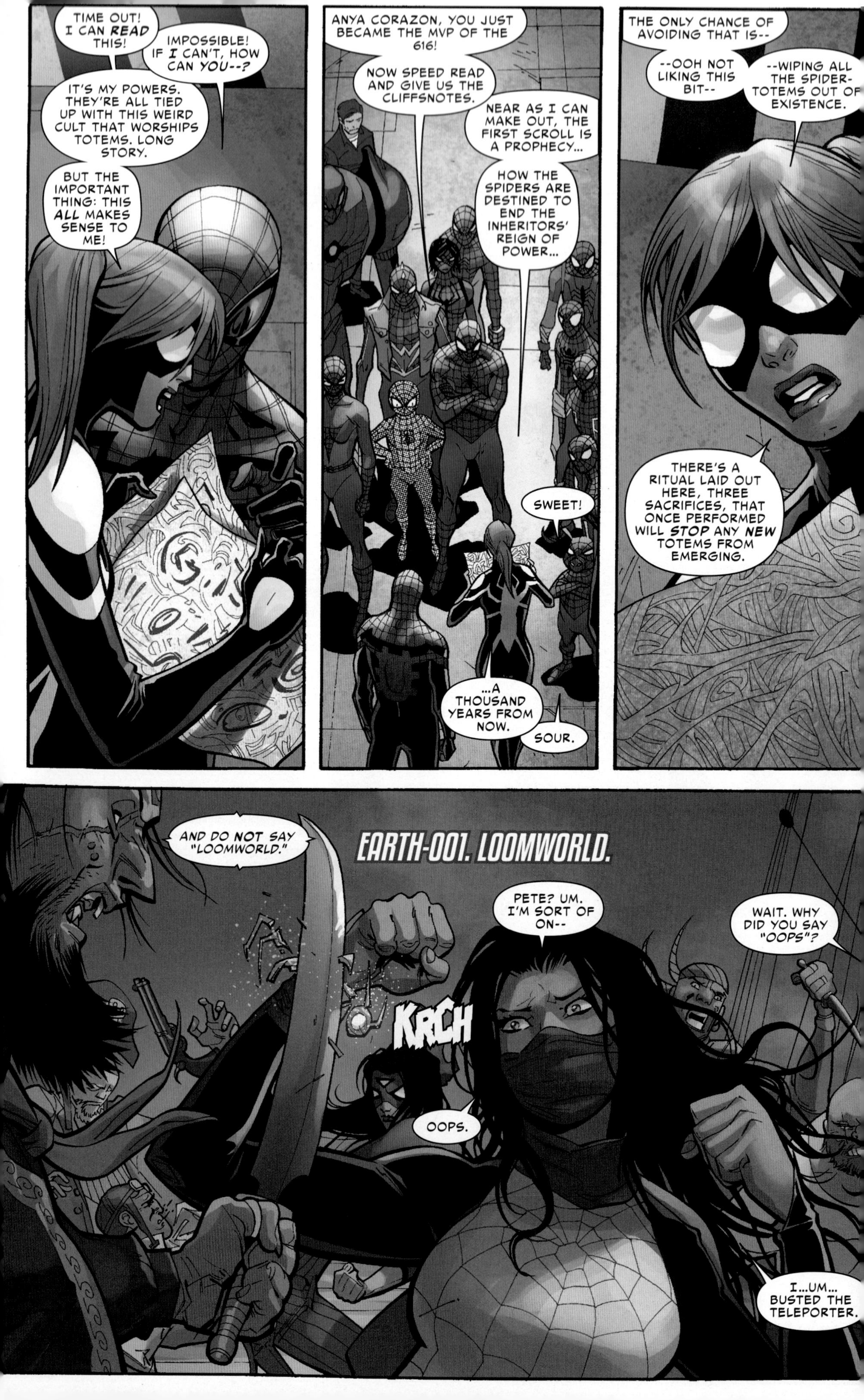
TIME OUT! I CAN READ THIS!
IMPOSSIBLE! IF I CAN'T, HOW CAN YOU--?
IT'S MY POWERS. THEY'RE ALL TIED UP WITH THIS WEIRD CULT THAT WORSHIPS TOTEMS. LONG STORY.
BUT THE IMPORTANT THING: THIS ALL MAKES SENSE TO ME!
ANYA CORAZON, YOU JUST BECAME THE MVP OF THE 616!
NOW SPEED READ AND GIVE US THE CLIFFSNOTES.
NEAR AS I CAN MAKE OUT, THE FIRST SCROLL IS A PROPHECY...
HOW THE SPIDERS ARE DESTINED TO END THE INHERITORS' REIGN OF POWER...
SWEET!
...A THOUSAND YEARS FROM NOW.
SOUR.
THE ONLY CHANCE OF AVOIDING THAT IS--
--OOH NOT LIKING THIS BIT--
--WIPING ALL THE SPIDER-TOTEMS OUT OF EXISTENCE.
THERE'S A RITUAL LAID OUT HERE, THREE SACRIFICES, THAT ONCE PERFORMED WILL STOP ANY NEW TOTEMS FROM EMERGING.
AND DO NOT SAY "LOOMWORLD."
EARTH-001. LOOMWORLD.
PETE? UM. I'M SORT OF ON--
WAIT. WHY DID YOU SAY "OOPS"?
KRCH
OOPS.
I...UM... BUSTED THE TELEPORTER.

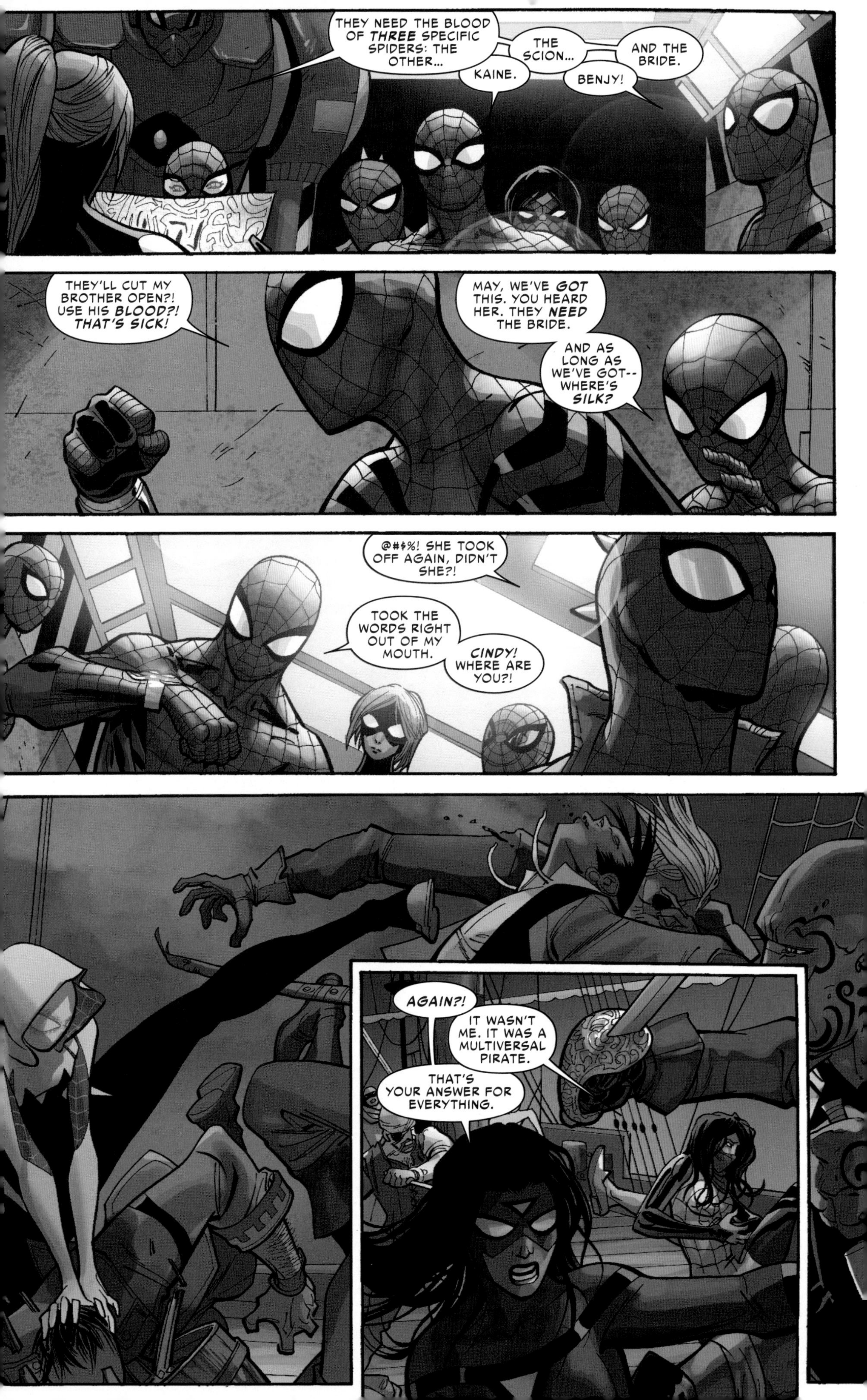
THEY NEED THE BLOOD OF *THREE* SPECIFIC SPIDERS: THE OTHER...
KAINE.
THE SCION...
BENJY!
AND THE BRIDE.
THEY'LL CUT MY BROTHER OPEN?! USE HIS *BLOOD?! THAT'S SICK!*
MAY, WE'VE *GOT* THIS. YOU HEARD HER. THEY *NEED* THE BRIDE.
AND AS LONG AS WE'VE GOT-- WHERE'S *SILK?*
@#$%! SHE TOOK OFF AGAIN, DIDN'T SHE?!
TOOK THE WORDS RIGHT OUT OF MY MOUTH.
CINDY! WHERE ARE YOU?!
AGAIN?!
IT WASN'T ME. IT WAS A MULTIVERSAL PIRATE.
THAT'S YOUR ANSWER FOR EVERYTHING.

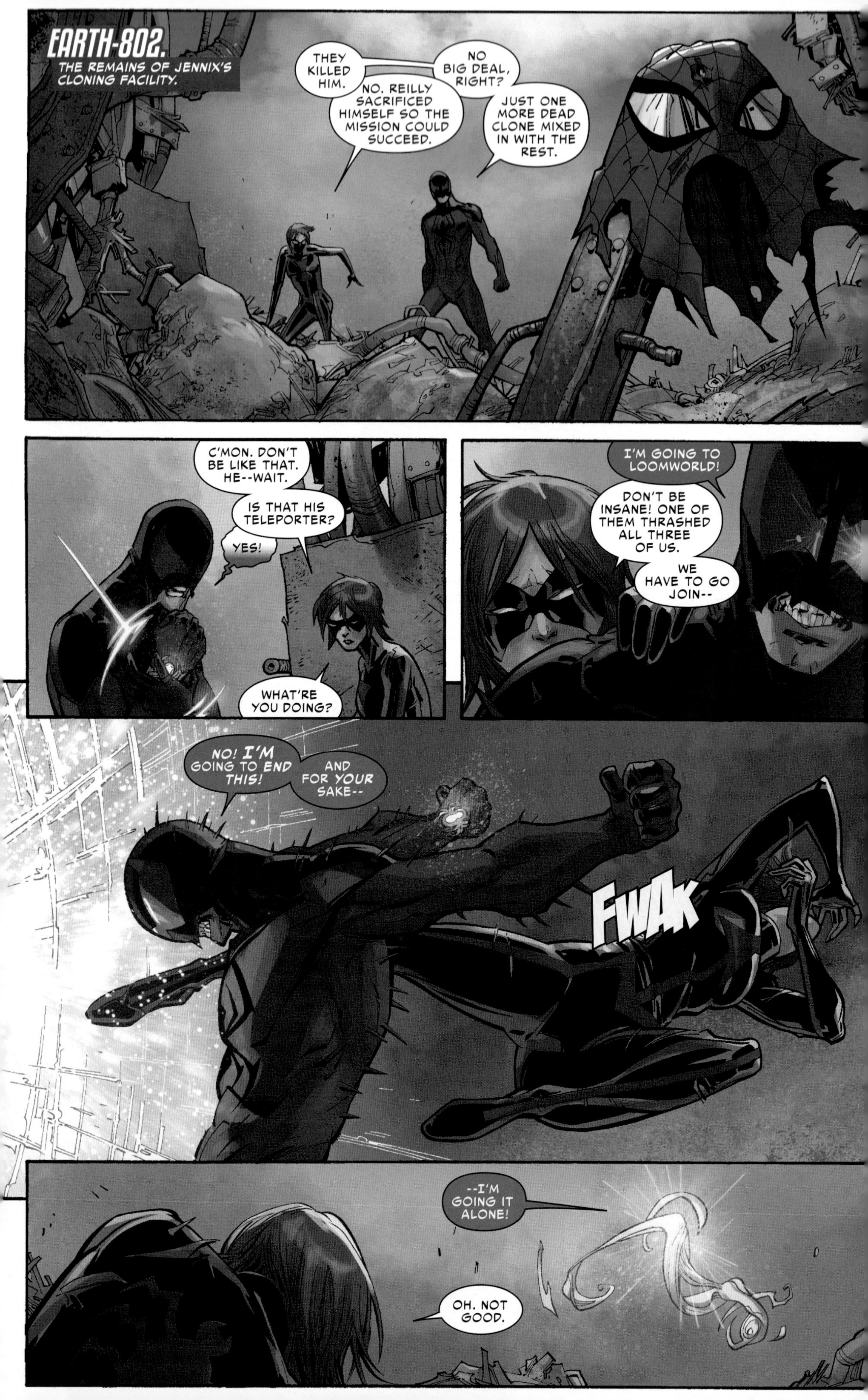
EARTH-802.
THE REMAINS OF JENNIX'S CLONING FACILITY.
THEY KILLED HIM.
NO BIG DEAL, RIGHT?
NO. REILLY SACRIFICED HIMSELF SO THE MISSION COULD SUCCEED.
JUST ONE MORE DEAD CLONE MIXED IN WITH THE REST.
C'MON. DON'T BE LIKE THAT. HE--WAIT.
IS THAT HIS TELEPORTER?
YES!
WHAT'RE YOU DOING?
I'M GOING TO LOOMWORLD!
DON'T BE INSANE! ONE OF THEM THRASHED ALL THREE OF US.
WE HAVE TO GO JOIN--
NO! I'M GOING TO END THIS!
AND FOR YOUR SAKE--
FWAK
--I'M GOING IT ALONE!
OH. NOT GOOD.

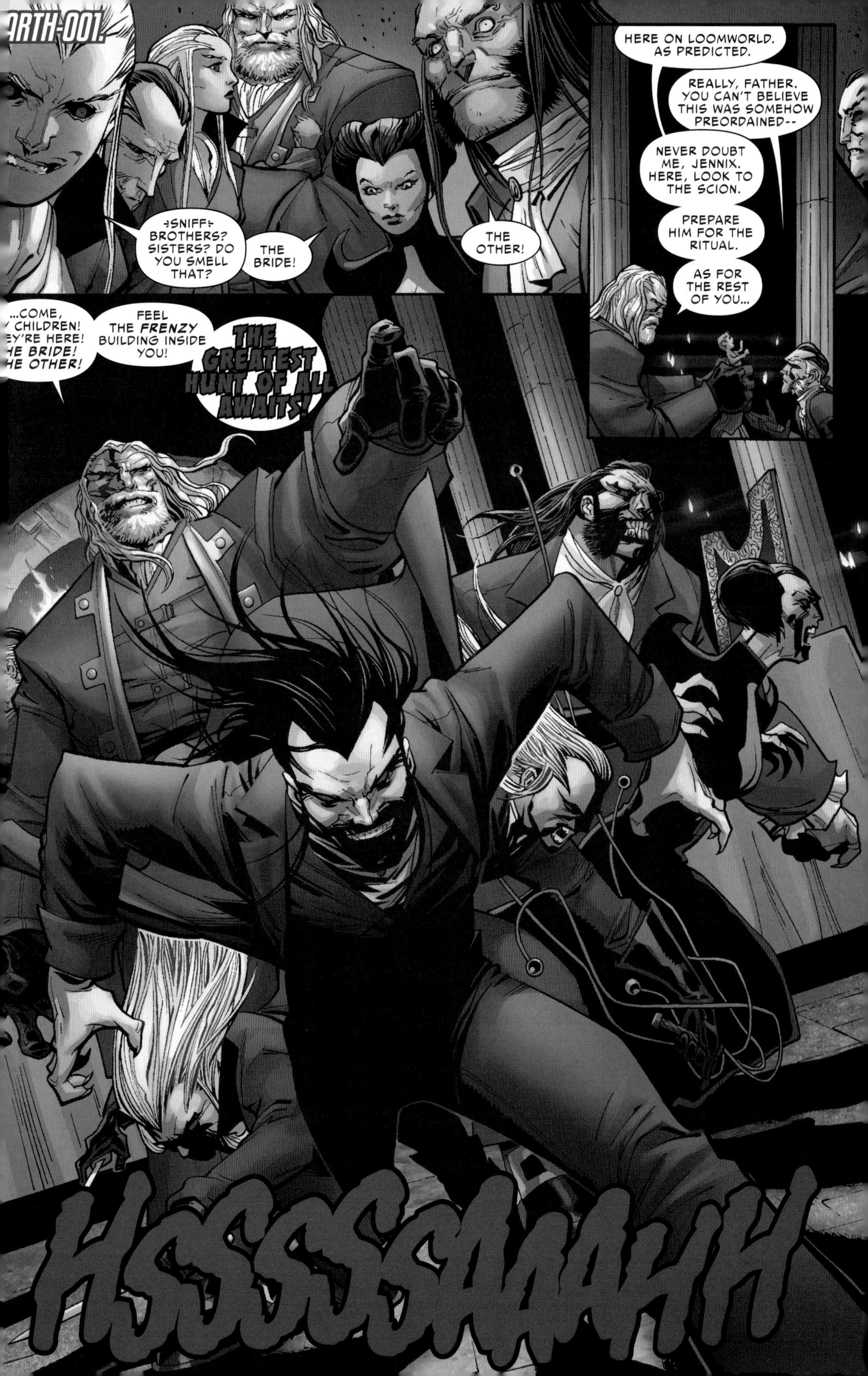

ARTH-001.
HERE ON LOOMWORLD. AS PREDICTED.
REALLY, FATHER. YOU CAN'T BELIEVE THIS WAS SOMEHOW PREORDAINED--
NEVER DOUBT ME, JENNIX. HERE, LOOK TO THE SCION.
PREPARE HIM FOR THE RITUAL.
AS FOR THE REST OF YOU...
SNIFF BROTHERS? SISTERS? DO YOU SMELL THAT?
THE BRIDE!
THE OTHER!
...COME, CHILDREN! EY'RE HERE! HE BRIDE! HE OTHER!
FEEL THE FRENZY BUILDING INSIDE YOU!
THE GREATEST HUNT OF ALL AWAITS!
HSSSSAAAHH

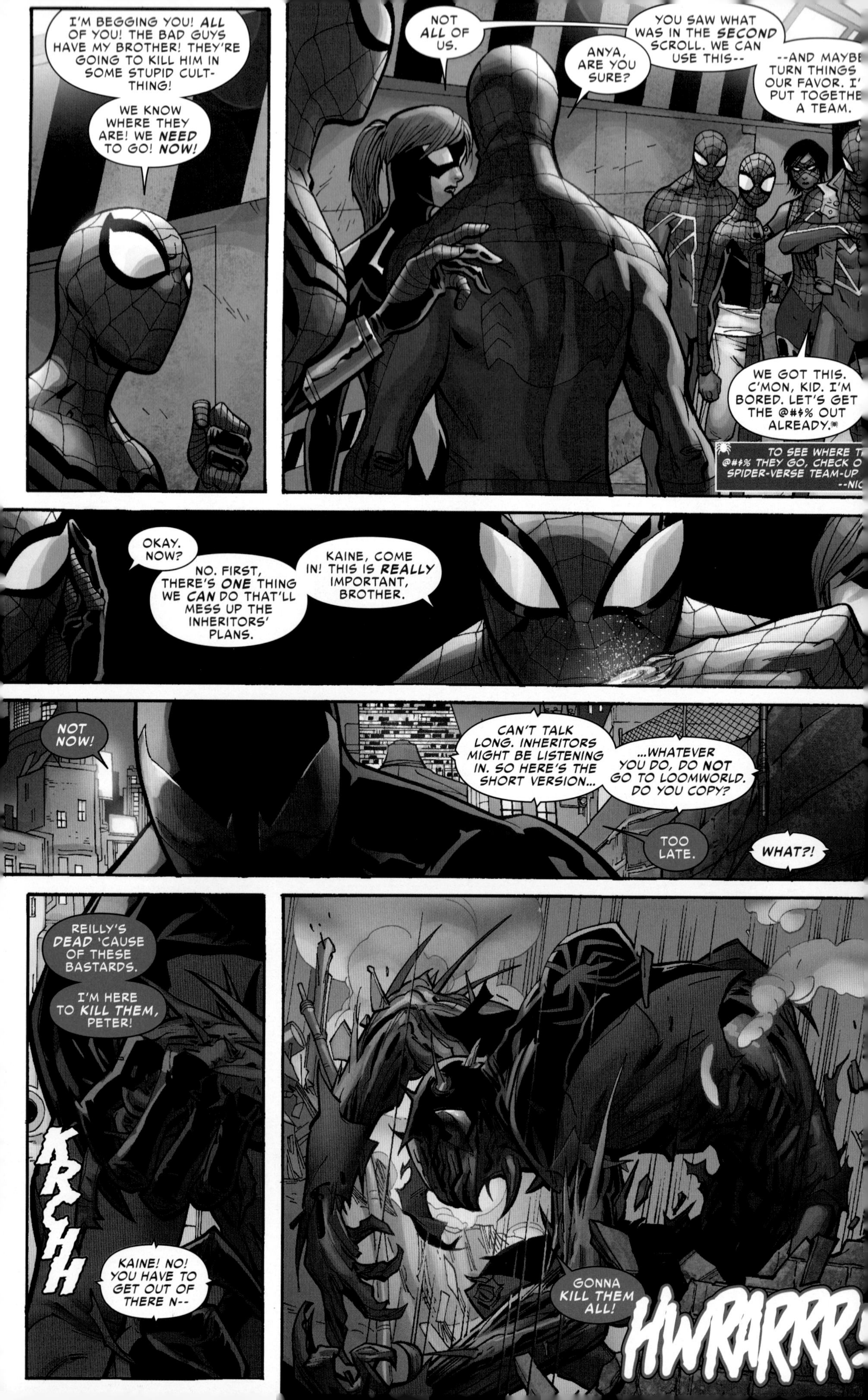
I'M BEGGING YOU! ALL OF YOU! THE BAD GUYS HAVE MY BROTHER! THEY'RE GOING TO KILL HIM IN SOME STUPID CULT-THING!
WE KNOW WHERE THEY ARE! WE NEED TO GO! NOW!
NOT ALL OF US.
ANYA, ARE YOU SURE?
YOU SAW WHAT WAS IN THE SECOND SCROLL. WE CAN USE THIS--
--AND MAYBE TURN THINGS OUR FAVOR. I' PUT TOGETHE A TEAM.
WE GOT THIS. C'MON, KID. I'M BORED. LET'S GET THE @#$% OUT ALREADY.
TO SEE WHERE T @#$% THEY GO, CHECK O SPIDER-VERSE TEAM-UP --NIC
OKAY. NOW?
NO. FIRST, THERE'S ONE THING WE CAN DO THAT'LL MESS UP THE INHERITORS' PLANS.
KAINE, COME IN! THIS IS REALLY IMPORTANT, BROTHER.
NOT NOW!
CAN'T TALK LONG. INHERITORS MIGHT BE LISTENING IN. SO HERE'S THE SHORT VERSION...
...WHATEVER YOU DO, DO NOT GO TO LOOMWORLD. DO YOU COPY?
TOO LATE.
WHAT?!
REILLY'S DEAD 'CAUSE OF THESE BASTARDS.
I'M HERE TO KILL THEM, PETER!
KRCHH
KAINE! NO! YOU HAVE TO GET OUT OF THERE N--
GONNA KILL THEM ALL!
HWRARRR

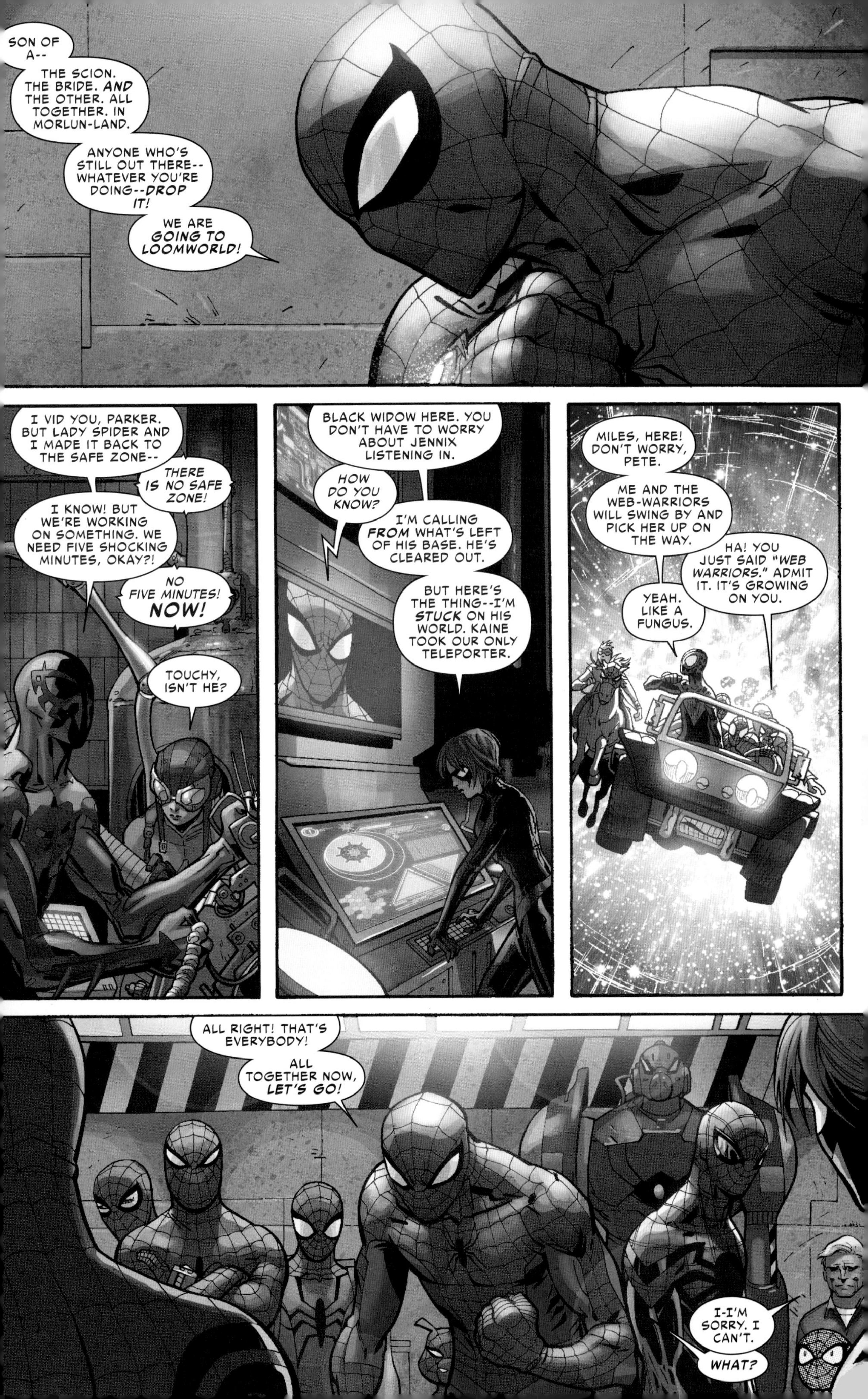
SON OF A--
THE SCION. THE BRIDE. AND THE OTHER. ALL TOGETHER. IN MORLUN-LAND.
ANYONE WHO'S STILL OUT THERE--WHATEVER YOU'RE DOING--DROP IT!
WE ARE GOING TO LOOMWORLD!
I VID YOU, PARKER. BUT LADY SPIDER AND I MADE IT BACK TO THE SAFE ZONE--
THERE IS NO SAFE ZONE!
I KNOW! BUT WE'RE WORKING ON SOMETHING. WE NEED FIVE SHOCKING MINUTES, OKAY?!
NO FIVE MINUTES! NOW!
TOUCHY, ISN'T HE?
BLACK WIDOW HERE. YOU DON'T HAVE TO WORRY ABOUT JENNIX LISTENING IN.
HOW DO YOU KNOW?
I'M CALLING FROM WHAT'S LEFT OF HIS BASE. HE'S CLEARED OUT.
BUT HERE'S THE THING--I'M STUCK ON HIS WORLD. KAINE TOOK OUR ONLY TELEPORTER.
MILES, HERE! DON'T WORRY, PETE.
ME AND THE WEB-WARRIORS WILL SWING BY AND PICK HER UP ON THE WAY.
HA! YOU JUST SAID "WEB WARRIORS." ADMIT IT. IT'S GROWING ON YOU.
YEAH. LIKE A FUNGUS.
ALL RIGHT! THAT'S EVERYBODY!
ALL TOGETHER NOW, LET'S GO!
I-I'M SORRY. I CAN'T.
WHAT?

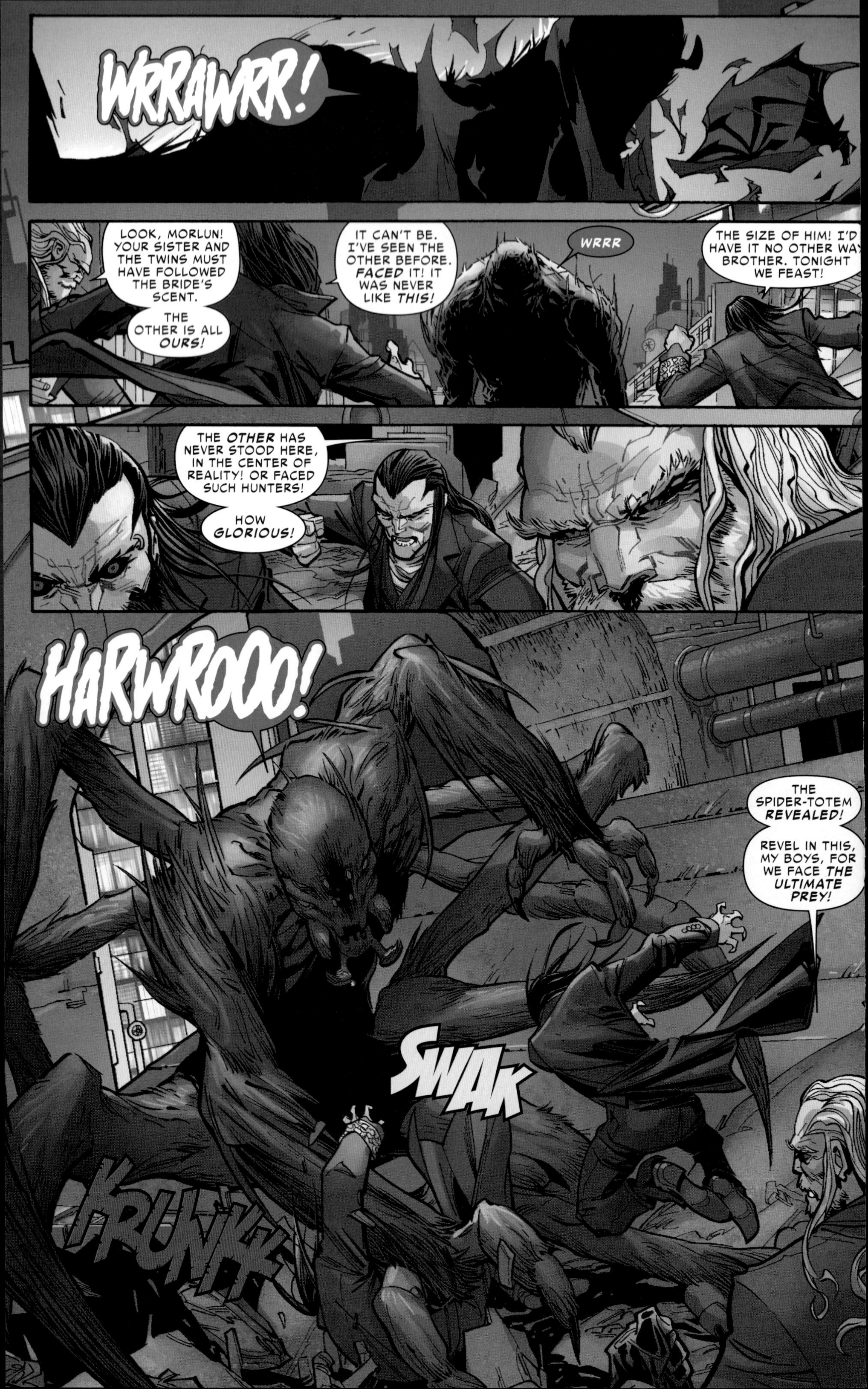
WRRAWRR!
LOOK, MORLUN! YOUR SISTER AND THE TWINS MUST HAVE FOLLOWED THE BRIDE'S SCENT.
THE OTHER IS ALL OURS!
IT CAN'T BE. I'VE SEEN THE OTHER BEFORE. FACED IT! IT WAS NEVER LIKE THIS!
WRRR
THE SIZE OF HIM! I'D HAVE IT NO OTHER WAY BROTHER. TONIGHT WE FEAST!
THE OTHER HAS NEVER STOOD HERE, IN THE CENTER OF REALITY! OR FACED SUCH HUNTERS!
HOW GLORIOUS!
HARWROOO!
THE SPIDER-TOTEM REVEALED!
REVEL IN THIS, MY BOYS, FOR WE FACE THE ULTIMATE PREY!
SWAK
KRUNK

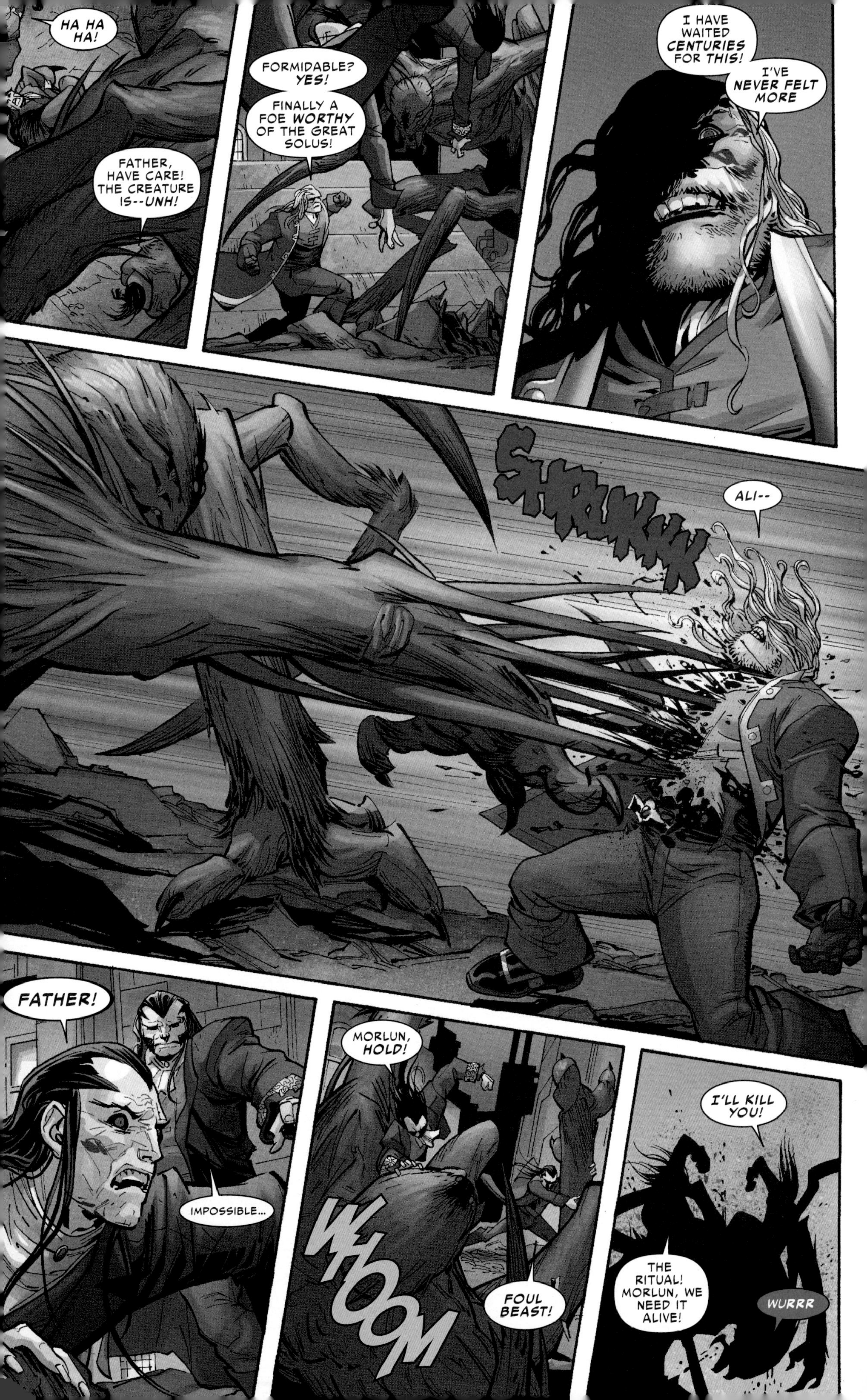
HA HA HA!
FATHER, HAVE CARE! THE CREATURE IS--UNH!
FORMIDABLE? YES!
FINALLY A FOE WORTHY OF THE GREAT SOLUS!
I HAVE WAITED CENTURIES FOR THIS!
I'VE NEVER FELT MORE
SHRUNKKK
ALI--
FATHER!
IMPOSSIBLE...
MORLUN, HOLD!
WHOOM
FOUL BEAST!
I'LL KILL YOU!
THE RITUAL! MORLUN, WE NEED IT ALIVE!
WURRR

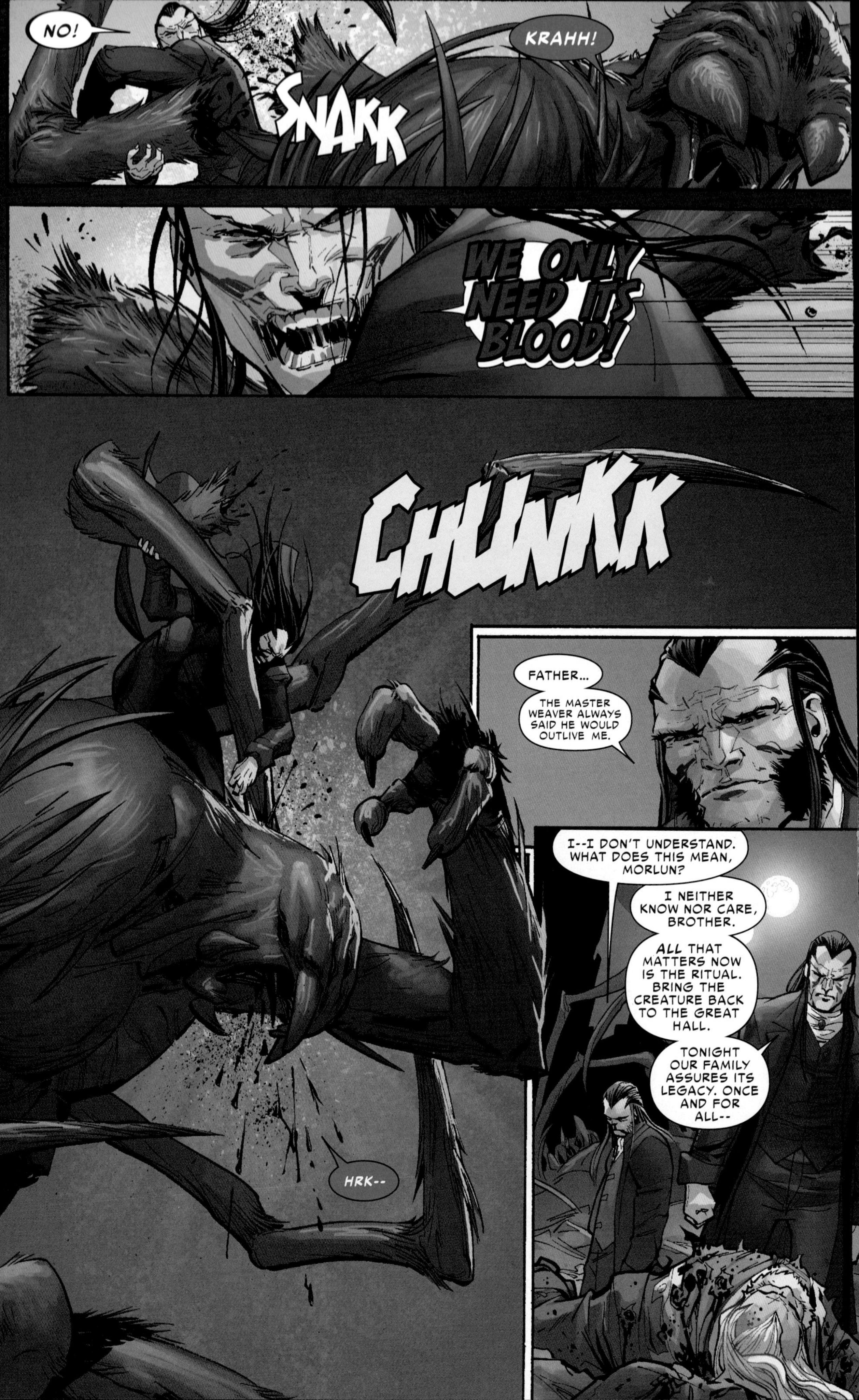
NO!
KRAHH!
SNAKK
WE ONLY NEED ITS BLOOD!
CHUNKK
HRK--
FATHER...
THE MASTER WEAVER ALWAYS SAID HE WOULD OUTLIVE ME.
I--I DON'T UNDERSTAND. WHAT DOES THIS MEAN, MORLUN?
I NEITHER KNOW NOR CARE, BROTHER.
ALL THAT MATTERS NOW IS THE RITUAL. BRING THE CREATURE BACK TO THE GREAT HALL.
TONIGHT OUR FAMILY ASSURES ITS LEGACY. ONCE AND FOR ALL--

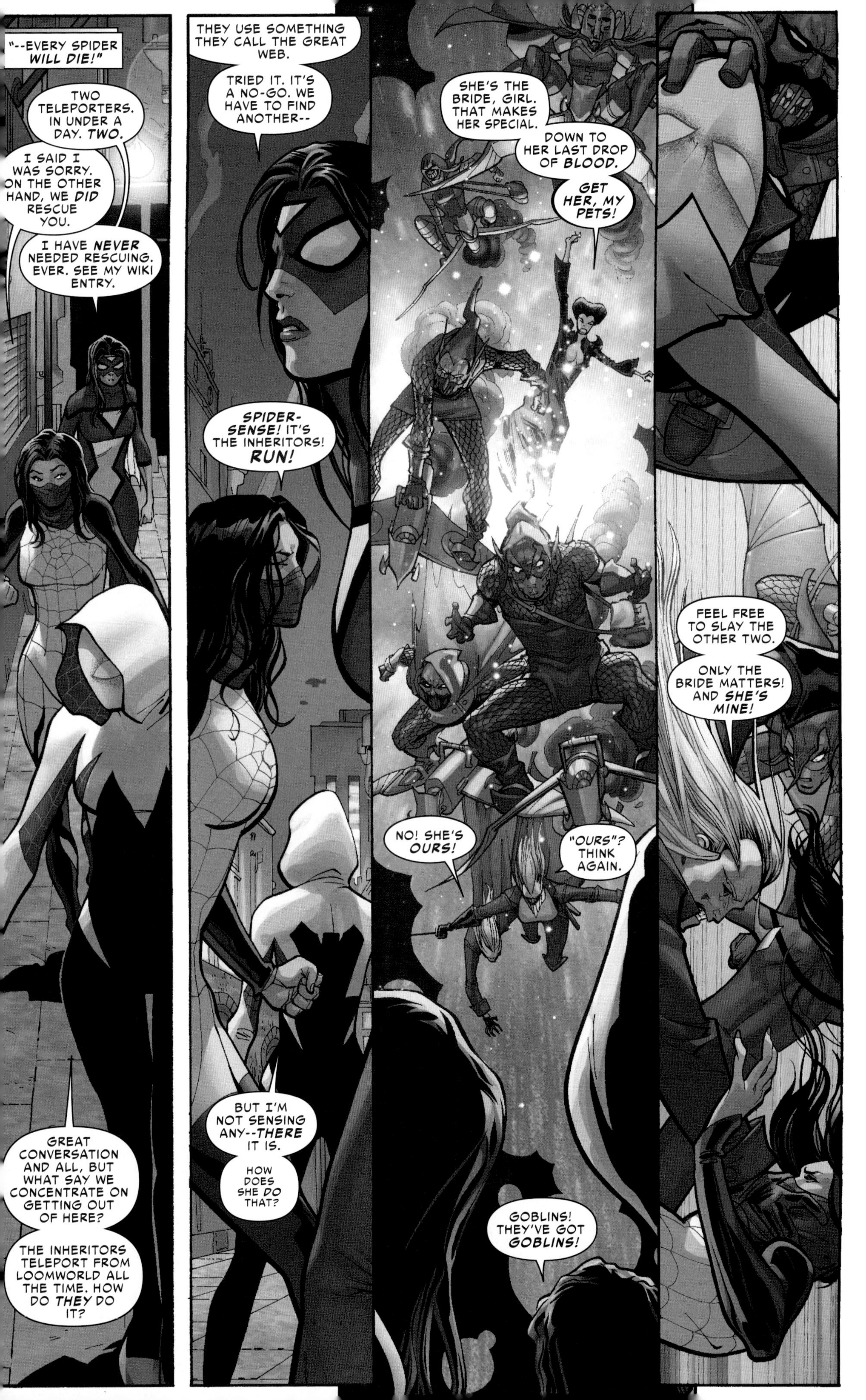
"--EVERY SPIDER WILL DIE!"
TWO TELEPORTERS. IN UNDER A DAY. TWO.
I SAID I WAS SORRY. ON THE OTHER HAND, WE DID RESCUE YOU.
I HAVE NEVER NEEDED RESCUING. EVER. SEE MY WIKI ENTRY.
GREAT CONVERSATION AND ALL, BUT WHAT SAY WE CONCENTRATE ON GETTING OUT OF HERE?
THE INHERITORS TELEPORT FROM LOOMWORLD ALL THE TIME. HOW DO THEY DO IT?
THEY USE SOMETHING THEY CALL THE GREAT WEB.
TRIED IT. IT'S A NO-GO. WE HAVE TO FIND ANOTHER--
SPIDER-SENSE! IT'S THE INHERITORS! RUN!
BUT I'M NOT SENSING ANY--THERE IT IS.
HOW DOES SHE DO THAT?
SHE'S THE BRIDE, GIRL. THAT MAKES HER SPECIAL.
DOWN TO HER LAST DROP OF BLOOD.
GET HER, MY PETS!
NO! SHE'S OURS!
"OURS"? THINK AGAIN.
GOBLINS! THEY'VE GOT GOBLINS!
FEEL FREE TO SLAY THE OTHER TWO.
ONLY THE BRIDE MATTERS! AND SHE'S MINE!

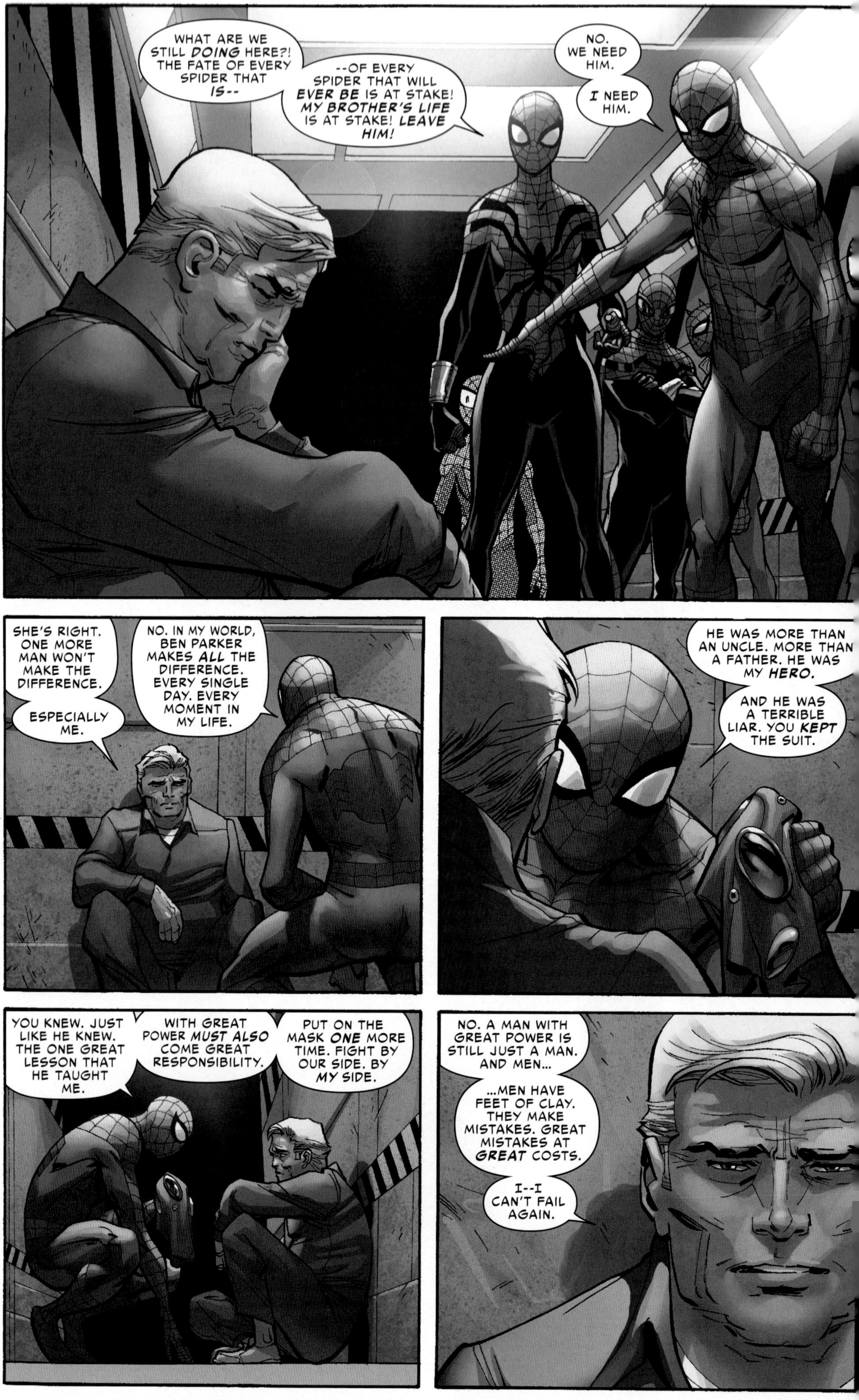
WHAT ARE WE STILL DOING HERE?! THE FATE OF EVERY SPIDER THAT IS--
--OF EVERY SPIDER THAT WILL EVER BE IS AT STAKE! MY BROTHER'S LIFE IS AT STAKE! LEAVE HIM!
NO. WE NEED HIM.
I NEED HIM.
SHE'S RIGHT. ONE MORE MAN WON'T MAKE THE DIFFERENCE.
ESPECIALLY ME.
NO. IN MY WORLD, BEN PARKER MAKES ALL THE DIFFERENCE. EVERY SINGLE DAY. EVERY MOMENT IN MY LIFE.
HE WAS MORE THAN AN UNCLE. MORE THAN A FATHER. HE WAS MY HERO.
AND HE WAS A TERRIBLE LIAR. YOU KEPT THE SUIT.
YOU KNEW. JUST LIKE HE KNEW. THE ONE GREAT LESSON THAT HE TAUGHT ME.
WITH GREAT POWER MUST ALSO COME GREAT RESPONSIBILITY.
PUT ON THE MASK ONE MORE TIME. FIGHT BY OUR SIDE. BY MY SIDE.
NO. A MAN WITH GREAT POWER IS STILL JUST A MAN. AND MEN...
...MEN HAVE FEET OF CLAY. THEY MAKE MISTAKES. GREAT MISTAKES AT GREAT COSTS.
I--I CAN'T FAIL AGAIN.

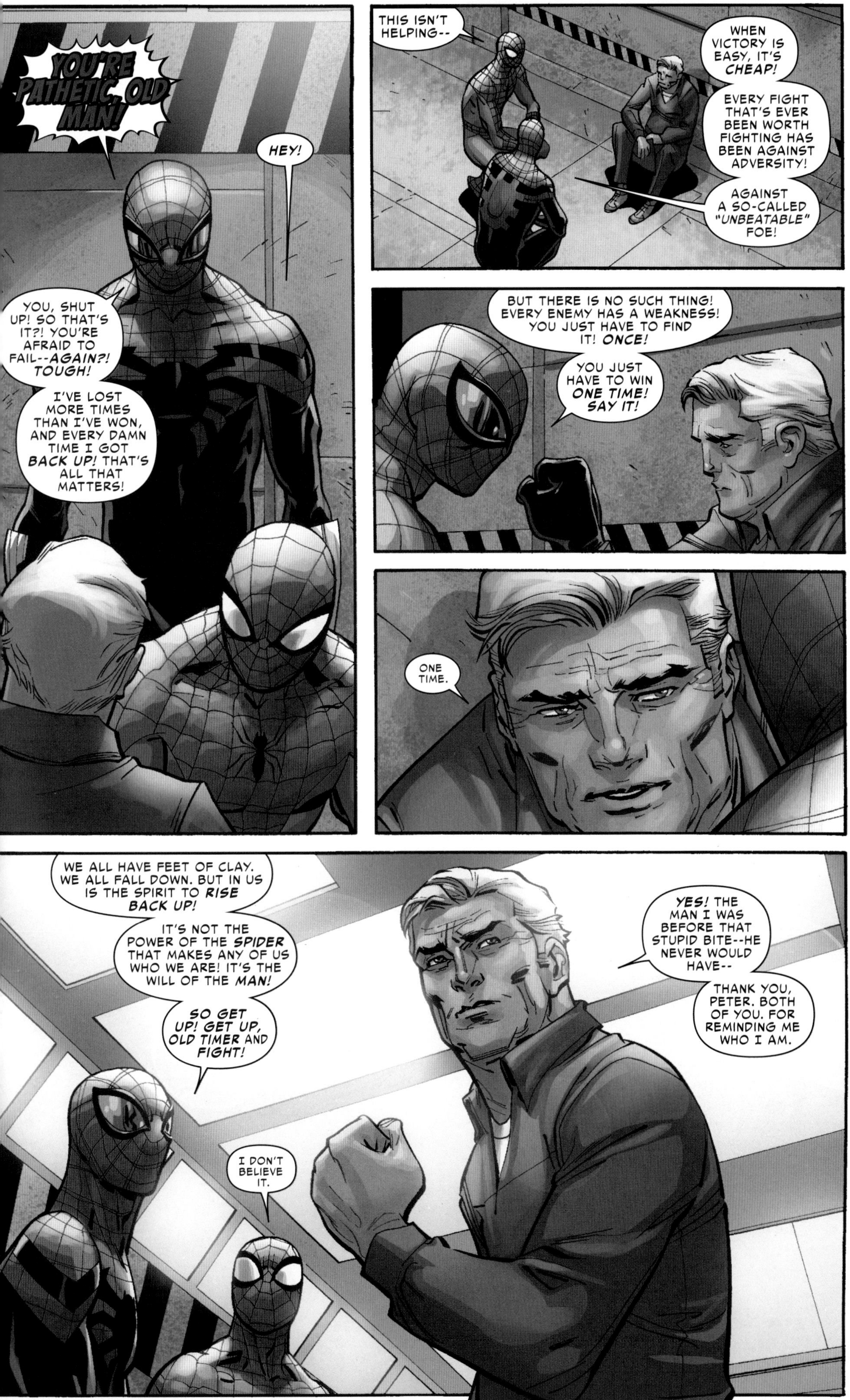
YOU'RE PATHETIC, OLD MAN!
HEY!
YOU, SHUT UP! SO THAT'S IT?! YOU'RE AFRAID TO FAIL--AGAIN?! TOUGH!
I'VE LOST MORE TIMES THAN I'VE WON, AND EVERY DAMN TIME I GOT BACK UP! THAT'S ALL THAT MATTERS!
THIS ISN'T HELPING--
WHEN VICTORY IS EASY, IT'S CHEAP!
EVERY FIGHT THAT'S EVER BEEN WORTH FIGHTING HAS BEEN AGAINST ADVERSITY!
AGAINST A SO-CALLED "UNBEATABLE" FOE!
BUT THERE IS NO SUCH THING! EVERY ENEMY HAS A WEAKNESS! YOU JUST HAVE TO FIND IT! ONCE!
YOU JUST HAVE TO WIN ONE TIME! SAY IT!
ONE TIME.
WE ALL HAVE FEET OF CLAY. WE ALL FALL DOWN. BUT IN US IS THE SPIRIT TO RISE BACK UP!
IT'S NOT THE POWER OF THE SPIDER THAT MAKES ANY OF US WHO WE ARE! IT'S THE WILL OF THE MAN!
SO GET UP! GET UP, OLD TIMER AND FIGHT!
I DON'T BELIEVE IT.
YES! THE MAN I WAS BEFORE THAT STUPID BITE--HE NEVER WOULD HAVE--
THANK YOU, PETER. BOTH OF YOU. FOR REMINDING ME WHO I AM.

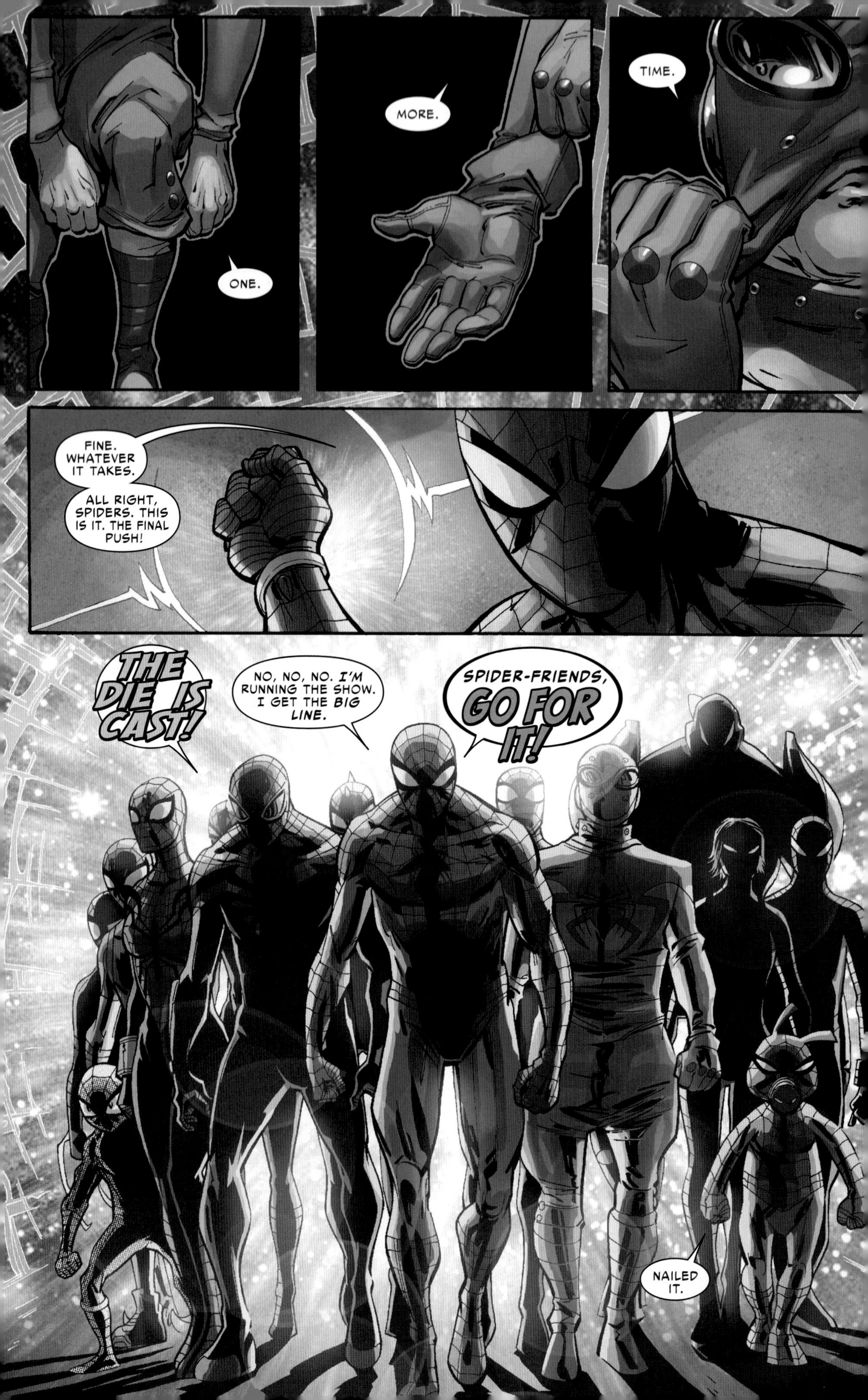
ONE.
MORE.
TIME.
FINE. WHATEVER IT TAKES.
ALL RIGHT, SPIDERS. THIS IS IT. THE FINAL PUSH!
THE DIE IS CAST!
NO, NO, NO. I'M RUNNING THE SHOW. I GET THE BIG LINE.
SPIDER-FRIENDS, GO FOR IT!
NAILED IT.

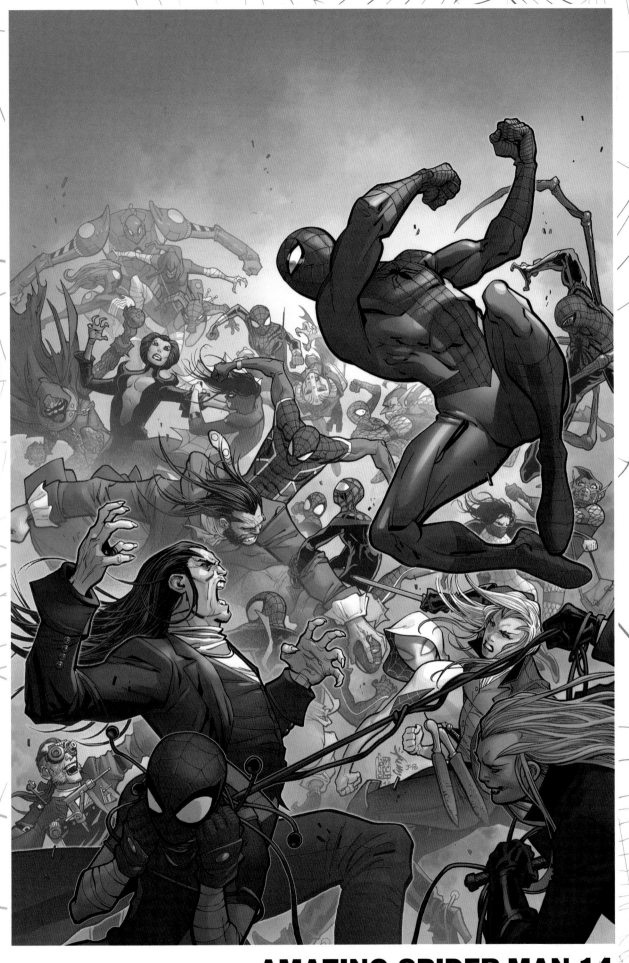

AMAZING SPIDER-MAN 14
SPIDER-VERSE, PART SIX: WEB WARRIORS

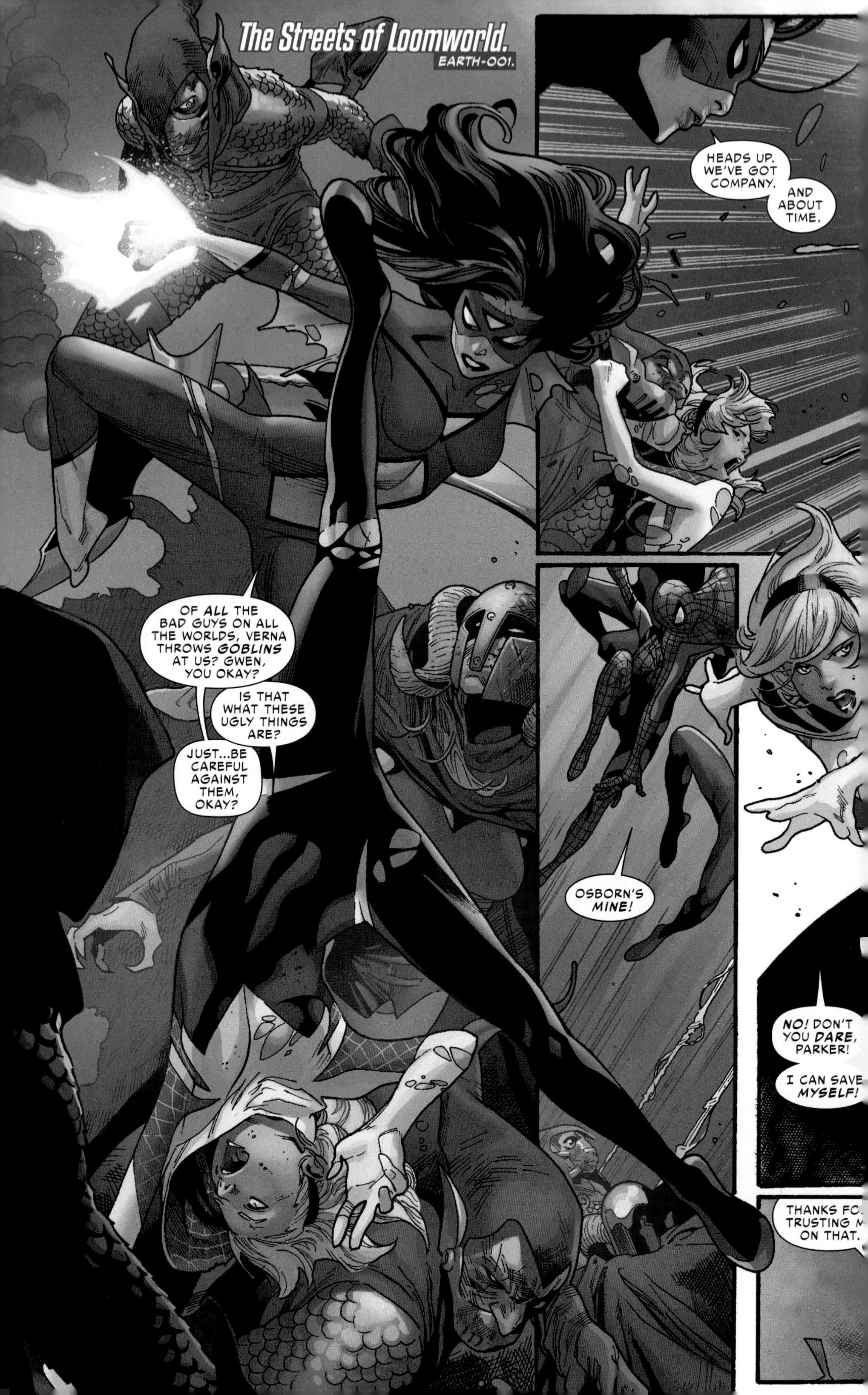

The Streets of Loomworld.
EARTH-001.
HEADS UP. WE'VE GOT COMPANY.
AND ABOUT TIME.
OF ALL THE BAD GUYS ON ALL THE WORLDS, VERNA THROWS GOBLINS AT US? GWEN, YOU OKAY?
IS THAT WHAT THESE UGLY THINGS ARE?
JUST...BE CAREFUL AGAINST THEM, OKAY?
OSBORN'S MINE!
NO! DON'T YOU DARE, PARKER!
I CAN SAVE MYSELF!

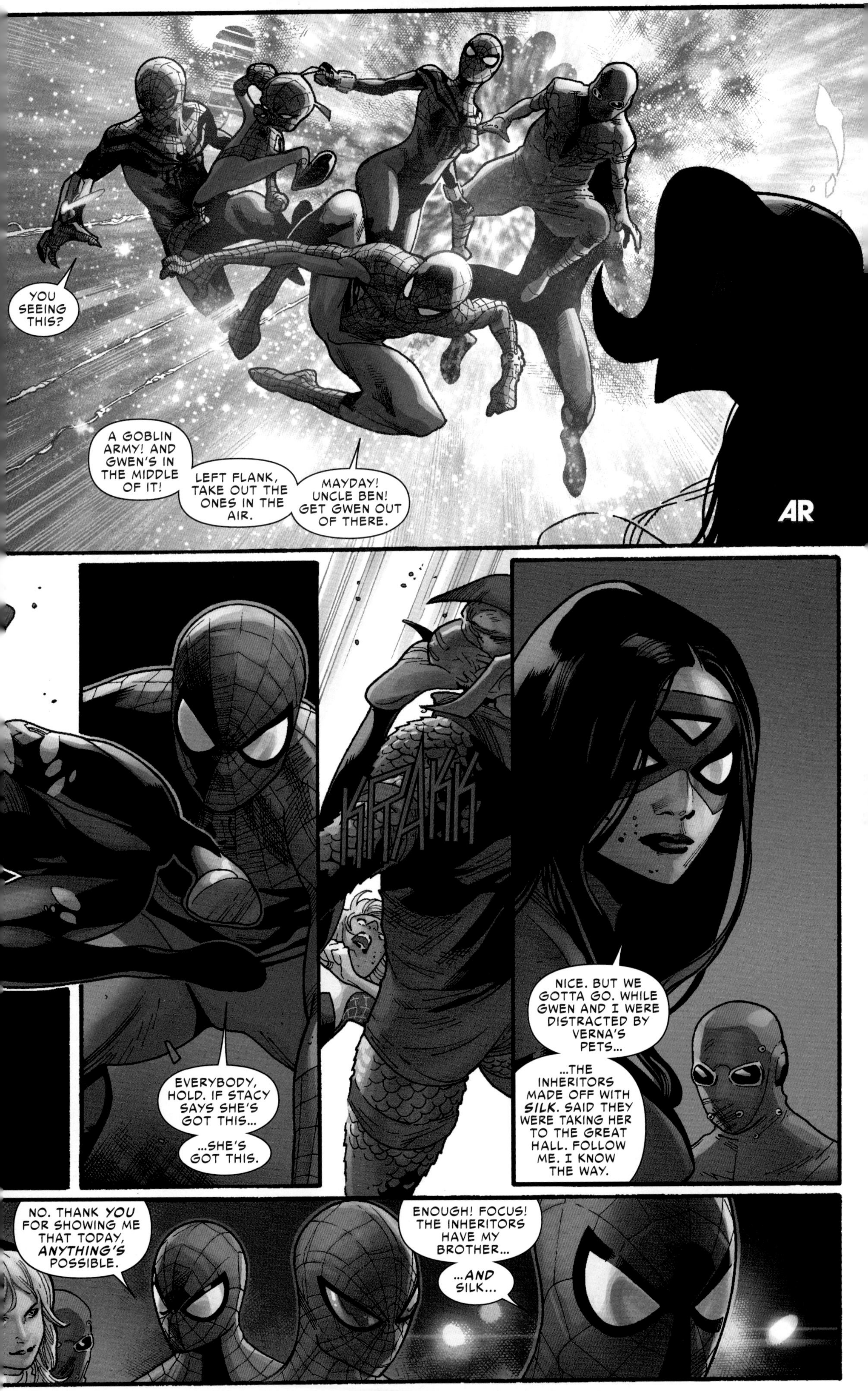
YOU SEEING THIS?
A GOBLIN ARMY! AND GWEN'S IN THE MIDDLE OF IT!
LEFT FLANK, TAKE OUT THE ONES IN THE AIR.
MAYDAY! UNCLE BEN! GET GWEN OUT OF THERE.
AR
KRAKK
EVERYBODY, HOLD. IF STACY SAYS SHE'S GOT THIS...
...SHE'S GOT THIS.
NICE. BUT WE GOTTA GO. WHILE GWEN AND I WERE DISTRACTED BY VERNA'S PETS...
...THE INHERITORS MADE OFF WITH *SILK*. SAID THEY WERE TAKING HER TO THE GREAT HALL. FOLLOW ME. I KNOW THE WAY.
NO. THANK *YOU* FOR SHOWING ME THAT TODAY, *ANYTHING'S* POSSIBLE.
ENOUGH! FOCUS! THE INHERITORS HAVE MY BROTHER...
...*AND* SILK...

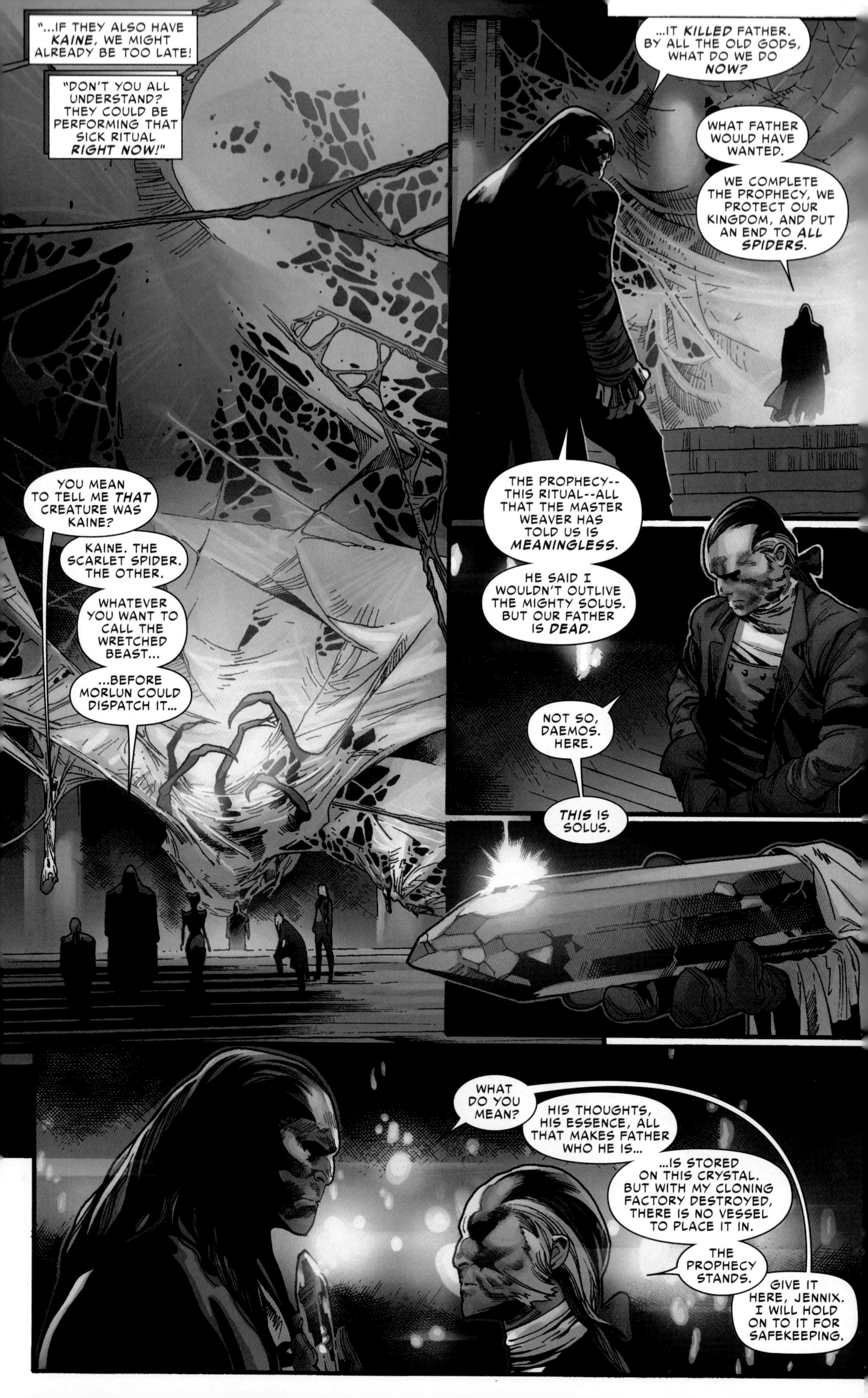
"...IF THEY ALSO HAVE KAINE, WE MIGHT ALREADY BE TOO LATE!
"DON'T YOU ALL UNDERSTAND? THEY COULD BE PERFORMING THAT SICK RITUAL RIGHT NOW!"
YOU MEAN TO TELL ME THAT CREATURE WAS KAINE?
KAINE. THE SCARLET SPIDER. THE OTHER.
WHATEVER YOU WANT TO CALL THE WRETCHED BEAST...
...BEFORE MORLUN COULD DISPATCH IT...
...IT KILLED FATHER. BY ALL THE OLD GODS, WHAT DO WE DO NOW?
WHAT FATHER WOULD HAVE WANTED.
WE COMPLETE THE PROPHECY, WE PROTECT OUR KINGDOM, AND PUT AN END TO ALL SPIDERS.
THE PROPHECY-- THIS RITUAL--ALL THAT THE MASTER WEAVER HAS TOLD US IS MEANINGLESS.
HE SAID I WOULDN'T OUTLIVE THE MIGHTY SOLUS. BUT OUR FATHER IS DEAD.
NOT SO, DAEMOS. HERE.
THIS IS SOLUS.
WHAT DO YOU MEAN?
HIS THOUGHTS, HIS ESSENCE, ALL THAT MAKES FATHER WHO HE IS...
...IS STORED ON THIS CRYSTAL. BUT WITH MY CLONING FACTORY DESTROYED, THERE IS NO VESSEL TO PLACE IT IN.
THE PROPHECY STANDS.
GIVE IT HERE, JENNIX. I WILL HOLD ON TO IT FOR SAFEKEEPING.

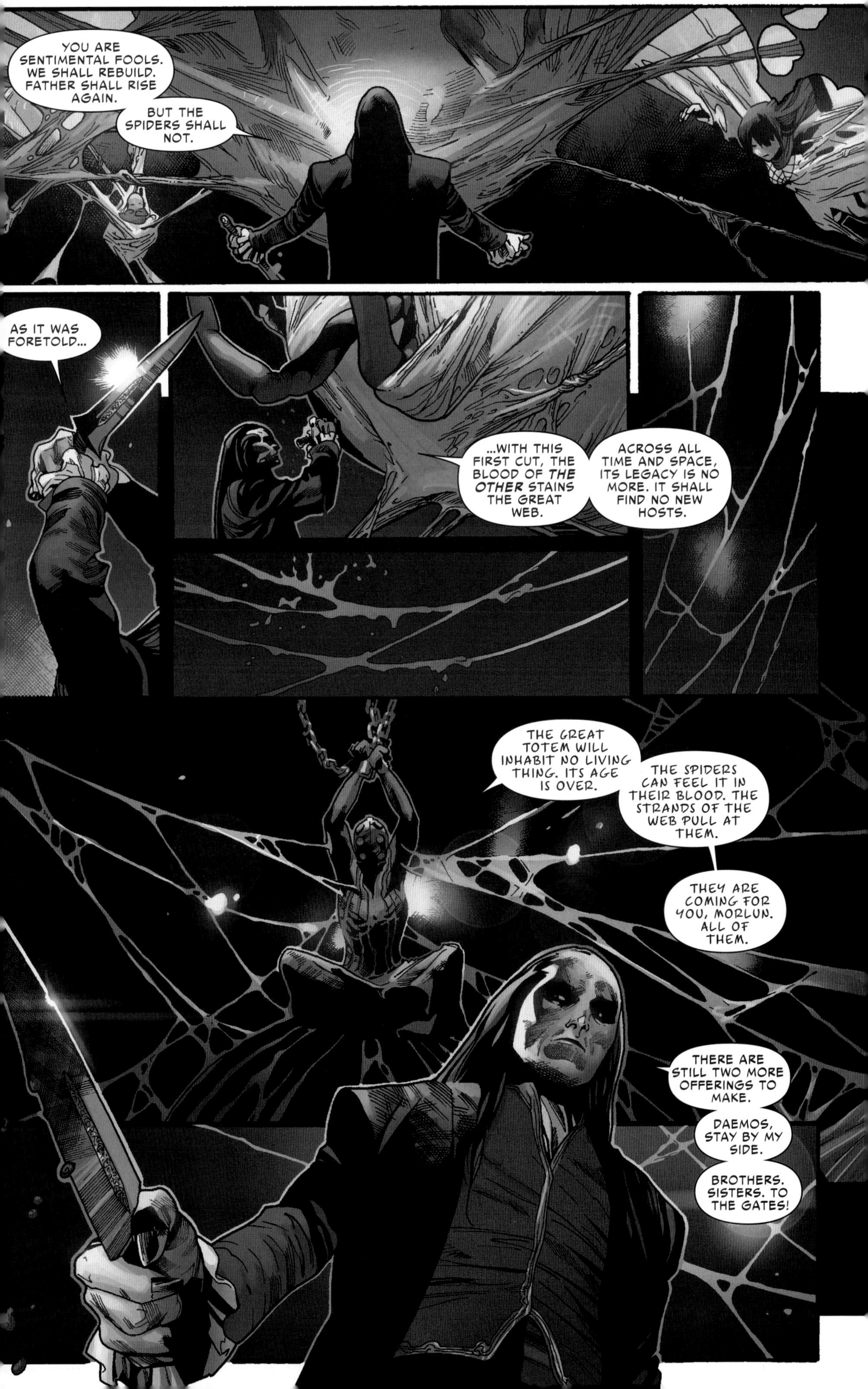
YOU ARE SENTIMENTAL FOOLS. WE SHALL REBUILD. FATHER SHALL RISE AGAIN.
BUT THE SPIDERS SHALL NOT.
AS IT WAS FORETOLD...
...WITH THIS FIRST CUT, THE BLOOD OF *THE OTHER* STAINS THE GREAT WEB.
ACROSS ALL TIME AND SPACE, ITS LEGACY IS NO MORE. IT SHALL FIND NO NEW HOSTS.
THE GREAT TOTEM WILL INHABIT NO LIVING THING. ITS AGE IS OVER.
THE SPIDERS CAN FEEL IT IN THEIR BLOOD. THE STRANDS OF THE WEB PULL AT THEM.
THEY ARE COMING FOR YOU, MORLUN. ALL OF THEM.
THERE ARE STILL TWO MORE OFFERINGS TO MAKE.
DAEMOS, STAY BY MY SIDE.
BROTHERS. SISTERS. TO THE GATES!

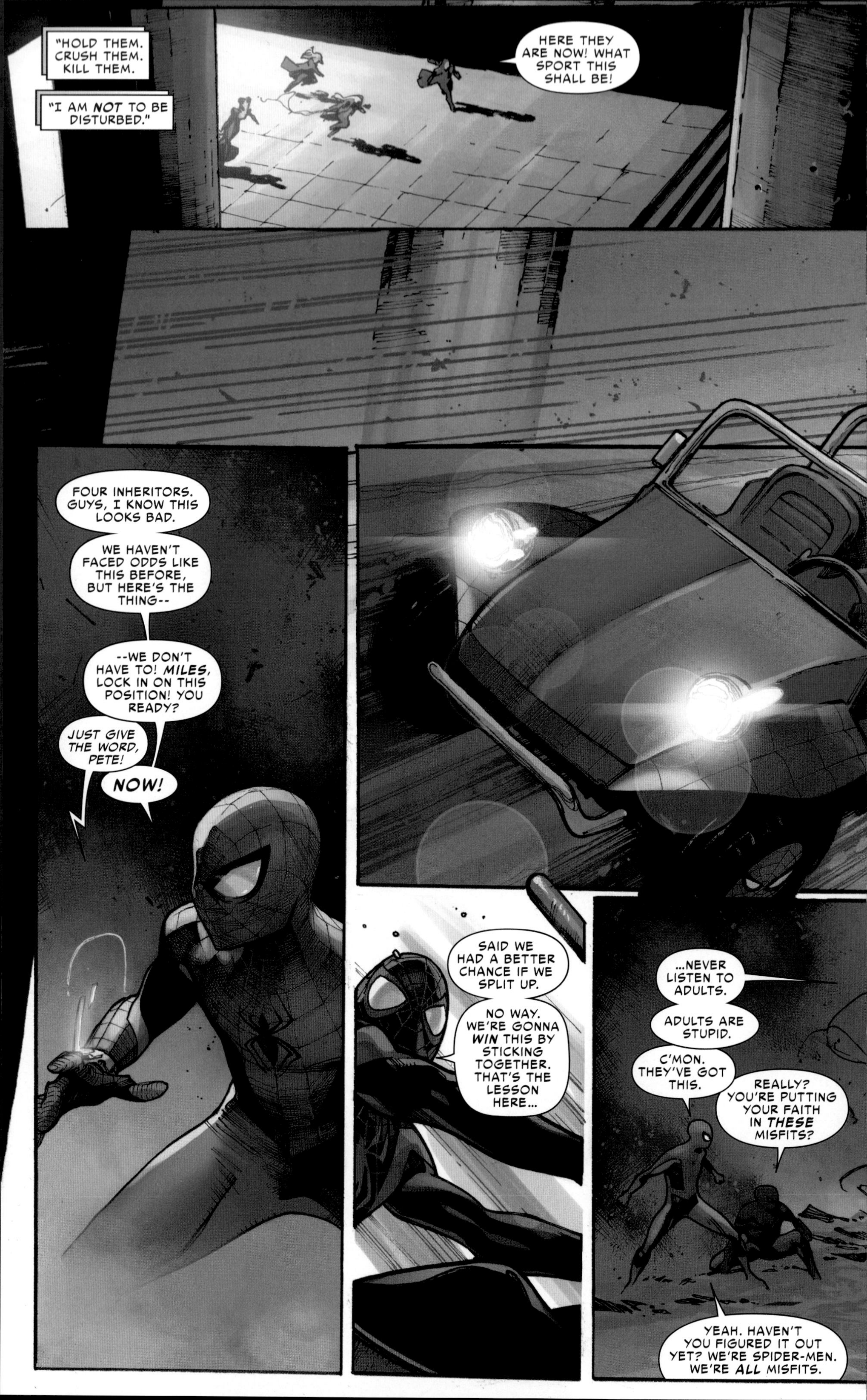
"HOLD THEM. CRUSH THEM. KILL THEM.
"I AM *NOT* TO BE DISTURBED."
HERE THEY ARE NOW! WHAT SPORT THIS SHALL BE!
FOUR INHERITORS. GUYS, I KNOW THIS LOOKS BAD.
WE HAVEN'T FACED ODDS LIKE THIS BEFORE, BUT HERE'S THE THING--
--WE DON'T HAVE TO! *MILES*, LOCK IN ON THIS POSITION! YOU READY?
JUST GIVE THE WORD, PETE!
NOW!
SAID WE HAD A BETTER CHANCE IF WE SPLIT UP.
NO WAY. WE'RE GONNA ***WIN*** THIS BY STICKING TOGETHER. THAT'S THE LESSON HERE...
...NEVER LISTEN TO ADULTS.
ADULTS ARE STUPID.
C'MON. THEY'VE GOT THIS.
REALLY? YOU'RE PUTTING YOUR FAITH IN ***THESE*** MISFITS?
YEAH. HAVEN'T YOU FIGURED IT OUT YET? WE'RE SPIDER-MEN. WE'RE ***ALL*** MISFITS.

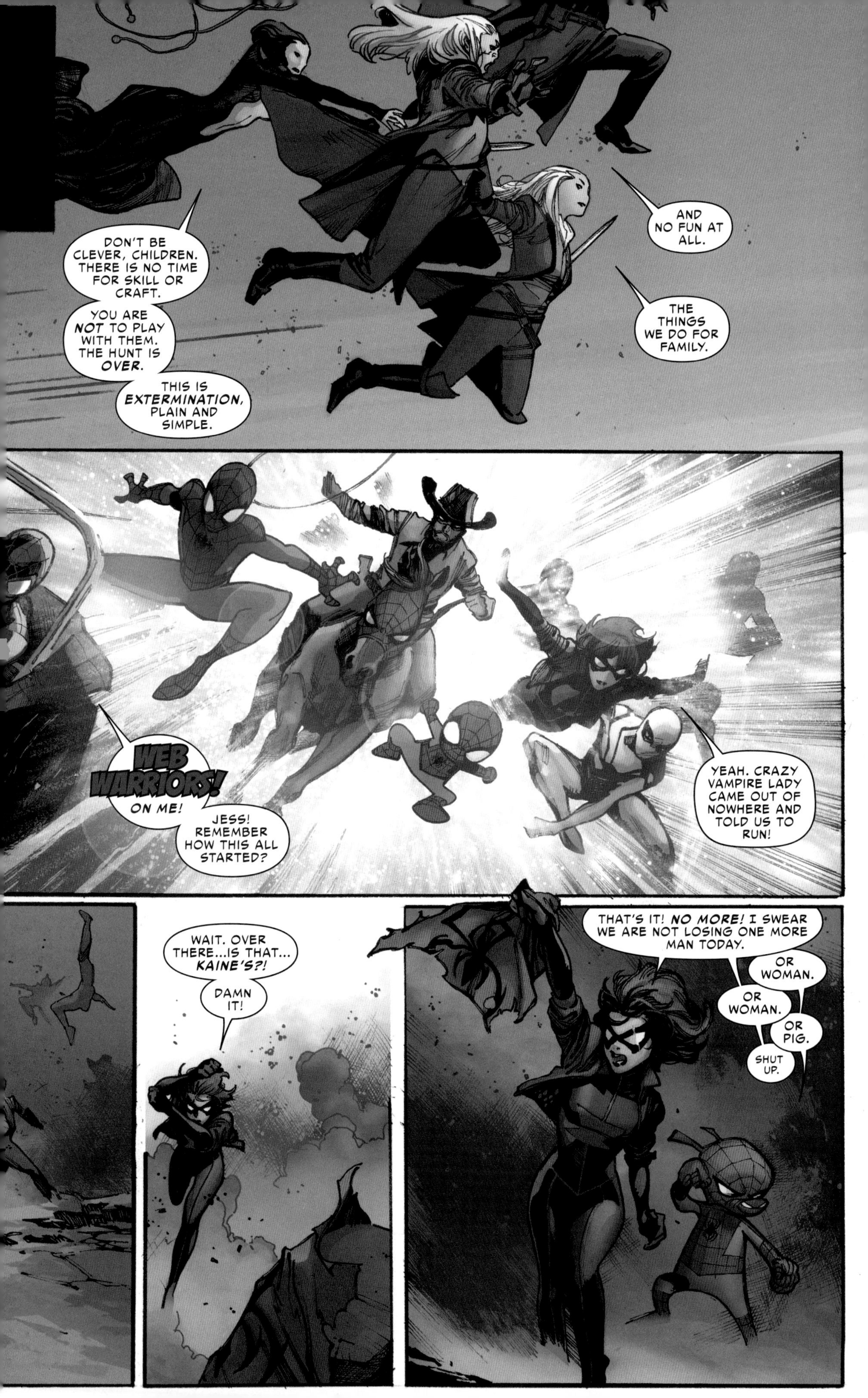
DON'T BE CLEVER, CHILDREN. THERE IS NO TIME FOR SKILL OR CRAFT.
YOU ARE NOT TO PLAY WITH THEM. THE HUNT IS OVER.
THIS IS EXTERMINATION, PLAIN AND SIMPLE.
AND NO FUN AT ALL.
THE THINGS WE DO FOR FAMILY.
WEB WARRIORS! ON ME!
JESS! REMEMBER HOW THIS ALL STARTED?
YEAH. CRAZY VAMPIRE LADY CAME OUT OF NOWHERE AND TOLD US TO RUN!
WAIT. OVER THERE...IS THAT... KAINE'S?!
DAMN IT!
THAT'S IT! NO MORE! I SWEAR WE ARE NOT LOSING ONE MORE MAN TODAY.
OR WOMAN.
OR WOMAN.
OR PIG.
SHUT UP.

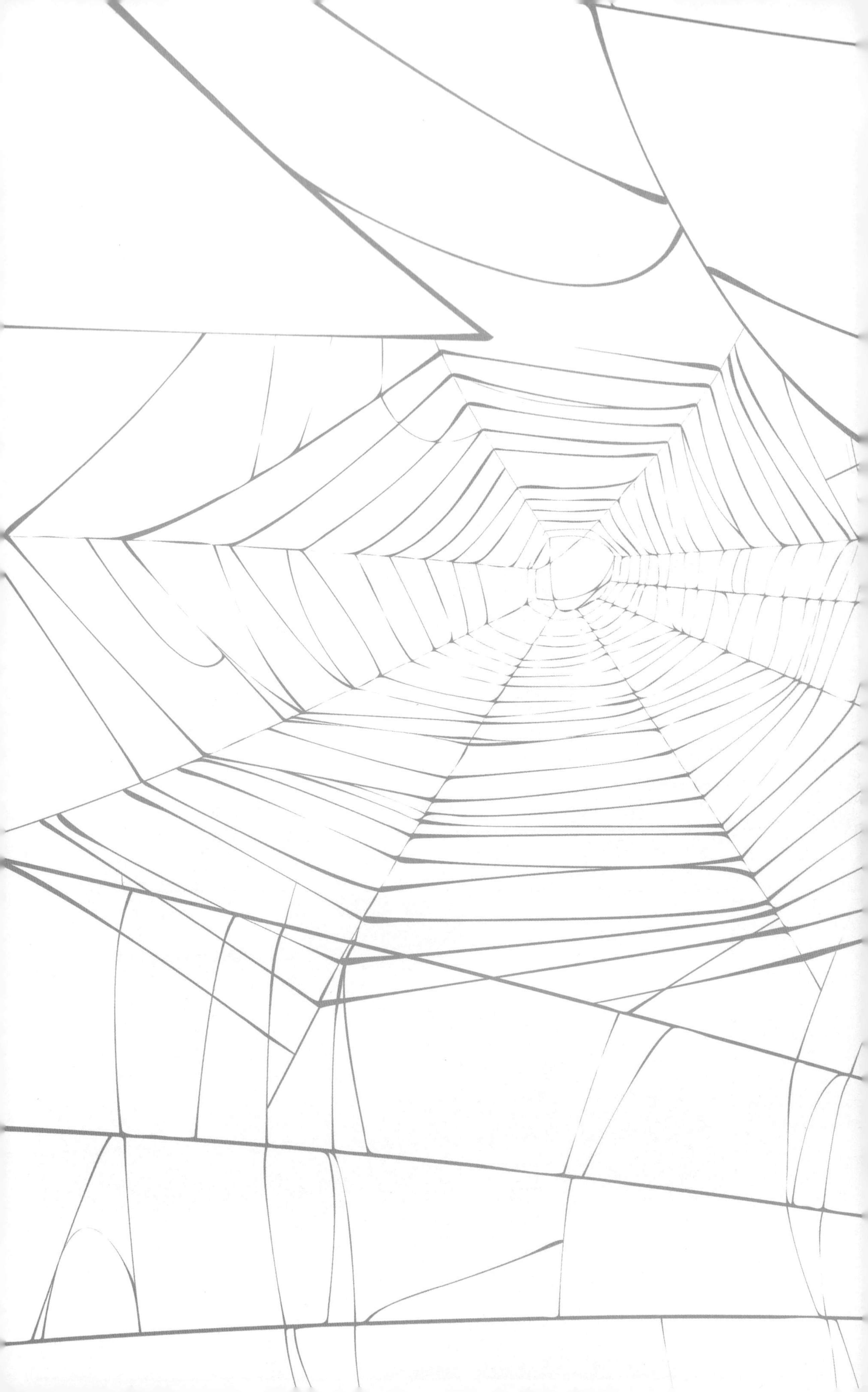

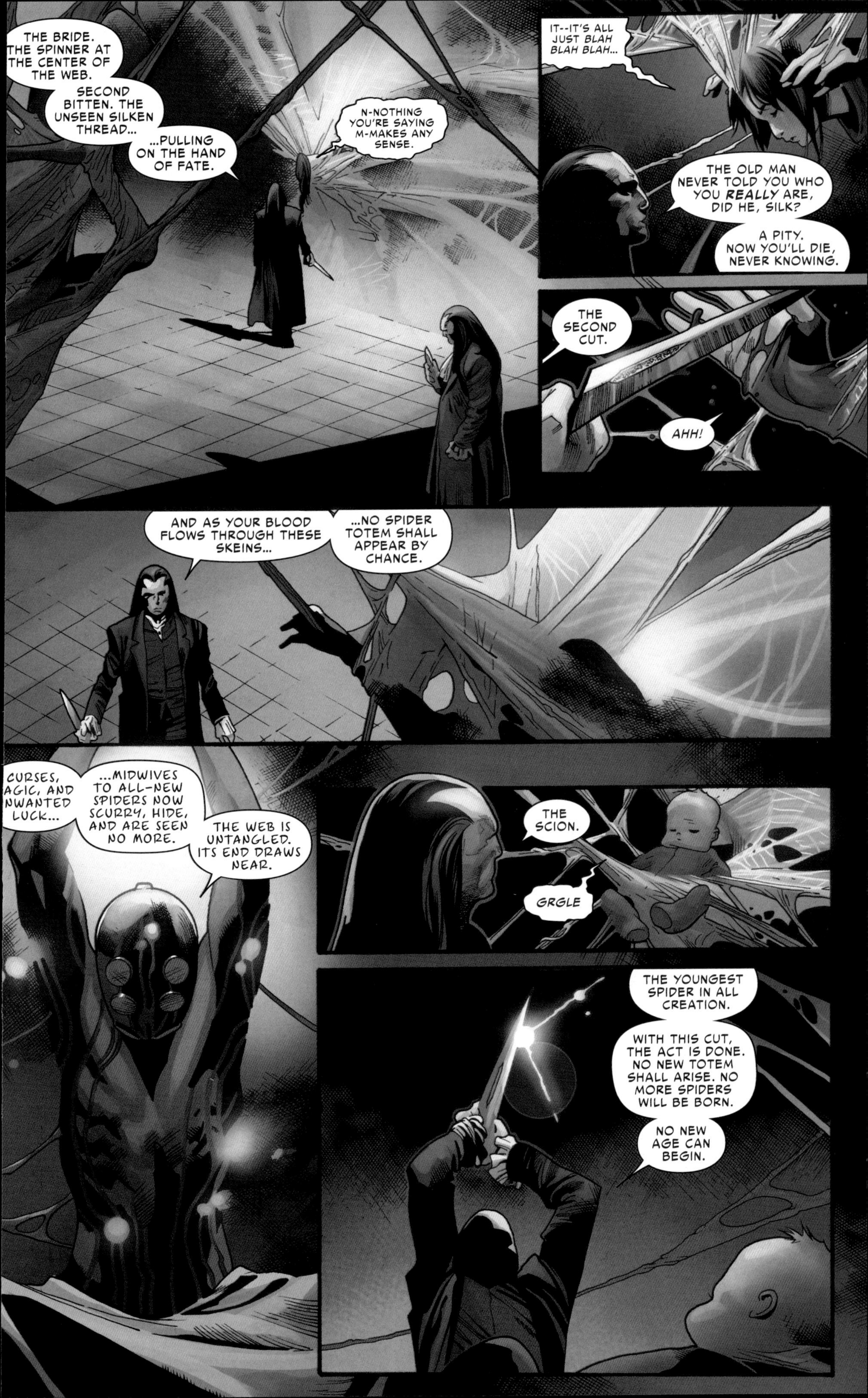
THE BRIDE. THE SPINNER AT THE CENTER OF THE WEB.
SECOND BITTEN. THE UNSEEN SILKEN THREAD...
...PULLING ON THE HAND OF FATE.
N-NOTHING YOU'RE SAYING M-MAKES ANY SENSE.
IT--IT'S ALL JUST *BLAH BLAH BLAH*...
THE OLD MAN NEVER TOLD YOU WHO YOU ***REALLY*** ARE, DID HE, SILK?
A PITY. NOW YOU'LL DIE, NEVER KNOWING.
THE SECOND CUT.
AHH!
AND AS YOUR BLOOD FLOWS THROUGH THESE SKEINS...
...NO SPIDER TOTEM SHALL APPEAR BY CHANCE.
CURSES, AGIC, AND NWANTED LUCK...
...MIDWIVES TO ALL-NEW SPIDERS NOW SCURRY, HIDE, AND ARE SEEN NO MORE.
THE WEB IS UNTANGLED. ITS END DRAWS NEAR.
THE SCION.
GRGLE
THE YOUNGEST SPIDER IN ALL CREATION.
WITH THIS CUT, THE ACT IS DONE. NO NEW TOTEM SHALL ARISE. NO MORE SPIDERS WILL BE BORN.
NO NEW AGE CAN BEGIN.

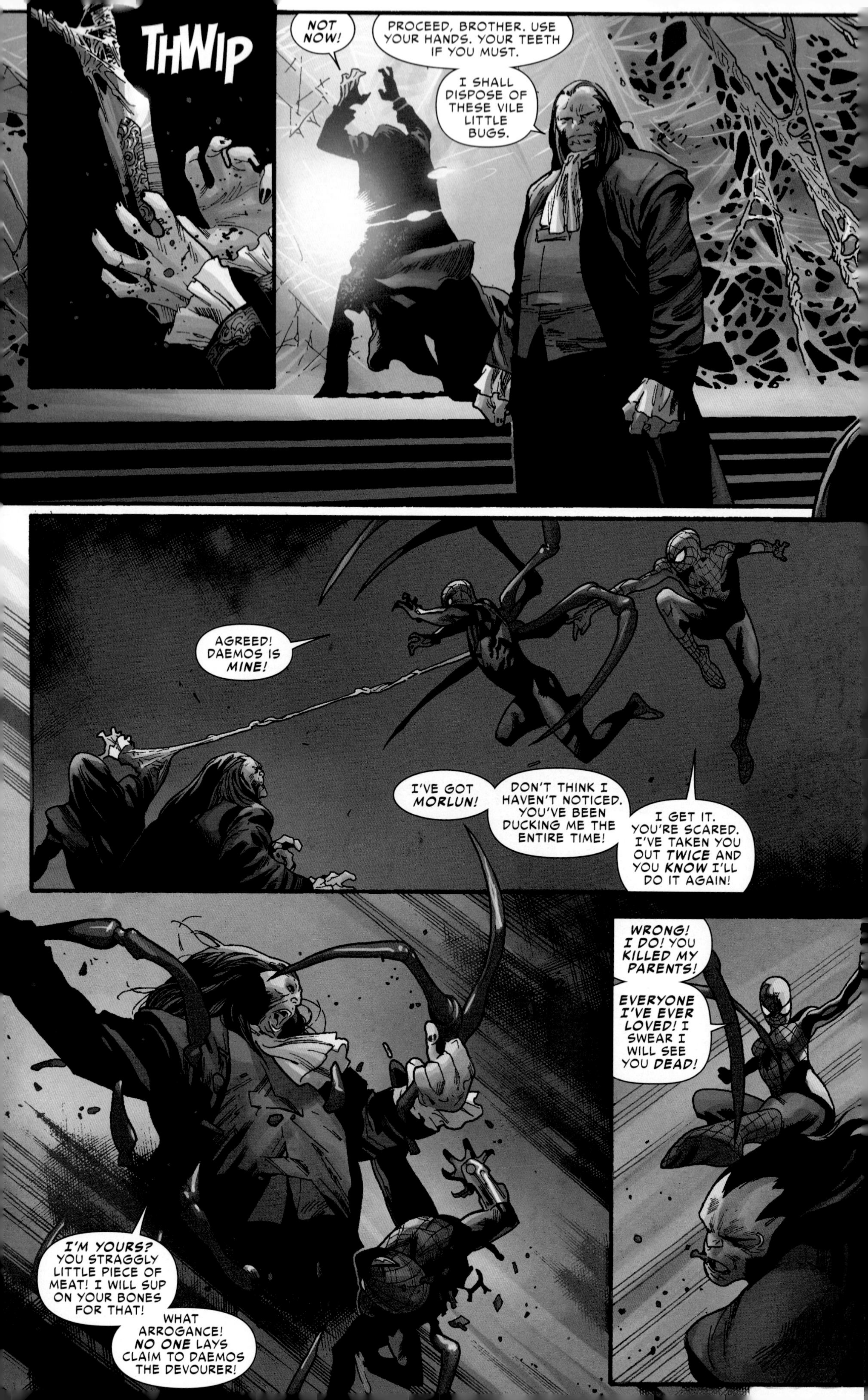
THWIP
NOT NOW!
PROCEED, BROTHER. USE YOUR HANDS. YOUR TEETH IF YOU MUST.
I SHALL DISPOSE OF THESE VILE LITTLE BUGS.
AGREED! DAEMOS IS MINE!
I'VE GOT MORLUN!
DON'T THINK I HAVEN'T NOTICED. YOU'VE BEEN DUCKING ME THE ENTIRE TIME!
I GET IT. YOU'RE SCARED. I'VE TAKEN YOU OUT TWICE AND YOU KNOW I'LL DO IT AGAIN!
I'M YOURS? YOU STRAGGLY LITTLE PIECE OF MEAT! I WILL SUP ON YOUR BONES FOR THAT!
WHAT ARROGANCE! NO ONE LAYS CLAIM TO DAEMOS THE DEVOURER!
WRONG! I DO! YOU KILLED MY PARENTS!
EVERYONE I'VE EVER LOVED! I SWEAR I WILL SEE YOU DEAD!

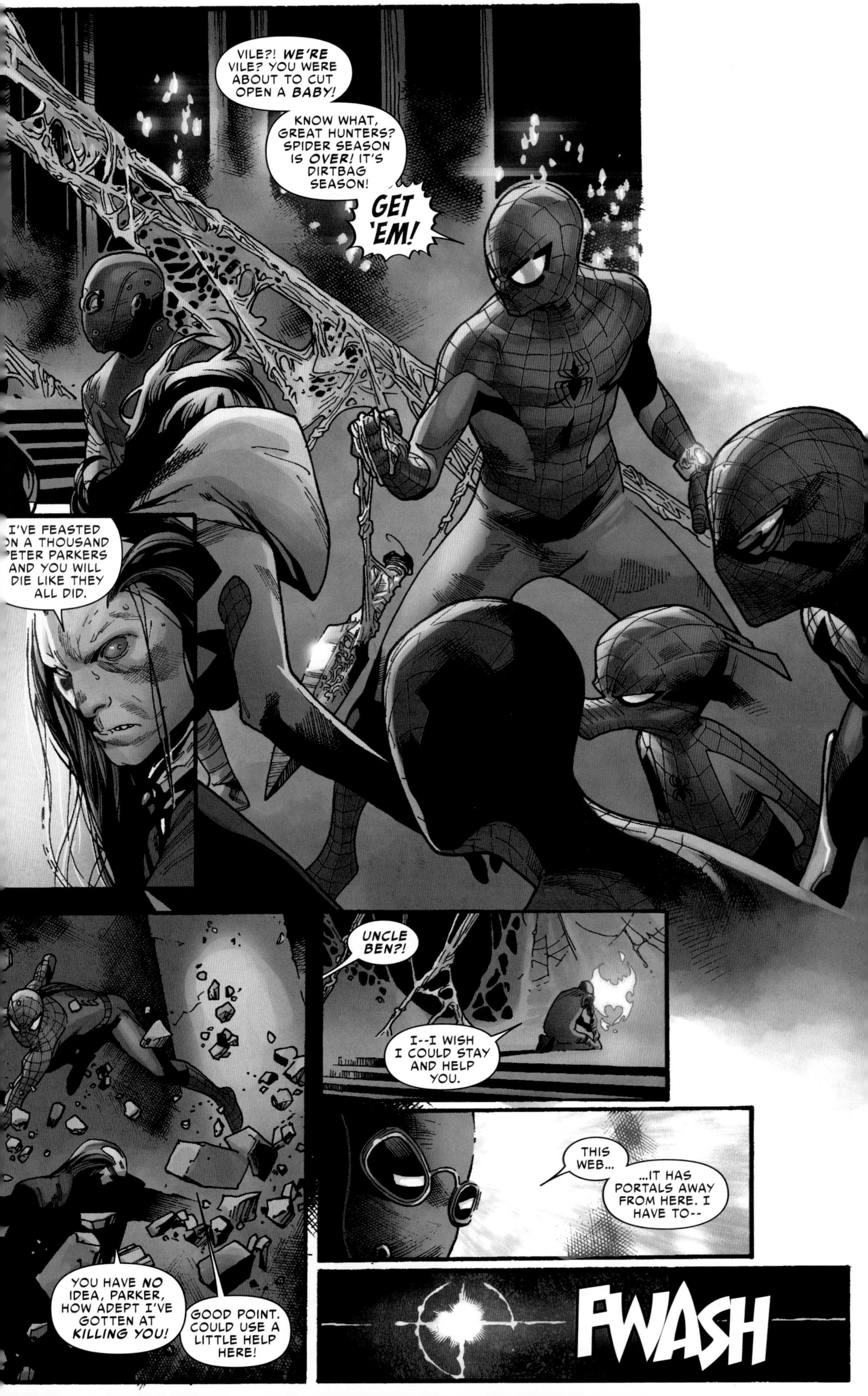
VILE?! WE'RE VILE? YOU WERE ABOUT TO CUT OPEN A BABY!
KNOW WHAT, GREAT HUNTERS? SPIDER SEASON IS OVER! IT'S DIRTBAG SEASON!
GET 'EM!
I'VE FEASTED ON A THOUSAND PETER PARKERS AND YOU WILL DIE LIKE THEY ALL DID.
YOU HAVE NO IDEA, PARKER, HOW ADEPT I'VE GOTTEN AT KILLING YOU!
GOOD POINT. COULD USE A LITTLE HELP HERE!
UNCLE BEN?!
I--I WISH I COULD STAY AND HELP YOU.
THIS WEB...
...IT HAS PORTALS AWAY FROM HERE. I HAVE TO--
FWASH

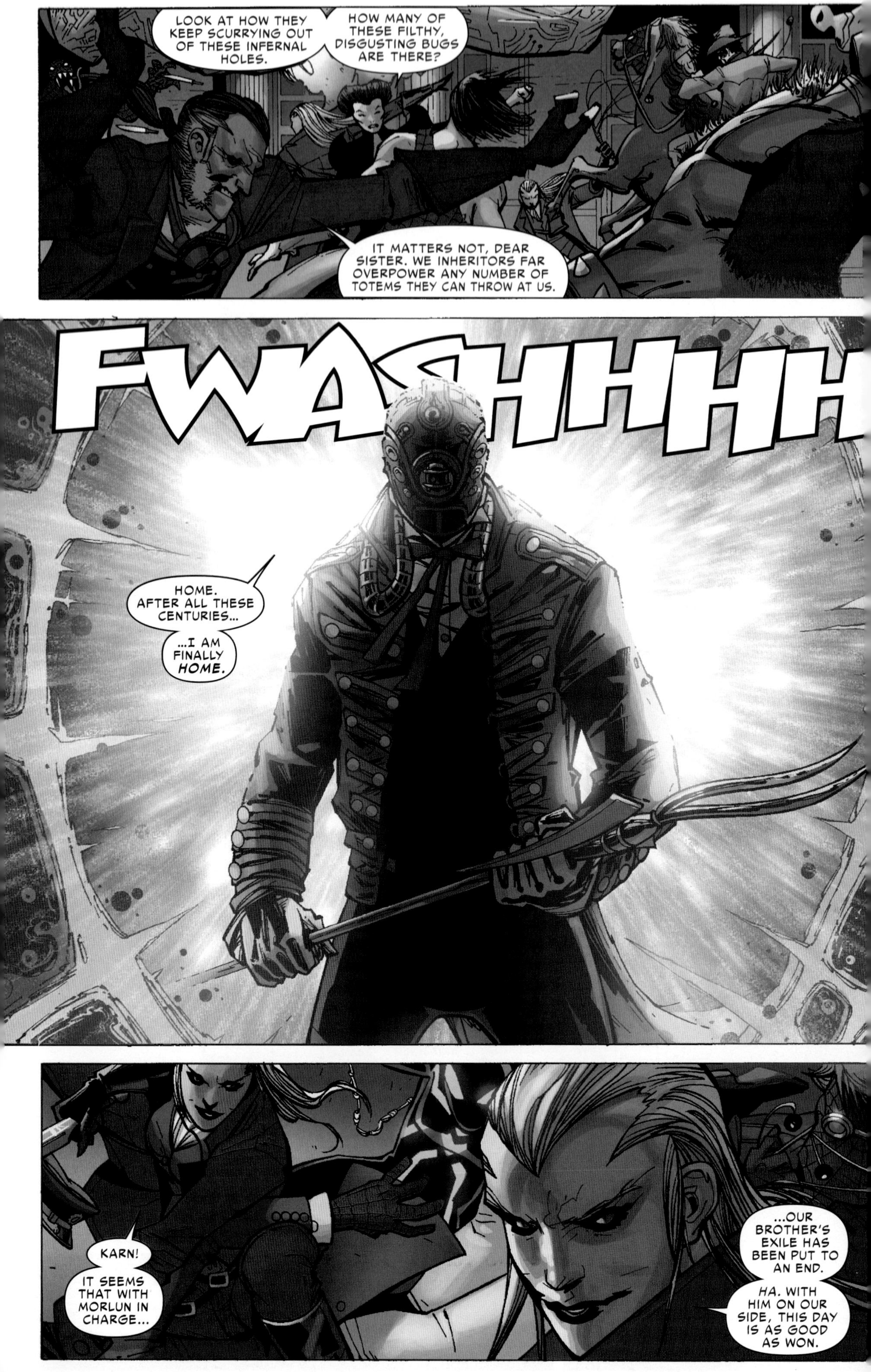
LOOK AT HOW THEY KEEP SCURRYING OUT OF THESE INFERNAL HOLES.
HOW MANY OF THESE FILTHY, DISGUSTING BUGS ARE THERE?
IT MATTERS NOT, DEAR SISTER. WE INHERITORS FAR OVERPOWER ANY NUMBER OF TOTEMS THEY CAN THROW AT US.
FWASHHHH
HOME. AFTER ALL THESE CENTURIES...
...I AM FINALLY *HOME.*
KARN!
IT SEEMS THAT WITH MORLUN IN CHARGE...
...OUR BROTHER'S EXILE HAS BEEN PUT TO AN END.
HA. WITH HIM ON OUR SIDE, THIS DAY IS AS GOOD AS WON.

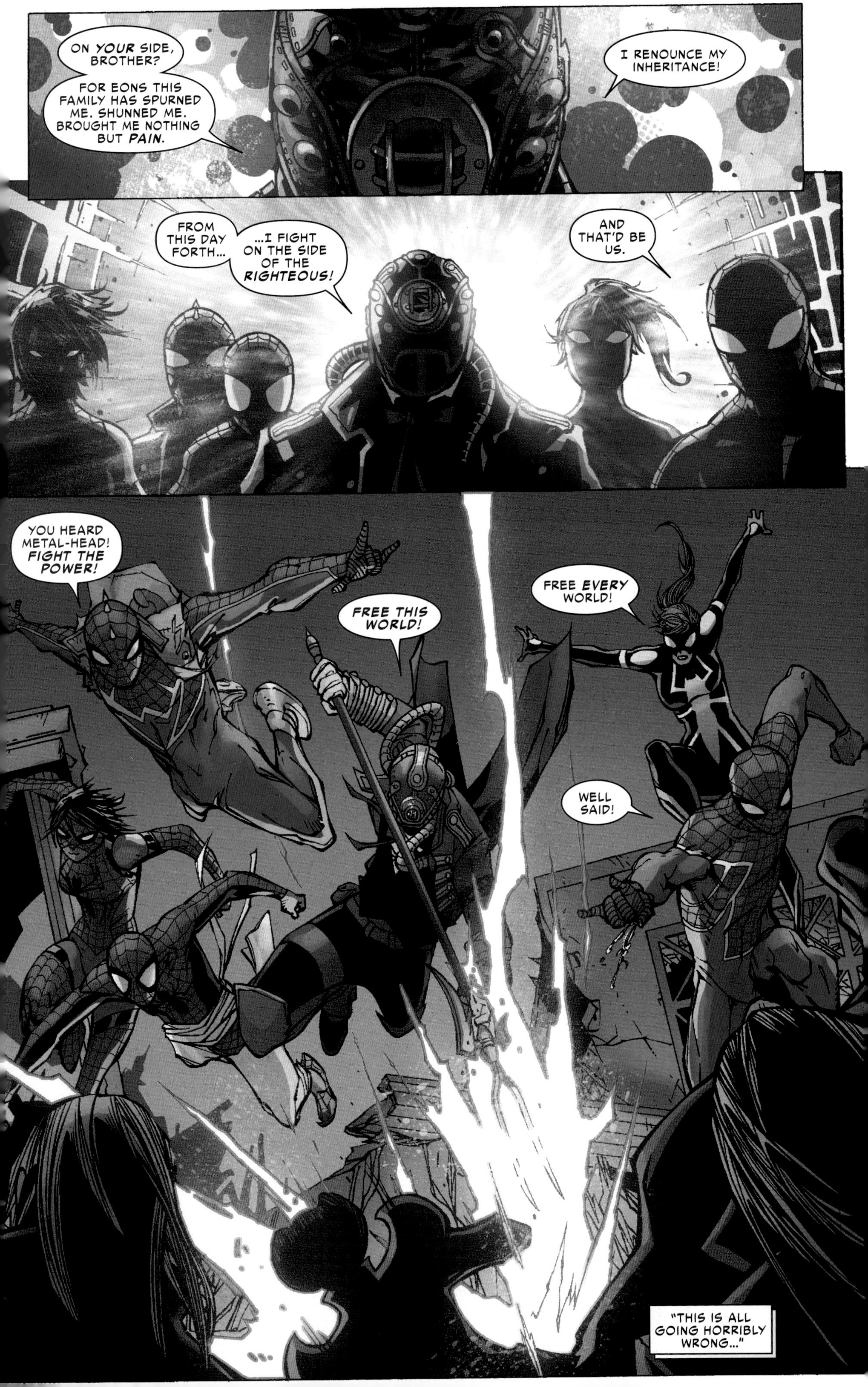

ON YOUR SIDE, BROTHER?
FOR EONS THIS FAMILY HAS SPURNED ME. SHUNNED ME. BROUGHT ME NOTHING BUT PAIN.
I RENOUNCE MY INHERITANCE!
FROM THIS DAY FORTH...
...I FIGHT ON THE SIDE OF THE RIGHTEOUS!
AND THAT'D BE US.
YOU HEARD METAL-HEAD! FIGHT THE POWER!
FREE THIS WORLD!
FREE EVERY WORLD!
WELL SAID!
"THIS IS ALL GOING HORRIBLY WRONG..."

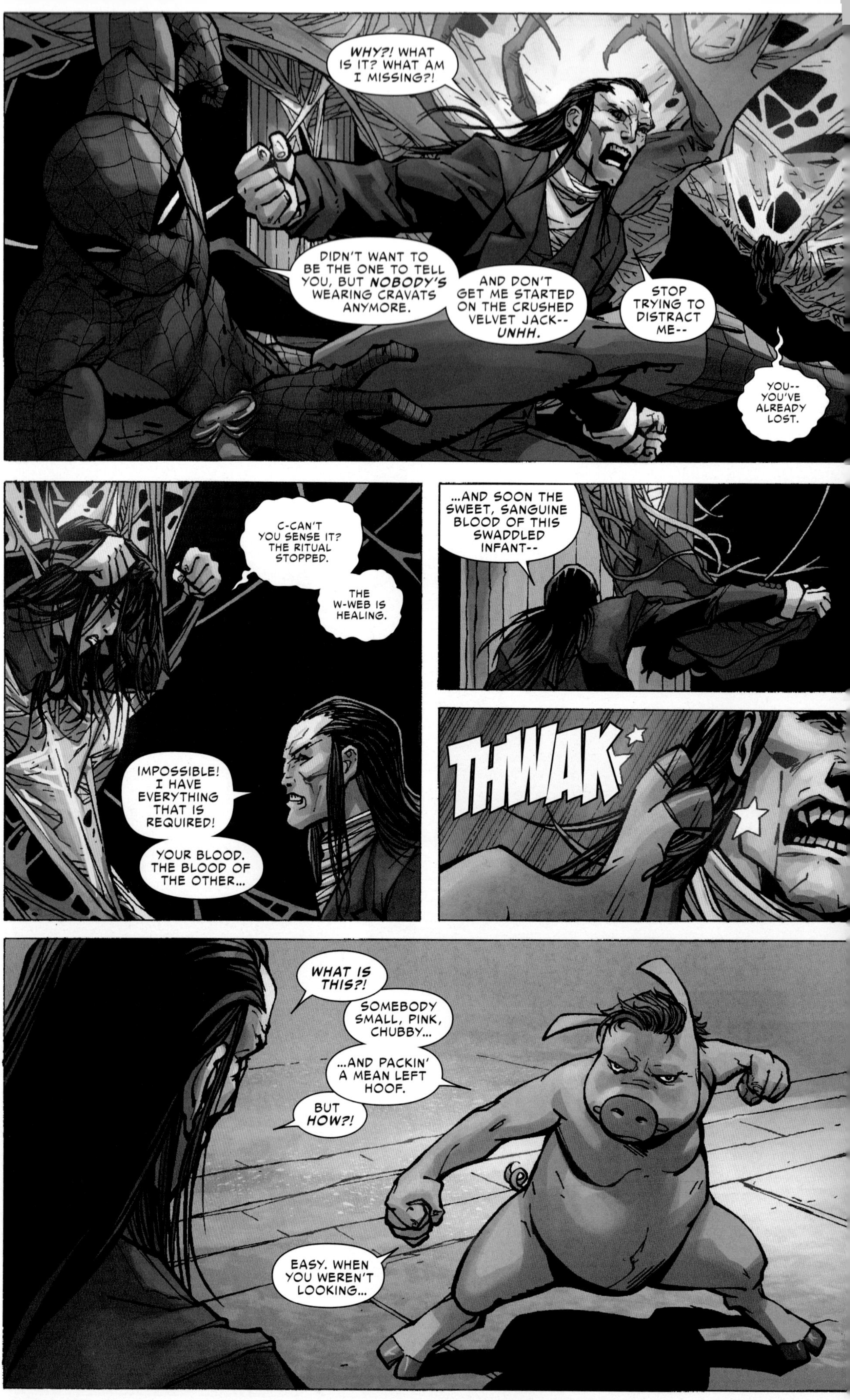

WHY?! WHAT IS IT? WHAT AM I MISSING?!
DIDN'T WANT TO BE THE ONE TO TELL YOU, BUT NOBODY'S WEARING CRAVATS ANYMORE.
AND DON'T GET ME STARTED ON THE CRUSHED VELVET JACK-- UNHH.
STOP TRYING TO DISTRACT ME--
YOU-- YOU'VE ALREADY LOST.
C-CAN'T YOU SENSE IT? THE RITUAL STOPPED.
THE W-WEB IS HEALING.
IMPOSSIBLE! I HAVE EVERYTHING THAT IS REQUIRED!
YOUR BLOOD. THE BLOOD OF THE OTHER...
...AND SOON THE SWEET, SANGUINE BLOOD OF THIS SWADDLED INFANT--
THWAK
WHAT IS THIS?!
SOMEBODY SMALL, PINK, CHUBBY...
...AND PACKIN' A MEAN LEFT HOOF.
BUT HOW?!
EASY. WHEN YOU WEREN'T LOOKING...

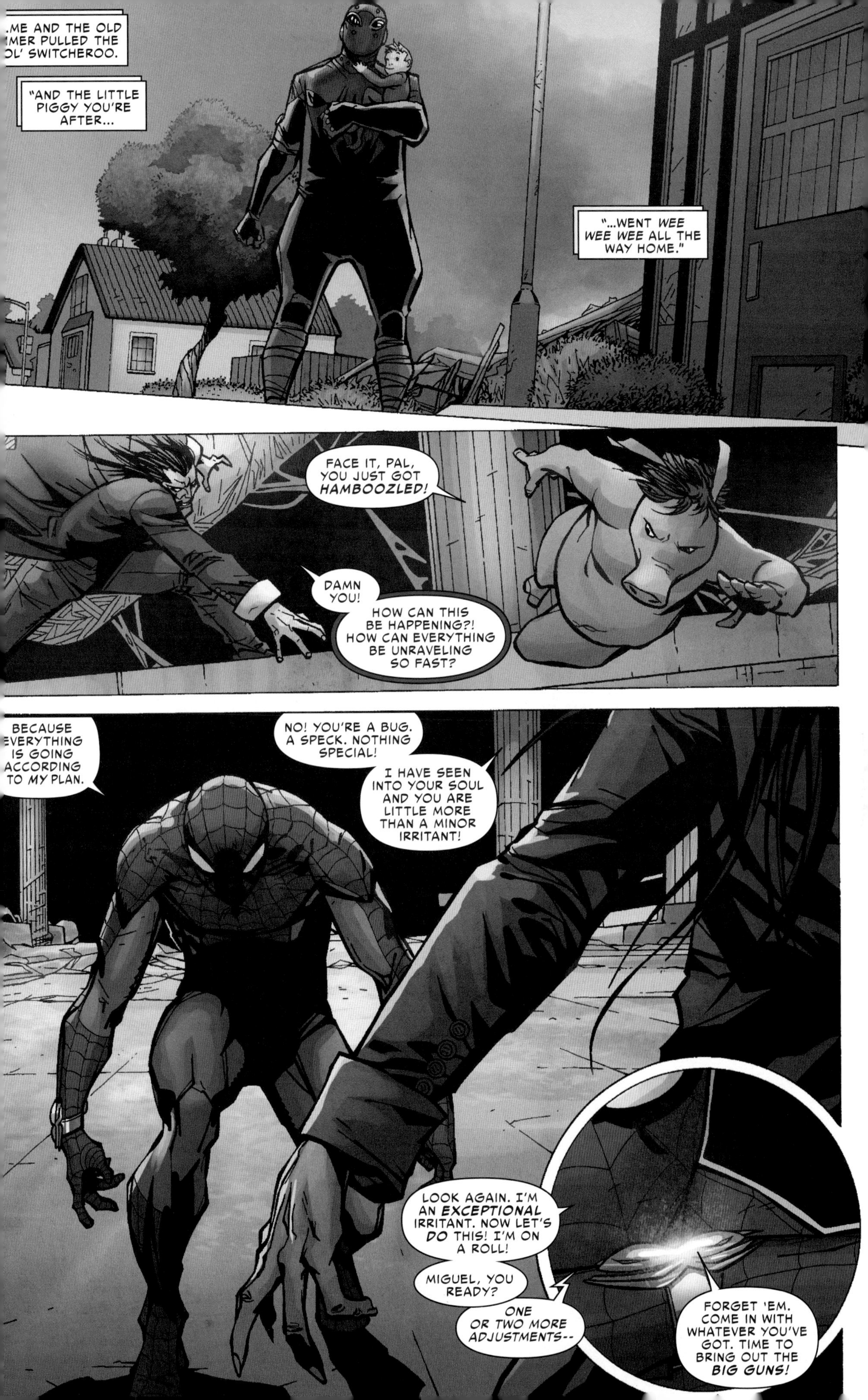

..ME AND THE OLD ..MER PULLED THE ..OL' SWITCHEROO.
"AND THE LITTLE PIGGY YOU'RE AFTER...
"...WENT WEE WEE WEE ALL THE WAY HOME."
FACE IT, PAL, YOU JUST GOT HAMBOOZLED!
DAMN YOU!
HOW CAN THIS BE HAPPENING?! HOW CAN EVERYTHING BE UNRAVELING SO FAST?
BECAUSE EVERYTHING IS GOING ACCORDING TO MY PLAN.
NO! YOU'RE A BUG. A SPECK. NOTHING SPECIAL!
I HAVE SEEN INTO YOUR SOUL AND YOU ARE LITTLE MORE THAN A MINOR IRRITANT!
LOOK AGAIN. I'M AN EXCEPTIONAL IRRITANT. NOW LET'S DO THIS! I'M ON A ROLL!
MIGUEL, YOU READY?
ONE OR TWO MORE ADJUSTMENTS--
FORGET 'EM. COME IN WITH WHATEVER YOU'VE GOT. TIME TO BRING OUT THE BIG GUNS!

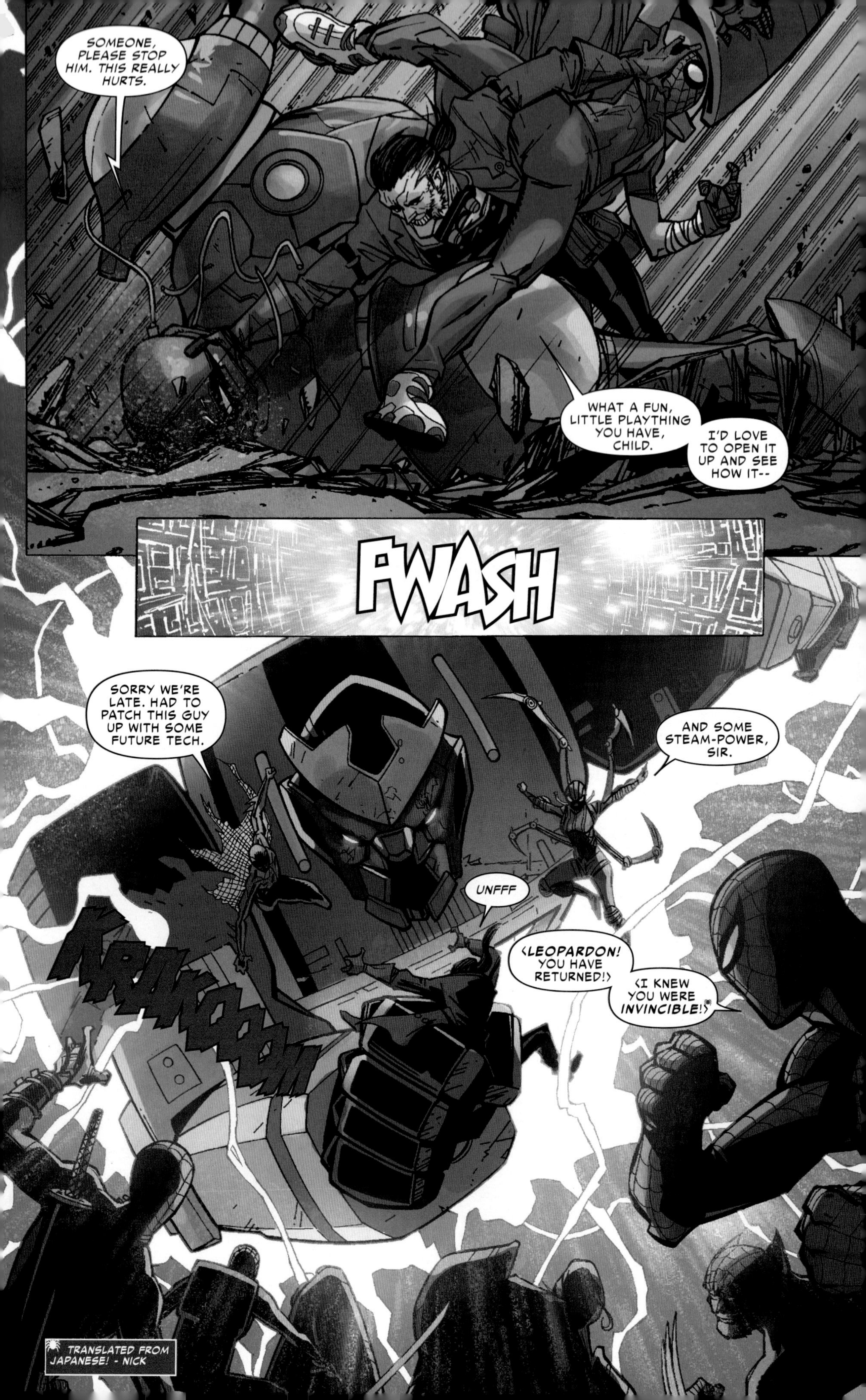
SOMEONE, PLEASE STOP HIM. THIS REALLY HURTS.
WHAT A FUN, LITTLE PLAYTHING YOU HAVE, CHILD.
I'D LOVE TO OPEN IT UP AND SEE HOW IT--
FWASH
SORRY WE'RE LATE. HAD TO PATCH THIS GUY UP WITH SOME FUTURE TECH.
AND SOME STEAM-POWER, SIR.
KRAKOOOM
UNFFF
‹LEOPARDON! YOU HAVE RETURNED!›
‹I KNEW YOU WERE INVINCIBLE!›
TRANSLATED FROM JAPANESE! - NICK

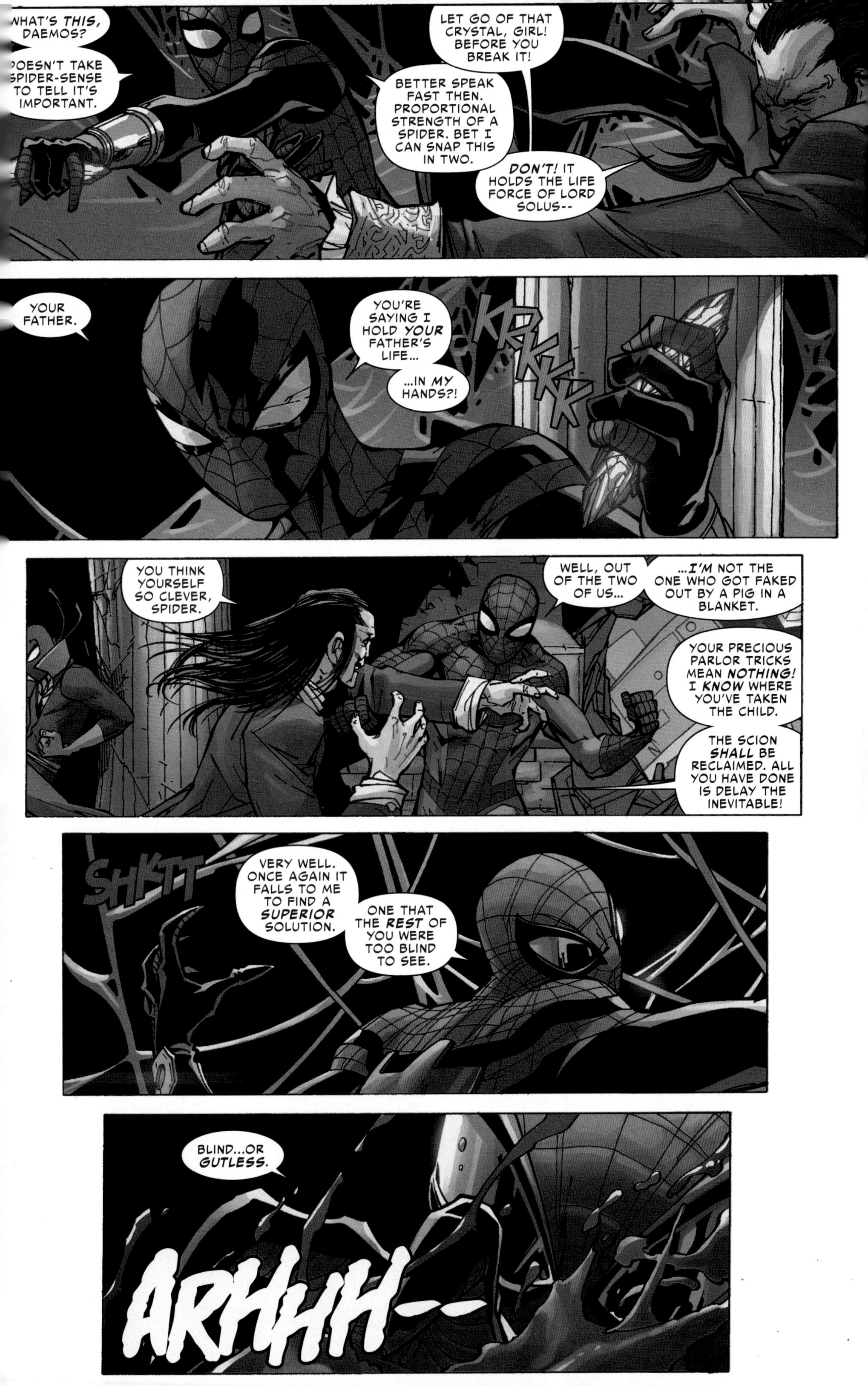
WHAT'S THIS, DAEMOS?
DOESN'T TAKE SPIDER-SENSE TO TELL IT'S IMPORTANT.
LET GO OF THAT CRYSTAL, GIRL! BEFORE YOU BREAK IT!
BETTER SPEAK FAST THEN. PROPORTIONAL STRENGTH OF A SPIDER. BET I CAN SNAP THIS IN TWO.
DON'T! IT HOLDS THE LIFE FORCE OF LORD SOLUS--
YOUR FATHER.
YOU'RE SAYING I HOLD YOUR FATHER'S LIFE...
...IN MY HANDS?!
KRKKK
YOU THINK YOURSELF SO CLEVER, SPIDER.
WELL, OUT OF THE TWO OF US...
...I'M NOT THE ONE WHO GOT FAKED OUT BY A PIG IN A BLANKET.
YOUR PRECIOUS PARLOR TRICKS MEAN NOTHING! I KNOW WHERE YOU'VE TAKEN THE CHILD.
THE SCION SHALL BE RECLAIMED. ALL YOU HAVE DONE IS DELAY THE INEVITABLE!
SHKTT
VERY WELL. ONCE AGAIN IT FALLS TO ME TO FIND A SUPERIOR SOLUTION.
ONE THAT THE REST OF YOU WERE TOO BLIND TO SEE.
BLIND...OR GUTLESS.
ARHHH--

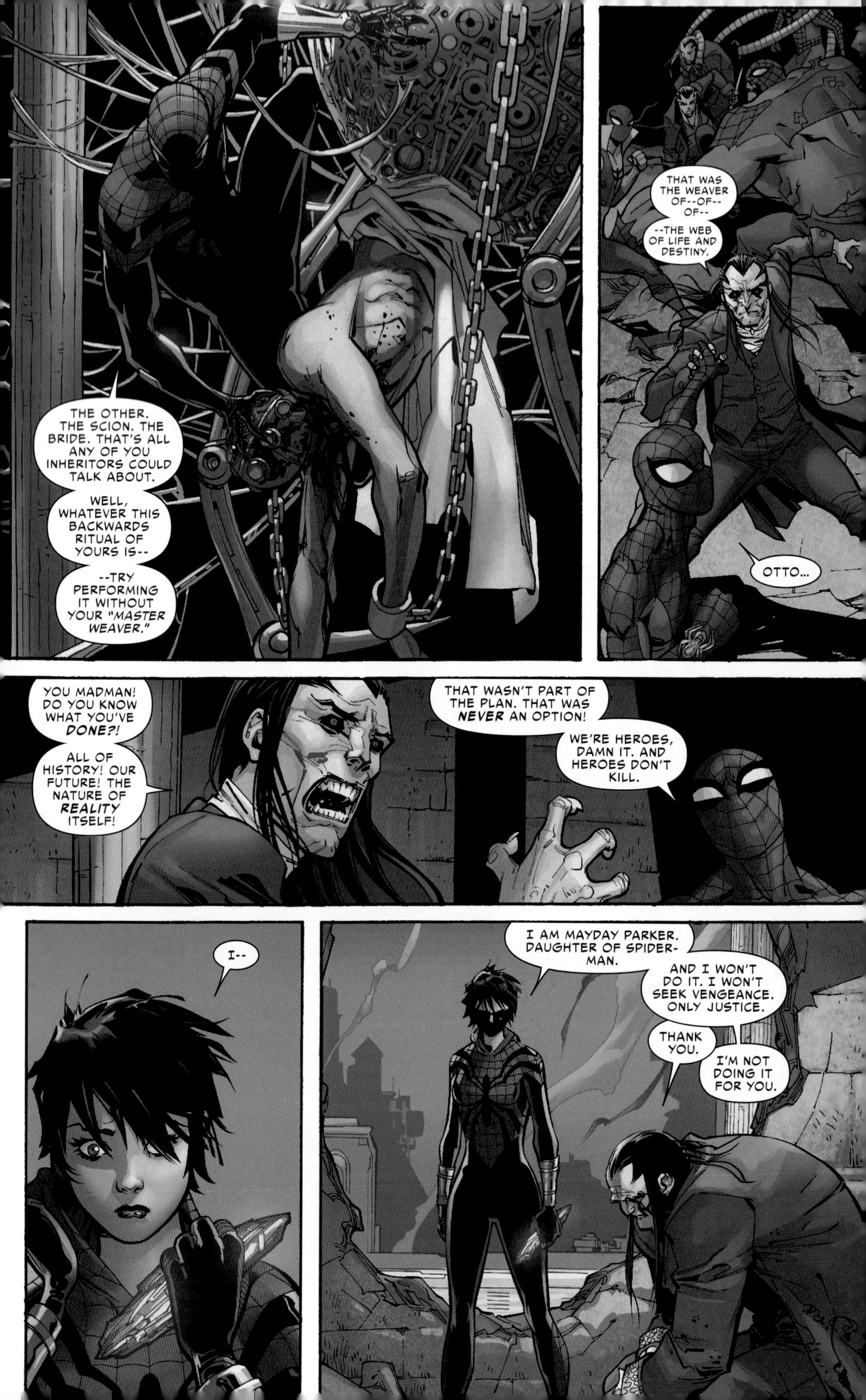
THE OTHER. THE SCION. THE BRIDE. THAT'S ALL ANY OF YOU INHERITORS COULD TALK ABOUT.
WELL, WHATEVER THIS BACKWARDS RITUAL OF YOURS IS--
--TRY PERFORMING IT WITHOUT YOUR "*MASTER WEAVER.*"
THAT WAS THE WEAVER OF--OF--OF--
--THE WEB OF LIFE AND DESTINY.
OTTO...
YOU MADMAN! DO YOU KNOW WHAT YOU'VE ***DONE?!***
ALL OF HISTORY! OUR FUTURE! THE NATURE OF ***REALITY*** ITSELF!
THAT WASN'T PART OF THE PLAN. THAT WAS ***NEVER*** AN OPTION!
WE'RE HEROES, DAMN IT. AND HEROES DON'T KILL.
I--
I AM MAYDAY PARKER. DAUGHTER OF SPIDER-MAN.
AND I WON'T DO IT. I WON'T SEEK VENGEANCE. ONLY JUSTICE.
THANK YOU.
I'M NOT DOING IT FOR YOU.

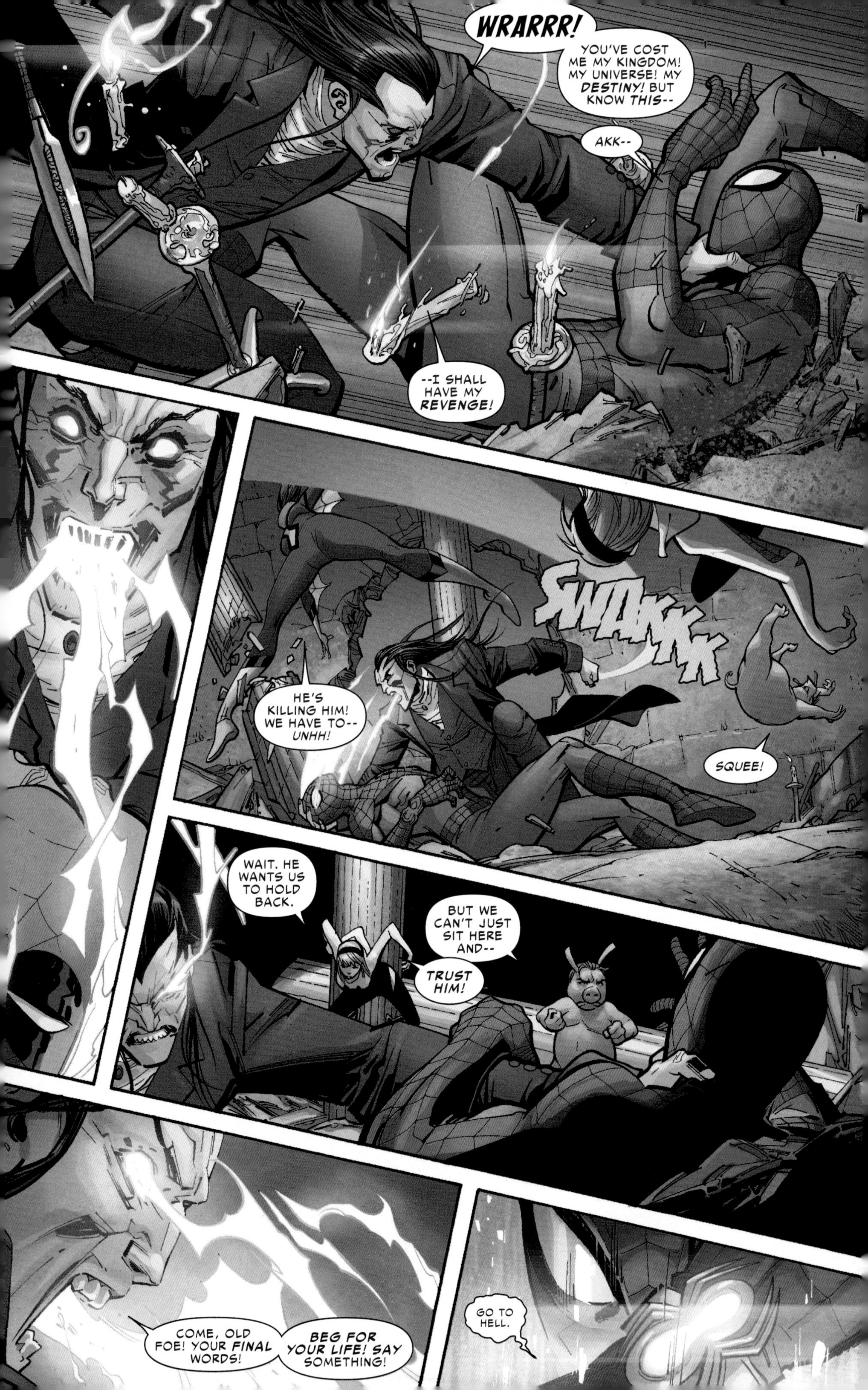
WRARRR!
YOU'VE COST ME MY KINGDOM! MY UNIVERSE! MY DESTINY! BUT KNOW THIS--
AKK--
--I SHALL HAVE MY REVENGE!
SWAKKK
HE'S KILLING HIM! WE HAVE TO-- UNHH!
SQUEE!
WAIT. HE WANTS US TO HOLD BACK.
BUT WE CAN'T JUST SIT HERE AND--
TRUST HIM!
COME, OLD FOE! YOUR FINAL WORDS!
BEG FOR YOUR LIFE! SAY SOMETHING!
GO TO HELL.

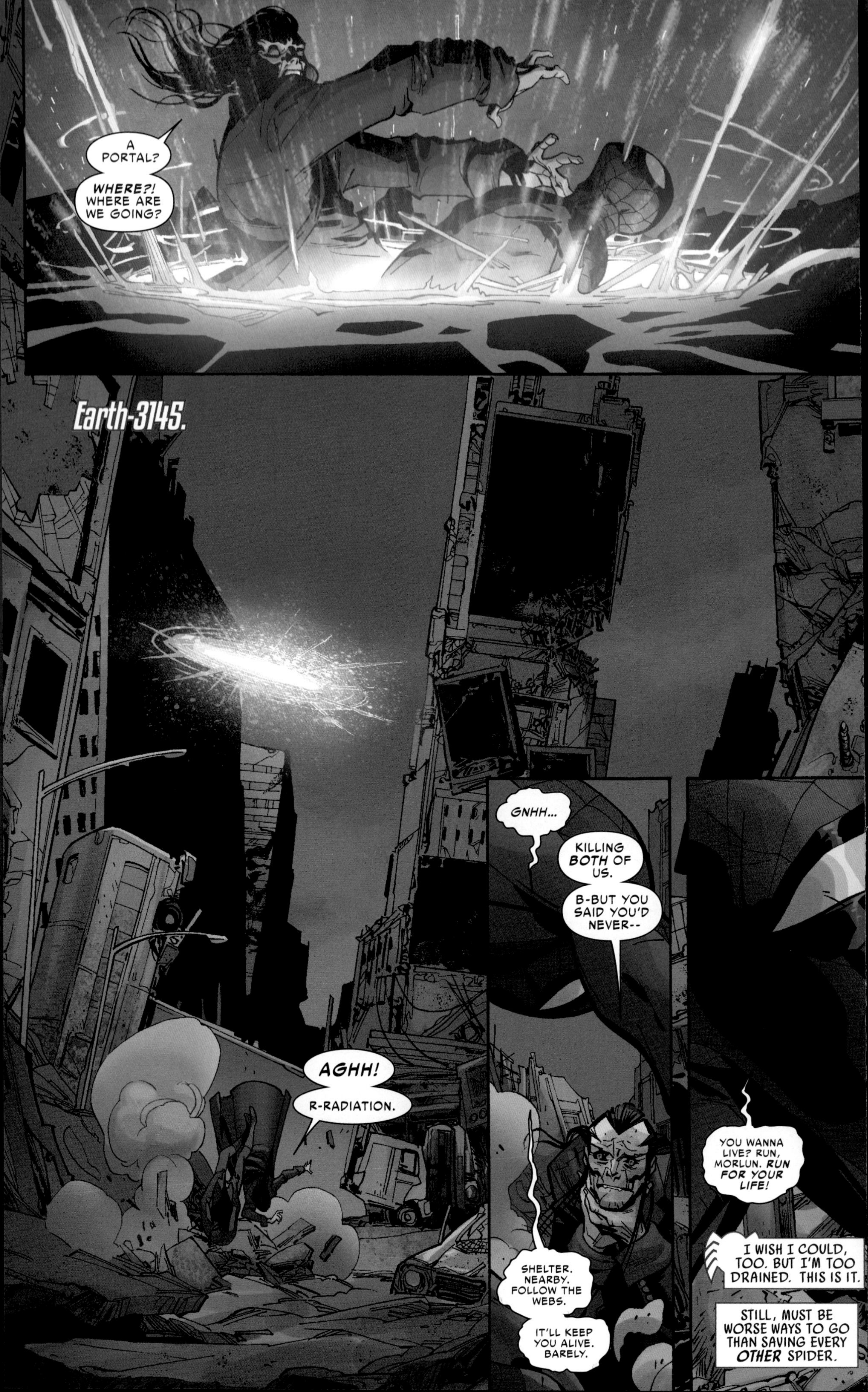
A PORTAL?
WHERE?! WHERE ARE WE GOING?
Earth-3145.
AGHH!
R-RADIATION.
GNHH...
KILLING BOTH OF US.
B-BUT YOU SAID YOU'D NEVER--
SHELTER. NEARBY. FOLLOW THE WEBS.
IT'LL KEEP YOU ALIVE. BARELY.
YOU WANNA LIVE? RUN, MORLUN. RUN FOR YOUR LIFE!
I WISH I COULD, TOO. BUT I'M TOO DRAINED. THIS IS IT.
STILL, MUST BE WORSE WAYS TO GO THAN SAVING EVERY OTHER SPIDER.

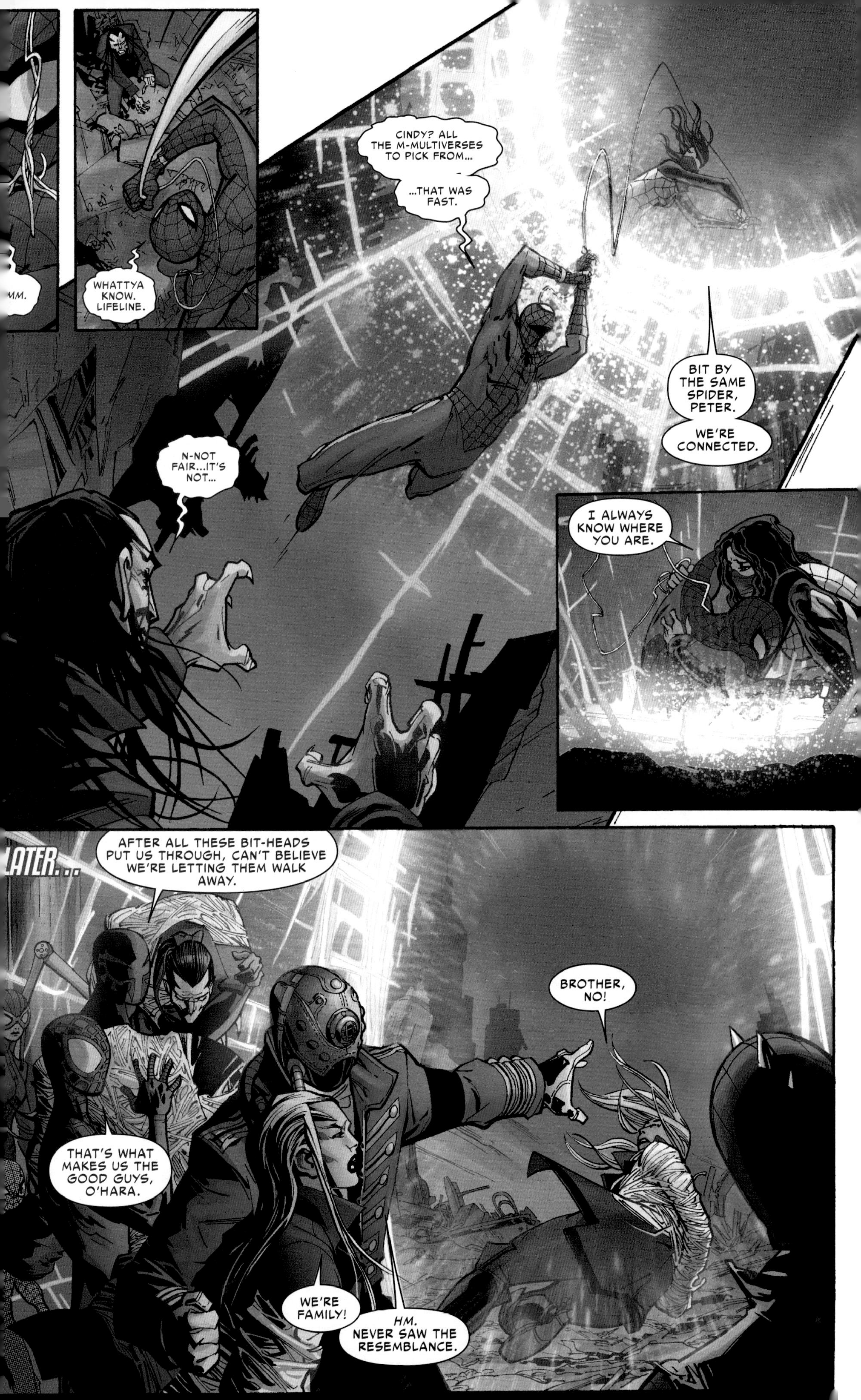

...MM.
WHATTYA KNOW. LIFELINE.
CINDY? ALL THE M-MULTIVERSES TO PICK FROM...
...THAT WAS FAST.
BIT BY THE SAME SPIDER, PETER.
WE'RE CONNECTED.
N-NOT FAIR...IT'S NOT...
I ALWAYS KNOW WHERE YOU ARE.
LATER...
AFTER ALL THESE BIT-HEADS PUT US THROUGH, CAN'T BELIEVE WE'RE LETTING THEM WALK AWAY.
THAT'S WHAT MAKES US THE GOOD GUYS, O'HARA.
BROTHER, NO!
WE'RE FAMILY!
HM. NEVER SAW THE RESEMBLANCE.

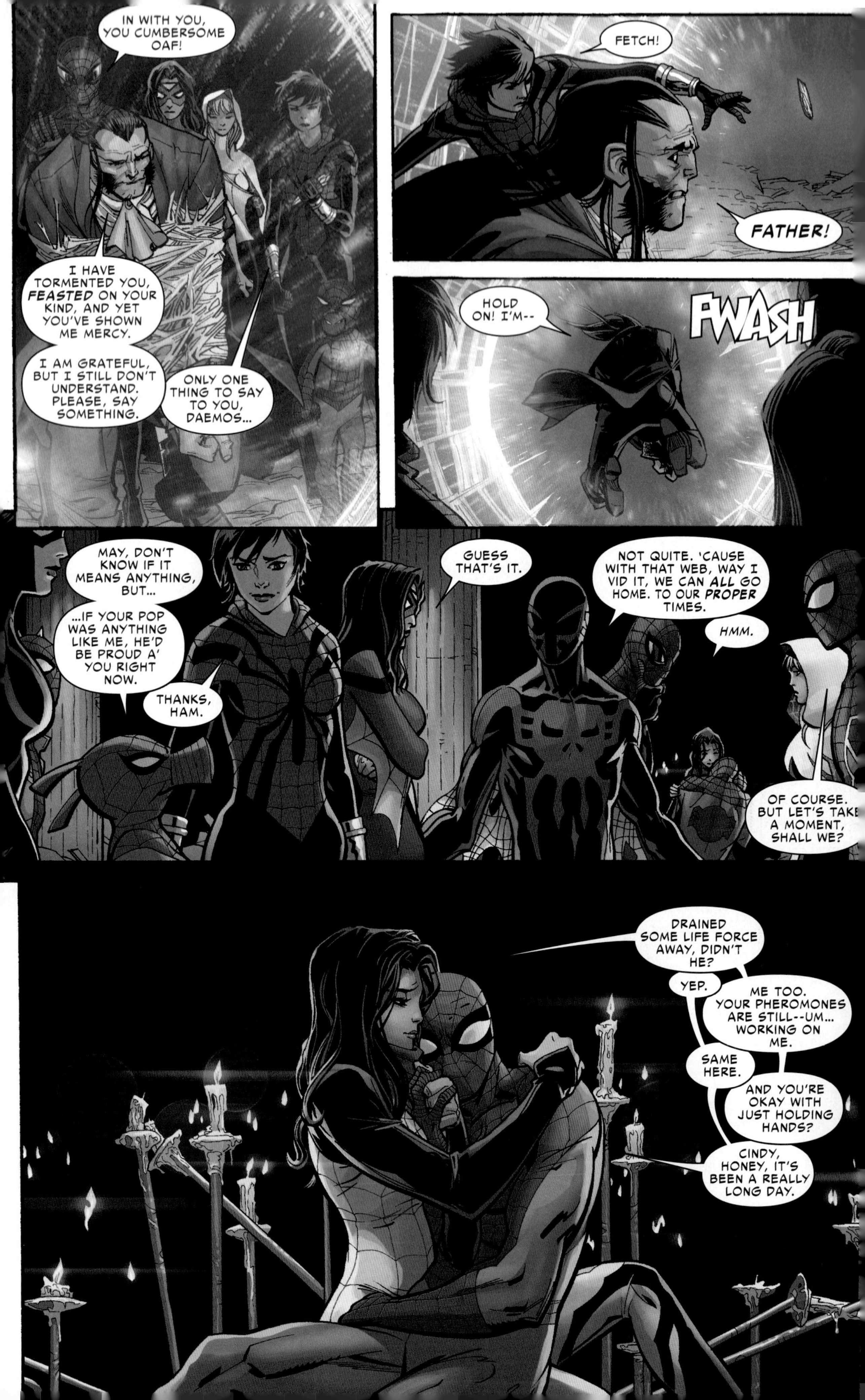
IN WITH YOU, YOU CUMBERSOME OAF!
I HAVE TORMENTED YOU, FEASTED ON YOUR KIND, AND YET YOU'VE SHOWN ME MERCY.
I AM GRATEFUL, BUT I STILL DON'T UNDERSTAND. PLEASE, SAY SOMETHING.
ONLY ONE THING TO SAY TO YOU, DAEMOS...
FETCH!
FATHER!
HOLD ON! I'M--
FWASH
MAY, DON'T KNOW IF IT MEANS ANYTHING, BUT...
...IF YOUR POP WAS ANYTHING LIKE ME, HE'D BE PROUD A' YOU RIGHT NOW.
THANKS, HAM.
GUESS THAT'S IT.
NOT QUITE. 'CAUSE WITH THAT WEB, WAY I VID IT, WE CAN ALL GO HOME. TO OUR PROPER TIMES.
HMM.
OF COURSE. BUT LET'S TAKE A MOMENT, SHALL WE?
DRAINED SOME LIFE FORCE AWAY, DIDN'T HE?
YEP.
ME TOO. YOUR PHEROMONES ARE STILL--UM... WORKING ON ME.
SAME HERE.
AND YOU'RE OKAY WITH JUST HOLDING HANDS?
CINDY, HONEY, IT'S BEEN A REALLY LONG DAY.

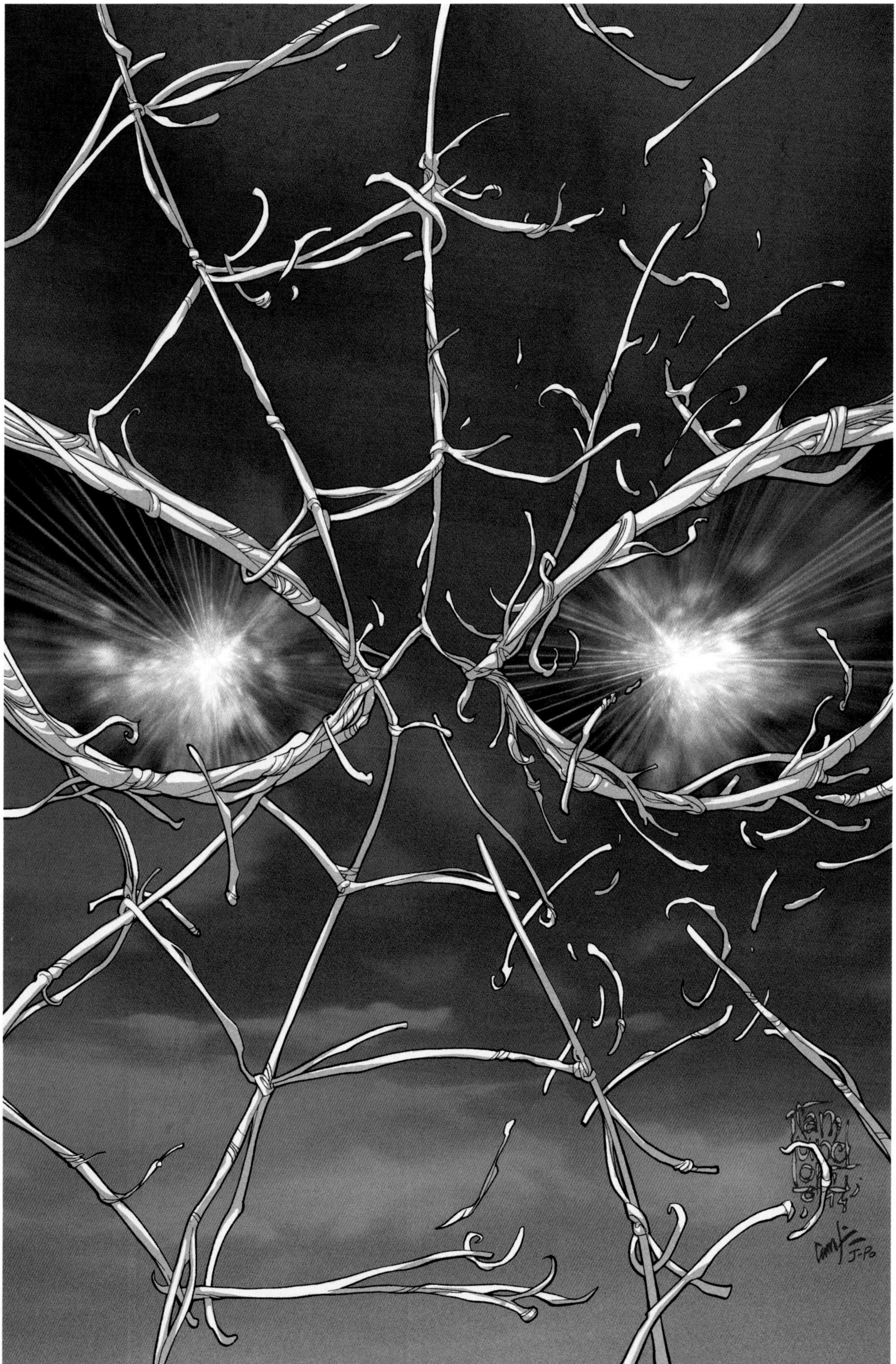

AMAZING SPIDER-MAN 15
SPIDER-VERSE EPILOGUE

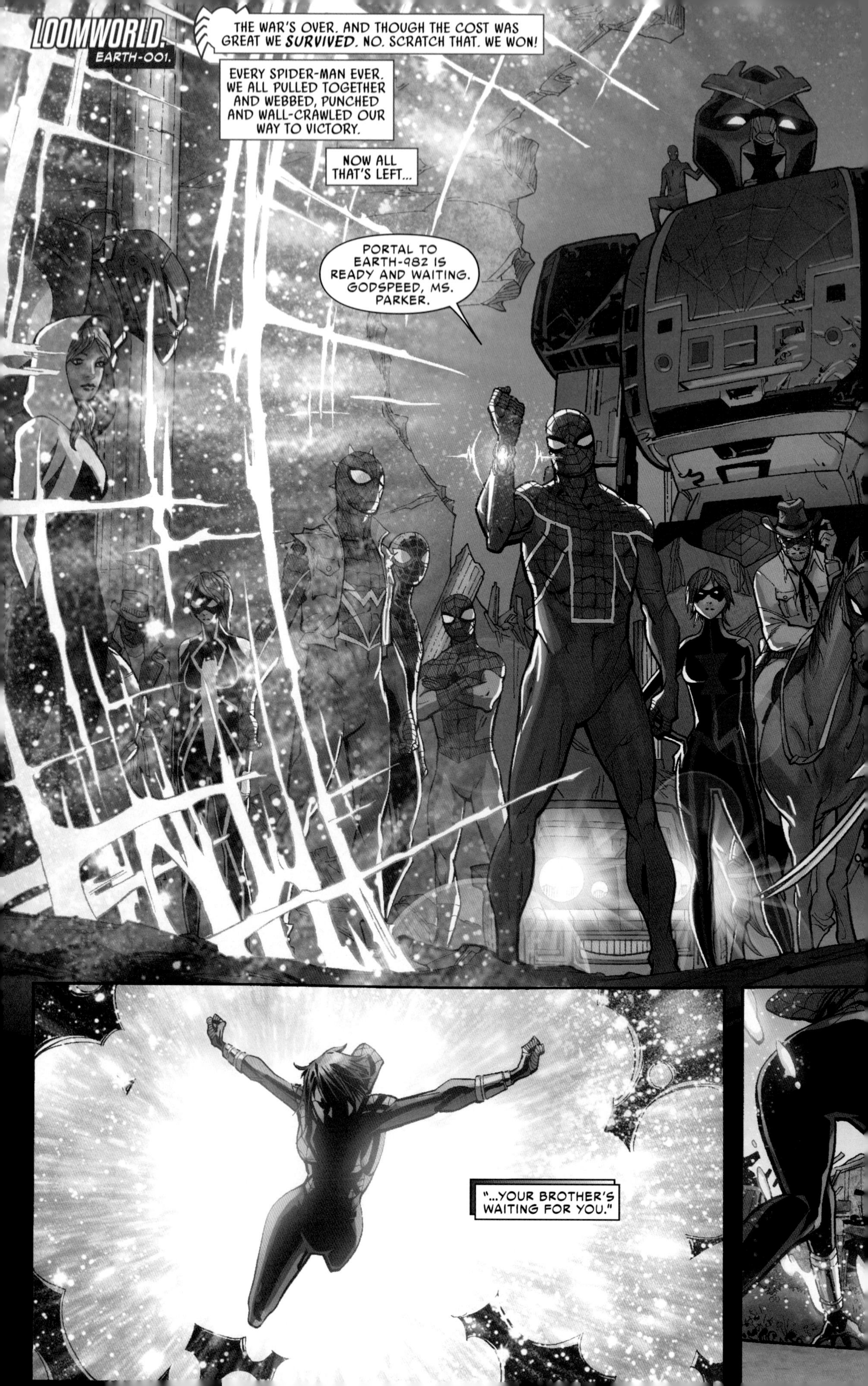
LOOMWORLD. EARTH-001.
THE WAR'S OVER. AND THOUGH THE COST WAS GREAT WE SURVIVED. NO. SCRATCH THAT. WE WON!
EVERY SPIDER-MAN EVER. WE ALL PULLED TOGETHER AND WEBBED, PUNCHED AND WALL-CRAWLED OUR WAY TO VICTORY.
NOW ALL THAT'S LEFT...
PORTAL TO EARTH-982 IS READY AND WAITING. GODSPEED, MS. PARKER.
"...YOUR BROTHER'S WAITING FOR YOU."

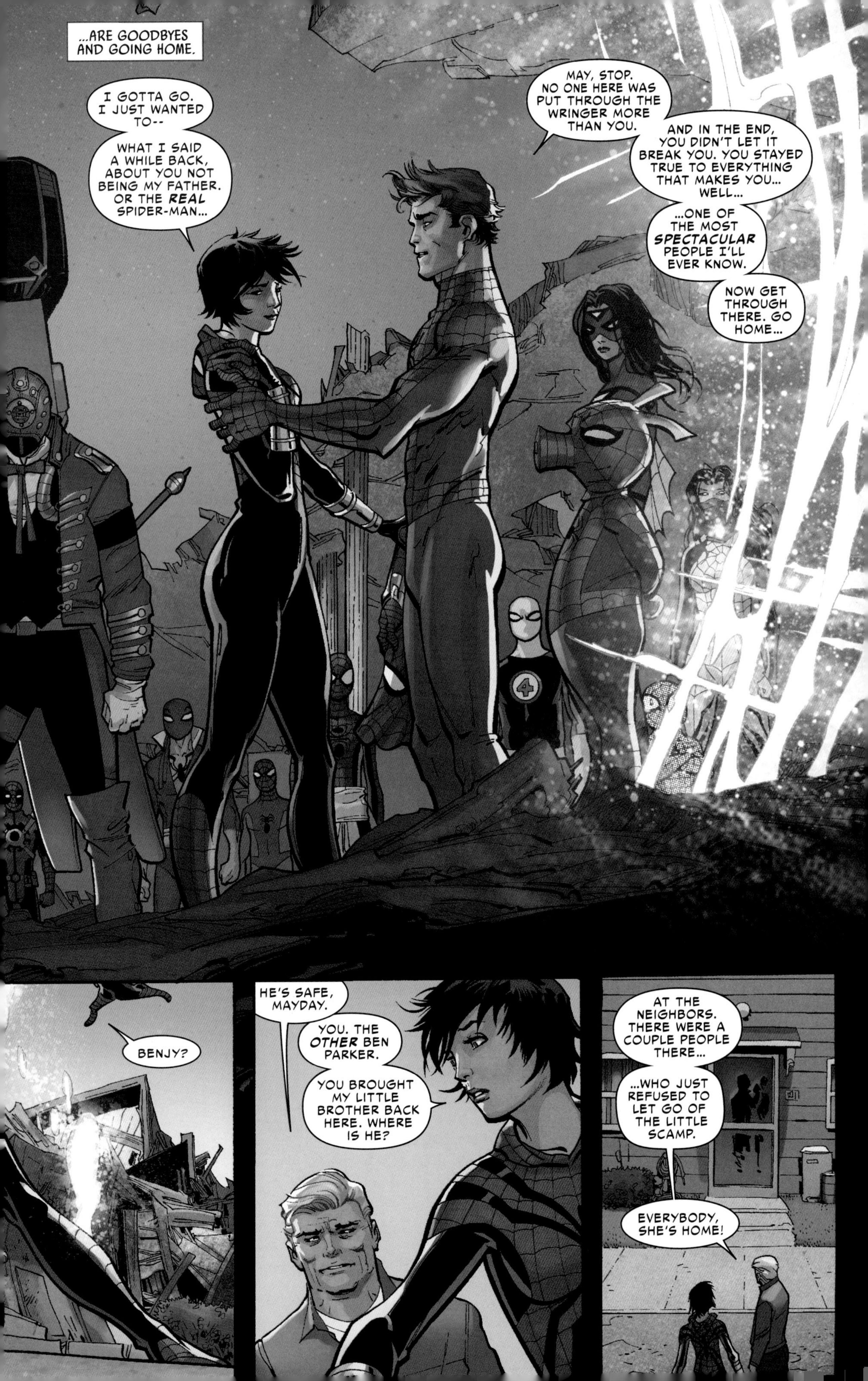
...ARE GOODBYES AND GOING HOME.
I GOTTA GO. I JUST WANTED TO--
WHAT I SAID A WHILE BACK, ABOUT YOU NOT BEING MY FATHER. OR THE *REAL* SPIDER-MAN...
MAY, STOP. NO ONE HERE WAS PUT THROUGH THE WRINGER MORE THAN YOU.
AND IN THE END, YOU DIDN'T LET IT BREAK YOU. YOU STAYED TRUE TO EVERYTHING THAT MAKES YOU... WELL...
...ONE OF THE MOST *SPECTACULAR* PEOPLE I'LL EVER KNOW.
NOW GET THROUGH THERE. GO HOME...
BENJY?
HE'S SAFE, MAYDAY.
YOU. THE *OTHER* BEN PARKER.
YOU BROUGHT MY LITTLE BROTHER BACK HERE. WHERE IS HE?
AT THE NEIGHBORS. THERE WERE A COUPLE PEOPLE THERE...
...WHO JUST REFUSED TO LET GO OF THE LITTLE SCAMP.
EVERYBODY, SHE'S HOME!

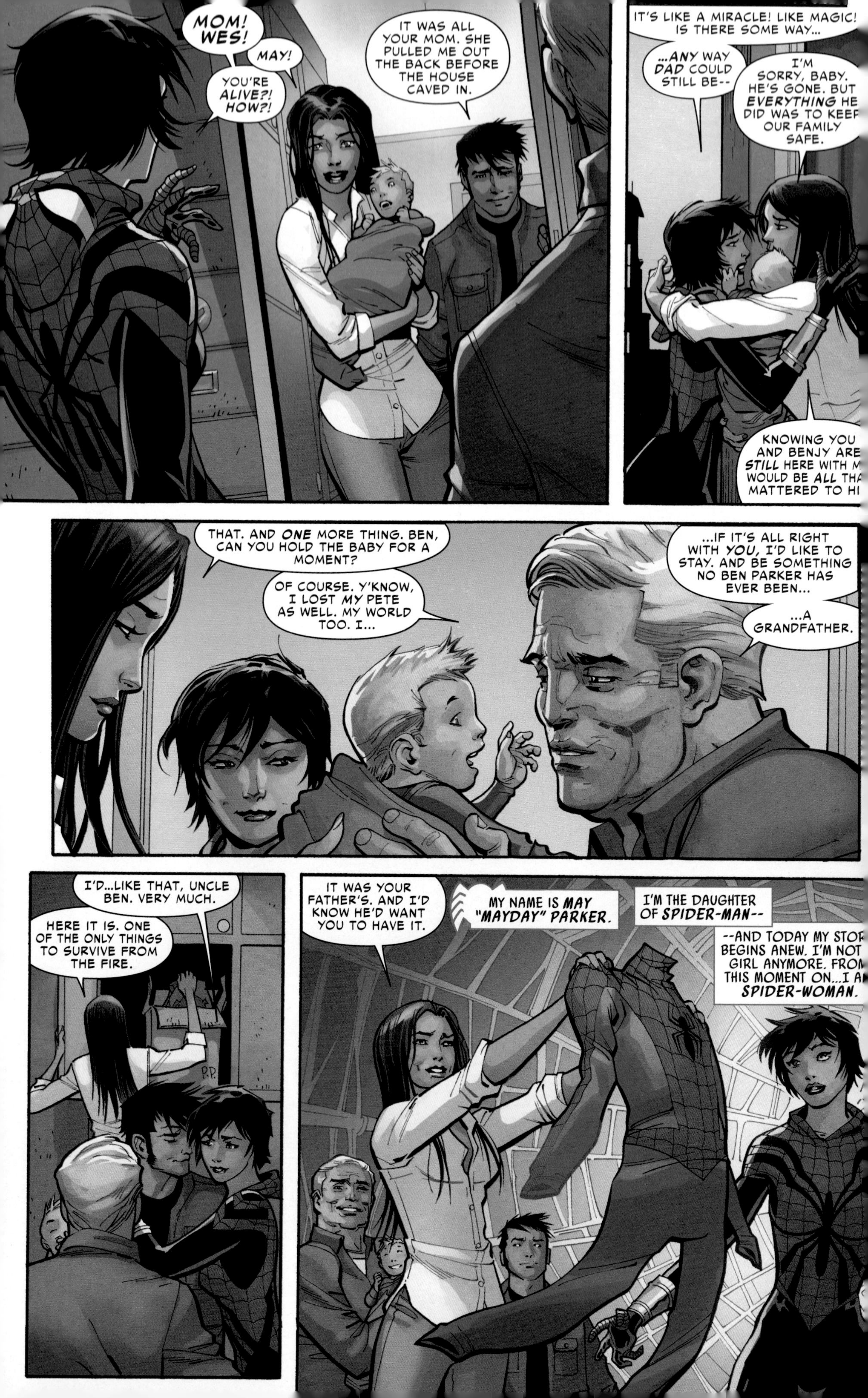
MOM! WES!
MAY!
YOU'RE ALIVE?! HOW?!
IT WAS ALL YOUR MOM. SHE PULLED ME OUT THE BACK BEFORE THE HOUSE CAVED IN.
IT'S LIKE A MIRACLE! LIKE MAGIC! IS THERE SOME WAY...
...ANY WAY DAD COULD STILL BE--
I'M SORRY, BABY. HE'S GONE. BUT EVERYTHING HE DID WAS TO KEEP OUR FAMILY SAFE.
KNOWING YOU AND BENJY ARE STILL HERE WITH M WOULD BE ALL THA MATTERED TO HI
THAT. AND ONE MORE THING. BEN, CAN YOU HOLD THE BABY FOR A MOMENT?
OF COURSE. Y'KNOW, I LOST MY PETE AS WELL. MY WORLD TOO. I...
...IF IT'S ALL RIGHT WITH YOU, I'D LIKE TO STAY. AND BE SOMETHING NO BEN PARKER HAS EVER BEEN...
...A GRANDFATHER.
I'D...LIKE THAT, UNCLE BEN. VERY MUCH.
HERE IT IS. ONE OF THE ONLY THINGS TO SURVIVE FROM THE FIRE.
P.P.
IT WAS YOUR FATHER'S. AND I'D KNOW HE'D WANT YOU TO HAVE IT.
MY NAME IS MAY "MAYDAY" PARKER.
I'M THE DAUGHTER OF SPIDER-MAN--
--AND TODAY MY STOR BEGINS ANEW. I'M NOT GIRL ANYMORE. FROM THIS MOMENT ON...I A SPIDER-WOMAN.

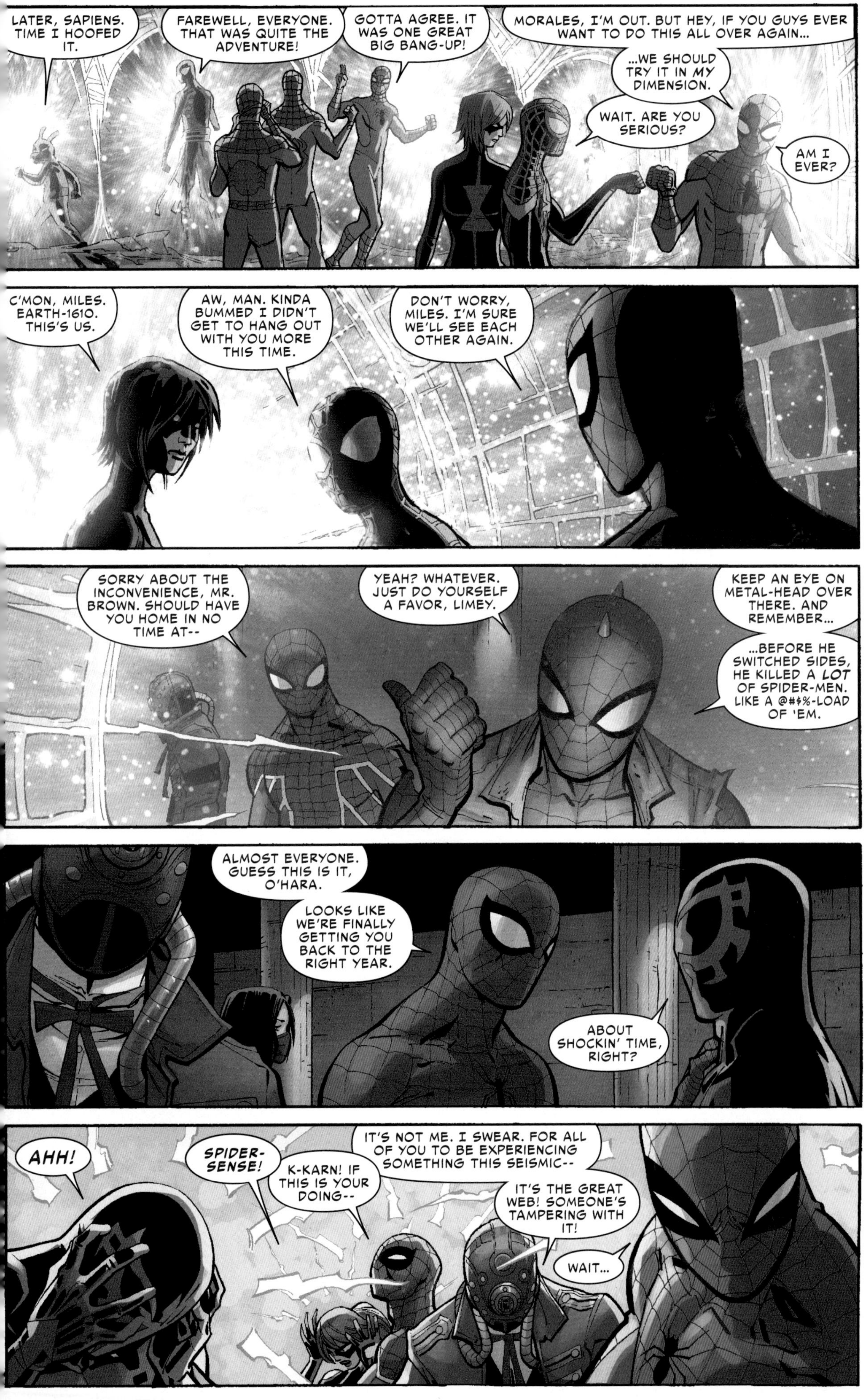

LATER, SAPIENS. TIME I HOOFED IT.
FAREWELL, EVERYONE. THAT WAS QUITE THE ADVENTURE!
GOTTA AGREE. IT WAS ONE GREAT BIG BANG-UP!
MORALES, I'M OUT. BUT HEY, IF YOU GUYS EVER WANT TO DO THIS ALL OVER AGAIN...
...WE SHOULD TRY IT IN MY DIMENSION.
WAIT. ARE YOU SERIOUS?
AM I EVER?
C'MON, MILES. EARTH-1610. THIS'S US.
AW, MAN. KINDA BUMMED I DIDN'T GET TO HANG OUT WITH YOU MORE THIS TIME.
DON'T WORRY, MILES. I'M SURE WE'LL SEE EACH OTHER AGAIN.
SORRY ABOUT THE INCONVENIENCE, MR. BROWN. SHOULD HAVE YOU HOME IN NO TIME AT--
YEAH? WHATEVER. JUST DO YOURSELF A FAVOR, LIMEY.
KEEP AN EYE ON METAL-HEAD OVER THERE. AND REMEMBER...
...BEFORE HE SWITCHED SIDES, HE KILLED A LOT OF SPIDER-MEN. LIKE A @#$%-LOAD OF 'EM.
ALMOST EVERYONE. GUESS THIS IS IT, O'HARA.
LOOKS LIKE WE'RE FINALLY GETTING YOU BACK TO THE RIGHT YEAR.
ABOUT SHOCKIN' TIME, RIGHT?
AHH!
SPIDER-SENSE!
K-KARN! IF THIS IS YOUR DOING--
IT'S NOT ME. I SWEAR. FOR ALL OF YOU TO BE EXPERIENCING SOMETHING THIS SEISMIC--
IT'S THE GREAT WEB! SOMEONE'S TAMPERING WITH IT!
WAIT...

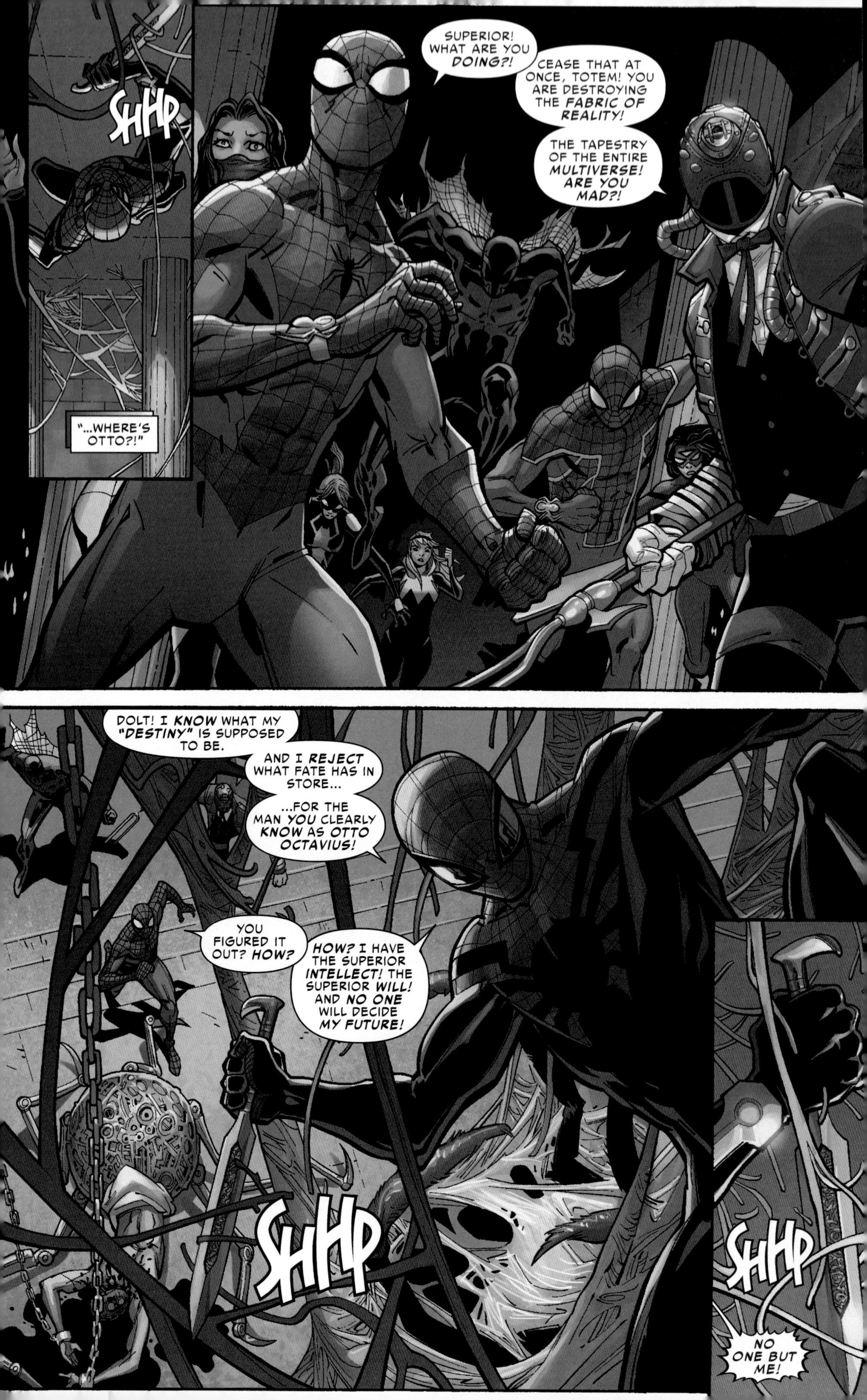
SHHP
"...WHERE'S OTTO?!"
SUPERIOR! WHAT ARE YOU DOING?!
CEASE THAT AT ONCE, TOTEM! YOU ARE DESTROYING THE FABRIC OF REALITY!
THE TAPESTRY OF THE ENTIRE MULTIVERSE! ARE YOU MAD?!
DOLT! I KNOW WHAT MY "DESTINY" IS SUPPOSED TO BE.
AND I REJECT WHAT FATE HAS IN STORE...
...FOR THE MAN YOU CLEARLY KNOW AS OTTO OCTAVIUS!
YOU FIGURED IT OUT? HOW?
HOW? I HAVE THE SUPERIOR INTELLECT! THE SUPERIOR WILL! AND NO ONE WILL DECIDE MY FUTURE!
SHHP
SHHP
NO ONE BUT ME!

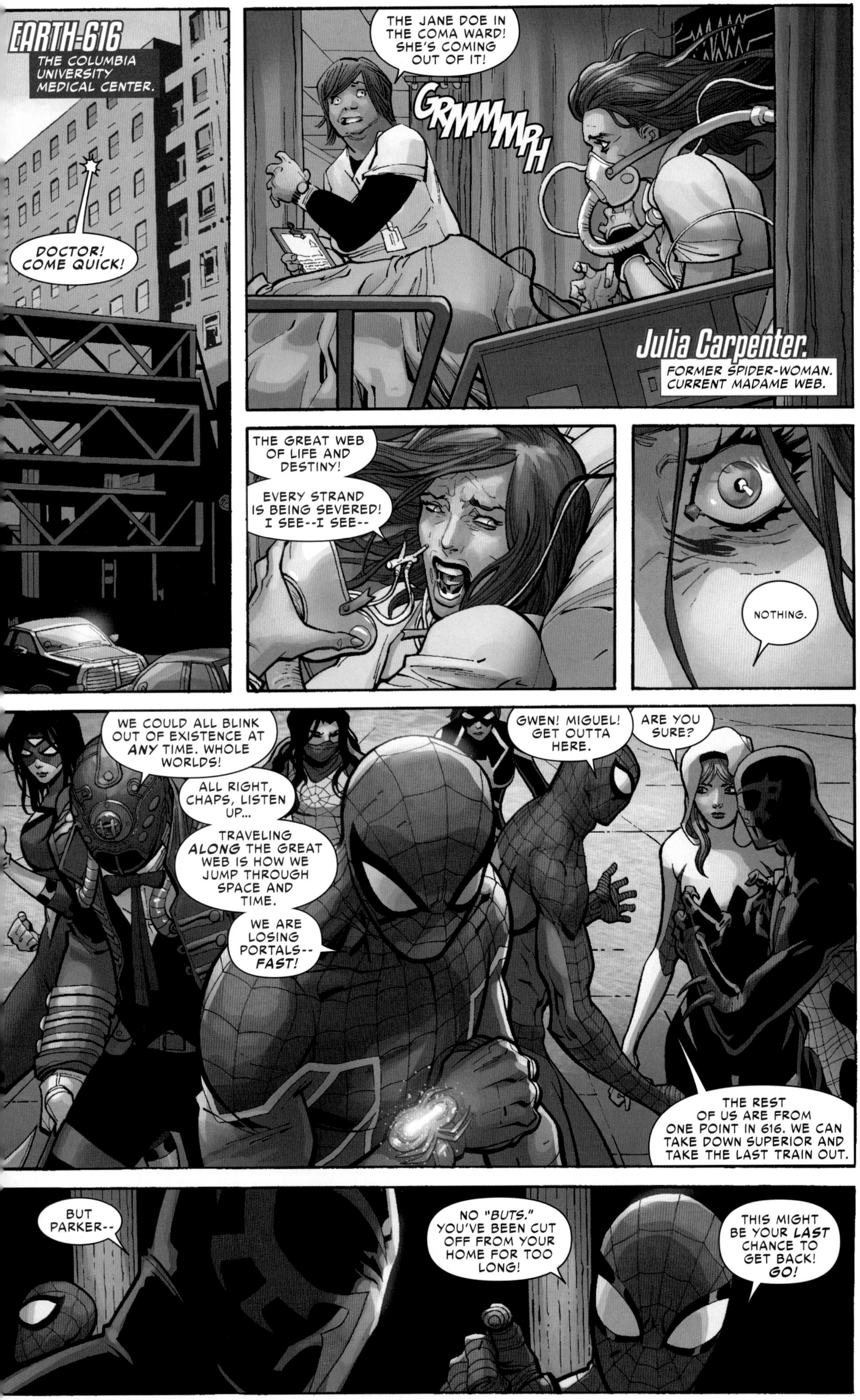
EARTH-616
THE COLUMBIA UNIVERSITY MEDICAL CENTER.
DOCTOR! COME QUICK!
THE JANE DOE IN THE COMA WARD! SHE'S COMING OUT OF IT!
GRMMMPH
Julia Carpenter.
FORMER SPIDER-WOMAN. CURRENT MADAME WEB.
THE GREAT WEB OF LIFE AND DESTINY!
EVERY STRAND IS BEING SEVERED! I SEE--I SEE--
NOTHING.
WE COULD ALL BLINK OUT OF EXISTENCE AT ANY TIME. WHOLE WORLDS!
ALL RIGHT, CHAPS, LISTEN UP...
TRAVELING ALONG THE GREAT WEB IS HOW WE JUMP THROUGH SPACE AND TIME.
WE ARE LOSING PORTALS--FAST!
GWEN! MIGUEL! GET OUTTA HERE.
ARE YOU SURE?
THE REST OF US ARE FROM ONE POINT IN 616. WE CAN TAKE DOWN SUPERIOR AND TAKE THE LAST TRAIN OUT.
BUT PARKER--
NO "BUTS." YOU'VE BEEN CUT OFF FROM YOUR HOME FOR TOO LONG!
THIS MIGHT BE YOUR LAST CHANCE TO GET BACK! GO!

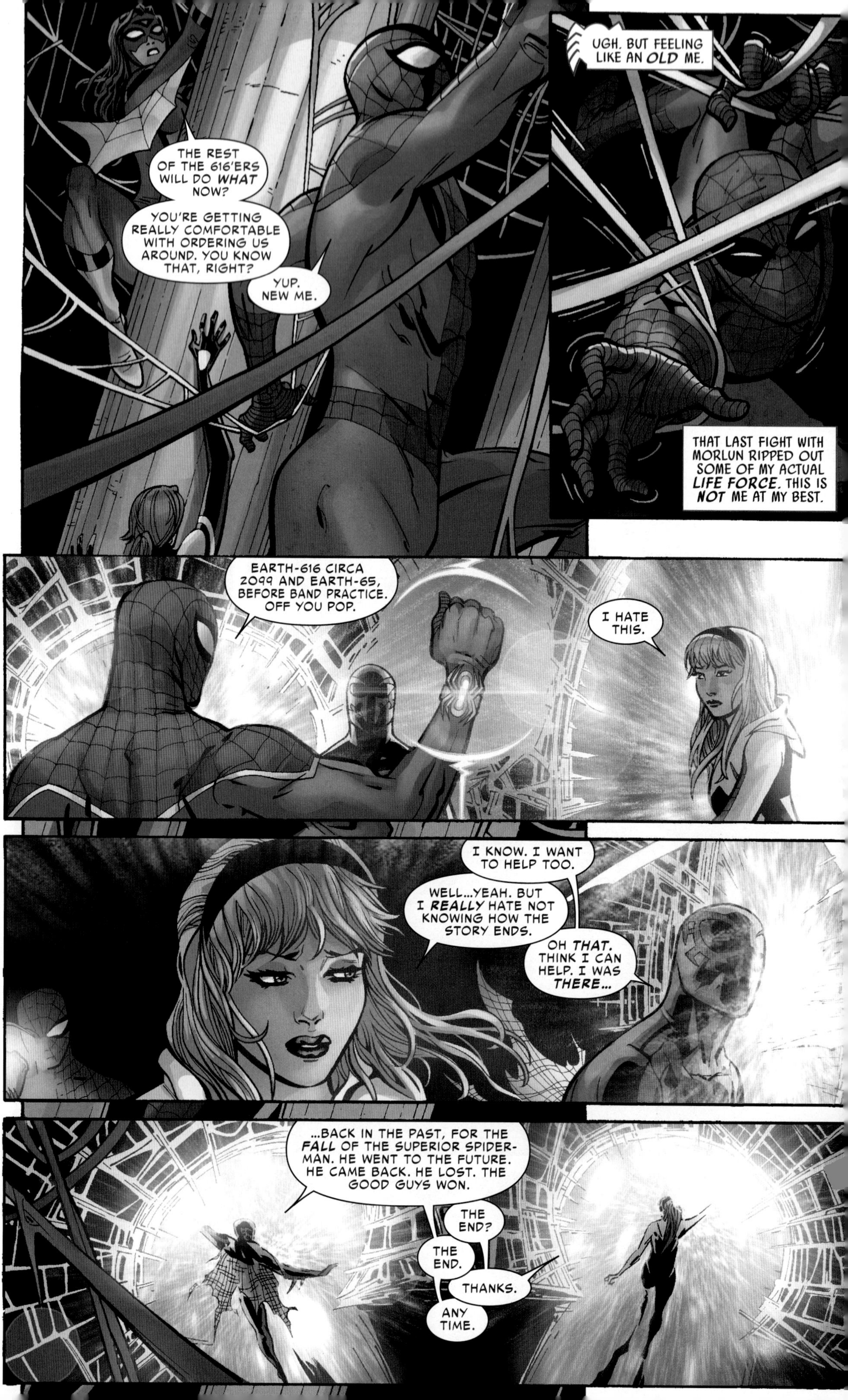
THE REST OF THE 616'ERS WILL DO WHAT NOW?
YOU'RE GETTING REALLY COMFORTABLE WITH ORDERING US AROUND. YOU KNOW THAT, RIGHT?
YUP. NEW ME.
UGH. BUT FEELING LIKE AN OLD ME.
THAT LAST FIGHT WITH MORLUN RIPPED OUT SOME OF MY ACTUAL LIFE FORCE. THIS IS NOT ME AT MY BEST.
EARTH-616 CIRCA 2099 AND EARTH-65, BEFORE BAND PRACTICE. OFF YOU POP.
I HATE THIS.
I KNOW. I WANT TO HELP TOO.
WELL...YEAH. BUT I REALLY HATE NOT KNOWING HOW THE STORY ENDS.
OH THAT. THINK I CAN HELP. I WAS THERE...
...BACK IN THE PAST, FOR THE FALL OF THE SUPERIOR SPIDER-MAN. HE WENT TO THE FUTURE. HE CAME BACK. HE LOST. THE GOOD GUYS WON.
THE END?
THE END.
THANKS.
ANY TIME.

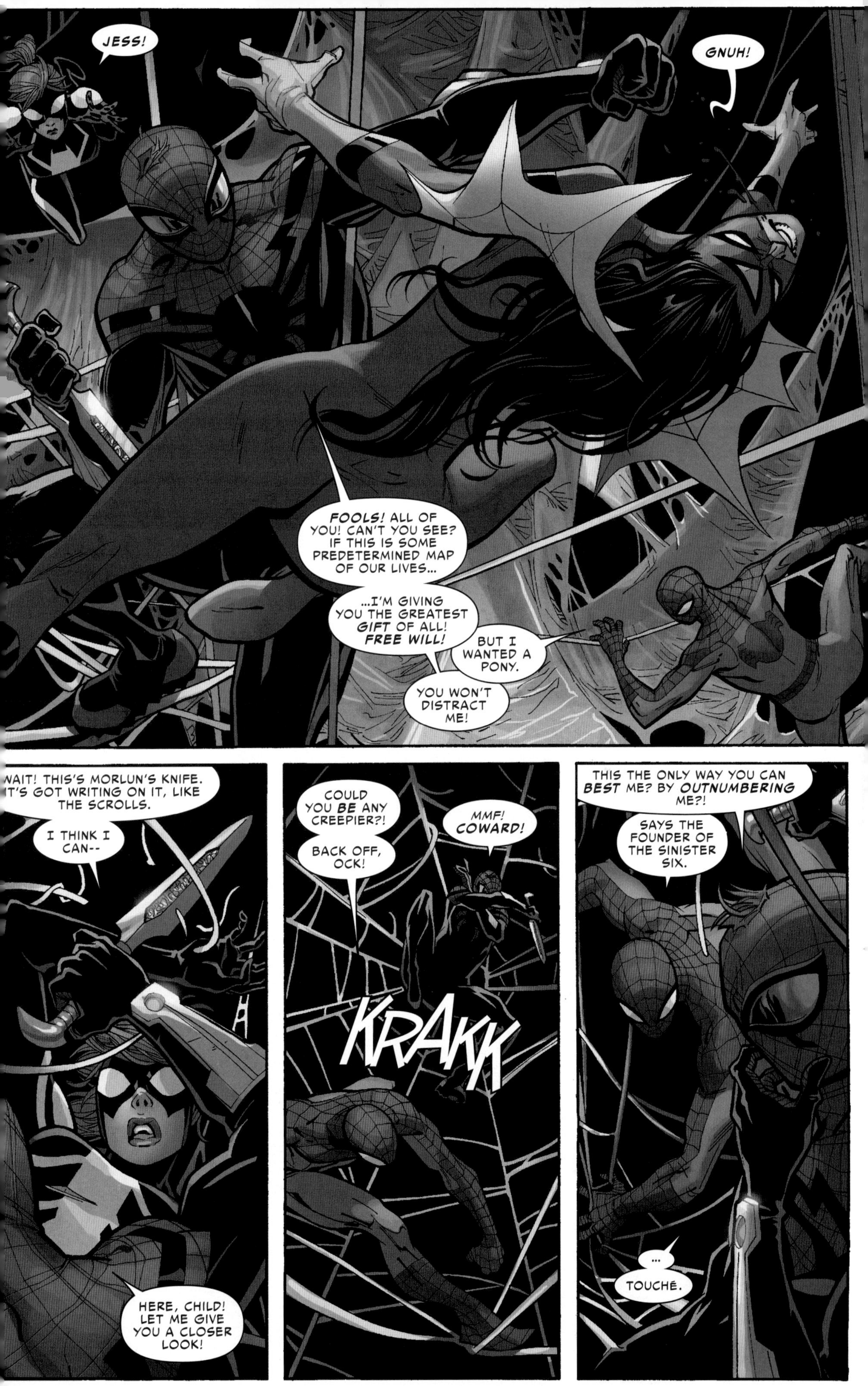
JESS!
GNUH!
FOOLS! ALL OF YOU! CAN'T YOU SEE? IF THIS IS SOME PREDETERMINED MAP OF OUR LIVES...
...I'M GIVING YOU THE GREATEST GIFT OF ALL! FREE WILL!
BUT I WANTED A PONY.
YOU WON'T DISTRACT ME!
WAIT! THIS'S MORLUN'S KNIFE. IT'S GOT WRITING ON IT, LIKE THE SCROLLS.
I THINK I CAN--
HERE, CHILD! LET ME GIVE YOU A CLOSER LOOK!
COULD YOU BE ANY CREEPIER?!
BACK OFF, OCK!
MMF! COWARD!
KRAKK
THIS THE ONLY WAY YOU CAN BEST ME? BY OUTNUMBERING ME?!
SAYS THE FOUNDER OF THE SINISTER SIX.
...
TOUCHÉ.

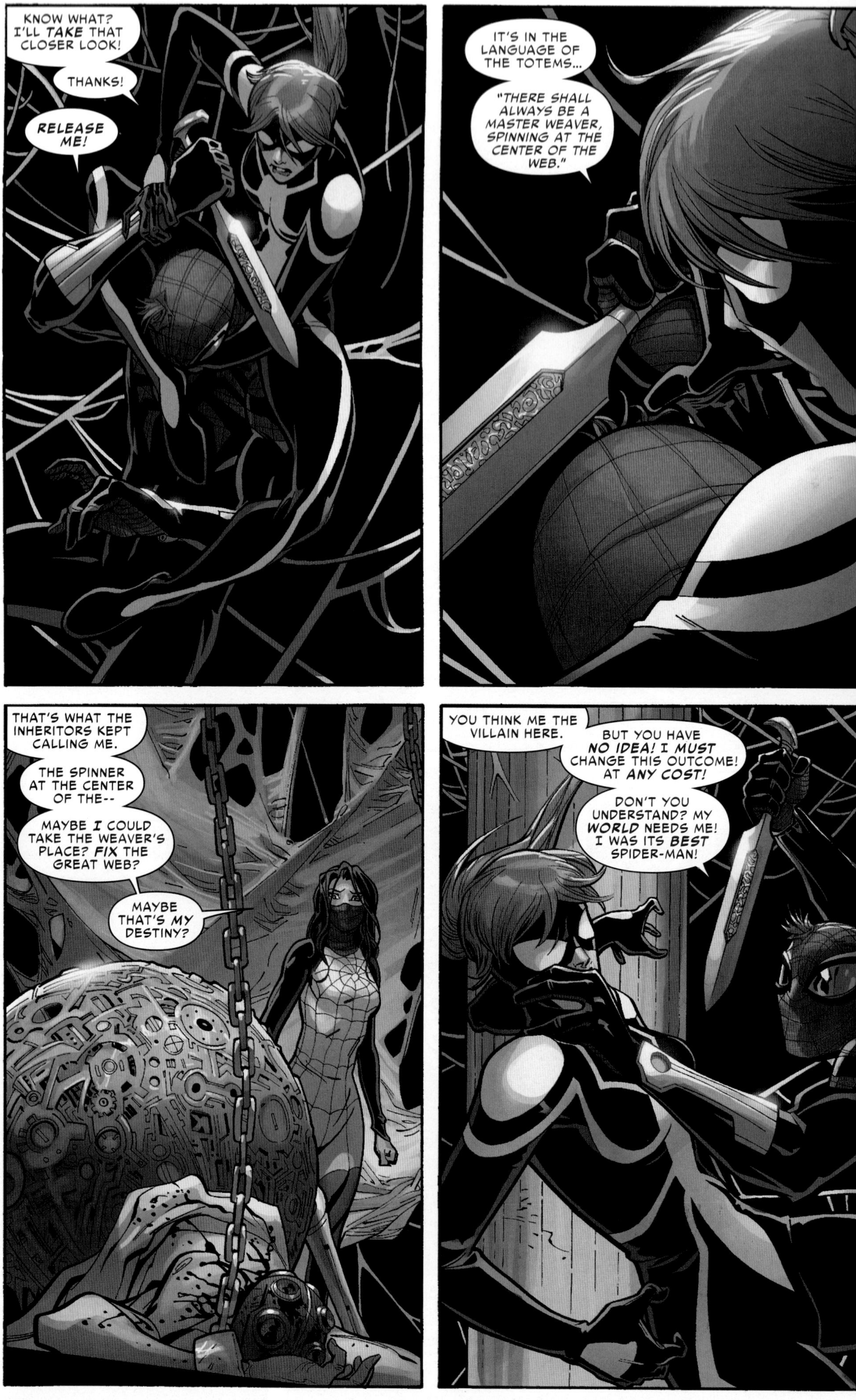

KNOW WHAT? I'LL *TAKE* THAT CLOSER LOOK!
THANKS!
RELEASE ME!
IT'S IN THE LANGUAGE OF THE TOTEMS...
"THERE SHALL ALWAYS BE A MASTER WEAVER, SPINNING AT THE CENTER OF THE WEB."
THAT'S WHAT THE INHERITORS KEPT CALLING ME.
THE SPINNER AT THE CENTER OF THE--
MAYBE *I* COULD TAKE THE WEAVER'S PLACE? *FIX* THE GREAT WEB?
MAYBE THAT'S *MY* DESTINY?
YOU THINK ME THE VILLAIN HERE.
BUT YOU HAVE *NO IDEA!* I *MUST* CHANGE THIS OUTCOME! AT *ANY COST!*
DON'T YOU UNDERSTAND? MY *WORLD* NEEDS ME! I WAS ITS *BEST* SPIDER-MAN!

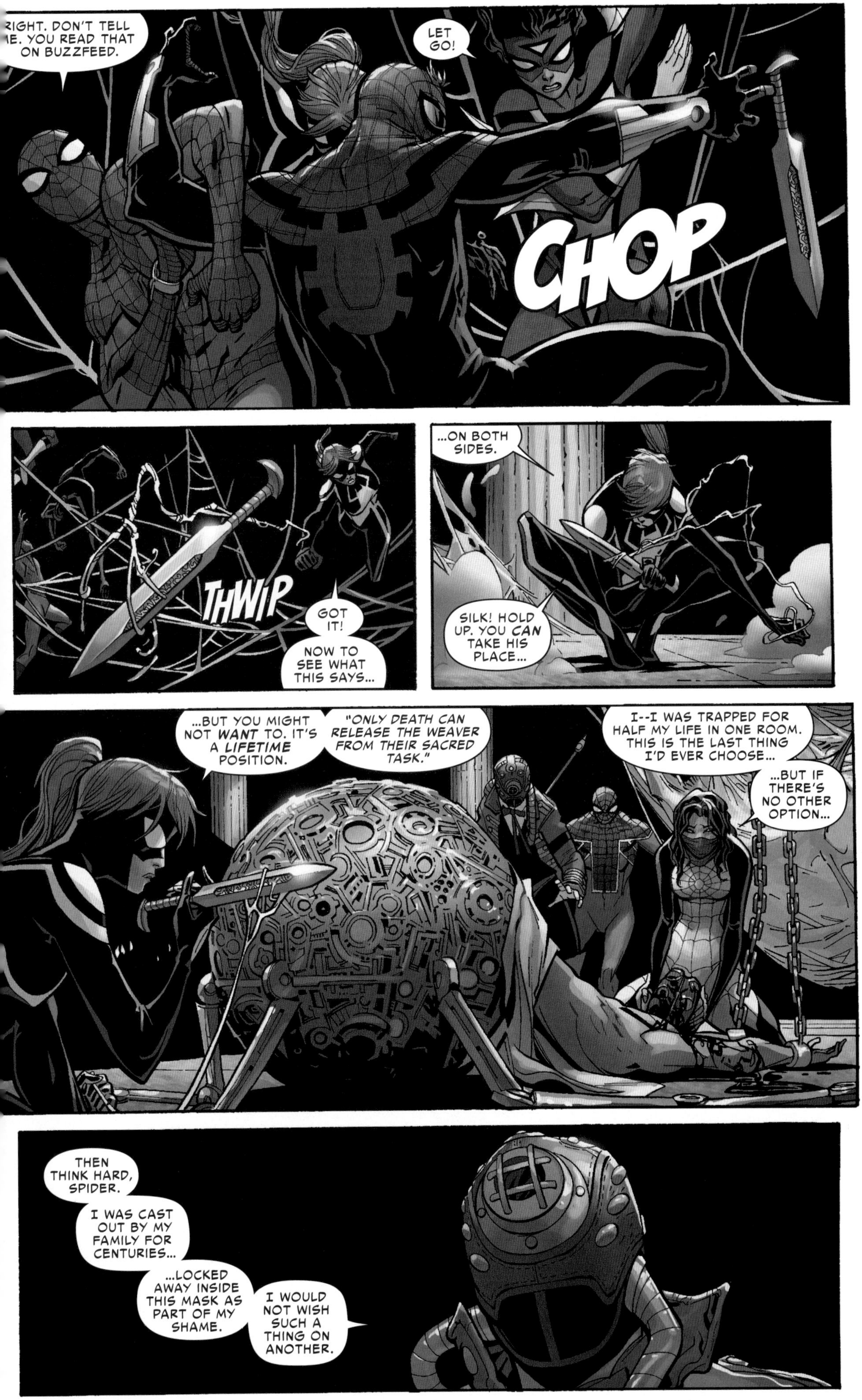
RIGHT. DON'T TELL ME. YOU READ THAT ON BUZZFEED.
LET GO!
CHOP
THWIP
GOT IT!
NOW TO SEE WHAT THIS SAYS...
...ON BOTH SIDES.
SILK! HOLD UP. YOU CAN TAKE HIS PLACE...
...BUT YOU MIGHT NOT WANT TO. IT'S A LIFETIME POSITION.
"ONLY DEATH CAN RELEASE THE WEAVER FROM THEIR SACRED TASK."
I--I WAS TRAPPED FOR HALF MY LIFE IN ONE ROOM. THIS IS THE LAST THING I'D EVER CHOOSE...
...BUT IF THERE'S NO OTHER OPTION...
THEN THINK HARD, SPIDER.
I WAS CAST OUT BY MY FAMILY FOR CENTURIES...
...LOCKED AWAY INSIDE THIS MASK AS PART OF MY SHAME.
I WOULD NOT WISH SUCH A THING ON ANOTHER.

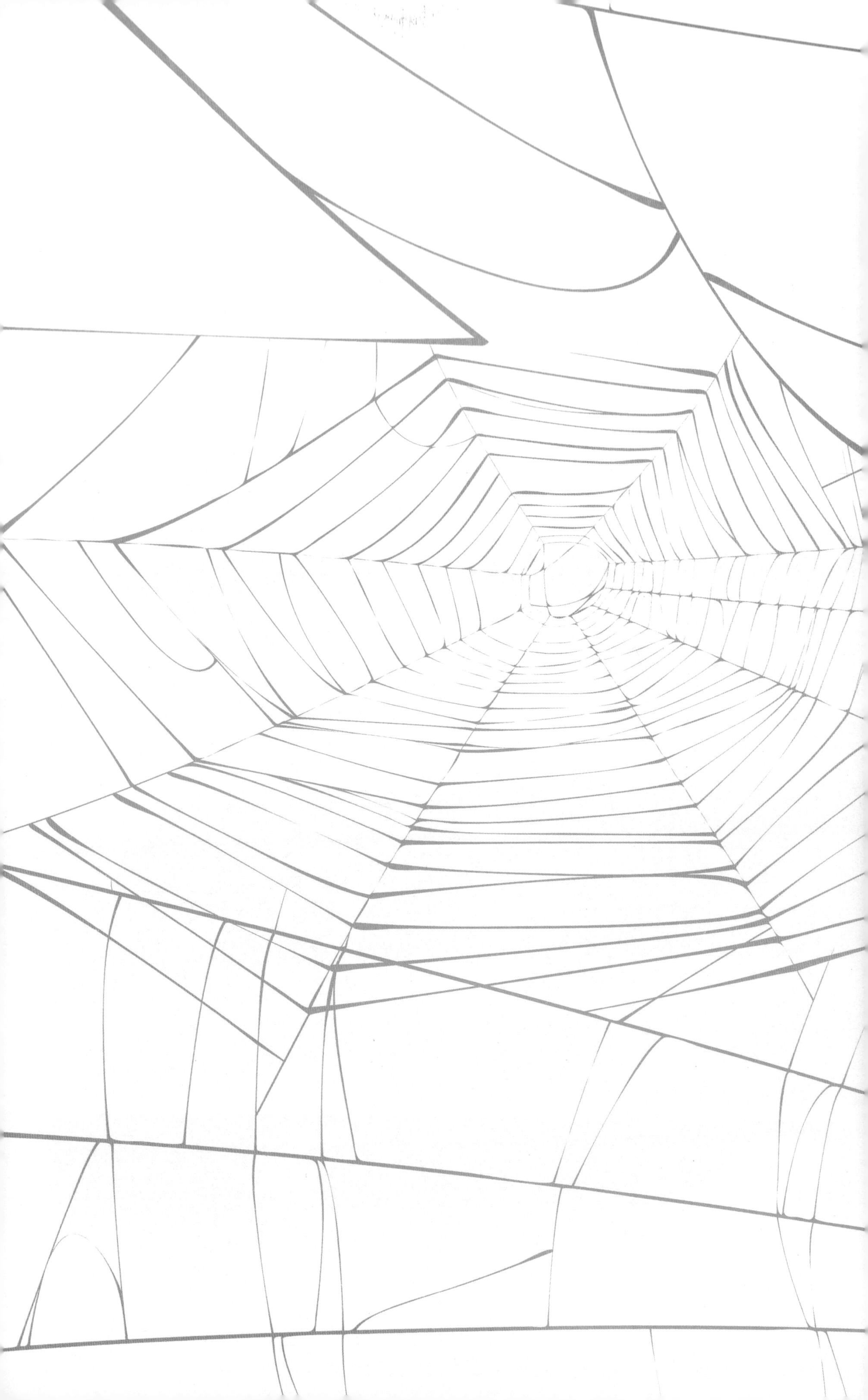

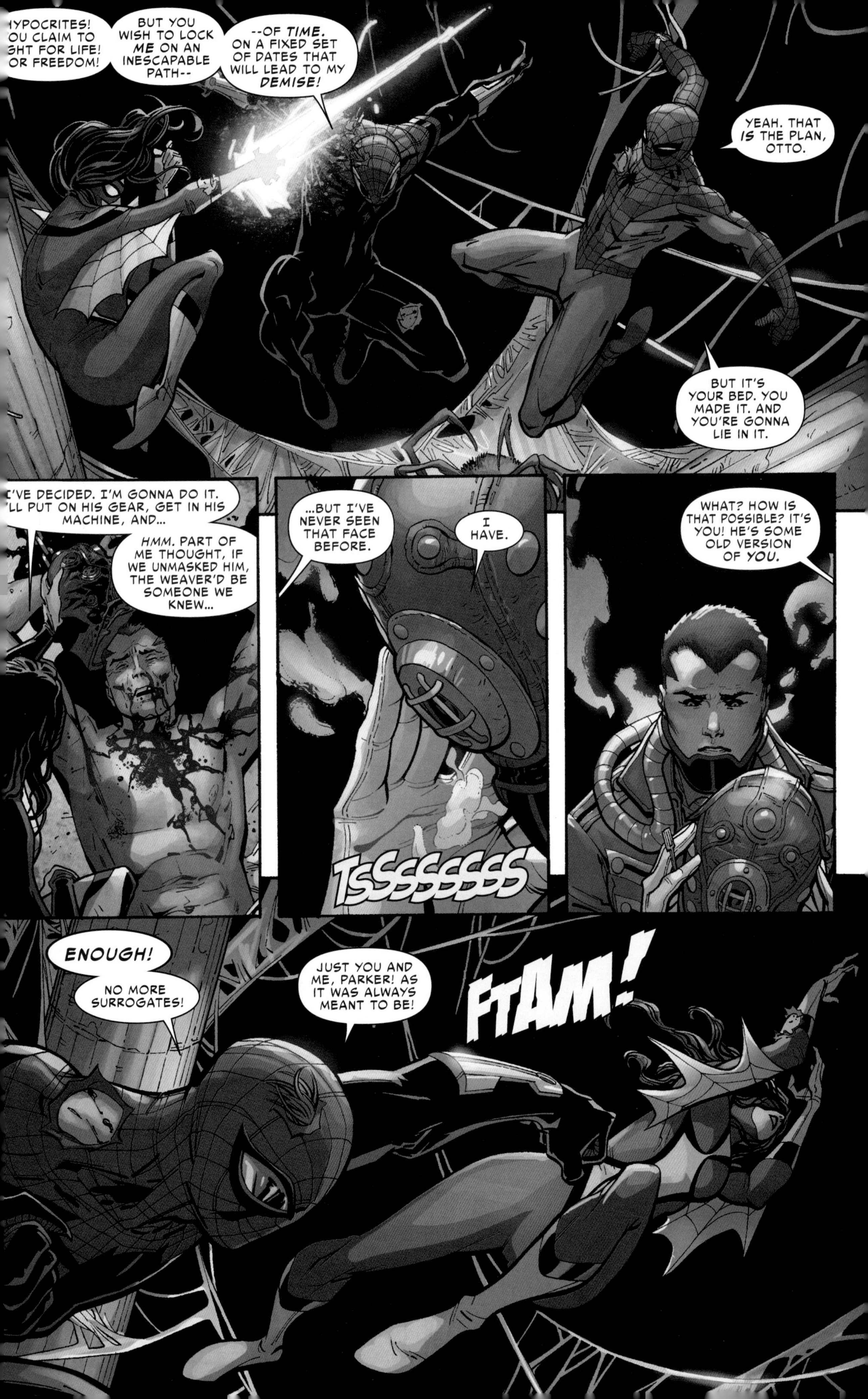
HYPOCRITES! YOU CLAIM TO FIGHT FOR LIFE! FOR FREEDOM!
BUT YOU WISH TO LOCK ME ON AN INESCAPABLE PATH--
--OF TIME. ON A FIXED SET OF DATES THAT WILL LEAD TO MY DEMISE!
YEAH. THAT IS THE PLAN, OTTO.
BUT IT'S YOUR BED. YOU MADE IT. AND YOU'RE GONNA LIE IN IT.
I'VE DECIDED. I'M GONNA DO IT. I'LL PUT ON HIS GEAR, GET IN HIS MACHINE, AND...
HMM. PART OF ME THOUGHT, IF WE UNMASKED HIM, THE WEAVER'D BE SOMEONE WE KNEW...
...BUT I'VE NEVER SEEN THAT FACE BEFORE.
I HAVE.
TSSSSSSSS
WHAT? HOW IS THAT POSSIBLE? IT'S YOU! HE'S SOME OLD VERSION OF YOU.
ENOUGH!
NO MORE SURROGATES!
JUST YOU AND ME, PARKER! AS IT WAS ALWAYS MEANT TO BE!
FTAM!

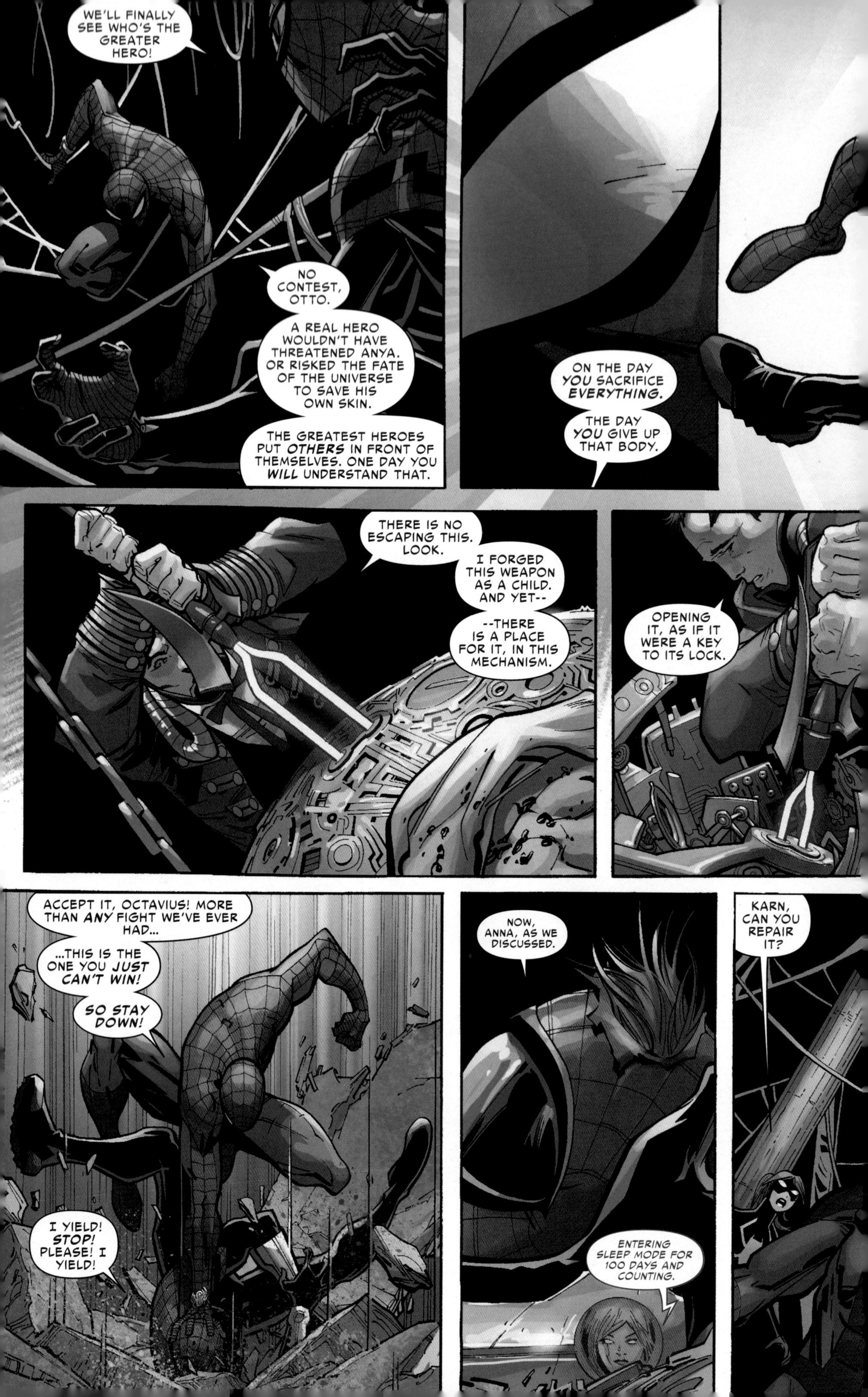
WE'LL FINALLY SEE WHO'S THE GREATER HERO!
NO CONTEST, OTTO.
A REAL HERO WOULDN'T HAVE THREATENED ANYA. OR RISKED THE FATE OF THE UNIVERSE TO SAVE HIS OWN SKIN.
THE GREATEST HEROES PUT OTHERS IN FRONT OF THEMSELVES. ONE DAY YOU WILL UNDERSTAND THAT.
ON THE DAY YOU SACRIFICE EVERYTHING.
THE DAY YOU GIVE UP THAT BODY.
THERE IS NO ESCAPING THIS. LOOK.
I FORGED THIS WEAPON AS A CHILD. AND YET--
--THERE IS A PLACE FOR IT, IN THIS MECHANISM.
OPENING IT, AS IF IT WERE A KEY TO ITS LOCK.
ACCEPT IT, OCTAVIUS! MORE THAN ANY FIGHT WE'VE EVER HAD...
...THIS IS THE ONE YOU JUST CAN'T WIN!
SO STAY DOWN!
I YIELD! STOP! PLEASE! I YIELD!
NOW, ANNA, AS WE DISCUSSED.
ENTERING SLEEP MODE FOR 100 DAYS AND COUNTING.
KARN, CAN YOU REPAIR IT?

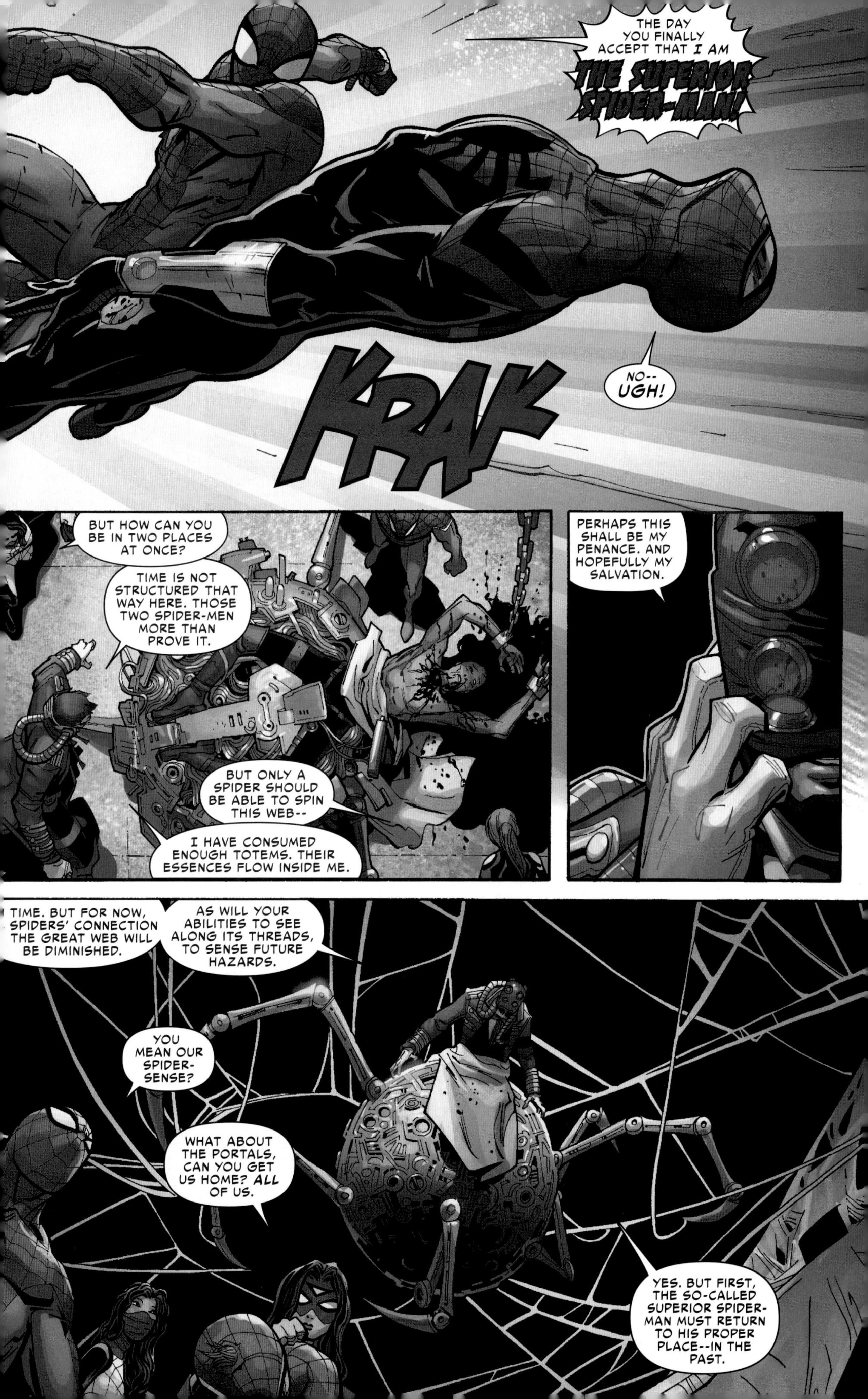
THE DAY YOU FINALLY ACCEPT THAT I AM THE SUPERIOR SPIDER-MAN!
KRAK
NO-- UGH!
BUT HOW CAN YOU BE IN TWO PLACES AT ONCE?
TIME IS NOT STRUCTURED THAT WAY HERE. THOSE TWO SPIDER-MEN MORE THAN PROVE IT.
BUT ONLY A SPIDER SHOULD BE ABLE TO SPIN THIS WEB--
I HAVE CONSUMED ENOUGH TOTEMS. THEIR ESSENCES FLOW INSIDE ME.
PERHAPS THIS SHALL BE MY PENANCE. AND HOPEFULLY MY SALVATION.
TIME. BUT FOR NOW, SPIDERS' CONNECTION THE GREAT WEB WILL BE DIMINISHED.
AS WILL YOUR ABILITIES TO SEE ALONG ITS THREADS, TO SENSE FUTURE HAZARDS.
YOU MEAN OUR SPIDER-SENSE?
WHAT ABOUT THE PORTALS, CAN YOU GET US HOME? ALL OF US.
YES. BUT FIRST, THE SO-CALLED SUPERIOR SPIDER-MAN MUST RETURN TO HIS PROPER PLACE--IN THE PAST.

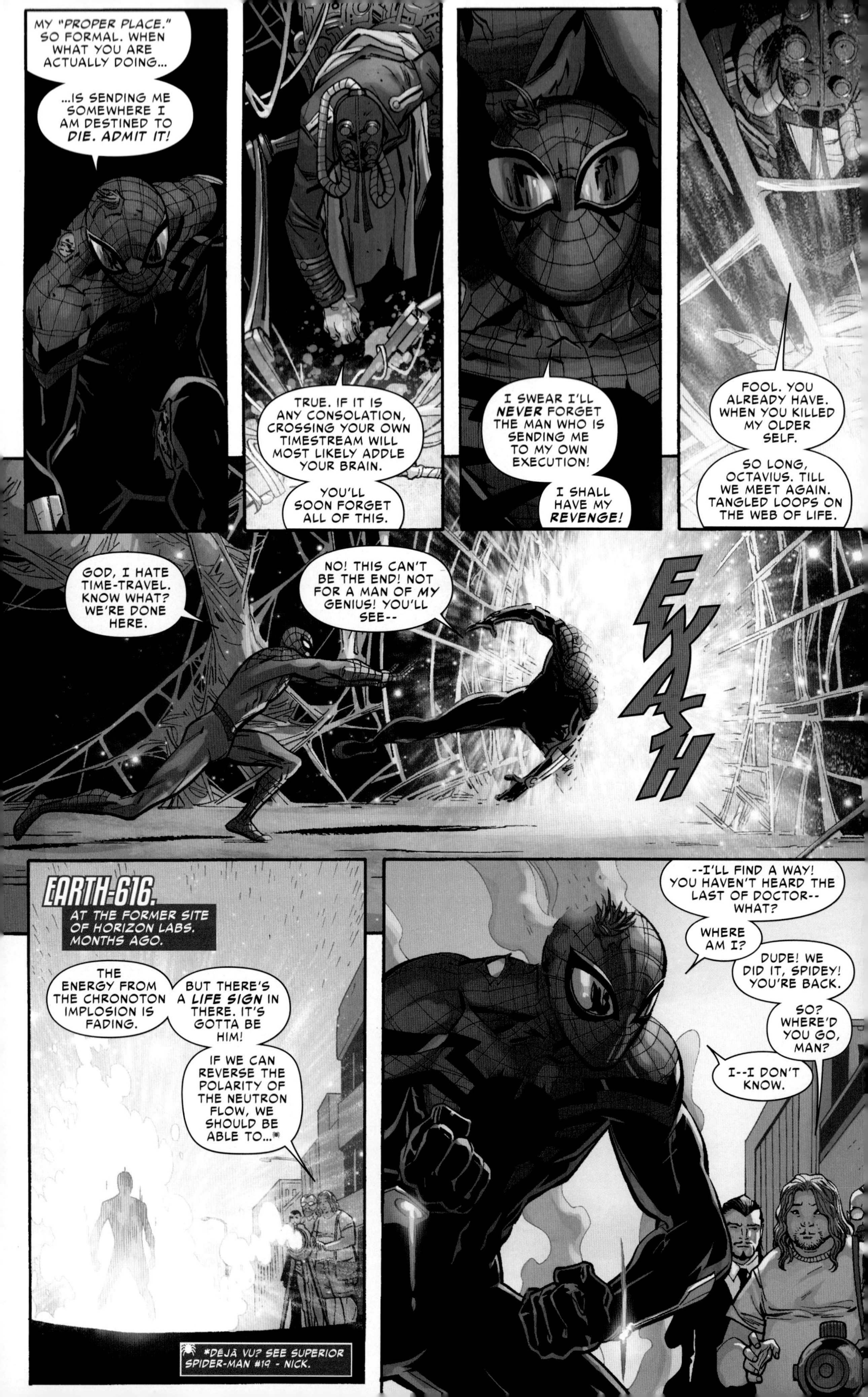

MY "PROPER PLACE." SO FORMAL. WHEN WHAT YOU ARE ACTUALLY DOING...
...IS SENDING ME SOMEWHERE I AM DESTINED TO DIE. ADMIT IT!
TRUE. IF IT IS ANY CONSOLATION, CROSSING YOUR OWN TIMESTREAM WILL MOST LIKELY ADDLE YOUR BRAIN.
YOU'LL SOON FORGET ALL OF THIS.
I SWEAR I'LL NEVER FORGET THE MAN WHO IS SENDING ME TO MY OWN EXECUTION!
I SHALL HAVE MY REVENGE!
FOOL. YOU ALREADY HAVE. WHEN YOU KILLED MY OLDER SELF.
SO LONG, OCTAVIUS. TILL WE MEET AGAIN. TANGLED LOOPS ON THE WEB OF LIFE.
GOD, I HATE TIME-TRAVEL. KNOW WHAT? WE'RE DONE HERE.
NO! THIS CAN'T BE THE END! NOT FOR A MAN OF MY GENIUS! YOU'LL SEE--
EWAH
EARTH-616.
AT THE FORMER SITE OF HORIZON LABS. MONTHS AGO.
THE ENERGY FROM THE CHRONOTON IMPLOSION IS FADING.
BUT THERE'S A LIFE SIGN IN THERE. IT'S GOTTA BE HIM!
IF WE CAN REVERSE THE POLARITY OF THE NEUTRON FLOW, WE SHOULD BE ABLE TO...*
*DÉJÀ VU? SEE SUPERIOR SPIDER-MAN #19 - NICK.
--I'LL FIND A WAY! YOU HAVEN'T HEARD THE LAST OF DOCTOR-- WHAT?
WHERE AM I?
DUDE! WE DID IT, SPIDEY! YOU'RE BACK.
SO? WHERE'D YOU GO, MAN?
I--I DON'T KNOW.

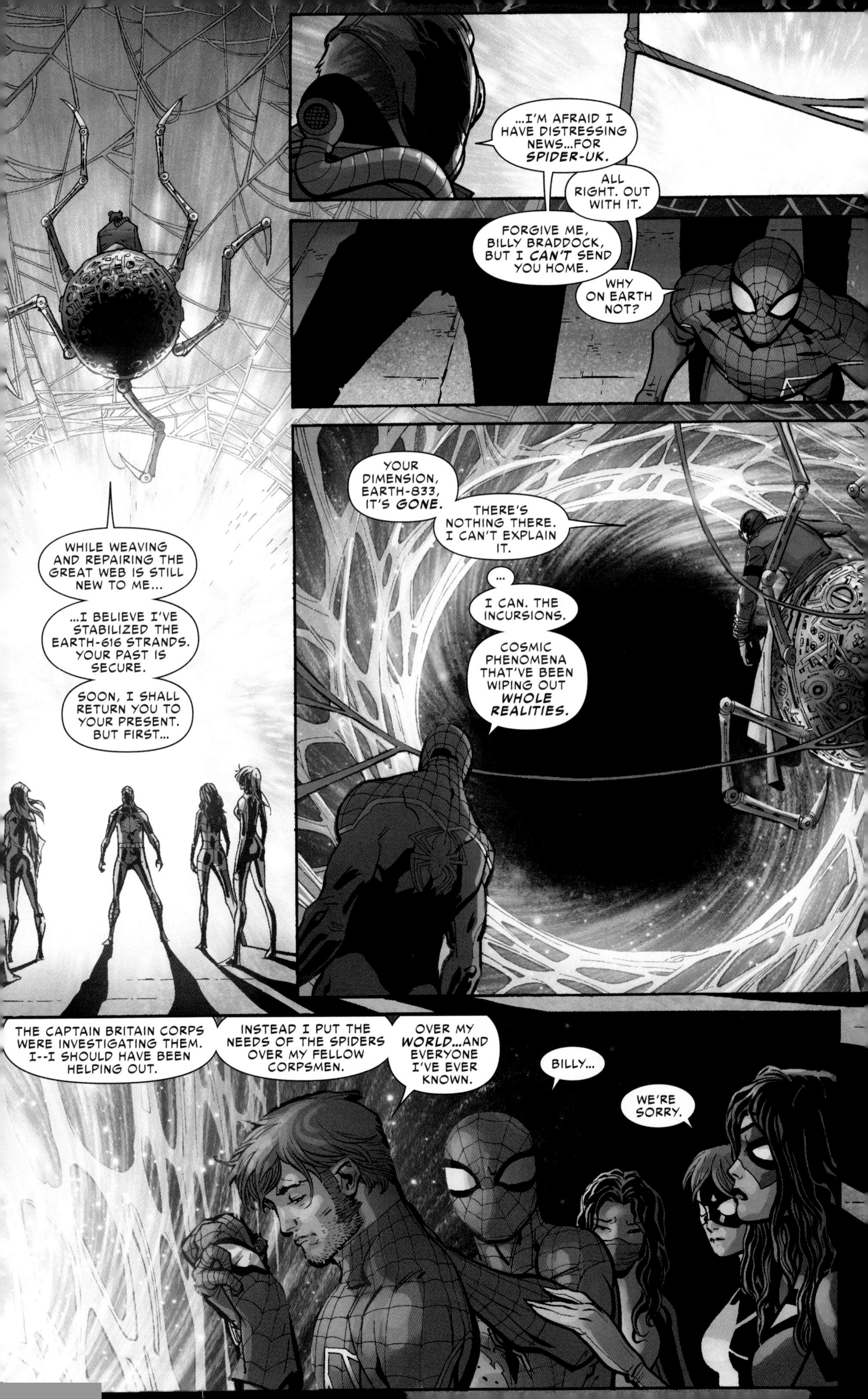
...I'M AFRAID I HAVE DISTRESSING NEWS...FOR SPIDER-UK.
ALL RIGHT. OUT WITH IT.
FORGIVE ME, BILLY BRADDOCK, BUT I CAN'T SEND YOU HOME.
WHY ON EARTH NOT?
WHILE WEAVING AND REPAIRING THE GREAT WEB IS STILL NEW TO ME...
...I BELIEVE I'VE STABILIZED THE EARTH-616 STRANDS. YOUR PAST IS SECURE.
SOON, I SHALL RETURN YOU TO YOUR PRESENT. BUT FIRST...
YOUR DIMENSION, EARTH-833, IT'S GONE.
THERE'S NOTHING THERE. I CAN'T EXPLAIN IT.
...
I CAN. THE INCURSIONS.
COSMIC PHENOMENA THAT'VE BEEN WIPING OUT WHOLE REALITIES.
THE CAPTAIN BRITAIN CORPS WERE INVESTIGATING THEM. I--I SHOULD HAVE BEEN HELPING OUT.
INSTEAD I PUT THE NEEDS OF THE SPIDERS OVER MY FELLOW CORPSMEN.
OVER MY WORLD...AND EVERYONE I'VE EVER KNOWN.
BILLY...
WE'RE SORRY.

I KNOW IT DOESN'T COMPARE, BUT WITHOUT *YOU* BRINGING US ALL TOGETHER...

...WE SPIDERS WOULDN'T HAVE STOOD A CHANCE AGAINST THE INHERITORS.

THANKS, MATE.

SPEAKING OF THE BIG BAD GUYS...

...WE'RE SURE THAT RADIOACTIVE WORLD CAN HOLD 'EM?

AND *NOT*... Y'KNOW...*KILL* THEM? I MEAN, DON'T THEY NEED TO EAT SPIDER TOTEMS TO LIVE?

NOT TRUE. MY KIND CAN FEAST OFF *ANY* ANIMAL-TOTEMS. ANY *ANIMAL* REALLY.

AND *FORTUNATELY* FOR THEM, THE BUNKER YOU LEFT FOR THEM ON EARTH-3145...

...WAS TEEMING WITH *ONE* FORM OF LIFE. SEE?

MORE THAN ENOUGH TO *SUSTAIN* THEM *IF* THEY CAN STOMACH IT.

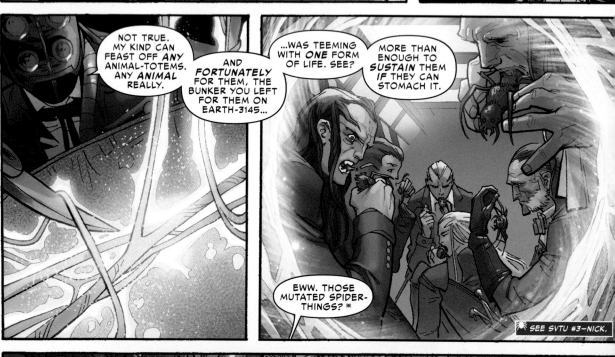

EWW. THOSE MUTATED SPIDER-THINGS? *

SEE SVTU #3—NICK.

GOOD. IT'S MORE THAN THEY DESERVE.

WE LOST A LOT OF GOOD SPIDER-MEN BECAUSE OF THEM.

INCLUDING MY FRIEND, MY BROTHER, *KAINE.*

HE DESERVED BETTER THAN TO GO OUT LIKE...*THAT.*

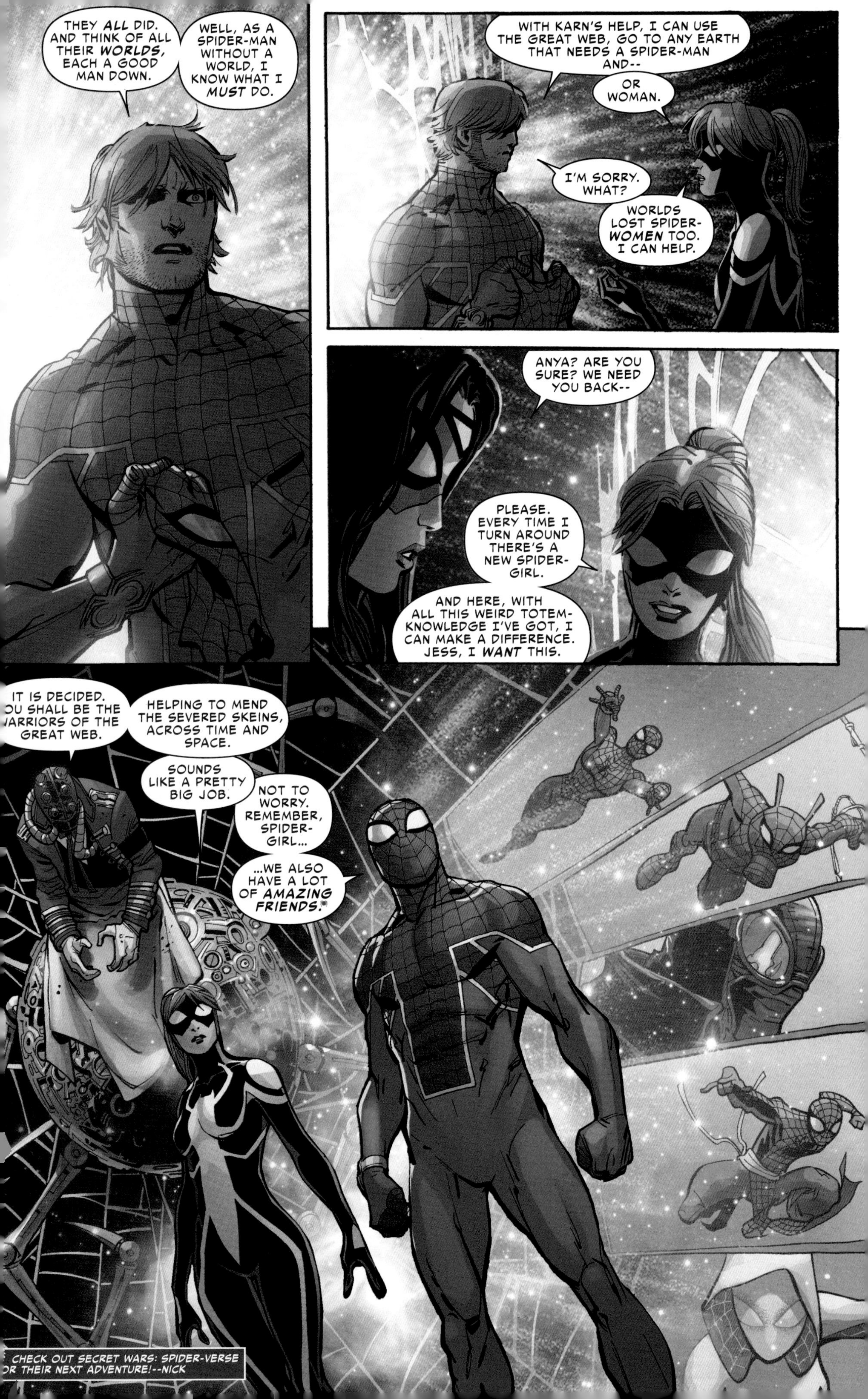

THEY ALL DID. AND THINK OF ALL THEIR WORLDS, EACH A GOOD MAN DOWN.
WELL, AS A SPIDER-MAN WITHOUT A WORLD, I KNOW WHAT I MUST DO.
WITH KARN'S HELP, I CAN USE THE GREAT WEB, GO TO ANY EARTH THAT NEEDS A SPIDER-MAN AND--
OR WOMAN.
I'M SORRY. WHAT?
WORLDS LOST SPIDER-WOMEN TOO. I CAN HELP.
ANYA? ARE YOU SURE? WE NEED YOU BACK--
PLEASE. EVERY TIME I TURN AROUND THERE'S A NEW SPIDER-GIRL.
AND HERE, WITH ALL THIS WEIRD TOTEM-KNOWLEDGE I'VE GOT, I CAN MAKE A DIFFERENCE. JESS, I WANT THIS.
IT IS DECIDED. OU SHALL BE THE ARRIORS OF THE GREAT WEB.
HELPING TO MEND THE SEVERED SKEINS, ACROSS TIME AND SPACE.
SOUNDS LIKE A PRETTY BIG JOB.
NOT TO WORRY. REMEMBER, SPIDER-GIRL...
...WE ALSO HAVE A LOT OF AMAZING FRIENDS.
CHECK OUT SECRET WARS: SPIDER-VERSE OR THEIR NEXT ADVENTURE!--NICK

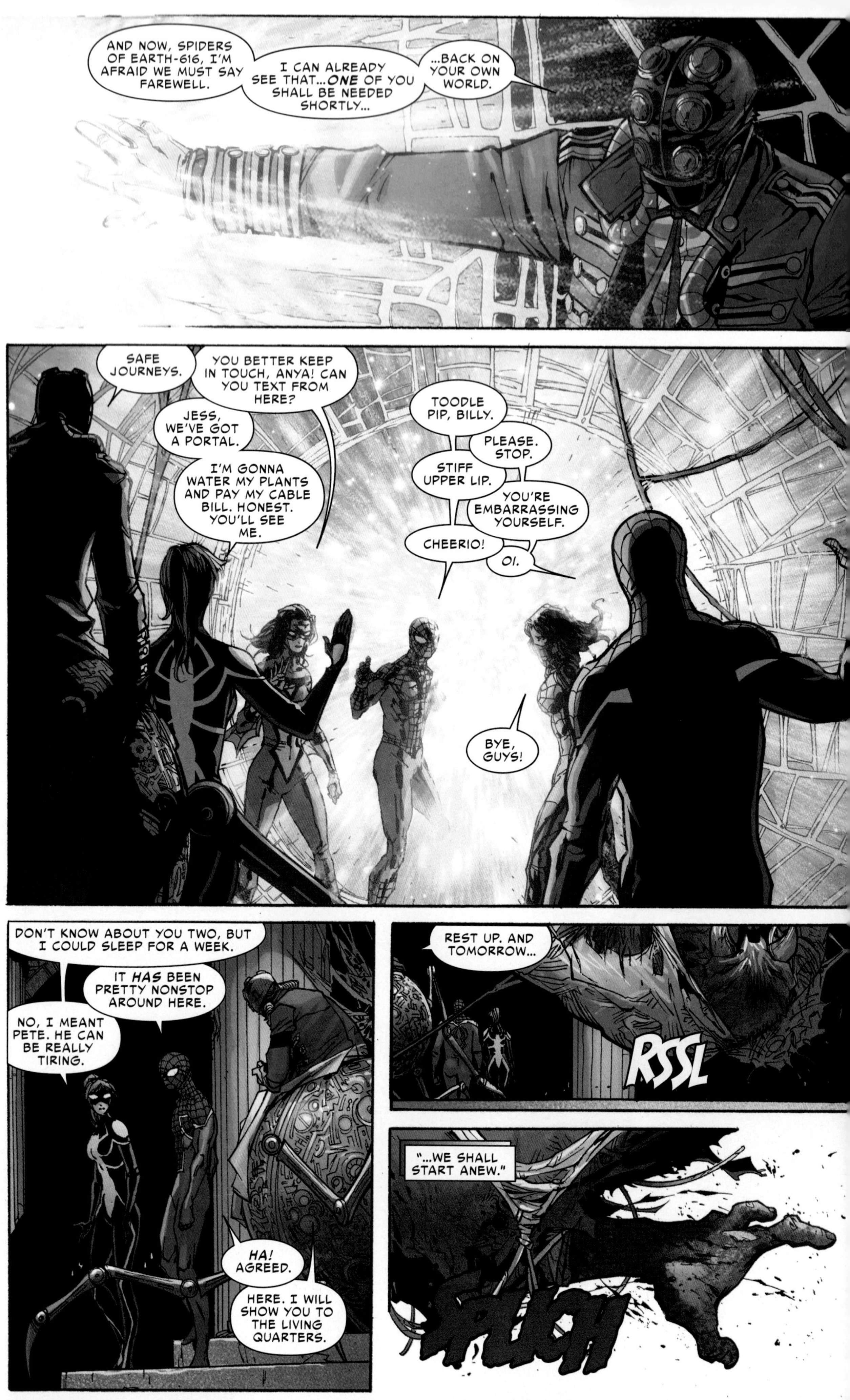
AND NOW, SPIDERS OF EARTH-616, I'M AFRAID WE MUST SAY FAREWELL.
I CAN ALREADY SEE THAT...ONE OF YOU SHALL BE NEEDED SHORTLY...
...BACK ON YOUR OWN WORLD.
SAFE JOURNEYS.
YOU BETTER KEEP IN TOUCH, ANYA! CAN YOU TEXT FROM HERE?
JESS, WE'VE GOT A PORTAL.
I'M GONNA WATER MY PLANTS AND PAY MY CABLE BILL. HONEST. YOU'LL SEE ME.
TOODLE PIP, BILLY.
PLEASE. STOP.
STIFF UPPER LIP.
YOU'RE EMBARRASSING YOURSELF.
CHEERIO!
OI.
BYE, GUYS!
DON'T KNOW ABOUT YOU TWO, BUT I COULD SLEEP FOR A WEEK.
IT HAS BEEN PRETTY NONSTOP AROUND HERE.
NO, I MEANT PETE. HE CAN BE REALLY TIRING.
HA! AGREED.
HERE. I WILL SHOW YOU TO THE LIVING QUARTERS.
REST UP. AND TOMORROW...
RSSL
"...WE SHALL START ANEW."
SPLUCH

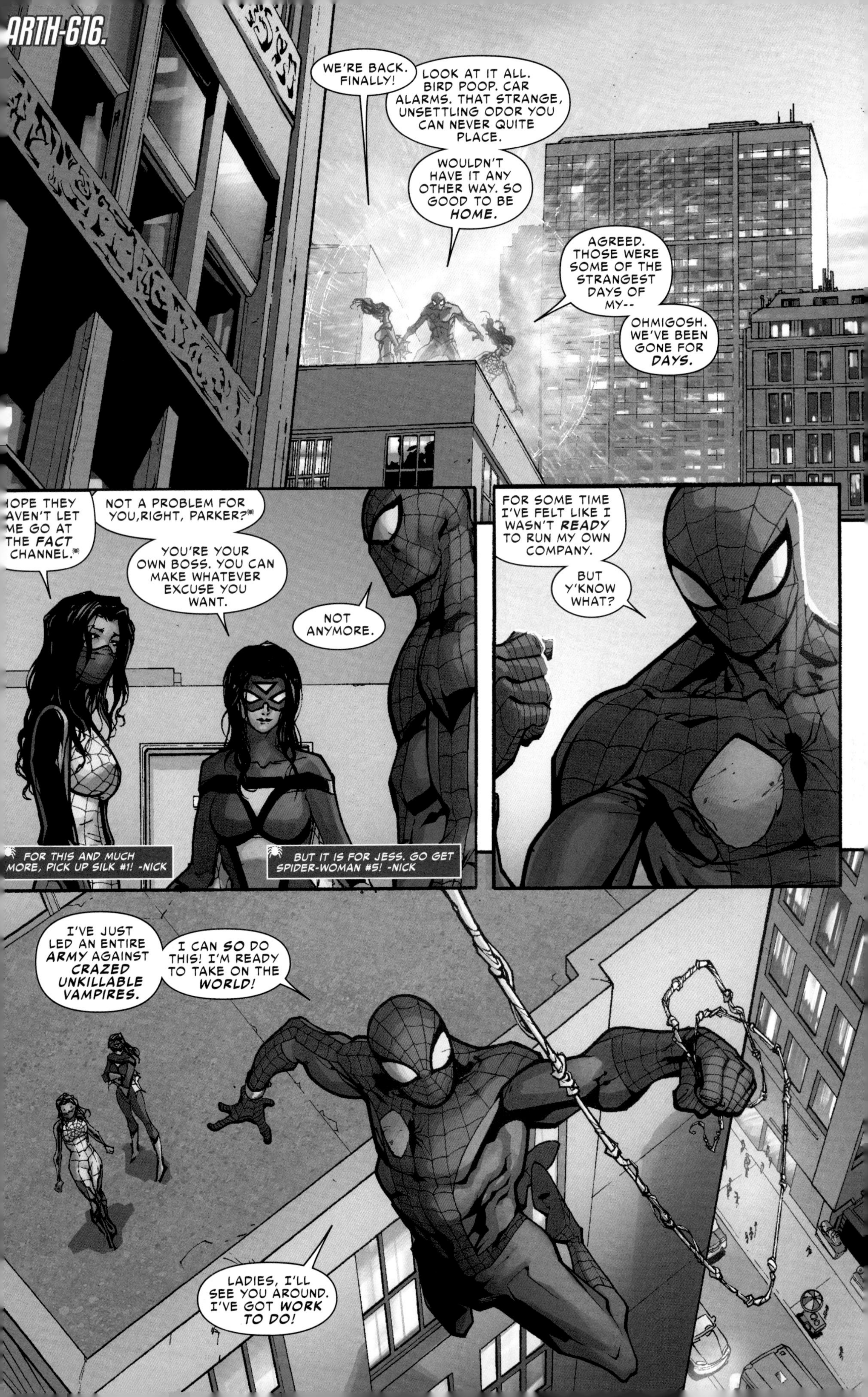
ARTH-616.
WE'RE BACK. FINALLY!
LOOK AT IT ALL. BIRD POOP. CAR ALARMS. THAT STRANGE, UNSETTLING ODOR YOU CAN NEVER QUITE PLACE.
WOULDN'T HAVE IT ANY OTHER WAY. SO GOOD TO BE HOME.
AGREED. THOSE WERE SOME OF THE STRANGEST DAYS OF MY--
OHMIGOSH. WE'VE BEEN GONE FOR DAYS.
HOPE THEY HAVEN'T LET ME GO AT THE FACT CHANNEL.
NOT A PROBLEM FOR YOU,RIGHT, PARKER?
YOU'RE YOUR OWN BOSS. YOU CAN MAKE WHATEVER EXCUSE YOU WANT.
NOT ANYMORE.
FOR THIS AND MUCH MORE, PICK UP SILK #1! -NICK
BUT IT IS FOR JESS. GO GET SPIDER-WOMAN #5! -NICK
FOR SOME TIME I'VE FELT LIKE I WASN'T READY TO RUN MY OWN COMPANY.
BUT Y'KNOW WHAT?
I'VE JUST LED AN ENTIRE ARMY AGAINST CRAZED UNKILLABLE VAMPIRES.
I CAN SO DO THIS! I'M READY TO TAKE ON THE WORLD!
LADIES, I'LL SEE YOU AROUND. I'VE GOT WORK TO DO!

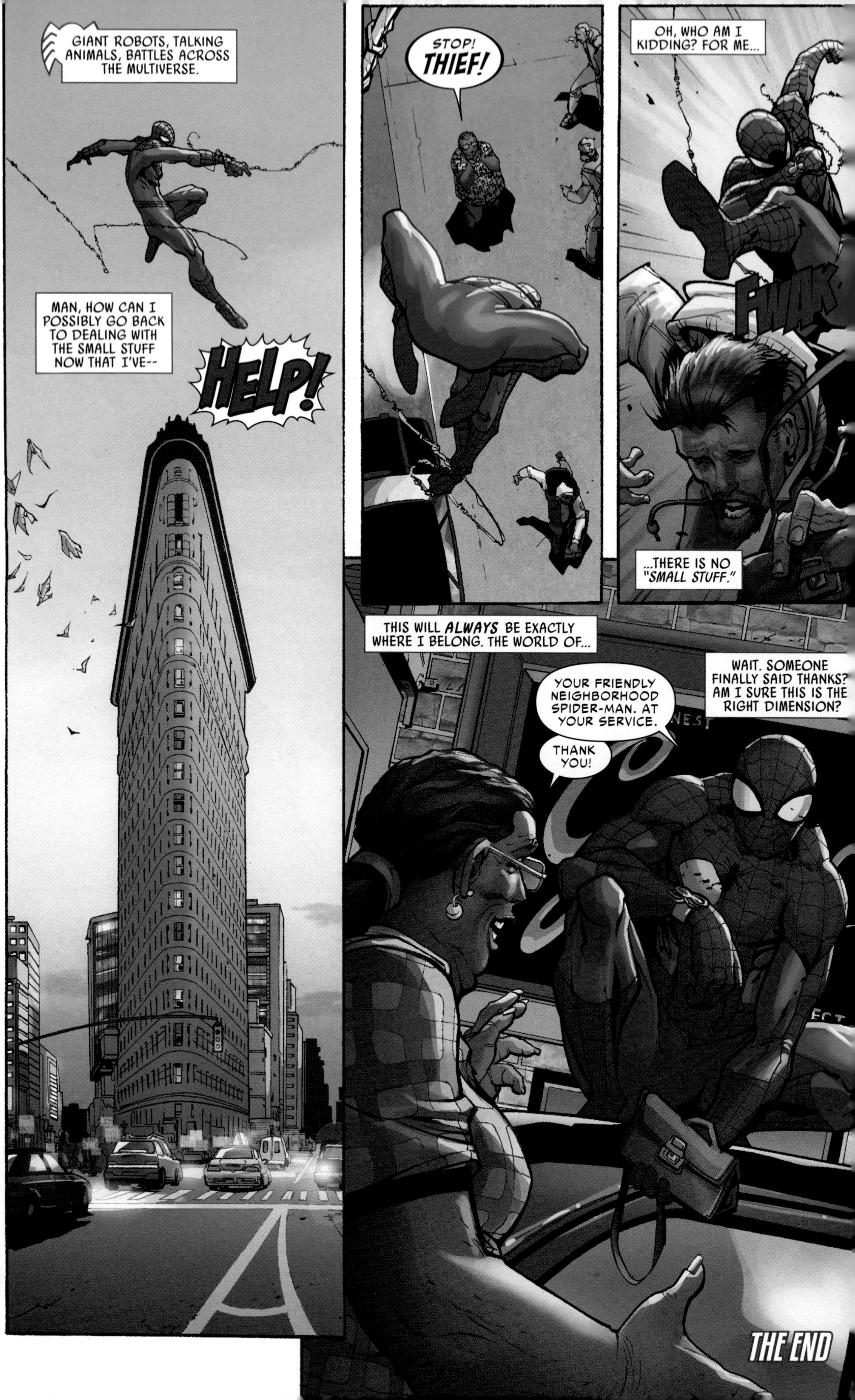
GIANT ROBOTS, TALKING ANIMALS, BATTLES ACROSS THE MULTIVERSE.
MAN, HOW CAN I POSSIBLY GO BACK TO DEALING WITH THE SMALL STUFF NOW THAT I'VE--
HELP!
STOP! THIEF!
OH, WHO AM I KIDDING? FOR ME...
FWAK
...THERE IS NO "SMALL STUFF."
THIS WILL ALWAYS BE EXACTLY WHERE I BELONG. THE WORLD OF...
YOUR FRIENDLY NEIGHBORHOOD SPIDER-MAN. AT YOUR SERVICE.
THANK YOU!
WAIT. SOMEONE FINALLY SAID THANKS? AM I SURE THIS IS THE RIGHT DIMENSION?
THE END

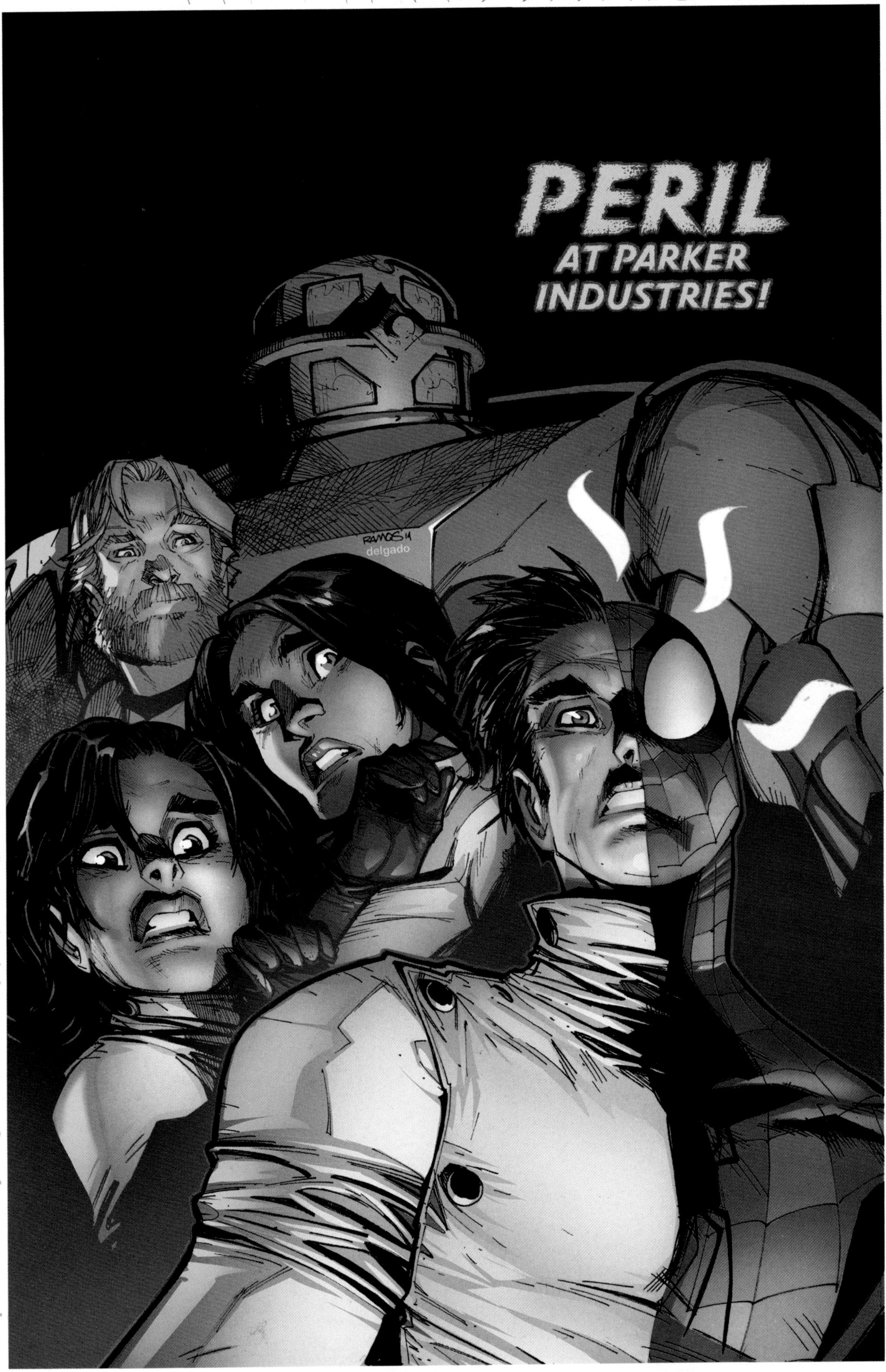
PERIL
AT PARKER
INDUSTRIES!

AMAZING SPIDER-MAN 16
GRAVEYARD SHIFT, PART ONE: THE LATE, LATE MR. PARKER

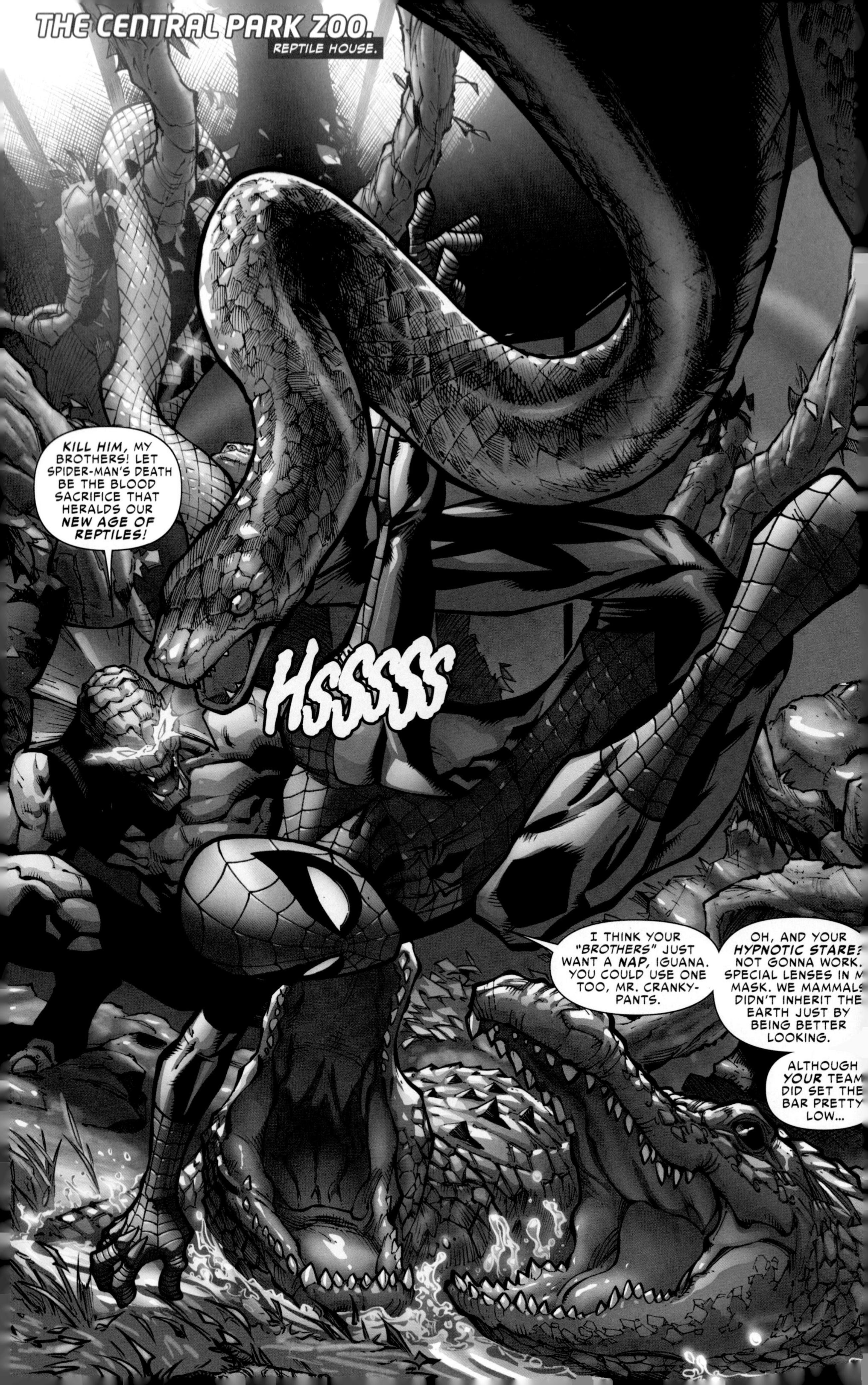
THE CENTRAL PARK ZOO.
REPTILE HOUSE.
KILL HIM, MY BROTHERS! LET SPIDER-MAN'S DEATH BE THE BLOOD SACRIFICE THAT HERALDS OUR NEW AGE OF REPTILES!
HSSSSS
I THINK YOUR "BROTHERS" JUST WANT A NAP, IGUANA. YOU COULD USE ONE TOO, MR. CRANKY-PANTS.
OH, AND YOUR HYPNOTIC STARE? NOT GONNA WORK. SPECIAL LENSES IN MY MASK. WE MAMMALS DIDN'T INHERIT THE EARTH JUST BY BEING BETTER LOOKING.
ALTHOUGH YOUR TEAM DID SET THE BAR PRETTY LOW...

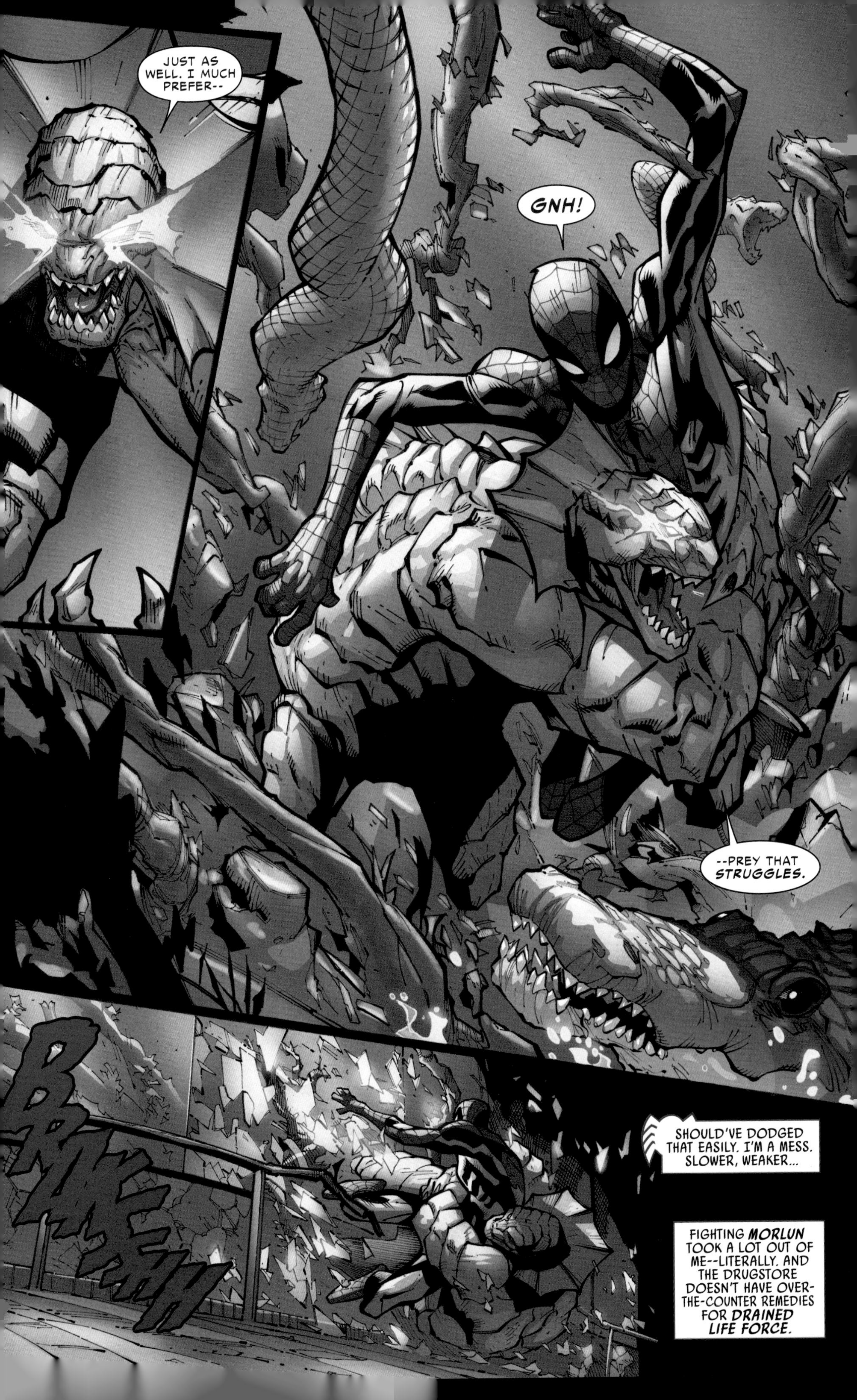
JUST AS WELL. I MUCH PREFER--
GNH!
--PREY THAT STRUGGLES.
SHOULD'VE DODGED THAT EASILY. I'M A MESS. SLOWER, WEAKER...
FIGHTING MORLUN TOOK A LOT OUT OF ME--LITERALLY. AND THE DRUGSTORE DOESN'T HAVE OVER-THE-COUNTER REMEDIES FOR DRAINED LIFE FORCE.

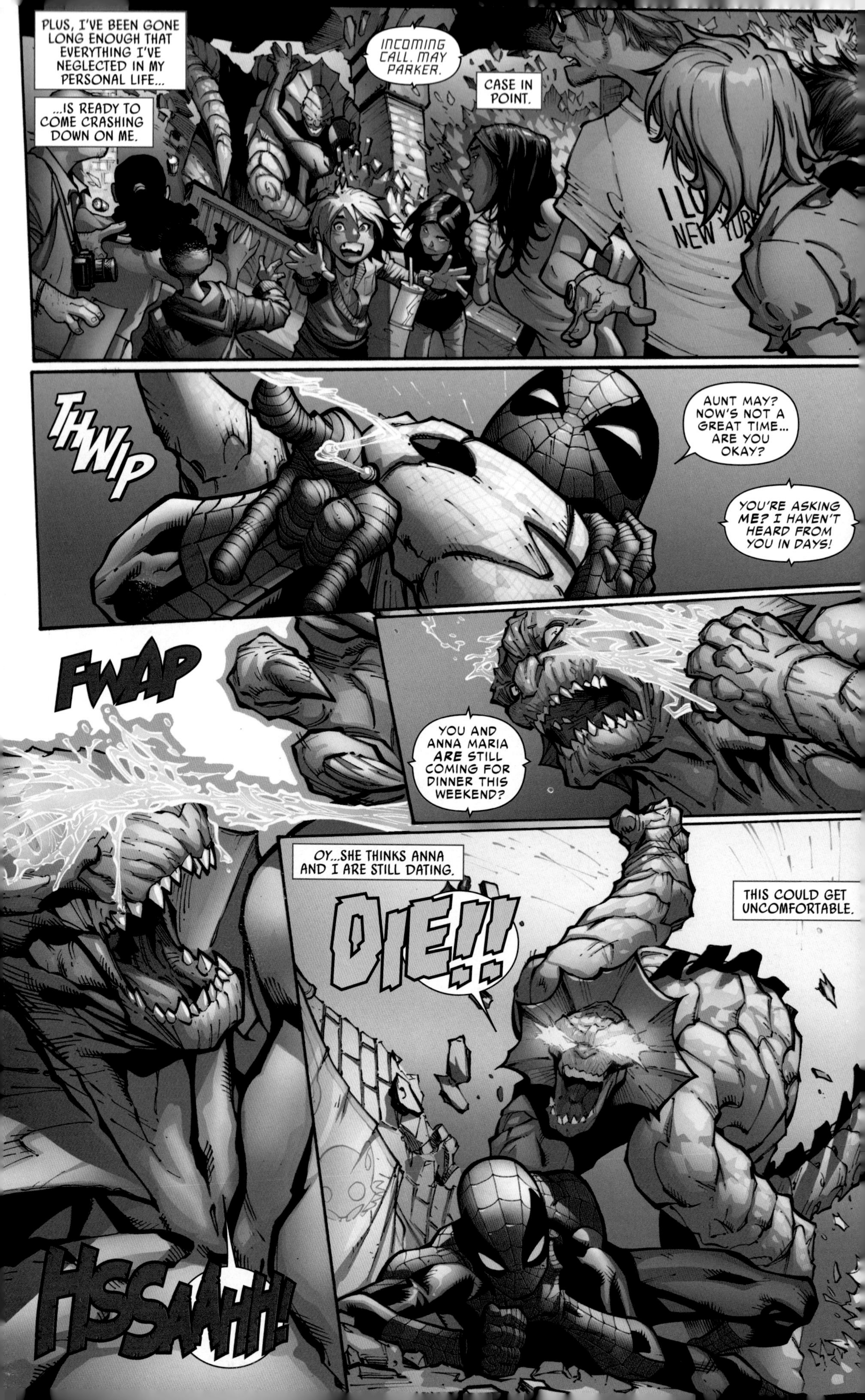

PLUS, I'VE BEEN GONE LONG ENOUGH THAT EVERYTHING I'VE NEGLECTED IN MY PERSONAL LIFE...
...IS READY TO COME CRASHING DOWN ON ME.
INCOMING CALL. MAY PARKER.
CASE IN POINT.
I LO... NEW YOR...
THWIP
AUNT MAY? NOW'S NOT A GREAT TIME... ARE YOU OKAY?
YOU'RE ASKING ME? I HAVEN'T HEARD FROM YOU IN DAYS!
FWAP
YOU AND ANNA MARIA ARE STILL COMING FOR DINNER THIS WEEKEND?
OY...SHE THINKS ANNA AND I ARE STILL DATING.
THIS COULD GET UNCOMFORTABLE.
DIE!!
HSSAHH!

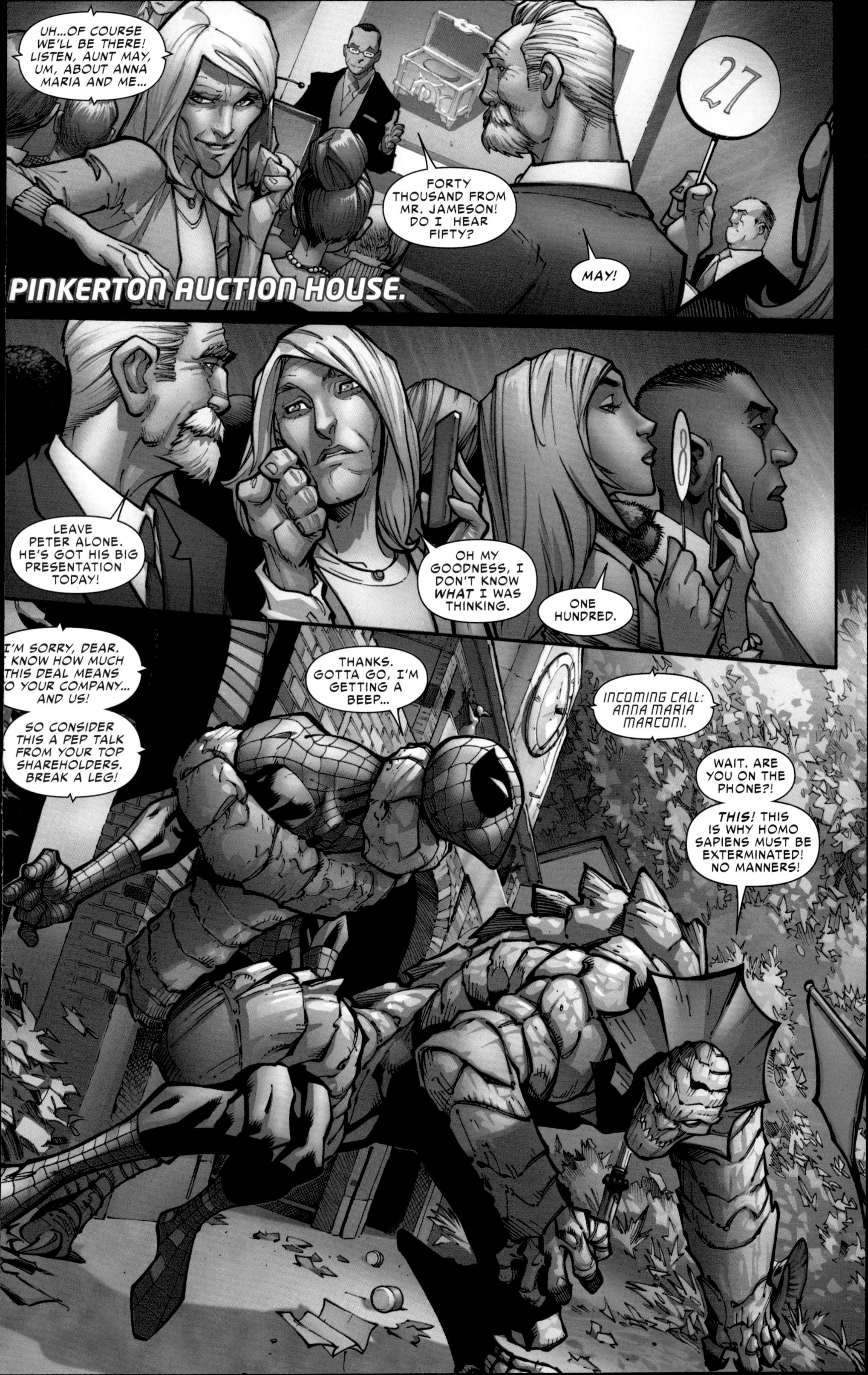
UH...OF COURSE WE'LL BE THERE! LISTEN, AUNT MAY, UM, ABOUT ANNA MARIA AND ME...
FORTY THOUSAND FROM MR. JAMESON! DO I HEAR FIFTY?
27
MAY!
PINKERTON AUCTION HOUSE.
LEAVE PETER ALONE. HE'S GOT HIS BIG PRESENTATION TODAY!
OH MY GOODNESS, I DON'T KNOW WHAT I WAS THINKING.
8
ONE HUNDRED.
I'M SORRY, DEAR. I KNOW HOW MUCH THIS DEAL MEANS TO YOUR COMPANY... AND US!
SO CONSIDER THIS A PEP TALK FROM YOUR TOP SHAREHOLDERS. BREAK A LEG!
THANKS. GOTTA GO, I'M GETTING A BEEP...
INCOMING CALL: ANNA MARIA MARCONI.
WAIT. ARE YOU ON THE PHONE?!
THIS! THIS IS WHY HOMO SAPIENS MUST BE EXTERMINATED! NO MANNERS!

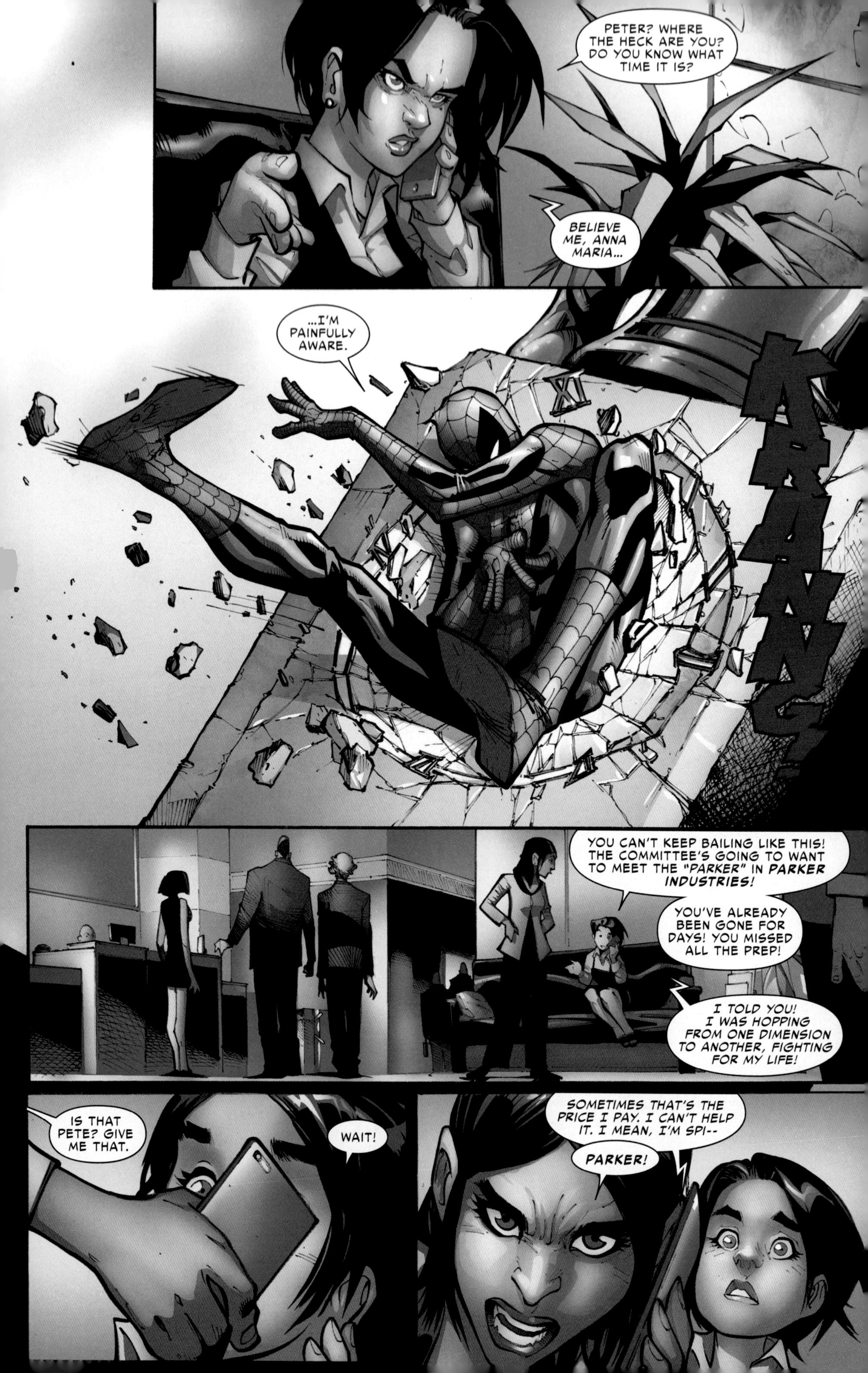
PETER? WHERE THE HECK ARE YOU? DO YOU KNOW WHAT TIME IT IS?
BELIEVE ME, ANNA MARIA...
...I'M PAINFULLY AWARE.
KRANNG!
YOU CAN'T KEEP BAILING LIKE THIS! THE COMMITTEE'S GOING TO WANT TO MEET THE "PARKER" IN PARKER INDUSTRIES!
YOU'VE ALREADY BEEN GONE FOR DAYS! YOU MISSED ALL THE PREP!
I TOLD YOU! I WAS HOPPING FROM ONE DIMENSION TO ANOTHER, FIGHTING FOR MY LIFE!
IS THAT PETE? GIVE ME THAT.
WAIT!
SOMETIMES THAT'S THE PRICE I PAY. I CAN'T HELP IT. I MEAN, I'M SPI--
PARKER!

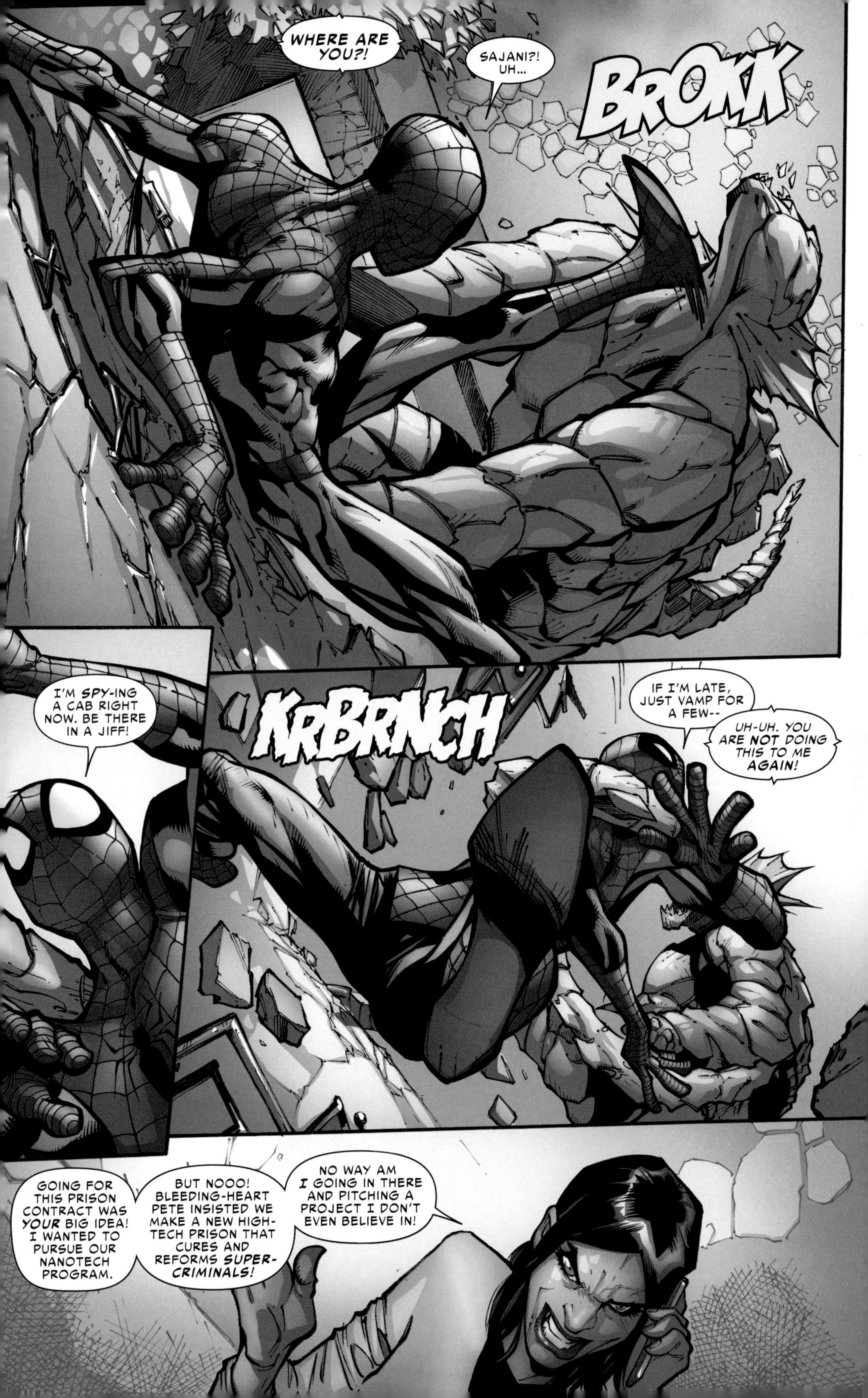
WHERE ARE YOU?!
SAJANI?! UH...
BROKK
I'M SPY-ING A CAB RIGHT NOW. BE THERE IN A JIFF!
KRBRNCH
IF I'M LATE, JUST VAMP FOR A FEW--
UH-UH. YOU ARE NOT DOING THIS TO ME AGAIN!
GOING FOR THIS PRISON CONTRACT WAS YOUR BIG IDEA! I WANTED TO PURSUE OUR NANOTECH PROGRAM.
BUT NOOO! BLEEDING-HEART PETE INSISTED WE MAKE A NEW HIGH-TECH PRISON THAT CURES AND REFORMS SUPER-CRIMINALS!
NO WAY AM I GOING IN THERE AND PITCHING A PROJECT I DON'T EVEN BELIEVE IN!

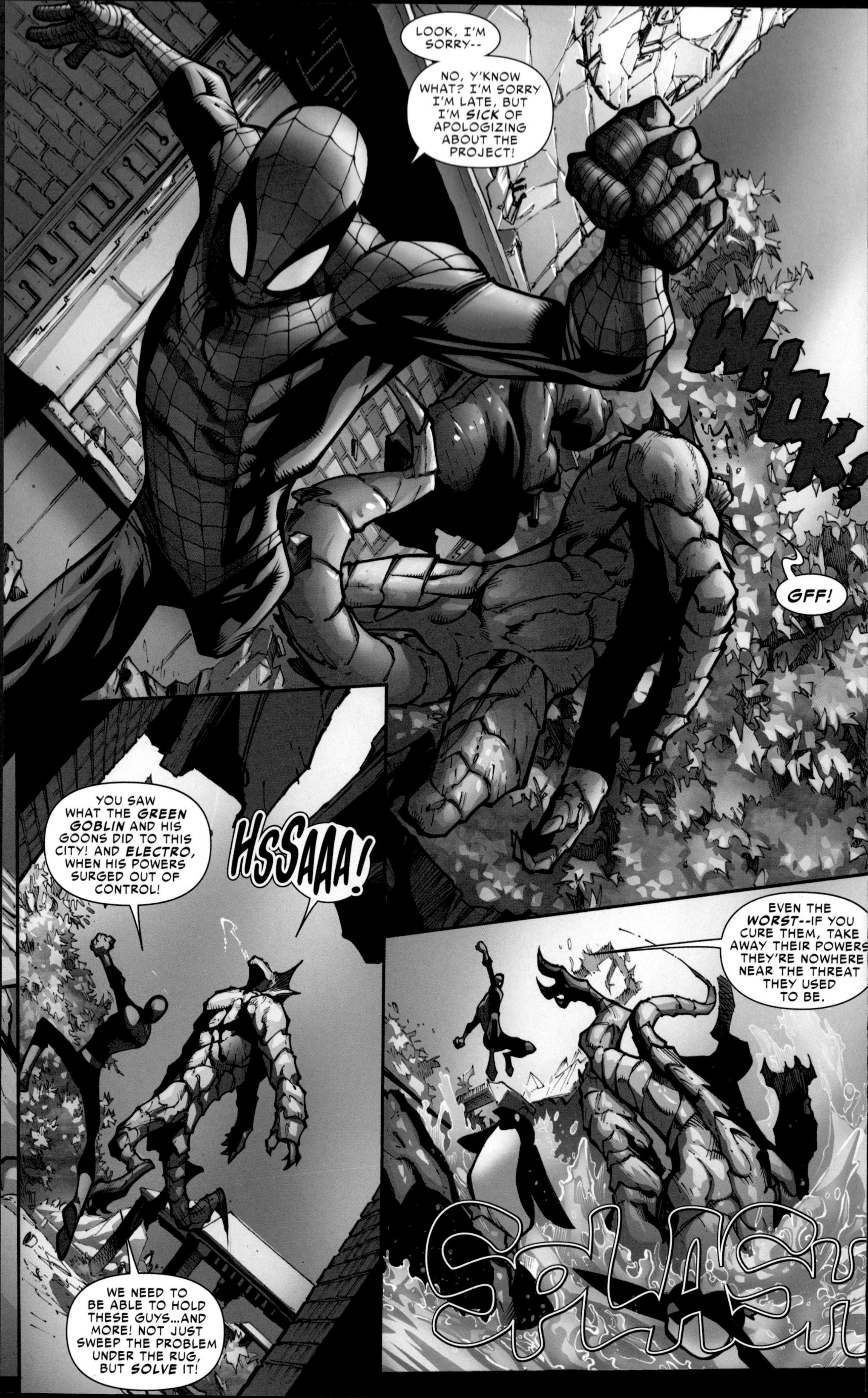
LOOK, I'M SORRY--
NO, Y'KNOW WHAT? I'M SORRY I'M LATE, BUT I'M SICK OF APOLOGIZING ABOUT THE PROJECT!
WHAK!
GFF!
YOU SAW WHAT THE GREEN GOBLIN AND HIS GOONS DID TO THIS CITY! AND ELECTRO, WHEN HIS POWERS SURGED OUT OF CONTROL!
HSSAAA!
WE NEED TO BE ABLE TO HOLD THESE GUYS...AND MORE! NOT JUST SWEEP THE PROBLEM UNDER THE RUG, BUT SOLVE IT!
EVEN THE WORST--IF YOU CURE THEM, TAKE AWAY THEIR POWERS THEY'RE NOWHERE NEAR THE THREAT THEY USED TO BE.
SPLASH

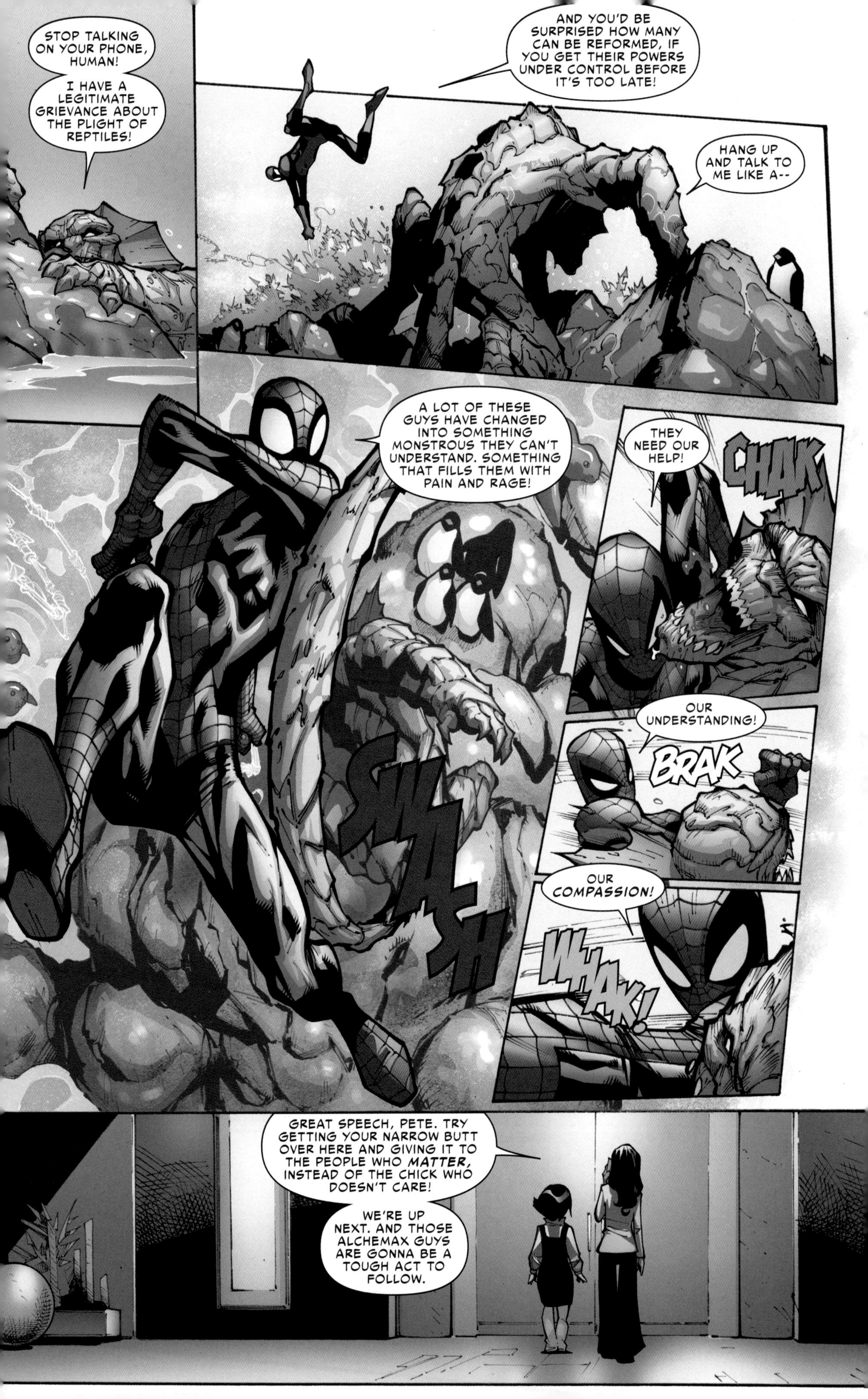

STOP TALKING ON YOUR PHONE, HUMAN!
I HAVE A LEGITIMATE GRIEVANCE ABOUT THE PLIGHT OF REPTILES!
AND YOU'D BE SURPRISED HOW MANY CAN BE REFORMED, IF YOU GET THEIR POWERS UNDER CONTROL BEFORE IT'S TOO LATE!
HANG UP AND TALK TO ME LIKE A--
A LOT OF THESE GUYS HAVE CHANGED INTO SOMETHING MONSTROUS THEY CAN'T UNDERSTAND. SOMETHING THAT FILLS THEM WITH PAIN AND RAGE!
SMASH
THEY NEED OUR HELP!
CHAK
OUR UNDERSTANDING!
BRAK
OUR COMPASSION!
WHAK!
GREAT SPEECH, PETE. TRY GETTING YOUR NARROW BUTT OVER HERE AND GIVING IT TO THE PEOPLE WHO *MATTER*, INSTEAD OF THE CHICK WHO DOESN'T CARE!
WE'RE UP NEXT. AND THOSE ALCHEMAX GUYS ARE GONNA BE A TOUGH ACT TO FOLLOW.

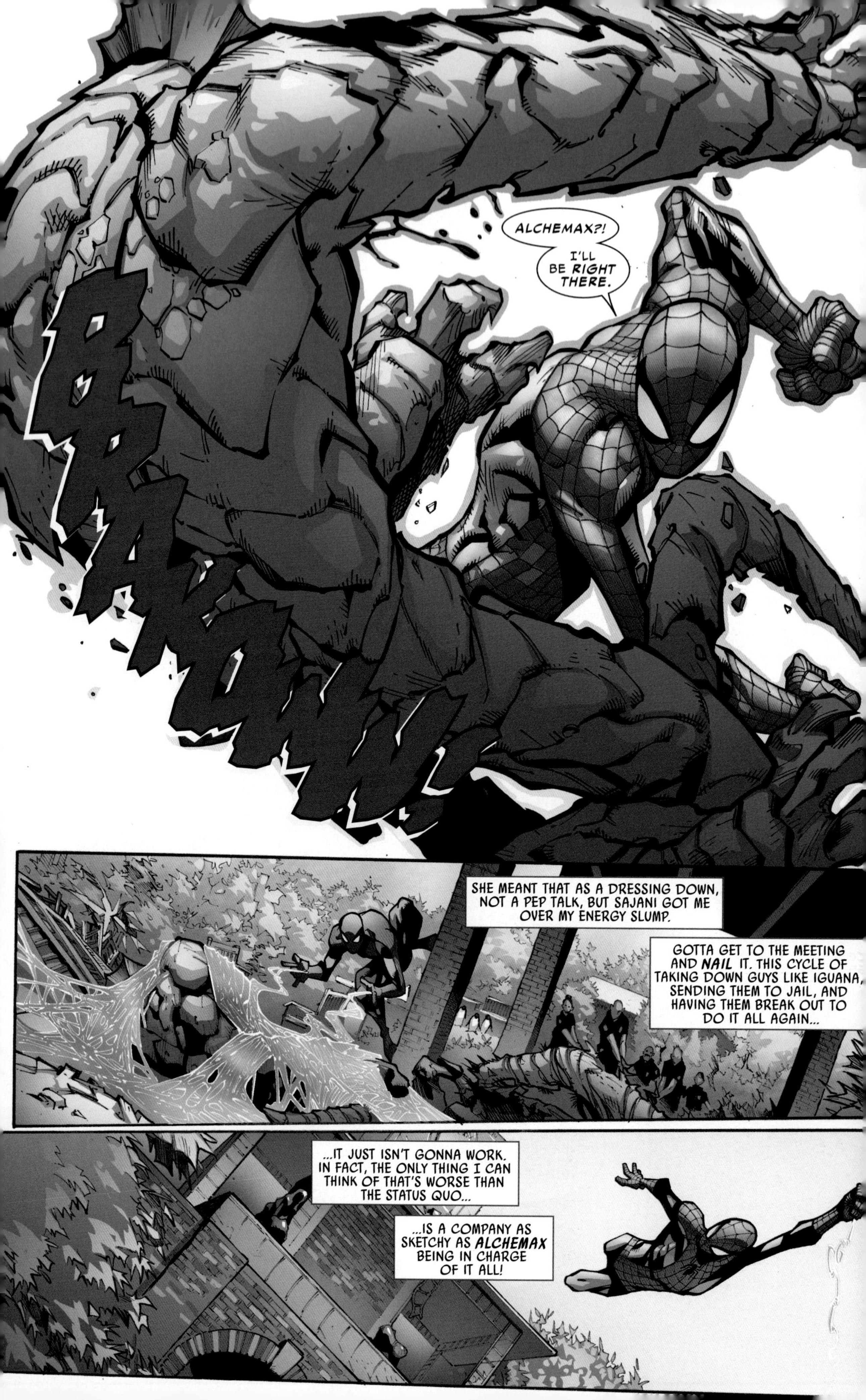
ALCHEMAX?!
I'LL BE RIGHT THERE.
SHE MEANT THAT AS A DRESSING DOWN, NOT A PEP TALK, BUT SAJANI GOT ME OVER MY ENERGY SLUMP.
GOTTA GET TO THE MEETING AND NAIL IT. THIS CYCLE OF TAKING DOWN GUYS LIKE IGUANA, SENDING THEM TO JAIL, AND HAVING THEM BREAK OUT TO DO IT ALL AGAIN...
...IT JUST ISN'T GONNA WORK. IN FACT, THE ONLY THING I CAN THINK OF THAT'S WORSE THAN THE STATUS QUO...
...IS A COMPANY AS SKETCHY AS ALCHEMAX BEING IN CHARGE OF IT ALL!

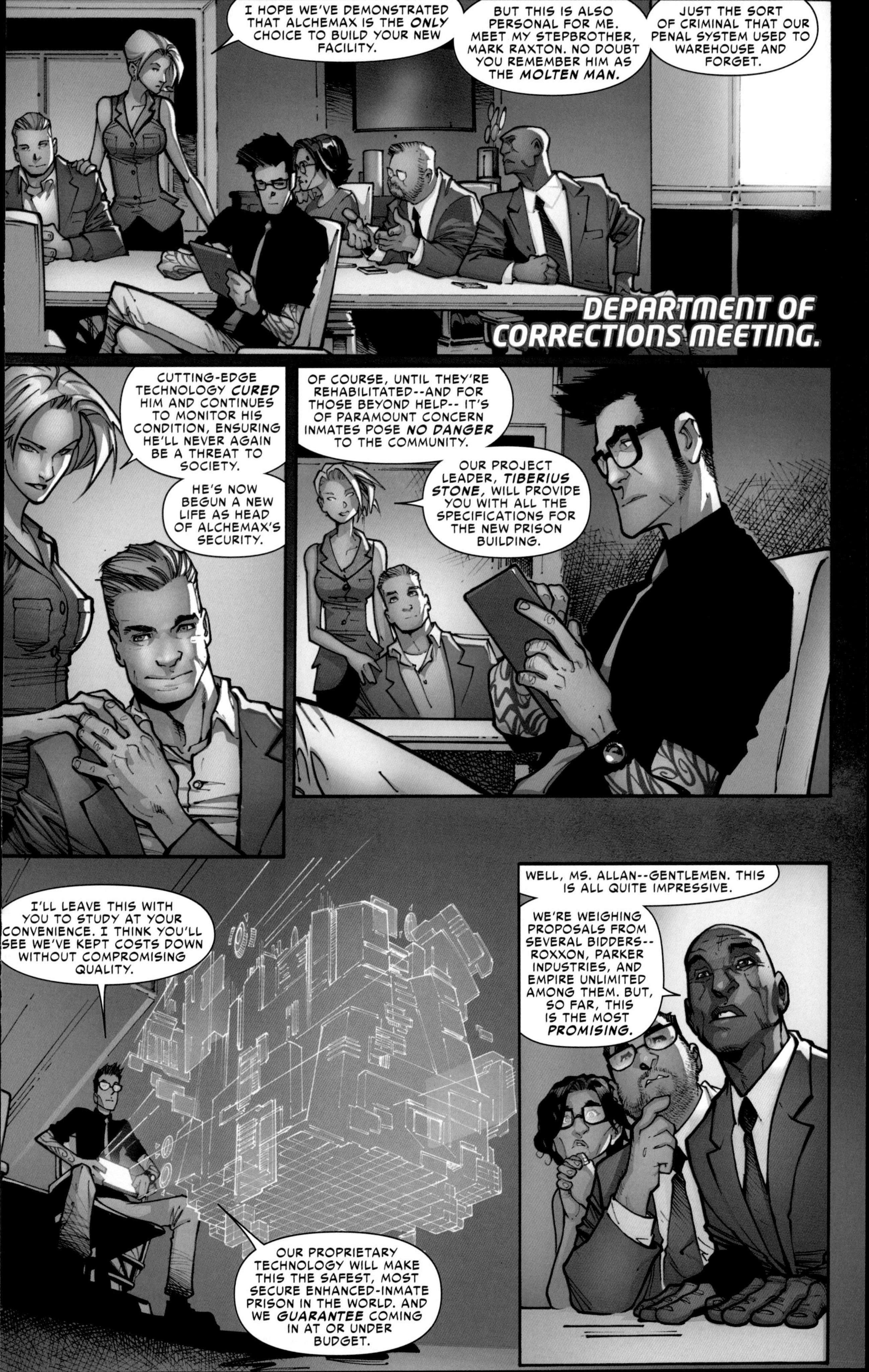

I HOPE WE'VE DEMONSTRATED THAT ALCHEMAX IS THE ONLY CHOICE TO BUILD YOUR NEW FACILITY.
BUT THIS IS ALSO PERSONAL FOR ME. MEET MY STEPBROTHER, MARK RAXTON. NO DOUBT YOU REMEMBER HIM AS THE MOLTEN MAN.
JUST THE SORT OF CRIMINAL THAT OUR PENAL SYSTEM USED TO WAREHOUSE AND FORGET.
DEPARTMENT OF CORRECTIONS MEETING.
CUTTING-EDGE TECHNOLOGY CURED HIM AND CONTINUES TO MONITOR HIS CONDITION, ENSURING HE'LL NEVER AGAIN BE A THREAT TO SOCIETY.
HE'S NOW BEGUN A NEW LIFE AS HEAD OF ALCHEMAX'S SECURITY.
OF COURSE, UNTIL THEY'RE REHABILITATED--AND FOR THOSE BEYOND HELP-- IT'S OF PARAMOUNT CONCERN INMATES POSE NO DANGER TO THE COMMUNITY.
OUR PROJECT LEADER, TIBERIUS STONE, WILL PROVIDE YOU WITH ALL THE SPECIFICATIONS FOR THE NEW PRISON BUILDING.
I'LL LEAVE THIS WITH YOU TO STUDY AT YOUR CONVENIENCE. I THINK YOU'LL SEE WE'VE KEPT COSTS DOWN WITHOUT COMPROMISING QUALITY.
OUR PROPRIETARY TECHNOLOGY WILL MAKE THIS THE SAFEST, MOST SECURE ENHANCED-INMATE PRISON IN THE WORLD. AND WE GUARANTEE COMING IN AT OR UNDER BUDGET.
WELL, MS. ALLAN--GENTLEMEN. THIS IS ALL QUITE IMPRESSIVE.
WE'RE WEIGHING PROPOSALS FROM SEVERAL BIDDERS-- ROXXON, PARKER INDUSTRIES, AND EMPIRE UNLIMITED AMONG THEM. BUT, SO FAR, THIS IS THE MOST PROMISING.

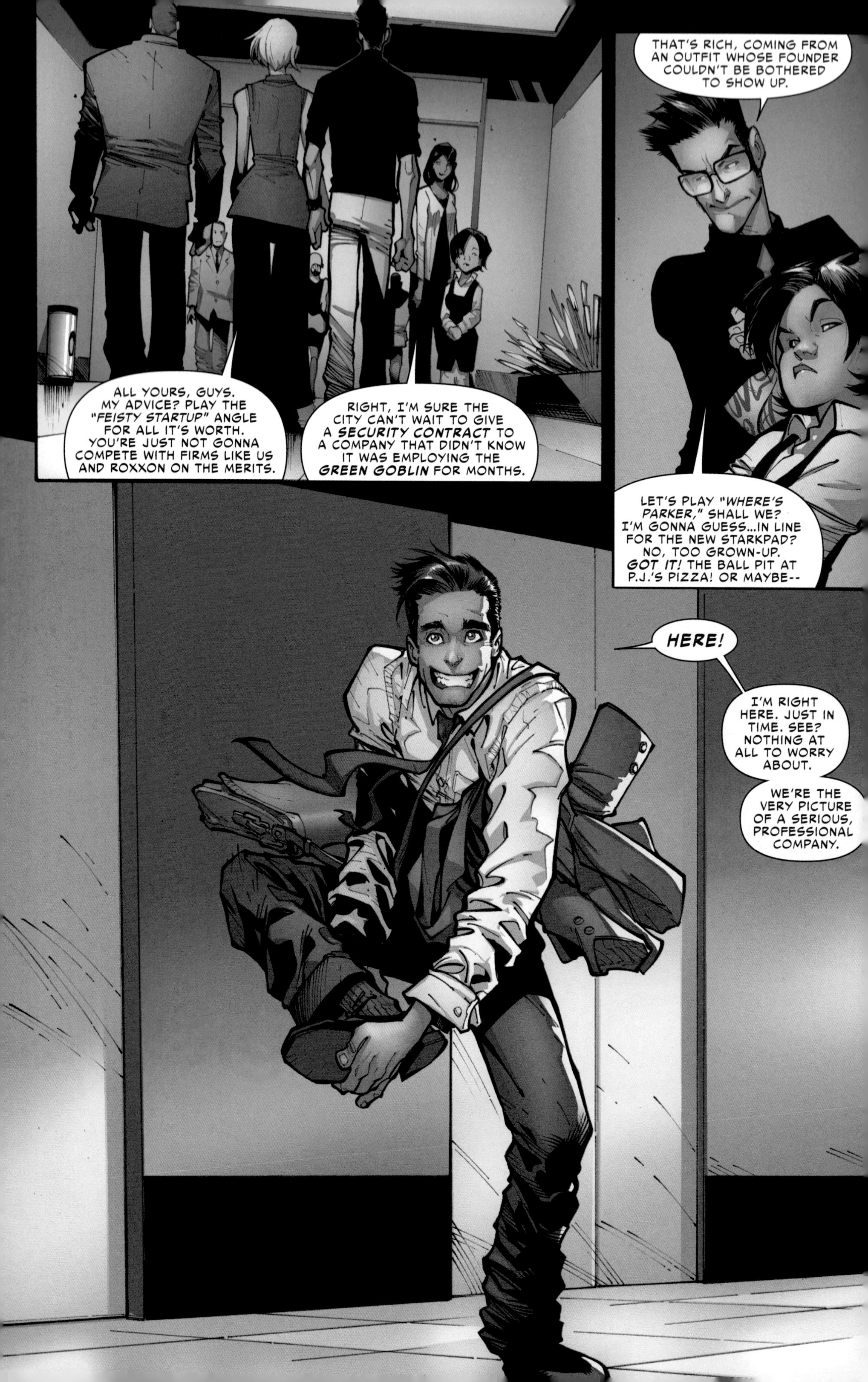
ALL YOURS, GUYS. MY ADVICE? PLAY THE "FEISTY STARTUP" ANGLE FOR ALL IT'S WORTH. YOU'RE JUST NOT GONNA COMPETE WITH FIRMS LIKE US AND ROXXON ON THE MERITS.
RIGHT, I'M SURE THE CITY CAN'T WAIT TO GIVE A SECURITY CONTRACT TO A COMPANY THAT DIDN'T KNOW IT WAS EMPLOYING THE GREEN GOBLIN FOR MONTHS.
THAT'S RICH, COMING FROM AN OUTFIT WHOSE FOUNDER COULDN'T BE BOTHERED TO SHOW UP.
LET'S PLAY "WHERE'S PARKER," SHALL WE? I'M GONNA GUESS...IN LINE FOR THE NEW STARKPAD? NO, TOO GROWN-UP. GOT IT! THE BALL PIT AT P.J.'S PIZZA! OR MAYBE--
HERE!
I'M RIGHT HERE. JUST IN TIME. SEE? NOTHING AT ALL TO WORRY ABOUT.
WE'RE THE VERY PICTURE OF A SERIOUS, PROFESSIONAL COMPANY.

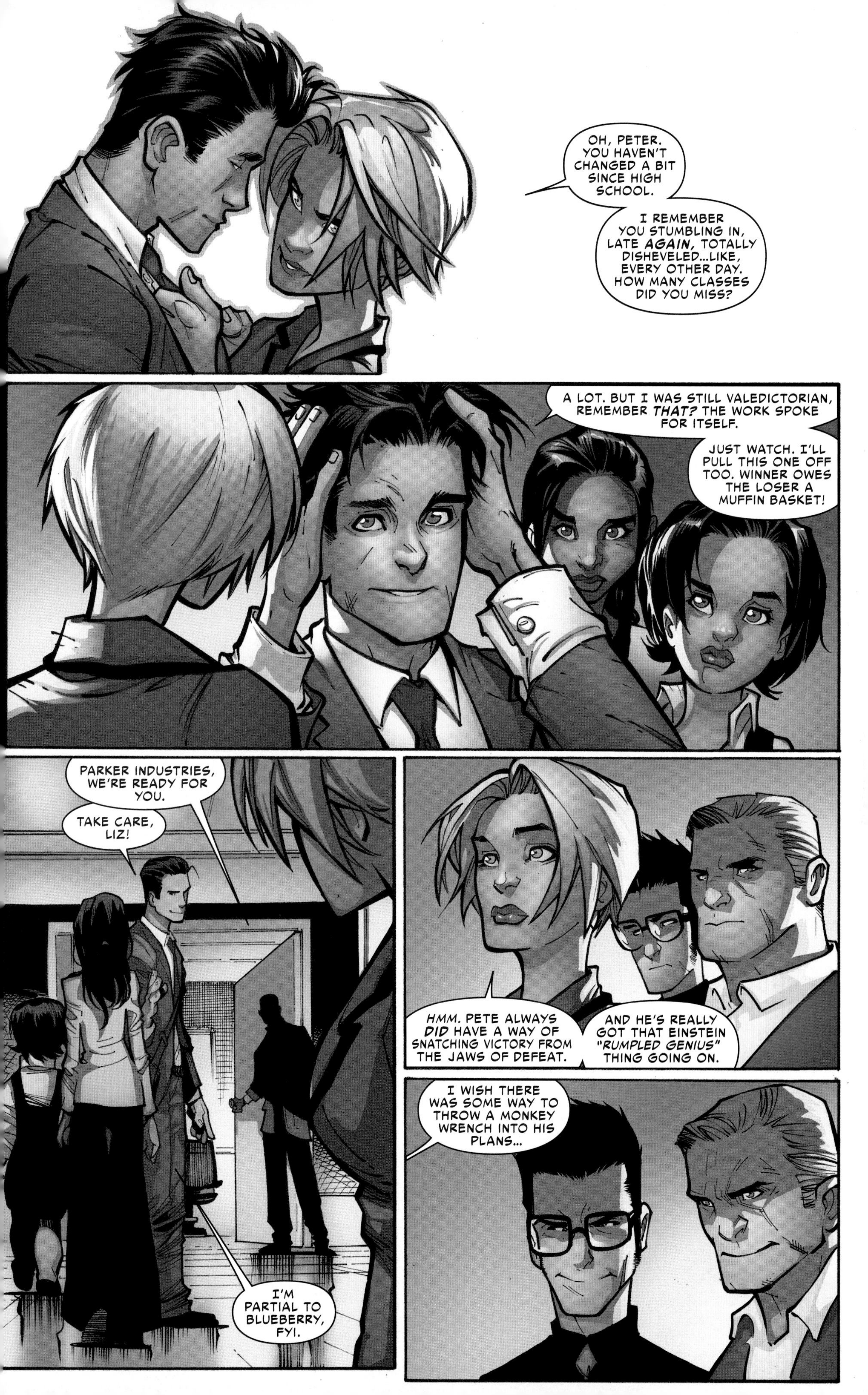
OH, PETER. YOU HAVEN'T CHANGED A BIT SINCE HIGH SCHOOL.
I REMEMBER YOU STUMBLING IN, LATE *AGAIN*, TOTALLY DISHEVELED...LIKE, EVERY OTHER DAY. HOW MANY CLASSES DID YOU MISS?
A LOT. BUT I WAS STILL VALEDICTORIAN, REMEMBER *THAT?* THE WORK SPOKE FOR ITSELF.
JUST WATCH. I'LL PULL THIS ONE OFF TOO. WINNER OWES THE LOSER A MUFFIN BASKET!
PARKER INDUSTRIES, WE'RE READY FOR YOU.
TAKE CARE, LIZ!
I'M PARTIAL TO BLUEBERRY, FYI.
HMM. PETE ALWAYS *DID* HAVE A WAY OF SNATCHING VICTORY FROM THE JAWS OF DEFEAT.
AND HE'S REALLY GOT THAT EINSTEIN *"RUMPLED GENIUS"* THING GOING ON.
I WISH THERE WAS SOME WAY TO THROW A MONKEY WRENCH INTO HIS PLANS...

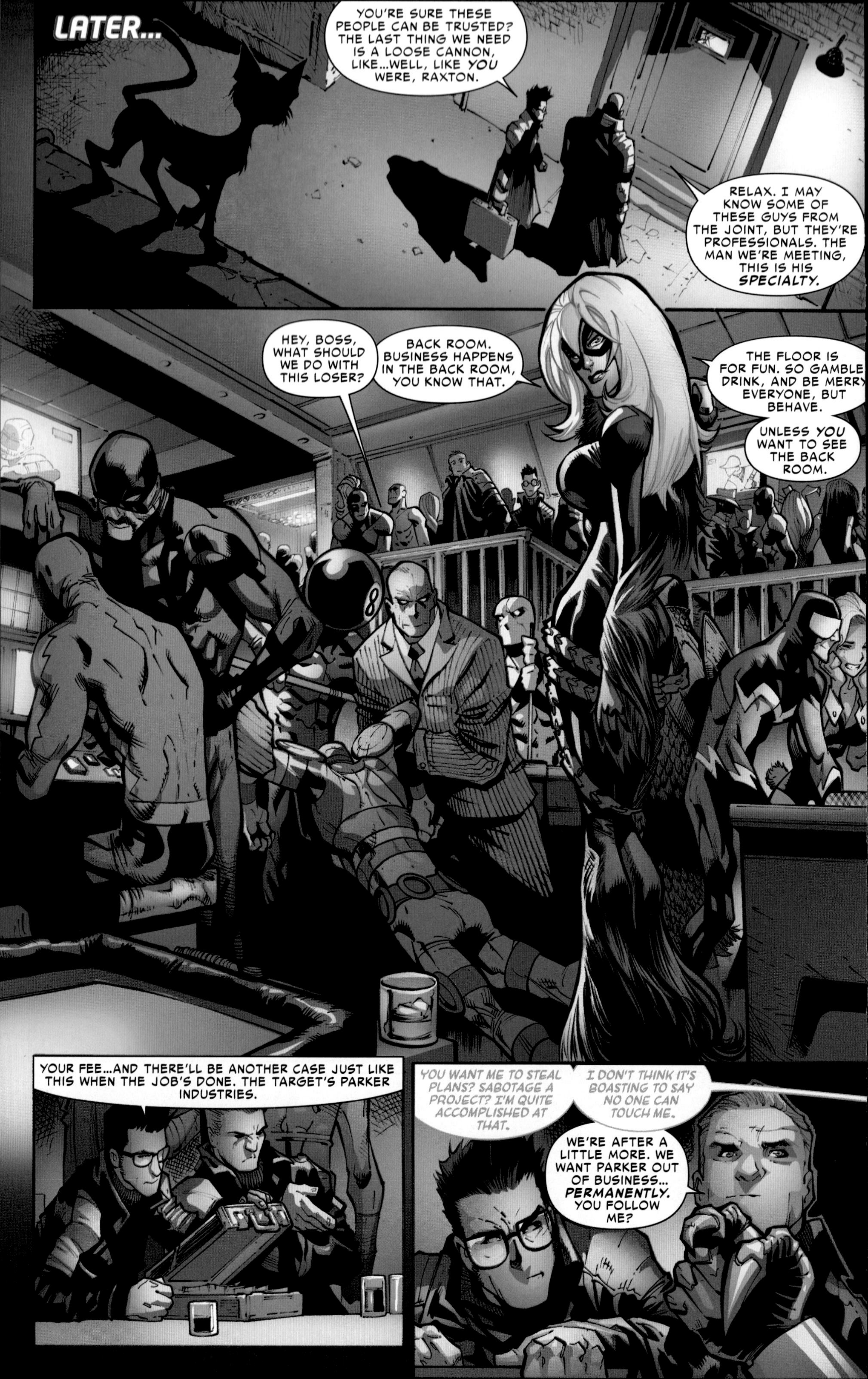
LATER...
YOU'RE SURE THESE PEOPLE CAN BE TRUSTED? THE LAST THING WE NEED IS A LOOSE CANNON, LIKE...WELL, LIKE YOU WERE, RAXTON.
RELAX. I MAY KNOW SOME OF THESE GUYS FROM THE JOINT, BUT THEY'RE PROFESSIONALS. THE MAN WE'RE MEETING, THIS IS HIS SPECIALTY.
HEY, BOSS, WHAT SHOULD WE DO WITH THIS LOSER?
BACK ROOM. BUSINESS HAPPENS IN THE BACK ROOM, YOU KNOW THAT.
THE FLOOR IS FOR FUN. SO GAMBLE DRINK, AND BE MERRY EVERYONE, BUT BEHAVE.
UNLESS YOU WANT TO SEE THE BACK ROOM.
YOUR FEE...AND THERE'LL BE ANOTHER CASE JUST LIKE THIS WHEN THE JOB'S DONE. THE TARGET'S PARKER INDUSTRIES.
YOU WANT ME TO STEAL PLANS? SABOTAGE A PROJECT? I'M QUITE ACCOMPLISHED AT THAT.
I DON'T THINK IT'S BOASTING TO SAY NO ONE CAN TOUCH ME.
WE'RE AFTER A LITTLE MORE. WE WANT PARKER OUT OF BUSINESS... PERMANENTLY. YOU FOLLOW ME?

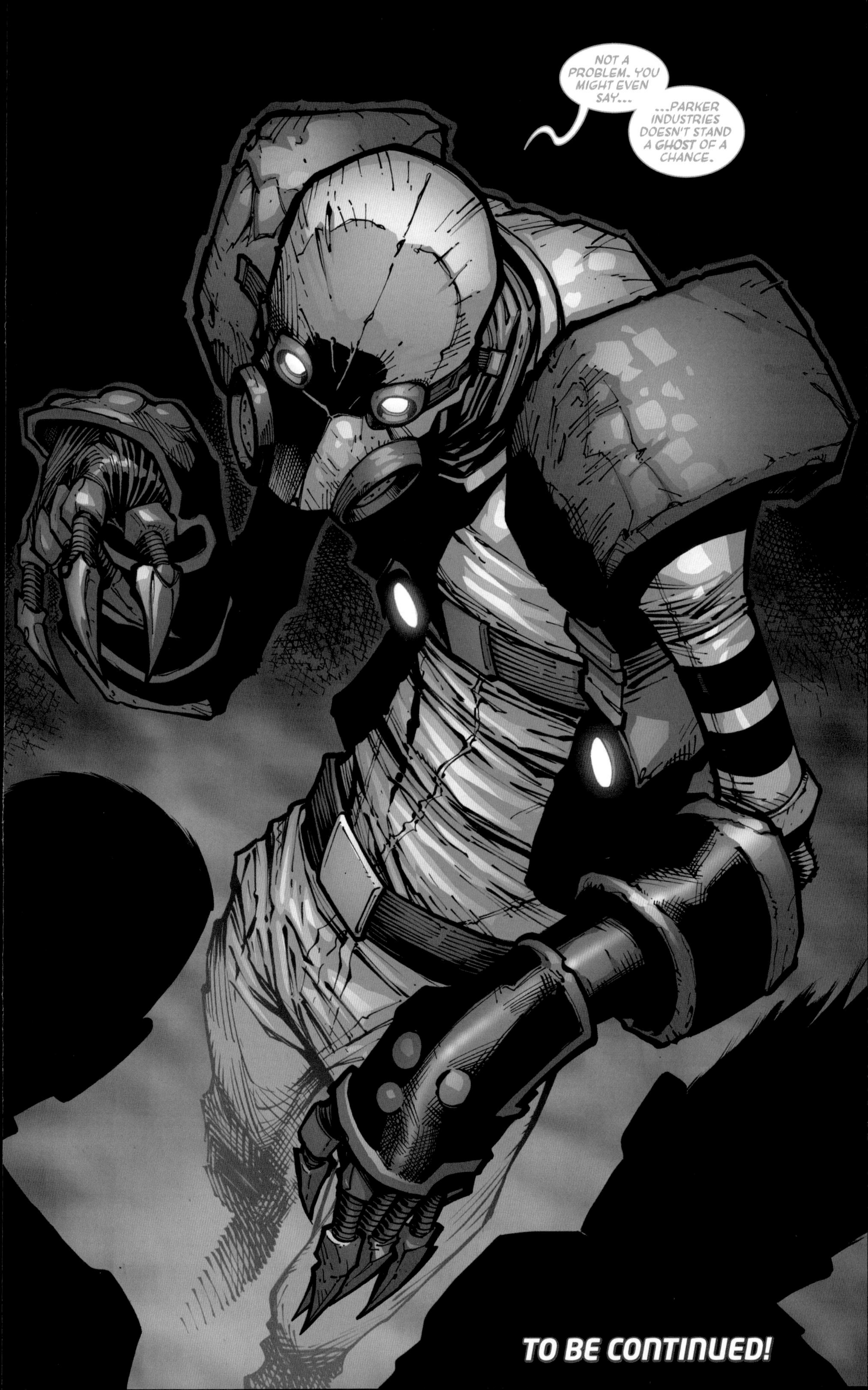
NOT A PROBLEM. YOU MIGHT EVEN SAY...
...PARKER INDUSTRIES DOESN'T STAND A GHOST OF A CHANCE.
TO BE CONTINUED!

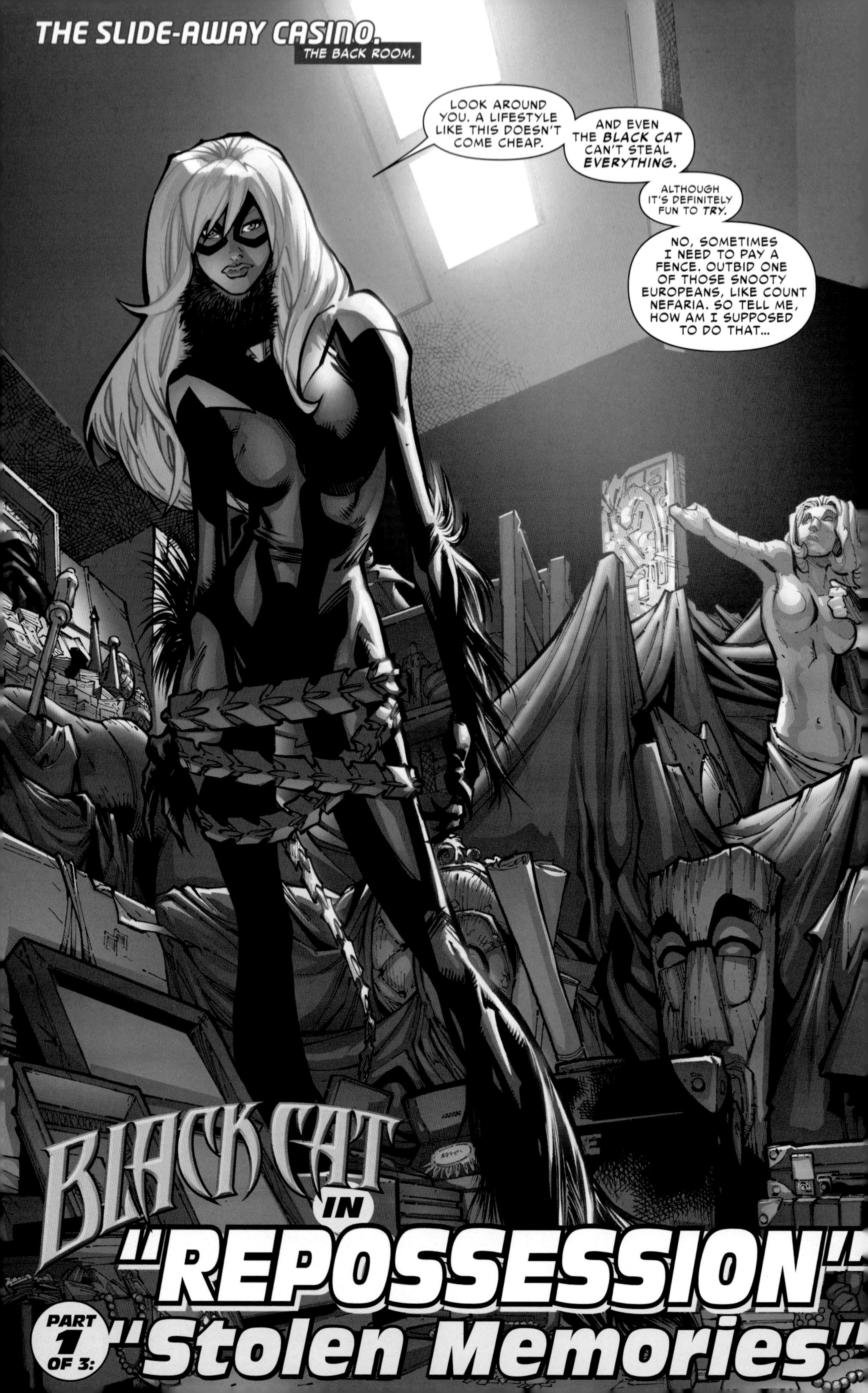
THE SLIDE-AWAY CASINO.
THE BACK ROOM.
LOOK AROUND YOU. A LIFESTYLE LIKE THIS DOESN'T COME CHEAP.
AND EVEN THE BLACK CAT CAN'T STEAL EVERYTHING.
ALTHOUGH IT'S DEFINITELY FUN TO TRY.
NO, SOMETIMES I NEED TO PAY A FENCE. OUTBID ONE OF THOSE SNOOTY EUROPEANS, LIKE COUNT NEFARIA. SO TELL ME, HOW AM I SUPPOSED TO DO THAT...
BLACK CAT
IN
"REPOSSESSION"
PART 1 OF 3: "Stolen Memories"

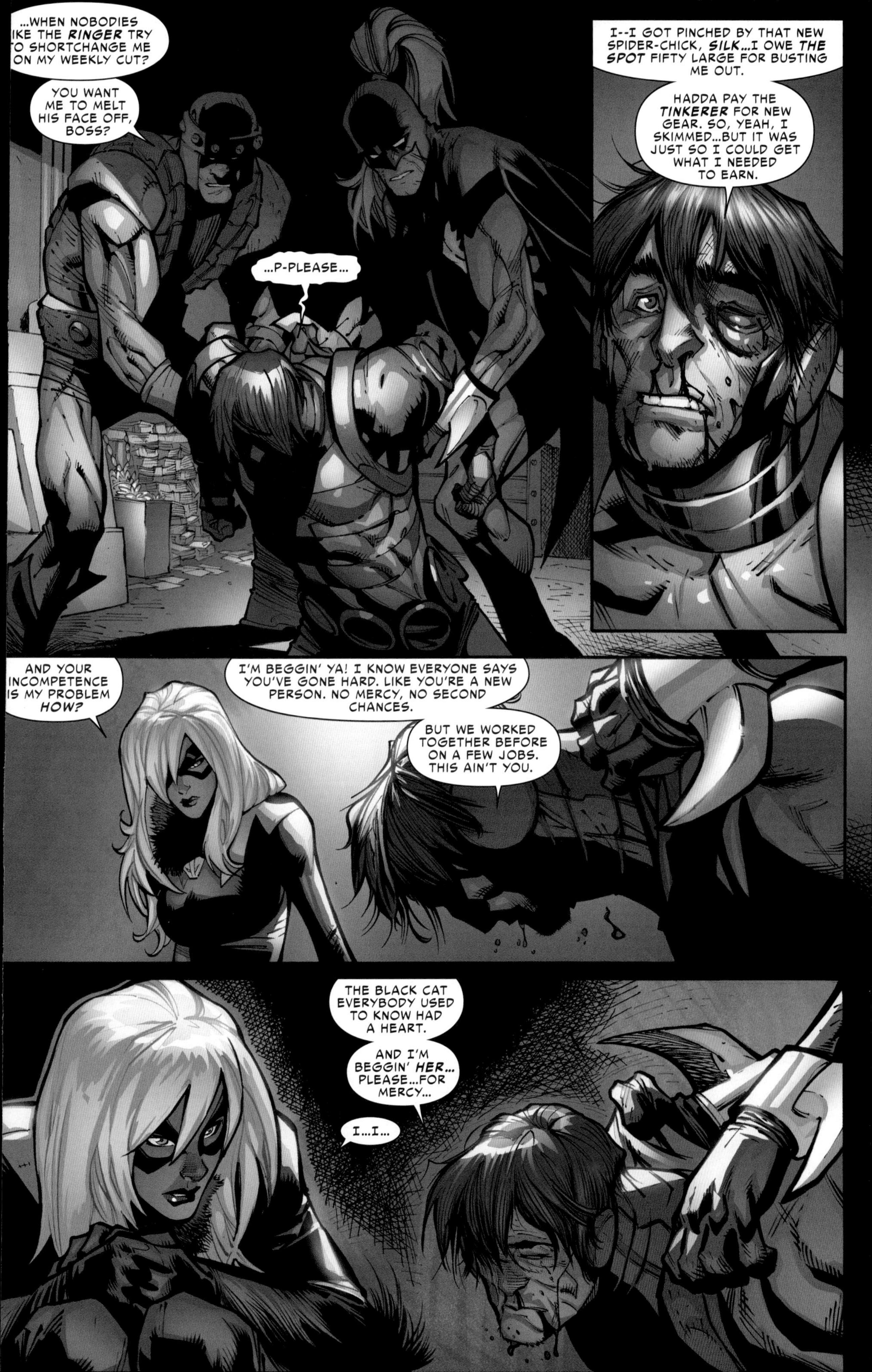
...WHEN NOBODIES LIKE THE RINGER TRY TO SHORTCHANGE ME ON MY WEEKLY CUT?
YOU WANT ME TO MELT HIS FACE OFF, BOSS?
...P-PLEASE...
I--I GOT PINCHED BY THAT NEW SPIDER-CHICK, SILK...I OWE THE SPOT FIFTY LARGE FOR BUSTING ME OUT.
HADDA PAY THE TINKERER FOR NEW GEAR. SO, YEAH, I SKIMMED...BUT IT WAS JUST SO I COULD GET WHAT I NEEDED TO EARN.
AND YOUR INCOMPETENCE IS MY PROBLEM HOW?
I'M BEGGIN' YA! I KNOW EVERYONE SAYS YOU'VE GONE HARD. LIKE YOU'RE A NEW PERSON. NO MERCY, NO SECOND CHANCES.
BUT WE WORKED TOGETHER BEFORE ON A FEW JOBS. THIS AIN'T YOU.
THE BLACK CAT EVERYBODY USED TO KNOW HAD A HEART.
AND I'M BEGGIN' HER... PLEASE...FOR MERCY...
I...I...

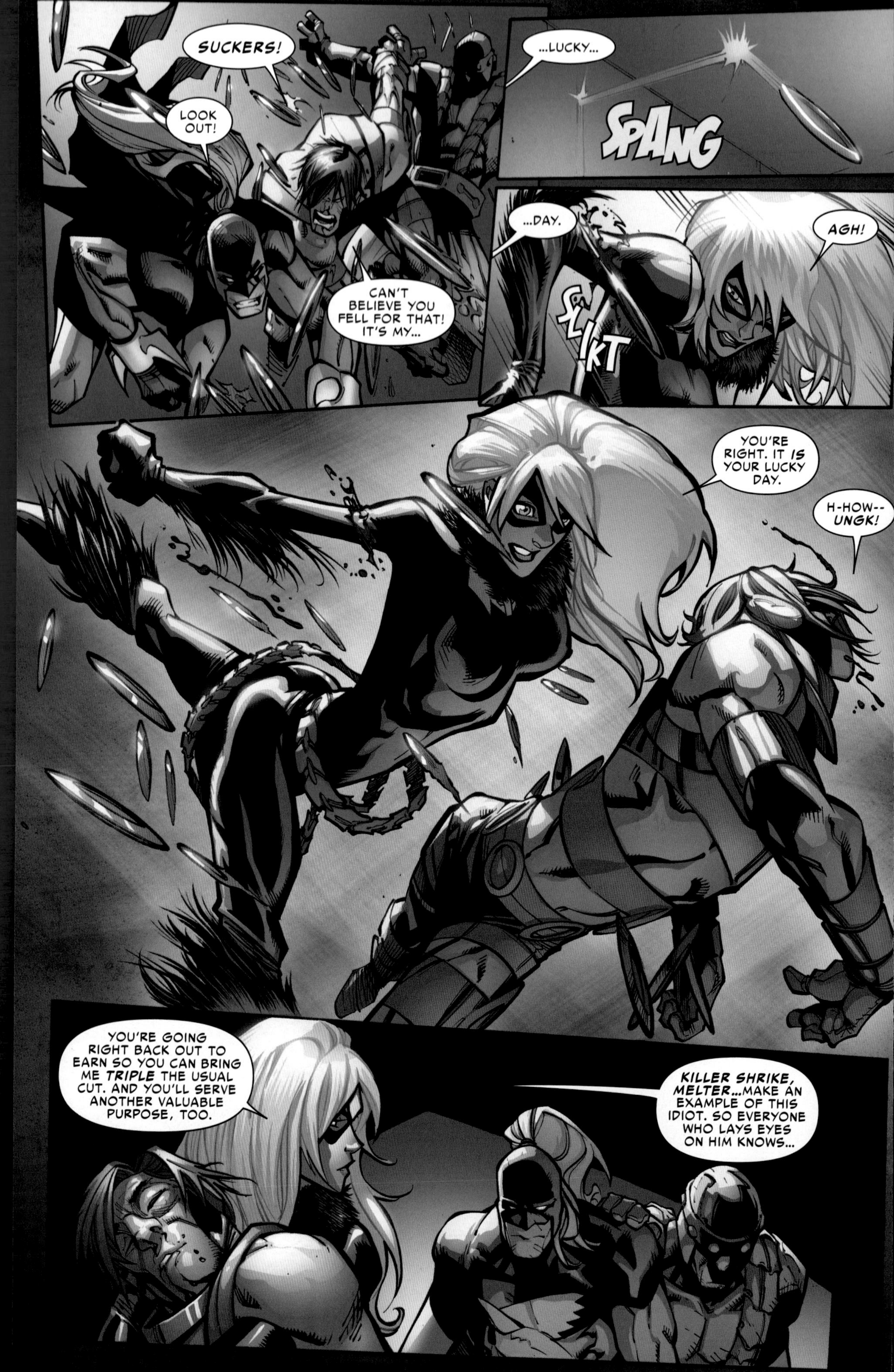
SUCKERS!
LOOK OUT!
CAN'T BELIEVE YOU FELL FOR THAT! IT'S MY...
...LUCKY...
SPANG
...DAY.
AGH!
SLIKT
YOU'RE RIGHT. IT IS YOUR LUCKY DAY.
H-HOW-- UNGK!
YOU'RE GOING RIGHT BACK OUT TO EARN SO YOU CAN BRING ME TRIPLE THE USUAL CUT. AND YOU'LL SERVE ANOTHER VALUABLE PURPOSE, TOO.
KILLER SHRIKE, MELTER...MAKE AN EXAMPLE OF THIS IDIOT. SO EVERYONE WHO LAYS EYES ON HIM KNOWS...

...YOU DON'T CROSS THE BLACK CAT.

OUR PLEASURE, BOSS.

SHZZZ

GGAAAIIEEE!

CAN'T BELIEVE HE TAGGED ME. I'M USUALLY NOT THAT UNLUCKY. UNLESS...THAT *WAS* LUCKY. TO REMIND ME WHO I AM NOW.

WELL, THERE'S AN EASY WAY TO FIND OUT. THE REASON I SET UP SHOP IN A CASINO: I NEVER HAVE TO GO FAR...

...TO TEST MY LUCK.

CHUNG

WHIRRRR

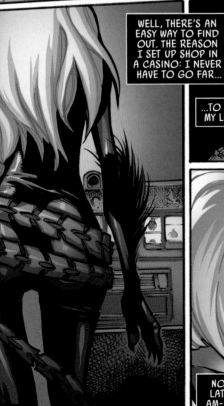

NOTICED SOMETHING LATELY. THE HARDER I AM--THE MORE I LISTEN TO THE PART OF ME THAT SAYS NOT TO LET ANYONE OR ANYTHING *EVER* PUT ME DOWN AGAIN--

--THE MORE MY LUCK POWERS GO OFF THE CHARTS.

DING DING DING

JACKPOT JACKPOT JACKPOT JACKPOT

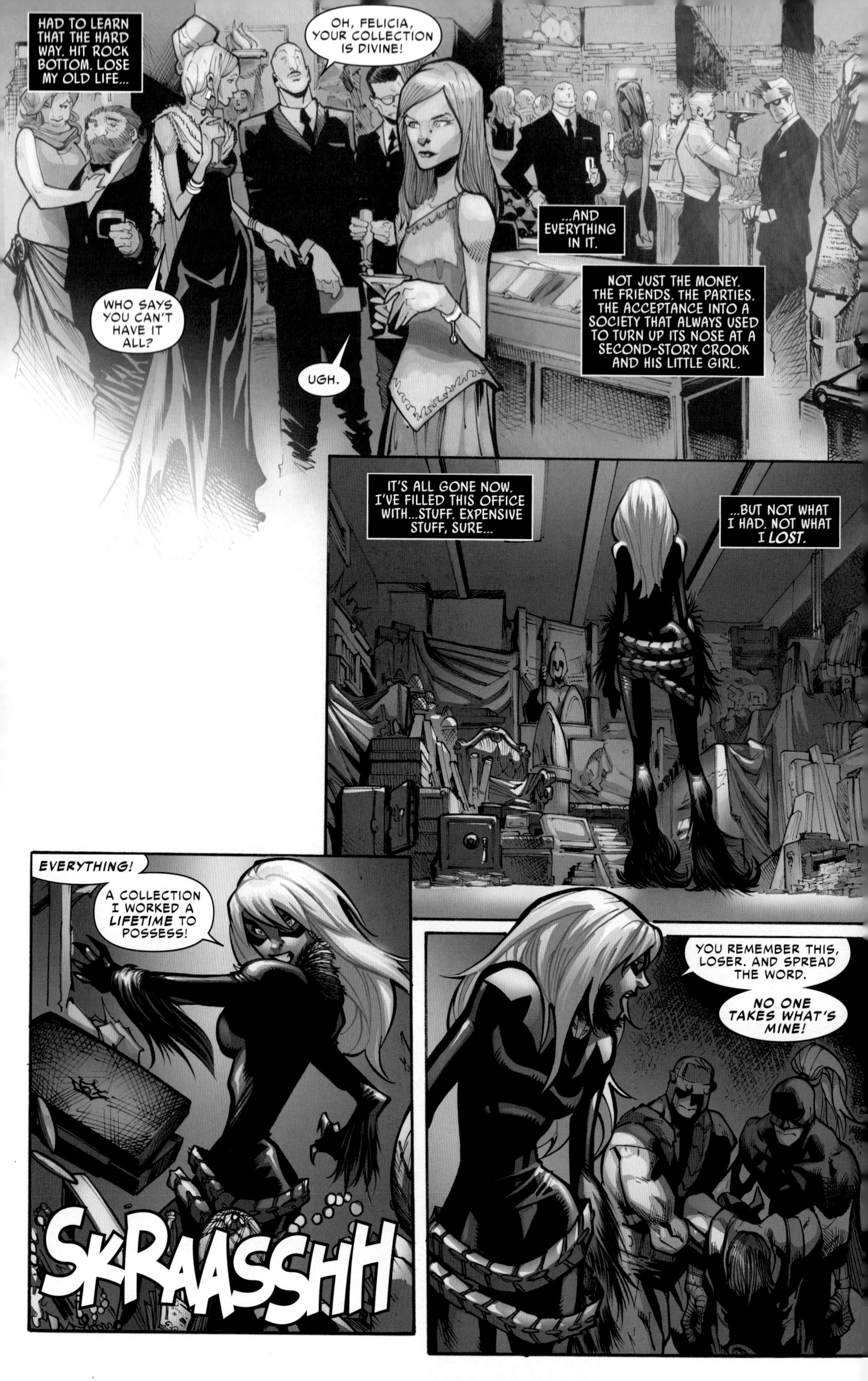
HAD TO LEARN THAT THE HARD WAY. HIT ROCK BOTTOM. LOSE MY OLD LIFE...
OH, FELICIA, YOUR COLLECTION IS DIVINE!
WHO SAYS YOU CAN'T HAVE IT ALL?
UGH.
...AND EVERYTHING IN IT.
NOT JUST THE MONEY. THE FRIENDS. THE PARTIES. THE ACCEPTANCE INTO A SOCIETY THAT ALWAYS USED TO TURN UP ITS NOSE AT A SECOND-STORY CROOK AND HIS LITTLE GIRL.
IT'S ALL GONE NOW. I'VE FILLED THIS OFFICE WITH...STUFF. EXPENSIVE STUFF, SURE...
...BUT NOT WHAT I HAD. NOT WHAT I LOST.
EVERYTHING!
A COLLECTION I WORKED A LIFETIME TO POSSESS!
SKRAASSHH
YOU REMEMBER THIS, LOSER. AND SPREAD THE WORD.
NO ONE TAKES WHAT'S MINE!

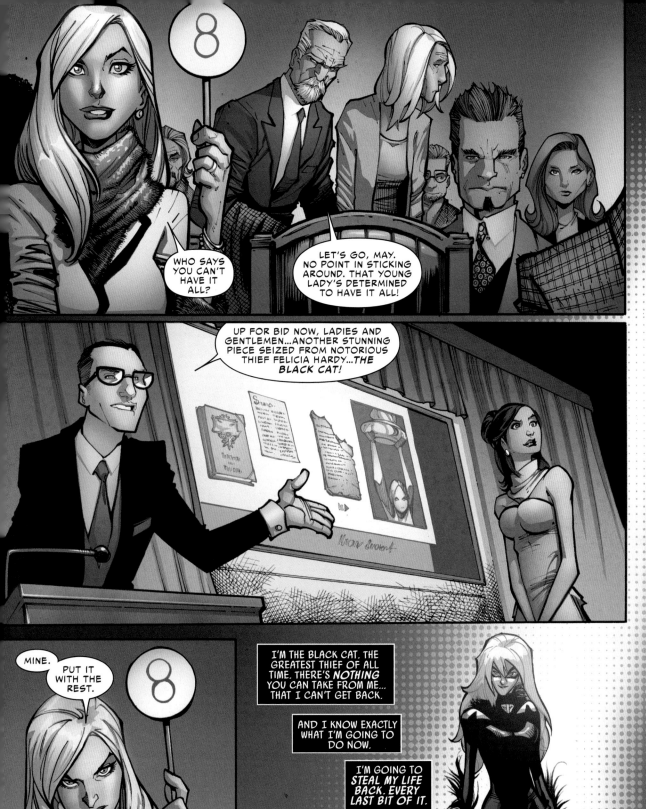

WHO SAYS YOU CAN'T HAVE IT ALL?

LET'S GO, MAY. NO POINT IN STICKING AROUND. THAT YOUNG LADY'S DETERMINED TO HAVE IT ALL!

UP FOR BID NOW, LADIES AND GENTLEMEN...ANOTHER STUNNING PIECE SEIZED FROM NOTORIOUS THIEF FELICIA HARDY...*THE BLACK CAT!*

MINE.

PUT IT WITH THE REST.

I'M THE BLACK CAT. THE GREATEST THIEF OF ALL TIME. THERE'S *NOTHING* YOU CAN TAKE FROM ME... THAT I CAN'T GET BACK.

AND I KNOW EXACTLY WHAT I'M GOING TO DO NOW.

I'M GOING TO *STEAL MY LIFE BACK. EVERY LAST BIT OF IT.*

TO BE CONTINUED!

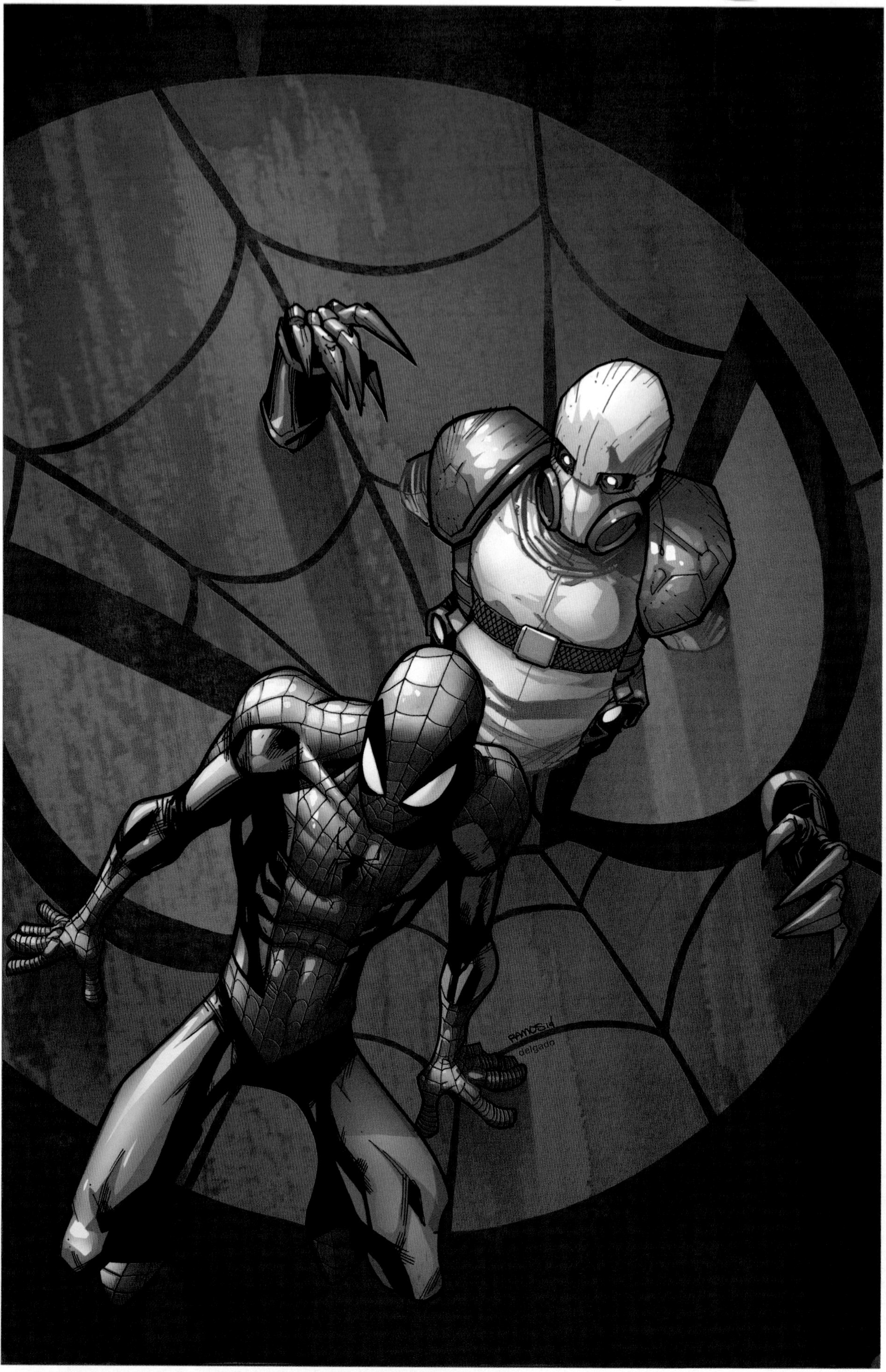

AMAZING SPIDER-MAN 17
GRAVEYARD SHIFT, PART TWO: TRUST ISSUES

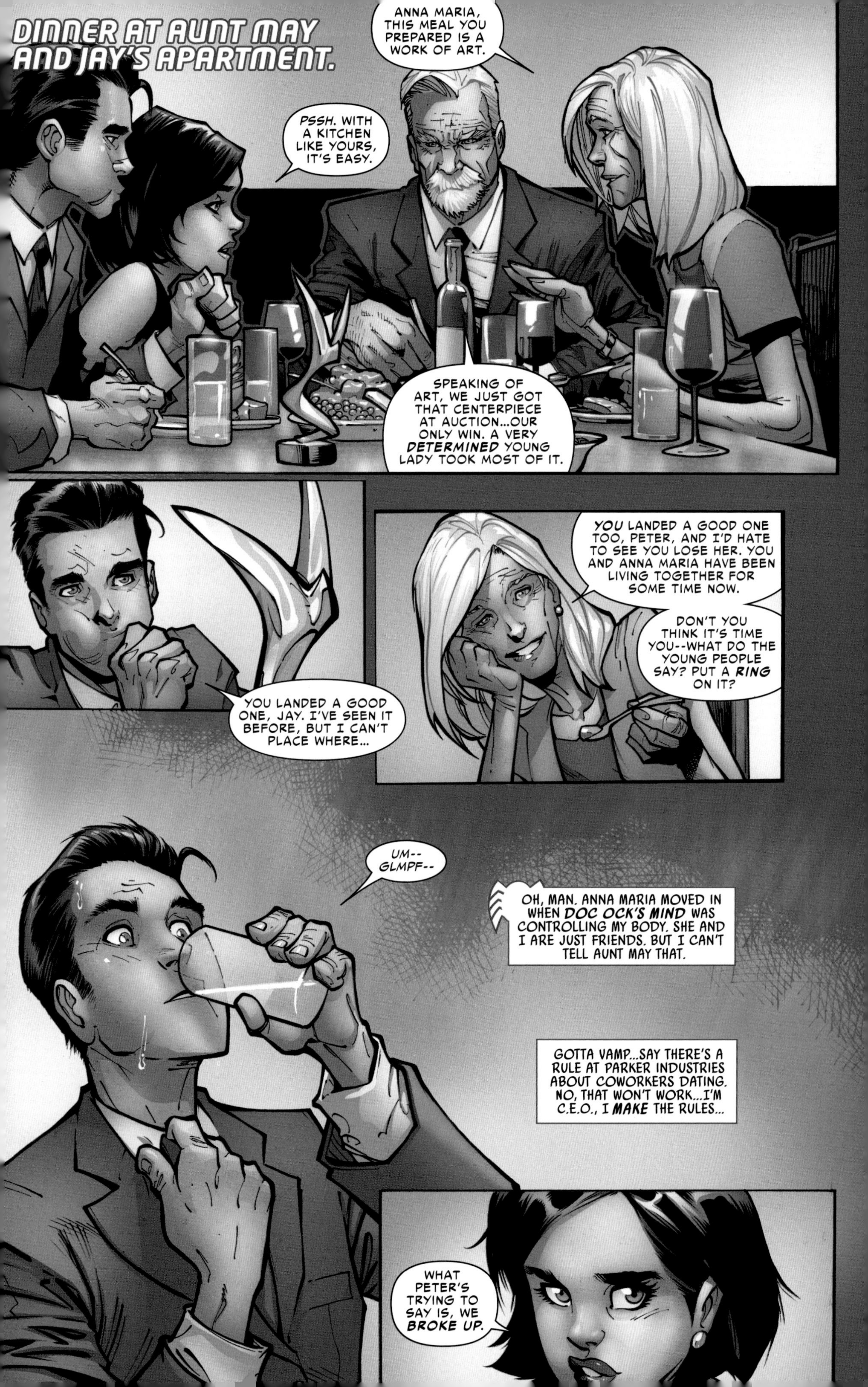
DINNER AT AUNT MAY AND JAY'S APARTMENT.
ANNA MARIA, THIS MEAL YOU PREPARED IS A WORK OF ART.
PSSH. WITH A KITCHEN LIKE YOURS, IT'S EASY.
SPEAKING OF ART, WE JUST GOT THAT CENTERPIECE AT AUCTION...OUR ONLY WIN. A VERY DETERMINED YOUNG LADY TOOK MOST OF IT.
YOU LANDED A GOOD ONE, JAY. I'VE SEEN IT BEFORE, BUT I CAN'T PLACE WHERE...
YOU LANDED A GOOD ONE TOO, PETER, AND I'D HATE TO SEE YOU LOSE HER. YOU AND ANNA MARIA HAVE BEEN LIVING TOGETHER FOR SOME TIME NOW.
DON'T YOU THINK IT'S TIME YOU--WHAT DO THE YOUNG PEOPLE SAY? PUT A RING ON IT?
UM-- GLMPF--
OH, MAN. ANNA MARIA MOVED IN WHEN DOC OCK'S MIND WAS CONTROLLING MY BODY. SHE AND I ARE JUST FRIENDS. BUT I CAN'T TELL AUNT MAY THAT.
GOTTA VAMP...SAY THERE'S A RULE AT PARKER INDUSTRIES ABOUT COWORKERS DATING. NO, THAT WON'T WORK...I'M C.E.O., I MAKE THE RULES...
WHAT PETER'S TRYING TO SAY IS, WE BROKE UP.

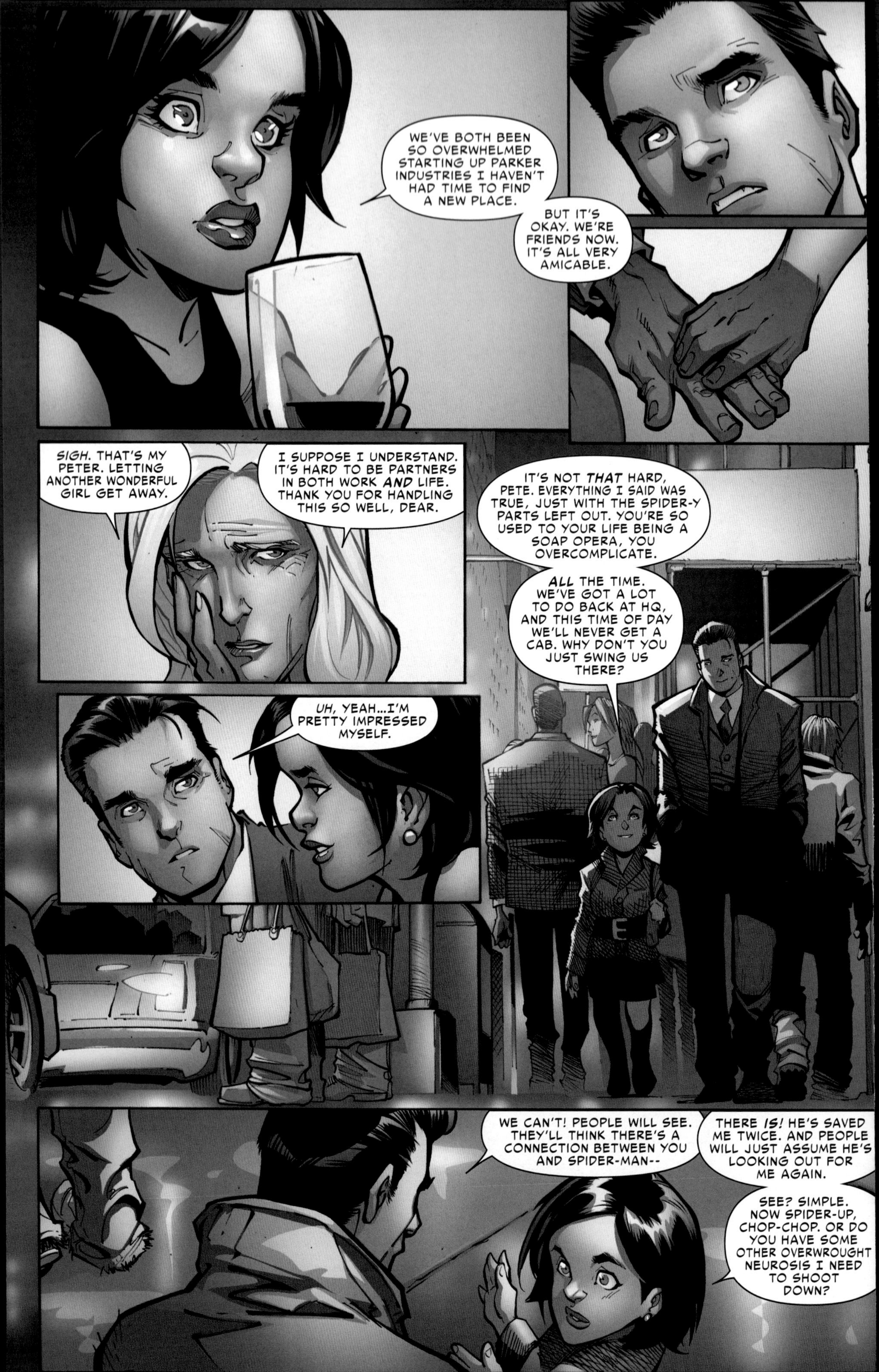
WE'VE BOTH BEEN SO OVERWHELMED STARTING UP PARKER INDUSTRIES I HAVEN'T HAD TIME TO FIND A NEW PLACE.
BUT IT'S OKAY. WE'RE FRIENDS NOW. IT'S ALL VERY AMICABLE.
SIGH. THAT'S MY PETER. LETTING ANOTHER WONDERFUL GIRL GET AWAY.
I SUPPOSE I UNDERSTAND. IT'S HARD TO BE PARTNERS IN BOTH WORK AND LIFE. THANK YOU FOR HANDLING THIS SO WELL, DEAR.
UH, YEAH...I'M PRETTY IMPRESSED MYSELF.
IT'S NOT THAT HARD, PETE. EVERYTHING I SAID WAS TRUE, JUST WITH THE SPIDER-Y PARTS LEFT OUT. YOU'RE SO USED TO YOUR LIFE BEING A SOAP OPERA, YOU OVERCOMPLICATE.
ALL THE TIME. WE'VE GOT A LOT TO DO BACK AT HQ, AND THIS TIME OF DAY WE'LL NEVER GET A CAB. WHY DON'T YOU JUST SWING US THERE?
WE CAN'T! PEOPLE WILL SEE. THEY'LL THINK THERE'S A CONNECTION BETWEEN YOU AND SPIDER-MAN--
THERE IS! HE'S SAVED ME TWICE. AND PEOPLE WILL JUST ASSUME HE'S LOOKING OUT FOR ME AGAIN.
SEE? SIMPLE. NOW SPIDER-UP, CHOP-CHOP. OR DO YOU HAVE SOME OTHER OVERWROUGHT NEUROSIS I NEED TO SHOOT DOWN?

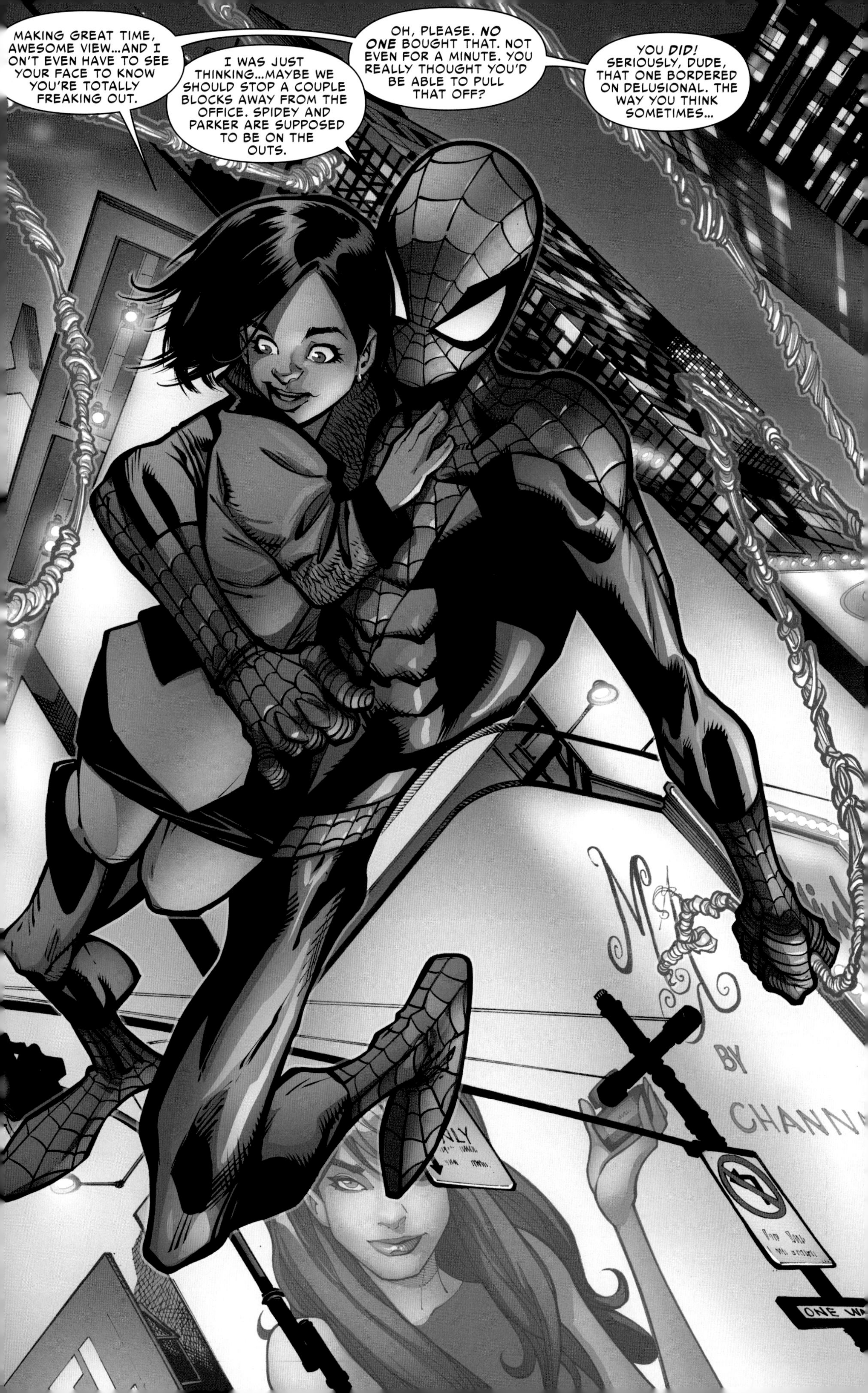
MAKING GREAT TIME, AWESOME VIEW...AND I ON'T EVEN HAVE TO SEE YOUR FACE TO KNOW YOU'RE TOTALLY FREAKING OUT.
I WAS JUST THINKING...MAYBE WE SHOULD STOP A COUPLE BLOCKS AWAY FROM THE OFFICE. SPIDEY AND PARKER ARE SUPPOSED TO BE ON THE OUTS.
OH, PLEASE. ***NO ONE*** BOUGHT THAT. NOT EVEN FOR A MINUTE. YOU REALLY THOUGHT YOU'D BE ABLE TO PULL THAT OFF?
YOU ***DID!*** SERIOUSLY, DUDE, THAT ONE BORDERED ON DELUSIONAL. THE WAY YOU THINK SOMETIMES...

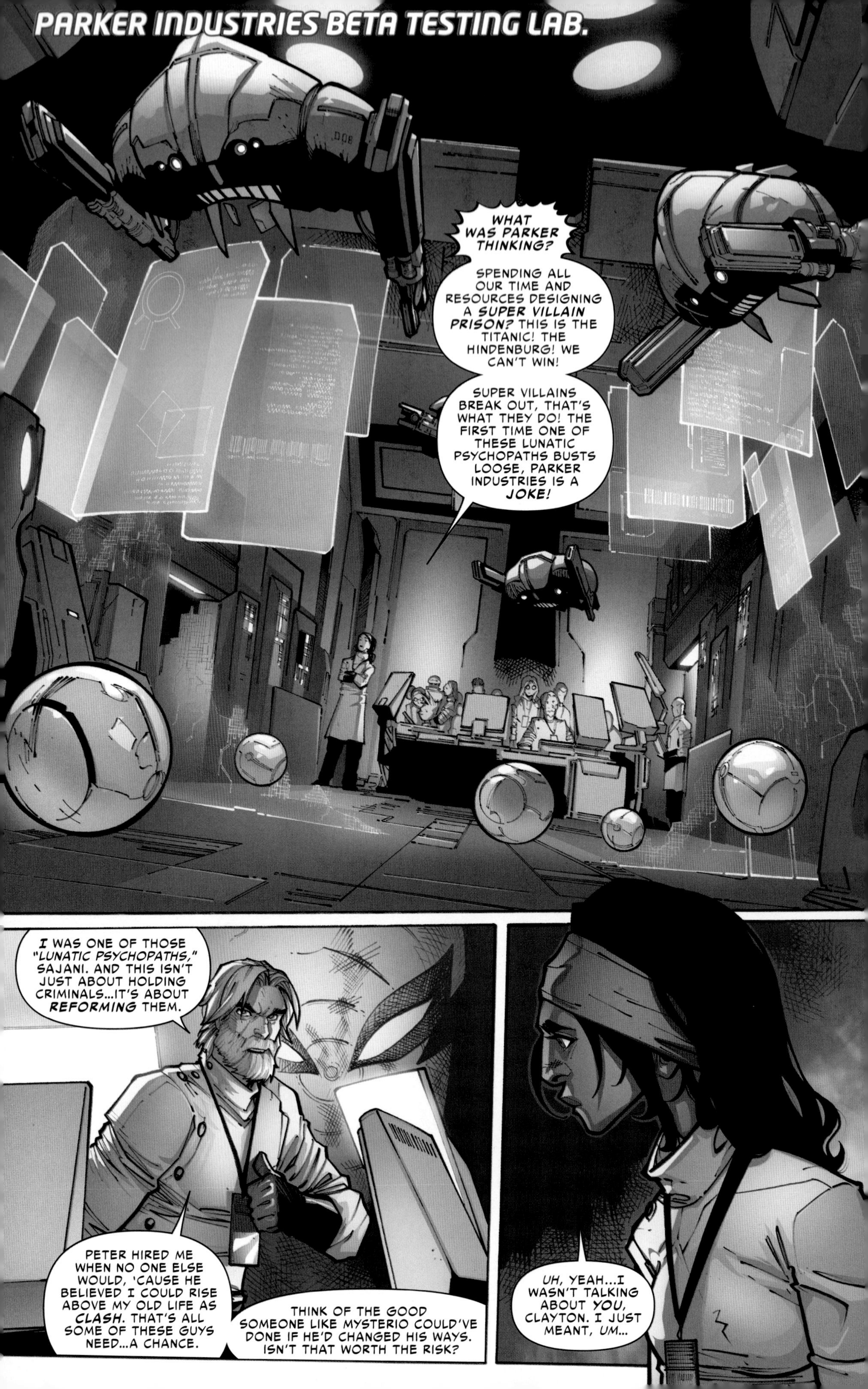
PARKER INDUSTRIES BETA TESTING LAB.
WHAT WAS PARKER THINKING?
SPENDING ALL OUR TIME AND RESOURCES DESIGNING A SUPER VILLAIN PRISON? THIS IS THE TITANIC! THE HINDENBURG! WE CAN'T WIN!
SUPER VILLAINS BREAK OUT, THAT'S WHAT THEY DO! THE FIRST TIME ONE OF THESE LUNATIC PSYCHOPATHS BUSTS LOOSE, PARKER INDUSTRIES IS A JOKE!
I WAS ONE OF THOSE "LUNATIC PSYCHOPATHS," SAJANI. AND THIS ISN'T JUST ABOUT HOLDING CRIMINALS...IT'S ABOUT REFORMING THEM.
PETER HIRED ME WHEN NO ONE ELSE WOULD, 'CAUSE HE BELIEVED I COULD RISE ABOVE MY OLD LIFE AS CLASH. THAT'S ALL SOME OF THESE GUYS NEED...A CHANCE.
THINK OF THE GOOD SOMEONE LIKE MYSTERIO COULD'VE DONE IF HE'D CHANGED HIS WAYS. ISN'T THAT WORTH THE RISK?
UH, YEAH...I WASN'T TALKING ABOUT YOU, CLAYTON. I JUST MEANT, UM...

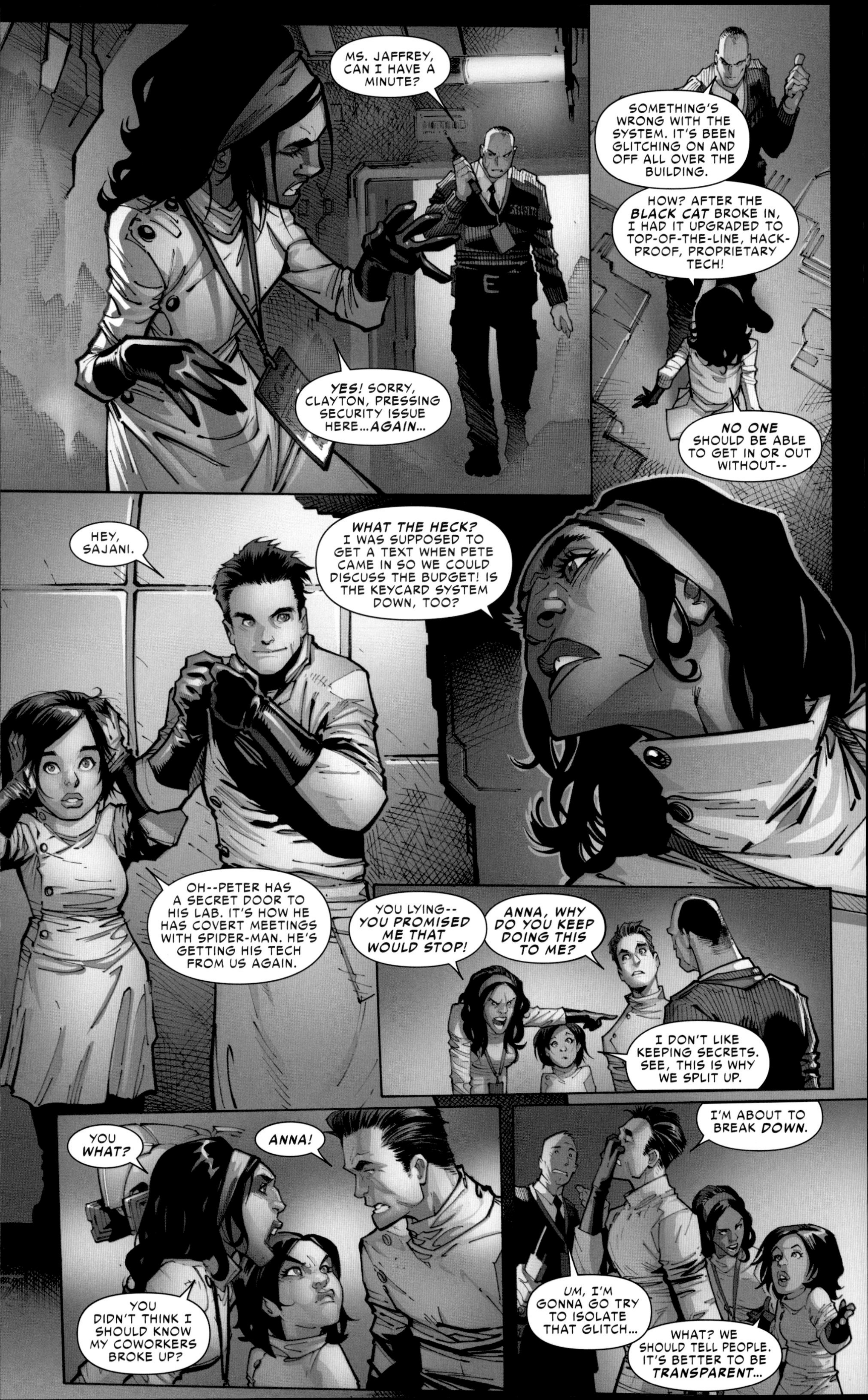

MS. JAFFREY, CAN I HAVE A MINUTE?
YES! SORRY, CLAYTON, PRESSING SECURITY ISSUE HERE...AGAIN...
SOMETHING'S WRONG WITH THE SYSTEM. IT'S BEEN GLITCHING ON AND OFF ALL OVER THE BUILDING.
HOW? AFTER THE BLACK CAT BROKE IN, I HAD IT UPGRADED TO TOP-OF-THE-LINE, HACK-PROOF, PROPRIETARY TECH!
NO ONE SHOULD BE ABLE TO GET IN OR OUT WITHOUT--
HEY, SAJANI.
WHAT THE HECK? I WAS SUPPOSED TO GET A TEXT WHEN PETE CAME IN SO WE COULD DISCUSS THE BUDGET! IS THE KEYCARD SYSTEM DOWN, TOO?
OH--PETER HAS A SECRET DOOR TO HIS LAB. IT'S HOW HE HAS COVERT MEETINGS WITH SPIDER-MAN. HE'S GETTING HIS TECH FROM US AGAIN.
YOU LYING-- YOU PROMISED ME THAT WOULD STOP!
ANNA, WHY DO YOU KEEP DOING THIS TO ME?
I DON'T LIKE KEEPING SECRETS. SEE, THIS IS WHY WE SPLIT UP.
YOU WHAT?
ANNA!
YOU DIDN'T THINK I SHOULD KNOW MY COWORKERS BROKE UP?
I'M ABOUT TO BREAK DOWN.
UM, I'M GONNA GO TRY TO ISOLATE THAT GLITCH...
WHAT? WE SHOULD TELL PEOPLE. IT'S BETTER TO BE TRANSPARENT...

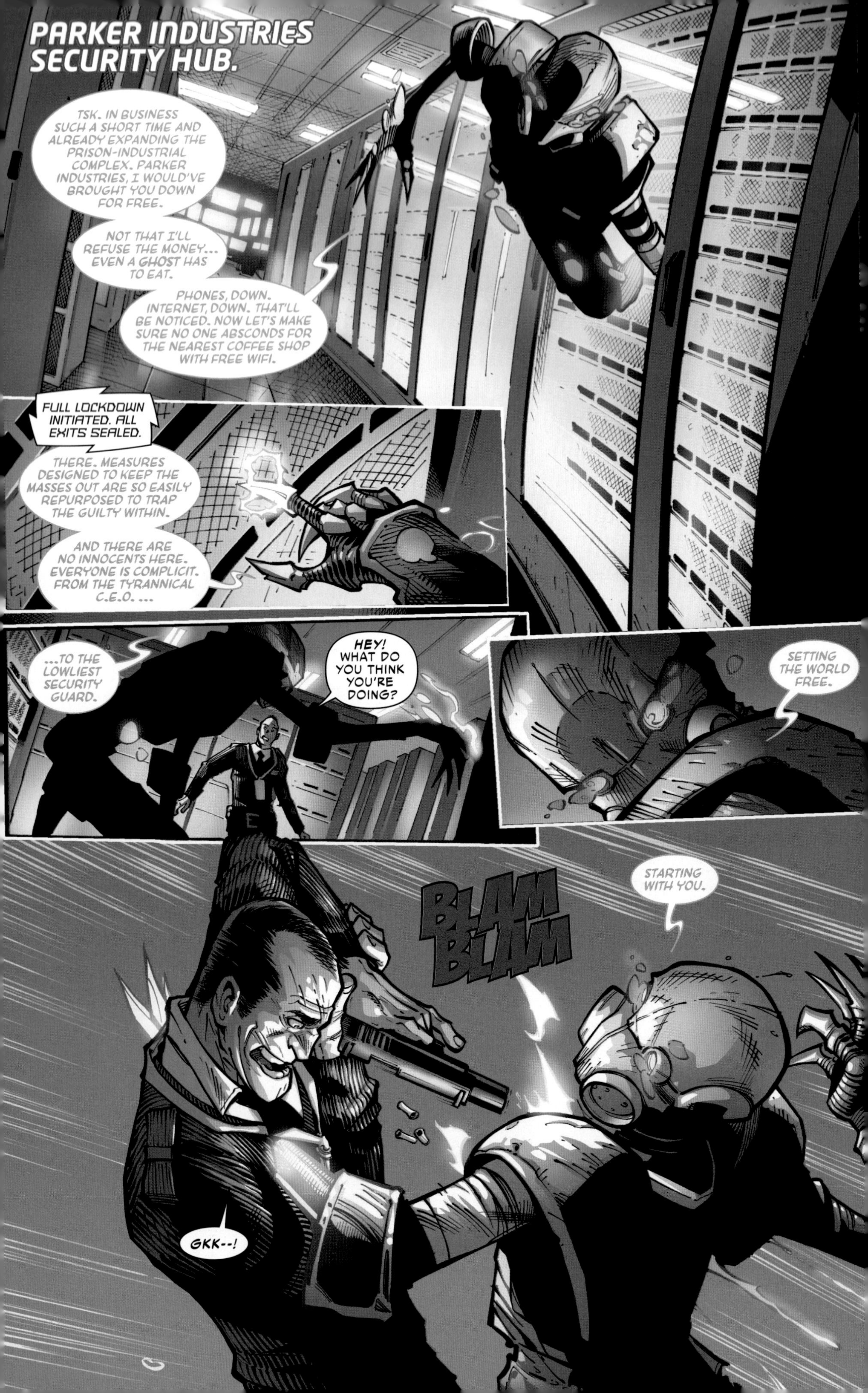
PARKER INDUSTRIES SECURITY HUB.
TSK. IN BUSINESS SUCH A SHORT TIME AND ALREADY EXPANDING THE PRISON-INDUSTRIAL COMPLEX. PARKER INDUSTRIES, I WOULD'VE BROUGHT YOU DOWN FOR FREE.
NOT THAT I'LL REFUSE THE MONEY... EVEN A GHOST HAS TO EAT.
PHONES, DOWN. INTERNET, DOWN. THAT'LL BE NOTICED. NOW LET'S MAKE SURE NO ONE ABSCONDS FOR THE NEAREST COFFEE SHOP WITH FREE WIFI.
FULL LOCKDOWN INITIATED. ALL EXITS SEALED.
THERE. MEASURES DESIGNED TO KEEP THE MASSES OUT ARE SO EASILY REPURPOSED TO TRAP THE GUILTY WITHIN.
AND THERE ARE NO INNOCENTS HERE. EVERYONE IS COMPLICIT. FROM THE TYRANNICAL C.E.O. ...
...TO THE LOWLIEST SECURITY GUARD.
HEY! WHAT DO YOU THINK YOU'RE DOING?
SETTING THE WORLD FREE.
STARTING WITH YOU.
BLAM BLAM
GKK--!

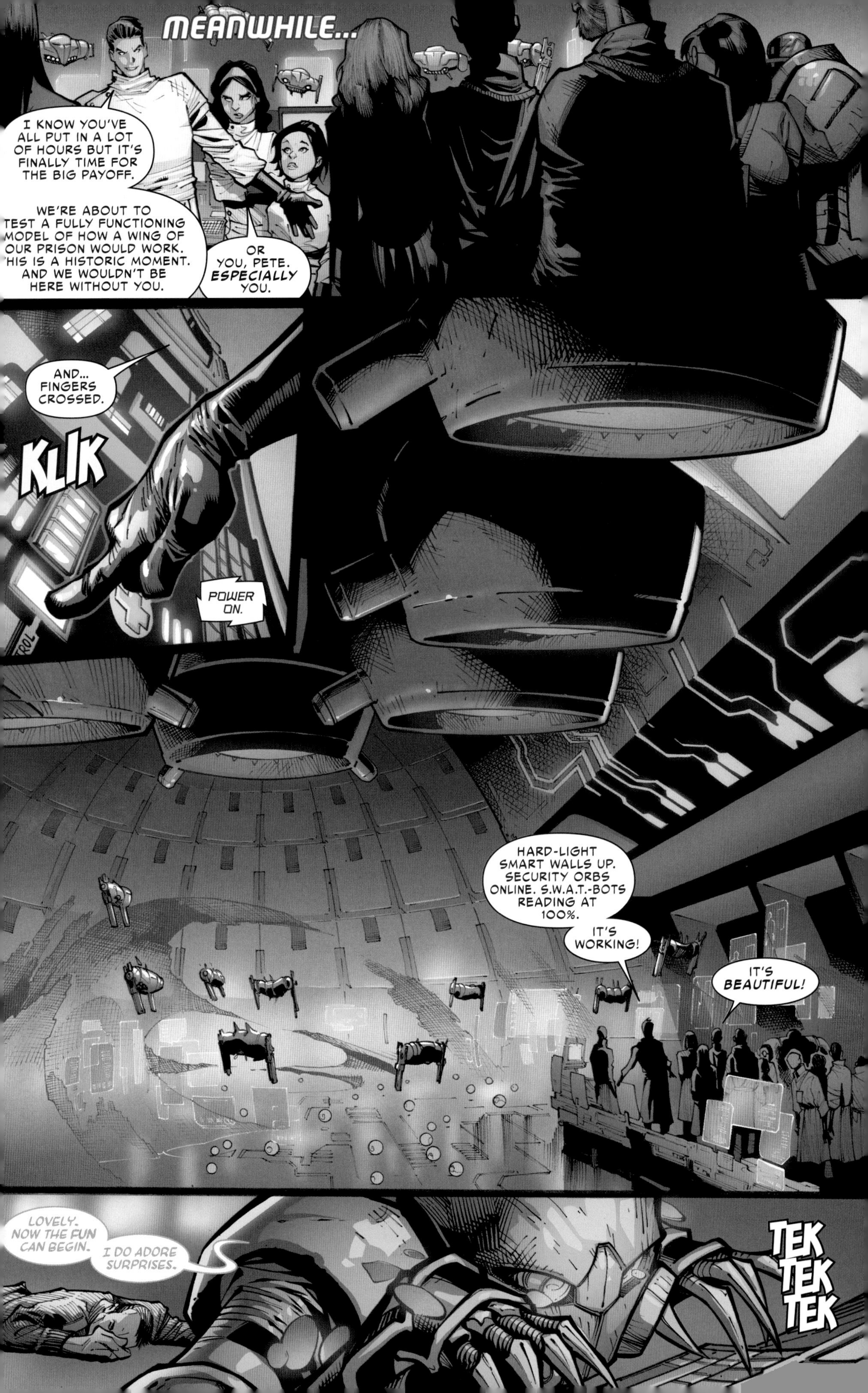
MEANWHILE...
I KNOW YOU'VE ALL PUT IN A LOT OF HOURS BUT IT'S FINALLY TIME FOR THE BIG PAYOFF.
WE'RE ABOUT TO TEST A FULLY FUNCTIONING MODEL OF HOW A WING OF OUR PRISON WOULD WORK. THIS IS A HISTORIC MOMENT. AND WE WOULDN'T BE HERE WITHOUT YOU.
OR YOU, PETE. ESPECIALLY YOU.
AND... FINGERS CROSSED.
KLIK
POWER ON.
HARD-LIGHT SMART WALLS UP. SECURITY ORBS ONLINE. S.W.A.T.-BOTS READING AT 100%.
IT'S WORKING!
IT'S BEAUTIFUL!
LOVELY. NOW THE FUN CAN BEGIN.
I DO ADORE SURPRISES.
TEK TEK TEK

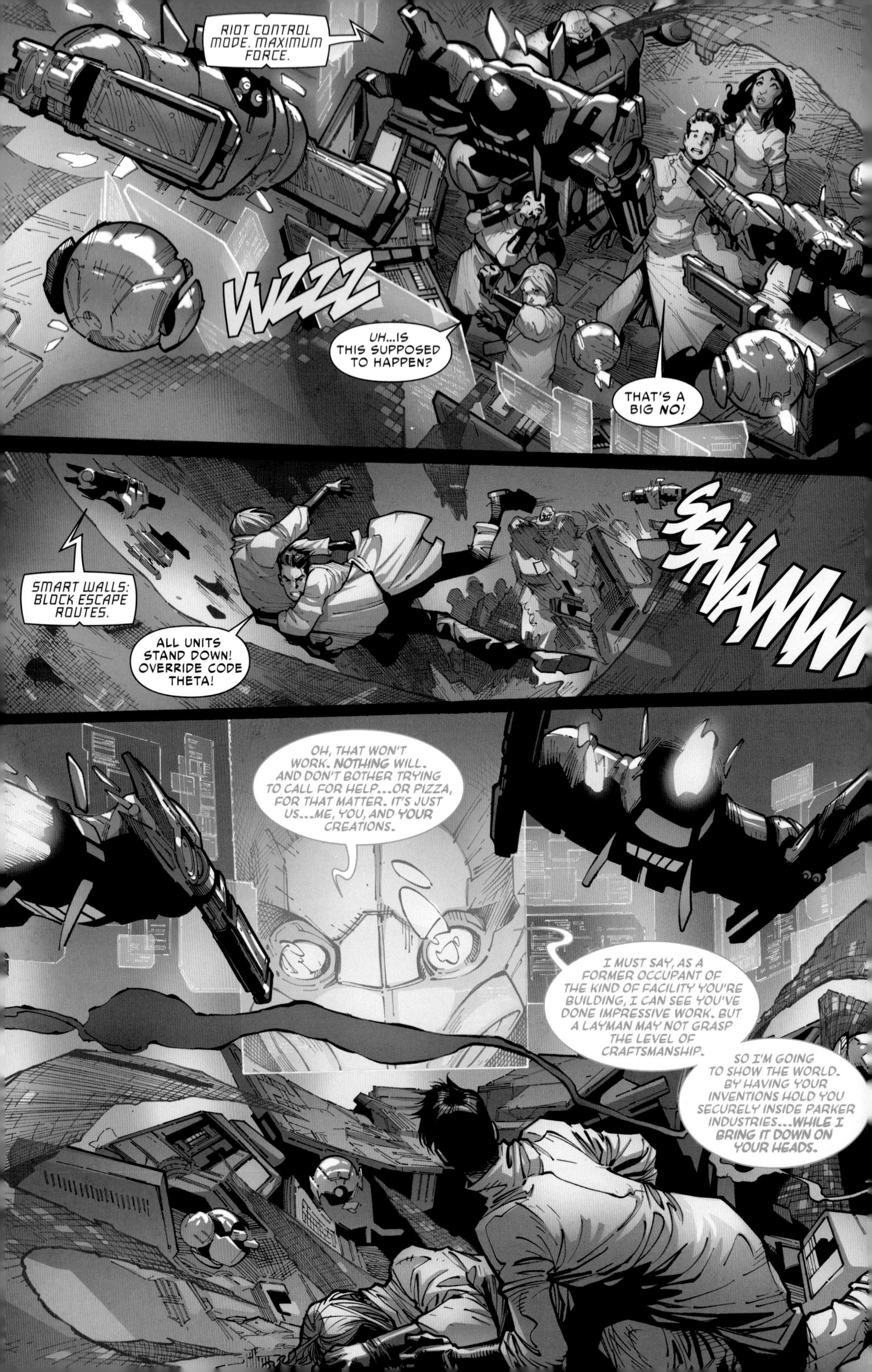
RIOT CONTROL MODE. MAXIMUM FORCE.
VWZZZ
UH...IS THIS SUPPOSED TO HAPPEN?
THAT'S A BIG NO!
SMART WALLS: BLOCK ESCAPE ROUTES.
ALL UNITS STAND DOWN! OVERRIDE CODE THETA!
SCHVANNN
OH, THAT WON'T WORK. NOTHING WILL. AND DON'T BOTHER TRYING TO CALL FOR HELP...OR PIZZA, FOR THAT MATTER. IT'S JUST US...ME, YOU, AND YOUR CREATIONS.
I MUST SAY, AS A FORMER OCCUPANT OF THE KIND OF FACILITY YOU'RE BUILDING, I CAN SEE YOU'VE DONE IMPRESSIVE WORK. BUT A LAYMAN MAY NOT GRASP THE LEVEL OF CRAFTSMANSHIP.
SO I'M GOING TO SHOW THE WORLD. BY HAVING YOUR INVENTIONS HOLD YOU SECURELY INSIDE PARKER INDUSTRIES...WHILE I BRING IT DOWN ON YOUR HEADS.

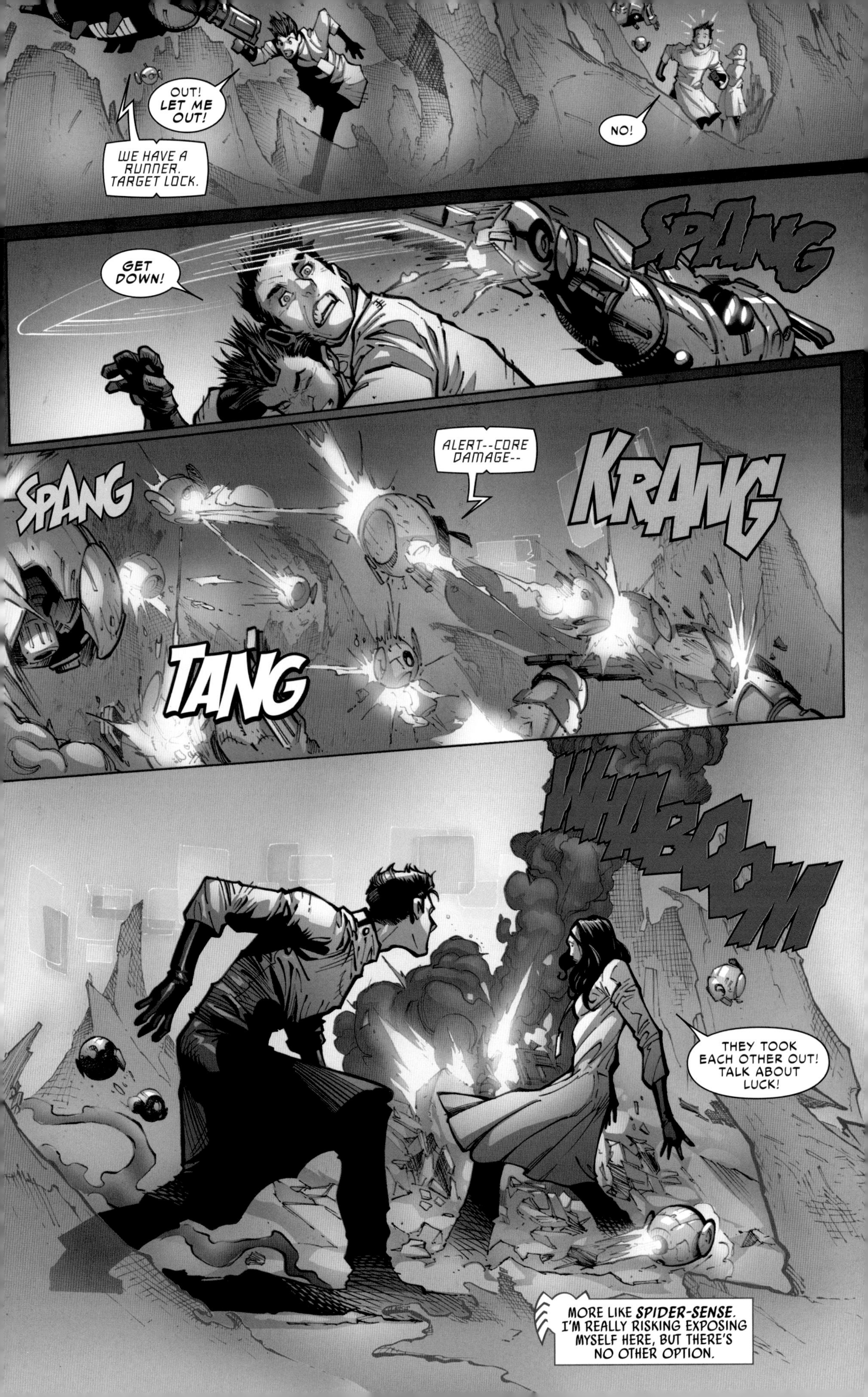
OUT! LET ME OUT!
WE HAVE A RUNNER. TARGET LOCK.
NO!
SPANG
GET DOWN!
ALERT--CORE DAMAGE--
SPANG
KRANG
TANG
WHABOOM
THEY TOOK EACH OTHER OUT! TALK ABOUT LUCK!
MORE LIKE SPIDER-SENSE. I'M REALLY RISKING EXPOSING MYSELF HERE, BUT THERE'S NO OTHER OPTION.

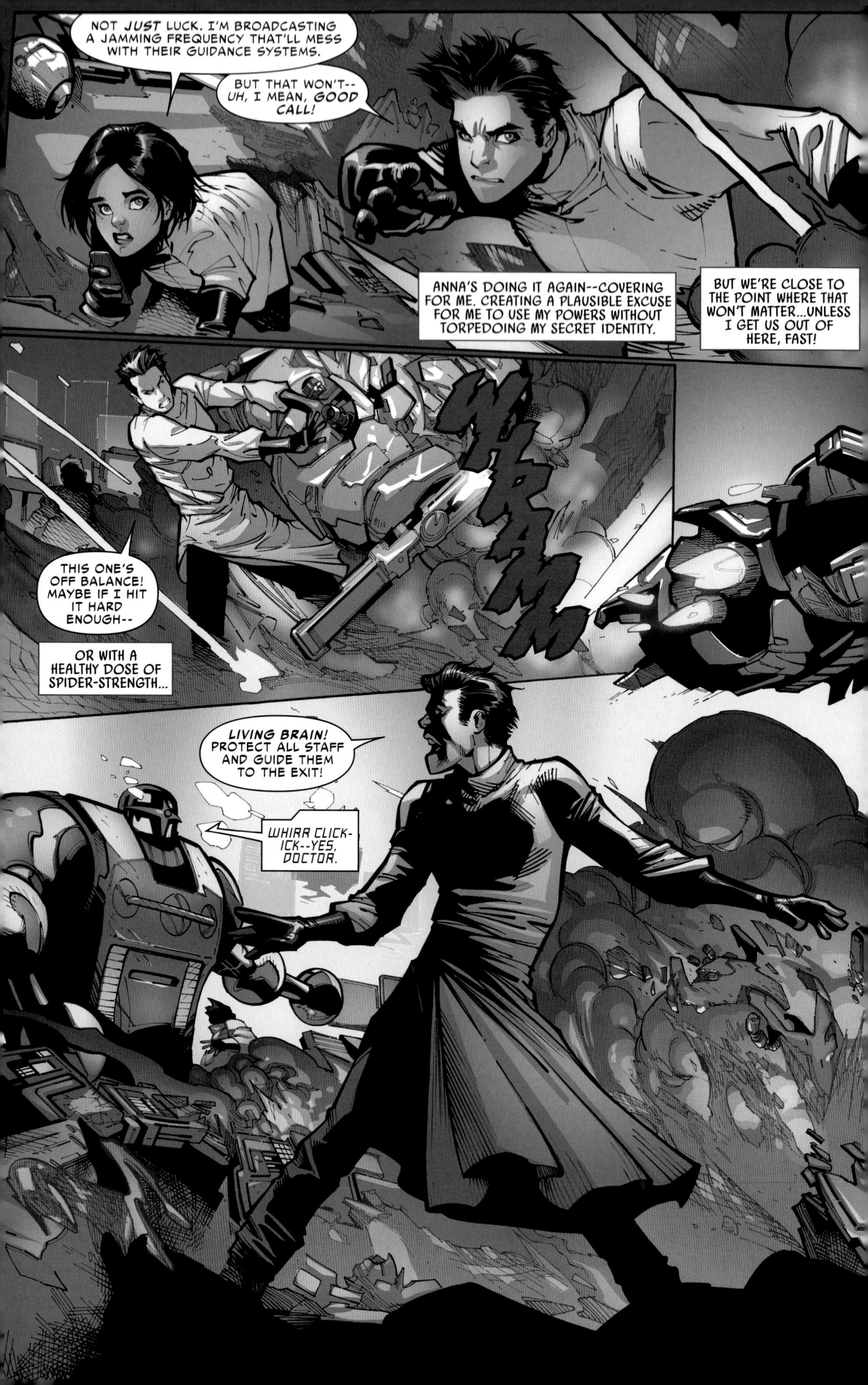

NOT JUST LUCK. I'M BROADCASTING A JAMMING FREQUENCY THAT'LL MESS WITH THEIR GUIDANCE SYSTEMS.
BUT THAT WON'T-- UH, I MEAN, GOOD CALL!
ANNA'S DOING IT AGAIN--COVERING FOR ME. CREATING A PLAUSIBLE EXCUSE FOR ME TO USE MY POWERS WITHOUT TORPEDOING MY SECRET IDENTITY.
BUT WE'RE CLOSE TO THE POINT WHERE THAT WON'T MATTER...UNLESS I GET US OUT OF HERE, FAST!
THIS ONE'S OFF BALANCE! MAYBE IF I HIT IT HARD ENOUGH--
OR WITH A HEALTHY DOSE OF SPIDER-STRENGTH...
WHRAMM
LIVING BRAIN! PROTECT ALL STAFF AND GUIDE THEM TO THE EXIT!
WHIRR CLICK-ICK--YES, DOCTOR.

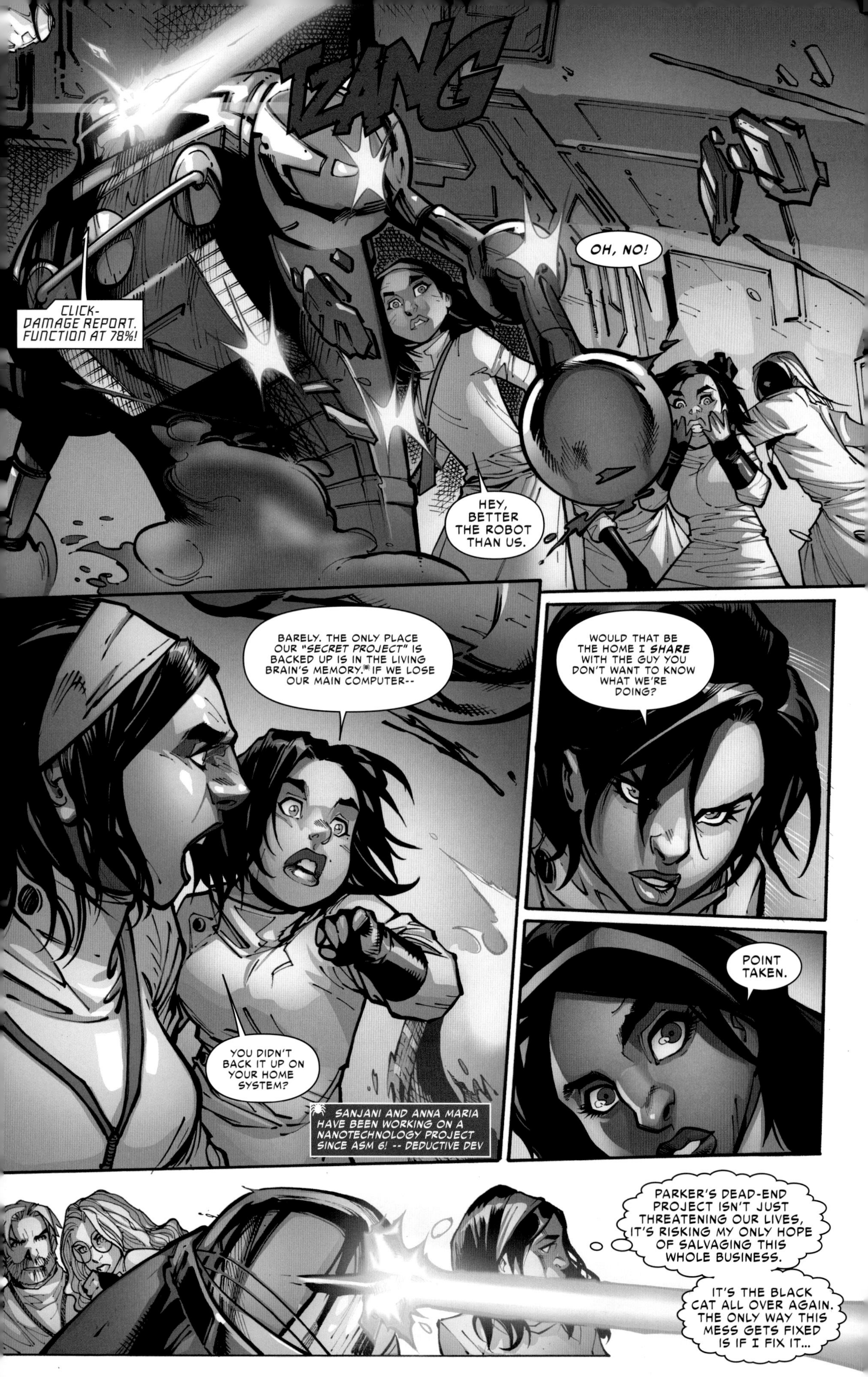
TZANG
CLICK- DAMAGE REPORT. FUNCTION AT 78%!
OH, NO!
HEY, BETTER THE ROBOT THAN US.
BARELY. THE ONLY PLACE OUR "SECRET PROJECT" IS BACKED UP IS IN THE LIVING BRAIN'S MEMORY.* IF WE LOSE OUR MAIN COMPUTER--
YOU DIDN'T BACK IT UP ON YOUR HOME SYSTEM?
*SANJANI AND ANNA MARIA HAVE BEEN WORKING ON A NANOTECHNOLOGY PROJECT SINCE ASM 6! -- DEDUCTIVE DEV
WOULD THAT BE THE HOME I SHARE WITH THE GUY YOU DON'T WANT TO KNOW WHAT WE'RE DOING?
POINT TAKEN.
PARKER'S DEAD-END PROJECT ISN'T JUST THREATENING OUR LIVES, IT'S RISKING MY ONLY HOPE OF SALVAGING THIS WHOLE BUSINESS.
IT'S THE BLACK CAT ALL OVER AGAIN. THE ONLY WAY THIS MESS GETS FIXED IS IF I FIX IT...

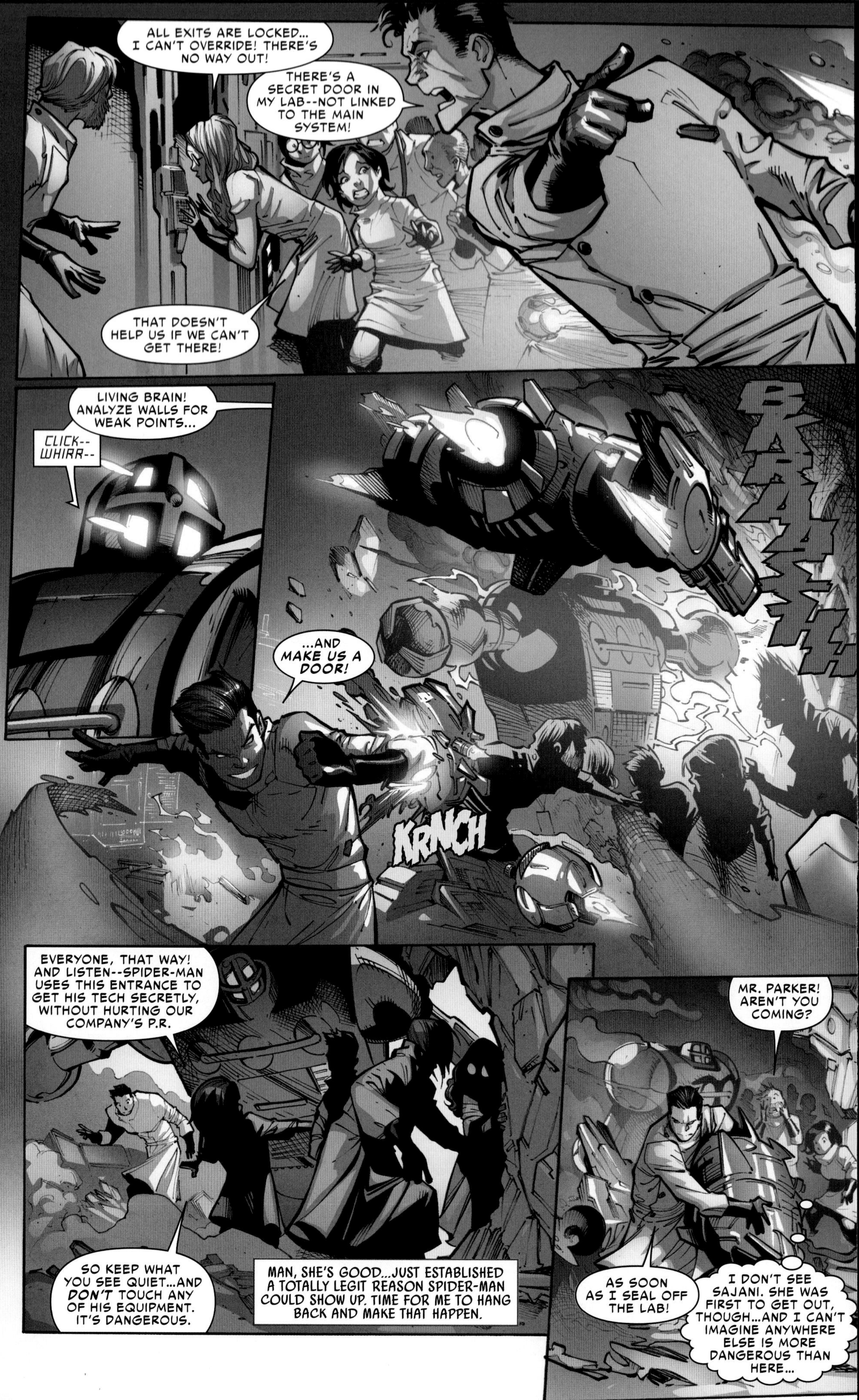
ALL EXITS ARE LOCKED... I CAN'T OVERRIDE! THERE'S NO WAY OUT!
THERE'S A SECRET DOOR IN MY LAB--NOT LINKED TO THE MAIN SYSTEM!
THAT DOESN'T HELP US IF WE CAN'T GET THERE!
LIVING BRAIN! ANALYZE WALLS FOR WEAK POINTS...
CLICK-- WHIRR--
...AND MAKE US A DOOR!
KRNCH
EVERYONE, THAT WAY! AND LISTEN--SPIDER-MAN USES THIS ENTRANCE TO GET HIS TECH SECRETLY, WITHOUT HURTING OUR COMPANY'S P.R.
SO KEEP WHAT YOU SEE QUIET...AND DON'T TOUCH ANY OF HIS EQUIPMENT. IT'S DANGEROUS.
MAN, SHE'S GOOD...JUST ESTABLISHED A TOTALLY LEGIT REASON SPIDER-MAN COULD SHOW UP. TIME FOR ME TO HANG BACK AND MAKE THAT HAPPEN.
MR. PARKER! AREN'T YOU COMING?
AS SOON AS I SEAL OFF THE LAB!
I DON'T SEE SAJANI. SHE WAS FIRST TO GET OUT, THOUGH...AND I CAN'T IMAGINE ANYWHERE ELSE IS MORE DANGEROUS THAN HERE...

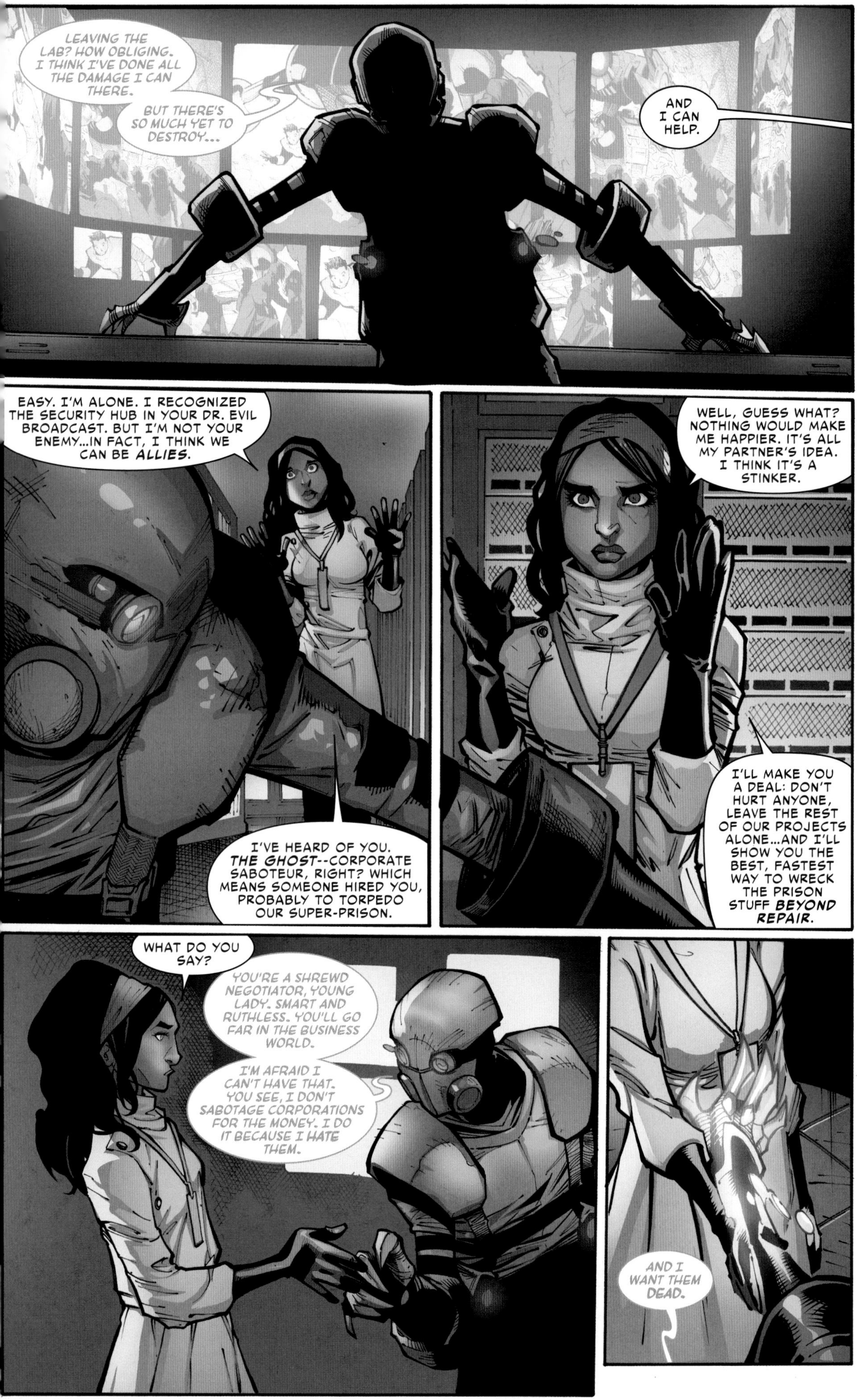
LEAVING THE LAB? HOW OBLIGING. I THINK I'VE DONE ALL THE DAMAGE I CAN THERE.
BUT THERE'S SO MUCH YET TO DESTROY...
AND I CAN HELP.
EASY. I'M ALONE. I RECOGNIZED THE SECURITY HUB IN YOUR DR. EVIL BROADCAST. BUT I'M NOT YOUR ENEMY...IN FACT, I THINK WE CAN BE ALLIES.
I'VE HEARD OF YOU. THE GHOST--CORPORATE SABOTEUR, RIGHT? WHICH MEANS SOMEONE HIRED YOU, PROBABLY TO TORPEDO OUR SUPER-PRISON.
WELL, GUESS WHAT? NOTHING WOULD MAKE ME HAPPIER. IT'S ALL MY PARTNER'S IDEA. I THINK IT'S A STINKER.
I'LL MAKE YOU A DEAL: DON'T HURT ANYONE, LEAVE THE REST OF OUR PROJECTS ALONE...AND I'LL SHOW YOU THE BEST, FASTEST WAY TO WRECK THE PRISON STUFF BEYOND REPAIR.
WHAT DO YOU SAY?
YOU'RE A SHREWD NEGOTIATOR, YOUNG LADY. SMART AND RUTHLESS. YOU'LL GO FAR IN THE BUSINESS WORLD.
I'M AFRAID I CAN'T HAVE THAT. YOU SEE, I DON'T SABOTAGE CORPORATIONS FOR THE MONEY. I DO IT BECAUSE I HATE THEM.
AND I WANT THEM DEAD.

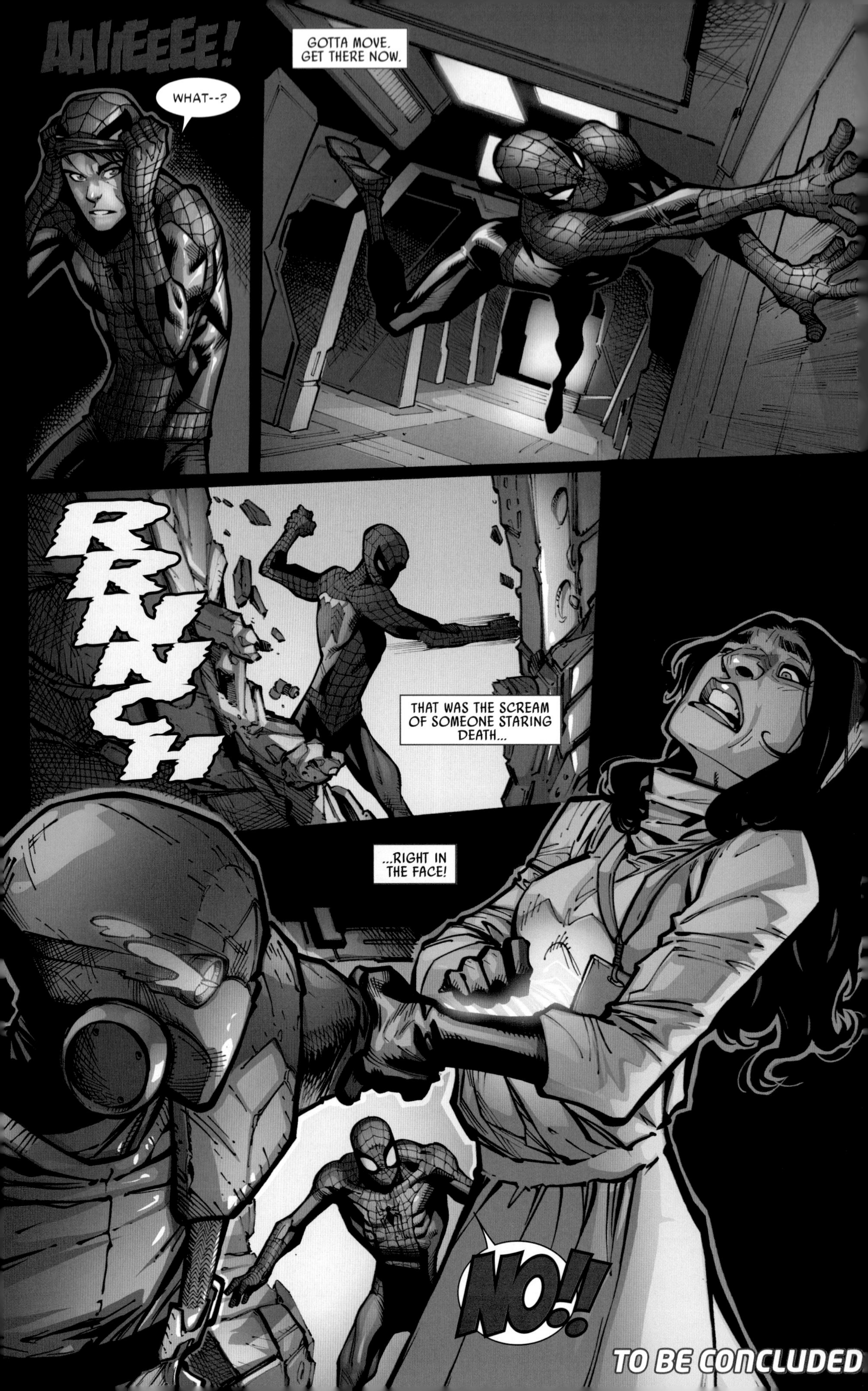
AAIIEEEE!
WHAT--?
GOTTA MOVE. GET THERE NOW.
RRNCH
THAT WAS THE SCREAM OF SOMEONE STARING DEATH...
...RIGHT IN THE FACE!
NO!!
TO BE CONCLUDED

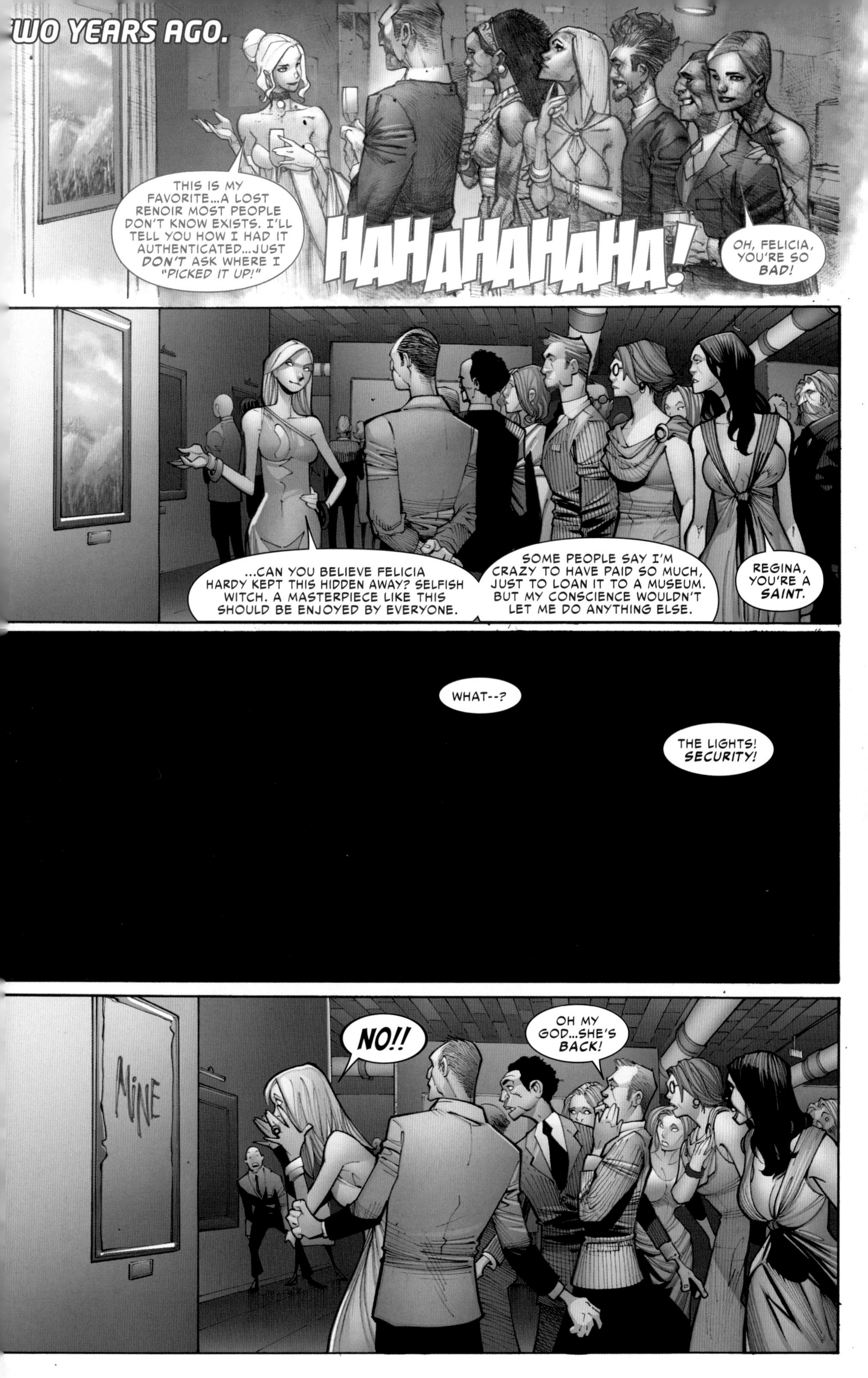
WO YEARS AGO.
THIS IS MY FAVORITE...A LOST RENOIR MOST PEOPLE DON'T KNOW EXISTS. I'LL TELL YOU HOW I HAD IT AUTHENTICATED...JUST DON'T ASK WHERE I "PICKED IT UP!"
HAHAHAHAHAHA!
OH, FELICIA, YOU'RE SO BAD!
...CAN YOU BELIEVE FELICIA HARDY KEPT THIS HIDDEN AWAY? SELFISH WITCH. A MASTERPIECE LIKE THIS SHOULD BE ENJOYED BY EVERYONE.
SOME PEOPLE SAY I'M CRAZY TO HAVE PAID SO MUCH, JUST TO LOAN IT TO A MUSEUM. BUT MY CONSCIENCE WOULDN'T LET ME DO ANYTHING ELSE.
REGINA, YOU'RE A SAINT.
WHAT--?
THE LIGHTS! SECURITY!
MINE
NO!!
OH MY GOD...SHE'S BACK!

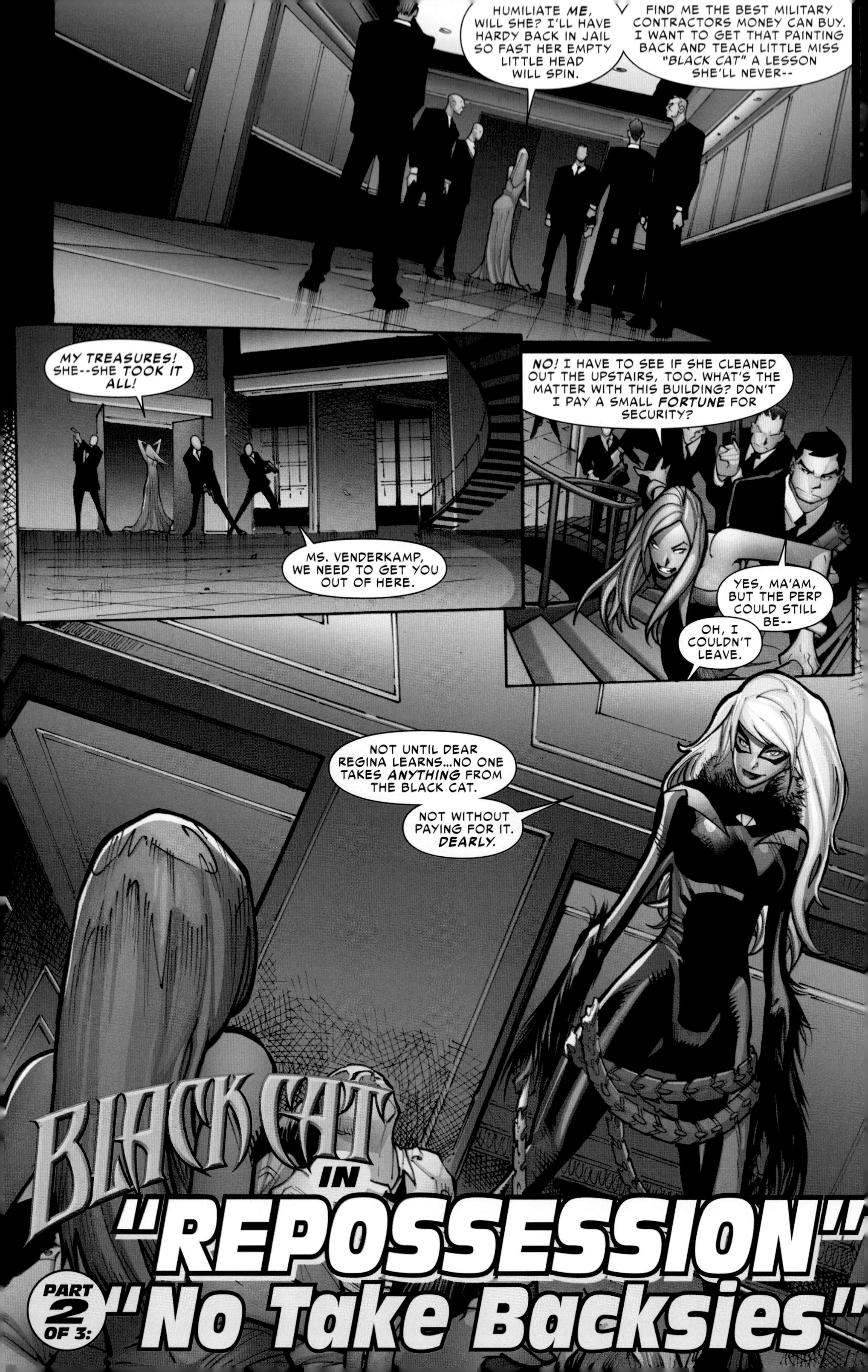
HUMILIATE ME, WILL SHE? I'LL HAVE HARDY BACK IN JAIL SO FAST HER EMPTY LITTLE HEAD WILL SPIN.
FIND ME THE BEST MILITARY CONTRACTORS MONEY CAN BUY. I WANT TO GET THAT PAINTING BACK AND TEACH LITTLE MISS "BLACK CAT" A LESSON SHE'LL NEVER--
MY TREASURES! SHE--SHE TOOK IT ALL!
MS. VENDERKAMP, WE NEED TO GET YOU OUT OF HERE.
NO! I HAVE TO SEE IF SHE CLEANED OUT THE UPSTAIRS, TOO. WHAT'S THE MATTER WITH THIS BUILDING? DON'T I PAY A SMALL FORTUNE FOR SECURITY?
YES, MA'AM, BUT THE PERP COULD STILL BE--
OH, I COULDN'T LEAVE.
NOT UNTIL DEAR REGINA LEARNS...NO ONE TAKES ANYTHING FROM THE BLACK CAT.
NOT WITHOUT PAYING FOR IT. DEARLY.
BLACK CAT
IN
"REPOSSESSION"
PART 2 OF 3:
"No Take Backsies"

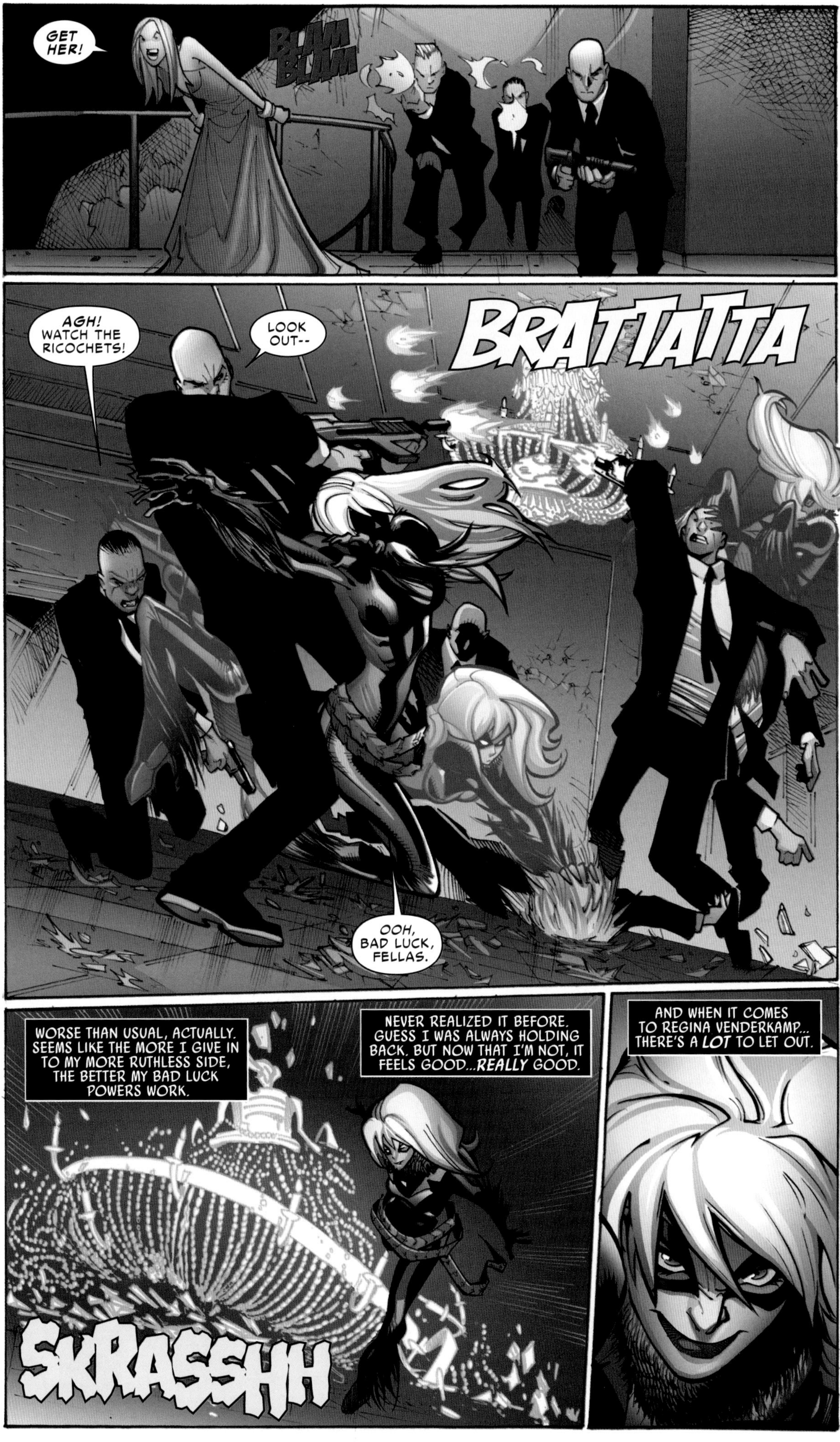
GET HER!
BLAM BLAM
AGH! WATCH THE RICOCHETS!
LOOK OUT--
BRATTATTA
OOH, BAD LUCK, FELLAS.
WORSE THAN USUAL, ACTUALLY. SEEMS LIKE THE MORE I GIVE IN TO MY MORE RUTHLESS SIDE, THE BETTER MY BAD LUCK POWERS WORK.
NEVER REALIZED IT BEFORE. GUESS I WAS ALWAYS HOLDING BACK. BUT NOW THAT I'M NOT, IT FEELS GOOD...REALLY GOOD.
SKRASSHH
AND WHEN IT COMES TO REGINA VENDERKAMP... THERE'S A LOT TO LET OUT.

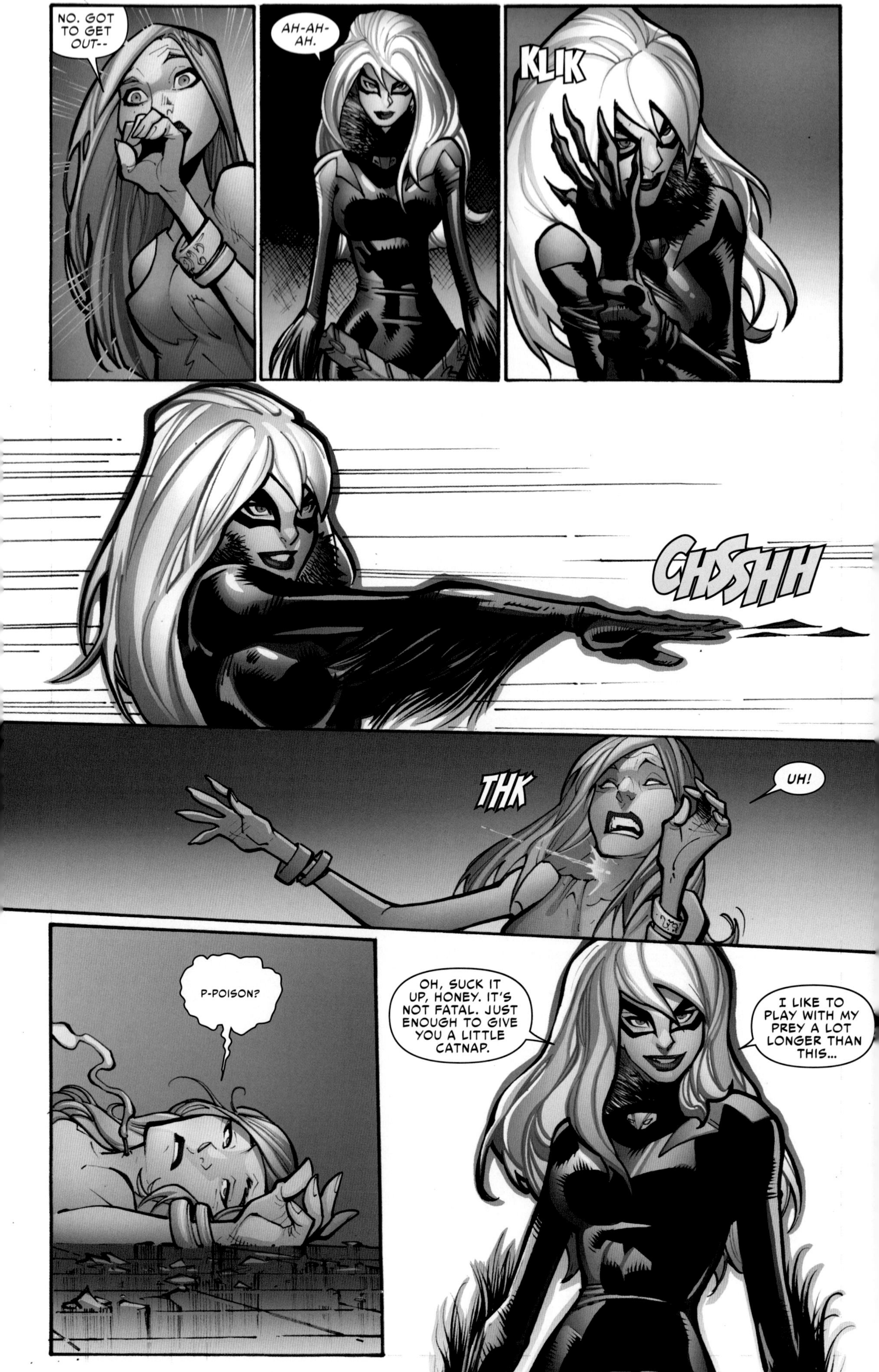
NO. GOT TO GET OUT--
AH-AH-AH.
KLIK
CHSHH
THK
UH!
P-POISON?
OH, SUCK IT UP, HONEY. IT'S NOT FATAL. JUST ENOUGH TO GIVE YOU A LITTLE CATNAP.
I LIKE TO PLAY WITH MY PREY A LOT LONGER THAN THIS...

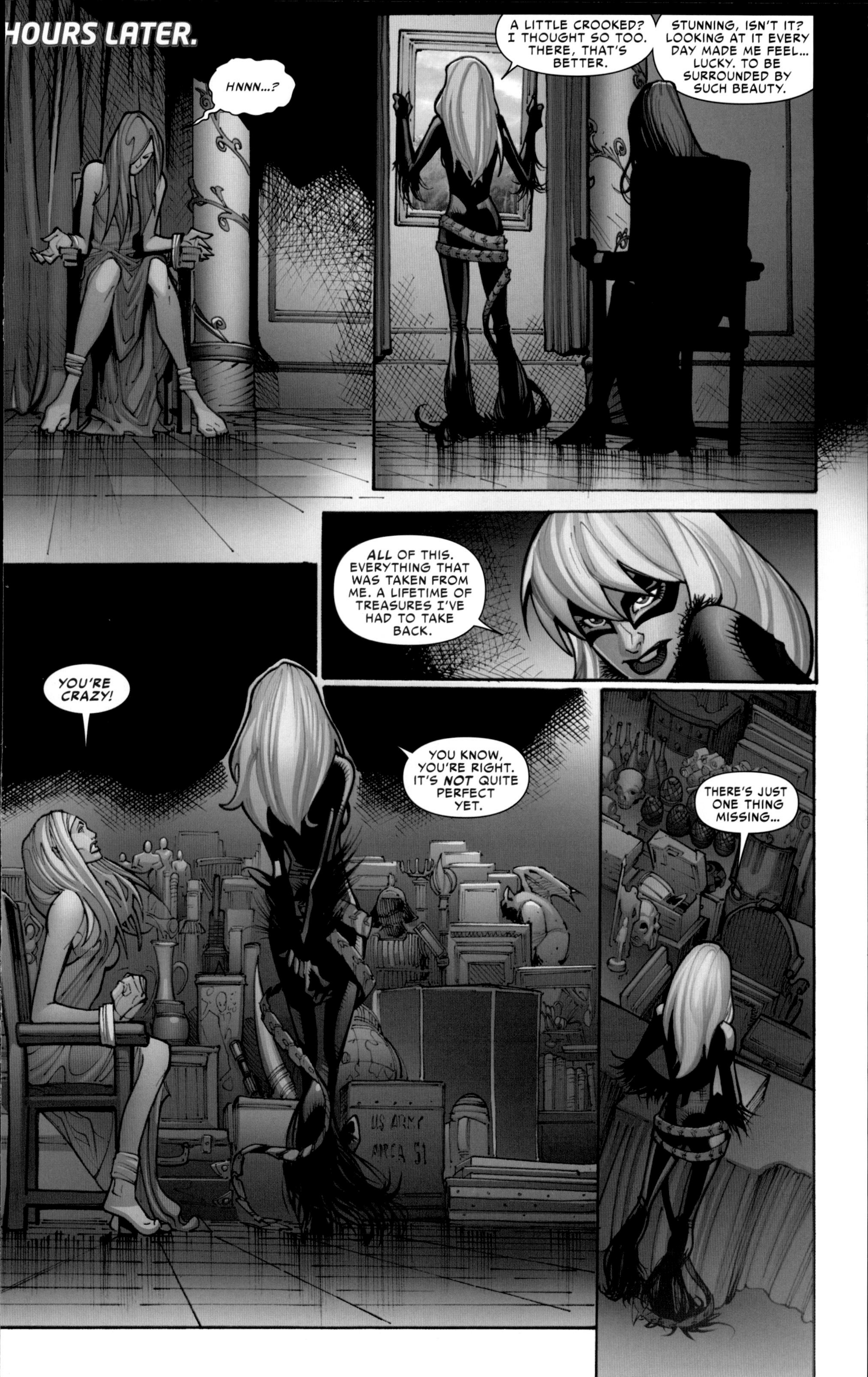
HOURS LATER.
HNNN...?
A LITTLE CROOKED? I THOUGHT SO TOO. THERE, THAT'S BETTER.
STUNNING, ISN'T IT? LOOKING AT IT EVERY DAY MADE ME FEEL... LUCKY. TO BE SURROUNDED BY SUCH BEAUTY.
ALL OF THIS. EVERYTHING THAT WAS TAKEN FROM ME. A LIFETIME OF TREASURES I'VE HAD TO TAKE BACK.
YOU'RE CRAZY!
YOU KNOW, YOU'RE RIGHT. IT'S NOT QUITE PERFECT YET.
THERE'S JUST ONE THING MISSING...

THAT'S IT.

IT DOES LOOK NICE ON THE MANTEL, DOESN'T IT?

SO MUCH BETTER THAN THE TABLE. ALL THROUGH DINNER, I WORRIED PETER WOULD KNOCK IT OVER. I ADORE THAT BOY, BUT HE CAN BE A BIT KLUTZY.

IT'S SO SAD ABOUT HIM AND ANNA MARIA. I'M ABOUT TO GIVE UP ON EVER SEEING HIM MARRIED BEFORE I DIE.

NOW, MAY, YOU'RE HEALTHY AS A HORSE. PETER WILL FIND THE RIGHT GIRL IN HIS OWN TIME. DO YOU WANT TO GO OUT, SEE A MOVIE? TAKE YOUR MIND OFF IT?

THANK YOU, JAY, BUT IT'S GETTING LATE. I'D RATHER STAY IN.

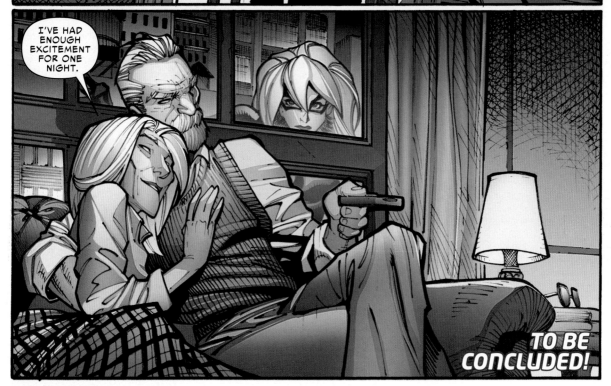

I'VE HAD ENOUGH EXCITEMENT FOR ONE NIGHT.

TO BE CONCLUDED!

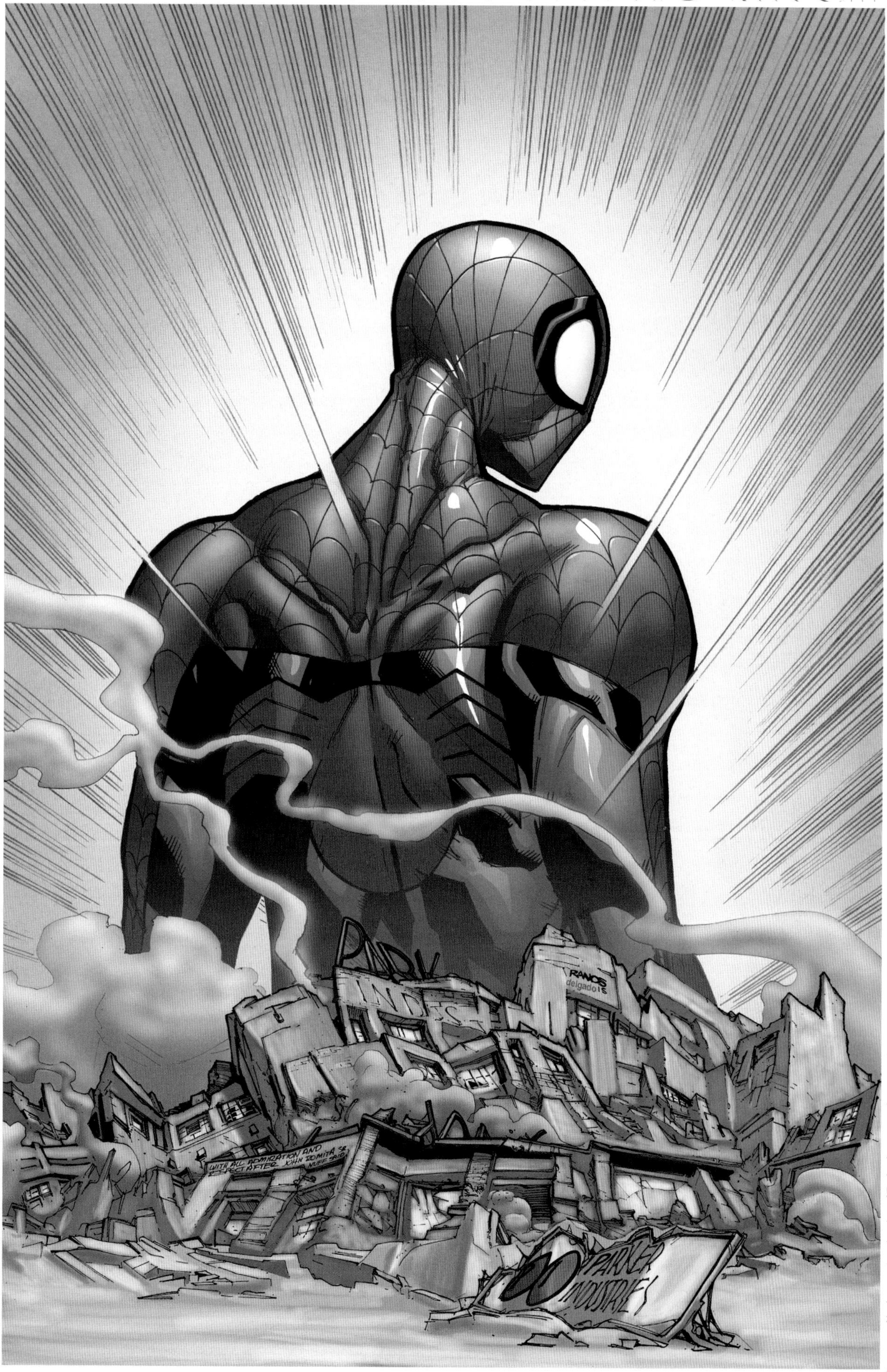
RANOS
delgado's
WITH ALL ADMIRATION AND RESPECT AFTER JOHN ROMITA SR. NUFF SAID!

AMAZING SPIDER-MAN 18

GRAVEYARD SHIFT, PART THREE: TRADE SECRETS

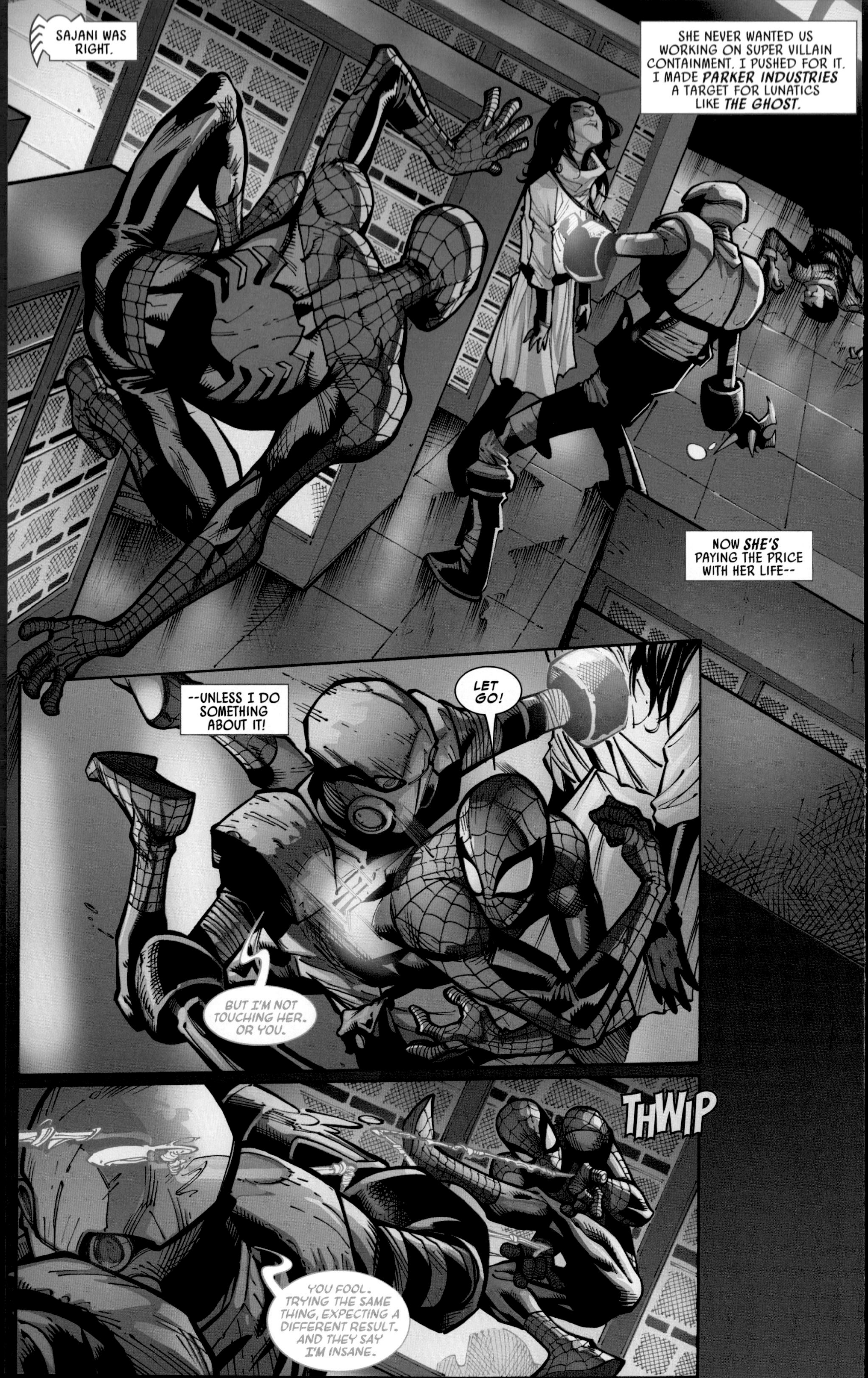
SAJANI WAS RIGHT.
SHE NEVER WANTED US WORKING ON SUPER VILLAIN CONTAINMENT. I PUSHED FOR IT. I MADE PARKER INDUSTRIES A TARGET FOR LUNATICS LIKE THE GHOST.
NOW SHE'S PAYING THE PRICE WITH HER LIFE--
--UNLESS I DO SOMETHING ABOUT IT!
LET GO!
BUT I'M NOT TOUCHING HER. OR YOU.
THWIP
YOU FOOL. TRYING THE SAME THING, EXPECTING A DIFFERENT RESULT. AND THEY SAY I'M INSANE.

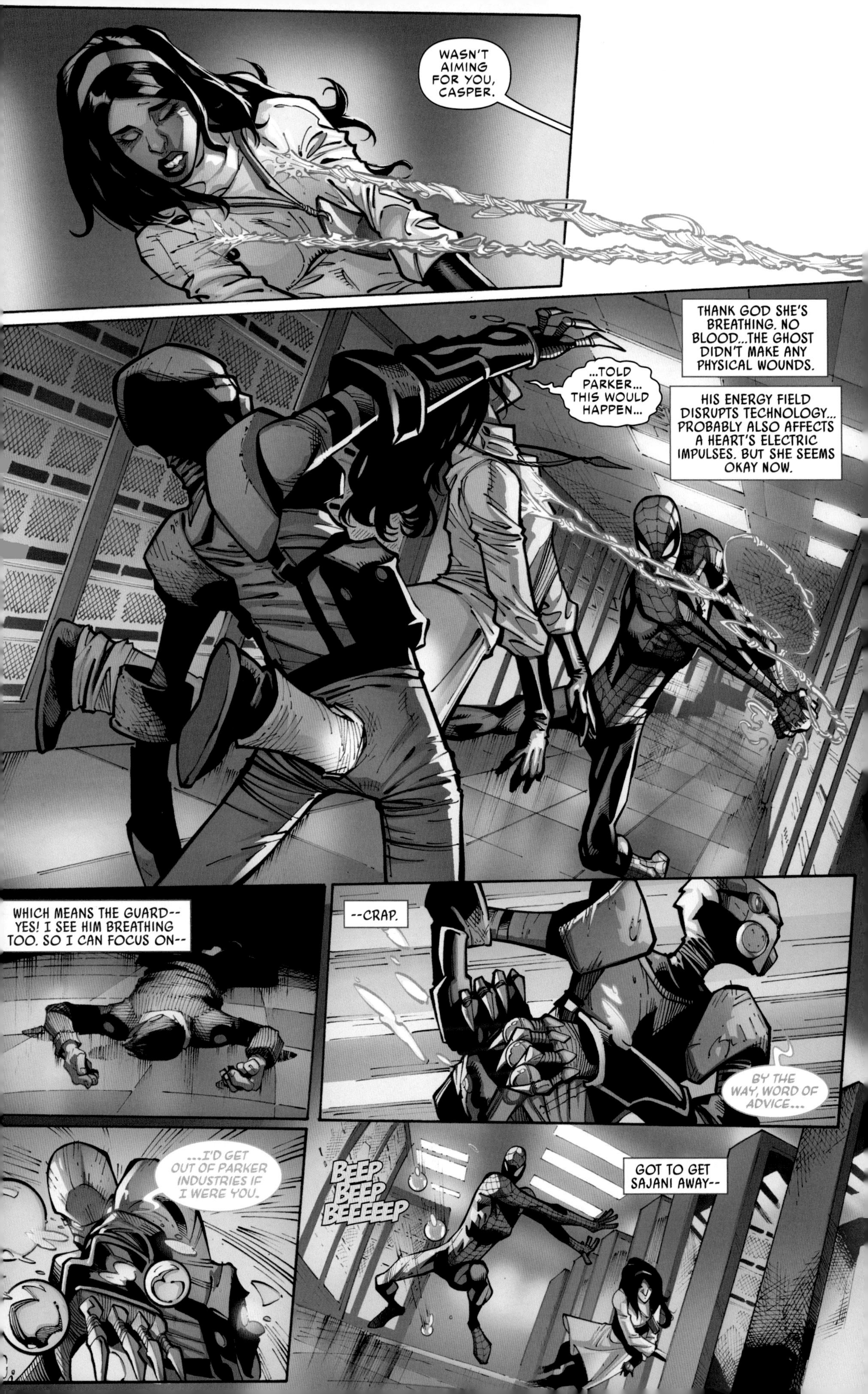
WASN'T AIMING FOR YOU, CASPER.
THANK GOD SHE'S BREATHING. NO BLOOD...THE GHOST DIDN'T MAKE ANY PHYSICAL WOUNDS.
...TOLD PARKER... THIS WOULD HAPPEN...
HIS ENERGY FIELD DISRUPTS TECHNOLOGY... PROBABLY ALSO AFFECTS A HEART'S ELECTRIC IMPULSES. BUT SHE SEEMS OKAY NOW.
WHICH MEANS THE GUARD-- YES! I SEE HIM BREATHING TOO. SO I CAN FOCUS ON--
--CRAP.
BY THE WAY, WORD OF ADVICE...
...I'D GET OUT OF PARKER INDUSTRIES IF I WERE YOU.
BEEP BEEP BEEEEEP
GOT TO GET SAJANI AWAY--

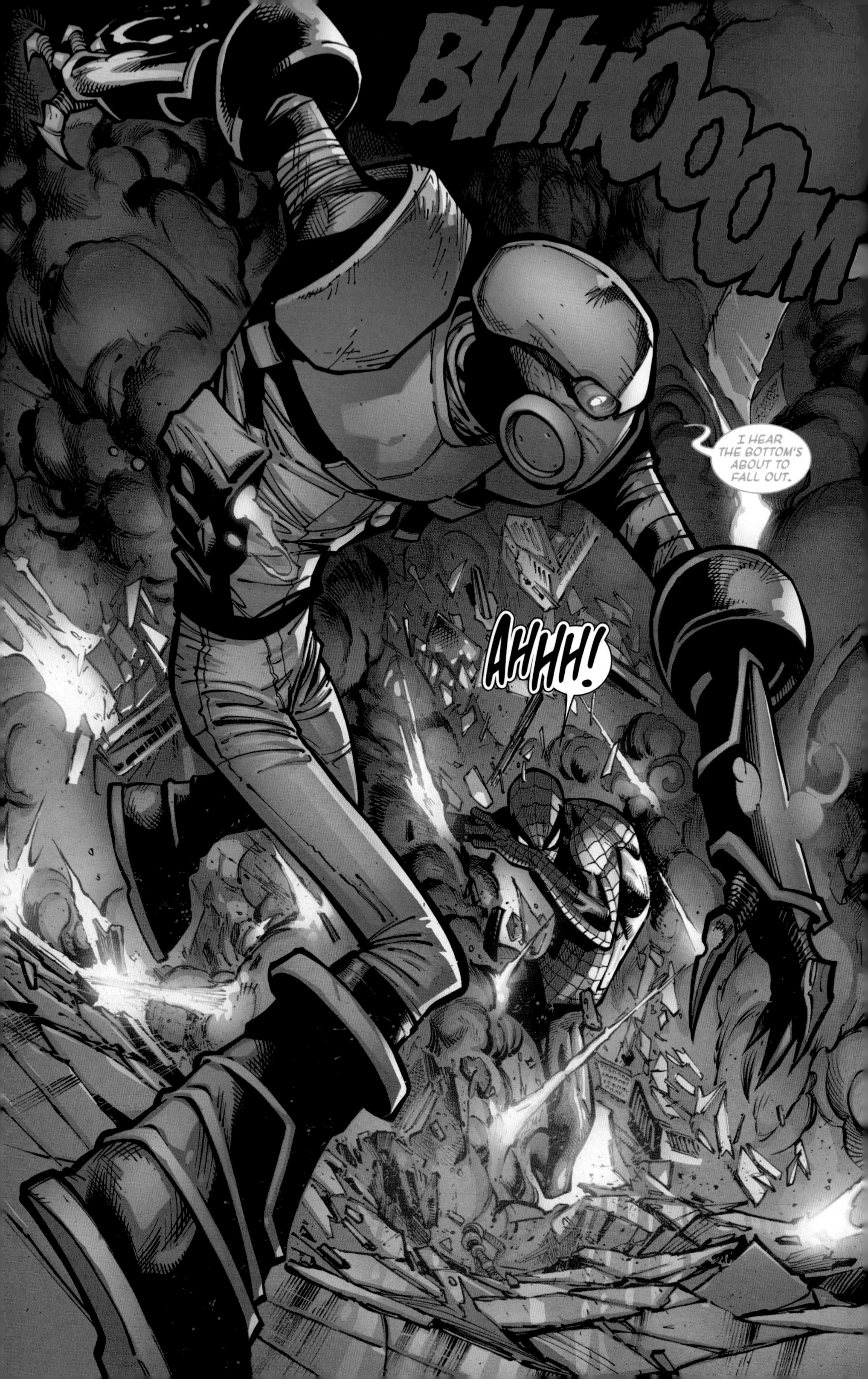
BWHOOOOM!
I HEAR THE BOTTOM'S ABOUT TO FALL OUT.
AHHH!

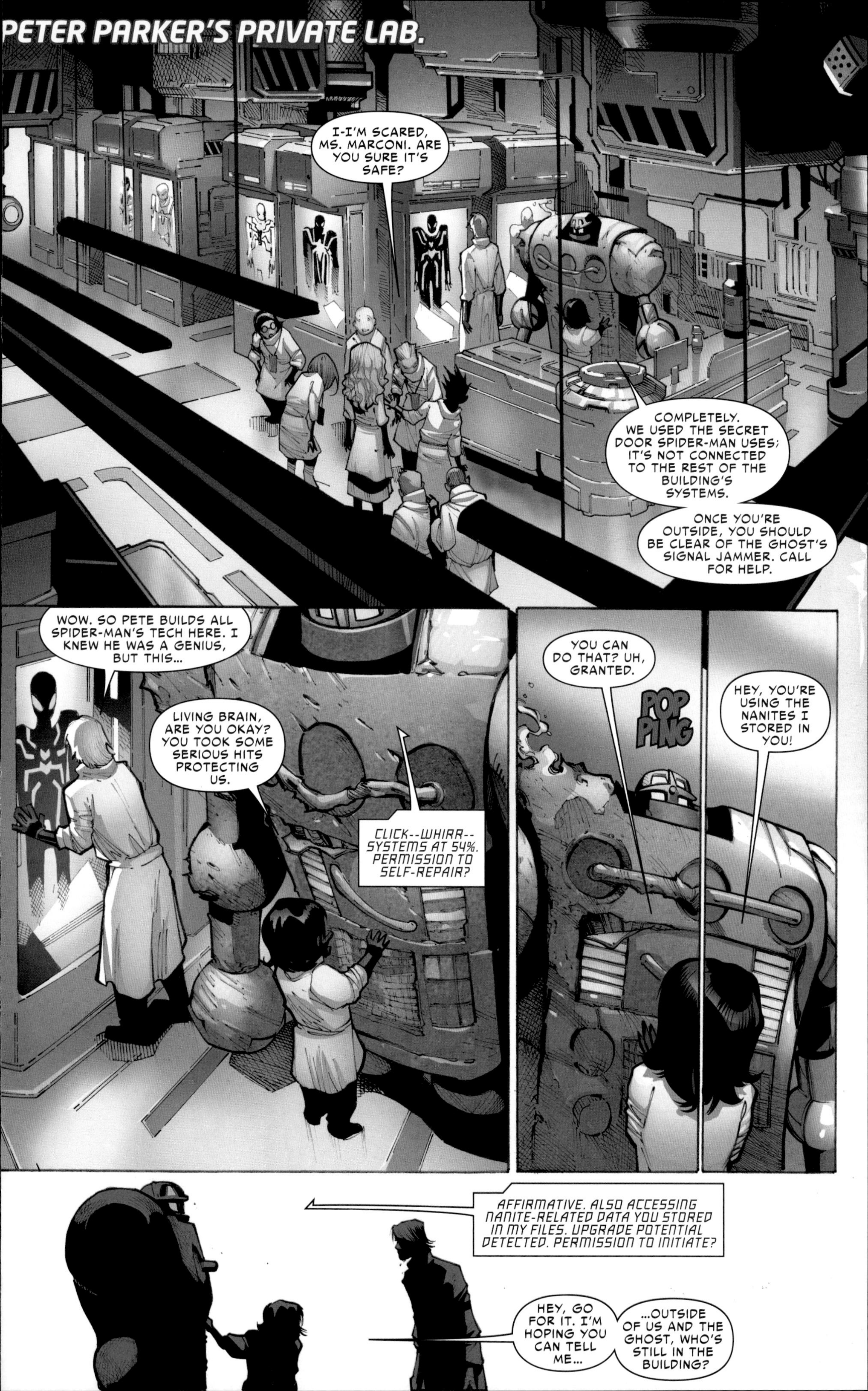
PETER PARKER'S PRIVATE LAB.
I-I'M SCARED, MS. MARCONI. ARE YOU SURE IT'S SAFE?
COMPLETELY. WE USED THE SECRET DOOR SPIDER-MAN USES; IT'S NOT CONNECTED TO THE REST OF THE BUILDING'S SYSTEMS.
ONCE YOU'RE OUTSIDE, YOU SHOULD BE CLEAR OF THE GHOST'S SIGNAL JAMMER. CALL FOR HELP.
WOW. SO PETE BUILDS ALL SPIDER-MAN'S TECH HERE. I KNEW HE WAS A GENIUS, BUT THIS...
LIVING BRAIN, ARE YOU OKAY? YOU TOOK SOME SERIOUS HITS PROTECTING US.
CLICK--WHIRR-- SYSTEMS AT 54%. PERMISSION TO SELF-REPAIR?
YOU CAN DO THAT? UH, GRANTED.
POP
PING
HEY, YOU'RE USING THE NANITES I STORED IN YOU!
AFFIRMATIVE. ALSO ACCESSING NANITE-RELATED DATA YOU STORED IN MY FILES. UPGRADE POTENTIAL DETECTED. PERMISSION TO INITIATE?
HEY, GO FOR IT. I'M HOPING YOU CAN TELL ME...
...OUTSIDE OF US AND THE GHOST, WHO'S STILL IN THE BUILDING?

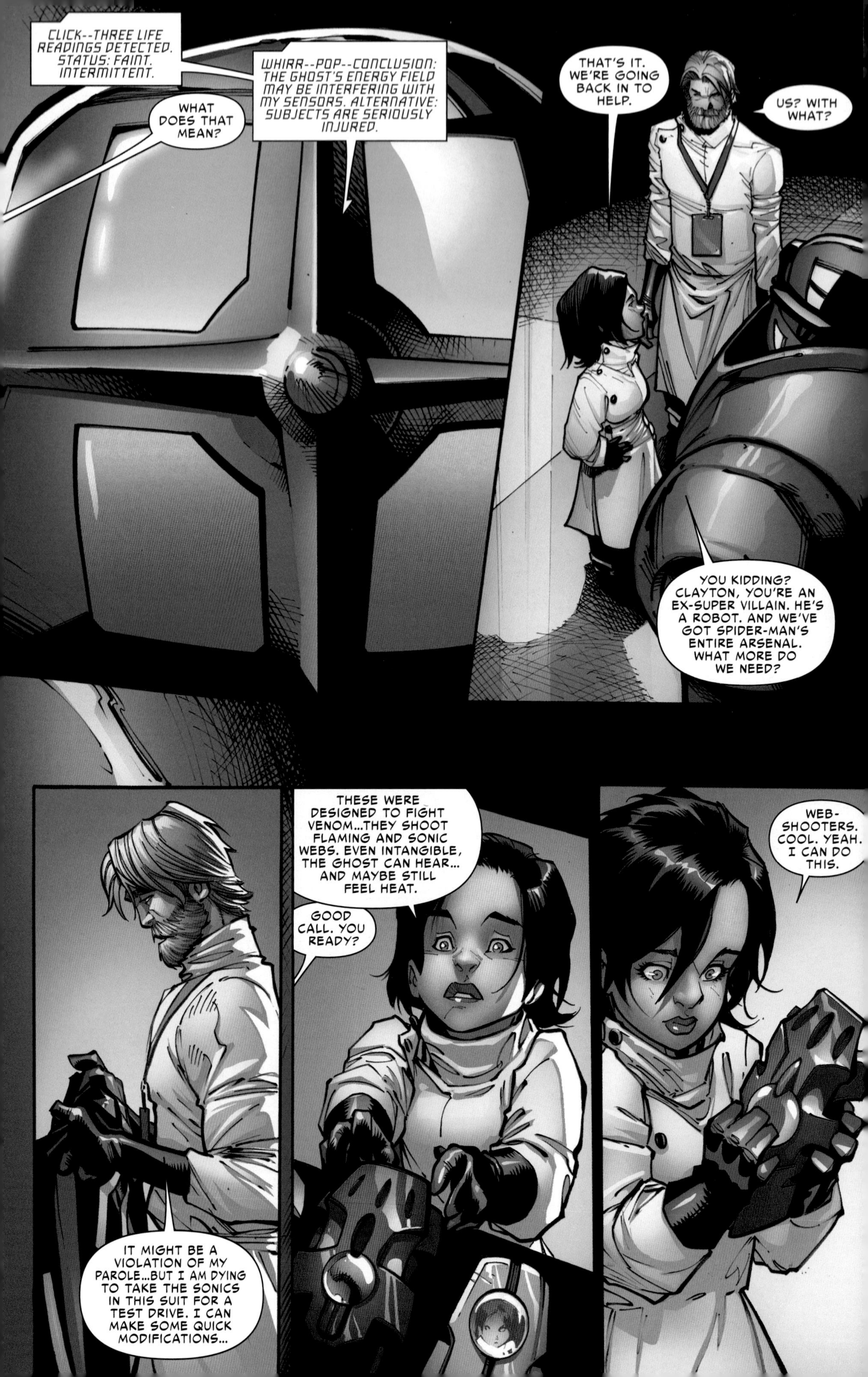
CLICK--THREE LIFE READINGS DETECTED. STATUS: FAINT. INTERMITTENT.
WHAT DOES THAT MEAN?
WHIRR--POP--CONCLUSION: THE GHOST'S ENERGY FIELD MAY BE INTERFERING WITH MY SENSORS. ALTERNATIVE: SUBJECTS ARE SERIOUSLY INJURED.
THAT'S IT. WE'RE GOING BACK IN TO HELP.
US? WITH WHAT?
YOU KIDDING? CLAYTON, YOU'RE AN EX-SUPER VILLAIN. HE'S A ROBOT. AND WE'VE GOT SPIDER-MAN'S ENTIRE ARSENAL. WHAT MORE DO WE NEED?
IT MIGHT BE A VIOLATION OF MY PAROLE...BUT I AM DYING TO TAKE THE SONICS IN THIS SUIT FOR A TEST DRIVE. I CAN MAKE SOME QUICK MODIFICATIONS...
THESE WERE DESIGNED TO FIGHT VENOM...THEY SHOOT FLAMING AND SONIC WEBS. EVEN INTANGIBLE, THE GHOST CAN HEAR... AND MAYBE STILL FEEL HEAT.
GOOD CALL. YOU READY?
WEB-SHOOTERS. COOL. YEAH. I CAN DO THIS.

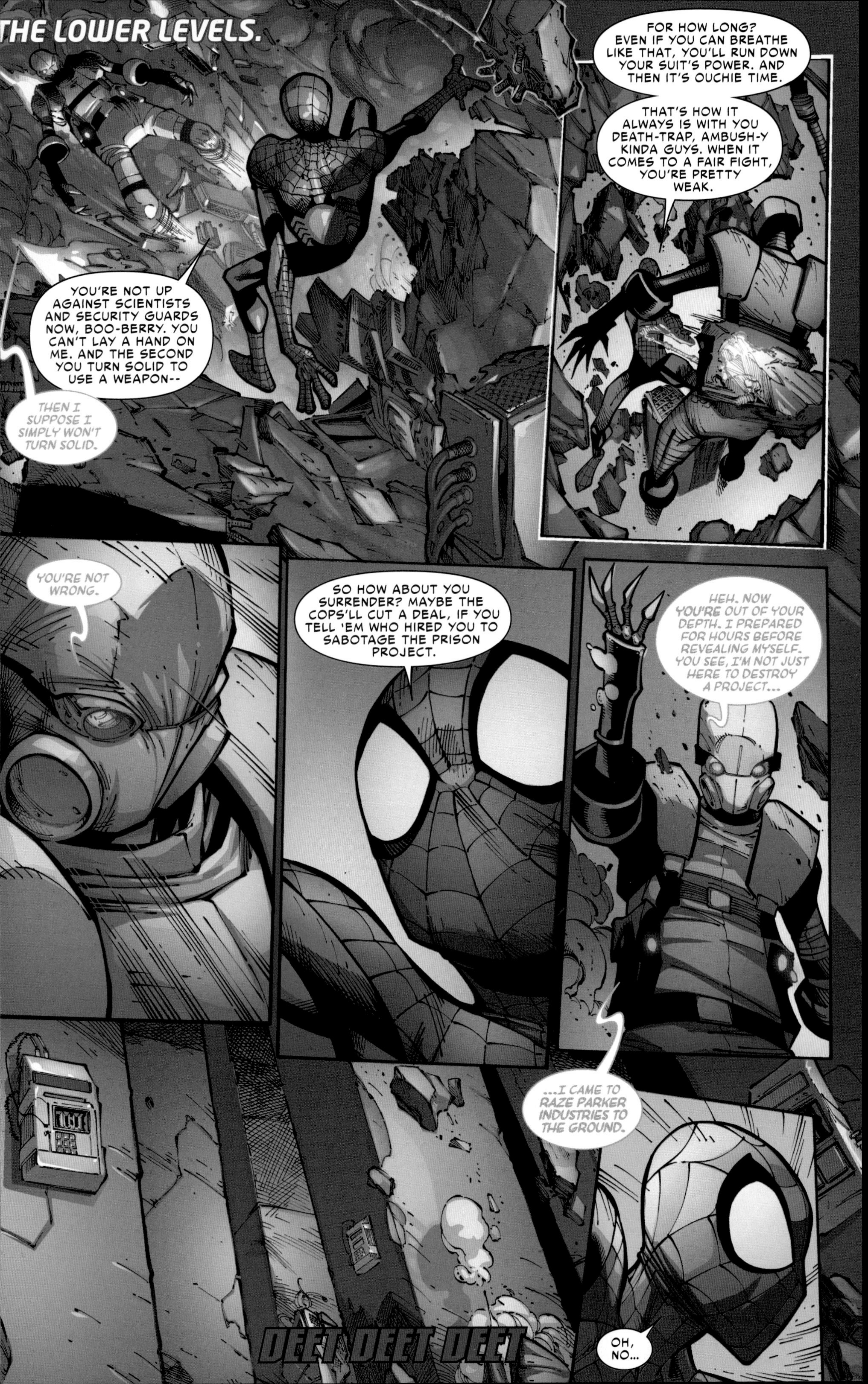
THE LOWER LEVELS.
YOU'RE NOT UP AGAINST SCIENTISTS AND SECURITY GUARDS NOW, BOO-BERRY. YOU CAN'T LAY A HAND ON ME. AND THE SECOND YOU TURN SOLID TO USE A WEAPON--
THEN I SUPPOSE I SIMPLY WON'T TURN SOLID.
FOR HOW LONG? EVEN IF YOU CAN BREATHE LIKE THAT, YOU'LL RUN DOWN YOUR SUIT'S POWER. AND THEN IT'S OUCHIE TIME.
THAT'S HOW IT ALWAYS IS WITH YOU DEATH-TRAP, AMBUSH-Y KINDA GUYS. WHEN IT COMES TO A FAIR FIGHT, YOU'RE PRETTY WEAK.
YOU'RE NOT WRONG.
SO HOW ABOUT YOU SURRENDER? MAYBE THE COPS'LL CUT A DEAL, IF YOU TELL 'EM WHO HIRED YOU TO SABOTAGE THE PRISON PROJECT.
HEH. NOW YOU'RE OUT OF YOUR DEPTH. I PREPARED FOR HOURS BEFORE REVEALING MYSELF. YOU SEE, I'M NOT JUST HERE TO DESTROY A PROJECT...
...I CAME TO RAZE PARKER INDUSTRIES TO THE GROUND.
DEET DEET DEET
OH, NO...

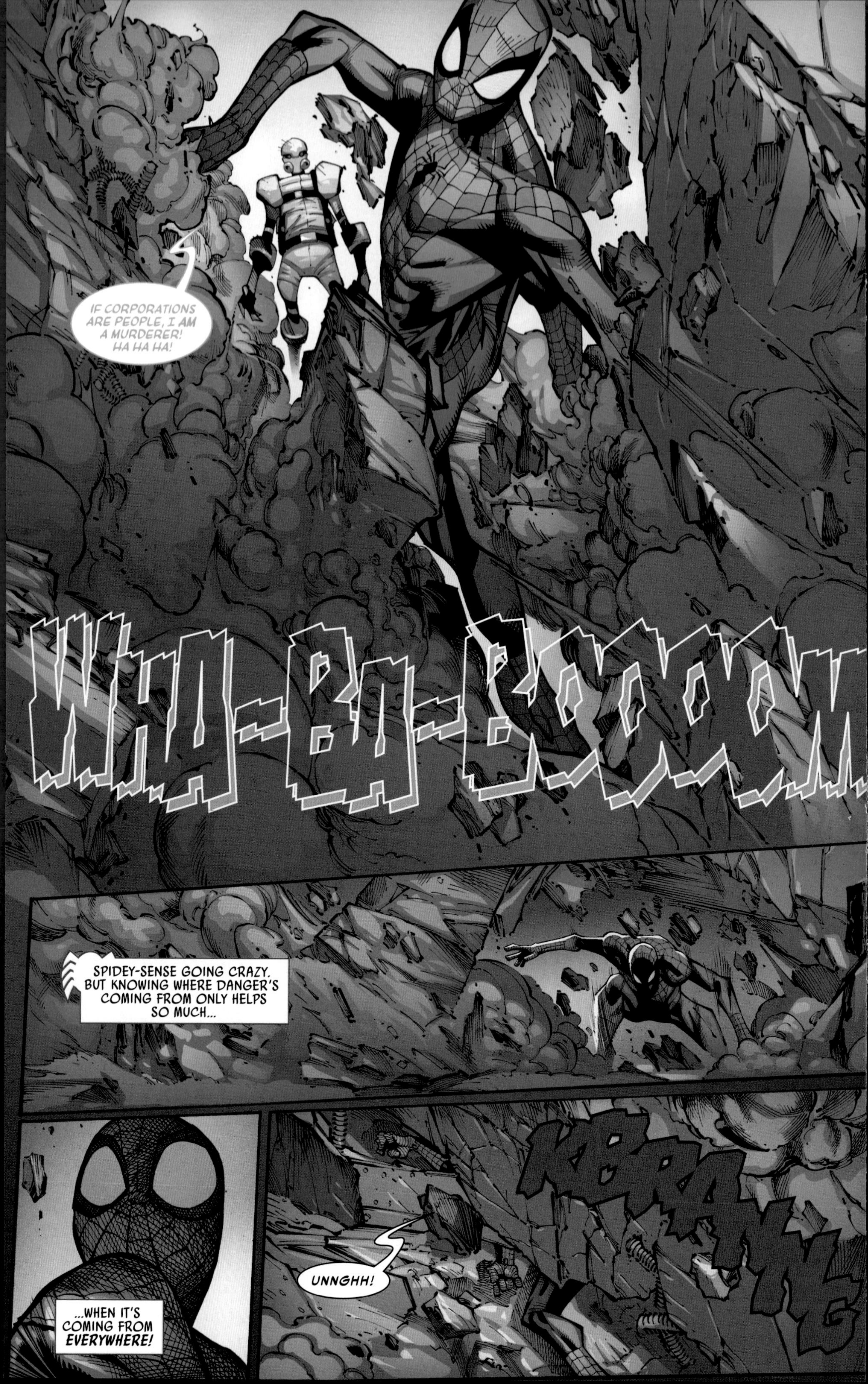
IF CORPORATIONS ARE PEOPLE, I AM A MURDERER! HA HA HA!
WHA-BA-BOOOM
SPIDEY-SENSE GOING CRAZY. BUT KNOWING WHERE DANGER'S COMING FROM ONLY HELPS SO MUCH...
...WHEN IT'S COMING FROM EVERYWHERE!
KBRAANG
UNNGHH!

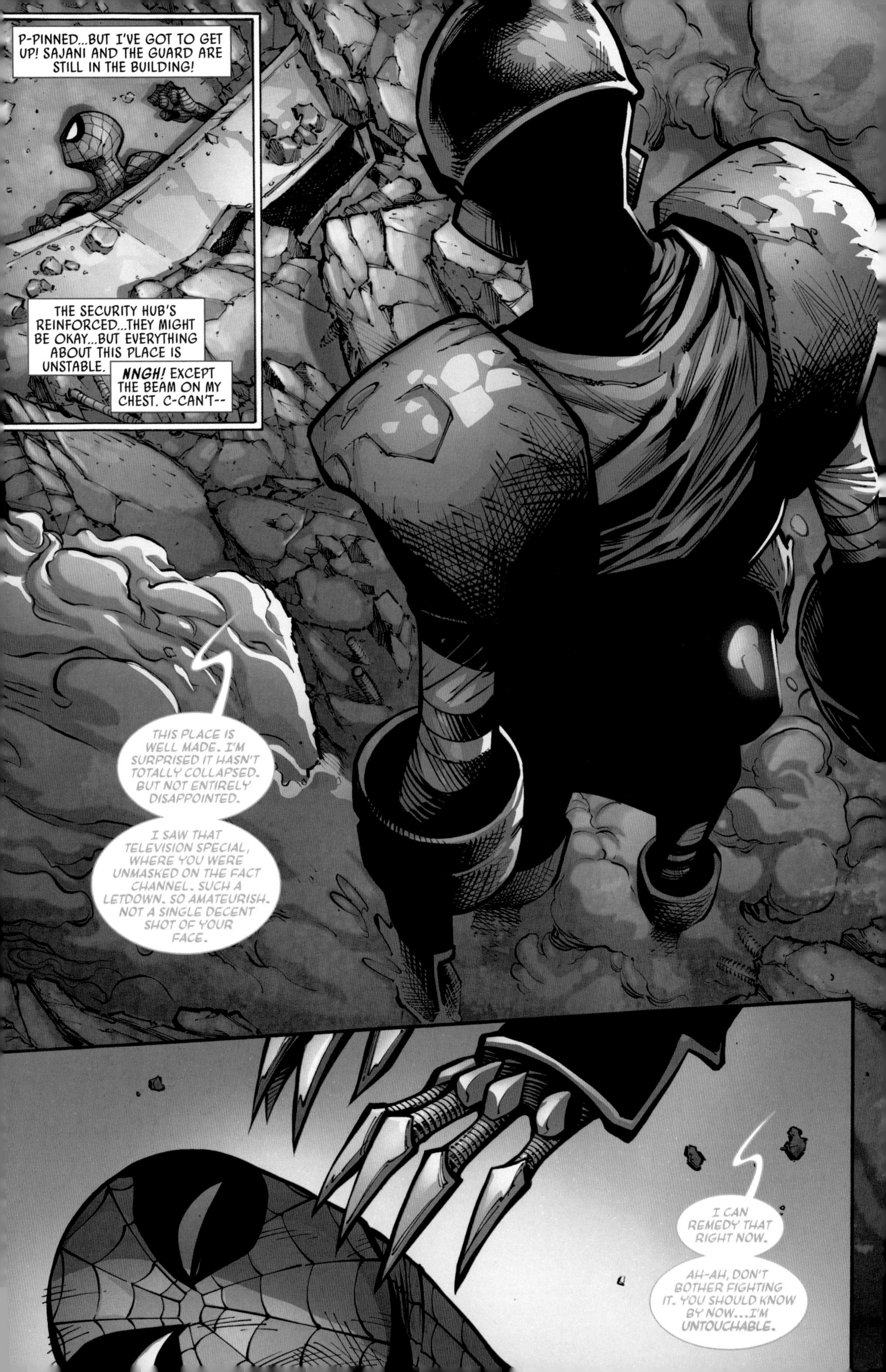
P-PINNED...BUT I'VE GOT TO GET UP! SAJANI AND THE GUARD ARE STILL IN THE BUILDING!
THE SECURITY HUB'S REINFORCED...THEY MIGHT BE OKAY...BUT EVERYTHING ABOUT THIS PLACE IS UNSTABLE.
NNGH! EXCEPT THE BEAM ON MY CHEST. C-CAN'T--
THIS PLACE IS WELL MADE. I'M SURPRISED IT HASN'T TOTALLY COLLAPSED. BUT NOT ENTIRELY DISAPPOINTED.
I SAW THAT TELEVISION SPECIAL, WHERE YOU WERE UNMASKED ON THE FACT CHANNEL. SUCH A LETDOWN. SO AMATEURISH. NOT A SINGLE DECENT SHOT OF YOUR FACE.
I CAN REMEDY THAT RIGHT NOW.
AH-AH, DON'T BOTHER FIGHTING IT. YOU SHOULD KNOW BY NOW...I'M UNTOUCHABLE.

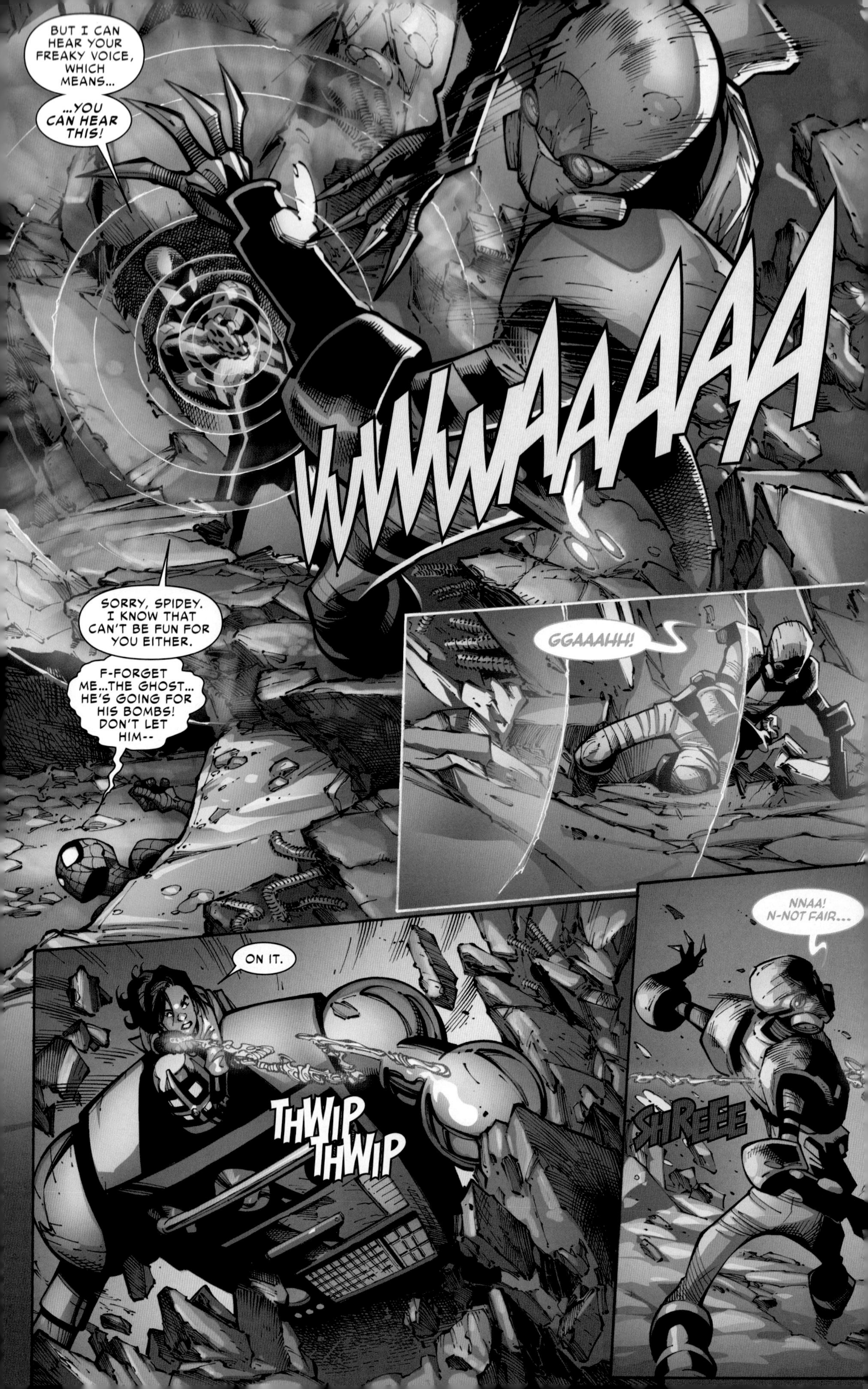
BUT I CAN HEAR YOUR FREAKY VOICE, WHICH MEANS...
...YOU CAN HEAR THIS!
VVVVVAAAAAA
SORRY, SPIDEY. I KNOW THAT CAN'T BE FUN FOR YOU EITHER.
F-FORGET ME...THE GHOST... HE'S GOING FOR HIS BOMBS! DON'T LET HIM--
GGAAAHH!
ON IT.
THWIP THWIP
NNAA! N-NOT FAIR...
SHREEE

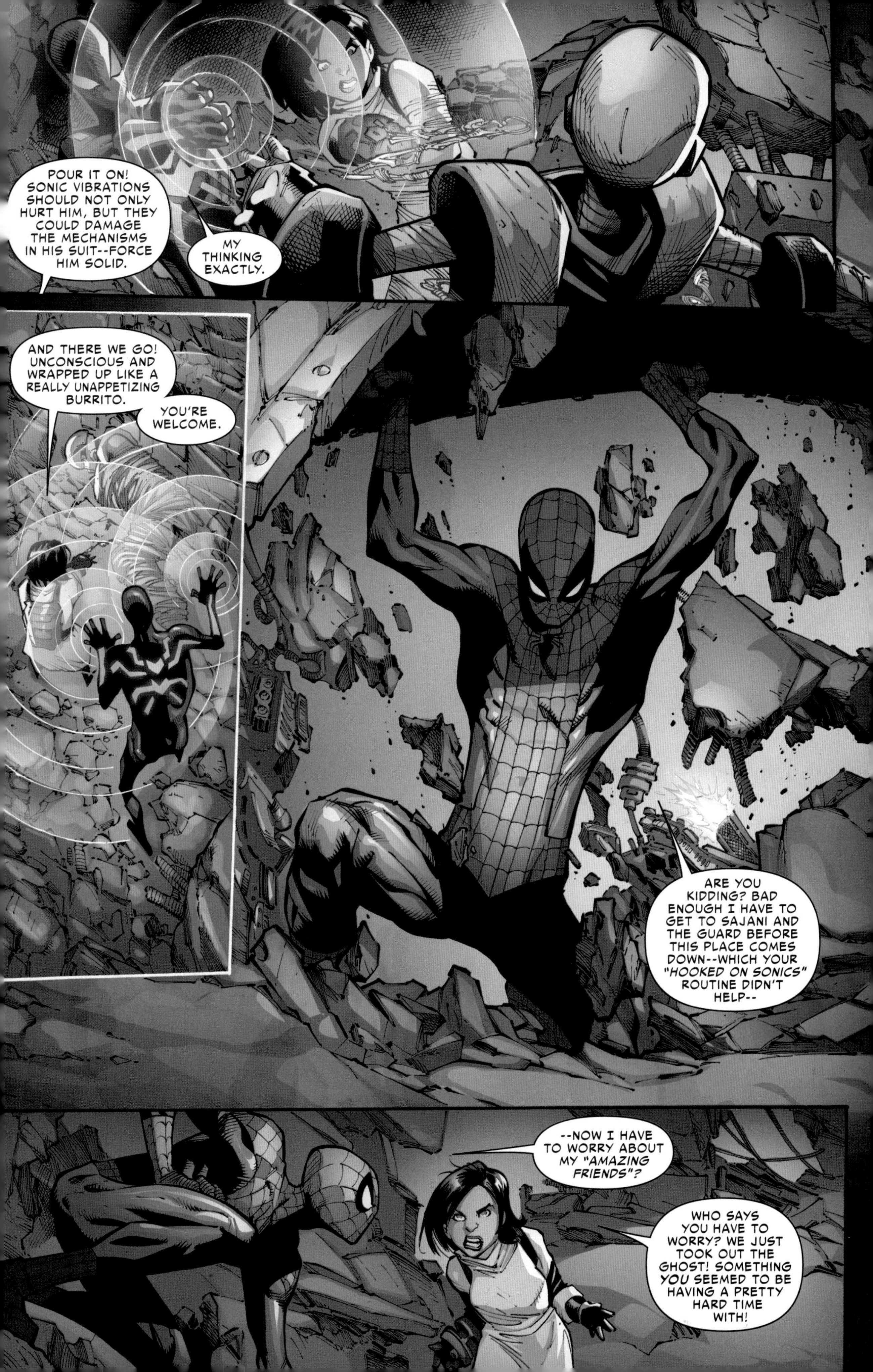

POUR IT ON! SONIC VIBRATIONS SHOULD NOT ONLY HURT HIM, BUT THEY COULD DAMAGE THE MECHANISMS IN HIS SUIT--FORCE HIM SOLID.
MY THINKING EXACTLY.
AND THERE WE GO! UNCONSCIOUS AND WRAPPED UP LIKE A REALLY UNAPPETIZING BURRITO.
YOU'RE WELCOME.
ARE YOU KIDDING? BAD ENOUGH I HAVE TO GET TO SAJANI AND THE GUARD BEFORE THIS PLACE COMES DOWN--WHICH YOUR "*HOOKED ON SONICS*" ROUTINE DIDN'T HELP--
--NOW I HAVE TO WORRY ABOUT MY "*AMAZING FRIENDS*"?
WHO SAYS YOU HAVE TO WORRY? WE JUST TOOK OUT THE GHOST! SOMETHING *YOU* SEEMED TO BE HAVING A PRETTY HARD TIME WITH!

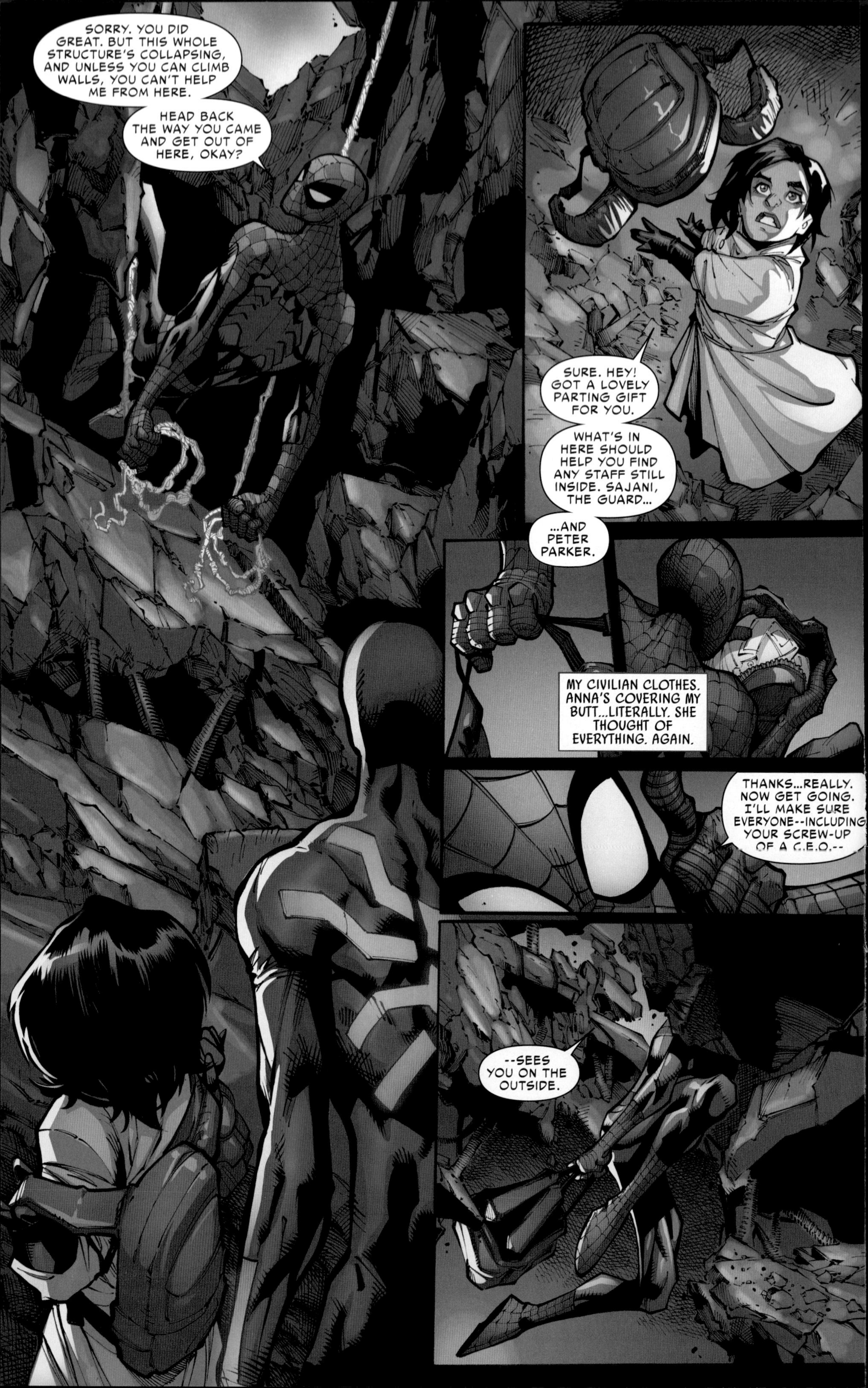
SORRY. YOU DID GREAT. BUT THIS WHOLE STRUCTURE'S COLLAPSING, AND UNLESS YOU CAN CLIMB WALLS, YOU CAN'T HELP ME FROM HERE.
HEAD BACK THE WAY YOU CAME AND GET OUT OF HERE, OKAY?
SURE. HEY! GOT A LOVELY PARTING GIFT FOR YOU.
WHAT'S IN HERE SHOULD HELP YOU FIND ANY STAFF STILL INSIDE. SAJANI, THE GUARD...
...AND PETER PARKER.
MY CIVILIAN CLOTHES. ANNA'S COVERING MY BUTT...LITERALLY. SHE THOUGHT OF EVERYTHING. AGAIN.
THANKS...REALLY. NOW GET GOING. I'LL MAKE SURE EVERYONE--INCLUDING YOUR SCREW-UP OF A C.E.O.--
--SEES YOU ON THE OUTSIDE.

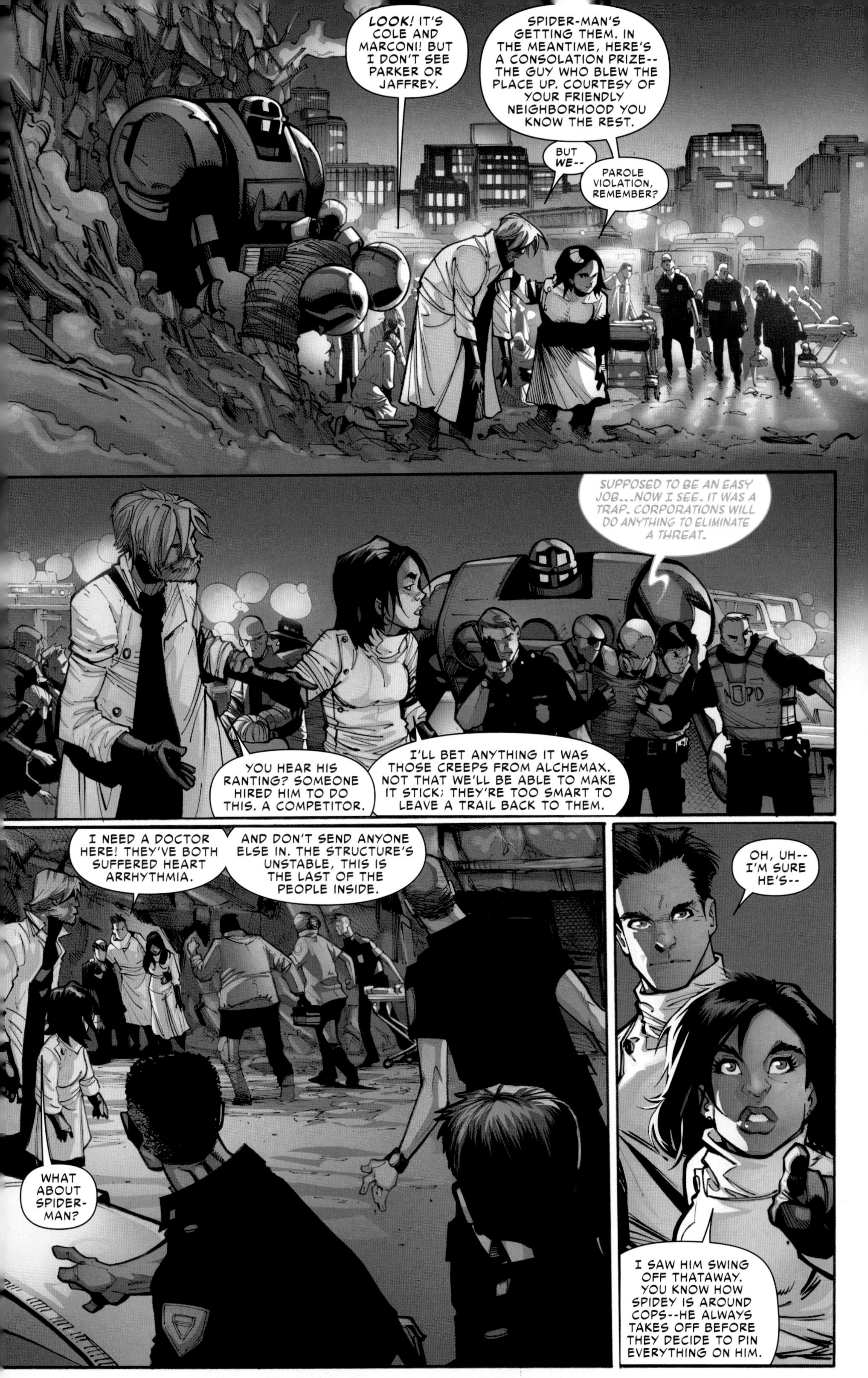
LOOK! IT'S COLE AND MARCONI! BUT I DON'T SEE PARKER OR JAFFREY.
SPIDER-MAN'S GETTING THEM. IN THE MEANTIME, HERE'S A CONSOLATION PRIZE-- THE GUY WHO BLEW THE PLACE UP. COURTESY OF YOUR FRIENDLY NEIGHBORHOOD YOU KNOW THE REST.
BUT WE--
PAROLE VIOLATION, REMEMBER?
SUPPOSED TO BE AN EASY JOB...NOW I SEE. IT WAS A TRAP. CORPORATIONS WILL DO ANYTHING TO ELIMINATE A THREAT.
YOU HEAR HIS RANTING? SOMEONE HIRED HIM TO DO THIS. A COMPETITOR.
I'LL BET ANYTHING IT WAS THOSE CREEPS FROM ALCHEMAX. NOT THAT WE'LL BE ABLE TO MAKE IT STICK; THEY'RE TOO SMART TO LEAVE A TRAIL BACK TO THEM.
I NEED A DOCTOR HERE! THEY'VE BOTH SUFFERED HEART ARRHYTHMIA.
AND DON'T SEND ANYONE ELSE IN. THE STRUCTURE'S UNSTABLE, THIS IS THE LAST OF THE PEOPLE INSIDE.
WHAT ABOUT SPIDER-MAN?
OH, UH-- I'M SURE HE'S--
I SAW HIM SWING OFF THATAWAY. YOU KNOW HOW SPIDEY IS AROUND COPS--HE ALWAYS TAKES OFF BEFORE THEY DECIDE TO PIN EVERYTHING ON HIM.

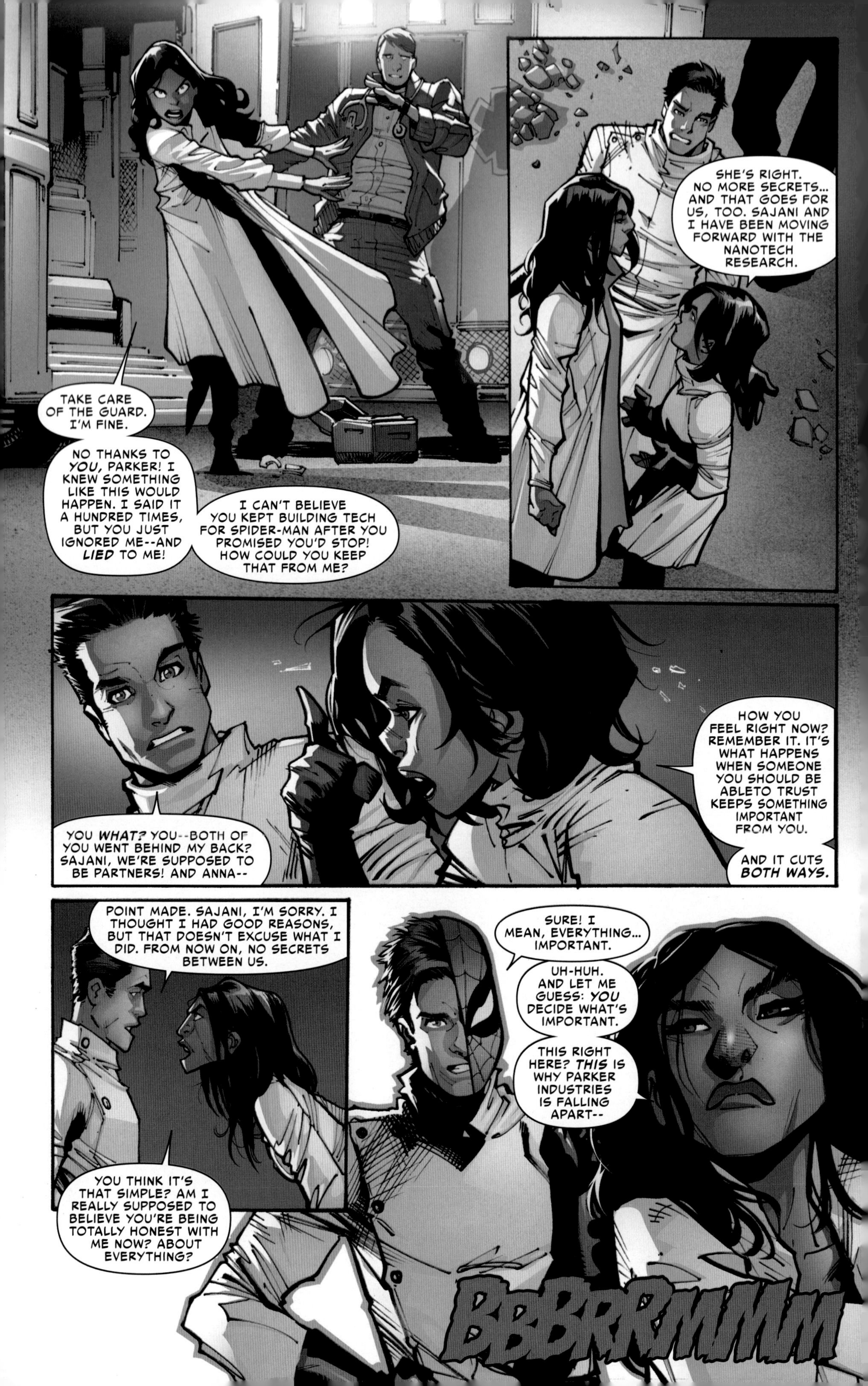

TAKE CARE OF THE GUARD. I'M FINE.
NO THANKS TO *YOU*, PARKER! I KNEW SOMETHING LIKE THIS WOULD HAPPEN. I SAID IT A HUNDRED TIMES, BUT YOU JUST IGNORED ME--AND *LIED* TO ME!
I CAN'T BELIEVE YOU KEPT BUILDING TECH FOR SPIDER-MAN AFTER YOU PROMISED YOU'D STOP! HOW COULD YOU KEEP THAT FROM ME?
SHE'S RIGHT. NO MORE SECRETS... AND THAT GOES FOR US, TOO. SAJANI AND I HAVE BEEN MOVING FORWARD WITH THE NANOTECH RESEARCH.
YOU *WHAT?* YOU--BOTH OF YOU WENT BEHIND MY BACK? SAJANI, WE'RE SUPPOSED TO BE PARTNERS! AND ANNA--
HOW YOU FEEL RIGHT NOW? REMEMBER IT. IT'S WHAT HAPPENS WHEN SOMEONE YOU SHOULD BE ABLETO TRUST KEEPS SOMETHING IMPORTANT FROM YOU.
AND IT CUTS *BOTH WAYS.*
POINT MADE. SAJANI, I'M SORRY. I THOUGHT I HAD GOOD REASONS, BUT THAT DOESN'T EXCUSE WHAT I DID. FROM NOW ON, NO SECRETS BETWEEN US.
YOU THINK IT'S THAT SIMPLE? AM I REALLY SUPPOSED TO BELIEVE YOU'RE BEING TOTALLY HONEST WITH ME NOW? ABOUT EVERYTHING?
SURE! I MEAN, EVERYTHING... IMPORTANT.
UH-HUH. AND LET ME GUESS: *YOU* DECIDE WHAT'S IMPORTANT.
THIS RIGHT HERE? *THIS* IS WHY PARKER INDUSTRIES IS FALLING APART--
BBBRRRMMMM

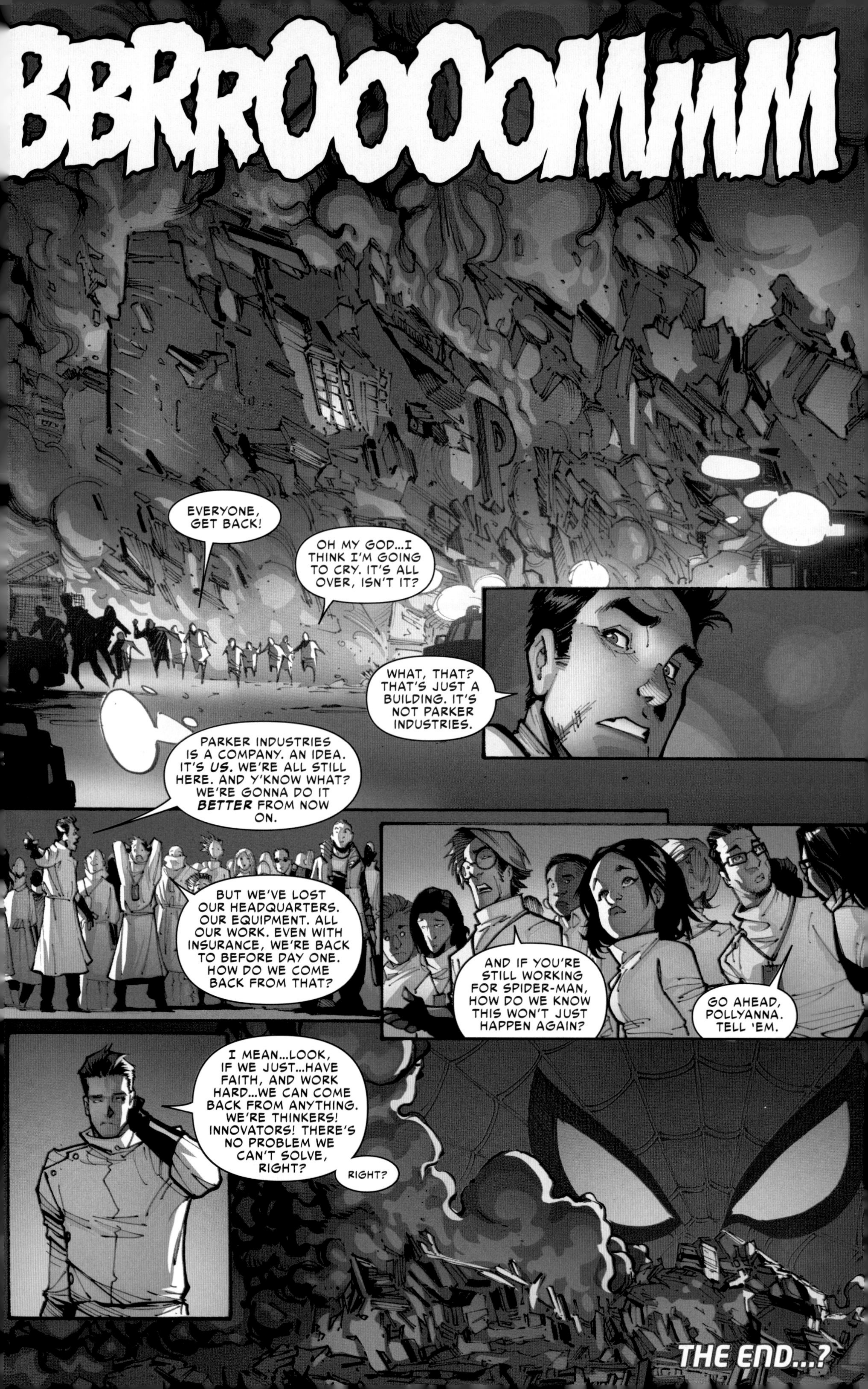
BBRROOOOMMM
EVERYONE, GET BACK!
OH MY GOD...I THINK I'M GOING TO CRY. IT'S ALL OVER, ISN'T IT?
WHAT, THAT? THAT'S JUST A BUILDING. IT'S NOT PARKER INDUSTRIES.
PARKER INDUSTRIES IS A COMPANY. AN IDEA. IT'S US. WE'RE ALL STILL HERE. AND Y'KNOW WHAT? WE'RE GONNA DO IT BETTER FROM NOW ON.
BUT WE'VE LOST OUR HEADQUARTERS. OUR EQUIPMENT. ALL OUR WORK. EVEN WITH INSURANCE, WE'RE BACK TO BEFORE DAY ONE. HOW DO WE COME BACK FROM THAT?
AND IF YOU'RE STILL WORKING FOR SPIDER-MAN, HOW DO WE KNOW THIS WON'T JUST HAPPEN AGAIN?
GO AHEAD, POLLYANNA. TELL 'EM.
I MEAN...LOOK, IF WE JUST...HAVE FAITH, AND WORK HARD...WE CAN COME BACK FROM ANYTHING. WE'RE THINKERS! INNOVATORS! THERE'S NO PROBLEM WE CAN'T SOLVE, RIGHT?
RIGHT?
THE END...?

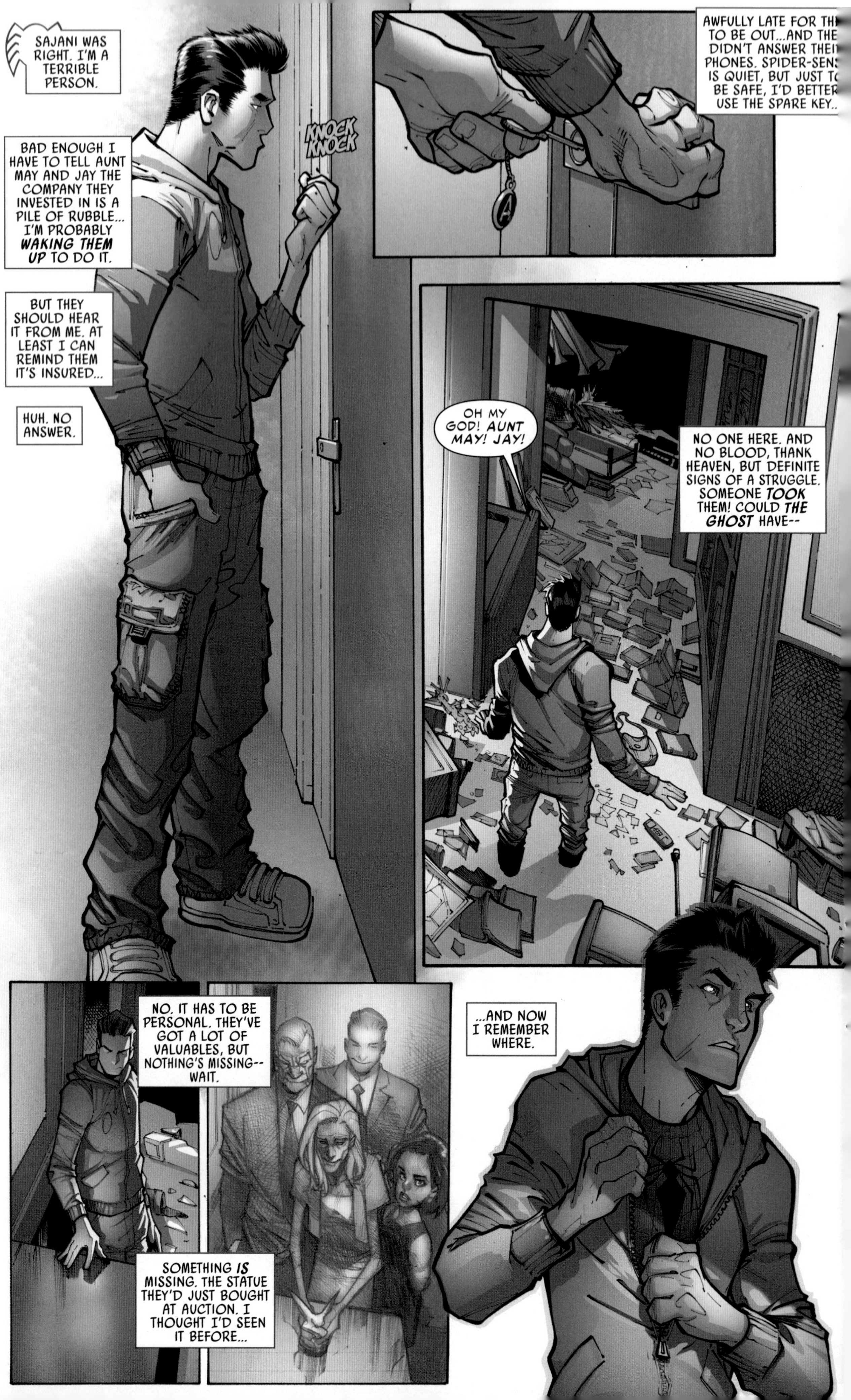
SAJANI WAS RIGHT. I'M A TERRIBLE PERSON.
BAD ENOUGH I HAVE TO TELL AUNT MAY AND JAY THE COMPANY THEY INVESTED IN IS A PILE OF RUBBLE... I'M PROBABLY WAKING THEM UP TO DO IT.
KNOCK KNOCK
BUT THEY SHOULD HEAR IT FROM ME. AT LEAST I CAN REMIND THEM IT'S INSURED...
HUH. NO ANSWER.
AWFULLY LATE FOR TH TO BE OUT...AND THE DIDN'T ANSWER THEI PHONES. SPIDER-SENS IS QUIET, BUT JUST T BE SAFE, I'D BETTER USE THE SPARE KEY..
OH MY GOD! AUNT MAY! JAY!
NO ONE HERE. AND NO BLOOD, THANK HEAVEN, BUT DEFINITE SIGNS OF A STRUGGLE. SOMEONE TOOK THEM! COULD THE GHOST HAVE--
NO. IT HAS TO BE PERSONAL. THEY'VE GOT A LOT OF VALUABLES, BUT NOTHING'S MISSING-- WAIT.
SOMETHING IS MISSING. THE STATUE THEY'D JUST BOUGHT AT AUCTION. I THOUGHT I'D SEEN IT BEFORE...
...AND NOW I REMEMBER WHERE.

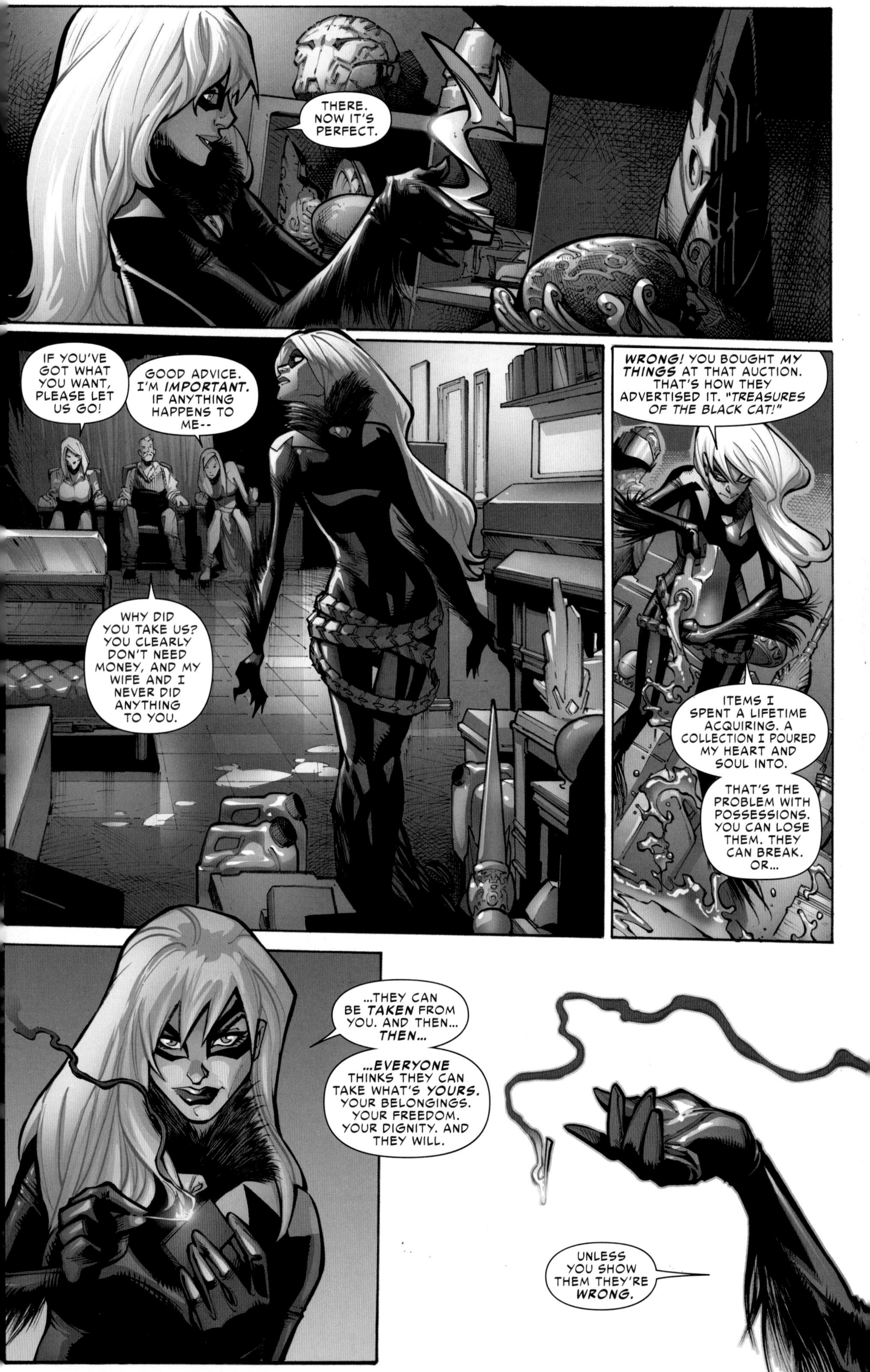
THERE. NOW IT'S PERFECT.
IF YOU'VE GOT WHAT YOU WANT, PLEASE LET US GO!
GOOD ADVICE. I'M *IMPORTANT.* IF ANYTHING HAPPENS TO ME--
WHY DID YOU TAKE US? YOU CLEARLY DON'T NEED MONEY, AND MY WIFE AND I NEVER DID ANYTHING TO YOU.
WRONG! YOU BOUGHT *MY THINGS* AT THAT AUCTION. THAT'S HOW THEY ADVERTISED IT. "*TREASURES OF THE BLACK CAT!*"
ITEMS I SPENT A LIFETIME ACQUIRING. A COLLECTION I POURED MY HEART AND SOUL INTO.
THAT'S THE PROBLEM WITH POSSESSIONS. YOU CAN LOSE THEM. THEY CAN BREAK. OR...
...THEY CAN BE *TAKEN* FROM YOU. AND THEN... *THEN...*
...EVERYONE THINKS THEY CAN TAKE WHAT'S *YOURS.* YOUR BELONGINGS. YOUR FREEDOM. YOUR DIGNITY. AND THEY WILL.
UNLESS YOU SHOW THEM THEY'RE *WRONG.*

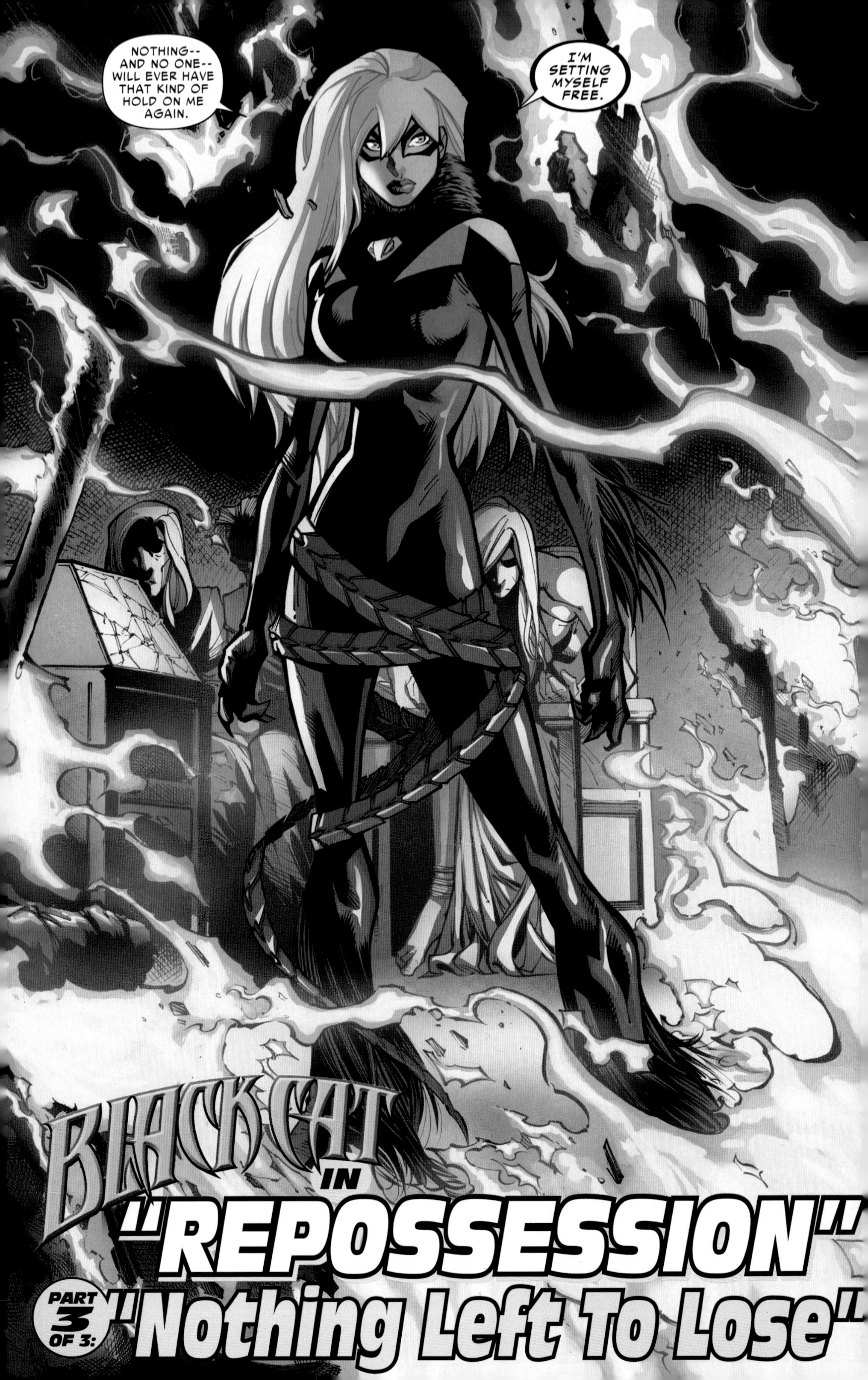
NOTHING-- AND NO ONE-- WILL EVER HAVE THAT KIND OF HOLD ON ME AGAIN.
I'M SETTING MYSELF FREE.
BLACK CAT
IN
"REPOSSESSION"
PART 3 OF 3:
"Nothing Left To Lose"

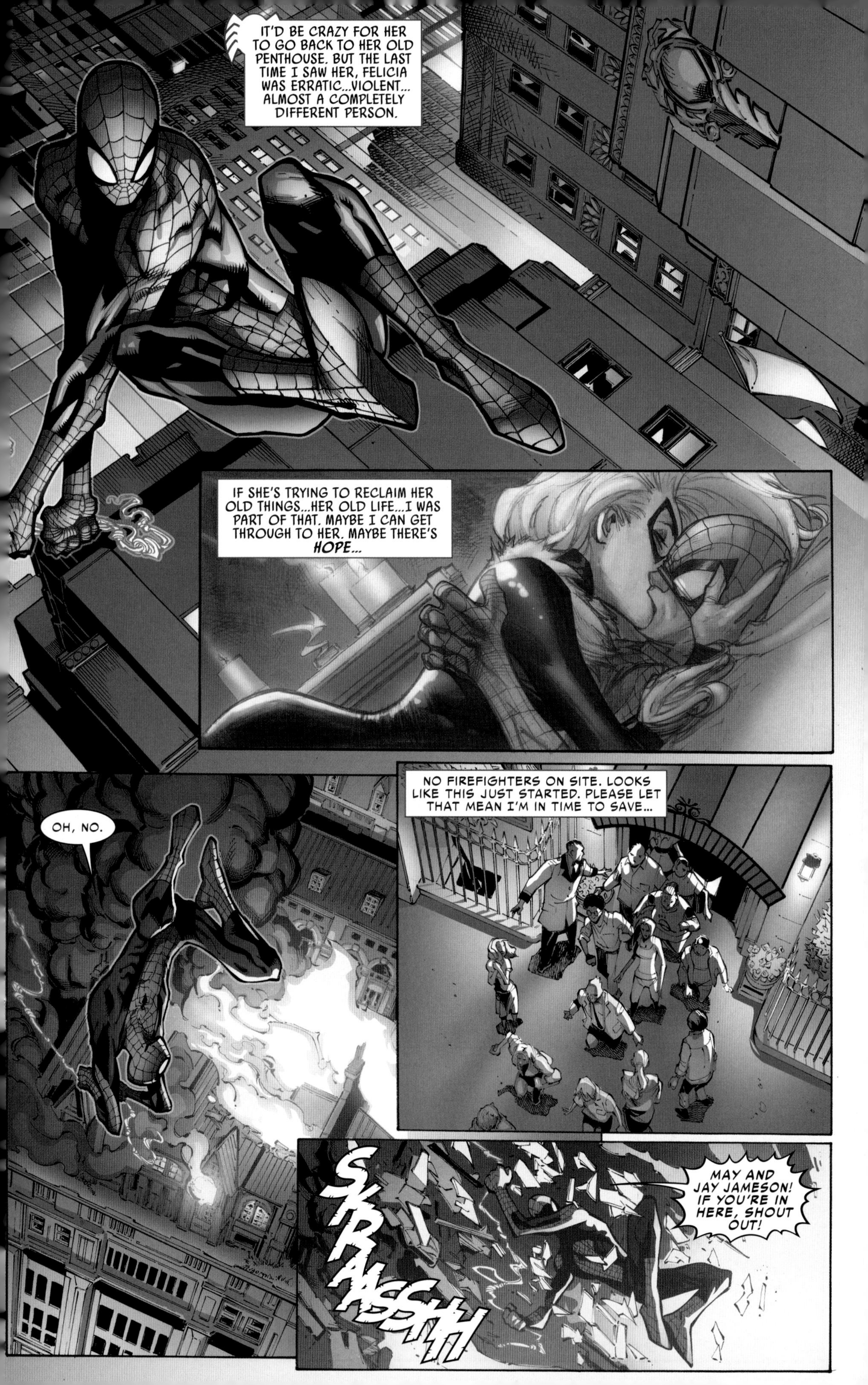
IT'D BE CRAZY FOR HER TO GO BACK TO HER OLD PENTHOUSE. BUT THE LAST TIME I SAW HER, FELICIA WAS ERRATIC...VIOLENT... ALMOST A COMPLETELY DIFFERENT PERSON.
IF SHE'S TRYING TO RECLAIM HER OLD THINGS...HER OLD LIFE...I WAS PART OF THAT. MAYBE I CAN GET THROUGH TO HER. MAYBE THERE'S *HOPE*...
OH, NO.
NO FIREFIGHTERS ON SITE. LOOKS LIKE THIS JUST STARTED. PLEASE LET THAT MEAN I'M IN TIME TO SAVE...
SKRASSHH
MAY AND JAY JAMESON! IF YOU'RE IN HERE, SHOUT OUT!

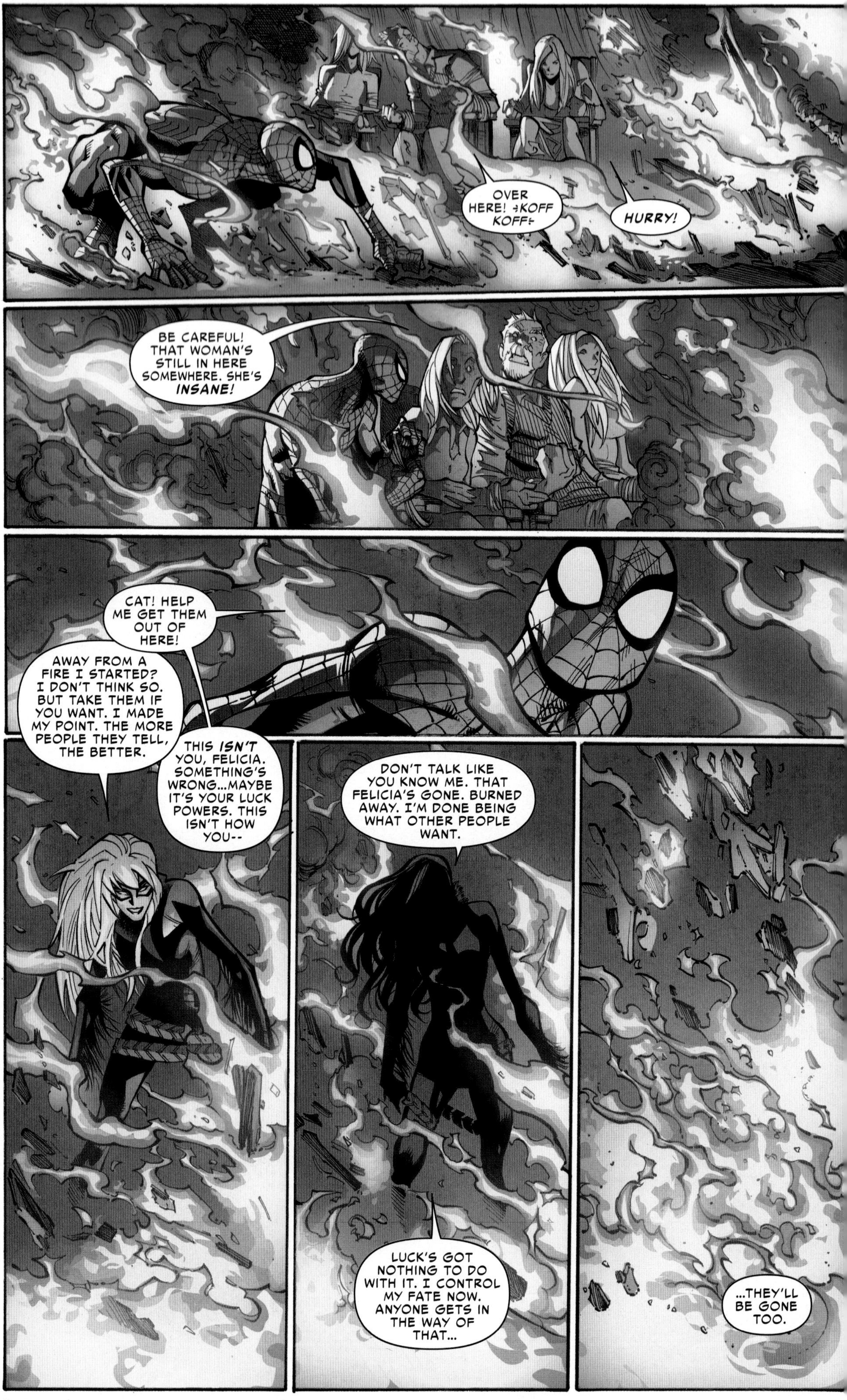
OVER HERE! ⸗KOFF KOFF⸗
HURRY!
BE CAREFUL! THAT WOMAN'S STILL IN HERE SOMEWHERE. SHE'S INSANE!
CAT! HELP ME GET THEM OUT OF HERE!
AWAY FROM A FIRE I STARTED? I DON'T THINK SO. BUT TAKE THEM IF YOU WANT. I MADE MY POINT. THE MORE PEOPLE THEY TELL, THE BETTER.
THIS ISN'T YOU, FELICIA. SOMETHING'S WRONG...MAYBE IT'S YOUR LUCK POWERS. THIS ISN'T HOW YOU--
DON'T TALK LIKE YOU KNOW ME. THAT FELICIA'S GONE. BURNED AWAY. I'M DONE BEING WHAT OTHER PEOPLE WANT.
LUCK'S GOT NOTHING TO DO WITH IT. I CONTROL MY FATE NOW. ANYONE GETS IN THE WAY OF THAT...
...THEY'LL BE GONE TOO.

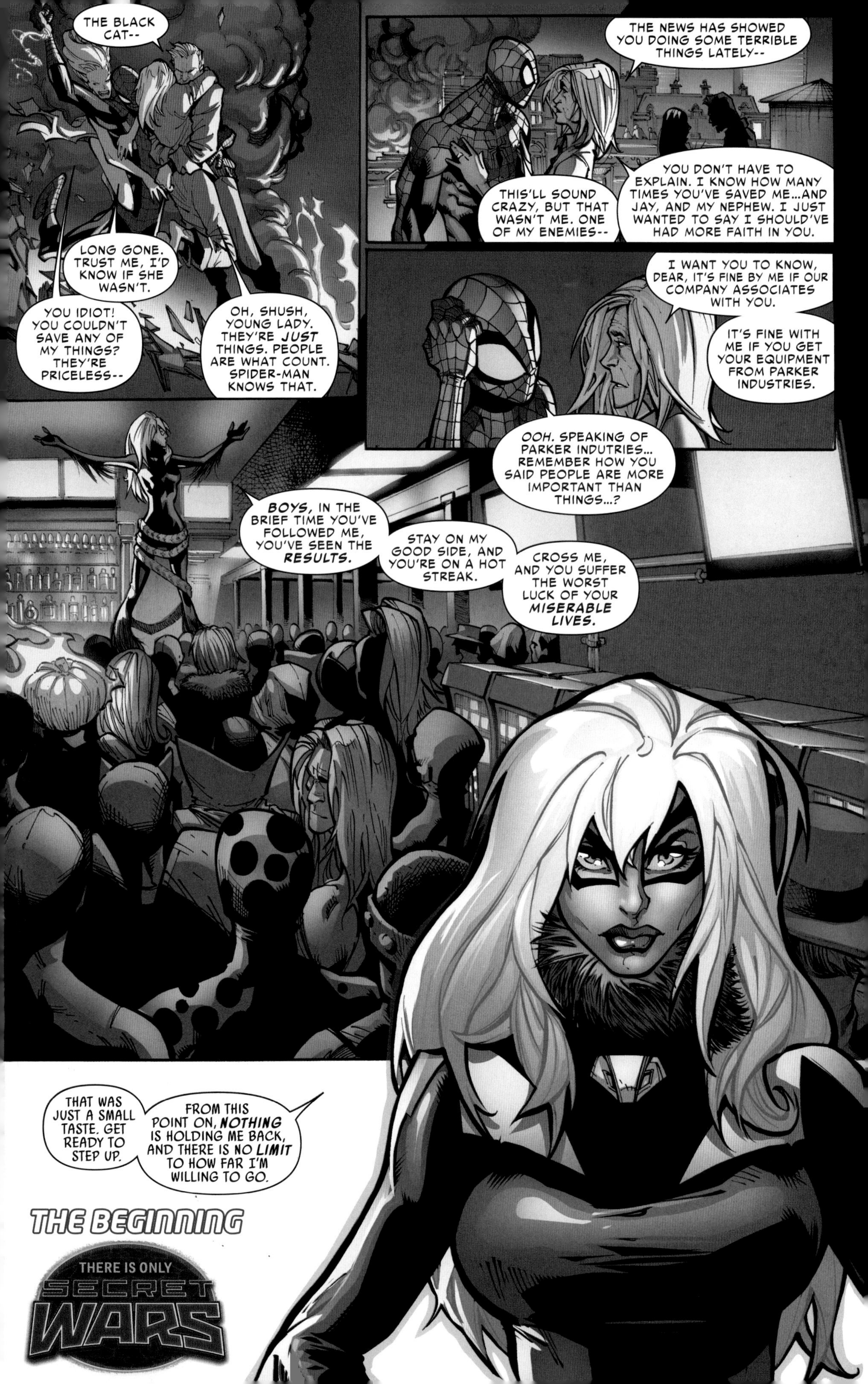

THE BLACK CAT--
LONG GONE. TRUST ME, I'D KNOW IF SHE WASN'T.
YOU IDIOT! YOU COULDN'T SAVE ANY OF MY THINGS? THEY'RE PRICELESS--
OH, SHUSH, YOUNG LADY. THEY'RE JUST THINGS. PEOPLE ARE WHAT COUNT. SPIDER-MAN KNOWS THAT.
THE NEWS HAS SHOWED YOU DOING SOME TERRIBLE THINGS LATELY--
THIS'LL SOUND CRAZY, BUT THAT WASN'T ME. ONE OF MY ENEMIES--
YOU DON'T HAVE TO EXPLAIN. I KNOW HOW MANY TIMES YOU'VE SAVED ME...AND JAY, AND MY NEPHEW. I JUST WANTED TO SAY I SHOULD'VE HAD MORE FAITH IN YOU.
I WANT YOU TO KNOW, DEAR, IT'S FINE BY ME IF OUR COMPANY ASSOCIATES WITH YOU.
IT'S FINE WITH ME IF YOU GET YOUR EQUIPMENT FROM PARKER INDUSTRIES.
OOH. SPEAKING OF PARKER INDUTRIES... REMEMBER HOW YOU SAID PEOPLE ARE MORE IMPORTANT THAN THINGS...?
BOYS, IN THE BRIEF TIME YOU'VE FOLLOWED ME, YOU'VE SEEN THE RESULTS.
STAY ON MY GOOD SIDE, AND YOU'RE ON A HOT STREAK.
CROSS ME, AND YOU SUFFER THE WORST LUCK OF YOUR MISERABLE LIVES.
THAT WAS JUST A SMALL TASTE. GET READY TO STEP UP.
FROM THIS POINT ON, NOTHING IS HOLDING ME BACK, AND THERE IS NO LIMIT TO HOW FAR I'M WILLING TO GO.
THE BEGINNING
THERE IS ONLY
SECRET WARS

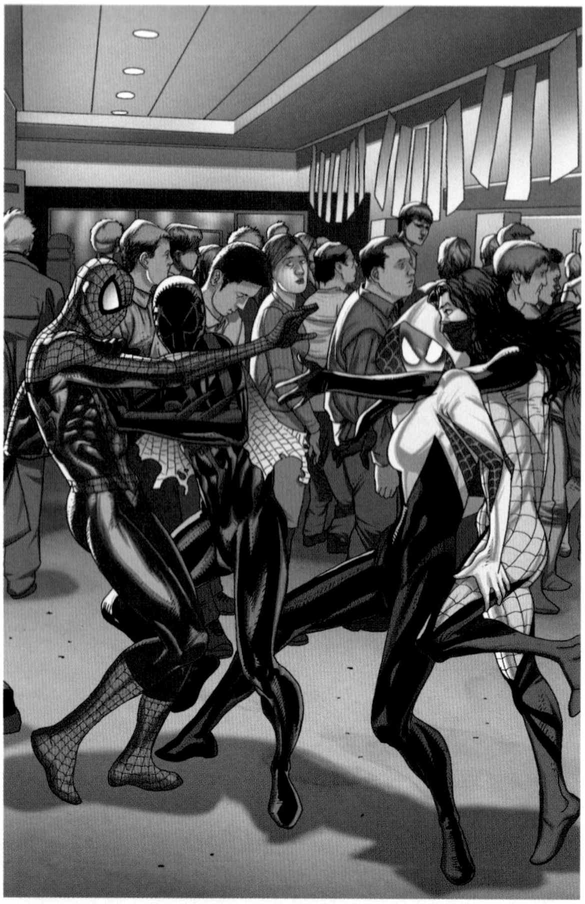

AMAZING SPIDER-MAN 13 VARIANT
BY SALVADOR LARROCA & ISRAEL SILVA

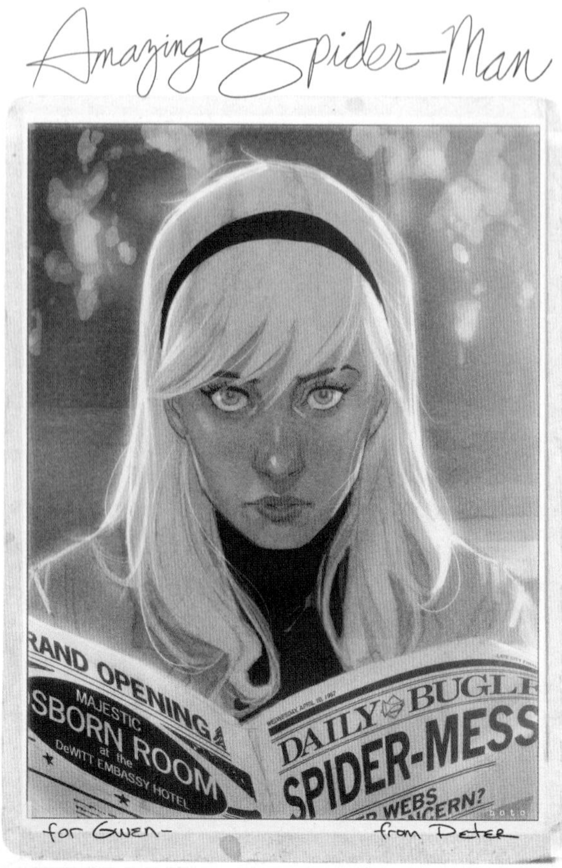
Amazing Spider-Man
RAND OPENING
MAJESTIC
SBORN ROOM
at the
DeWITT EMBASSY HOTEL
DAILY BUGLE
SPIDER-MESS
for Gwen-
from Peter

AMAZING SPIDER-MAN 14 VARIANT
BY PHIL NOTO

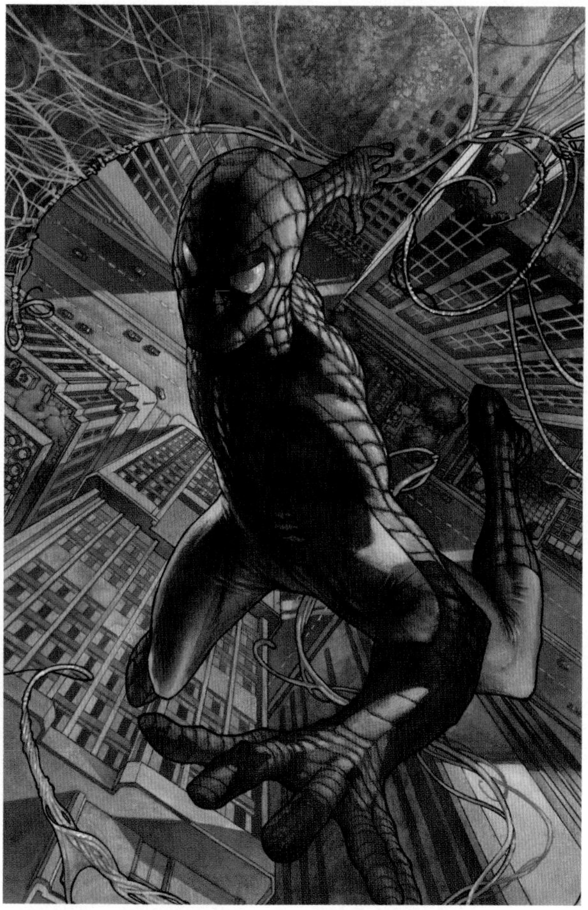

AMAZING SPIDER-MAN 15 VARIANT
BY SIMONE BIANCHI

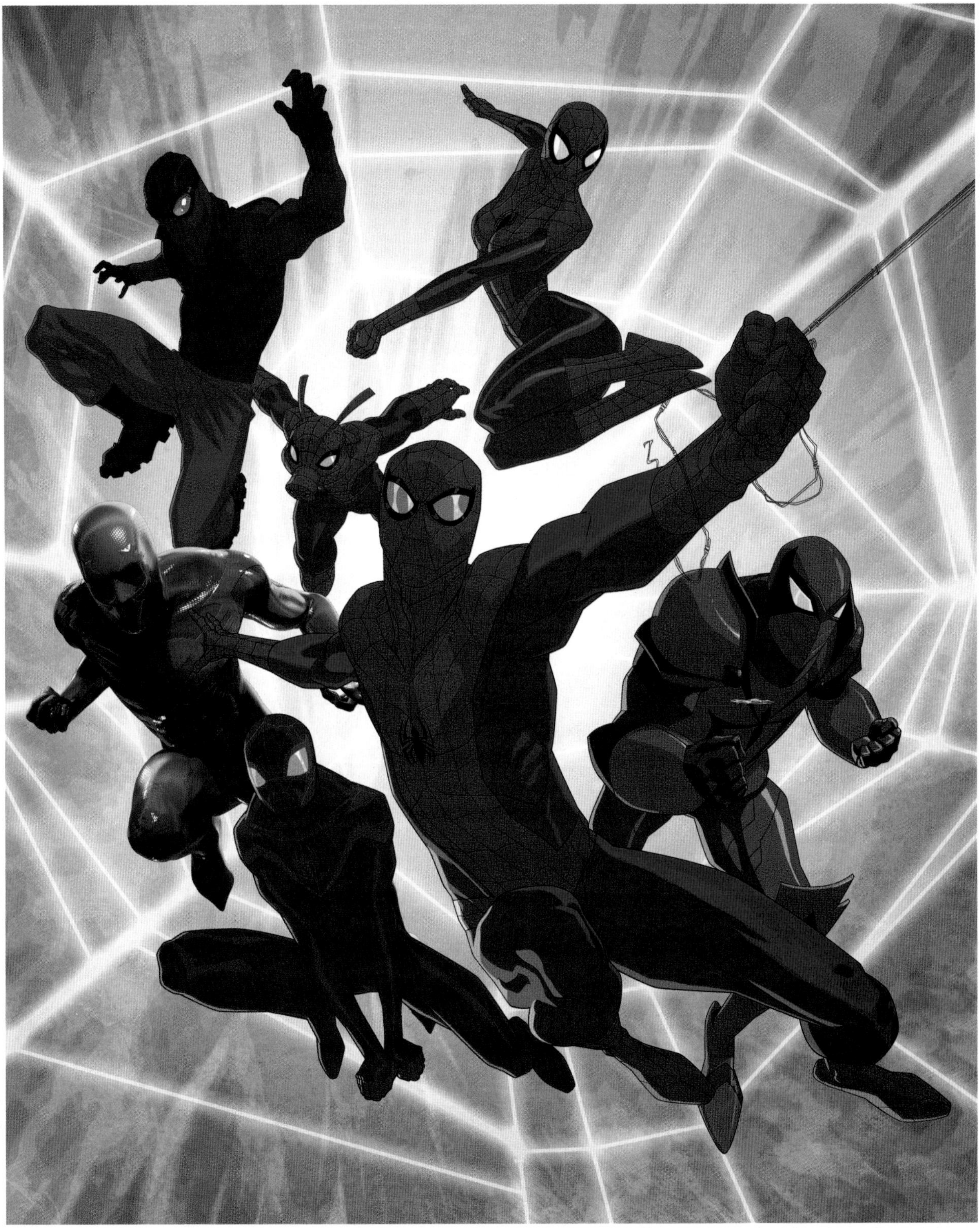

AMAZING SPIDER-MAN 9-14 MARVEL ANIMATION SPIDER-VERSE COMBINED VARIANTS

BY JEFF WAMESTER

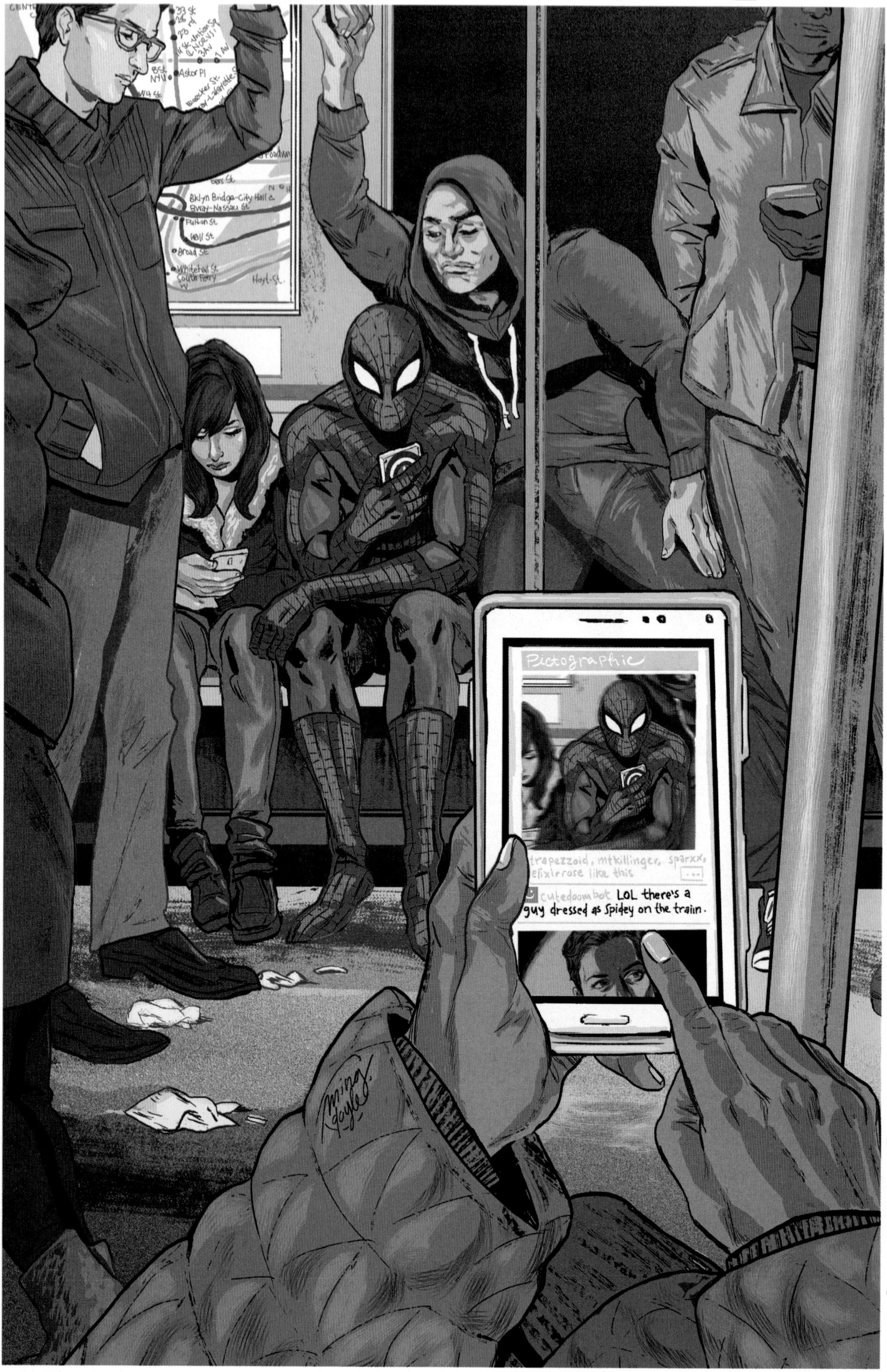
Astor Pl
Bklyn Bridge-City Hall
Bway-Nassau St
Fulton St
Wall St
Broad St
Whitehall St
South Ferry
Hoyt-St.
Pictographic
trapezzoid, mtkillinger, sparxx, elixirrose like this
cutedoombot LOL there's a guy dressed as Spidey on the train.
ming doyle

AMAZING SPIDER-MAN 17 WOMEN OF MARVEL VARIANT

BY MING DOYLE

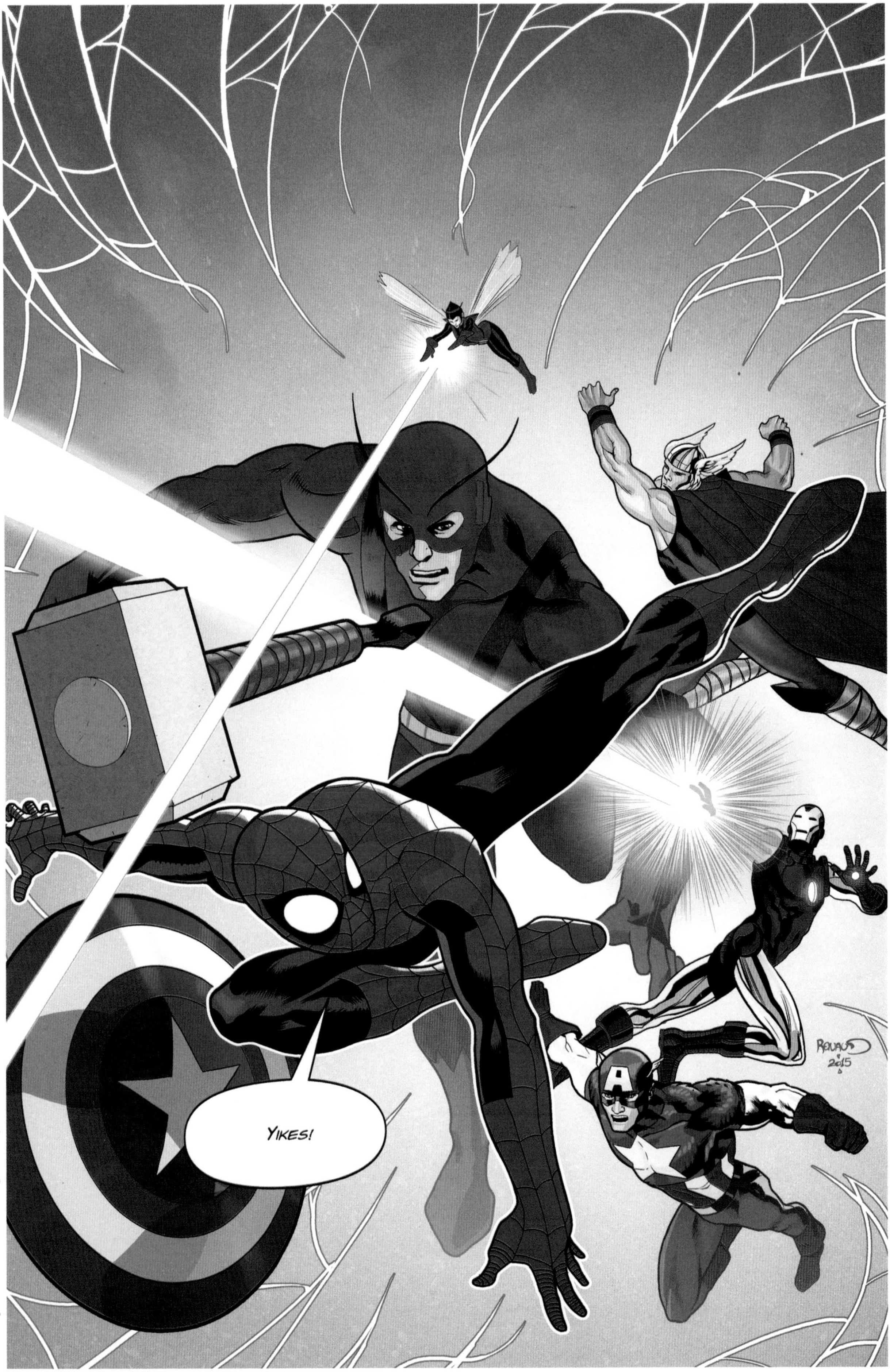
YIKES!
RENAUD 2015

AMAZING SPIDER-MAN 17 VARIANT

BY PAUL RENAUD

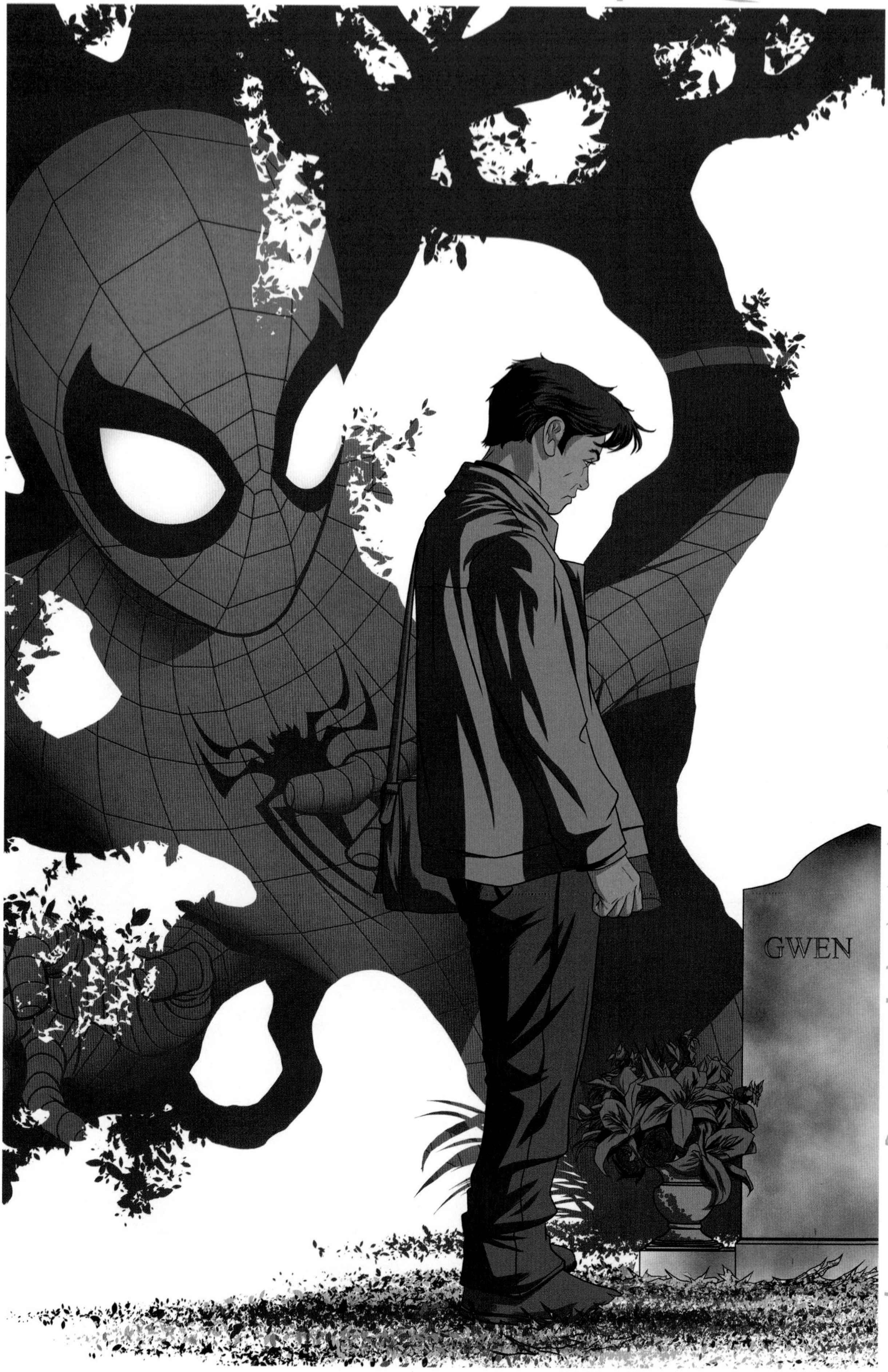
GWEN

AMAZING SPIDER-MAN 17 VARIANT

BY MIKE McKONE

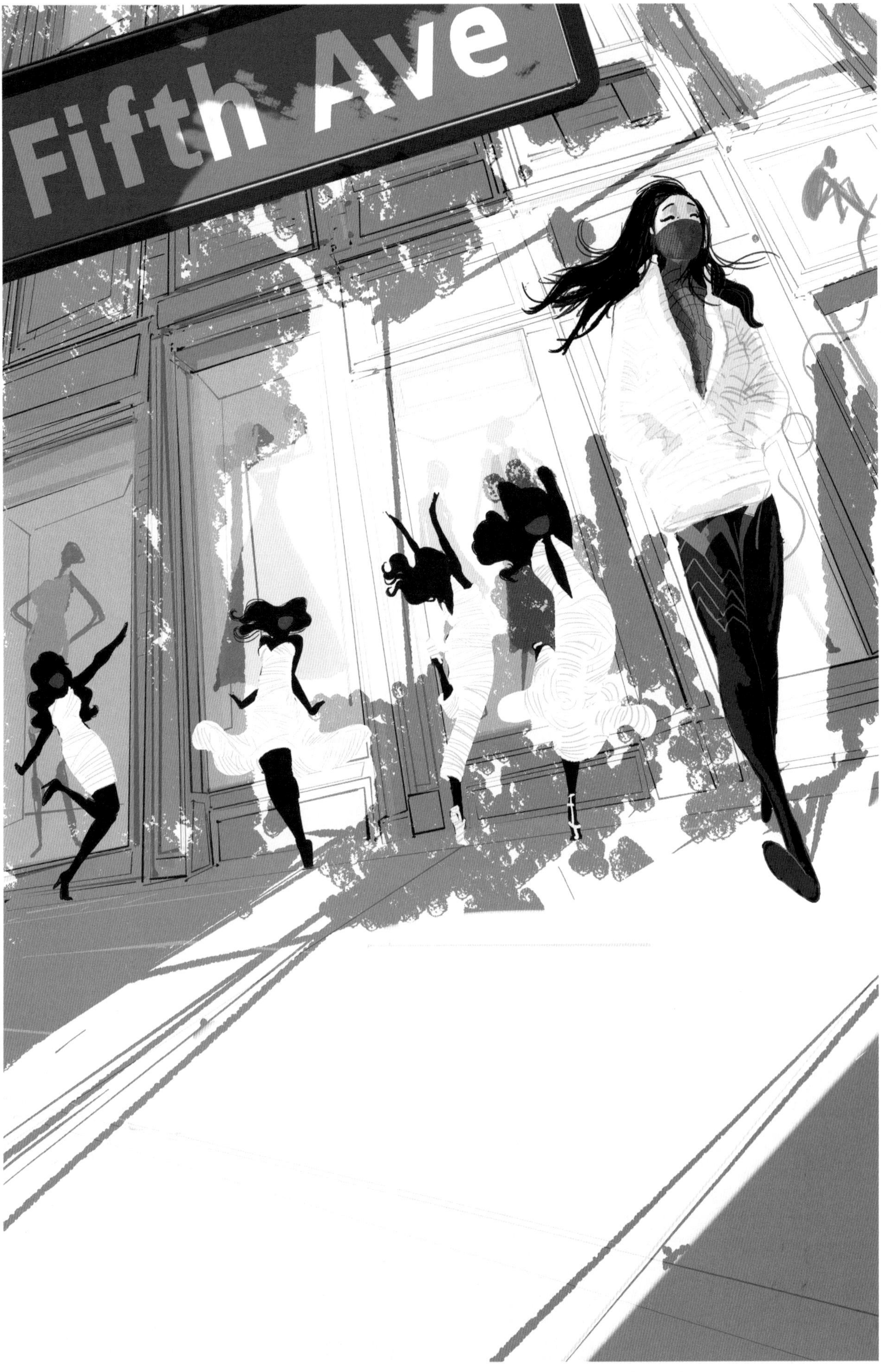
Fifth Ave

AMAZING SPIDER-MAN 18 NYC VARIANT

BY PASCAL CAMPION

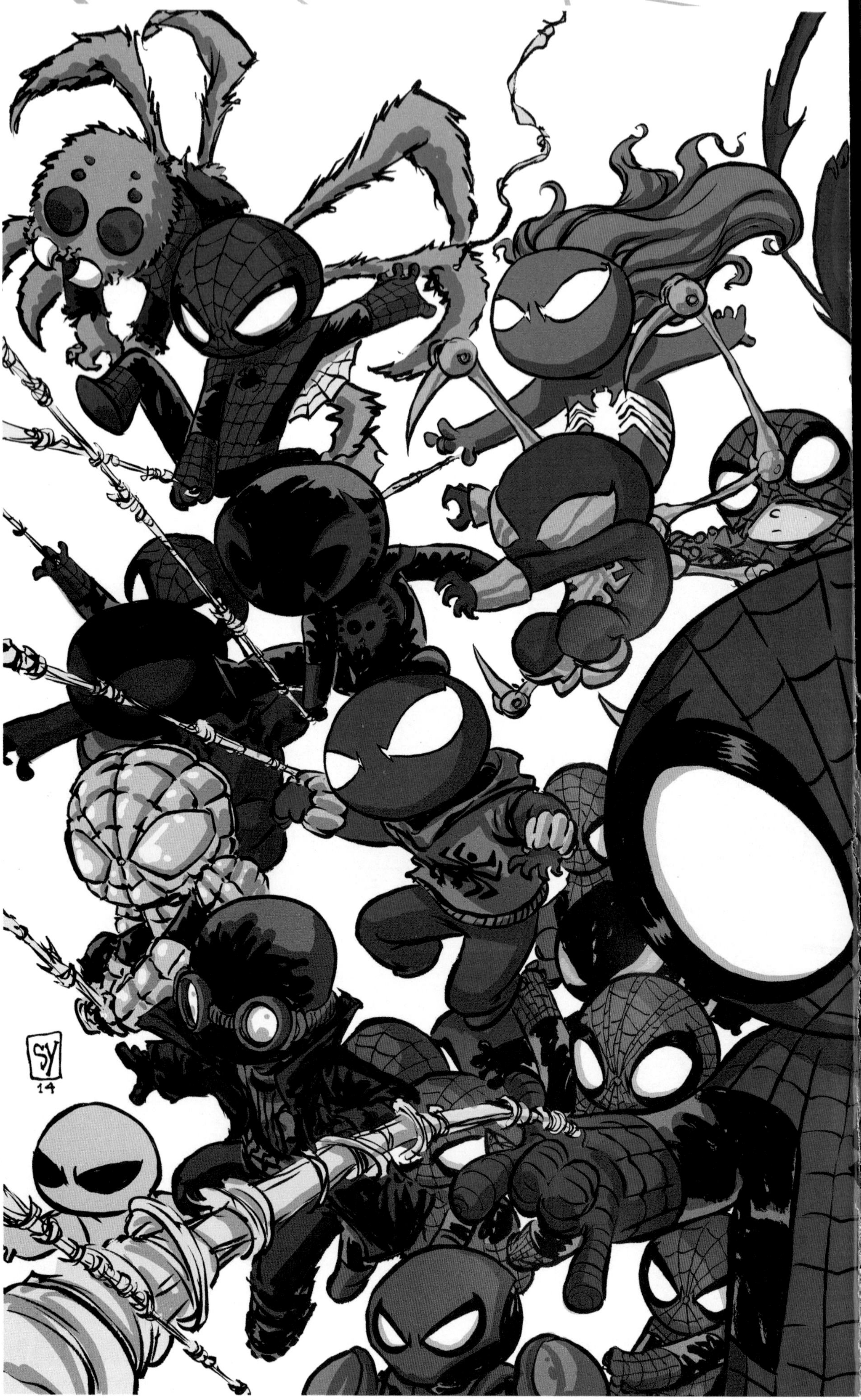
SY
14

SUPERIOR SPIDER-MAN 32 & AMAZING SPIDER-MAN 9 COMBINED VARIANTS BY SKOTTIE YOUNG

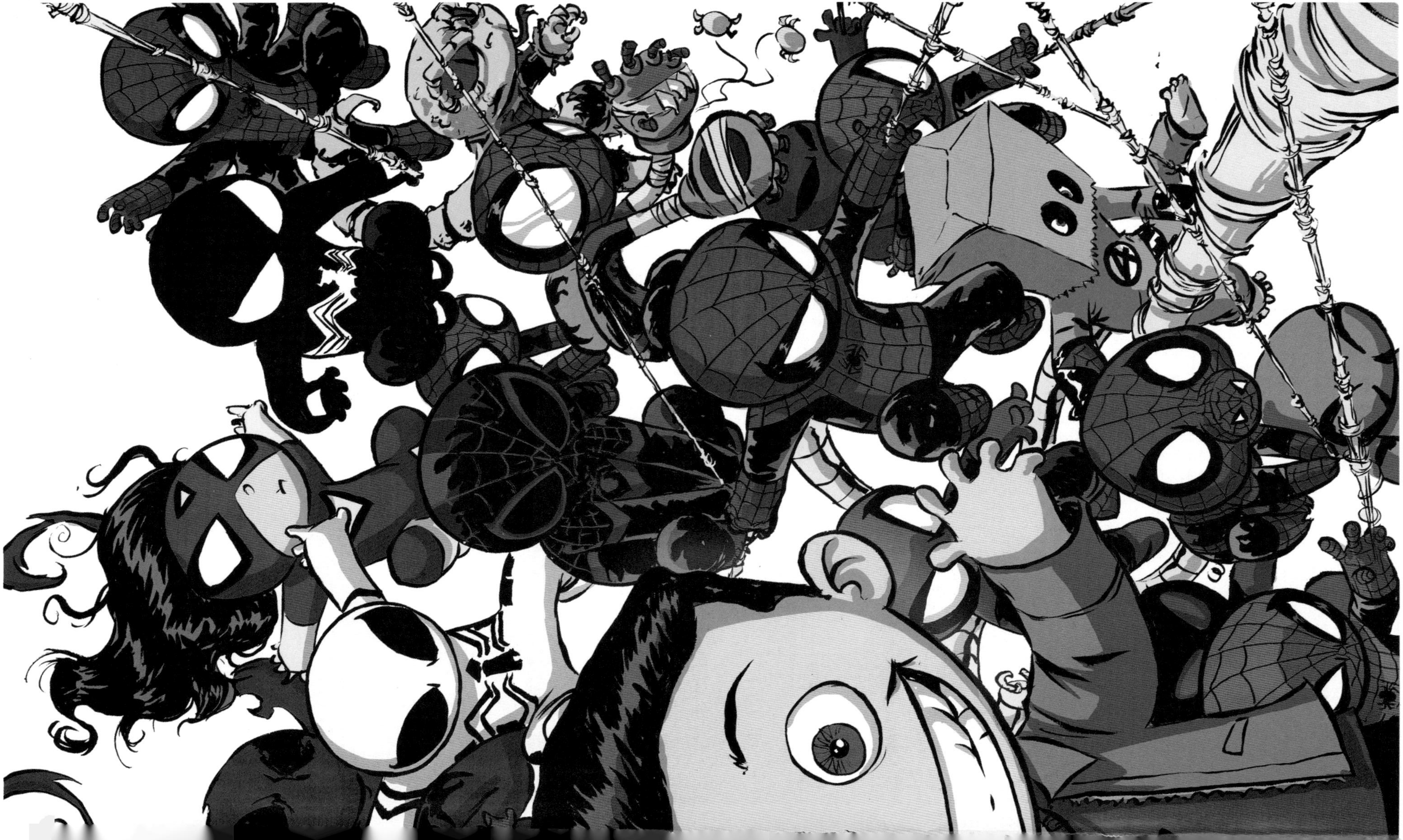

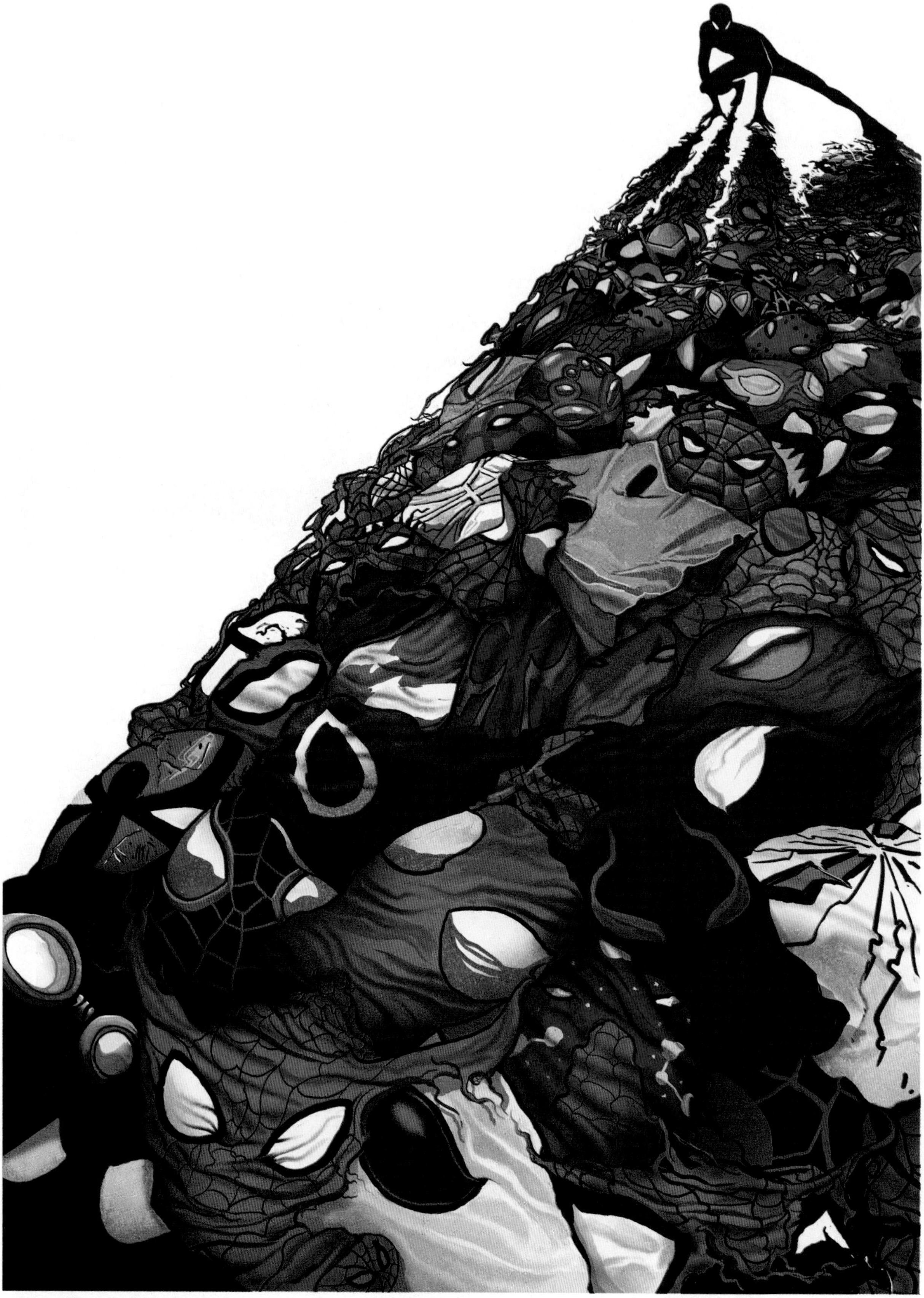

SUPERIOR SPIDER-MAN 33 VARIANT

BY MICHAEL DEL MUNDO